GOD'S PLAYGROUND
A History of Poland

II

GOD'S PLAYGROUND

A History of Poland

IN TWO VOLUMES
VOLUME II
1795 TO THE PRESENT

by

NORMAN DAVIES

COLUMBIA UNIVERSITY PRESS
NEW YORK

Copyright © 1982 Norman Davies

Printed in the United States of America

Library of Congress Cataloging in Publication Data
Davies, Norman.
 A history of Poland, God's playground.
 Bibliography: p.
 Includes indexes.
 Contents: v. 1. The origins to 1795 —
v. 2. 1795 to the present.
 1. Poland — History. I. Title. II. Title: Gods playground.
DK4140.D38   943.8   81-10241
ISBN 0-231-04326-0 (set)   (cloth)
ISBN 0-231-05350-9 (v. 1)   (cloth)   AACR2
ISBN 0-231-05352-5 (v. 2)   (cloth)
ISBN 0-231-04327-9 (set)   (paper)
ISBN 0-231-05351-7 (v. 1)   (paper)
ISBN 0-231-05353-3 (v. 2)   (paper)

Set in IBM Press Roman
in Great Britain by
Express Litho Service (Oxford)

p 10 9 8 7 6 5 4
c 10 9 8 7 6 5 4

Preface to Volume Two

This second volume, which takes the History of Poland from the late eighteenth century to the present day, continues the pattern adopted in the first one. The main narrative chapters (12–21) are preceded by a block of thematic essays, and are followed by a concluding section which summarises developments since 1945. The dominant tenor of the two volumes is quite different, however. Polish History in the earlier period saw the gradual rise and sudden fall of a unique civilisation, whose culture and institutions reflected an eccentric mixture of Western values injected into the Slavonic East. Polish History in the subsequent period saw the protracted struggle of the peoples of the defunct Republic to outlast the upstart Empires of Eastern Europe, and, by furnishing themselves with new identities, to find a new place in the world.

Nonetheless, the memory of an ancient heritage has coloured Polish perceptions of their predicament throughout modern times. Unlike many national movements, whose separate consciousness was manufactured from scratch in the course of the nineteenth century, the Poles have always had the image of the old Republic before their eyes, and through the fertile medium of their literature, have used it to perpetuate their sense of indestructibility and of moral superiority. Although they could not claim to share the decades of military glory, political power, or economic prosperity which came the way of their German or Russian neighbours, they were bound to consider themselves one of the 'historic nations' of Europe, and did not figure among the lesser breeds who (without mentioning any names), were frequently obliged to invent the greater part of their alleged histories. Poland may well be 'a country on wheels' both in regard to its geographical location and also to its exits and entrances on the political stage, but, as a cultural community with deep and lasting traditions, it has shown itself to be a permanent fixture of the European scene.

v

In political terms, of course, Poland's recent history is a tragic one. The task of reconstituting the old Republic proved quite insuperable, and the Polish states which have been created in the twentieth century have been but pale imitations, not to say, stunted parodies, of the original model. Although the long sought goal of national sovereignty has twice been achieved, in 1918 and again in 1945, the achievement has turned sour on both occasions. The Second Republic (1918–39) was extinguished in less than a generation; the People's Republic formed under Soviet auspices in 1944–45, lacks many of the essential attributes of independence. The old Republic at least knew victory in defeat – in that its spirit long survived its physical destruction. Contemporary Poland, in contrast, may be said to have experienced defeat in victory, in that the re-establishment of the state has failed to eliminate many of the humiliations and oppressions of the past.

Yet Poland's interminable defeats must always be viewed in proportion. In 1797, the Partitioning Powers, who had just destroyed the old Republic, solemnly swore to banish the very name of 'Poland' from the record. There have been several moments – after the insurrections of 1830 and 1863, and, above all, during the Nazi-Soviet Pact of 1939–41 – when it appeared that their oath might be fulfilled. But nowadays anyone can see that Poland does exist both in body and soul. This country seems to be inseparable from the catastrophes and crises, on which, paradoxically, it thrives. Poland is permanently on the brink of collapse. But somehow, Poland has never failed to revive, and, in spheres perhaps more important than the political and economic, to flourish.

* * * * *

The final preparation of a large typescript further increases an author's indebtedness to collaborators and patrons. In this regard, I wish to acknowledge the assistance of Mr. Ken Wass of University College, London, who undertook the technical drawing of most of my maps and diagrams: of Andrzej Suchcitz and Marek Siemaszko, who compiled the index: of the Publications Committee of the School of Slavonic and East European Studies: and especially of the De Brzezie Lanckoroński Foundation, which provided a generous subsidy.

Norman Davies.

Wolvercote, 3 May 1979.

CONTENTS

MAPS AND DIAGRAMS

LIST OF ILLUSTRATIONS

Plates follow page 356

NOTES ON THE ILLUSTRATIONS

Volume II

Plate I Paul Delaroche (1797–1856), potrait of *Prince Adam Jerzy Czartoryski* in exile in Paris, c. 1848. *Muzeum Narodowe (Wilanów)*.

Franciszek Paderewski (1767–1819), posthumous portrait of *Prince Józef Poniatowski* as Marshal of France, painted in 1814 from an earlier portrait by Bacciarelli. *Muzeum Narodowe (Wilanów)*.

Plate II W. Wodzinowski, *Odpoczynek żniwiarzy* (The Harvesters' Rest). *Muzeum Narodowe (Warsaw)*.

(Anon.) *Peasant Devotions at Easter.* *Biblioteka Narodowa (Warsaw)*.

Plate III Stanisław Witkiewicz (1851–1915), founder of the so-called 'Zakopane Style', father of the painter and dramatist of the same name. *Ranny powstaniec* (The Wounded Insurrectionary) – a scene from the January Rising (1863). *Muzeum Narodowe (Warsaw)*.

Aleksander Gierymski (1850–1902), together with his brother Maksymilian, worked with the Munich School. His Warsaw period, 1879–84 produced many memorable scenes of Jewish life. His *Święto trąbek* (Feast of the Trumpets, 1884) shows the *Tashlikh* ceremony of the Jewish New Year in the Powiśle district. Following the text of Micah vii, 19, 'Thou shalt cast all their sins into the depth of the sea', orthodox Jews sang and prayed beside the nearest stretch of water, in this case the River Vistula. Note the Kerbedź Bridge, and the accordionist. *Muzeum Narodowe (Warsaw)*.

Plate IV Walenty Wańkowicz (1800–42), portrait painter active first in Minsk, later in Paris. One of several versions of his allegory, *Mickiewicz na Judahu skale*. (Adam Mickiewicz on the Rock of Judah, 1840), which likens the role of poet after the suppression of the November Rising by

the Russians to that of the biblical prophets after the destruction of Jerusalem by the Babylonians.
Muzeum Narodowe (Warsaw).

Plate IV   Aleksander Lesser (1814–84), *Smierć Wandy* (The Death of Wanda). Wanda, the daughter of the legendary King Krak, refused to marry a German prince, and then, in order to avoid a tribal war, drowned herself in the Vistula. A popular patriotic tale in the late nineteenth century.
Muzeum Narodowe (Warsaw).

Plate V   Kazimierz Sichulski (1879–1942), painter and caricaturist from Lwów. This sketch of *Józef Piłsudski* places the Marshał in the company of Stańczyk, the court jester of Sigismund I, and of Piotr Skarga, the confessor of Sigismund III – both of them severe critics of their compatriots.
Biblioteka Narodowa (Warsaw).

Plate VI   L. Wintorowski, *Taczanki naprzód!* (Gun-carriages ahead!) – an incident from the Polish–Soviet War of 1920 where a detachment of the 13th Krechowiecki Uhlans cuts down a Bolshevik artillery unit. (The *tachanka* was a horse-drawn heavy machine-gun battery.)
Sikorski Museum (London).

E. Mesjasz, *Bitwa pod Mokrą* (The Battle of River Mokra) – an eye-witness reconstruction of a fierce frontier action near Częstochowa on 1 September 1939 when the dismounted Volhynian Cavalry Brigade repulsed the 4th Panzer Division with the loss of twenty tanks.
Sikorski Museum (London).

Plate VII   W. Siwek, *Entry to Block II,* Auschwitz, 1943. A naive sketch of the infamous punishment and experimentation block of the Nazi death-camp at Auschwitz (Oświęcim).
Sikorski Museum (London).

Long Live the Government of National Unity – a photograph despite appearances. Bydgoszcz, June 1945 – a political rally in support of the coalition government (TRJN). Platform speakers in Polish uniforms surrounded by the flags of Great Britain and the USA, and by portraits of Mikołajczyk and Bierut.

Plate VIII   Aleksander Kobzdej (1920–72), *Podaj cegłę* (Pass the brick, 1952). An evocation of postwar Reconstruction in the obligatory Socialist Realist style of the early 1950s.
Muzeum Narodowe (Warsaw).

Plate VIII   Vlastimil HOFMAN (1881–1970), symbolist painter associated with the Academy of Fine Arts (ASP) in Cracow. *Spowiedź* (Confession) contrasts the simple devotion of the Polish peasant in the timeless countryside with the ambivalent attitudes of the Church.
Muzeum Narodowe (Warsaw).

ABBREVIATIONS

AK	*Armia Krajowa*	(Home Army, 1942–5, continuator of SZP, ZWZ and SZK)
AL	*Armia Ludowa*	(People's Army, 1944–5)
BBWR	*Bezpartyjny Blok dla Współpracy z Rządem*	(Non-Party Bloc for Co-operation with the Government, 1928–35)
BCh	*Bataliony Chłopskie*	(Peasant Battalions, 1940–4)
BMN	*Blok Mniejszości Narodowych 1922–9*	(Bloc of National Minorities)
BNR	–	(Byelorussian National Republic, 1918)
CAP	*Centralna Agencja Prasowa*	(Central Press Agency, 1915–18)
CBKP	*Centralne Biuro Komunistów Polskich*	(Central Bureau of Polish Communists, Moscow, 1943–5)
ChD	*Chrześcijańska Demokracja (Chadecja)*	(Christian Democratic (Party), 1902–37)
CK	*Centralny Komitet*	(Central Committee)
CKL	*Centralny Komitet Ludowy*	(Central People's Committee, 1943–4)
CKO	*Centralny Komitet Obywatelski*	(Central Citizens' Committee)
CKR	*Centralna Komisja Rewizyjna*	(Central Review Commission)
COP	*Centralny Okręg Przemysłowy*	(Central Industrial Area, 1936–9)
CPSU	–	(Communist Party of the Soviet Union)
CUP	*Centralny Urząd Planowania*	(Central Planning Office, 1945–9)
d.	*Denar*	(Penny)

FJN	*Front Jedności Narodowej*	(Front of National Unity, 1956–)
GG	*Generalna Gubernia*	(General-Gouvernement – Nazi Government in occupied Poland 1939–45)
GL	*Gwardia Ludowa*	(People's Guard, 1943–4)
gr.	*Groszy*	(Polish groat)
GUKPPiW	*Główny Urząd Kontroli Prasy, Przedstawień i Widowisk*	(Main Office for the Control of the Press, Theatre, and Cultural Spectacles [Censorship])
KBW	*Korpus Bezpieczeństwa Wewnętrznego*	(Internal Security Corps 1945–)
KNAPP	*Komitet Narodowy Amerykanów Pochodzenia Polskiego*	(National Committee of Americans of Polish Origin, 1944–)
KNP	*Komitet Narodowy Polski*	(Polish National Committee, 1831–2, 1914–15, 1917–19)
KP	*Królestwo Polskie*	(Kingdom of Poland, 1815–64(74))
KP	*Komisja Planowania*	(Planning Commission, 1949–)
KPP	*Komunistyczna Partia Polski*	(Communist Party of Poland, 1926–38)
KPRP	*Komunistyczna Partia Robotnicza Polska*	(Polish Communist Workers' Party, 1918–26)
KRN	*Krajowa Rada Narodowa*	(National Home Council, 1944)
KRP	*Krajowa Reprezentacja Polityczna*	(Home Political Representative Body, 1943–5; continuator of PKP)
KUL	*Katolicki Uniwersytet Lubelski*	(Catholic University of Lublin, 1918–)
KWC	*Kierownictwo Walki Cywilnej*	(Directorship of the Civilian Struggle, 1941–3)
KWP	*Kierownictwo Walki Podziemnej*	(Directorship of the Underground Struggle, 1943–5: continuator of KWC)
LOT	(LOT = Flight)	(Polish Airlines, 1929–)

m.	–	(Mark)
MO	*Milicja Obywatelska*	(Citizens' Militia, 1945–)
ND	*Narodowa Demokracja* (*Endecja*)	(*See* SN-D)
NIK	*Naczelna Izba Kontroli*	(Supreme Chamber of Control, 1957–)
NKL	*Naczelny Komitet Ludowy*	(Supreme People's Committee, 1944–5: continuator of CKL)
NKN	*Naczelny Komitet Narodowy*	(Supreme National Committee, Cracow, 1914–17)
NOW	*Narodowa Organizacja Wojskowa*	(National Military Organization, 1940–2)
NPR	*Narodowa Partia Robotnicza*	(National Workers' Party, 1920–37)
NRL	*Naczelna Rada Ludowa*	(Supreme People's Council, Poznań, 1918–19)
NSR	*Narodowe Stronnictwo Robotników*	(National Workers' Party, 1920)
NSZ	*Narodowe Siły Zbrojne*	(National Armed Forces, 1942–4)
NZR	*Narodowy Związek Robotniczy*	(National Workers' Union, 1905–20)
ORMO	*Ochotnicza Rezerwa Milicji Obywatelskiej*	(Volunteer Reserve of the People's Militia, 1946–)
OWP	*Obóz Wielkiej Polski*	(Camp of Great Poland, 1926–33)
OZON	*Obóz Zjednoczenia Narodowego*	(Camp of National Unification, 1937–9)
PAL	*Polska Armia Ludowa*	(Polish People's Army, 1943–4)
PAN	*Polska Akademia Nauk*	(Polish Academy of Sciences, 1951–)
(P)AU	*(Polska) Akademia Umiejętności*	(Polish Academy of Learning, 1872–1951)
PGR	*Państwowe gospodarstwo rolne*	(State agricultural unit – collective farm)
PKI	*Polski Komitet Informacyjny*	(Polish Information Committee, London, 1915–17)

PKP	1. *Polskie Koleje Państwowe*	(Polish State Railways, 1918–)
	2. *Polityczny Komitet Porozumiewawczy*	(Political Liaison Committee, 1940–3)
PKL	*Polski Komitet Likwidacyjny*	(Polish Liquidation Committee, Cracow, 1918)
PKO	*Powszechna Kasa Oszczędności*	(Universal Savings Bank)
PKWN	*Polski Komitet Wyzwolenia Narodowego*	(Polish Committee of National Liberation, 1944)
PON	*Polska Organizacja Narodowa*	(Polish National Organization, 1914)
POP	*Pełniący Obowiązki Polaków*	([Soviet Citizens] executing the functions of Poles, 1945–)
POW	*Polska Organizacja Wojskowa*	(Polish Military Organization, 1914–18)
POWN	*Polska Organizacja Walki i Niepodległości*	(Polish Organization of Struggle and Independence, 1944–5)
PPR	*Polska Partia Robotnicza*	(Polish Workers' Party, 1942–8)
PPS	*Polska Partia Socjalistyczna*	(Polish Socialist Party, 1892–1948)
PPSD	*Polska Partia Socjaldemokratyczna Galicji i Śląska*	(Polish Social-Democratic Party, 1892–1918)
PS	*Polscy Socjaliści*	(Polish Socialists, 1940–3)
PSL	*Polskie Stronnictwo Ludowe*	(Polish People's [Peasant] Movement, 1895–1947)
PTH	*Polskie Towarzystwo Historyczne*	(Polish Historical Society, 1886–)
PUR	*Państwowy Urząd Repatriacyjny*	(State Repatriation Office, 1944–50)
PZPR	*Polska Zjednoczona Partia Robotnicza*	(Polish United Workers' Party, 1948–)
RGO	*Rada Główna Opiekuńcza,*	(Main Welfare Council 1916–18, 1940–44)
RJN	*Rada Jedności Narodowej*	(Council of National Unity, 1943–4)
RM	*Reichsmark*	—

RPPS	*Robotnicza Partia Polskich Socjalistów*	(Workers' Party of Polish Socialists, 1943–5, continuator of PS)
RPZ	*Rada Pomocy Żydom*	(Council of Help for the Jews, (1942–4)
RTRP	*Rząd Tymczasowy Rzeczypospolitej Polskiej*	(Provisional Government of the Polish Republic, 1945)
SSC	*Stronnictwo Społeczno-Chrześcijańskie*	(Christian Social Movement)
SCh	*Stronnictwo Chłopskie*	(Peasant Movement, 1926–31)
SChD	*Stronnictwo Chrześcijańsko-Demokratyczne (Chadecja)*	(Christian Democratic Movement, 1902–37)
SD	*Stronnictwo Demokratyczne*	(Democratic Movement, 1938–)
SDKPiL	*Socjal-demokracja Królestwa Polskiego i Litwy*	(Social Democracy of the Kingdom of Poland and Lithuania, 1898–1918)
SL	*Stronnictwo Ludowe*	(People's [Peasant] Movement, an offshoot of the PSL, 1935–45)
SN	*Stronnictwo Narodowe*	(National Movement, 1928–44, continuator of ZL-N)
SN-D	*Stronnictwo Narodowo-Demokratyczne*	(National Democratic Movement, forerunner of ZLN, 1897–1919)
SP	*Stronnictwo Pracy*	(Labour Movement, 1937–50)
SRC	*Stowarzyszenie Robotników Chrześcijańskich*	(Association of Christian Workers)
SZK	*Siły Zbrojne w Kraju*	(Home Armed Forces, 1940–2)
SZP	*Służba Zwycięstwa Polskiego*	(Polish Victory Service, 1939)
TCL	*Towarzystwo Czytelni Ludowych*	(Society for Popular Reading-rooms, 1880–1939)
TDP	*Towarzystwo Demokratyczne Polskie*	(Polish Democratic Society, 1832–62)
TNP	*Towarzystwo Nauki Polskiej*	(Polish Scientific Society)

TOL	*Towarzystwo Oświaty Ludowej*	(Society for Popular Education)
TON	*Tajna Organizacja Nauczycielska*	(Secret Teachers' Organization, 1939–45)
TOR	*Towarzystwo Osiedli Robotniczych*	(Society for Workers' Housing Estates, 1934–44)
TRS	*Tymczasowa Rada Stanu*	(Provisional Council of State, 1916–18)
UB	*Urząd Bezpieczeństwa*	(Security Office)
UNR	–	(Ukrainian National Republic, 1918–20)
USW	*Urząd do Spraw Wyznań*	(Office for Denominational Affairs)
WiN	*Wolność i Niezawisłość*	(Freedom and Independence, 1945–7)
WOP	*Wojsko Ochrony Pogranicza*	(Frontier Defence Force, 1945–)
WP	*Wojsko Polskie*	(Polish Army)
WRN	*Wolność, Równość, Niepodległość*	(Freedom, Equality, Independence, 1940–5, off shoot of PPS)
WTD	*Warszawskie Towarzystwo Dobroczynne*	(Warsaw Charitable Society)
WVHA	*Wirtschafts – und Verwaltungs Hauptamt:*	(Nazi Chief Economic and Administrative Office)
WZO	–	(World Zionist Organization)
ZEP	*Zjednoczenie Emigracji Polskiej*	(Amalgamation of the Polish Emigration, 1837–46)
Zet	*Związek Młodzieży Polskiej*	(Union of Polish Youth, 1887–)
ZHP	*Zwiazek Harcerstwa Polskiego*	(Polish Scouts Association, 1910–48)
ZL-N	*Związek Ludowo-Narodowy*	(People's National Union, 1919–28, continuator of SN-D, and forerunner of SN)
ZLP	*Związek Ludu Polskiego*	(Polish People's Union, 1872–80)
zł.	*Złoty*	(Originally gold crown)
złp	*Złoty polski*	(Polish złoty)

ZMW	*Związek Młodzieży Wiejskiej, Wici*	(Union of Rural Youth, 'Beacon Fires', 1928–48)
ZSL	*Zjednoczone Stronnictwo Ludowe*	(United People's [Peasant] Movement, 1949–)
(S) ZSP	*(Socjalistyczne) Zrzeszenie Studentów Polskich*	((Socialist) Association of Polish Students, 1950–)
ZURL	–	(People's Republic of the Western Ukraine, 1918–19)
ZWC	*Związek Walki Czynnej*	(Union of Active Struggle, 1908–14)
ZWZ	*Związek Walki Zbrojnej*	(Union for the Armed Struggle, 1939–42)
ZZZ	*Zrzeszenie Związków Zawodowych*	(Trade Unions Organization, 1949)
ZZZ(P)	*Zjednoczenie Związków Zawodowych (Polskich)*	(Amalgamation of (Polish) Trade Unions)

CHRONOLOGY

1795–1918 PERIOD OF THE PARTITIONS
1797–1802   Polish Legions in French Service
1807–1813(–15) Duchy of Warsaw
1815   Congress Kingdom of Poland formed (suspended 1832–61, abolished 1874)
1815   Grand Duchy of Posen formed (abolished 1848)
1815   Republic of Cracow formed (abolished 1846)
1830–1831   November Rising: Russo-Polish War: Great Emigration
1846   Galician Jacquerie: Cracow Revolution
1848   Posnanian Rising: emancipation of serfs in Austria
1855   Death of Adam Mickiewicz
1861–3   Administration of Alexander Wielopolski in Congress Kingdom
1863–1864   January Rising: final abolition of serfdom (1864) in Russian Poland
1867   Galician Autonomy established (to 1918)
1872   Polish Academy of Sciences founded in Cracow
1905–1907   Revolution in Russian Poland
1914   Emergence of Piłsudski's Polish Legions (disbanded 1917)
1915   Russian occupation ended by German victory on Eastern Front
1916   Restoration of Kingdom of Poland by Germany
1917   President Wilson's Fourteen Points
1918   Allied Governments recognize principle of Polish Independence (3 June)

1918–1945 PERIOD OF INDEPENDENCE (Second Republic)

1918	Joseph Piłsudski assumes power in Warsaw (11 November)
1918–1921	Six border wars fought against neighbouring powers.
1919	Treaty of Versailles with Germany
1920	Battle of Warsaw (13–19 August)
1921	Treaty of Riga (18 March) with Soviet Russia
	March Constitution enacted (21 March)
1926	Piłsudski's Coup d'État (12 May): Sanacja Regime begins
1932	Pact of Non-aggression with USSR (25 July)
1934	Pact of Non-aggression with Germany (5 January)
1935	New Constitution enacted (23 March)
	Death of J. Piłsudski (12 May)
1936	Launching of Central Industrial Region
1939	British Guarantee of Poland (31 March)
	Nazi–Soviet Pact (23 August):
1939–1945	Second World War
1939	September Campaign: Poland partitioned by Germany and USSR (28 September)
1941	German invasion of USSR: Polish–Soviet Treaty
	Implementation of Nazi 'Final Solution' begins
1943	USSR severs diplomatic relations with Polish Government-in-Exile:
	Warsaw Ghetto Rising (April)
1944	Warsaw Rising (1 August–2 October)
1944–5	Liberation: complete occupation of Polish lands by Soviet Army
1945	Transfer of international recognition from Polish Government-in-Exile in London to Provisional Government of National Unity in Warsaw (28 June)
	Potsdam Conference (July)

Since 1944 PEOPLE'S POLAND

1944	Lublin Committee formed by Soviet patronage (22 July)
1944–1947	Civil War: liquidation of all resistance to Soviet supremacy
1945	Formation of Provisional Government of National Unity
1946	Referendum (30 June)
1947	First Elections to Sejm (19 January): Allied protest
1948	Formation of Polish United Workers' Party: One-Party State launched
1948–1956	Period of Stalinism
1952	Constitution of Polish People's Republic (22 July)
1955	Formation of Warsaw Pact by USSR
1956	VIII Plenum of Party independently elects W. Gomułka as First Secretary
Since 1956	Poland governed by national communist regime
1958	Re-constitution of COMECON (23 May)
1966	Celebration of the Polish Millennium
1968	March events:
1970	Baltic Riots: Fall of Gomułka: E. Gierek First Secretary
1976	Constitutional amendments
	June events: rise of political opposition
1978	Cardinal Karol Wojtyła elected Pope John Paul II (16 October)

PART ONE
Poland Destroyed and Reconstructed,
1795–1945

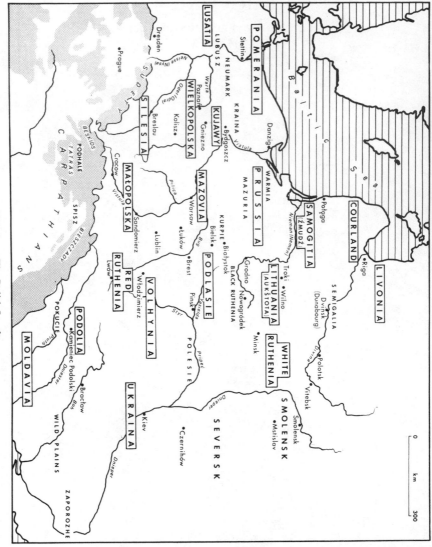

Map 1.   The Polish Lands

CHAPTER ONE

NARÓD:

The Growth of the Modern Nation (1772-1945)

In the western democracies, Nationalism has rarely commanded much respect or sympathy. In the two centuries since the concepts of nationality, of national sovereignty, and of national liberation first found coherent expression in the French Revolution, they have spread to all parts of Europe and thence to all corners of the globe; but they have carried less conviction in the English-speaking world than in most other areas. In the established political communities of Britain and America in particular, where democratic institutions have been solidly based on the consent of the majority for longer than anyone remembers, there has been no great incentive to question the legitimacy of the state or to worry unduly about the rights of minorities. Until recently, the separate interests of the Scots, the Welsh, the English, or even the Irish, aroused little more than intermittent bouts of irritation amongst the British public, as did those of the Blacks, the Amerindians, the Chicanos, or the Quebecois in North America. Supremely confident of the universal benefits of Freedom and Democracy as enshrined in the Westminster tradition or in the American Constitution, the leaders of liberal opinion usually saw Nationalism as an unnecessary diversion from their main purposes, and tended to think of it as inherently illiberal and undemocratic. In many liberal eyes, 'nations' are selfish, irrational, and disruptive, almost by definition; whilst 'states', whatever their present defects, are all at least potentially reformable. Traditional Anglo-American priorities in this matter were clearly formulated long ago by that doyen of Victorian historians, Lord Acton. 'A state can sometimes create a nation,' wrote Acton; 'but for a nation to create a state is going against nature.'[1]

This viewpoint, which permeates much historical writing in English, obviously stands opposed to developments in Eastern Europe, where the growth of Nationalism, of nations, and of

3

national states, has generated the most significant changes of the last two hundred years. On the one hand, it refuses to contemplate the possibility that in certain circumstances dictatorship may enjoy popular support or that democracies may entertain malevolent or aggressive designs. In this, it contradicts much practical evidence. On the other hand, through a characteristic obsession with legal rules and procedures, it places unwarranted faith in the efficacy of constitutional reforms which may bear little relevance to prevailing social and cultural conditions. Hence, in areas such as Eastern Europe where the rule of Law has usually been subordinated to the dictates of political convenience, western statesmen have usually set greater store on the reform of existing states than on the creation of new ones. Incorrigibly sanguine about the willingness of autocrats and totalitarians to confess their faults and to mend their ways, they hope eternally against hope that the status quo can somehow be saved without recourse to violence and revolution. They long as earnestly today for the 'liberalization' of the Soviet Union as their predecessors once longed for the reform of Tsarist Russia and for the preservation of Austria–Hungary. Fearful that the new national states might prove to be just as repressive as the dynastic empires, they have accepted their formation with reluctance and with no small scepticism. Paradoxically therefore, and in clear contradiction of their supposedly liberal principles, they have never hastened to give active support to the protracted struggles of national movements against autocracy and tyranny.

In Eastern Europe, where the prevailing political environment has differed widely from that in the west, attitudes towards Nationalism have been very different. So long as the dynastic empires remained in place, the main struggle for power lay between the ultra-conservative champions of the ruling establishment and the motley ranks of revolutionaries who saw no possible hope of progress until the imperial regimes had been replaced by some new, more equitable form of state-entity. Reformism of the western kind was the preserve of a small, intellectual, and middle-class minority. In this context, the adherents of the numerous national movements, whose ultimate goal of forming independent national states was fundamentally incompatible with the integrity of the empires, must be counted among the revolutionary elements, even though they may often have recoiled from the use of revolutionary methods. They saw no contradiction whatsoever between Nationalism and Democracy, preferring to view the one as the natural guarantor of the other. Inevitably, they always included a hard core of activists devoted to the classic paradox of fighting democracy by undemocratic means. For the activists, recourse to violence had no necessary connection with their own philosophies or aspirations, but was dictated by the violent nature of regimes against which they were pitted. In situations where all political life had been frozen solid by generations of autocratic controls, the idea of gradual reform or of 'political evolution', like that of melting butter in a refrigerator, has always been unrealistic. What is more, the spectacle of western liberals comfortably reproving the conduct of people whose ideals were repeatedly tested in the fire, is as ridiculous as it is offensive. It is depressing to realize that western liberals have an unfortunate tendency to take the side of the powers-that-be against the very people in Eastern Europe who most nearly share their own principles.

In the last analysis, of course, differences of opinion about the ethics of Nationalism cannot be resolved. Like Democracy or Autocracy, Nationalism in itself is neither virtuous nor vicious. It can only be judged in relation to the particular motives of its particular adherents. According to circumstance, it has been espoused both by noble idealists and also by scoundrels for whom the means is an end in itself. There can be democratic nationalists and undemocratic nationalists, magnanimous nationalists and mean nationalists, nationalist moderates and nationalist fanatics. The only thing that they have in common is the conviction that their nations have an inalienable right to control their own destiny. For the historian, Nationalism, and the nations which Nationalism has brought into being, are objective phenomena whose doings have to be logged and described. Their ultimate morality must be left for others to decide. In this, the history of Polish Nationalism, and of the Polish nation, is no exception.

* * * * *

For most of the 150 years, from the abdication of Stanisław-August on 25 November 1795 to the retreat of the German Army from Warsaw on 17 January 1945, 'Poland' was little more than a name. Like Armenia or Macedonia today, names redolent of ancient kings and empires, it often had no practical significance beyond that of a cultural, linguistic, or administrative area lying in the territories of three separate states. None of the states which were constructed on the lands of the former Polish–Lithuanian Republic could claim to be its successor. Few included even the greater part of the people who might have called themselves 'Poles'. The Duchy of Warsaw (1807–15) barely disguised the reality of Napoleonic occupation. The Grand Duchy of Posen in Prussia (1815–49) and the Kingdom of Galicia and Lodomeria (1772–1918) in Austria gave fine titles to imperial provinces. The former was suppressed for demanding the fully autonomous status which the latter did not receive till 1867. The Congress Kingdom of Poland, the *Kongresówka* (1815–74), and the Republic of Cracow (1815–46), were both abolished in defiance of the international statutes which had brought them into existence. The revival of the 'Kingdom of Poland' under German auspices in November 1916 was entirely embryonic, and that, too, miscarried. Like most of the other experiments in Polish statehood over the previous century, it mocked the intelligence of those it sought to satisfy. In this light, the Second Republic (1918–39) of the inter-war period, must be viewed as a brief interlude in the over-all stream of statelessness. Its government, which was driven into exile in September 1939, is still in existence in London nearly forty years later, and might still be regarded in terms of Polish law as the repository of constitutional legality. But it has never regained control of its territory, and in June 1945 lost the formal recognition of most foreign powers. Even the People's Republic of Poland (founded in 1945, formally constituted in 1952) which has exercised effective authority since the Second World War, bears serious limitations on its sovereignty. Thus, for the greater part of modern history, statelessness has been the Poles' normal condition. Genuine independence has rarely been more than a pipe-dream. (See Diagram A.)

During the five or six generations when it had no concrete

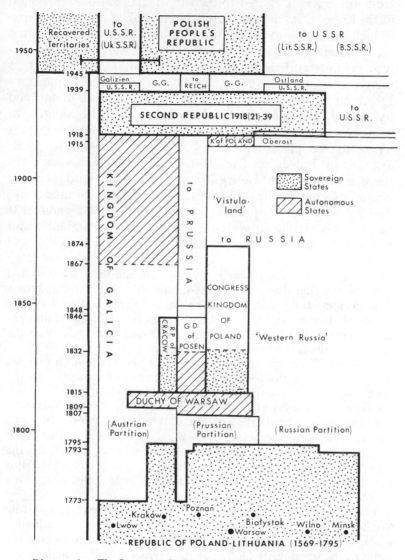

Diagram A. The Successor States of Poland–Lithuania, (1772–1945)

existence, 'Poland', as an abstraction, could be remembered from the past, or aspired to for the future, but only imagined in the present. It had not merely been broken into three parts; it had been vaporized, transposed into thin air, fragmented into millions of invisible particles. There were as many different Polands as there were people who cared to perceive it, as many 'kings of Poland' as cared to reign in their imaginary kingdoms. Its essentially spiritual nature has been underlined by all the most sensitive foreign observers of the nineteenth century — from Helmuth von Moltke, who took an instant liking to the place during his visit in 1828–31, to J. H. Sutherland Edwards, *The Times* correspondent, who was there in 1861–2, and Georg Brandes, the Dane, who recorded his impressions in the 1880s and 1890s.[2] Its attributes could best be described by poetry, by metaphor, and by parable. It presented a challenge which exercised all the romantic and patriotic poets, but none so effectively as Adam Mickiewicz:

In the beginning, there was belief in one God, and there was Freedom in the world. And there were no laws, only the will of God, and there were no lords and slaves, only patriarchs and their children. But later the people turned aside from the Lord their God, and made themselves graven images, and bowed down . . . Thus God sent upon them the greatest punishment which is Slavery . . .

Then the Kings, renouncing Christ, made new idols which they set up in the sight of the people, and bade them bow down . . . So the kings made an idol for the French and called it HONOUR; and this was the same that was called . . . the Golden Calf. And for the Spaniards, their king made an idol called POLITICAL POWER; and this was the same that the Assyrians worshipped as Baal . . . And for the English, their king made an idol called SEA POWER AND COMMERCE, which was the same as Mammon . . . And for the Germans, an idol was made called BROTSINN or Prosperity which was the same as Moloch . . . And the nations forgot they had sprung from one Father . . .

Finally, in idolatrous Europe there rose three rulers . . . a Satanic Trinity, Frederick, whose name signifieth 'Friend of Peace' . . . Catherine, which in Greek signifieth 'pure' . . . and Maria Theresa, who bore the name of the immaculate Mother of the Saviour . . . Their names were thus three blasphemies, their lives three crimes, their memory three curses . . . And this Trinity fashioned a new idol, which was unknown to the ancients, and they called it INTEREST . . .

But the Polish nation alone did not bow down . . . And finally Poland said: 'Whosoever will come to me shall be free and equal, for I am FREEDOM'. But the Kings when they heard were frightened in their hearts, and said . . . 'Come, let us slay this nation'. And they conspired together . . . And they crucified the Polish Nation, and laid it in its grave, and cried out 'We have slain and buried Freedom'. But they cried out foolishly . . .

For the Polish Nation did not die. Its body lieth in the grave; but its spirit has descended into the abyss, that is into the private lives of people who suffer slavery in their country . . . But on the third day the soul shall return again to the body, and the Nation shall arise, and free all the peoples of Europe from slavery.[3]

Kazimierz Brodziński (1791—1835) expressed the same thoughts in simpler words:

> Hail, O Christ, Thou Lord of Men!
> Poland, in Thy footsteps treading
> Like Thee suffers, at Thy bidding;
> Like Thee, too, shall rise again. [4]

The implications of Poland's 'Descent into the Tomb' affect the historian's task most profoundly. Many of the social, economic, constitutional, and diplomatic themes which dominate studies of the pre-Partition period, come to an abrupt end. In so far as the descendants of the citizens of the Polish—Lithuanian Republic were incorporated into the states of Russia, Prussia, or Austria, the material aspects of their lives form subjects not for Polish History but for Russian, Prussian, or Austrian History. At the same time, new themes assume unprecedented importance. In the realm of political and international action, Poland emerged at the most in sporadic fits. But in the realm of political ideas, it occupied a position of uninterrupted importance. For Poland was now an Idea. It existed in men's minds, even if it could not always be observed on the ground or in the material world. Henceforward, the historian of Poland must focus his attention more on men's beliefs and aspirations. In particular, in political affairs, he must examine the central phenomenon of the growth of the Polish nation — a theme to which, in the absence of a Polish state, all others must be subordinated.

For *Nationality* is essentially a belief — a deep sense of conviction concerning one's personal identity. It is not inherent in human kind, and in European life is hard to discover at any period prior to the French Revolution. In the nine-teenth and twentieth centuries, it has developed out of all previous proportions, and in some areas of the world, such as Eastern Europe, has come to dominate all aspects of political and social life. Unfortunately, if the cynics are to be trusted, it is a belief which is based on mistaken criteria. As Ernest Renan once remarked, 'a nation is a community united by common error with regard to its origins, and by common aversion with regard to its neighbours.' At all events, the modern *Nation* can only be effectively defined as a social group whose individual members, being convinced rightly or wrongly of their common descent and destiny, share that common sense of identity. *National consciousness* relates to the degree of people's awareness of belonging to their nation. *Nationalism,* in consequence, is a doctrine shared by all political movements which seek to create a nation by arousing people's awareness of their nationality, and to mobilize their feelings into a vehicle for political action. In this sense, a *nationalist* is someone who approves or advocates the aims of Nationalism.[5]

Anglo-Saxon readers need to be warned against the com-plexities which beset the terminology of this subject. Leaving aside the fact that many writers use terms such as 'nation', 'nationality', 'people', 'race', and 'state' indiscriminately, with no thought for their precise meanings, it is essential to realize that usage varies widely. Both the British and the Americans belong to political communities where the growth of the modern nation has been patronized by the ruling authorities of the state, and where as a result, 'nationality' has been systematically confused with 'citizenship'. Americans in particular tend to talk of 'the nation' as a synonym for the 'citizens', the 'inhabitants of the country', the 'population', or even 'the territory' of the state. In the English language, 'nationality' refers less to an individual's private convictions, but rather to officialdom's estimate of his fitness to acquire the legal status of a citizen. It is something which one acquires not by reflecting on one's personal beliefs, but by applying to the Home Office or to the Department of Immigration. In this sense, a 'British national' is coterminous with official labels such as 'HM Subject' or 'Citizen of the United Kingdom and Colonies'; an 'American national' refers to anyone who possesses the legal status of a citizen of the United States of America.

The Poles, in contrast, belong to a community which has acquired its modern sense of nationality in active opposition to the policies of the states in which they lived. Polish nationality is a belief which at various times officialdom of the partitioning powers strove to suppress. The Polish nation was recruited from people who, whilst conceding that they were Russian, Prussian, or Austrian subjects, steadfastly refused to admit that they were 'Russians', 'Prussians', or 'Austrians'. In such circumstances, Polish Nationalism was largely propagated by activists who sought to use national consciousness for political purposes entirely contrary to those of the state authorities. To this extent, the Poles have shared the experience of many stateless nations in Europe — from the Bulgars and the Basques, to the Walloons, the Wends, or the Welsh. (In this connection, it is interesting to note how precise is the official terminology of present-day Eastern Europe, where the distinction between 'citizenship' and 'nationality' is always made. In Soviet documents, for example, all residents of the USSR are described as 'Soviet citizens', whilst leaving them free to declare their own nationality as 'Russian', 'Byelorussian', 'Georgian', 'Jewish', 'Uzbek', 'Yakut', or whatever. Unfortunately, English usage habitually refers to all Soviet citizens as 'Russians' irrespective of their nationality, thereby smudging one of the most important features of East European life.)

The Polish case is specially complicated by the fact that Polish statehood, though intermittent, was not completely absent. In the old Republic, prior to 1795, Polish nationality could indeed be defined in terms of loyalty to the state. The 'Polish nation' was usually reserved as an appellation for those inhabitants who enjoyed full civil and political rights, and thus for the nobility alone. It did not refer to a man's native language, his religion, or ethnic origin. Hence, in this context, there were many 'Poles', who in modern terms might not be so described; and there were masses of Polish-speaking inhabitants, in the peasantry or bourgeoisie, who did not regard themselves as Poles. In extreme instances, as in the case of a seventeenth-century cleric, a man might describe himself as *canonicus cracoviensis, natione Polonus, gente Ruthenus, origine Judaeus* – 'a Canon of Cracow, a member of the Polish nation, of the Ruthenian people, of Jewish origin'. Once the Republic was destroyed, however, the old terms gradually lost their validity. Old words assumed new meanings, and were used by different people in different ways and for different purposes. The word 'nation' shed its former political connotation and increasingly assumed its modern cultural and ethnic overtones. The word 'Pole' was abandoned in relation to those peoples of the former Republic who were now developing their separate national identities as Germans, Jews, Ukrainians, Byelorussians, or Lithuanians; whilst it was commonly expanded to embrace everyone who could speak the Polish language.

Even so, many ambiguities persisted. Each of the bureaucracies of the partitioning powers had their own terminological conventions. In Russian official usage, a man living on the left bank of the River Bug might be called a 'Pole', in that he was a citizen of the Congress Kingdom of Poland; his neighbour on the right bank of the river, even if he were the other man's brother, was a 'Russian'. After 1874, when the Congress Kingdom was abolished, they were all classified 'Russians', whether they liked it or not. Even among the Poles themselves, wide variations prevailed. People who looked for the restoration of a state resembling the old Republic, continued to think of Polishness in non-national terms. Mickiewicz, for one, saw no reason why he should not be a 'Pole' and a 'Lithuanian' at one and the same time. This apostle of Polish culture began his most famous poem with an invocation not to 'Poland', but to 'Lithuania': *Litwo! Ojczyzno moja! ty jesteś jak zdrowie* (O Lithuania, my Fatherland! You are like health to me).[6] At a later date, Józef Piłsudski expressed the same sort of sentiment. Other people, whose aspirations departed completely from all historical precedents, came to think of Polishness as a quality reserved exclusively for Polish-speakers, or even for Polish Catholics.

So, here again, great caution is necessary. Nationalists, no less than state officials have a strong propensity for turning terminology to their own uses. For one thing, since the term 'nationalist' quickly acquires from official usage a pejorative sense equivalent to 'separatist' or 'troublemaker', they prefer to describe themselves as 'patriots' or 'activists'. For another, they adopt their own private criteria to raise the concept of the nation into that of an exclusive community, projecting modern standards of national cohesion into the past, disregarding the differing degrees of identification which individuals may have professed, and ignoring the complicated web of conflicting loyalties to which everyone was subjected. Thus, in nationalist argument, a Polish-speaking peasant or a man with a Polish-sounding name will often be described as 'Poles' whether they have any sense of belonging to the Polish community or not, 'a true Pole' cannot at one and the same time be the loyal servant of an 'alien' state; and the Polish nation is viewed as a compact community manfully defending itself against 'enemies', 'aliens', foreign 'oppressors', and 'occupiers'. In nationalist minds, the idea that the Prussian sergeant, the Russian bureaucrat, or the Austrian Count might easily have been no less Polish than the people he was allegedly tormenting, is entirely unacceptable. Reality, of course, was rather different. Many individuals are identified with more than one nation; and no nation can fairly claim to enjoy the undivided allegiance of all its nationals. When talking of 'the Poles', it is important to remember that one is using a form of shorthand to define the common denominator in a variegated collection of human beings who might separately be better described as 'potential Poles', 'possible Poles', 'proto-Poles', 'part-Poles', 'semi-Poles', 'hyper-Poles', 'super-Poles', 'non-Poles', 'pro-Poles', 'anti-Poles', 'crypto-Poles', 'pseudo-Poles', 'ex-Poles', 'good Poles', 'bad Poles', 'Austro-Poles', 'Russo-Poles', 'Prusso-Poles', or, most historically, 'Polish Austrians', 'Polish Russians', or 'Polish Prussians'.

The fact is: the modern Polish nation is the end-product of modern Polish Nationalism. Its growth has proceeded erratically for nearly two centuries, and its ultimate success was far from certain for most of recent history. The exact date at which it assumed a preponderant role in the affairs of the Polish lands is a matter for dispute. Some historians see the decisive moment in 1864, when a measure of social emancipation attended the national demonstration of the January Rising. Others would delay it to the Rebirth of the Polish state in 1918. The most rigorous observers would argue that the national process could not be regarded as complete until a homogeneous Polish population, uniformly conscious of their national identity, took undivided control of their own national territory. That point was not reached until 1945.[7]

*   *   *   *   *

In so far as general histories of modern Europe mention Poland at all, they usually turn their attention to the one and only theme which ever exercised the minds of the statesmen of the day, namely to 'The Polish Question'. Like its partner, 'The Eastern Question', this subject has appeared on countless conference agendas, and on all students' examination papers, of the last two centuries. In Polish minds, too, it assumed overbearing proportions. According to the oldest joke in the ambassadors' repertoire, the Polish candidate at an international essay competition on 'Elephants' produces a piece entitled 'The Elephant and the Polish Question'. One can say without exaggeration that of all the animals to be found in the diplomatic garden of modern Europe 'The Polish Question' is indeed the elephant, if not the dodo.

For diplomats, of course, and for those who supplied the diplomats with their information, the disposition of the former Polish lands was not without significance. During each of the great continental wars, the territory of partitioned Poland formed an area of actual or potential instability, whose ultimate fate was repeatedly called into question. At each of the main peace conferences – at Vienna in 1814–15, at Paris in 1919–20, and at Yalta and Potsdam in 1945 – Poland's future was discussed and debated at great length. In between the wars and conferences, from Prince Czartoryski's Memorial in 1803 to the project for Polish–Czechoslavak Federation in 1943, formula after ill-fated formula was invented in attempts to reconcile the demands of the Polish people with the interests of the ruling Powers. For 150 years, the Polish Question was a conundrum that could not be solved, a circle that could never be squared. In that time, it generated mountains of archival material and oceans of secondary literature.[8]

For the historian of Poland, however, the Polish Question is a singularly barren subject. Very few, if any, of the diplomatic memoranda concerning Poland's future ever exerted a decisive influence on the course of events. Many of them, like Prince Czartoryski's Memorandum, remained a dead letter.[9] Some, like the Polish–Czechoslovak Project, were killed by the politicians.[10] Others were simply ignored: The most important of them did nothing but express the pious aspirations of their authors or confirm the details of political settlements already accomplished. At Vienna, for example, there was no way that the statesmen could have persuaded the Tsar to relinquish control of a country long since occupied by his victorious army. At Paris, there was no way that the Allied leaders could have induced Józef Piłsudski to follow their policies. At Yalta and Potsdam, there was no way that Churchill or Roosevelt, by diplomatic means, could have deflected Stalin from his chosen solution. At each of these critical moments, matters were not decided at the conference table, but by the situation on the ground and by the men who held the reins of practical power. At moments of less importance, diplomatic action counted for even less. Throughout the modern period, in fact, notes, protests, and rejoinders about Poland fell thick as autumn leaves, whilst life in Eastern Europe continued unruffled. The Polish nation grew from infancy to maturity regardless of the diplomats, and it owes them no debt of gratitude.

* * * * *

Certain forms of Polish national consciousness were much older than the Partitions, of course. But there is little point in tracing their manifestations back into the Renaissance or the Middle Ages, when nationality played little significant part in social or political affairs. Yet certainly in 'the Deluge' of the seventeenth century, and more acutely in the civil wars of the eighteenth, the citizens of the Polish–Lithuanian Republic were bound to question the age-old traditions of loyalty and identity. Political allegiances, which had always assumed that 'to be a Pole' was to be a loyal subject of the Polish King and the Republic, were undermined. In the situation which prevailed after 1717, where King and Republic were puppets of the Russian Tsar, 'loyalty' was gradually confused with 'collaboration' and 'careerism'. In its place, religious and cultural bonds were strengthened. Henceforth, for men of integrity, the 'good citizen' also included the one who was prepared to protest and to resist, the one who, secure in the Church's promise of eternal salvation, thought light of laying down his life in resistance to the established order. These ideas were already current among the Confederates of Bar. They provide a precocious example of the revolutionary nationalism which swept America and Europe in the subsequent era. From the very beginning, Polish patriotism was associated with dissidence and insurrection.

For the Poles, however, the Revolutionary Era proved a bitter disappointment. In theory, the French Revolution was supposed to replace the corrupt and oppressive rule of the old monarchies with an age of national liberation. In practice, the old tyrants were exchanged for new, more efficient ones. In terms of money and blood, Napoleon's exploitation of Poland was as blatant as anything which the Tsar had achieved. For those Poles who flocked to the Napoleonic armies, there was no reward. They were seduced by the banners of 'Liberté, Egalité, Fraternité', as surely as the beautiful Maria Walewska was seduced by the Emperor himself. Dąbrowski's Polish Legions raised in 1798 for the Army of Italy, were sent in 1801 to Haiti, to crush the rebellion of Negro slaves. They perished to a man, struck down by swamp-fever, which thereby achieved for Haiti what Poland could not enjoy for more than a century. Their hymn, sung with abandon to a spritely *mazurek*, is marvellously expressive of their desperate plight:

Jeszcze Polska nie zginęła	Poland has not perished yet
Póki My żyjemy.	So long as we still live.
Co nam obca przemoc wzięła	That which alien force has seized
Szablą odbijemy.	We at swordpoint shall retrieve.
Marsz, marsz, Dąbrowski!	March, march, Dąbrowski!
Z ziemi włoskiej do Polski!	From Italy to Poland!
Za Twoim przewodem	Let us now rejoin the nation
Złączym się z narodem.	Under thy command. *

* The hymn, with these words, has formed the national anthem since Piłsudski's Coup in 1926. In the original version, composed in 1797 by Józef Wybicki to a popular folk-tune, the first line read: *Jeszcze Polska nie umarła* (Poland has not yet died); but the implication that the Polish state might have died from natural causes as distinct from assault and battery, later proved unacceptable. Once *umarła* had been replaced by *zginęła*, other minor changes were necessary to maintain the rhyme and rhythm.[11]

The Army of the Duchy of Warsaw was no more fortunate. Splendidly devoted in distant parts, notably in the charge of Samosierra in the Peninsula in 1808, it was decimated in Russia in 1812 and annihilated at the Battle of the Nations near Leipzig in 1813. Despite these sacrifices, or perhaps because of them, Polish independence was not restored. At the Congress of Vienna, the principle of Legitimacy was supreme. Attempts to press Polish claims were dismissed. The territorial acquisitions of 'the Satanic Trinity' were confirmed and sanctified. The Congress Kingdom, created by way of compromise, had nothing but a paper guarantee to protect it from Russia manipulations. The three partitioning powers — Russia, Prussia, and Austria — now victorious, were to dominate the continent of Europe for the duration. (See Chapter 12.)

In these revolutionary years, Polish Nationalism had the misfortune to run counter to the general direction of political development in Eastern Europe. Inspired by the example of France, where the *ancien régime* was in full retreat, it was surrounded by expansive dynastic empires, where the *ancien régime* was triumphant. Political scientists might describe it as 'asynchronic development'. In human terms, it frequently led to tragedy.

In the circumstances, it was inevitable that Polish aspirations should have been widely misunderstood. Once the partitioning powers were firmly in control, the Poles could never obtain elementary justice, as they saw it, by peaceful methods. They could only hope to change their predicament by recruiting assistance from outside, or by causing a major disruption. Treason and violence often seemed inseparable from justice. The relief of twenty million Poles could only be effected by the discomfort of two hundred million fellow-Europeans. As Lord Brougham once remarked, 'The Polish Cause is opposed to the wishes of all the other powers. They all want peace, whilst to take up the cause of Poland means War.' There was the rub. If supporting Polish claims meant going to war, few responsible people in Europe were ready to pay the price. Indeed, the mere repetition of Polish claims was enough to arouse the spectre of war and to evoke from frightened leaders the most hysterical denunciations of the Polish 'trouble-makers'. For the Poles, this mechanism was incomprehensible.

When a British parliamentarian, or a Russian liberal denounced the iniquities of the reigning establishment; when a German or an Italian nationalist campaigned against the petty tyrannies of their oppressors, they were widely acclaimed as reformers, progressives, and men of vision. They were seen to be ironing out the inconsistencies in the established order, but not to be threatening it. When a Pole presumed to express exactly the same opinions, or to demand the same rights for the Poles as other nations enjoyed, he was regularly treated as a 'rebel', a 'dreamer', an 'extremist', a 'fanatic'. By challenging the authority of the major continental empires, he provoked much greater hostility, and a very special response. Thus, whereas the nineteenth century was the Age of Reform and Improvement for Britain, of Expansion for America, of Might and Empire for Prussia and Russia, and of national liberation for the Germans and Italians, it was, for the Poles, an era of defeat, isolation, and humiliation. It was the 'Babylonian Captivity', 'the Sojourn in the Wilderness', the 'Descent into the Tomb', the 'Journey through Hell', 'the Time on the Cross'.

In the British Isles, the only comparable experience was that suffered by the Irish, whose own loss of statehood lasted from 1800 to 1921 and who strove to preserve their own sense of identity from within another rich, confident, and expansive empire. But if the Irish were faced with one imperial 'enemy', the Poles were faced with three. When Julian Ursyn Niemcewicz visited Ireland in 1833, he admitted that there were many similarities, adding 'I would willingly exchange our condition today for Ireland's.'[12]

In the absence of a national state, Polish national consciousness drew on four fundamental sources of inspiration — Church, Language, History, and Race.

The Roman Catholic Church had never enjoyed a monopoly in the religious affairs of the old Republic. Yet its influence had gradually increased in response to the depredations of Swedish and Prussian Protestants, and Orthodox Muscovites. In the eastern provinces, it had long been known as 'the Polish religion' to distinguish its adherents from the Uniates and the Orthodox. In these areas a Catholic peasant would often be called 'a Pole' even though he said his prayers in Latin and spoke to his family in Byelorussian or Ukrainian. The Confederates of Bar, who took to the field in 1768 as much in defence of Catholicism as of their Golden Freedom, put Faith and Fatherland, the service of the Virgin and that of Poland, into one and the same breath:

> I stand on Parade
> As God has bidden,
> My Commission defray'd
> For leave in Heaven.
> For Freedom, I'll die;
> My Faith not deny.
> That is my Hazard.

> The Cross is my Shield,
> Salvation my Loot,
> I'll stay in the Field
> Though Death be afoot.
> My Safety is nought.
> My Soul's rest is sought
> In the Fatherland.

> It's nothing novel
> When Poland's Fate
> Is to enter the Battle
> As Mary's Breastplate.
> In the thick of the Fight
> She succours her Knight,
> And Thee, Sweet Fatherland.[13]

After the Partitions, for the Poles in Russia and Prussia, and to a lesser extent in Catholic Austria, these associations assumed capital importance. Ever since, the celebration of the Mass has traditionally ended with the singing of the same patriotic hymn:

> O God who through the ages
> Hast girded Poland with power and fame,
> Whose shield hath kept Her in Thy care
> From evils that would cause her harm.
> Before Thy altars, we bring our entreaty:
> Restore, O Lord, our free country.*

---

* *Boże coś Polskę* was composed in 1816 by the Revd Alojzy Feliński (1771–1820) as a 'Hymn on the Anniversary of the Declaration of the Congress Kingdom', and was later adapted. In 1918–39, and again after 1945, the last line was changed at official request to read 'Bless, O Lord, our free country'; but many people still keep to the traditional words.[14]

Hymn writing in this period occupied an important branch of literature, and hymn-singing a prominent place in popular culture. The hymns of Franciszek Karpiński (1741–1825) were learned by generations of churchgoers. At Christmas time, Karpiński's carols enjoyed universal acclaim.

Some scholars have chosen to minimize the Catholic contribution to Polish nationhood. They point to the fact that devout Catholics frequently struck entirely passive attitudes towards political and social reform, and that the hierarchy of the Church was consistently hostile to nationalist aims. Certainly, the situation was not free from ambiguity. The tendency to identify Catholics as Poles, and non-Catholics as non-Poles, was more common in border areas of mixed religious affiliations than in solidly Catholic neighbourhoods. But to deny that Catholicism acted as one of the major spurs to national consciousness is as absurd as to maintain that Polishness and Catholicism were identical. It was often the case that fervent nationalists would reject their Catholicity in protest against the political lethargy of the supposedly 'priest-ridden' community from which they originated. But their actions only underlined the significance of Catholicism in defining the Polish national community which they so desperately hoped to arouse.[15] (See Chapter 7.)

The Polish language expanded its horizons enormously, especially in conjunction with the spread of mass education. Under the old Republic, it had been obliged to take second place. The royal court had been Italianate, Francophile, and Germanophone by turns; and both Church and state promoted Latin as the best vehicle for communicating with a heterodox population which spoke anything from Low German or Ruthenian to Armenian or Yiddish. The advocates of vernacular culture, from Kochanowski onwards, achieved considerable results; but they had sought to put Polish on an equal footing with Latin, not to replace it. They were generally regarded as the enemies of traditional education methods, and never gained the ascendancy until the establishment of the National Education Commission in 1770. Oddly enough, Polish had been stronger as a cultural medium in Lithuania than in Poland. In contrast to the Latinized nobility of the Kingdom, the nobility of the Grand Duchy had cultivated the

Polish language as a means of setting themselves apart from the Lithuanian or Ruthenian peasantry. After 1697, when *Ruski* was finally abolished as the official language of the Grand Duchy's courts, the supremacy of Polish in social and political life was complete. In the Kingdom, the decisive change did not occur till after 1795, when the partitioning powers removed Latin as the official language, and tried to impose Russian or German. In this situation, Polish was thrust into a role to which it had never pretended. It now became a great force for unity, where previously it had divided. It united the nobility with the peasantry, pushing them together towards a common cultural heritage. It united Catholics and non-Catholics. It linked the Polonized gentry of Lithuania, who in the early years produced almost all its literary exponents of genius, with the farmers of Poznania, the assimilated Jews of the cities, the professors of Cracow, the peasants of Silesia and Pomerania, and the citizens of Warsaw. It crossed all frontiers with impunity, and quickly became a vehicle for all those ideas and feelings which the authorities wished to suppress. For those who continued to oppose the effects of the Partitions, it became the 'language of freedom'. Indeed, with time, it became an essential touchstone of Polish nationality. In strict contrast to the English-speaking world, where Irish, Scots, Australian, or American nationalisms have less to do with language, families who ceased to speak Polish, ceased to be regarded as Poles. The 'homeland' was indistinguishable from the language. In Julian Tuwim's memorable phrase, it was *'Ojczyzna-Polszczyzna'* (The Fatherland of the Polish tongue).[16]

The Polish language provided the gateway to unofficial literature and to independent interpretations of History. In the Romantic period, both these activities found ample support from the prevailing intellectual fashions of the day. In the hands of Adam Mickiewicz (1798–1855), Juliusz Słowacki (1809–49), and Zygmunt Krasiński (1812–59), Polish poetry and drama flourished as never before. These authors applied the usual Romantic obsessions with agony, horror, separation, and death to specifically national subjects. To the foreign reader, their brand of Messianism sometimes seems ridiculous, or even 'immorally proud'. Yet as exiles their feelings were genuine enough; their knowledge of their audience was exact; and their mastery of words supreme. Moreover, their work was by no means confined to messianic outbursts. The poems of Mickiewicz contain as many classical elements as romantic ones, whilst his epic masterpiece *Pan Tadeusz* (1834) is filled with a lyrical serenity of truly universal appeal. These men, the pioneers of modern Polish letters, ensured that nineteenth-century Polish literature rapidly acquired traditions as strong, and a treasure-house as vast and as varied, as the better-known cultures of Germany and Russia, not to say of Western Europe. Henceforth, Polish Literature could always supply the nation's needs whenever Polish politics was found wanting.[17]

Polish History enjoyed its greatest success in artistic and imaginative forms. In the world of literature, Julian Ursyn Niemcewicz, already an established author before the Third Partition, paid great attention to historical subjects after his return from America in 1807. His *Śpiewy historyczne* (Historical Ballads), first published in 1816 with words, music, and illustrations, became one of the most popular books of the century. He also launched the vogue for historical novels in the style of Walter Scott. His novel *Dwaj panowie Sieciechowie* (The Two Mr Sieciechóws, 1815) is notable for its sympathetic treatment of the problem of the generations in the life of the nobility; *Lejbe i Siora* (1821) for its satirical descriptions of Chassidic Jewry and its appeal for Polish—Jewish assimilation; and *Jan z Tęczyna* (1825) for its vivid portrayal of the Court of Zygmunt-August. In the hands of Józef Ignacy Kraszewski (1812—87), the historical novel assumed the proportions of a mass industry. In a lifetime of unparalleled productivity, Kraszewski wrote over five hundred works, which touched on every conceivable aspect of Poland's past. He made heroes of the peasants, no less than of nobles and soldiers, and in his middle age, was fascinated by the contemporary problems of insurrection and subterfuge as suggested by the January Rising. In the last decade of his life, he composed a cycle of seventy-six volumes forming a chronological survey of events from prehistoric times — in *Stara baśń* (An Old Tale, 1876) — to the eighteenth century — in *Saskie ostatki* (Saxon Remnants, 1890). He completed this extraordinary achievement undeterred by his arrest in Berlin in 1883 on a charge of treason, and his imprisonment in Magdeburg Castle. His death in Switzerland coincided with the completion of the masterwork of his literary heir, Henryk Sienkiewicz (1846—1916), whose *Trylogia* (Trilogy, 1883—8) represented the zenith of popular literature in Poland. In the eyes of his Polish readership, Sienkiewicz's chivalric tales of the Cossack Wars of the 1650s, and, in *Krzyżacy* (1900), of the medieval struggle against the Teutonic Order, lacked nothing in comparison to his world-wide success with *Quo Vadis?* (1896). In the same era, the Cracovian dramatist and designer Stanisław Wyspiański (1869—1907) used the theatrical stage to explore the theme of national liberation in a series of highly colourful, eccentric, and symbolic dramas on historical subjects. In *Warszawianka* (La Varsovienne, 1898), *Lelewel* (1899), *Legion* (The Legion, 1900), *Kazimierz Wielki* (Casimir the Great, 1900), *Wyzwolenie* (Liberation, 1903), *Bolesław Śmiały* (Bolesław the Bold, 1903), and *Zygmunt August* (1907), and above all in *Wesele* (The Wedding Feast, 1901), which evokes the historical memories of Galicians, and in *Noc listopadowa* (The November Night, 1903), which fantasizes on the outbreak of the Rising of 1830, he conjured up a body of images which are infinitely more forceful and memorable than any documentary or factual historical record. In the world of painting, Jan Matejko (1838—93) devoted his later years to a marvellously tendentious sequence of heroic historical scenes. His vast canvases of *The Battle of Grunwald, The Prussian Homage,* and *Rejtan's Defiance,* and his *Poczet Królów Polskich* (Portraits of the Polish Kings, 1890—2) have been known ever since to every Polish school child. In the world of music, Stanisław Moniuszko (1819—72) drew heavily on History and Folklore to amass a large and very popular repertoire of operas and songs. All these artists had numerous admirers and imitators, who pursued the same goals and interests. For them, as for all patriots, the love of their country's heritage overrode any scruples of objectivity or factual accuracy. For them, it was sufficient that Polish History should not be forgotten, and that its dead champions and heroes should provide a living force of inspiration. Such indeed was their success that the poetic, imaginative, and enthusiastic approach to History is still more common among Poles than the critical, reflective, or analytical approach. In the Polish tradition, the historical image has proved far more convincing than the historical fact.[18]

The Poles also drew on, and contributed to, fashionable racial theories. In the world of scholarship, the work of the ethnographer, the Revd Franciszek Duchiński (1817–93), had repercussions far beyond the Slavonic orbit. His *Peuples Aryas et Tourans* (Aryan and Turanian Peoples, 1864) was written in response to Pan-slav concepts emanating from Russia, where official policy was urging all the Slavonic nations to think of themselves as 'brothers of the one blood'. Its point of departure was the debate surrounding Alexander II's unveiling in 1861 of a monument in Novgorod celebrating the supposed Millennium of the Russian State; and its specific target was the ideology which has since become known as 'The Russian Scheme of History'. According to Duchiński, the origins of peoples cannot be reduced to simple factors such as Language or Religion, but can only be determined by reference to twenty-eight points of differentiation varying from Hydrography and Pedology to Epidemiology, Nutrition, Folklore, and the status of women. On this basis, he argued that the origins of the Great Russians lay not with the Indo-European Slavs but rather with the Finnic and Hunnic peoples of Asia. The connection between the Slavonic–Christian state of Kiev Rus and the later Grand Duchy of Moscow and its successor, the Empire of all the Russias, was, in his view, a political fabrication. The ancestral home of the Slavs lay between the Vistula and the Dnieper, and in its eastern reaches contained the lands of the Poles and the Ruthenes, but not of the Muscovites. In short, the Poles are not related to the Russians in any natural way. Duchiński's ideas have inspired numerous continuators, not least the Ukrainian historian, Hrushevsky. Yet, in the words of his Russian critics, whose views have since gained a virtual monopoly in the world at large, they were nothing more than 'an ancient Polish song'.[19]

In the popular mind, Polish racial concepts assumed much cruder form. Under pressure from German racialists on the one hand and from Pan-slav racialists on the other, Poles were driven to invent fantasies of their own ethnic exclusiveness, and to reject all thoughts of kinship with other peoples of the area. In view of the ban on intermarriage recommended by Catholic priests and Jewish rabbis alike, they were tempted to swell the rising tide of anti-Semitism, and of Jewish anti-Polonism. In this way, a fundamental rift began to appear in the ranks of Polish Nationalism. Henceforth, one branch of opinion began to imagine the nation to be a distinct ethnic group, biologically unique. The other branch held to the older view whereby the nation was seen to be made up of all those individuals who shared the same political, social, and cultural traditions. The former opinion, which believes that Poles are born, not created, has always been able to find common language with sympathetic elements in Russia. The latter which holds that anyone is a Pole who feels himself to be one, has invariably found support among the intelligentsia, where people of variegated origins frequently intermixed. Strangely enough, the most devoted disciples of Polish nationalism often came from families of mixed origin. Lelewel, whose family was of German origin, and Chopin, who was half French, are obvious examples of men whose sense of Polish identity was reinforced by the need to compensate for their genealogy. Assimilated Jews, in particular, were noted for their tendency to become more Polish than the Poles.

National pride was generated no less from achievements which had no immediate connection with nationality. Great efforts were made to prove and exaggerate the 'Polishness' of men and women whose achievements were thought to bolster the self-esteem of the emergent nation. The two primary candidates for this treatment in the scientific field were Marie Curie-Skłodowska and Nicholas Copernicus: in the literary field, the English writer of Polish extraction, Joseph Conrad, and in music, Frederyk Chopin. In 1873, for example, immense resentment was aroused by preparations in Germany to celebrate the fourth centenary of the great German scientist 'Nikolaus Koppernik', for the Poles were themselves preparing to honour the great Polish scientist 'Mikołaj Kopernik'. Połkowski's biography published in Warsaw set out to challenge the conclusions of Von Hipler's biography published in Berlin, initiating a debate which has raged with pointless fury every since. The fact that Copernicus

himself and Copernicus's contemporaries, were largely indifferent to nationality, disappeared under the deluge of charge
and counter-charge. As a native of Royal Prussia, he never
admitted to anything other than a local patriotism, whereby
he described himself as a 'Prussian'. He was a loyal subject of
the Jagiellonian Kings, and a lifelong opponent of the
Teutonic Knights and of Albrecht von Hohenzollern. From
the cultural point of view, he came from a family whose
connections in Silesia, and in the bourgeoisie of fifteenth-
century Cracow, in Thorn, and in Frauenberg, were with the
German-speaking rather than with the Polish-speaking element;
but there is ample evidence that he knew the Polish language.
In his scientific work, like all scholars of this time, he thought
and wrote exclusively in Latin. Taking everything into consideration, there is good reason to regard him both as a
German and as a Pole: and yet, in the sense that modern
nationalists understand it, he was neither. Objective observers
might look with admiration on the fact that in Jagiellonian
times a prominent German churchman and scientist was able
to show such marked loyalty to the Polish kingdom. But in a
later world, where Germans and Poles were doing everything
to destroy the bonds of mutual respect and harmony, Polish
scholars have felt obliged to follow the German example and
to mount exclusive claims over a generous man who would
turn in his grave to hear their bickerings.[20]

Strong emotions have also been generated in interpretations
of the works of Frederyk Chopin (1810–49). Although the
French have been slightly less proprietorial towards Chopin
than the Germans towards Copernicus, the same debates and
disagreements concerning the extent and significance of his
'Polishness' have regularly recurred. Born at Żelazowa Wola
in the Duchy of Warsaw, the son of a French musician, he
spent the greater part of his creative life by choice in Paris,
in cosmopolitan artistic circles. He maintained close emotional
ties with his family in Poland, writing to his father in French
and to his mother and sisters in Polish. But what this means
for his music is difficult to say. Anglo-Saxon critics with no
vested interest in the matter, have tended to discount the
national factor. 'The Polish element in Chopin's music is as
urbane as the Hungarian in Liszt', wrote one critic, 'and . . . is

not of paramount artistic importance.' 'Nothing in the outside world', wrote another, 'exercised the slightest influence
on his work, either for good or evil.' To most Polish listeners,
and to people familiar with the Polish way of thinking, such
comments are incomprehensible. For them, Chopin's works
were based on his experiences in the formative years in
Warsaw, distilled from the Polish melodies, harmonies, and
rhythms that he heard in his youth, and inspired by a bitter-
sweet nostalgia for the land of his birth; they represent the
quintessence of 'Polishness'. Who is to say? Listening to the
Mazurkas in C Minor (Op. 30, no. 4; Op. 41, no. 1; Op. 50,
no. 3), one listener recognizes 'a common mood . . . of regal
bitterness over the passing of Poland's glory', another, while
feeling the power of the music with equal sensibility, recognizes nothing more than the 'feverish, morbid, diseased
fantasies' of a diminutive and consumptive bachelor. On
hearing the so-called 'Revolutionary Study' in C Minor
(Op. 10, no. 12), the man who knows that it was written in
September 1831 during the climax of the Russo-Polish War,
may sense the composer's fury at Poland's defeat, 'full of
conspiracy and sedition'; the next man who knows that the
'revolutionary' title was not Chopin's own, may choose to
ignore the historical context altogether. On hearing the
famous Polonaise in A Major (Op. 40, no. 1) – Le Militaire,
with its 'cannon buried in the flowers', as Robert Schumann
once remarked, a Pole may well feel that he is hearing the
purest possible distillation of Polish culture; a Japanese or a
Jamaican, who knows nothing at all about Poland, will appreciate the piece none the less. Chopin's musical genius is
universal. His nationality gains overriding relevance only to
those who need to harness his unique talents to their own
purposes. Certainly for the Poles in their mutilated political
condition, it has been of the utmost solace, not merely to
share the subtle emotions of Chopin's music, but also to
claim it as their very own. For most of the world, Chopin is
just a composer of supreme genius; for Poland, he is also 'a
national poet' and a 'national prophet'.[21]

Surely, Polish national consciousness must also have been
encouraged by contact with other emergent nations. In the
Napoleonic Era, the Poles were thoroughly infected with the

ideas of the French Revolution which could never be fully
eradicated, even if they could not be realized. In this connection, their experiences resembled those of the Germans and
the Italians, whose strivings for long followed a path similar
to their own. In the first half of the nineteenth century,
Poland was generally classified as a historic nation, whose
chances of reuniting its scattered parts and of asserting its
independence were broadly similar to those of Germany and
Italy. Poles came to know the Italian Carbonari during the
Napoleonic wars in Italy, and later were much impressed by
Mazzini.[22] But they had much more intimate ties with
Germany. The German universities attracted large numbers of
Polish students, and it is inconceivable that the nationalist
ideas which flourished there should not have been absorbed
and translated into Polish terms. In so far as thinkers such as
Herder, Fichte, Schelling, or at a later date, Nietzsche, played
a prominent part in the development of Nationalism in
Germany, it is not usual to consider them as prophets of the
Polish cause. Yet the connection is undeniable. Lelewel's
concept of the primitive democracy of the Slavs came straight
from Herder, whilst the obvious similarities between Fichte's
concepts on the moral and cultural regeneration of the nation,
and those professed by his Polish pupils at Berlin, are too
close to be purely accidental. Fichte's ideas of the *Urvolk* or
'Primordial people', and of the mystical union of the nation
with its native soil, are still alive, completely unattributed, in
Poland today. It would be a nice paradox, therefore, to stress
the German character of Polish Nationalism; but an objective
study of the dissemination of nationalist ideas in an era when
'Poland' and 'Germany' were still thought to be comple-
mentary ideals, would probably bring some surprising results.[23]

Inevitably, however, the strongest single spur to Polish
national consciousness derived from political frustrations. It
is a basic feature of human nature that people will develop an
intense desire for whatever is denied them. They desire it,
irrespective of their material needs, or of their original intentions. In strict contrast to the state-sponsored nationalisms
of Britain and America which have fed on a diet of confidence
and prosperity, Polish national consciousness fed on deprivation and want. Like most of the other nationalisms of Eastern

Europe, it may be seen as a negative function of the reigning tyrannies, and as such has frequently assumed a militant, even a truculent air.

* * * * *

The politics of Polish Nationalism were conditioned from the start by the uncompromising nature of the established order. At no time did the authorities of the partitioning powers look with favour on the re-creation of a sovereign and fully independent Polish state. Their original willingness to grant a measure of autonomy to their Polish provinces declined steadily, and in Russia and Prussia was abandoned altogether. As a result, the politically conscious Pole was faced with a very limited choice of action. If he loyally acquiesced in the policies of his government, he was tempted to surrender his Polish nationality in favour of the official nationalisms of the imperial regime. By pursuing a career in the Tsarist, Prussian, or Royal-and-Imperial service, the chances are that he would adopt the culture and the outlook of the ruling élite, and would come to think of himself not as a Pole but as a Russian, a German, or an Austrian. In the second half of the nineteenth century, it was only in Austria that he could openly profess loyalty both to the state and to the Polish cause, and even there the possibilities were strictly circumscribed. If, however, he were to give priority to Polish aims, he was immediately confronted with a fundamental dilemma. He had either to work with the authorities, or against them. In the context of autocratic, authoritarian, or absolutist regimes, where pluralist political aims were not permitted, there was no middle way: there was no concept of a 'loyal opposition'. In the eyes of authority, one was a faithful subject, or an unfaithful one. Ineluctably therefore, those Poles who refused to work with the authorities, were immediately thrown into the world of subterfuge, conspiracy, and terrorism. They were obliged to resort to violent methods, and to pit the feeble resources of their individual minds and muscles against the massed cohorts of the regime with little hope of victory. These 'Insurrectionaries' were maximalists by nature, risking all, and as often as not, losing all. In contrast to them, those who chose to work with the authorities, were obliged to adopt a deferential posture towards powerful and essentially unsympathetic officials. At the cost of much humiliation, and by risking the disgust of patriotic constituents, they could only hope to extract concessions of a perfunctory nature, mainly in the social, economic, or cultural fields. These 'Conciliators' were in the nature of things minimalists. Hence, from the mid-eighteenth century to the present day, Polish politics have been dominated by three distinct traditions, those of Loyalism, Insurrection, and Conciliation.* From the nationalist point of view, they represent the roads respectively of Treason, of Idealism, and of Realism. In the eyes of the ruling Empires, they followed the paths of Duty, of Rebellion, and of Moderation. As always, each side in the political arena had its own vocabulary for describing the positions of its opponents in relation to itself.

Loyalism persisted at every level. Its clearest formulation was made shortly after the Third Partition by Stanisław Szczęsny Potocki, the Confederate of Targowica. 'I no longer speak of Polishness and the Poles,' he said. 'That state, that name, have vanished, as have many others in the history of the world. Poles should abandon all memory of their fatherland. I myself am a Russian forever.'24 In the course of the next century and more, many Poles followed where Potocki had led, and not all of them for the same opportunist motives. General Wincenty Krasiński (1782–1858), for instance, the father of the poet, was a man of unbending conservative principles, who consistently opposed all forms of nationalist politics and served for twenty years on the Russian Council of State. In that same generation Tadeusz Bulgarin

---

* Loyalism (*Lojalizm*), Insurrection (*Powstanie*), and Conciliation (*Ugoda*) are all translations of specific Polish terms, and cannot be divorced from their specific Polish context. Polish Loyalism has something in common with American Loyalism of the Revolutionary Era and also with Irish Loyalism, but not with loyalism as generally understood in England. The Polish concept of Insurrection used to be equated with political 'Revolution'; but the appearance in the later nineteenth century of social revolutionaries, who were strongly opposed to national insurrections, made nonsense of the equation. 'Conciliation' often appears as 'Realism' or 'compromise'. The Polish word from which it derives, *ugodzić się*, literally means 'to strike a bargain'.

(1789—1859), editor of *The Northern Bee,* and Osip-Julian Senkowski (1800—58), Professor of Oriental Languages at St. Petersburg, both of them from Polish families, may be regarded as leading ideologues of official *Russian* Nationalism. As neophytes to Russian values, they showed zeal beyond the call of duty. In Prussia, a similar role was played by Bogdan Hutten-Czapski (1851—1937), a close associate of Bismarck, and in Austria by Kazimierz Badeni (1846—1909), who for two years served as President of the Imperial Council of Ministers. These men, whilst in no way denying their Polish origins, placed full political confidence in the governments of St. Petersburg, Berlin, or Vienna. In this sense, they were Central European counterparts of Scots, Welsh, or Irish politicians who made their fortunes with the British government in London. They were nothing unusual.

Loyalism commanded the support of several prominent writers and philosophers. Henryk Rzewuski (1791—1866) had the misfortune to be born on 3 May 1791 and spent the rest of his life combating all the liberal ideals which the defunct Constitution symbolized. As the author of *Pamiątki Soplicy* (Memoirs of Soplica, 1839), he was widely admired for his sentimental, nostalgic evocations of old Polish society; and as a disciple of de Maistre, the advocate of universal papal theocracy, he was seen to be a pillar of conservative Catholicism. Yet as the devoted son of a family closely tied to the Confederacy of Targowica, he also gave whole-hearted support to the political supremacy of the Russian Empire, under whose benevolent aegis the entire Slav world was supposed to unite. In his way, Rzewuski was certainly a Polish patriot, but one so attached to traditional social and cultural principles that he automatically opposed all forms of political change. His congenital hatred of conspiracies inspired him, in his *Mieszaniny obyczajowe* (A Miscellany of Manners, 1842) to write that 'Poland is a corpse which is being eaten by worms.' He made an ideal aide to Prince Paskievitch, the Russian Viceroy in Warsaw, in the darkest days of Nicholas I's reign. Rzewuski's contemporary, Adam Gurowski (1805—66), was led to similar conclusions by a very different road. Gurowski's philosophy was as radical as Rzewuski's was reactionary; but he, too, came to believe in Poland's spiritual bankruptcy and in Russia's providential mission. Having studied under Hegel at the University of Berlin, he returned to Warsaw as one of the firebrands of the 1820s, hatching an abortive plot to assassinate Nicholas I and, during the November Rising, initiating the demands to dethrone the Tsar. In Paris, he helped found the Polish Democratic Society (TDP). Three years later, however, he experienced a total change of heart, abandoned all his former views on the national issue, and abjectly pleaded with the Tsarist authorities for a pardon. In the following period, as a self-confessed admirer of Saint-Simon and Fourier, he somehow saw Russian autocracy as an ideal instrument for social and cultural modernization. He savagely denounced the conceited, uncaring individualism of the Polish nobles, and gave practical proof of his sincerity by denouncing his disaffected neighbours to the Tsarist police. He even submitted a memorandum on educational reform, which proposed that the Polish language — 'a degenerate dialect of Russian' — should be replaced in Polish schools by Old Church Slavonic. His major works — *La Civilisation et la Russie* (1840) and *Le Panslavisme* (1848) — systematically advocated loyalist politics. But they failed to win him the prominent position which he hoped for, and in 1847 he fled to Germany, and thence to the United States. In later life, he became a doughty champion of the abolition of slavery and a prophet of America's 'Manifest Destiny'. His *America and Europe* (1857) elaborated de Tocqueville's earlier thesis that America and Russia were destined to overtake the decayed European powers and that they would divide the world between them. In America, Gurowski is well remembered. In his native Poland, as a 'national apostate', he has been cast to oblivion.

Loyalism, moreover, was not the preserve of a few peripheral eccentrics. Nowadays it is often forgotten that large numbers of people in the Polish lands were either indifferent to Polish politics or else were categorically opposed to them. In the first half of the nineteenth century, these 'non-Poles' included not only whole ethnic groups who were preoccupied with separate nationalist movements of their own, but also a significant sector of the educated classes, who identified increasingly with German or Russian culture. They also included the broad masses of the Polish peasantry, who were as yet largely illiterate and apolitical. In later decades, they were joined by an assortment of interests which viewed Nationalism as the express enemy of their chosen designs. Apart from the Polish Slavophiles such as Kazimierz Krzywicki (1820–83), who wanted to replace the particular Russian or Polish nationalisms by the brotherhood of all Slav peoples, these included both Marxists on the Left and ultra-Catholic conservatives on the Right. All for their various purposes sought to preserve the established framework of European sovereignty and to stifle all thoughts of Polish Independence. They were abetted by the formidable accomplices of inertia and apathy. In the Bismarckian Era, 'Triloyalism' enjoyed considerable respectability. This was a new variation on the older idea that the best interests of the Polish nation could only be maintained by fostering harmonious relations between all three partitioning powers. It declined in the years before the First World War when mounting international tensions revived the more usual Polish game of trying to play off one of the partitioning powers against the others. With Polish loyalists in Germany and Austria denouncing the imperialism of Russia, and Polish loyalists in Russia denouncing the imperialism of the Central Powers, the over-all balance was not disturbed. Hence, both by design and by accident, Loyalism acted as a powerful buttress of the status quo.

At the other end of the political scale, the Polish Insurrectionary Tradition was firmly rooted in the principles and practices of the old Republic. Every Pole who wished to take up arms against the partitioning powers was conscious to a greater or lesser degree of the ancient Right of Resistance and the example of the confederations. If the noblemen of Poland–Lithuania had once felt justified in their frequent resort to arms against their own, highly democratic government, how much more could their sons and grandsons sense the justice of their struggles against foreign tyranny. The new insurrectionary was the old *rokoszanin* writ large. Resolved to overthrow the established order by force, he invariably made demands for the re-creation of an independent Polish state. It was natural that the insurrectionary movement should have been strong in the first half of the nineteenth century, when memories of independence were still alive, and that thereafter it should have declined.

The pedigree of the Polish insurrectionary, therefore, was as old and as noble as any in Europe. In the 1820s the numerous Polish patriotic societies may have formed part of a widespread international network which included the German *'Bursenschaften'*, the Italian Carbonari, and the Russian Decembrists. But their main source of inspiration lay in the legends of Kościuszko and his National Rising of 1794 and of Bonaparte's Polish Legions. In the ultra-conservative world of Metternich and the dynastic empires, their activities could never be legalized or condoned, and they could easily be branded as disturbers of the peace or enemies of social progress and stability. As a result, they could never obtain the active support of the masses who in ideal circumstances might otherwise have sympathized with their aims. They remained a brilliant, impractical, and tiny minority. Like Kościuszko before them, they entertained exaggerated hopes both as to the prospects for foreign support and to the vulnerability of the imperial regimes. They knew few moments of success; and each of their abortive adventures provoked waves of repression which vastly multiplied the injustices they were seeking to remove.

The leading advocates of insurrectionary nationalism included the 'Belvedere Group' of November 1830; the Polish Democratic Society (TDP), which co-ordinated conspiratorial enterprises from abroad between 1832 and 1846; the 'Reds' of Warsaw's City Committee, who launched the Rising of 1863; the 'revolutionary wing' of the Polish Socialist Party, whose fighting squads played such a prominent role in 1905–7; the Polish Legions of the First World War, and the Home Army (AK) of the Second World War. As militants devoted to their cause, their lives tended to be intense, principled, and short. These men, whose views of social issues were often as radical as on the national issue, were the prototypes of *'Les Justes'* – the terrorists, revolutionaries, and 'anarchists' who appeared in many parts of Eastern Europe at the end of the century.

Understandably enough, insurrectionary nationalism was specially influential abroad. The Polish Cause provided the natural preoccupation of political *émigrés,* who had nothing more to lose, and was espoused by a variety of European liberals ever ready for a cheap crusade in distant parts. 'Poland' became a symbol of other people's frustrations. It sprang to the lips of Heine, and especially of Victor Hugo who in 1847 addressed the National Assembly in Paris where in the following year the gallery rang to shouts of 'Vive la Pologne!' It attracted multitudes of well-wishers, but few active supporters of consequence. It inspired a stream of diplomatic notes, but not a single demonstration of intent by the Powers. One of the strongest elements of its appeal lay in the fact that its cause was thought to be 'lost'. When Alexander II talked of Polish 'rêveries' and Bismarck of *'Polonismus',* they had exactly the same thing in mind — the virulent concoction of misguided hopes and false sentimentality. Meanwhile, Polish *émigrés* were cheerfully exploited on other people's business. The fate of Bonaparte's Polish Legions in Haiti was far from unique. Poles have appeared, like Irishmen, in all of Europe's revolutionary confrontations with great regularity. They fought in large numbers on the barricades in Paris in 1848; in Italy and in Hungary in 1848—9 and in 1859—60; and in the Paris Commune of 1871. Like Adam Mickiewicz, who died in Turkey in 1854 whilst trying to organize a Legion for service against Russia in the Crimea, they often sought a hero's death in distant parts; and some of them, like Jarosław Dąbrowski (1836—71), Commander-in-chief of the forces of the Paris Commune, actually found it. Others lived out their lives in loneliness and isolation. Józef Bem (1794—1850), one-time Commander of the Hungarian Insurrectionary Army, died in Syria, in the Turkish service; Henryk Kamieński (1813—66), theoretician of the People's War, died in Algiers; Ryszard Berwiński (1819—79), Mickiewicz's assistant and fellow-poet, died alone in Constantinople.

Of these insurrectionists, none was more typical than Ludwik Mierosławski (1814—78). As a youth he fought in the November Rising. As an *émigré,* he joined the Carbonari, and belonged to a 'Young Poland' in the image of Mazzini's Young Italy. As a principal officer of the TDP's *Centralizacja,* or 'Co-ordinating Committee' he had been designated to lead the abortive insurrection of 1846, but appeared instead as the chief defendant of the Berlin Trial. He was sentenced to death, but was reprieved at the eleventh hour by the outbreak of revolution in Prussia. In 1848−9, he headed the insurrectionary forces first in Posen, then in Sicily, and later in Baden. In the 1850s he fomented a schism in the Polish Democratic Society, antagonizing the left-wing revolutionary democrats no less than the conservative Hotel Lambert. In 1863, he returned to Poland, fought in Kujawy, and briefly acted as 'dictator' of the Rising. Thereafter he earned a meagre living in exile, writing as a historian and publicist. His lifetime of conspiracy and sacrifice brought no definable benefits to Poland. In the words of a respected historian of the period, 'Mierosławski loved his country dearly, and caused it untold harm.'[25]

In one sense, however − and some would say the most important sense − the insurrectionists were eminently successful. Their sacrifices created the sentiment of moral superiority against which the forces of the partitioning states would not be brought to bear. If they suffered in the flesh, they raised 'the Word' to a position of supreme respect in the Polish tradition. They inspired the myths and poetry on which future generations could feed. They generated fierce emotions, both of admiration and of revulsion, which perpetuated memories of their deeds, even among those who would have preferred to forget. They showed that 'Poland', whatever it was, was still alive. Paradoxically enough, the men who chose physical violence as their expression of defiance, even in the face of certain defeat, ensured that the battle of minds could be sustained on a much more equal footing. By provoking the authorities into decades of active repression, they stimulated the other, spiritual contest which could not be waged with batons and bullets, and where the deployment of soldiers and policemen was both ridiculous and self-defeating:

> Ogromne wojska, bitne generały,
> Policje − tajne, widne, i dwupłciowe.
> Przeciwko komuż tak się pojednały?
> Przeciwko kilku myślom . . . co nie nowe.*

---

*Enormous armies, brave generals,
 Police forces − secret, or open, and of both sexes,
 Against whom are they ranged?
 Against a few ideas . . . which is nothing new.[26]

During the century of statelessness and beyond, every single Polish generation has produced men careless of their own survival, who have risen with desperate courage against their tormentors. The Warsaw Rising of August 1944 was but the last performance of a drama which was also enacted in 1733, 1768, 1794, 1830, 1846, 1848, 1863, 1905, and 1920. On each occasion, if asked what they were fighting for, their reply might well have been the same: for 'a few ideas . . . which is nothing new'.

Active conspiracy was for the few, however. Much more typical for Poles who shared the same convictions, if not the same courage, was the mental habit of withdrawing from the public world altogether. In the mid-nineteenth century, especially in Russian Poland, public life was so overborne by the interminable brutalities and humiliations of censorship, police surveillance, arrests, imprisonments, and exiles, that many Poles simply refused to participate. Instead, they withdrew into the 'poetico-political dream world' of literature. There, they could read of triumphs and satisfactions which were denied them elsewhere. Their cultivation of the inner spiritual life, where aesthetic and moral values hold sway over all manifestations of reality, marks one of the abiding characteristics of Polish culture. In this sense, all the great writers were profoundly political; and politics was saturated in literature. Mickiewicz, in *Konrad Wallenrod* (1828) and *Dziady* (Forefathers' Eve, 1832) explored the theme of vengeance; Krasiński, in *Nieboska komedia* (The Undivine Comedy, 1835) and *Irydion* (1836), preached the gospel of submission and of private spiritual mastery; Słowacki, in the play *Kordian* (1834), in the prose-poem *Anhelli* (1838), in the epic *Beniowski* (1841), and in the symbolic *Król-Duch* (King-Spirit, 1847), explored political, historical, and historiosophic subjects and made some notable forays into the realm of satire. Perhaps more than any of his great contemporaries, he agonized in the present in order to inspire the happier generations of the future:

> Oh Poland, Poland, sacred and godly,
> Sometime perhaps in calm and serenity
> You may turn the gaze of your re-awakened eyes
> Onto our graves, where we rot, and the worm pries:

Where, like sleepy swans in the Spring, our ashes
Lie wrapped in thought beneath the willows.
Oh Poland mine! Remember us
When we can feel no longer; remember
How we framed and fashioned your cause
Both as a prayer of sorrow and as a flash of thunder.
Then, it will suffice that you ponder awhile
Beside our sepulchres, and, in the deathly quiet,
Accursed, as it were, by God, and vile,
That you, oh Holy One, should not forget.[27]

The conscious link between Romantic literature and insurrectionary politics was forged at an early date by Maurycy
Mochnacki (1804–34) whose activities as a militant critic in
the one field were expressly designed to redeem his failures in
the other. As a youth of 17, he had been expelled from Warsaw
University for striking a policeman who ordered him to extinguish his pipe, and two years later was arrested for belonging to a secret society. In the Carmelite Prison, his resistance
was broken. He was induced to write a letter condemning the
irresponsibility of Polish youth, and was released on the condition of working for the Tsarist censorship. The rest of his
short life was spent in expiation. Already in 1825 in a long
essay entitled *On the spirit and sources of poetry in Poland,*
he was arguing that true poetry is born from 'the infinity of
feeling' and that a national literature could only grow from
Romanticism. Between 1827 and 1829, as editor of *Kurier
Polski,* he attacked the established writers who were still calling for 'classical' restraint. In 1828, his anonymous *'Głos
obywatela z zabranego kraju'* (The Voice of a Citizen from a
Captured Country) was judged to have influenced the outcome of the trial of Łukasiński and his fellow-conspirators
from the Patriotic Society. By this time, his characteristic
outlook was firmly set. Deeply absorbed in the study of
German philosophy, and in particular of Schiller and Schlegel,
he was initiated into the preparations of the November Rising.
He was wrestling with the problems of harmonizing literature
with the needs of political action and of giving it a coherent
philosophical base. It was no accident that the Preface to his
cardinal work, *O literaturze polskiej* (On Polish Literature),
was composed at a moment when the fate of the November

Rising was uncertain, and when its management was slipping into the hands of saner, weaker men. 'It is time to stop writing about art,' he said. 'Now we have something rather different in our hearts and minds . . . Our life is already poetry. From now on, our metre will be the clash of swords and our rhyme the roar of the guns.' Within three years he was dead. But his writings were remembered as a basic guide for all those who dabbled in insurrectionary politics and those who might have done so if they could.[28]

Better known to the world at large were Mickiewicz's lectures delivered at the Collège de France and published as his *Cours des littératures slaves.*

Joachim Lelewel's role in Polish historiography closely matched that of Mochnacki and Mickiewicz in Polish literature. By idealizing the themes of Liberty and Democracy in Poland's past, his writings acted as a powerful spur to attack the Servitude of the present. (See Vol. I, Chapter 1.)

Polish Romanticism and Messianism were built on strong philosophical foundations. The first figure of note in this regard was Józef Maria Hoehne-Wroński (1778–1853), who, having fought in Kościuszko's Rising, then in the Russian army and eventually in Napoleon's Polish Legions, lived thereafter in Paris and published in French. As a onetime student at Königsberg, he started from a fulsome admiration of Kant, and later worked his way to an extreme rationalist position. He attempted to construct a complete metaphysical system on the basis of a fundamental 'law of creation' whose dichotomous mechanism somewhat resembled Hegelian trichotomy. He saw his own day and age as a transitory period which would soon give way to the 'Intellectual Age' where former conflicts would be resolved and Man would achieve complete fulfilment and immortality. His main works included *Prodrome du Messianisme* (1831), *Métapolitique messianique* (1839), and *Messianisme ou réforme absolue du savoir humain* (1847). The second figure, Józef Gołuchowski (1797–1858), stayed closer to Polish affairs, and exercised a greater influence on his literary contemporaries. A disciple of Schelling, at whose feet he had studied at Erlangen, he was removed from the Chair of Philosophy at Wilno after only one year's tenure. His lectures, which coincided with those of Lelewel on Polish

History, had found a strong rapport with the political enterprises of his students, and alarmed the Russian authorities. His one work of stature, *Die Philosophie in ihrem Verhaltniss zum Leben ganzer Volker und einzelner Menschen* (1822), continued to be read long after he took to farming his estates. In it, he raised intuition to the same prominence which Wroński gave to intelligence, and used it to prove the existence of God and the indestructibility of the soul. His brand of Romantic metaphysics added little to the work of his German predecessors, but his fervour and manner of exposition effectively translated their outlook into Polish terms. The third figure, Andrzej Towiański (1799–1878), born in Wilno, appeared in Paris in the 1840s, and in the guise of a mystic-prophet attracted a considerable following. Having organized one of the Adventist sects fashionable in intellectual *émigré* circles, he is best remembered in Polish history as the mentor of Mickiewicz's later years. August Cieszkowski (1814–94) was the most original of all. A Hegelian by training, and a contemporary of Karl Marx at the University of Berlin, he consciously directed his philosophical inquiries towards social and political ends. Firmly believing in the divine mission of the Catholic Church and of the Polish nation, he stressed the irrational factors in the sources of knowledge, and recognized the will as the essence of human existence. In his *Prologomena zur Historisophie* (1838) and *Gott und Palingenesie* (1842), he argued that utopias should be designed for implementation, and predicted an 'Era of the Holy Spirit' – a Catholic version of Wroński's intellectual utopia. During his stay in Paris in the 1840s he seems to have exercised a strong influence both on Proudhon, who acknowledged his debt, and on Marx, who did not. Certainly, as a left-Hegelian philosopher who turned metaphysics to the service of social action, he must be regarded as one of the precursors of Marxism.[29] Having spent the middle decades of his career in practical pursuits, as collaborator of the first agricultural Credit Bank in France, and then as a Posnanian deputy in the Prussian parliament, he began to compose his chief work, *Ojcze Nasz* (Our Father), published posthumously in 1900. This enormous undertaking, inspired by the text: 'Thy Kingdom Come', stands as a monument of European Messianism. It argued that radical politics were not incompatible with Catholic belief, and need not necessarily be associated with violent methods. In this way, the philosophy of insurrectionary Nationalism developed many complex trends and variations, which in the hands of numerous disciples and continuators, such as Bronisław Trentowski at Freiburg and Józef Kremer at Cracow, amassed a resilient body of ideas which could weather the storms of political adversity.[30]

The strength of the Insurrectionary Tradition, therefore, bore no relation to the numbers of its adherents or to the outcome of its political programme. It reflected not the support of the masses, but the intense dedication of its devotees, whose obstinate temper, conspiratorial habits, and unfailing guardianship of the Romantic approach to Literature and History was effectively transmitted from generation to generation. The mechanism of this transmission owed a great deal to a particular breed of courageous and strong-minded women. The memoirs of revolutionaries rarely fail to pay tribute to the mother or grandmother who first instilled them with their lifelong political faith:

My grandmother was a woman of great intelligence and strength of character, and in the breadth of her mind and reading undoubtedly excelled the majority of her contemporaries. After her husband's death, she ran the estate herself, controlling the servants and the workmen with an iron hand . . .

Patriotism was the main motor of her life. The entire passion of her intense and powerful nature was devoted to the cause of her country's freedom . . . and in the conspiratorial work of the January Rising she played a prominent part in the neighbourhood, chairing secret meetings in the house, and carrying guns. She took on danger with utter contempt. The failure of the Rising provoked the greatest trauma of her whole life. Henceforward, she always wore the same black dress with its thin white lace at the neck and cuffs, and on her finger a ring decorated with a white cross in pearls on black enamel . . .

I was perhaps seven years old when one evening I asked her about that ring. We were alone in the drawing-room . . . and the rays of the oil-lamp flickered on the pearls.
— 'It's a ring of mourning for those who died', she said . . .
But when I asked her to put it on my finger, she shook her head.
— 'You can only wear it when you're a real patriot, my child . . .'
— 'And what does that mean, Grandma, "being a patriot"? . . .'

- 'A patriot is someone who loves Poland above everything else in the world', she replied, 'and who will abandon everything, even life itself, for her Freedom . . .'
- 'I want to fight for Poland, Grandma', I said, only half comprehending what I meant . . .
  After a while, my grandmother's eyes flashed.
- 'Yes, I believe that's what you do want. Do you *promise* to fight for Poland, my child?'
- 'I promise, Grandma', I repeated, enthralled by the ominous feeling and power in her voice.
  Then she drew me towards her, caressed me, and placing the ring on my finger, held it there tightly.
- 'Now, there, run along and play with your sisters. But don't forget, and don't tell a soul . . .'[31]

Thus was the young Aleksandra Szczerbińska initiated at her home in Suwałki into a revolutionary career which was destined to involve her in the same sort of conspiracies and gun-running escapades that had preoccupied her grandmother. Thirty years later, as Mme Piłsudska, she entered respectable politics as consort of the Chief-of-State of the Polish Republic.

In many homes, in an atmosphere of supercharged patriotism, no formal initiation was necessary. A youngster who listened to his grandmother playing one of Chopin's Mazurkas, could not fail to notice the further implications:

> And she played it for me
> On an old piano,
> In the room with the portraits
> Of her two executed brothers.[32]

Children such as these were won over to the Polish Cause for life, irrespective of its objective merits. They were taught to serve, and to resist, with no expectation of personal advantage, and with no consolation except that of poetry:

Behind you, soldier of Poland, when you hang on the gallows, or when you perish in the slow agony of the Siberian desert, there wave no mighty banners . . . When you die, no one will feed your children: your fellow-citizens will disown you; your compatriots will forget you . . . Your offspring will be reared in the gutter . . . and cut-throats will be their guardians . . . All is against you: reticence, fear, hatred, the protests of the ruling class, the jangling of factory bells, the intrigues of cowards, and the dark ignorance of poverty. The frightened eyes of national self-bondage peer at you through cracks and holes, from behind buildings and corners . . . Your destiny is death for holy ideals, death without consolation, death without fame . . . You crept out in the darkness of the autumn night, with the wild wind moaning and the rain beating down, whilst the rest of us, twenty million strong, slept in our beds, sunk in the deep slumber of slaves . . . And yet, soldier, your steps resound with a lonely echo in the secret hearts of the people . . . Legends will arise from the pools of congealed blood — legends such as Poland has not yet heard . . . For the poetry of Poland will not forsake you, will not betray or insult you . . . Poetry alone will be faithful, however lost your cause . . . Poetry will cover your corpse . . . with a mantle of nobility . . . Between your deathly, stiffened hands, she will place her golden dream — the dream of a knight-errant's lance![33]

The moderates of Polish politics dismissed such statements as so much romantic slush: but each generation had its sons and daughters who took them seriously, and followed their bidding.

The catastrophes of insurrectionary-Nationalism regularly encouraged the opposite forces of compromise and Conciliation. These forces had always been present, and they, too, can be traced to the traditions of the pre-Partition era. They were embodied in the convictions of people who believed that more could be achieved by striking a bargain with the powers-that-be than by confronting them. They calculated that proof of political loyalty would be rewarded by a licence of limited autonomy or at least of control over social and cultural affairs. Their attitude to the ruling Empires may be summed up in the phrase attributed to Staszic: 'We are ready to be your brothers, but not your slaves.' Their advice to their hot-blooded compatriots was to abandon the negative and distructive exercises of Insurrection, Resistance, or Conspiracy, and to throw themselves into all forms of enterprise that were positive and constructive. In their view, the Polish nation could never secure its position in the world until it was as well educated, as prosperous, and as united, as its neighbours. Hence the emphasis on Education, on Self-improvement, on Science, on Economy, on Social Reform, and above all, on Work. In this context, the stance of Stanisław-August should be contrasted with that of Kościuszko, the career of Staszic or of Wawrzyniec Surowiecki (1769–1827), the economist, with that of Hugo Kołłątaj. In Russian Poland, the road of Conciliation was followed by Xawery Drucki-Lubecki (1778–1848), by Aleksandr Wielopolski (1803–77), and at the end of the century by Roman Dmowski (1864–1939). Their policies ran parallel to those of Prince Antoni Radziwiłł (1775–1833), Viceroy of the Grand Duchy of Posen in Prussia, and of a long line of Kaisertreu Galicians in Austria. After the January Rising of 1863, Conciliation became the dominant trend in Polish politics for almost half a century. It found its first serious ideologues in the Stańczyk Group in Cracow, and was elaborated by a formidable array of writers including Piotr Chmielowski (1848–1904), Aleksander Świętochowski (1849–1938), Julian Klaczko (1825–1906), Adam Wiślicki (1836–1912), Włodzimierz Spasowicz (1829–1906), and above all by the novelist, Bolesław Prus (1847–1912). It was connected with a variety of related cultural and intellectual movements which carried labels such as 'Organic Work', 'Sobriety', 'Warsaw Positivism', and 'Literary Realism'. Its leading organ in the later decades of the century was the *Przegląd Tygodniowy* (Weekly Review), edited throughout its existence by Wiślicki from 1866 to 1905.

Predictably enough, the most fervent advocates of Conciliation were drawn from the ranks of disillusioned insurrectionists — from men and women who had followed the revolutionary road in their youth and who had seen its limitations with their own eyes. Karol Świdziński (1841–77) was exactly such a figure. As a youngster, he joined the radical 'Reds' of the January Rising, served as Dąbrowski's adjutant on the barricades of the Paris Commune, and had passed his term of political exile in England. Yet when he returned home, he composed the verse which is often remembered as the manifesto of the Conciliatory camp:

> FORWARD THROUGH WORK
> . . .
> The strains of the harp are not for you,
> No cavalry charge, no flashes of lightning,
> No eagles soaring on the wing,
> Neither sabre, nor spear, nor arrow.
> What you need is unremitting toil,
> The food of the mind, the bread of the soul.
> . . .

What have you ever gained from your whirling swords?
Just a few notches in the mildew of History.
What benefit came from your lutes and your poetry?
The world will doze through a million chords.

Young comrade, one fights
Not with the sword, but by other lights,
Head down, poring over the page
Of wisdom. There your heart can gauge
The true current of affairs;
And from the harvest of our forebears
You will learn to understand and to love
Everything which makes it good to live.
. . .
Surely you see, my young confrères,
There is nothing much in dreams and swordplay.
It is all a waste of time and energy.
The sabre snaps; and the song fades away.

Take instead a different road,
And count on gains that are lasting,
On triumphs quiet and unassuming
Which give your children bread

And so to the work-bench, to the trowel
To the plough, and to the spirit-level!
Although the work is hard and long
We will come through it, bold and strong.[34]

Świdziński's aversion to poetry may be apparent in the quality
of his verse; but his priorities were perfectly clear — Work
before Battle, Science before Art, Careful Thought before
Rash Action. This sober, practical programme was particularly
admired in the second half of the nineteenth century when
Positivism and Scientism were sweeping Europe. But it has
had its counterparts in Poland on many occasions, both before
and after.

In so far as the Conciliators were sceptical about demands
for Polish Independence, and opposed to the violent designs
of the insurrectionists, they are sometimes characterized as
being passive, if not downright reactionary. In fact, they possessed a highly developed sense of national duty, and not
infrequently a genuine commitment to radical social change.
They strove to restrain not only the conspirators on the one
side but also the unashamed loyalists, careerists, and 'castle

Catholics' on the other. They concentrated their efforts on cultural, economic, and social enterprises, preferring to ensure gradual advance in these spheres at the cost of limited political progress. In their own view, they were practising 'the art of the possible', and as such were the only real politicians. Their achievements, though piecemeal, were considerable. Staszic, for example, who freed the serfs on his private estate at Hrubieszów and gave them the land in communal tenure, was the first man to survey Poland's mineral deposits and to open a colliery at Dąbrowa. From 1808, he was president of the Society of Friends of Science in Warsaw, disseminating the benefits of the scientific and agricultural revolutions, and from 1815, a member of the Commission of Education and Religion, which founded the University of Warsaw. His colleague, Drucki-Lubecki, was equally energetic. As Minister of Finance, in the Congress Kingdom, he launched the Bank of Poland, and planned the country's first steps towards industrialization. His faith was pinned on the liberal proclivities of Alexander I. Wielopolski, who took office as head of the Civil Administration of the Congress Kingdom forty years later, entertained similar hopes about Tsar Alexander II. He initiated the rentification of serf tenures and set aside the civil disabilities on Jews and the barriers to the promotion of Poles in the Tsarist bureaucracy. In particular, he restored the system of Polish language schools and established the *Szkoła Główna,* or 'Main School' in Warsaw. None of these men was successful in any absolute sense. Their moments of effective control were almost as brief as those of the insurrectionists. Especially in Russia, they were handicapped by the absence of any matching generosity of spirit on the part of the authorities. In the last analysis, they could never pursue a lasting policy of Conciliation with imperial superiors who did not understand what compromise meant, and who only made concessions as tactical gestures dictated by temporary weakness. Their work was invariably cut short by political failure. Yet it was they, and men like them, who gave the Polish Nation the wherewithal to survive once independence was finally obtained. If the Insurrectionists were the high-priests of the nation's Soul, the Conciliators were the guardians of its Body.

Wielopolski for instance, was never popular. Square-jawed and grimly determined, he did his duty as he saw it, and ignored criticism. Having served in his twenties as the envoy of the Revolutionary Government to London, he was deeply affected by its failure, and convinced not only of Poland's inability to escape from bondage single-handed, but also of the futility of hoping for foreign assistance. In 1846, appalled by the conduct of the Viennese authorities during the Galician *jacquerie,* he made a public appeal to the Tsar to accept the willing submission of the Polish nation:

We are reaching the point where we can submit, since you are the most high-minded of our opponents. Once we were yours by right of conquest and from fear, like slaves. We despised the oaths of allegiance which were extracted by force. But today, you accede to a new title. We submit to you as a free people, voluntarily and by God's favour, and we accept His sentence. We reject all the self-interested and seductive sentiments, the cheap phrases and everything which is pompously called 'the right of nations'. We cast off the tattered rags in which European charity has clothed us but which do not hide our wounds or clothe our loved ones. We make no conditions . . . [35]

Nicholas I did not even read this appeal. But Wielopolski persevered, and after another decade in the political wilderness, eventually won the confidence of Alexander II. His brief tenure of office preceded the January Rising, and, in the eyes of his critics, provoked it. (See Chapter 16.)

Yet Wielopolski had his admirers, and Włodzimierz Spasowicz was one who consistently defended his reputation over the next forty years. Spasowicz's views are particularly interesting since he was the offspring of a mixed Russo–Polish marriage who, as Professor of Criminal Law at St. Petersburg and later as a lawyer and publicist, spent most of his life in Russia and expressed his ideas in the Russian language. On the political front, he was categorically opposed to all nationalist adventures and to all forms of Polish separatism. Yet on the cultural front, he waged a ceaseless campaign for Polish rights and for the promotion of Polish authors. As a leading contributor to the *Vestnik Evropy,* he battled the cultural chauvinists of the day, and as founder of the journal *Ateneum* and editor of *Kraj* (The Land) he commanded a large readership. His works included a biography of Wielopolski and the

full-scale *Obzor istorii polskoi literatury* (Survey of the
History of Polish Literature, 1880). His concept of nationality,
first formulated in 1872, remained clear and unequivocal to
the end of his life. 'A historical nationality, severed from the
state which had been its cradle, can still have a full right to
exist . . .', he wrote; for 'nationality is a moral treasure, pains-
takingly amassed by a nation and destined for the welfare of
all humanity.'[36]

The literature of Conciliation had no simple programme.
Its one common denominator lay in the widely felt revulsion
from conspiratorial politics. Thus, while seeking to dispel the
mystique of nationality fostered by the Romantics and
Messianists, it strove to 'normalize' and to 'modernize' the
Polish arts: that is, to replace the one-sided obsession with
the Polish cause by a full range of genres and interests, as
exhibited in the cultural life of other European nations. It
was as much concerned with the Fine Arts as with national
politics. Its chief exponent was Aleksander Głowacki (1847—
1912), the 'Polish Dickens', better known by his pen-name of
Bolesław Prus. His career spanned the Risings of 1863—4 and
of 1905—6, and was deeply affected by them. In the former,
he was wounded and arrested; and he reacted sharply against
the latter. His early works avoided overtly political themes,
concentrating instead on psychological observation and social
criticism. *Wieś i miasto* (Town and Country, 1875), and
Anielka (1880) — a powerful attack on the land-owning class
— were written in optimistic mood, whilst he was still searching for a more definite 'positivist' programme. Yet the older
he grew, the more sombre and the more political he became.
His masterwork, *Lalka* (The Doll, 1890), contains the clear
message that proud people who, like its central figure, Wokul-
ski, succumb to over-lofty ambitions, will suffer a fall. *Faraon*
(Pharaoh, 1897) is a study of power, with the scenario of
Ancient Egypt thinly disguising allusions to contemporary
Russia. *Dzieci* (Children, 1908) is a purely political study of
revolutionary conspirators.

The posture which Prus adopted towards the end of his
career was one of profound dismay, not to say cynicism. He
had described the evils of capitalism in convincing detail. Yet
he criticized the socialists and progressives no less. Poland's

international position was all but hopeless. Wilhelmian Germany was 'a fortress of bandits and cut-throats', where 'the new chemistry' was to be used to poison inconvenient citizens, and 'where very unpleasant concoctions are being prepared'; it was 'born in blood, lives on blood, and may one day drown in blood'. Russia, on the other hand, offered only minimal prospects for compromise. Prus judged Polish independence to be a harmful daydream which could only end tragically. Autonomy was to be the absolute limit of all distant national aspirations. 'The Day of Freedom! . . . The Day of Freedom! . . . If we have to play with metaphors, I myself cannot see any daylight at all,' he wrote, 'It's barely dawn, and a bloody one at that . . . and the Devil only knows what sort of Day will follow.' A century of insurrectionary nationalism had produced nothing of value.

We are, as it were, a field on which nothing can ever mature, since everything falls under the sickle before its time; as soon as an ear of corn appears, it is cut down immediately . . . If all the blood spilled by Poles in the cause of freedom were poured together, it would fill the biggest lake in the country; and if all the bones of those who have died in battles, on the gallows, in the camps, or in exile were collected in one heap, they would make another Wawel. But what benefit has there been? None, and there never can be any, since Polish patriotism is made up from violent explosions of emotion which are not illumined by understanding and are not transformed into acts of creative will.[37]

The drift of *Dzieci* is unmistakable. It examines the experiences of Kazimierz Świrski, a youth of integrity and courage, the Commander of a revolutionary society called the 'Knights of Freedom'. It tells a tale of unrelieved waste and mismanagement, which ends in Świrski's futile suicide. Control of the Society passes remorselessly into the hands of a group of common sadists. The characters of Zając, the fearless criminal who thrives on the chaos of a revolutionary crisis; of Starka, his alcoholic associate, who specializes in street hangings; and of Regen, the tubercular Jew, who cannot grasp why the police chief is less frightened of him, than he of the police chief — constitute a merciless denunciation of the people who had launched the Rising of 1905 and who were still conspiring in the underground. In the last resort, Świrski's death was quite unnecessary, and entirely unheroic. On his way to the Galician frontier, the fugitive Commander is asleep in a barn and is awoken by the approach of marching feet:

Suddenly, he imagined that the elegant Cossack was seizing him by the scruff of the neck and dragging him across the snow to the officers, like a piece of carrion. His whole body was shaking. He placed the Brauning to his right ear, and squeezed the trigger lightly. In his head, the bells of all the world rang out. The earth exploded in fiery fragments . . .

Meanwhile, the Cossacks did not even know that Świrski was in the barn, and did not come to arrest him. Their officers had sent them to requisition supplies. Finding the door closed, and their knocking unanswered, they marched on to some other houses.

As usual poor Kazimierz had been in too much of a hurry.[38]

Historians played a prominent role in the Conciliatory camp, especially when they began to apply positivist concepts to their methods of investigation. In this regard, it is interesting to note that Henry Buckle's seminal *History of Civilization in England* (1861) was translated into Polish within a year of its appearance in London. Like Buckle, the Polish positivists were fascinated by Darwinism and by evolutionary biology; and in their haste to jettison all immediate political considerations, they threw themselves into the task of amassing data and documents on all the neglected, non-political aspects of their subject. The clearest formulation of their ideals appeared in the polemics of Władysław Smoleński. On the general issue of whether or not the historian should direct his knowledge to practical purposes, Smoleński took an unequivocal stand. 'The question is determined by one's over-all concept of Science,' he wrote; 'and Science has no other task than the verification and explanation of phenomena. For the botanist, it is quite irrelevant whether the characteristics of a particular plant may be applied in medicine or in gastronomy. Similarly, the historian is not obliged to draw lessons from the past. Kitchen chefs may well benefit from botanical investigations, and statesmen from historical studies, if they so wish. None the less, the practical benefits are an incidental, not a necessary, result of the scientific exercise.' Having said that, Smoleński passed to his famous denunciation of political history, which in Poland was still obsessed with the cause and effects of the Partitions:

To take the fall of Poland as the foundation for one's view of the past is a complete and utter error . . . The fact that the state disappeared is important for the history of the nineteenth century; but there is no scientific reason why it should be seen as the cardinal event of our entire history. Was the whole of Polish History nothing but a prelude to the Partitions? Were there not other factors other than the defective nature of the state? . . . It would be understandable for the theme of decline and fall to dominate the history of the state, but not the history of the nation, which is the primary subject of historical research and which did not cease to exist because of the loss of political independence . . . The organism we call the state is not the centre of all aspects of life, and its history is not the quintessence of the past. In addition to creating its own state, the Polish nation left a contribution to civilization that survived the fall, and this is the main theme of history.[39]

The positivist historians would have strenuously denied that their studies were influenced by political considerations. But by defusing the supercharged themes of Independence and Statehood, they inevitably tranquillized the intellectual atmosphere in which Conciliatory politics were trying to operate. (See Vol. I, Chapter 1.)

The philosophical underpinning of Conciliation took many forms. Yet in its efforts to avoid the specifically Polish character of Messianism, it frequently lapsed into mere imitation of foreign trends. The 'minimalists' had always been represented in Poland, ever since the eighteenth century, in thinkers such as Jan Śniadecki (1756–1830), an exponent of the ideas of the French Enlightenment, or Michał Wiszniewski (1794–1865), a disciple of the Scottish 'common sense' school; and even at the height of the Romantic craze, there were Catholic philosophers at work like Eleonora Ziemięcka (1819–69), and in Cracow, the Revd Stefan Pawlicki (1839–1916). After 1863, the Positivists gained the upper hand, though by no means a monopoly. Their leader, Julian Ochorowicz (1850–1917), a graduate of Leipzig, and the leader of 'the new direction', as he was acclaimed in Warsaw, can be counted a follower of Comte. 'A Positivist', he wrote, 'is a name we give to anyone whose statements are supported by evidence which can be checked – a person who does not discuss doubtful matters without qualifications and who never talks of things which are inaccessible.' In alliance with the Neo-Kantians, he battled against the remnants of the preceding fashion. In each of their different ways, all these philosophers served to deflect Polish intellectual circles from revolutionary fantasies and dreams of revenge.[40]

Roman Dmowski, founder in 1897 of the National Democratic Movement, carried the ideals of Conciliation into the realm of modern party politics. Yet his posture was conciliatory only on the practical question of political methods. On many other issues, his style was aggressive, and his programme radical. He had early decided that the principal threat to the survival of the Polish nation lay in German Imperialism, and he looked for protection to Russia. In return for loyalty to the Tsar, he expected the widest concessions. He enjoyed the support of Russian liberals, and in the Duma in 1907–12 was working his way towards demands for Polish autonomy. In Poland itself, he aroused the economic aspirations of the urban bourgeoisie, and did not shrink from inflaming their latent antipathies towards Polish Jewry. He organized the attempted boycott of Jewish enterprises in 1911, and as a result lost the next election. He was equally opposed both to the old landowning conservatism and to the new class-based movements of the peasant and socialist parties. His ideas, set out in *La Question polonaise* (1906) and *Myśli nowoczesnego Polaka* (Thoughts of an Up-to-Date Pole, 1909) stressed the virtues of individualism and constitutionalism, and drew attention to his name in Western Europe. In the First World War, he was the natural candidate for liaison with the Allied Powers. From 1916 he headed the Polish National Committee in Paris and in 1919 the Polish Delegation to the Peace Conference. In terms of political attitudes, he was probably the single most significant figure in modern Polish politics. But he never grasped the reins of power. He was the lifelong rival and detractor of Józef Piłsudski.[41]

The organizations with which Dmowski was associated tended to be rather ephemeral. Being formed in the first instance under generalized slogans of a national revival, they attracted a wide range of incompatible interests and personalities, and often developed in directions unintended by their original founders. The Polish League, which took the name of an earlier body which had appeared briefly in Prussian

Poland in 1848–50, was founded in Switzerland in 1887 in co-operation with Zygmunt Miłkowski (1824–1915), a veteran *émigré* and novelist of a distinctly liberal persuasion. Finding it tinged with revolutionary elements unsympathetic to his taste, Dmowski abandoned it in April 1893 in favour of his own breakaway National League, which, together with its militant youth section called *Zet* (Union of Polish Youth), had a more right-wing flavour. Over the next three decades, the National League spawned a stream of political parties – the National Democratic Movement (SN-D) in 1897; the People's National Union (ZL-N) in 1919; and the National Movement (SN) in 1928. Taken together, Dmowski's organizations earned the popular name of the *Endecja* or 'National Democracy'. Their special contribution to nationalist politics was to propagate their aims in all three partitions – whereas most of their predecessors had limited their activities to one of the Empires – and thus to put debates on the national issue back on to the 'all-Polish' level. Although for political reasons, the National Democracy was overtly opposed to national independence, it was pressing for a reunion of the Polish lands which could not have been accommodated within the existing framework of the Empires. To this extent, its preferred solution of a 'separate and autonomous Poland', as opposed to a 'sovereign and independent' one, involved upheavals in the established order hardly less profound than those designed by the national revolutionaries. Apart from Dmowski, its spiritual fathers included the journalist Jan Ludwig Popławski (1854–1908), and Zygmunt Balicki (1858–1916), author of the influential *Egoizm narodowy wobec etyki* (National Egoism and Ethics, 1902).

Piłsudski (1867–1935) was an Insurrectionary in a generation of Conciliators, a Romantic in the age of Positivism. He was born in Lithuania, and lived most of his early life in Wilno. He was the second son of an old Polish family living in straitened circumstances. He was strongly influenced by a fiercely patriotic mother, and from an early age resisted the mood of dejection which, in the aftermath of the January Rising, affected most of his contemporaries. At the age of 20, he was arrested by Tsarist police investigating the attempt to assassinate Alexander III; and for a conspiracy in which he and his elder brother Bronisław were little more than unwitting accomplices, he spent five years of penal exile in eastern Siberia. In this first period of his political career, he was closely associated with the socialist movement. He was the founding editor of *Robotnik* (The Worker), the journal of the Polish Socialist Party, and worked in the underground as an agitator and party organizer. He spent some time among the revolutionary exiles in London. His second arrest in 1900 led to incarceration in a mental hospital in St. Petersburg whence he escaped with the help of a Polish doctor. In 1904—5 he was in Japan, vying with Dmowski for the political crumbs of the Russo-Japanese War. In 1905—7 he was back in Poland, in Łódź, in the thick of the revolutionary terror and strikes. Although he only dabbled with Marxism, and never belonged to any Bolshevik organization, his origins were much the same as those of the Bolshevik leaders. Like Lenin, whose own elder brother had been executed for that same attempt on the Tsar in 1887, he found the emotional drive for his activities in the adolescent humiliation which punished him for a crime which he did not commit. Like Feliks Dzierżyński, who attended the same school in Wilno until expelled for speaking Polish in class, he did not distinguish at first between 'Nationalism' and 'Socialism'. He used any idea, any instrument to hand, for fighting the hated regime. The second period of his career began in 1908 and lasted until 1921. It was the period of force, and of military action. It was inspired by the crushing defeat which by then had been imposed on all the revolutionary factions in Russia. As he wrote to a veteran socialist friend:

Let others play at throwing bouquets to socialism or to Polonism or to anything they like . . . I can't, not in this present atmosphere of a latrine . . . I want to conquer. My latest idea is to create . . . an organization of brute force — to use an expression which is unsupportable to the humanitarians. I have sworn to realize it, or to perish.[42]

Like the Bolsheviks, he denounced the prevarications of mainstream Social Democracy, and concluded that an élite, disciplined organization offered the only chance of combating the force which was ranged against them. He raised his funds by highway robbery; and in April 1908 at Bezdany, near Wilno, pulled off a highly successful mail-train raid. Unlike the Bolsheviks, however, he also turned to soldiering, and to an unashamedly nationalist campaign, believing that the loyalty of his Polish compatriots was a sounder basis for action than calls for class warfare. From then on, his one aim was for an independent Poland. He formed his Legions in Austria, first in the guise of 'Riflemen's Clubs', and later in the open. He persuaded the Central Powers that he might be of use in the event of war. He was given the rank of Brigadier-General, and allowed to train in the Carpathians. Between 1914 and 1917 he fought under Austrian Command on the Eastern Front. He briefly served as Minister of War in the Regency government, but was imprisoned by the Germans for refusing the proffered oath to the Kaiser. From July 1917 to November 1918, he remained in Magdeburg Castle. After ten years of unremitting effort, there was little forewarning of the triumph which was soon to be his. (See Chapter 18.)

To understand the extraordinary turns of fortune which marked Piłsudski's career, it is necessary to ponder three outstanding features of his complex personality. Firstly, he was a conspirator, not a statesman. His habits of mind were formed by the harsh realities of the Russian underground. He knew little of compromise or patient accommodation, and had little in common with politicians like Daszyński, the socialist, Witos, the peasant leader, or Dmowski, with whom he was later expected to co-operate. Secondly, he was a fighter. His natural instinct when faced with an impasse, was to shoot his way out. This was to be the hallmark of his diplomacy, and in 1926, of his approach to constitutional problems. Thirdly, he was a rogue elephant. He possessed all the political vices in full measure: he was wayward, reckless, rude, vindictive, childish, taciturn, and unpredictable. He was embarrassing to his colleagues, and offensive to his opponents. He was incapable of observing Party discipline, or of founding a coherent political movement. But in 1918–21, he played a part in Polish History which no one can fairly deny. Like that of Churchill twenty years later, his 'Finest Hour' stood in the midst of a lifetime strewn with blunders and failures. Yet such was the force of his personality, the strength of his nerve, and the obstinacy of his resolution that he imposed his will on the lesser and more cautious men around him. There is no other figure in the recent history of Poland to whom Józef Piłsudski can be compared.[43]

In the last decade before the First World War Polish political life was polarizing rapidly. The two main strands of the national movement, Dmowski's *Narodowcy* or 'Nationalists' and Piłsudski's *Niepodległościowcy* or 'Independence-ites', were operating in all three Partitions, and were stealing the limelight from all the other organizations. They shared the common insistence on the absolute priority of the national question over all other issues; but in philosophy, tactics, and temperament, they differed diametrically. The Nationalists conceived of the nation as a distinct ethnic community which possessed an inalienable right to the exclusive enjoyment of its ancestral territory; the Independence Camp, in contrast, favoured the concept of a spiritual community, united by bonds of culture and history, and looking to some form of association with the other oppressed nations of the area. The Nationalists saw the principal international menace in the rise of the German Empire, and were obliged to consider a tactical alliance with Russia. The Independence Camp thought of Russia as the historic enemy, and looked forward to the time when they could take up arms against Russia in the company of the Germans and Austrians. The Nationalists assumed that their necessary alliance with Russia ruled out any real hopes of independence, and were prepared to settle instead for national autonomy under Russian patronage. From the same premises, the Independence Camp argued that demands for national independence would necessarily involve an armed struggle against Russia in the grand insurrectionary tradition. The Nationalists are often classed as 'realists' on the basis of their willingness to compromise with the great powers, whilst the Independence Camp, with its determination to fight all-comers irrespective of the odds, are classed as 'Romantics'. In the domestic arena, however, the attitude of the Nationalists was harsh, intolerant, and strident, especially with regard to other national groups; whilst the attitude of the Independence Camp was relatively mild and tolerant. The Nationalists saved their venom for the enemies within; the Independence Camp sharpened their swords for the enemy without.

In describing the clear-cut traditions of Loyalism, Insurrection, and Conciliation, it is necessary to emphasize that one is dealing with ideas that cut across all forms of political organization. At any given moment, they rarely coincided exactly with the attitudes of individuals or with the declared programmes of the Parties. Yet as reflections of pressures which were felt in all sectors of Polish political life, they can all be observed in different combinations and degrees in almost everyone's thinking. When, towards the end of the nineteenth century, the dynastic Empires permitted the creation of political movements, most such movements contained a loyalist, an insurrectionary and a conciliatory wing. The leaders of the Peasant Movement, for example, were eternally debating whether the best advantage for the Polish peasant could be obtained by trying to please the authorities, by fighting them, or by bargaining with them. The Socialist Movement, too, was split from the very beginning between the internationalist (or anti-nationalist) wing; the revolutionary nationalist wing; and the moderate centre, which hoped to give equal priority to both social and national goals. In Germany they were faced by state-sponsored Socialism, and in Russia by so-called Police Socialism — both in their different ways variations on the Loyalist theme. The positions of individual politicians were equally complicated. Although, in a few extreme instances, it is possible to point to men who held to a consistent line throughout their careers, it is more usual to watch how they shifted their ground in response to changing events. It is often said that the best gamekeepers are recruited from the ranks of repentant poachers. By analogy, it is not surprising to find that the most fervent Loyalists were drawn from Poles who had entertained revolutionary fantasies in their youth. The career of General Józef Zajączek (1752–1826), who began as a Jacobin on Kościuszko's staff and ended up after 1815 as the Prince-Viceroy of the Tsar in Warsaw, is a case in point. The critics of Józef Piłsudski have said that he too was a 'Jacobin turned chauvinist' and that on the assumption of power he abandoned all the ideals which he had nurtured in opposition. Conversely, the most effective revolutionaries were often to be found among converted loyalists. There is no doubt that the Officer Corps of the Russian army acted as the most fertile ground for nurturing and training Polish revolutionaries. In the centre of Polish politics, away from these extremes, political figures who strove to reconcile contradictory pressures were most easily misunderstood. In examining the career of Prince Adam Jerzy Czartoryski, for instance, it would be simple to say that as Foreign Minister of Russia in 1804–6 he was a 'Loyalist'; as Curator of the Wilno School District from 1803 and promoter of Polish schooling, he was a 'Conciliator'; and in 1831 as President of the National Government which dethroned the Tsar, that he was an Insurrectionary. In effect, Czartoryski's changing fortunes were not instigated by any dramatic convulsions in his personal attitudes, but rather by fundamental changes in the poltical situation, and by striking differences in the policies of Alexander I and Nicholas I.[44] As always, the history of Political Ideas, which exist in the abstract, is logical and coherent: the history of real men and women, who have to operate in fluid circumstances, is infernally complicated.

Political life in the Polish lands was further characterized by the existence of powerful and independent institutions which, whilst denying any overtly political purpose, have always exercised a distinct political influence. These institutions have always come to the fore in periods of repression when the free right of political organization was not admitted. First and foremost were the Christian churches, and in particular the Roman Catholic Church, which was directed by the Vatican from a point beyond the control of the ruling governments. (See Chapter 7.)

Secondly, and more surprisingly perhaps, came Polish Freemasonry, whose continuing existence is proved by the frequent appeals and decrees for its abolition. Officially abolished in the old Republic in 1734, it re-emerged in the reign of Stanisław-August and claimed the King as one of its devoted members. Henceforth the Masonic Lodges, which rejected the religious absolutism of the Church and the political oppression of the governments alike, thrived on the established conspiratorial habits of their members, and played a prominent and little acknowledged role in nationalist history. In Prussian Poland, their activities were almost completely Germanized in the course of time, and were associated with German liberal movements. But in the Congress Kingdom, and again in Russian Poland after the revolution of 1905, they attracted a large following among the Polish liberal intelligentsia. Some aspects of their history, such as the foundation of a movement for National Freemasonry by the ill-starred Walerian Łukasiński (1786–1868) in 1819, are well known. But research in depth is still in its infancy; and a full list of Polish Freemasons in the nineteenth and early twentieth centuries might well contain a surprising number of the champions of the national cause.[45]

Lastly, it should be remembered that Polish Nationalism formed only part of political life. In view of its ultimate success, it is sometimes awarded a degree of attention which it did not always merit. Although the construction of the Polish nation must obviously command the limelight, the parallel growth of Russian, German, Ukrainian, Lithuanian, and Jewish nationalisms, and of populism, socialism, liberalism, and conservatism in these same Polish lands was no less important. Polish History in this period does not consist of a simple story describing the onward march of the Polish nation towards Independence. Rather, it relates a complex series of conflicts which, at the time, offerred little prospect of easy resolution.

Some of the most fearless and enlightened figures of their day have escaped general recognition, simply because they opposed all the reigning political fashions without exception. Such a figure, indeed, was Jan Ignacy Baudouin de Courtenay (Ivan Alexandrovitch Boduen de Kurtené, 1845–1929). A philologist by profession, he was constantly refused employment in his native Warsaw, but as Professor at Kazan, Dorpat, Cracow, and St. Petersburg, he established himself as one of the pioneers of modern linguistics. A pacifist, an environmentalist, a feminist, a progressive educationist, and a freethinker, he defied most of the social and intellectual conventions of his contemporaries. He was particularly incensed by the current cant of Nationalism of all sorts. From his fieldwork researching the dialects of the 'minor' Slav peoples such as the Sorbs, the Silesians, and the Slovenes, he was perfectly well aware that the individual's right to a cultural identity of his own was no less threatened by the modern nationalist movements than by the imperialist regimes. In his view, the politician from Warsaw who wanted to turn the Kashubs, the Silesians, or the Byelorussians into Poles could hardly claim to be aggrieved when Tsarist officialdom tried to turn Poles into Russians. In Hungary, Baudouin de Courtenay was denounced as a Tsarist spy, for interesting himself in the problems of the Slovaks. In Galicia, he found that his views on the Ukrainians were equally unwanted, and that his contract to teach at the Jagiellonian University was not renewed. In Russia, he was denounced as a degenerate and a traitor, and in 1913 was gaoled for expressing unacceptable opinions. After all that, having returned to Warsaw in 1918 to accept a professorial chair *honoris causa*, he outraged his compatriots by declaring in his inaugural lecture that 'Poland had not been resurrected in order to swell the tally of imperialist hyena-states.' As a candidate for the Presidency in 1922, he received the support of the minorities, and almost 20 per cent of the popular vote; but in the discussions on educational reform, he shocked many of his supporters by suggesting that Polish should be taught in all Jewish schools in Poland just as Yiddish ought to be taught in all Polish schools. There can be little doubt that Baudouin de Courtenay's ideals were grounded in the best of Polish individualist and libertarian traditions; but they could not be contained within the narrow limits of modern Polish nationalism. For this reason, they find little mention in modern histories. Yet without them, any survey of the Polish political scene would be far from complete.[46]

*   *   *   *   *

By the turn of the twentieth century, Polish independence looked as much a mirage as ever. In Germany and Russia, the Polish provinces were ruled from the centre, and played only a marginal role in policy-making. No nationalist politician held a responsible position in imperial counsels. In Austria, where Galicia had enjoyed political and cultural autonomy since 1867, the Poles formed one of the strongest pillars of the Habsburg regime. They gave little thought to all-Polish, as opposed to Galician interests, and even less to the proposition that they should combine with their compatriots in

Germany and Russia. The high degree of co-ordination between the police forces of the three Empires, assiduously engaged in combating nationalist movements, was never matched by the attempts at co-ordination among the multifarious Polish parties of the three Partitions.[47] On the diplomatic front, the Polish Question had long since disappeared from the active agenda of the powers. The impunity with which the provisions of the Treaty of Vienna were destroyed in the first half of the nineteenth century, had blunted the edge of foreign concern. By now, most statesmen had come to regard the Poles as just another minority, whose demands for fair treatment could not include the right to sovereignty. In a world of full-blown imperialism, they did not question the benefits of German or Russian rule in Poland, any more than those of their own rule in Ireland, Egypt, Algeria, or Panama. The diplomatic combinations of the last fifty years were consistently unfavourable. In the Bismarckian Era, the alliance of Prussia and Russia involved a close understanding on the suppression of Polish matters, and precluded all external interference. In 1888, it was enhanced by the accession of Austria—Hungary to the *Dreikaiserbund* (The Three Emperors' League). The fall of Bismarck, and the subsequent realignment of the Powers left certain room for manœuvre, especially during the Russo-Japanese War and the revolutionary years of 1905—6. But the Franco-Russian Alliance of 1891 neutralized one of the two western powers who might have exploited the Polish issue; whilst the Anglo-Russian Agreement of 1907 removed the other. To all intents and purposes, the Polish Question was dead.

Polish national consciousness was itself in a state of disarray. In Germany, the relative position of the Poles was much weaker than in the Kingdom of Prussia. It is true that their numbers were holding up in Pomerania and Posnania. They successfully resisted the *Kulturkampf* of the 1870s and the activities of the Prussian Land Commission, 1886—1913. Yet the relentless pressures of industrialization, of increasing social mobility, and of the virtual German monopoly in higher education took a heavy toll. The Polish element was in danger of relapsing into a residual, rural community. Posen alone, with its excellent educational institutions and its pool of skilled

Polish labour was the one place which stood to keep up with the times and stay Polish. In Silesia, second only to the Ruhr in industrial output, Germanization proceeded apace. Unlike the Posnanians, the indigenous population had no memories of former connections with the Polish state. Their designation by the Germans as *Wasserpolaken* or 'watered-down Poles' does great injustice to their highly individual characteristics; but it does reflect their limited interest in nationalist politics until the turn of the century. In Russian Poland, national consciousness was much stronger. 'Russification' campaigns had badly misfired. In contrast to Germany, the Russian state did not possess the means or the understanding to educate the Poles into new ways. Yet its massive powers of coercion were clear to all. It had survived the revolutionary years of 1905–7, and broken all political resistance. In the years before the War, it seemed to be entering on a period of constitutional reform, and of vast economic expansion. It seemed to offer great prospects for Polish enterprise, especially in the economic and intellectual spheres. Many educated Poles, despairing of any political progress, saw themselves as playing the part of the Greeks to this new Rome. In Galicia, the situation was different again. The pride of the Galician Poles in their strong Polish identity was mixed with deep gratitude to the Habsburgs. In all three partitions, changing social patterns strongly influenced political attitudes. The emancipation of the serfs and the growth of education awakened whole new sections of society to the national ideal. Jan Słomka (1842–1929), from Dzików on the Vistula, passed as he relates 'from serfdom to self-government'. As a young man, he had no idea that he was a Pole. The local peasants on that part of the Vistula called themselves *'Mazury'*, i.e. Mazovians. In the tradition of the old Republic, only gentlemen were thought of as Poles. On learning to read, however, and by participating in Galician politics, Słomka eventually became enthusiastically aware of his Polish identity.[48] The over-all picture, therefore, was exceedingly complicated. In quantitative terms, Polish national consciousness had not diminished. There were far more people who thought of themselves as Poles in 1914 than in 1814. But the understanding of their Polishness was so varied, so fragmented by competing loyalties

and by differing social and economic interests, that it provided
no certain basis for concerted political action. Polish nationalism was smouldering steadily, burning itself out in some areas,
whilst spreading into others. But it could not hope to burst
into general public flame so long as the stifling constrictions
of the three empires remained intact. No consensus existed
concerning Poland's future prospects. A handful of diehard
optimists continued to believe that their country would rise
once more, phoenix-like, from the flames. But most sanguine
observers, including many who were deeply sympathetic to
the Polish cause, felt it unlikely that Polish culture could
survive indefinitely. In 1886, Georg Brandes sensed an impending crisis. 'For a hundred years', he wrote, 'Poland has served
as the anvil of three great powers, and has borne the blows of
the enormous hammers without being crushed. Either before
very long, the hammers will be stopped, or this culture will
be annihilated.' Eight years later, in 1894, he likened the
conditions of the Poles to that of Harlequin in the story by
Prosper Mérimée when he fell from a fifth-storey window. As
Harlequin passed another window on the third floor, someone asked him how he felt. 'Pretty well,' he answered, 'provided that this continues.' 'We all know how the fall will end,'
Brandes concluded; 'but so long as one is in the air, it is not
so bad.'[49]

The limited achievement of Polish nationalism during the
nineteenth century was compounded by its signal failure to
make common cause with a wide variety of potential allies.
In theory, Polish nationalists considered themselves the
natural partners of all oppressed people in Eastern Europe, if
not in the world. Their illusion was shared by many idealists
of the age, from Marx to Macaulay. In practice, they found
that their demands for Polish independence monotonously
antagonized their would-be associates, causing bitter conflicts
and inconsolable rivalries.

One such conflict constantly recurred in connection with
social policy. Agrarian reform in the first half of the century,
industrialization and urbanization in the second, were always
thought to be problems of proper national concern. Emancipation of the serfs from the landlords, and later the liberation
of the working class from the capitalists were increasingly

regarded as the necessary adjunct to the deliverance of the nation from the partitioning powers. In an ideal world, the nation was to be liberated by the efforts of a united society. In reality, matters turned out rather differently. As shown by one of the best-known verses of the century composed in 1836 by Gustaw Ehrenberg (1818–95), social divisions continued to disrupt political unity:

> When the people went forth with the sword to the fray,
> The gentry were chatting in parliament.
> When the people declared 'We shall conquer or die',
> The nobles were counting their rent.
> The cannon at Stoczek were captured by youths
> Whose arms had been tanned at the plough,
> Whilst the gentry in town were smoking cheroots
> As they talked and debated and furrowed their brow
> On the problem of meeting their Muscovite friends,
> And of finding a formula of good common sense
> That could lead to a treaty and patch up a peace.
> So thanks very much, gentlemen, noble MPs!
> Many thanks indeed, you earls and you prelates,
> You counts and masters, you lords and magnates![50]

The idea that the peasants had done the fighting during the insurrections, whilst the noblemen stayed at home smoking their cigars is very wide of the mark. Most historians would agree that the risings were launched and supported by the nobility but that they failed, among other reasons, because the mass of the peasantry remained apathetic towards them. Even so, Ehrenberg was perfectly correct in stressing the gulf in social attitudes which separated the nobility from the peasantry and which hindered consolidated political action. His savage parodies of the landowning classes made him very popular in later times, and his own conspiratorial activities earned him half a lifetime spent in Siberian exile. His verse quoted above was set to music, and became one of favourite songs of the communist movement. It is a pity that few of the people who sing it today know that its author, Gustaw Ehrenberg, was the son of Alexander I, Tsar of Russia.

As successive Risings failed, noble leaders blamed the ignorance of the peasants; liberals blamed the conservatism of the nobility. Social reformers tended to view nationalist conspiracies as a threat to their own success, and were unwilling to defer their reforms until the time for concerted political action was ripe. The radical social legislation of the Risings, from Kościuszko's Manifesto of Połaniec to the emancipation decrees of 1863, was invariably overturned, often provoking episodes of rampant reaction. What is more, in moments of crisis, the authorities carefully exploited social reform as a means of winning back their disaffected Polish subjects. Legal equality in the Duchy of Warsaw, the rentification decree of 1823 in the Grand Duchy of Posen, the reforms undertaken in Prussia and Austria in 1848—50 and in Russian Poland in 1861 and 1864, were motivated as much by political considerations as by genuine social concern. Alexander II's *ukaz* of March 1864 on the emancipation of the Polish peasantry deliberately topped both the concessions already made in Russia as a whole, and those proposed by the leader of the January Rising. It was an expressly anti-nationalist initiative which successfully seduced the countryside from national politics for the next generation. (See Chapter 16.)

Similar disillusionment awaited the national movement when both Socialism and Marxism made their appearance. The first Polish socialist group, Ludwik Waryński's 'Proletariat', founded in Warsaw in 1882, was obsessively anti-nationalist. The main Polish Marxist party, the SDKPiL, actively opposed the union of the Polish lands. Its leading lights, Róża Luksemburg (Rosa Luxemburg), Feliks Dzierżynski, Julian Marchlewski, and Karol Radek, spent most of their energies in the service of the German or the Russian revolutions. The Polish Socialist Party (PPS), whose initial 'Paris Programme' placed equal emphasis on national and social justice, was constantly split by the incompatible aims of its twin interests. As Piłsudski himself was forced regretfully to admit, it was impossible to give equal priority to social and to nationalist policies. By the time he emerged in 1918 as the leader of the Polish Republic, he had ceased to regard himself as a socialist.

Another series of conflicts arose with regard to rival national movements. Russian and German liberals were all conspiring against the same partitioning powers. In the later nineteenth century, Lithuanians, Byelorussians, Ukrainians, Czechs, and Jews were all deprived and persecuted by the same imperial regimes. Common action against the common enemy was consistently pursued. But it was never achieved. (See Diagram B.)

The fitful Polish love-affair with the Russian dissidents was constantly racked by mutual recriminations, and ended in separation. The Polish patriotic societies of the 1820s had been in close contact with the Decembrists. Mickiewicz among others took trouble to tour Russia and make friends with dissident literary circles, Pushkin included. In 1831, it was a popular demonstration in honour of the Decembrists which steeled the Sejm to dethrone the Tsar. That beautiful slogan 'FOR YOUR FREEDOM AND OURS' was coined to express the contention that revolution in Russia and independence for Poland were essential to the overthrow of Tsarism. In 1863, Herzen was persuaded to praise the Poles, and to canvass an alliance not only with the Russian 'Zemlya i Volya', but also with the Italian and Hungarian exiles. All these contacts miscarried. Pushkin bitterly denounced the Poles, whose 'selfish' adventures presented an excellent pretext for strengthening autocracy in Russia. Mickiewicz likened Pushkin's protests to the 'barking of a mad dog'. Herzen's journal *Kolokol* lost half its supporters overnight. For those who had not known all along, most Russian revolutionaries wanted to keep Russia intact for the Revolution, and regarded Polish revolutionary nationalists as reactionaries and *provocateurs*. From 1863, anti-Polish tendencies prevailed in Russia, among Slavophiles and revolutionaries alike. In Poland, in the wake of the Risings, anti-Russian passions raged. Mutual antipathies, cemented the growing conviction in both countries that Polish and Russian cultures were incurably antagonistic. (See Chapter 2.)

The Polish—German alliance failed even earlier. In 1848, the Posnanian insurrectionists had appealed for support to the German Parliament at Frankfurt. They were promptly told to cease their occupation of the 'ancient German province of Posen'. There was to be no more sympathy from that quarter. German Nationalism of the Bismarckian Era was obsessively self-centred, and under Prussian auspices specifically hostile to Polish aims. (See Chapter 3.)

Relations with the Ukrainians, Byelorussians, and Lithuanians were no better. Polish territorial claims to Lwów, Minsk,

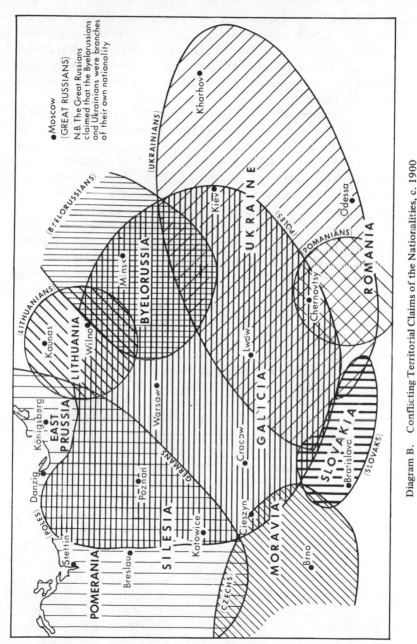

Diagram B. Conflicting Territorial Claims of the Nationalities, c. 1900

or Wilno, based on the frontiers and traditions of the old Republic were no longer acceptable. All were complicated by the arrival of militant Zionism. Thus it happened, that efforts designed to double the pressure on Tsarism, actually diminished it. The authorities divided their various enemies one from the other and ruled with equanimity.

The History of Polish Jewry provides an obvious case in point. In the course of the nineteenth century, the civil disabilities of the Jews were matched by mounting economic distress. A fivefold natural increase brought intolerable pressures on the Pale of Settlement and on Galicia, until mass emigration offered the only means of escape. For much of the century, the Polonization of Jewish culture, and their assimilation into Polish society were advocated both by Jewish reformers and by Polish liberals alike. Both in 1830–1 and in 1861–4, Poles and Jews stood side by side in the Risings against Russian tyranny. But from then on, attitudes hardened in both communities. Jewish nationalists of the new generation saw Assimilation as a threat to their own aspirations, and condemned co-operation with the Poles out of hand. In the Polish camp, the rise of militant nationalists of Dmowski's persuasion, with their slogan of 'Poland for the Poles' generated similar antipathies. Anti-Jewish themes reappeared in Polish literature – in Michał Bałucki's novel, *W żydowskich rękach* (In Jewish Hands, 1885), for example. One can only conclude that it is not possible to lead two tribes of Chosen People through the same desert. (See Chapter 9.)

Seen through the Jewish filter, the spectrum of Polish political life assumes an entirely different aspect.[51] As a result of rooted opposition to separate Jewish aspirations, a man like Staszic, who in Polish terms was considered a 'moderate', and a 'Conciliator', became an 'anti-semite' and therefore an 'extremist'. His pamphlet *Concerning the Reasons for the Obnoxiousness of the Jews* (1816) earned him the label of 'the old Jew-baiter'. Similarly, General Krasiński, who as a faithful servant of the Tsar and an unashamed Russifier was deemed by Poles to be a 'traitor', showed equal indifference to nationalist feelings of all sorts and became in Jewish terms a 'moderate'. It was only on the Far Left that Polish and Jewish politics tended to coincide. In the early decades, Lelewel or

Walerjan Łukasiński were classified both as Polish patriots and as 'pro-Semites'. At the end of the period, a number of progressive Jews, like Bernard Hausner joined Piłsudski's Legions, just as their forebears had joined Kościuszko or Poniatowski. Most typical, however, were those Polish and Jewish revolutionaries who, having rejected the bourgeois aspirations of their respective national communities came together in the internationalist Marxist movement.

To the north-east — that is, in the North Western Land of the Russian Empire — the Poles came into conflict with the national revivals of the Baltic Lithuanians, and of the Slavonic Byelorussians. Until the mid-nineteenth century, the separate identity of these two peoples had not been generally recognized, not even by themselves. Peter Kropotkin, writing in the first edition of the *Encyclopaedia Britannica* informed the world quite inaccurately that the peoples of the former Grand Duchy consisted of Baltic 'Zhmudi', i.e. Samogitians, and Slavic Lithuanians. No one seriously imagined that they could become a serious political factor. But they did.

For five hundred years, the Lithuanians had lived in political union with the Poles in a situation closely analogous to that of the Scots and English. Until 1793, their Grand Duchy had formed part of the united Republic of Poland–Lithuania. In the course of this long union, the Polish language, like English in Scotland, had been almost universally adopted by the ruling and educated classes. The Lithuanian language, like the Gælic language of the Scots in Scotland, had only survived in the remoter rural areas, and in certain segments of the peasantry. It was not normally spoken by any significant group in the country's capital, Vilnius (Wilno), whose Lithuanian population at the last Tsarist Census in 1897 reached only 2 per cent. It had no settled written form, and no literature of note. Its only centres of study and publication lay across the frontier in East Prussia, in so-called 'Little Lithuania', where the districts of Klajpeda (Memel) and Tylża (Tilsit) were inhabited by a Protestant Lithuanian minority. Lithuanian Nationalism developed in reaction on the one hand against the Polish assumption that Lithuania belonged to Poland, and on the other hand against the attempts of the Tsarist Government to impose Russian culture and Orthodox religion. The cultural revival was promoted in the first instance by the Catholic clergy, especially by successive Bishops of Samogitia, Joseph Giedroyć (1745–1838) and Matthias Valancius (1801–75). The publication in 1841 in Polish, of a multi-volume 'History of Lithuania' by Teodor Narbutt (1784–1864), and later translations into Lithuanian of works by that famous Lithuanian poet, 'Adomas Mickievičius', set the pace for native literary talent. Important cultural advances were provoked by the emancipation of the peasantry in 1861, and by the establishment of a Lithuanian orthography which, to spite the Poles, was based on the Czech alphabet. In the late nineteenth century, the Lithuanian national movement assumed an overtly political character, with its own loyalist, conciliatory, and revolutionary trends, its own parties, and its own *émigré* fund-raisers. As a result, the scope for Polish-oriented politics was confined to the Polish-speaking sector of the population, in particular to important segments of the land-owning class and of the urban bourgeoisie in Wilno, Grodno, Nowogródek, and elsewhere. The social and cultural situation was far more complex than either Polish or Lithuanian nationalists were willing to admit. Ethnographers who tried to investigate the area in a scientific manner encountered many baffling contradictions. An oral researcher, interviewing the local shoemaker in a village near Kaunas (Kowno) in 1885, recorded a most revealing conversation:

— What tribe do you belong to?
— I am a Catholic.
— That's not what I mean. I'm asking you whether you are a Pole or a Lithuanian.
— I am a Pole, and a Lithuanian as well.
— That is impossible. You have to be either one or the other.
— I speak Polish, the shoemaker said, and I also speak Lithuanian.
And that was the end of the interview.[52]

The shoemaker was better informed than the ethnographer. Many of the men who emerged as the leaders of the Lithuanian independence movement, and who in the course of the First World War, under German protection, formed the government of the *Taryba* or 'State Council' had intimate links with the Poles. For this very reason, they were especially mindful to conceal them. It is by no means exceptional that the first elected President of the Polish Republic, Gabriel Narutowicz (1865–1922) was the natural brother of a member of the *Taryba* and of the first government of the Lithuanian Republic, Stanislavas Narutavičius (1862–1932). In 1918, at the moment of independence, the population of Lithuania numbered some 3 million, of whom about 10 per cent were Poles.[53]

The Byelorussians were at odds not only with the Poles but also with the Russians, the Lithuanians, and the Ukrainians. Descendants of the Orthodox or Uniate Slavonic peasantry of central Lithuania, or 'White Ruthenia', they belonged to the least developed branch of the East Slavs. Their national movement, which in the disparaging words of Lewis Namier 'could have been seated on one small sofa', spent all its meagre resources proving to the world that it had no interest in Polish or Lithuanian political aspirations and no cultural or sentimental attachment to the Great Russians. For this purpose, some of their leaders revived the ancient tribal name of *Kryvicianie* (Kryvicians) – a label banned by Tsarist and Soviet censors alike. Their language, which had originally been classified by scholars both from St. Petersburg and from Warsaw as a *Polish* dialect, did not gain official recognition from the Tsarist authorities until 1906, and was written both in the Cyrillic and Latin forms. Their literature, like that of the Lithuanians, grew on Polish models, and was developed by writers like V. Dunin-Marcinkevic (1809–94) or F. Bohusevic (1840–1900) who wrote both in Polish and Byelorussian. Their national territory, as first defined by Rittich in 1875, was supposed to stretch from Białystok in the west to Smolensk in the east, and from the Dvina in the north to the Pripet in the south; their population, according to the same source, stood at 3,745,000. In Polesie, the primitive 'Poleshchuki', who had little consciousness of any national affiliation whatsoever, were claimed both by the Byelorussians and the Ukrainians. In Polish eyes, the Byelorussian movement was no more than a cultural curiosity, and a political irrelevance.[54]

To the south-east – that is, in the South-Western Land of the Russian Empire, and in Austrian Galicia – the Poles ran into conflict with the Ukrainian National Revival. The process

whereby this numerous branch of the East Slavs was meta-
morphosed from a motley assortment of 'Ruthenians' into a
coherent Ukranian nation was as long and as complex, as the
growth of the Polish Nation itself. It began in the Cossack
lands which were separated from Poland in 1667, and which,
until its suppression in 1787 had formed a semi-autonomous
'Hetman State' under Russian suzerainty. Later it spread to
the territories awarded to Russia and Austria by the Partitions.
In the late nineteenth century, the process was far from complete, and in the world at large, the essential distinction
between 'Ruthenians' and 'Russians' – analogous to that in
Western Europe between 'Dutch' and 'Deutsch' – was not
generally known. In the Tsarist Empire, where the Ruthenian
population was largely Orthodox, political separatism was
weak; but demands for the recognition and development of
the local language and literature were strong. It was here that
early Ruthenian leaders had first adopted the label of 'Ukrainian' as a means of avoiding their humiliating designation by
Tsarist officialdom as 'Little Russians'. (To western readers,
this new trade-mark can best be understood in the light of
the parallel adoption of the geographical label of 'Nether-
landers' by the Dutch population of the United Provinces. In
both cases, the crucial consideration was to avoid identification with their more numerous, and culturally expansive,
Russian or German neighbours.) In Tsarist Ukraine, the seminal
texts of the cultural renaissance were published by the
Brotherhood of Saints Cyril and Methodius prior to their
forcible dissolution in 1847. *The Books of the Genesis of the
Ukrainian Nation* of Mykola Kostomarov (1817–65) and the
powerful romantic poetry of Taras Shevchenko (1814–61)
served the same purpose for the Ukrainians as the works of
Mickiewicz, Słowacki, and Krasiński for the Poles, and to
some extent were modelled on them. The writings of the exiled
Professor of History from Kiev, Mykhailo Drahomaniv
(1841–95) encouraged a positivist, conciliatory brand of
nationalism. In Galicia, in contrast, the Ruthenian population was largely Uniate by religion, and political activism was
fuelled, among other things, by the prospect of forcible conversion to the Orthodoxy in the event of a Tsarist takeover.
The tolerant stance of the Austrian authorities permitted

extensive cultural developments. However, the prevalence of a numerous Polish community, even in eastern Galicia, led to bitter rivalry, and as in the case of the Lithuanians, to baffling contradictions. It was nothing exceptional that the most distinguished patron of the Ukrainian National Movement in Galicia, Count Andrei Sheptytsky (1865–1944), from 1900 Uniate Archbishop of Lemberg, was the loving elder brother of an active Polish nationalist, General Stanisław Szeptycki (1867–1946). Although most Ukrainians in Galicia had close connections with Polish culture, it was clear by the beginning of the twentieth century, that the interests of the Ukrainian National Movement diverged sharply from those of its Polish counterpart. Two fraternal slavonic nations, thirty and twenty million strong at this time, might in concert have exerted a powerful influence on European affairs. Instead, locked in fraternal combat, they cancelled out each other's efforts quite nicely.[55]

Elsewhere in the Austrian Empire, the Poles came into collision with the Czechs. Again, it might have been supposed that these two most developed of the Slav peoples, both predominantly Catholic and both possessed of long histories and rich cultures, would have worked together with gusto. Yet quite the opposite occurred. In the realm of Viennese politics, the outlook of the dissident bourgeois leaders of the Czech National Movement stood at marked variance with that of the loyalist, aristocratic Galician Poles. Their alignment with the Ukrainians and the South Slavs antagonized the traditional Polish alignment with the Magyars. The Czechs looked to Russia for support thereby both amazing and offending Poles. It is a sad fact, but Poles and Czechs have rarely practised the virtues of good neighbourliness.[56]

In the age of imperialism, when the world was full of Empires, it was natural that demands for national territories should have been discussed in imperialist terms. In revolutionary circles, the conduct of the partitioning powers in Eastern Europe had long since given Imperialism the bad name which Lenin later clothed with Marxist theory. That Russia, Germany, and Austria were guilty of 'Imperialism' in its most pejorative sense had been accepted doctrine for Polish radicals long since. But here was a game that more than one could play. Russians, Germans, and Austrians, smarting from Polish jibes against their holy empires, found that they could respond in kind. Demands for the restoration of a Polish national state, once supported by most European liberals, were now deliciously denounced as 'Polish Imperialism'. Socialists of all countries, opposed to the advent of Nationalism in principle, adopted the fashionable epithets with special glee. Hence the curious situation where British Socialists for example have consistently defended the integrity of the vast multi-national Russian Empire, the ally of the British Empire in two World Wars, whilst opposing the formation of an 'imperialist' Polish state in anything but its most abbreviated form. Yet the name-calling did not stop there. Lithuanians, Byelorussians, Ukrainians, and Czechs were all destined to join the common chorus against Polish Imperialism. For their part, the Polish imperialists decried 'Lithuanian Imperialism' in greater Lithuania, 'Ukrainian Imperialism' in Galicia, and 'Czech Imperialism' in Silesia. Eventually, the Poles took up with the Lithuanians and Ukrainians to denounce the advent of 'Byelorussian Imperialism' in Podlasie and Polesie. (It is not known whether Polesian imperialists ever recognized the mortal threat posed by the Jewish imperialists of Pinsk.) The ultimate point was reached at a meeting in the Kremlin on 13 October 1944, when Józef Stalin, of all people, accused the representative of the Polish Government-in-Exile, Stanisław Mikołajczyk, of being 'an imperialist'. 'Imperialism' had long since degenerated into an emotive catch-phrase, and everyone used it as they thought fit.

The divisive effects of Nationalism did not go unnoticed, of course, and there were many Polish leaders who tried to counteract them, Federalist ideas were especially strong in Piłsudski's camp, and found clear expression in the writings of Leon Wasilewski (1870–1936), editor of the theoretical socialist journal *Przedświt* (First Light) and author of *Litwa i Białoruś* (Lithuania and Byelorussia, 1912) and of *Ukraińska sprawa narodowa* (The Ukrainian National Cause, 1925). Whilst respecting the right of every nation to control its own destiny, Poles of this persuasion argued that some form of multi-national federation was essential in Eastern Europe, if the overwhelming military manpower and superior technical resources of the great empires were to be successfully opposed. The survival of all oppressed nations of the region demanded a measure of voluntary self-restraint from each and every one. These ideas are not yet dead, even today. The trouble was that the federalists were attacked not only by their more chauvinist compatriots at home, who charged them with selling Poland's birthright to foreigners, but also by their prospective Lithuanian, Byelorussian, and Ukrainian partners, who understandably mistook the modern federalist ideal for a revamped version of the old Polish *Rzeczpospolita*. Furthermore, it was a fact of political geography that the most uncompromising representatives of Polish Nationalism, namely Roman Dmowski and his National Democrats, drew their most fervent support from those cities, such as Poznań, Wilno, and Lwów, where compromise on the national issue would have been most desirable. To people unnerved by the constant anti-Polish sniping of local nationalist rivals, Dmowski's concept of Incorporation, which envisaged the future integration of all border areas into a completely unitary Polish state, proved much more attractive than Piłsudski's opposing concept of Federation. Moderation was most lacking in those places where it was most required. It is interesting to note, for instance, that Piłsudski probably counted fewer supporters among the Poles of his native Wilno, than among the city's Jews. For a man who laid great store by the Polish traditions of generosity and magnanimity, it was a bitter pill indeed. According to Wasilewski, the conquest of Wilno by the Red Army in July 1920, and its subsequent transfer to the Lithuanian National Republic, was the only event in his recollection which ever moved the taciturn Marshal to tears. Thus, in all the border provinces, fear was the father of extremism and discord, and the harbinger of tragedy.[57]

The proliferating profusion of possible political permutations among the pullulating peoples and parties of the Polish provinces in this period palpably prevented the propagation of permanent pacts between potential partners. It is easy to see that Dmowski's advocacy of an alliance with Russia against Germany was also designed to protect the Poles against Ukrainians, Lithuanians, Jews, *e tutti quanti;* and that his hopes were bound to be dashed by Piłsudski's rival scheme for a federation with the *tutti quanti* against both Russia and Germany. But that is only a beginning. It must also be realized that each of the national movements was itself fragmented not only in terms of political attitudes and of political parties, but also by the physical barriers of the state frontiers; and that each of the fragments had its own interests, traditions, and aspirations. It was common knowledge among Polish schoolboys that *Polonia,* like Caesar's *Gallia, est omnis divisa in partes tres.* But not everyone was aware that the Ukrainian, Lithuanian, German, and Jewish communities were trisected likewise. Apart from the Ukrainians in 'Little Russia' ruled from St. Petersburg, and the Ukrainians in Galicia ruled from Vienna, there were Ukrainians in Sub-Carpathian Ruthenia ruled from Budapest. The life of the Lithuanians in the North-Western Land of Russia and in the Congress Kingdom was enriched by the existence of the Lithuanians in East Prussia. The confident German majorities in Prussian Poland professed a very different outlook from that of the isolated German minorities in Russian Poland or in Galicia. In the same way, the assimilated Jew from Warsaw or Cracow was effectively alienated not only from the unassimilated, Yiddish-speaking Jews of the Pale, but also from the Russian-speaking Jews or *Litvaks,* who emigrated westwards from the 1880s onwards. Given the existence of the three partitioning powers, therefore, and of five main national movements each divided into three geographical sectors, into three main tactical groupings, and into at least three main parties, one reaches the astonishing conclusion that Polish politics at the turn of the century were faced with a total number of possible permutations of 3^8, or of rather more than nineteen thousand, if everyone was to be accommodated. Attempts were made at various moments to unite the Poles and the Russians against the Ukrainians; the Poles and the Ukrainians against the Germans; the Russians and the Ukrainians against the Poles and the Germans; and so on and so forth. But in every instance, the interests of a vocal minority were neglected or offended; a *rapproachement* in one direction invariably caused a rupture in another direction; and nothing substantial was ever achieved. (See Diagram B.)

Pressed on so many sides, it was perhaps inevitable that

Polish nationalism should have developed an assertive, exclusive nature. In this, it resembled all its rivals. Repelled by the prospect of a fixed alliance with his potential allies, the purist Pole was left dreaming about some special, poetical, but undefined Freedom of the future:

> Wolność w Polsce będzie inna –
> Nie szlachecka złota,
> Ni słomiana wolność gminna
> Od płota do płota:
>
> Ni słowiensko przepaścista
> O tatarskim czynie,
> Ni ta z której kabalista
> Śni o gilotynie.*

Cyprian Norwid (1821 83), who was so much in advance of his time in so many ways, had already formed these ideas in 1848. They were to prove increasingly convincing as political and social conflicts multiplied in succeeding years. The implications were bleak. If Poland could not find a form of government worthy of her traditions, it was better that she stayed as she was:

> Jeśli ma Polska pójść nie drogą mleczną
> W cało-ludzkości gromnym huraganie,
> Jeżeli ma być nie demokratyczną
> To niech pod carem na wieki zostanie.
>
> Jeśli mi Polska ma być anarchiczna
> Lub socjalizmu rozwinąć pytanie
> To ja już wolę tę panslawistyczną
> Co pod Moskalem na wieki zostanie!**

---

* Freedom in Poland will be different –/Not the noble-style Golden Freedom,/ Nor the thatched freedom of the peasant commune/From fence to fence:/Nor the fathomless freedom of Slav-style (anarchy)/Brought about by some (barbarous) Tartar outrage,/Nor yet the kind of Freedom where cabbalists/Dream of the guillotine.[58]

** If Poland is not to tread the Milky Way/In the thunderous hurricane of all-humanity;/If she is going to be undemocratic,/Then let her stay under the Tsar for centuries,/If Poland is to be anarchic/Or is to elaborate the question of Socialism,/Then I prefer that Pan-slav (system)/which would stay for centuries under the Muscovite.[59]

By the same token, the greatest dangers were not the obvious ones of oppression and exploitation, but the insidious advance of corruption and indifference:

> Z wszelkich kajdan, czy te są
> Powrozowe, złote czy stalne
> Przeciekłymi najbardziej krwią i łzami?
> Niewidzialne!*

Meanwhile, national salvation was to be found in work. As Norwid wrote in *Promethidion* (1852), 'It's a beautiful thing to be enchanted by work – work whose end is Resurrection.' Elsewhere he defined a nation as 'the internal union of inter-related races', in other words as a moral, not an ethnic or political community. 'The nation is formed of the spirit, of the will, of freedom, whereas the state is formed of the body or rather from the external things of this world, from slavery.' By this reckoning, Poland was a nation, whilst Russia was a *formalny stan,* a mere 'state of affairs', characterized by the complete divorce between the people and their rulers. In this way, he united both the 'Messianic' and the 'organic' trends in national life. Norwid's outlook was deeply Christian, and ultimately optimistic. But his immediate forecast was vague and ambiguous. Paradoxically, he hinted that the re-creation of a Polish state, might not be entirely desirable. By becoming as other nations are, with worldly responsibilities to fulfil and sordid compromises to consider, the Poles would lose their special calling. If the New Jerusalem were actually realized, the Messiah would become redundant. Perhaps, like many sinners, the Poles were praying for deliverance – but not just yet.[61]

Certainly, in Europe as a whole, there was no general expectation that Poland might be resurrected. In Paris in 1897, when the young Alfred Jarry staged the play which is often taken to be the starting-point of dramatic surrealism and of the Theatre of the Absurd, he expressly chose to give *Ubu Roi* a Polish setting. As he explained to a bemused audience, *'L'action se passe en Pologne, c'est-à-dire, nulle part'* (The action takes place in Poland, that is to say, Nowhere).[62] For

---

* Of all the sorts of shackles, which,/Cast iron, gold or steel,/Which are soaked the most in blood and tears?/The invisible ones![60]

the average educated European, 'Poland' had no more sub-stance than all the mythical realms of the past from Dipsodie to Camelot. Another persistent legend maintained that a similarly surrealist performance was regularly enacted in Constantinople with all the high seriousness of traditional ceremony. At the Court of the Sublime Porte, at the gather-ings of the Diplomatic Corps, the *chef de protocol* was said to call on His Excellency, the 'Ambassador of Lechistan' to present himself. An aide would then step forward to announce that the Polish ambassador presented his compliments and regretted his absence 'owing to temporary indisposition'.[63]

Thus the 'Third Day' dawned. And few were ready.

* * * * *

In the period since 1918, the earlier traditions of Polish Nationalism have survived largely intact. Although an inde-pendent Polish state was created, it did not last long enough to generate many new ideas of lasting importance. Although the partitioning powers were themselves destroyed, both Germany and Russia were soon reconstructed in new forms. On the international scene of the twentieth century, the Third Reich attempted to surpass the most expansive designs of the Central Powers whilst the Soviet Union has achieved the imperial supremacy in Eastern Europe of which the Tsarist Empire could only dream. Although the Poles obtained a large measure of control over their internal affairs, they were still forced to compete within the Second Republic and within the Soviet Block against rival nations. The cardinal problems of how to resist the overwhelming power of ruthless neigh-bours, and how to combine with suitable allies against them are, *mutatis mutandis,* as relevant today as they were a hundred years ago. In this sense, the predicament of the People's Republic after the Second World War resembles that of its many predecessors in the eighteenth and nineteenth centuries. Taking the Modern Era as a whole, the two decades of genuine national independence between 1918 and 1939 represent a brief and exceptional episode. To quote the phrase of S. Cat-Mackiewicz, 'unhappy is the nation for whom independence is nothing more than an adventure.'[64]

The events of the Second World War were incomparably

worse than anything which the Polish nation had suffered before. The conduct of the Nazis and the Soviets makes the misdeeds of their Prussian, Austrian, or Tsarist predecessors pale into insignificance. In the nineteenth century, the Poles had been faced with a life of deprivation. In the twentieth century, they were faced with extinction. If, somewhat fancifully, Poland had once been compared to Calvary, it now became, in reality, Golgotha.

CHAPTER TWO

ROSSIYA:

The Russian Partition (1772-1918)

'Russian Poland' is a name which appears neither in Russian nor in Polish history books. As a practical description of the territories of the former Polish—Lithuanian Republic annexed by the Russian Empire, it is apt enough, and as such is analogous to 'British Ireland', 'the Austrian Netherlands', 'Spanish Italy', or at an earlier period to the 'Polish Ukraine'. Yet it was unacceptable both to Russian officialdom and to the Tsar's new subjects. As far as official fictions were concerned, the Partitions restored to Russia an integral part of her ancient patrimony. In 1793, a medal was struck for Catherine II with the inscription: 'I have recovered what was torn away.'* Although expressions such as 'the Polish provinces' or 'the provinces detached from Poland and united with Russia' can still be found in the early nineteenth century, Russian officials were trained to think in terms of 'the Western Region' or 'the Recovered Territories'. In their eyes, 'Poland' had ceased to exist. It was a historical aberration which over the 800 years of its existence had somehow seduced the population from their true loyalties, and was best forgotten. Except for the interlude of the Congress Kingdom, in 1815—64, Russian officials were loath to concede that any part of their Empire had anything in common with a separate entity called Poland. Yet in the minds of the Poles, it was 'Poland' which remained the reality, whilst *'Rossiya'* (Russia) appeared as an alien imposition. For the patriots, Poland was Polish. 'Russian Poland' was a contradiction in terms, like 'Irish England' or 'French Germany' or 'Chinese Russia'. If they needed a label, they talked of *Zabór rosyjski* (The Russian Partition).

---

* Almost all the territorial depredations of modern times are justified by spurious historical claims of this sort. The Russians claimed that they were recovering the lands of Kievan Rus. The Prussians claimed to be reuniting the patrimony of the Teutonic Knights. The Austrians claimed to be restoring the Kingdom of Galicia, seized by the Poles (from Hungary) in 1390. In the twentieth century, the Poles have invented theories of their own about their 'Recovered Territories'.

The Russian Partition grew steadily from the base created by the lands ceded to Muscovy at the Truce of Andrusovo in 1667 — the middle Dnieper, the city of Kiev, and left-bank Ukraine. For practical purposes, from 1737 it included the Duchy of Courland whose ruling dynasty was casually replaced by a Russian appointee. At the First Partition of 1773, it was enlarged by the annexation of Semigalia, Polotsk, Witebsk, Mscisław, and the south-eastern area of the Palatinate of Minsk; at the Second Partition in 1793, by the right-bank Ukraine, including the Palatinates of Kiev, Bracław, Podolia, and Volhynia and by parts of Breść, Minsk, and Wilno; and at the Third Partition in 1795, by the remaining lands of the Grand Duchy up to the line of the Bug and Niemen. After 1864, it absorbed the Congress Kingdom of Poland, which, renamed Vistulaland, was ruled as part of the Empire.

The more easterly areas of Russian Poland were only 'Polish' in the pre-Partition sense: that is, that their traditions had developed within the multi-national community of the old Republic. The more westerly areas were Polish in the ethnic and linguistic sense also. Most of the cities, even in the east, such as Vilna, Dvinsk, Minsk, Pinsk, or Kamieniets, retained a strong Polish flavour. Yet to the outside world, the whole region was gradually dressed up as 'Western Russia'. By the end of the nineteenth century, no Russian was prepared to talk of 'Poland' except as an informal geographical area lying to the west of the Bug.

In later administrative terms, at its maximum extent Russian Poland comprised the *gubernias* of Vilna, Grodno, Kovno, Minsk, Vitebsk, Mohylev, Volynia, Podolia, Kiev, plus, from 1866, the ten *gubernias* (government districts) of Vistulaland — Warsaw, Kalisz, Płock, Piotrków, Radom, Kielce, Lublin, Siedlce, Łomża, and Suwałki.[1] (See Map 2.)

Russian political attitudes centred on the threefold principles of *Pravoslaviye* (Orthodoxy), *Samoderzhaviye* (Autocracy), and *Narodnost* (Nationality). They grew from deep roots in the Empire's Muscovite past, and inspired the institutions created during the reforms of Peter and Catherine the Great. In the reign of Nicholas I (1825–55), they crystallized in to a fixed ideology called 'Official Nationality'. Different Tsars gave different points of emphasis; and interpretation of

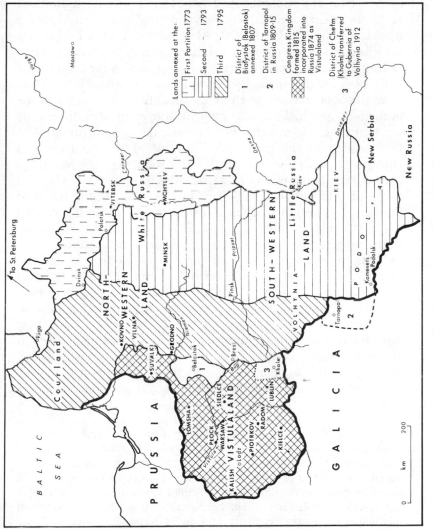

Map 2. The Russian Partition, (1773–1915)

the three principles meandered considerably with the times. Paul I (1796–1801) set a very different tone from his mother, Catherine (1763–96); Alexander I (1801–25); Alexander II (1855–81), and Nicholas II (1894–1917) have been pictured as liberal rulers who through bent or necessity introduced a degree of flexibility; whilst Alexander III (1881–94) has been seen as a reversion to the hard line of Nicholas I. Such judgements are purely relative, however, and refer only to the scale of Russian values. By European standards, all the Tsars were despots, varying in their outlook from the harsh to the humane. They had no interest whatsoever in liberalism in its western sense, where the will of the ruler is subordinated to the consent of the governed. They sat at the controls of a cumbrous governmental machine, which was staffed by a closed élite, animated by ideals decades if not centuries behind those of intellectual circles, and possessed of an inertia all of its own. In relation to their Polish subjects, they all accepted the desirability of the same, simple goals of ultimate assimilation, integration, conformity, and standardization. Their policies were designed to turn the Poles into 'true Christians, loyal subjects, and good Russians' – and varied only as to speed, tactics, and methods. They all stood for the programme of 'Faith, Throne, and Fatherland', whose most assiduous exponent was perhaps Sergei Uvarov, Nicholas I's long-serving Minister of Public Enlightenment. In 1843, after ten years in an office whose aim, as he saw it, was to turn the Tsar's subjects 'into worthy tools of the government', Uvarov surveyed the achievements of the decade in a report to the Tsar:

In the midst of the rapid collapse in Europe of religious and civil institutions, and at a time of the general spread of destructive ideas . . . it has been necessary to establish our Fatherland on firm foundations, on which the well-being, strength, and life of the people can be based. It has been necessary to find those principles which form the distinctive character of Russia, and which belong only to Russia: to gather into one whole the sacred remnants of Russian Nationality and to fasten them to the anchor of our salvation. Fortunately, Russia has retained a warm faith in the sacred principles without which she cannot prosper, gain in strength, or live. Sincerely and deeply attached to the Church of his fathers, the Russian has traditionally considered it to be the guarantor of social and family happiness. Without a love for the faith of its ancestors, a people, no less than an individual, must perish. A Russian devoted to his Fatherland, will agree as little to the loss of single dogma of our *Orthodoxy* as to the theft of a single pearl of the Tsar's Crown. *Autocracy* constitutes the main condition of Russia's political condition. The Russian giant stands on it, as on the cornerstone of his greatness . . . Together with these two principles, there is a third, no less important, no less powerful: the principle of *Nationality* . . .[2]

For his services, Uvarov was made a count, and received the words 'ORTHODOXY, AUTOCRACY, NATIONALITY' as his heraldic motto. But his ideas were far from original. They were a reformulation in more glowing terms of principles which had existed in Russia long before him, and which were to survive long afterwards.

The principle of Orthodoxy was derived from the special position given to Orthodox Christianity in the Russian political system. In Muscovite days, when the native population was overwhelmingly Great Russian and Orthodox, the Church had not been identified completely with the state. But in the later seventeenth and eighteenth centuries, when large non-Russian and non-Orthodox communities were being absorbed, the Church was consciously turned into a department of state and used as an agency of political coercion. A religion which had traditionally stressed the virtues of calm, contemplation, and tolerance, was systematically perverted, and put to work in the interests of uniformity and non-toleration. Indeed, its own code of spiritual submissiveness made it an easy victim to the designs of political manipulators, whilst the deep and mystical piety which permeated the highest circles of Court and bureaucracy, caused its most fervent adherents to be genuinely offended by the incidence of religious plurality. From 1721, when the old Patriarchate was abolished, the supreme organ of the Church, the Most Holy Synod, was directly subordinated to the Tsar, and to the Tsar's *Ober-Prokurator*. Henceforth, the purposes of God and Eternity were inextricable from those of the Russian Empire. Religious dissent was equated with treason. Stubborn schismatics or recalcitrant atheists were to be struck down and rooted out in the name of Charity, not merely as heretics, but as enemies of the established social and political order. As so often in the history of Russian civilization, the highest ideals were used to justify the most vulgar acts of violence.

For practical purposes, the principle of Orthodoxy fell heaviest on those people whose beliefs were closest to the dogmas of the official religion without actually coinciding with them. It left the Muslims largely alone, and came to a ready *modus vivendi* with the Protestants. It encouraged rather more suspicions about Jews and Roman Catholics, both of whom professed 'orthodoxies' of their own. But against the Greek Catholic Uniates it aroused feelings of unlimited hostility. Thus, whilst the Protestants of the former Republic found ready employment in the Tsarist service, and the Jews and the Roman Catholics suffered from sporadic discrimination, the Uniates were systematically persecuted. After the Third Partition, the Jews were confined to a Pale of Settlement whose eastern boundary coincided with the frontier of the old Republic; but it was only in brief periods, under Nicholas I and Alexander III, that any pressure was brought on them to submit to Christian baptism. The Catholics encountered constant obstacles to promotion in the Army or Bureaucracy. Their clergy were controlled, and deprived of their estates, their dioceses were reorganized; their contact with Rome was circumscribed. Papal bulls could not be published in Russia without the assent of St. Petersburg, and were often ignored or countermanded. Yet the Jesuit Order was not dissolved as elsewhere, and was recruited by the Empire for services in the educational sphere. The Uniates enjoyed no such ambiguities. As descendants of communities which had once adhered to the Orthodox faith, they were seen not as heretics but as renegades. Catherine deposed all but one of the Uniate bishops, and subordinated the ecclesiastical hierarchy to a Consistory entirely dependent on the State. In the 1770s and 1790s, and again in the 1830s and 1860s, the soldiery was called in to effect mass conversions. Books were burned; churches destroyed; priests murdered; services conducted according to the Orthodox rite under the shadow of bayonets. In 1839, all contact between the Uniate Church in Russia and the Vatican was severed. In 1875, the Union of Brest was itself officially annulled. By 1905, when a decree of religious toleration was finally exacted, no more than 200,000 Uniates were left to practise their faith openly. In all these religious policies, there is no doubt that the prime motivation was political. For this reason, the bogus 'Principle of Orthodoxy', as a state ideology, needs to be clearly distinguished from the genuine principles and practices of the Orthodox Church. Needless to say, it nicely contradicted the Polish traditions of plurality, individual conscience, and toleration. (See Chapter 7.)

The principle of Autocracy should not be confused with the general theory of Absolutism as known in Western Europe. Absolutism in France or Spain or Austria developed as an antidote to the excessively divisive tendencies of the estates and fiefs of the medieval period. Although divine blessing was invariably invoked for the new practices, there could never be any complete identity of interest between Church and State, between the Vatican in Rome and the Catholic monarchies at home. The very fact that Fénélon or Hobbes wrote elaborate and various treatises on absolutist theory is evidence in itself of a continuing debate with advocates of older and different doctrines. Despite the limitless pretensions of a Bourbon or a Habsburg, their real power was always limited to a greater or lesser degree by the residual resistance of regional or social groupings. Russian autocracy, in contrast, was the direct descendant of the primitive, patriarchal despotism of Muscovy. It reigned supreme in a country where feudal estates had never exercised any autonomous power, and where the separate role of the Church had been completely crushed. It was not only more absolute than Absolutism; it had different origins and different emanations. If it had any parallel in Western Europe, it was in the infallibility of the Roman Pope, whose politico-mystical regime in the Papal States was as puny as the Russian empire was vast.

As far as the Empire's Polish provinces were concerned, Autocracy brought at least six major changes to political life. Firstly, it abolished all the traditional democratic institutions of the old Republic. Secondly, it introduced a centralized administrative machine. The *Województwa* (Palatinates) were replaced by a new network of *gubernias,* where the Governor and the military commander acted as the direct vehicles of government policy. Thirdly, it reformed officialdom, whose

members henceforth were nominated not elected. From the
Governor down to the lowliest apparitor, their one duty was
to transmit orders from above, on pain of dismissal. Fourthly,
it introduced a vast and permanent military establishment
where previously a small mercenary force had been supplemented by voluntary service. Fifthly, it introduced elaborate
means of political coercion. Sixthly, and most importantly, it
sought to transform the relationship between the state and
the individual. As a result of St. Petersburgh's rooted suspicions, the Polish provinces did not benefit fully from such
limited measures of self-government as were extended to the
cities by Catherine in 1775, or to most of the Russian provinces by the *zemstva* (provincial councils) after 1864. Paradoxically, therefore, the Tsarist system called for a greater
degree of conformity and submissiveness from its wayward
Polish subjects than from its submissive Russian core. And it
called not merely for blind obedience, but for what in a later
age was to be called 'internal censorship'. The good citizen
could not rely on obeying instructions or on keeping his
private affairs within the limits of the law. He was taught to
discipline his thoughts actively, to cleanse from his mind all
trace of personal will. Politics were reduced to the point at
which the subject strove to divine the will of his superiors in
advance, as a form of spiritual exercise. The *Tsar-Otets,* the
'Little Father' was to be trusted implicitly; all criticism was
to be left to those whose advice was requested; all abuses
were to be borne patiently in gratitude for the 'Russian bread'
that one ate. People were encouraged to think communally,
denouncing and expelling all wilful elements from their midst,
as the individual seeks to purge sin from his soul. The ideal
was illustrated by a trivial incident at Vilna in the 1830s as
recorded by Uvarov himself:

When on the day of my departure, I ordered that all the students of the
institutions in Vilna under my authority, some one thousand persons in
number, be gathered in the palace courtyard, a pupil of the boarding
school for the gentry, Broński, stepped forward from the ranks, and in
the name of his comrades greeted me with a brief address. After saying,
in excellent Russian, that they thanked me for my visit and that they
thanked me for my fatherly treatment of them, he added in conclusion,
'Be also and always our protector before the Most Gracious Monarch.

Tell Him, that we remember Him, that we love Him, that we shall be worthy of Him, that we too are His good children . . .' Here, this thirteen-year-old youth dissolved in tears, and rushed to embrace me. Of course, not a single spectator remained unaffected by this expression of sentiment which was undoubtedly unfeigned and flowed straight from the heart.[3]

For the Minister, who had not expected such devotion during his visit to a fiercely Polish city, the incident was a sign of success. What he did not hear or record were the comments of Broński's Polish classmates after the visit was over.

The Principle of Nationality evolved in several important ways during the modern period. In the eighteenth century, it demanded little more than loyalty to the Tsar and to the established social order. As the instrument of a Court where French was the common language, and where Baltic Germans held positions of special prominence, it had none of the ethnic or cultural overtones of later decades. As late as 1840, Kankrin could suggest that the name of the Empire be changed from *Rossiya* to *Petrovia* in honour of its founder, Peter the Great, or to *Romanovia* in deference to the dynasty. 'An unusual idea', Bulgarin noted, 'but an essentially correct one.' Others stressed that 'Russian-ness' somehow involved an expression of social virtues, of submissiveness on the part of the people, and of dutiful service on the part of leaders. Serfdom came to be seen as a Russian practice *par excellence,* and as such an essential pillar of autocracy. Thus, it was not till the second quarter of the nineteenth century that Nationality was associated with any recognizable features of modern nationalism. By that time, the growth of a native intelligentsia naturally led to attacks on the Francophone and Prussophile court; and the government recognized the value of the Russian language in unifying the heterogeneous peoples of the realm. The Russian language was quickly raised to the touchstone of Nationality. Not only did Russian writers from Turgenev to Gogol extol the objective characteristics of their language; they implied that all other languages were markedly inferior. 'One can confidently affirm', wrote Grech, the grammarian, 'that our language is superior to all the modern European languages.' 'The Russian language', wrote Bulgarin, 'which without doubt holds first place in melodiousness and in the richness and ease of word construction, is the language of poetry and literature in all the countries of the globe.' Once these extreme views began to be officially propagated, the government was but one step removed from the idea that to speak a foreign language, or to promote a culture other than Russian, was to be unpatriotic, and politically disloyal. In mid-century, with the appearance of the Slavophil and Pan-Slav movements, racial overtones were introduced. 'We have a different climate from the West,' wrote Pogodin, 'a different landscape, a different temperament and character, a different blood, a different physiognomy, a different way of thinking, different beliefs, hopes, pleasures, different relations, different conditions, different history, everything different . . .' According to this notion, the Russians were the natural leaders of the Slav world, the bearers of a sacred mission to regenerate decadent European civilization, and to civilize Asia. Although Slavophilism led to a widening gulf in Russian intellectual circles, and eventually to democratic concepts which challenged the very foundations of Autocracy, it remained a constant theme in approved attitudes:

> Dawn is breaking over Warsaw;
> Kiev has opened its eyes;
> And Vysehrad has started to converse
> With Golden-domed Moscow.[4]

When, in response to repeated Polish Risings, Russification was adopted as a prime goal of offical policy throughout the Polish provinces, it lent the government a respectable intellectual justification for its proceedings. From 1864, when the *istniy russkiy chelovek,* 'the genuine Russian person', was taken as the sole criterion for candidates aspiring to serve the state, most Poles were automatically excluded. By that time, the principle of Russian Nationality was as emotional, as intense, and as exclusive as its Polish counterpart.

To many observers from the West, the miseries caused by Poland's incorporation into the Russian Empire were often thought to be essentially constitutional in nature. Since Russian Autocracy ran contrary to Poland's traditions, it was imagined that a few modifications in the form of government — a few concessions to local autonomy, a few gestures in the direction of democratization — would somehow eliminate Polish grievances. Hence, when Polish insurrections continued to occur in spite of the reforms of so-called 'liberal Tsars', western opinion tended to lose patience and to believe the Russian stereotype of the ungrateful, incorrigible, and anarchic Pole. In reality, the problem went much deeper. Muscovite social traditions, which demanded the total submission of the citizen to the ruler and the total effacement of the individual in the interests of the collective, were far too strong to be shaken by mere constitutional forms. Indeed, Russian History is full of instances where the most enlightened and apparently progressive constitutional declarations have coincided with the blackest periods of despotism. To the Muscovite way of thinking, any relaxation of the formal structures of Autocracy necessarily requires an intensified degree of vigilance and control on the part of the responsible authorities. By the same token, the prosecution of the most tyrannical policies can usually be masked by the promulgation of extremely libertarian, but completely inoperative, reforms. Outside commentators who have taken the Petrine Reforms or the Stalin Constitution at face value, and have interpreted them in the light of western conceptions of the rule of Law, or even of British ideas of fair play, invariably miss the point. The Poles under Russian rule learned the hard way. Whenever the Tsar was obliged to make constitutional concessions — as in 1815, 1861, and 1906 — the Poles were led to expect a genuine improvement in their condition. Instead, they found that the Tsarist bureaucracy, disturbed by the resultant restrictions on its freedom of action, would treat the concessions as a temporary withdrawal, and would then work assiduously to reassert its position, if necessary by ignoring the constitutional reforms, and to reimpose traditional methods of control. In the nineteenth, as in the eighteenth century, Reform was the harbinger not of calm, but of conflict; and for the Poles, of defeat. It was a situation, in which the constitutionalist or the democrat could never win. Either he submitted voluntarily, and surrendered his ideals from the start; or else he rebelled, and after a brief moment of liberty, was forced to submit involuntarily.

The point was well known in Russia, of course, and was

expounded for the benefit of the Poles by those few Russian dissidents with Polish sympathies. One such 'westerner', eventually declared insane by the authorities, was the writer Pyotr Chaadayev, who came to Poland as a young officer in the Napoleonic wars, and actually joined a Polish Masonic Lodge in Cracow. 'Speaking about Russia,' wrote Chaadayev, 'it is always imagined that one is just speaking about a particular form of government . . . This is not so. Russia is whole worlds apart – submissive to the will, the arbitrariness, the despotism of one man. Contrary to the laws of co-existence, Russia only moves in the direction of her own enslavement, and the enslavement of all neighbouring peoples.'[5]

The clearest example of the spiritual gulf separating the leaders of educated opinion on Poland from their Russian counterparts is to be found in the Polish connections of Feodor Mikhailovich Dostoevsky. Despite his Polish surname, Dostoevsky's upbringing in Moscow and his outlook were entirely Russian. Some critics have suggested that secret doubts about his Russian-ness may well have prompted the extreme, chauvinist attitudes which he cultivated. At all events, he felt compelled to combine an unstinting defence of everything Russian with a pathological hatred of everything Polish. Throughout the novels, his *Polyachishki* or 'Polish scoundrels' form a fantastic rogues' gallery of cheats, whores, liars, impostors, and monsters. The episode in *The Brothers Karamazov* where two silly Polish noblemen reluctantly drink a toast to 'Russia within the frontiers of 1772' and are then shown to be card-sharpers, is typical of many others. For the historian, however, it is interesting to learn that Dostoevsky's indisputable bias, unlike that of his readers, was not based on simple ignorance. Dostoevsky had a fluent command of Polish, and a detailed knowledge of Polish literature, especially of Mickiewicz. What is more, he spent several years under arrest in Siberia in the company of Polish prisoners, with whom he engaged in prolonged and heated conversations, and from whom, at a later date, he drew a number of his most vivid portraits. One of his fellow prisoners, Stanisław Tokarzewski (1821–91), recorded their encounters in some detail, and, it is a memorable picture which he paints. Dostoevsky, the Russian officer condemned to death for sedition, and reprieved from the firing squad at the last moment, and Tokarzewski, the Polish landowner and idealist, condemned to 2,000 lashes and ten years' penal servitude for promoting Father Ściegenny's crusade for the liberation of the peasants, might be supposed to have much in common. Here were two men of high principle, of good education, and of similar standing, who were both suffering gross injustice together for their integrity; and their mutual misunderstanding was complete:

Whenever he addressed us Poles, Dostojewski would always start with the phrase, 'We, the nobility . . .' So I would always interrupt him, 'Excuse me, sir', I would say, 'but I think that there are no gentlemen in this prison, only convicts, men deprived of their rights.' Then he would foam with anger, 'And you, sir, are evidently proud of being a convict! . . .

It was unfortunate that Dostojewski so hated the Poles, for judging by his traits and his name, one could recognize his Polish origins. He used to say that if ever he found a single drop of Polish blood in his veins he would have himself purged immediately. How painful it was to listen to this conspirator, this man sentenced for the cause of freedom and progress, who confessed that he would never be happy until all nations had fallen under Russian rule . . . According to him, the Russian nation alone was predestined for its magnificent mission in the World. 'The French' he insisted 'at least show some resemblance to men; but the English, Germans, and Spaniards are simply caricatures. In comparison to Russian literature, the literatures of other nations are mere parodies . . . Through what quirk, I wondered, had this son of the Russian Cadet Corps, found himself in penal servitude as a political prisoner . . .[5]

Needless to say, Tokarzewski, who was sent back to Siberia for a further twenty years after the January Rising, had as little love for Russia as Dostoevsky for Poland. The main difference between them lay in the fact that the Pole was an obscure political convict; the Russian was one of the supreme geniuses of world literature, who could propagate his prejudices to a world audience. In this sense, Dostoevsky has been described as 'the greatest enemy Poland ever had'.[7]

For most Polish readers, the incompatibility of the Russian and the Polish political traditions is so obvious, that many might question the place of an outline of the principles of Russian government in a survey of Polish History. Yet the need, and the relevance, is undeniable. It is quite inappropriate to conceive of the lands of the Russian Partition as being merely 'under Russian occupation'. They were not merely occupied, but were annexed and incorporated into the main body politic of Russia. Although they retained their own specific characteristics, as did all the provinces of the Empire, they were just as much part of Russia as was the Ukraine, the Crimea, or Transcaucasia. Except in the limited instance of the Congress Kingdom in 1815–32 and 1861–4, they could not be compared to the position of the Grand Duchy of Finland, which, though annexed in 1815 from Sweden, was never fully incorporated in the political or constitutional sense. It is a hard truth for Poles to grasp; but the largest element of the three parts of divided Poland did not enjoy even the nominal measure of separateness bestowed on the non-Russian Republics in the Soviet Union today. Contradictory though it may seem, Poland was an integral part of Russia; Warsaw and Wilno, as Varshava and Vilna, were Russian cities; and the Poles of Russia, whether they liked it or not, were subjects of the Tsar. They were not ruled by the Polish tradition, but by the Russian tradition, whose supremacy in the Polish provinces of the Empire was not effectively challenged between the First Partition and the First World War. What is more, the Russian tradition was not something which existed in the abstract. The threefold principles of Russian government were embodied in laws and institutions, and were operated by a host of officials, whose workings over more than one and a half centuries cannot possibly have left the people either indifferent or unscarred.

Of these institutions, the Russian Army was of capital importance. It was the ultimate reservoir of autocratic power, and made a constant impact on the life of all the Empire's inhabitants. Its influence, through the establishment of permanent garrisons and military districts, was particularly prominent in those Polish areas which formed the Empire's border with Europe. It offered an honourable career to the sons of noble families, and demanded 25 years' service from its peasant conscripts. Its role in domestic affairs was not inferior to that in external defence. Throughout the nineteenth century, it maintained the largest military establishment in the world, reaching a maximum in 1916 of some seven million men. It was a major instrument of social integration, throwing generation after generation of Russian and non-Russian soldiers together into the hardships and comradeship of army life. It was also the centre of an important sector of the economy. In Russian Poland, it maintained huge garrisons at Warsaw, Lublin, Vilna, Grodno, and Belostok (Białystok), and constructed major fortresses in Warsaw, at Novo Georgiyevsk (Modlin), at Ivangorod (Iwangród, Dęblin), at at Brest-Litovsk (Brześć Litewski), forming the so-called Polish Trilateral. Although care was taken to avoid forming regiments of exclusively Polish composition, many Poles served with distinction in all the Empire's wars. There were large numbers of Polish nobles in the 'Byelorussian Standards' of the Napoleonic period. There were Poles in Suvorov's army in Italy, Poles both with Kutuzov and against him, Poles in the Turkish wars, Poles in the Caucasus, Poles in the Crimea, Poles who reached the walls of Constantinople in 1878, Poles who fought in Manchuria against the Japanese in 1904–5, Poles who in the Russian army fought against Poles in the armies of the Central Powers on the Eastern Front of the First World War. There were Poles in each of the Russian armies which crushed each of the Polish Risings.

The civil bureaucracy of the Empire was organized on military lines. It consisted of fourteen hierarchical grades, each equivalent to a given military rank and each wearing its own distinctive uniform and insignia. Together with the army, it was considered the proper resort of the nobility, whose estates were supposed to be held less in private possession than in return for state service. In a centralized autocratic state, personal initiative was blighted; whilst the competence of petty officials extended into all spheres of everyday life. If Gogol's picture is to be believed, the *chinovnik,* the 'bureaucrat', the 'Inspector-General', was a figure of fun in Russian society, especially among the intelligentsia. But for most of the population, he was also a figure to be feared, and respected. In the Russian tradition, to have risen through the ranks of the Tsarist service was a sign of social success. In the Polish tradition, it was a sign of servility. The Polish nobles were used to running their own estates and their own affairs, and to electing their own officials. Quite apart from the disabilities

placed on Roman Catholics, and from the later policy of Russification, few self-respecting Poles were naturally disposed
either to serve in the bureaucracy or to heed its commands.
Many historians would agree that the cardinal vice of the
Russian bureaucracy was to create an unbridgeable gulf
between the governing class and the governed. Nowhere was
this more true than in the Western Region.

The Russian police system was inimitably elaborate, overlapping the competence of both civil and military authorities.
The civil Gendarmerie was supplemented by special formations of military police, and in the late nineteenth century by
the Cossack police regiments. From the accession of Nicholas
I, all their activities were supervised by the Third Department
of the Tsar's Private Chancery, which was the employer of
the so-called *Ochrana* or 'secret police'. The Third Department's terms of reference were contained in the Edict of
3 July 1826:

1. All orders and all reports in every case belonging to the higher police.
2. Information about the various sects and schisms which exist in the
   State.
3. Reports about discoveries of false banknotes, coins, documents,
   etc . . .
4. Information about all persons placed under police supervision . . .
5. Exile, distribution, and residence of all suspected and noxious
   individuals;
6. Superintendence and management of all places of incarceration.
7. All regulations and orders concerning foreigners who reside in Russia,
   or who enter or leave the state.
8. Reports about all occurrences without exception.
9. All statistical information which has police pertinence . . .[8]

In all cases of serious disturbance or political subversion, the
civil courts could be strengthened by the use of military tribunals. It is not surprising, therefore, that the Police Service
attracted the most ambitious individuals, and was itself
regarded as an élite branch of the public service. In Alexei
Arakchaev (1769–1834) under Alexander I, Benckendorff
and Orlov under Nicholas I, and K. P. Pobedonetsov under
Alexander III, it produced several of the Empire's most
powerful men and of the Tsar's most intimate advisers. Its
powers were all-prevailing, and limited only by the energy and

ingenuity of its countless agents. In time, it learned how to invent the problems which it was supposed to solve. Working on the fail-safe principle of *provokatsiya* (provocation), it fomented conspiracies in order to break them, and organized trade unions in order to penetrate them. Although it operated throughout the Empire, there are sound reasons why special vigilance was needed in the Western provinces, where 'schisms', 'sects', 'noxious individuals', 'foreigners', and 'frontiers', not to say 'false banknotes' or 'occurrences', were specially prevalent. In an Empire paranoid about security, the site of repeated Polish Risings was bound to attract special attention.

The police system was supported by a network of state fortresses and prisons. In Warsaw, the mighty Alexander Citadel, built in 1832–5 at the city's expense, soon became a symbol of Tsarist oppression. Its notorious Tenth Pavilion, the seat of the Permanent Investigatory Commission, was the first destination, and sometimes last resting-place, of all political prisoners.

The Empire's frontiers, whose European stretches ran through the middle of the former Polish lands, were guarded incessantly. Especially in the railway era, when the numbers of travellers increased rapidly, the precautions taken had no parallel anywhere in Europe. Here, the Army and Police were assisted by the green-coated Corps of Frontier Guards. They were deployed in three distinct zones. The first zone was manned by military detachments stationed at fixed intervals along the full length of the frontier line. At points of expected tension, there were soldiers posted every ten yards for mile after mile, as far as the eye could see. The second zone covered an area some two or three versts behind the frontier, and was patrolled by mobile mounted units. The third zone stretched for a further 150 versts from the frontier, and included almost all the main cities of Poland and Lithuania. All ports, roads, railway stations, and hotels were liable to peremptory search; all travellers were subject to investigation and questioning; all people with foreign contacts were treated as potential law-breakers. The Poles, whose cultural life spanned the three Partitions and who frequently possessed estates or relatives on all sides of the frontier came in for special suspicion, and responded in style. Villages and small towns near the frontier with East Prussia, Silesia, or Galicia developed thriving agencies for smuggling and illegal travel. Secret paths and dark nights were exploited to the full. Officials and soldiers could be bribed. Conspirators and revolutionary literature was brought in; Jews and other illegal emigrants were smuggled out. Every rabbi in Russia knew that the Jews of Płock or of Brody would see their co-religionists on their way to America along 'the moonlight road'. Every revolutionary knew that a platform ticket bought in the morning rush-hour at Sosnowiec, would see him safely across to Kattowitz in Germany. Every desperate refugee hoped that the helping hand of a Polish peasant would be waiting on the southern bank of the Vistula between Sandomierz and Cracow. Meanwhile, normal traffic was needlessly hindered. Baedeker warned western tourists that they should not line their suitcases with newspapers if they wished to avoid unnecessary delay.

The Censorship was equally elaborate. It had first been introduced by Peter the Great for theological works, and was raised into a general system in 1803. Under Nicholas I, and again at the end of the nineteenth century, it assumed the proportions of a major industry. It had twelve separate agencies – general, ecclesiastical, educational, military, theatrical, literary, press, postal, legal, international, foreign, and security – and a supreme secret committee charged with censoring the work of the censors. Its aim was to control all knowledge and all sources of information. In the Western provinces, it strangulated all works in non-Russian languages, and on non-approved subjects, such as politics, or sex, or Catholic theology. It was particularly harsh on all manifestations of Polish History, where any mention of the 'Golden Freedom', of 'Elections', the 'Constitution', the 'Republic' or, worst of all, of the 'Risings' was construed as an act of incitement. In all works of popular history, the 'King of Poland' had to be referred to as 'the Grand-Duke of Poland' so as not to offend the status of the Tsar. As a result, almost all the classics of Polish literature from the Romantic Era had to be published abroad – in Austria or Germany, if not in France or England. None of the dramas of Mickiewicz, Słowacki, or Krasiński were ever staged in Warsaw. The pettiness of the censors was proverbial. As early as 1784, the publication of the first volume of Naruszewicz's History of Poland was banned because Catherine's ambassador in Warsaw objected to the Poles being awarded a more prominent role in the prehistory of the Slavs than the Russians. A century later, in 1888, the first volume of Georg Brandes's two-volume Danish—English Dictionary was confiscated, on the grounds that one volume was insufficient to work the code.

To anyone unfamiliar with the Russian system, it is most surprising to learn that many of its most rigorous practices could be put into effect as mere administrative measures, at the whim of an official. The prisons were full, not of convicts, but of suspects 'waiting to assist the police with their inquiries'. Suspects had fewer known rights than condemned men. Deportation to Siberia could be ensured simply by withdrawing the victim's permission to continue at his place of residence. It was frequently applied to persons who could not be charged with a criminal offence, but whose temporary absence was desirable for official reasons. Surveillance and harassment could not be objected to, since every loyal citizen's duty was to co-operate with the authorities. In such circumstances, it was often a privilege and a relief to be brought to court, or sentenced to a term of imprisonment. Yet there again, many people did not enjoy that privilege. It was a punishable offence for a serf to complain to the authorities against his master, or for a soldier to report an officer for misconduct. (See pp. 286–7.)

Education played a key role in the Tsarist strategy; and the Ministry of Enlightenment in the work of the state. It was in the schools and universities that Polish pupils first came into contact with systematic efforts to change the attitudes and loyalties of their families. It was there that they met with the criticisms and conspiracies of the Russian intelligentsia. In the schools, the rote learning of the titles and birthdays of the endless imperial Grand Dukes and Grand Duchesses, and the unceasing controls of government inspectors, were outward signs of official policy. But nothing riled so much as the compulsory use of the Russian language. After 1864, the absurd situation was reached in Warsaw where Polish teachers had to use Russian as the means of instruction for teaching Polish to Polish children (in accordance with the official myth that Polish was a 'foreign' language). Under Aleksandr Apuchtin (1822–1904), Curator of the Warsaw School District from 1879 to 1897, political informers played an established part in the maintenance of student discipline. Among the higher institutions, the University of Wilno to 1822, the Liceum at Krzemieniec to 1832, the Main School in Warsaw, 1862–9, and from 1898, the Warsaw Polytechnic, were important centres of Polish learning. At Dorpat in Estonia, at Kharkhov from 1805, at St. Petersburg from 1819, at Kiev from 1834, at Odessa from 1865, and at Warsaw from 1869, Russian universities contained strong contingents of Poles among the staff and student body. In mid-century Kiev, two-thirds of the university students were Poles.

Russification caused sorry effects for everyone concerned. Its pettiness infuriated the Poles, and strengthened their sense of grievance; and its failures disheartened Tsarist officials. Its leading proponent was Field Marshal Iosif Hurko (1828–1911), Governor-General in Warsaw from 1883 to 1894. For a Pole, it was mildly annoying to arrive at the station in Warsaw or Wilno and see the platform signs written in Cyrillic characters, and to see all the street and shop signs in both Russian and Polish. It was much more shocking to realize that a person who did not learn Russian could not defend himself in the courts, or that thousands of literate Polish children could not follow the text of their native literature. Books printed in Polish were available from abroad, but would not be understood by children who had only been taught to read the Cyrillic alphabet. Under Russian auspices, increasing literacy was a threat to Polish nationality. Increasingly, Poles could only make good in the Tsarist service by rejecting their origins. A policy designed to promote assimilation generated a growing sense of mutual alienation. Maria Skłodowska, whose childhood was spent in Warsaw described the tension in her schoolroom in 1878:

On the threshold, laced into his fine uniform — yellow pantaloons and a blue tunic with shiny buttons — appeared M. Hornberg, inspector of private boarding-schools in the city of Warsaw. He was a thick-set fellow, sheared in the German fashion; his face was plump and his eyes piercing behind their gold-rimmed glasses . . . The delay had been too short today. The porter had just had time to sound the agreed signal when

Hornberg, going ahead of his guide, reached the landing and plunged into the classroom . . .

Hornberg advanced towards the teacher.

— You were reading aloud. What is the book, mademoiselle?

— Krylov's *Fairy Tales.* We began them today . . .

As if absent-mindedly, Hornberg opened the lid of the nearest desk. Nothing. Not a paper, not a book . . .

M. Hornberg, accepting the chair offered him by Melle Tupalska, seated himself heavily.

— Please call on one of these young people.

In the third row, Marya Sklodovska instinctively turned her frightened little face toward the window . . . But she knew very well that the choice would fall upon her. She knew that she was almost always chosen for the government inspector's questioning. At the sound of her name, she straightened up.

— Your prayer, snapped M. Hornberg.

Manya recited 'Our Father' in a voice without colour or expression. One of the subtlest humiliations the Tsar had discovered was to make the Polish children say their Catholic prayers every day in Russian . . .

— Name the Tsars who have reigned over our Holy Russia since Catherine II.

— Catherine II, Paul I, Alexander I, Nicholas I, Alexander II.

The inspector was satisfied. This child had a good memory . . .

— Tell me the names and titles of the members of the Imperial Family.

— Her Majesty the Empress, His Imperial Highness the Tsarevitch Alexander, His Imperial Highness the Grand Duke . . .

At the end of the enumeration, which was long, Hornberg smiled faintly . . .

— What is the title of the Tsar in the scale of dignities?

— *Vyelichestvo* (Majesty).

— And what is my title?

— *Vysokorodye* (High-born).

The inspector took pleasure in these hierarchic details, more important to his way of thinking than arithmetic or spelling. For his own simple pleasure he asked us again:

— Who rules over us?

To conceal the fire of their eyes, the directress and the superintendent stared hard at the registers they held before them. As the answer did not come quickly enough, Hornberg, annoyed, asked again in louder tones:

— Who rules over us?

— His Majesty Alexander II, Tsar of All the Russias, Manya articulated painfully. Her face had gone white.

The session was over. The functionary rose from his chair, and, after a brief nod, moved to the next room, followed by Melle Sikorska.

Then the teacher raised her head.

— Come here, my little soul.

Manya left her place and came up to the schoolmistress, who, without saying a word, kissed her on the forehead. And suddenly, in the classroom that was coming to life again, the Polish child, her nerves at an end, burst into tears.[9]

On the Russian side, anyone who dared to show sympathy for the Polish language or for Polish customs was asking for trouble. A certain Col. Krupsky, for instance, who had served as the commandant of a small Polish town after the suppression of the January Rising, was cashiered by the Army for exactly that reason. The charges against him mentioned that he had spoken in Polish in public, and that he had danced the Polonaise. The long struggle to clear his good name embittered the life of his entire family, and helped to turn his daughter, Nadzezhda Krupskaya, Lenin's consort, into a convinced revolutionary. In this way, the policy of Russification in Poland can be seen to have heightened the resolve of the Tsar's most doughty enemies. Relaxations introduced after 1905 had little time to repair the damage of previous decades.

None the less, it is undeniable that Russification did affect the scene in many important respects. To all outward appearances, Warsaw in the late nineteenth century became a cosmopolitan metropolis, whose local Polish colouring might modify but could not efface all those features common to cities throughout the Tsarist Empire:

WARSAW AND ENVIRONS

ARRIVAL. The larger hotels send carriages to meet the trains . . .

DEPARTURE. Tickets of the state-railways may be purchased at an advance of 10—20 cop., and baggage may be registered at an extra charge of not less than 50 cop. at Długa, No. 30 and Moniuszki, No. 2; open 9—4, on Sun. and holidays 9—12. The office of the International Sleeping Car Co. is in the Hotel Bristol . . .

RAILWAY STATIONS. Warsaw has five railway stations. On the left bank of the Vistula: 1. VIENNA STATION: (Foksal Varshavsko—Viedenski) for Cracow, Vienna, Thorn, Berlin, and Sosnowice. A policeman, posted at the exit, hands the traveller a metal ticket with the number of a cab. 2. KOVEL STATION: (Foksal Var.—Kovelski) to the S.W. of the citadel, for Mlawa (Marienburg) Lublin, Kovel (Kiev), and

Moscow (three express trains daily; the other Moscow trains start from the Brest station). 3. KALISZ STATION (Foksal Var.–Kaliski) near the Vienna Station, for Lodz and Kalisz (express from the Brest and Kovel stations). – On the right bank of the Vistula, in Praga: 4. ST. PETERS-BURG STATION (Foksal Var.–St. Petersburski) for Vilna, Dunaburg, and St. Petersburg. 5. BREST STATION (Foksal Var.–Brzeski) for Brest-Litovsk, Moscow, Kiev, Odessa, Granitza (Vienna) – The various stations are connected by a junction-line.

HOTELS. *HOTEL BRISTOL, Krakowskie Przedmieście 44, first-class, R. from 3, B. ¾, dej. (12–3 p.m.) 1½ D. (5–8 p.m.) 2, omn. 1 rb; *HOTEL DE L'EUROPE (Europejski) Krakowskie Przedmieście 13; GRAND-HOTEL BRUHL (Bruhlowski) Ulica hrabiego Kotzebue 12, POLONIA PALACE HOTEL, Aleje Jerozolimskie 53, new, opposite the Vienna Station, HOTEL DE ROME (Rzymski) Nowonsenatorska 1, frequented by country gentlemen . . .

Pension Wielhorska, Jasna 4. R. 1–4 board 1¼–1½ rb. The Home of the Protestant Association for Young Women (Jungfrauenverein), Widok 20, and the Home Français, Warecka 15 are intended for women-teachers and girls travelling alone.

RESTAURANTS. Hotel Bristol, *Hot, Bruhl (Munich or Pilsen beer on draught), *Hotel de l'Europe, Polonia Palace Hotel, Hot. de Rome, Versailles, Aleje Ujazdowskie;Hotel d'Angleterre: Cafe-Restaurant Ostrowski, Marszałkowska, corner of the Złota D. (1–5) 75 cop.; Wróbel, Mazowiecka 14, D. 50 cop., well spoken of. WINE. Lijewski, Krakowskie Przedmieście 8; Eremitage, at the corner of the Widok and Marszałkowska, near the Vienna Station, plat du jour, 40 cop.; Fukier, on the W. side of the Plac Stare Miasto (No. 27), an old establishment which has occupied its present unpretending quarters since 1590 . . .

CAFES AND CONFECTIONERS (Cukiernie) glass of coffee 15, tea 10–15, chocolate 20 cop.; also cold viands and beer. Lardelli, Nowy Świat 27 near the Aleje Jerozolimskie . . . Semadeni, in the Grand Theatre; . . . with dairy restaurant; . . . Warsaw pastry is good. Good milk can be obtained in the larger Dairy Restaurants (Mleczarnia).

THEATRES. Grand Theatre (Teatr Wielki) in the Plac Teatralny, for operas and ballets; box 6¾–14 rb., parquet from 1 rb. 40 to 4 rb. 75 cop.; closed in summer. Teatr Rozmaitości, in the W. wing of the Grand Theatre, for Polish dramas; Teatr Polski, . . . for comedies and dramas. Mały Teatr, Moniuszki, 5, in the building of the Philharmonic Society, for modern plays. – Second-class; Teatr Nowoczesny, Boduina 4, . . . for short dramas, comedies, and operettas (performances at 8 and 10 p.m.); New Theatre (Teatr Nowy), in summer only; Novelty Theatre (Teatr Nowości) operettas and comedies, in winter only. – Polish Summer Theatre in the Saxon Garden, parquet from 1 rb. 50 to

3 rb. 35 cop. — Variety Theatres. *Aquarium, Renaissance.* — Cabaret. *Oaza.* — Circus, in winter only.

PLEASURE RESORTS. *Vallée Suisse* (Dolina Szwajcarska) Ulica Szopena 5, with roller-skating rink, and good music on summer evenings (30 cop.), symphony concerts on Wed. and Sat. (50 cop.); *Bagatela,* operettas in summer; In winter the Philharmonic Orchestra gives concerts almost every day in the hall of the Philharmonic Society.

CABS (Dorożki). Per drive within the barriers (Rogatki) 20, at night (12–7 a.m.) 35, with two horses 35 and 50 cop.; Baggage 10 and 15 cop. per pud. — The ordinary one-horse cabs drive slowly, but the two-horse cabs, equipped with good horses, drive very fast. The drivers of the two-horse cabs with rubber tyres expect a gratuity of 20–50 cop. . . .

ELECTRIC TRAMWAYS (fare per section, 1st class 7, 2nd class 5 cop.). The chief intersecting points are the Krakowskie Przedmieście (Statue of Mickiewicz) for Nos. 0, 1, 3, 5, 7, 9, 17, 18, 22; Aleje Ujazdowskie; Vienna Station; St. Petersburg Station; Brest Station; Willanow Station 0 (circular line), from the Plac Zbawiciela, via the Marszałkowska, Złota, Karmelicka, Nalewki, Miodowa, Krakowskie Przedmieście, and Aleje Ujazdowskie to the Plac Zbawiciela; 7¼ M., in 62 min.

STEAMBOATS. Small passenger-steamboats (50 cop.); restaurant on board), starting from the Alexander Bridge, ply up and down the Vistula in summer (May–Oct), in the afternoon and evening . . .

BANKS. *Imperial Bank* (Bank Panstwa) Bielańska 10, open 10–3; *Commercial Bank,* Włodzimierska 27; *Discount Bank,* Ulica Hrabiego Kotzebue 8.

CONSULATES. British Consul, H. M. Grove, Służewska 3 (10–2). American Consul, T. E. Heenan, Aleje Ujazdowskie 18 (10–3). — Branch of the Russo-British Chamber of Commerce.

PHYSICIANS (English speaking) Dr. Horodyński, Nowogrodzka 34; Dr. Raum (surgeon), Bracka 5; Dr. Solman, Jerozolimska 63; Dr. Zaborowski (for ladies), Jerozolimska 58. — PROTESTANT HOSPITAL (*Szpital Ewangelicki*) Karmelicka 10. . . .

CHURCHES. English Church Service (11 a.m.) at Hortensja 3; Chaplain: Rev. H. C. Zimmerman — Lutheran Church — German Reformed Church — The Roman Catholic Churches are open all day.

COLLECTIONS ETC. — *Art Union.* Daily 10–7; adm. 30 cop. The Chojnowski Collection is open daily 10–3; adm. 30 cop.

Belvedere open in winter only, daily, except Sat., 10–3. All by tickets given out gratis at the Palace Office.

Łazienki open daily, except Sat., 10–6, holidays 1–6, in winter 10–3, or 1–3;

Museum of Industry and Commerce open daily, except Mon. 10–3; adm. 20 cop. Sun. 5 cop.

Palace, Royal open daily, except Sat., 1–6.
Picture Gallery open free, Tues., Thurs., & Sun. 11–3.
University Library open on week-days 10–4; during the vacation on Mon., Wed., & Fri., 11–2.
Willanow, Palace of, open on week-days 2–6.
PRINCIPAL ATTRACTIONS (1 day). Royal Palace; streets in the Krakowskie Przedmieście, the Marszałkowska, and the Saxon Garden; view from the lantern of the Lutheran Church; Aleje Ujazdowskie, especially towards evening; Imperial Chateau of Lazienki; Cathedral of St. John; Old Town; Alexander Bridge — Those who have a little more time should not omit a visit to Willanow.

Warsaw (Warszawa, Varshava; Ger. Warschau, Fr. Varsovie; 320 ft.), the capital of the General Government of Warsaw or Poland and an important railway centre, lies on the left bank of the Vistula, on the elevated edge (120–130 ft.) of a valley, descending abruptly to the river, here $\frac{1}{4}$–$\frac{1}{3}$M in width, and gradually merging on the W. in a wide and undulating plain. The city contains 872,500 inhab., including 15,000 Protestants, 300,000 Jews and a strong garrison. It is the intellectual centre of Poland, and its appearance is far more like that of West Europe than of Russia. Warsaw is the seat of the Governor-General of Warsaw, of a Civil Governor, of Archbishops of the Greek and Roman Catholic churches, of the Commandant of the Military District of Warsaw, and of those of the 15th, 19th and 23rd Army Corps, and of a Russian university and a Russian technical college. The city, which is divided into twelve police precincts (including Praga) consists of the Old Town (Stare Miasto), of the New Town (Nowe Miasto), to the N, and of Wola, Mokotow, and other suburbs. On the right bank of the Vistula lies Praga. The river is crossed by three bridges. The streets teem with activity; the great shopping district lies in the Marszałkowska and the Krakowskie Przedmieście. Whole quarters of the town are occupied by Jews, whose inattention to personal cleanliness has become proverbial. Warsaw is a flourishing industrial centre (machinery, wooden wares, leather, and tobacco) and carries on a considerable trade.[10]

* * * * *

If the infernal machine of Russian Government had ever worked as intended, there is no doubt that the future for the Poles, and for all other minorities, would have been completely hopeless. Fortunately for them, the machine had several built-in defects. The gap which separated the Autocrat's wish from its practical application was as vast as the Empire itself. Life was rendered tolerable by the interaction of inefficiency, caprice, and residual Christianity. Especially at the lower levels, the bureaucracy was radiantly corrupt. Inspectors could be counted on not to apply the rules too harshly unless the Chief Inspector happened to be in the offing. Service in the Polish *gubernias,* amidst a hostile population, was regarded with distaste. Ambitious men returned quickly to the capital. Laggards learned how to make themselves comfortable. Although Warsaw was not so remote from St. Petersburg in the geographical sense, it should certainly be counted among the *'gluchie provintsii'* from the administrative point of view, inexplicably 'deaf' to the voice of the Tsar. In a completely centralized empire, one faulty link in the chain of command was enough to paralyse action. Officials, whose only function was to interpret orders, would frequently interpret them in an eccentric way as an expression of their own individuality, or ignore them completely. Capricious decisions were everywhere observable. Extreme leniency was no less common than extreme brutality. Christian values were very much alive among the responsible classes. From the Tsar down to the humblest official, the political duty to act rigorously stood in severe conflict with the Christian duty to show mercy and forgiveness. Judges, who awarded exemplary sentences to the ringleaders of seditions and conspiracies, often commuted or annulled the punishment of their accomplices. Soldiers who were ordered to deal with rebels and traitors with bloody severity, were at the same time rewarded for acts of magnanimity and self-sacrifice. For reasons unknown to the ordinary citizen, one official would say 'Yes' and another say 'No'. Here was the timeless Russian paradox. Autocracy was justified and perpetuated to combat the very vices which it encouraged and which made it inoperative. It was a circle too vicious to be easily broken. Yet Tsarism was neither so monstrous nor so consistent as its later reputation suggests. Although capable of meaningless savagery on occasion, it was milder and more humane in practice than much that the twentieth century can boast of.

At the same time, the negative strength of the Russian Empire could not be underestimated. If the Tsar could not rule his Polish provinces with the degree of harmony that he wished for, he could easily prevent anyone else from interfering. The powers of denial were unlimited, and very effective.

The Army, police, frontiers, censors, fortresses, and prisons were not maintained for show. On the internal front, all the conspiracies and risings of a century and a half were suppressed without serious difficulty. On the international front, great advantages could be drawn from the Tsar's traditional role as the champion of Legitimacy. No European monarchy would tangle lightly with the giant Empire whose brute strength was a guarantee of international law and order. So long as the partitioning powers kept common cause, the Polish Question could not be raised. Diplomatic protests could be politely brushed aside. Of themselves, the Poles had no means to effect fundamental change. In Russia, nothing changed without the stimulus of an external defeat. It was the British and French whose campaign in the Crimea provoked the reforms of Alexander II. It was the Japanese whose victories in Manchuria made the 'Revolution' of 1905 possible and the consequent establishment of the *Duma*. It was the Germans who in 1915–16 drove the Tsarist authorities out of the Polish provinces for good, and who in the following year drove the subjects of the Tsar to revolution.

No amount of social and economic progress could alter the political situation. As the nineteenth century wore on, Russian Poland's share of the Empire's wealth and advancement grew rapidly. Industrialization and urbanization began much earlier than in central Russia. By 1914 Warsaw had grown to a city of 900,000, Łódź to 230,000, Wilno to 193,000, Sosnowiec to 100,000. After 1850, when the internal tariff barrier was removed, Polish producers were able to service the vast Russian market. After 1864, when serfdom was finally abolished, the rural masses could move freely to the towns. An urban working class appeared, and with it a seminal bourgeoisie, with strong German and Jewish connections. Together, they accounted for almost one-third of the population. The new social groups began to organize new political parties, some legal, some illegal. But in no way should these developments be seen as 'steps on the road towards independence'. Nicholas II was no more disposed to allow the Poles to secede than Nicholas I. And the Poles in Russia in 1914 had no better means of enforcing their demands than in 1814. It was the World War that eventually broke the Russian hold on Poland, not progress.

Despite its obvious faults, the Tsarist Government did not discriminate unduly against its Polish citizens. In Polish eyes, of course, it was supremely 'anti-Polish', just as in Jewish eyes, it was 'anti-Semitic', or in Ukrainian eyes it was 'anti-Ukrainian'. But that is only to say that it met all expressions of independent will with equal and total opposition. As a matter of fact, it was part of the Muscovite tradition that Russians should be treated worst of all. In the words of Mickiewicz, 'Cursed be this nation which kills its own prophets.'[11] The Government made a point of oppressing its own people first and foremost. No Pole or Jew or Ukrainian could claim that he was treated more harshly than the revolutionaries, sectarians, or conspirators among the Russian population at large. It is true that the Poles found no response to demands for independence. But they shared in such prosperity and suffering that was going. It was their expectations that were different, not their objective predicament. Unfortunately, Tsarism did not cater for expectations.

In the end, of course, the attempt to absorb the former Polish provinces into Russia failed gloriously. Political integration did not lead to social assimilation. On the contrary, it lead to increasing social polarization. Unlike the situation in Austria, or in Prussia before 1871, where the good citizen could reconcile his Polish patriotism to his loyalty to the Habsburgs or the Hohenzollerns, in Russia people were forced to choose between their conflicting loyalties. If a person continued to speak Polish, to practise the Catholic religion, and to cultivate Polish friends, he was automatically suspect in the eyes of the political authorities. In order to prove an acceptable degree of reliability and to qualify for a responsible position, a Pole had to abandon his native language, even in his home, to reject Catholicism or Judaism for Orthodoxy, and to shun his relatives and friends. Inevitably, in such an environment, Russians and Poles were forced to live separate lives. Social intercourse between the two nationalities diminished. In Warsaw, in Wilno, even in the smaller centres, the Poles kept to themselves. They formed their own closed societies, their own businesses, their own secret societies. Their children married amongst themselves, and looked with disfavour on any of their number who dared to break the unwritten rules of national solidarity. They were condemned by circumstances to love their country, and to hate their rulers. They pretended with all their heart and soul that Russia did not exist.

To people who have never experienced similar circumstances, it is difficult to explain what Russia meant to those disaffected Polish generations. Contemporary writers often expressed their predicament through metaphors and vivid images of active oppression which cannot always be taken at their face value. Having learned the lessons of successive Risings, the central government in St. Petersburg increasingly sought, not to thrash the Poles into submission in the Prussian fashion, but rather to wear them down by depriving them of all the spiritual and cultural resources which make life tolerable. In an autocratic Empire of 150 millions, which was increasingly preoccupied with the restless Russian heartland, 15 million Poles could not hope to assert their eccentric interests. Their resistance was to be overcome not by bullets and rawhide whips but by spiritual prescription, official ostracism, and 'internal exile'. For the most part, the warfare was psychological not physical. The longest confrontations took place not in the tumult of the barricades but in the quiet of private consciences. Here was a highly deceptive situation which inspired Józef Piłsudski to call Russia 'an Asiatic beast hidden behind a European mask'. Later, one of Piłsudski's successors, Marshal Śmigły-Rydz, fearing a choice between submission to Russia or to Germany, expressed a clear opinion. It was an opinion based on the Russian world in which most Poles grew up and with which many of them would have agreed. 'Germany will destroy our body' he said; 'Russia will destroy our soul.'[12]

The predominant mood in Russian Poland, therefore, was one of loneliness, emptiness, and frustration. For the government in St. Petersburg, the problems of Vistulaland, with its eternal grievances and its incurable *nieblagonadzhenost'* (unreliability) were of marginal concern. For the Poles, Russia was a wilderness in which nothing they held dear was ever given serious consideration. Adam Mickiewicz, travelling in Southern Russia in 1825, found an exact image for these sentiments:

The Steppes of Akkerman

I have sailed on to the expanse of a dry ocean.
The wagon is submerged in greenery, and like a boat, wanders
Through the rustling waves of the prairie, and glides among the flowers.
I pass coral islets of rank vegetation.
Already dusk is falling. No road here, no dolmen.
I look up, seeking the stars, my ship's couriers.
There, afar, a cloud gleams in the sky. The morning star glimmers.
There lies the glistening Dniester! There, the pharos of Akkerman.
Halt! How still! I can hear a flight of cranes
Which are invisible, even to the falcon's stare.
I listen to a butterfly snuggling in the grassy lanes,
And to a smooth-breasted snake nestling in the clover.
In such silence, my curious ear strains
To catch a voice from Lithuania . . . Drive on! No one's there.[13]

Russia rarely gave the Poles even an echo of what they wanted to hear. For them, Russia was a wilderness in more senses than one.

In Russia at large, Poland's plight continued to command little sympathy. In the great age of Russian literature which preceded the Revolution, frequent reference was made to Polish themes; but few comments were favourable. Dostoevsky's pathological hatred of Poland was no doubt exceptional in its virulence. Yet it found many echoes in the opinions of his literary confrères. In *Anna Karenina,* Tolstoy used the mouth of Karenin to express the prevalent attitude of educated Russians of his day. ' "The Poles", Karenin said, as if to inform his audience of a little known fact, "are not Russians; but now they are members of our nation, they ought to be Russified for their own benefit." ' It was a sharp mind indeed that could penetrate such overpowering ignorance and complacency, and see through the calm surface of Russia's Polish provinces to the underlying layers of frustration, contempt, and hatred. Alexander Blok, that most Russian of Russian poets, author of *The Scythians* and *The Twelve,* was one of the few to acquaint himself with Poland and to gain some sort of understanding. The poet's father, Alexander Lvovich Blok, was Professor of Public Law at Warsaw's Russian University, and when he died in November 1909, the son dutifully travelled from Moscow to attend the funeral. This winter journey to 'Russia's back-yard', this 'God-forsaken and lacerated country' 'burdened by insults and forced beneath the yoke of insolent violence' made a lasting impression, and supplied the direct inspiration for his poem *Voz'mediye* (Retribution).

> Gendarmes, Railway tracks, Gas lamps,
> Jargon, and old-fangled side curls —
> Just look in the rays of a sickly dawn
> How all that was, and all that is,
> Is inflated by a vengeful chimera.
> Even Copernicus, clutching a hollow globe
> Cries vengeance from his pedestal.
> Revenge! Revenge! it echoes
> Round Warsaw with the ring of cold iron.[14]

Less than six years after Blok's visit, Warsaw was captured by the German army. The Russian Partition was destroyed not by Polish vengeance, but by international war.

CHAPTER THREE
PREUSSEN:
The Prussian Partition (1772-1918)

'Prussian Poland', like 'Russian Poland', was a variable term. In official usage, it was generally confined to the one area, the Grand Duchy of Posen, which from 1815 to 1848 enjoyed a measure of autonomy. In this sense, and in the same period, it was the exact parallel to the restricted meaning of 'Russian Poland' in reference to the Congress Kingdom. In more popular usage, it referred to all the lands which the Kingdom of Prussia inherited from the former Polish—Lithuanian Republic, and as such included not only Posnania (Wielko-polska and Kujawy), but also West Prussia (Royal Prussia), and for a dozen years between 1795 and 1807 South Prussia (Mazovia), New Silesia (Częstochowa), and New East Prussia (Suwałki and Białystok). These are what Prussians used to call 'our Polish provinces'.* In Polish eyes, however, Prussian Poland was later thought to include every area of the Kingdom of Prussia which contained a predominantly Polish population or which in some way or another had been connected with Poland in the past. In this way, it came to refer both to Silesia and to Pomerania and even to East Prussia. (See Map 3.) For most of the nineteenth century, the Slav element in these provinces did not consider themselves to be Poles, and were widely classified as 'Polish-speaking Prussians'. At the beginning of the century, the Silesians, the Kashubs, and the Protestant Mazurians possessed a weaker sense of their Polishness than the German-speaking Danzigers.

The Kingdom of Prussia was in a state of flux throughout the modern period. It experienced several fundamental changes both to its territorial base and to its constitutional system.

---

* Despite subsequent changes of opinion, both Silesia and Pomerania were generally regarded at the time to be part of Germany, and both were included in the German League from 1815 to 1866. As from 1834, the *Zollverein* (German Customs Union), and as from 1867, the North German Confederation, included all the provinces of the Kingdom of Prussia.

Map 3.   The Prussian Partition, (1773–1918)

The Enlightened Despotism of Frederickian Prussia did not survive the death of its author in 1786. Under Frederick-William II (1786–97), and in the first half of the reign of Frederick-William III (1797–1819), the Revolutionary Era saw the decline of the monarchy and a series of political defeats and losses of territory. Prussia lost its Rhineland provinces and regained them; lost part of its Polish provinces and partly regained them; and was subjected to a whole series of constitutional and administrative experiments. But at the Congress of Vienna in 1815, Prussia was reconstituted, and emerged as a serious challenger to Austria's traditional supremacy in the German world. It played a prominent role in the German League, and the *Zollverein*. Under Frederick-William IV (1840–61), it passed from a period of conservative reaction to Reform and Revolution, and to the imposed constitution of 1850. Under Wilhelm I (1861–88), and in the hands of Bismarck, it became the organizer and central bastion of the German Empire. After 1871, though it retained its separate structure, many historians would argue that its separate interests and identity were effectively submerged in those of Germany as a whole. Certainly, the imperialism and chauvinism of Wilhelm II (1888–1918) were quite at odds with the older, more sober Prussian tradition.

Within the changing Prussian framework, the Polish element knew no settled existence. In 1800, when Warsaw was in Prussia, the Poles formed over 40 per cent of the total population. The prospect of a German–Slav state was briefly very real. After 1815, however, the Polish percentage dropped dramatically. Despite the steady growth in the absolute number of Poles, their relative strength against the German population steadily declined. By 1905, three million Poles formed a very small minority in a German Empire of 56 million people.[1]

The forum of Polish political activities shifted accordingly. Before 1848, the Diet and provincial institutions of the Grand Duchy of Posen formed a natural meeting-point. For a time, it looked as though the Grand Duchy might play a co-ordinating role for Poles from all three Partitions. Then, with the suppression of the Grand Duchy, attention moved to the 'Polish Circle' of the Prussian *Landtag* in Berlin, and after 1872, to the imperial *Reichstag*.

In German terminology, modern Prussia was an *Obrigkeits-staat*, an 'authoritarian state'. Although it failed to develop the mystical ideology of Autocracy or the streamlined machinery of Absolutism, it operated on the principle that the will of the ruler and of his government was supreme. Its system was typified less by rigid ideas or institutions than by that imprecise but ominous phrase, the Prussian Spirit. In the words of one of its least critical admirers, 'Prussianism was a life-style, an instinct, a compulsion . . . where the people desire and act as a super-personal whole . . . it is not a herd instinct, but something immensely strong and free which no one who does not belong can understand.'[2] It was a tradition created by the ceaseless struggle over three centuries to forge a kingdom from the scattered Hohenzollern possessions, and by the constant danger and insecurity which that struggle involved. For practical purposes, it reduced civil liberties to a minimum, and prevented democratic institutions, when they appeared, from being fully accountable to the people. In Prussia, as in Russia, the monarch was wont to command, and the people to obey.

In several important ways, therefore, Prussian authoritarianism closely matched Russian Autocracy. The Army, for example, occupied pride of place, and from the time of Frederick-William I and his *lange kerls,* or 'tall grenadiers', had acted as the principal instrument of Prussia's success. Its establishment was enormous, and its prowess, from Fehrbellin to Sedan, legendary. No one can deny that Prussian militarism was rather special. Whilst the Russian army practised methods of crude coercion against the civilian population and against its own ranks alike, the Prussians nurtured a genuine enthusiasm for the people-in-arms. Under the influence of Napoleonic France, Scharnhorst and Gneisenau abolished the press-ganging and brutal discipline of former times. In the nineteenth century, the Prussian soldier was not only the best drilled in Europe; he was the best led, the best fed, and the best armed; and he marched to the best military music in the world.

The bureaucracy, too, resembled its autocratic counterparts. The Prussian Inspector, with his pince-nez and rubber stamp, was no less a figure of fun and fear, than elsewhere. Unfortunately, he gained the reputation not only of petty-mindedness, but also of incorruptibility.

The Prussian Police mirrored the thoroughness of the bureaucracy as a whole. The Minister of the Interior combined his police duties with political functions, and till 1822 enjoyed the title of 'State-Chancellor' or premier. Wide-ranging powers of censorship and summary arrest were used against political opponents of all sorts, from lowly journalists like Karl Marx to lofty clerics such as the Archbishops of Cologne or Breslau. Marx's own revolutionary tendencies were undoubtedly strengthened by the knowledge that his father-in-law, Ferninand Henning von Westphalen, was Minister of the Interior in mid-century Berlin.

The Prussian army and administration rested on the support of a traditional caste of service aristocrats. The Junkers had enabled the Hohenzollerns to impose their rule on the multifarious cities and regions of the realm, and continued to fill the core of the 'military-authoritarian citadel'. From the old army of von Moltke to the new Reichswehr of von Seeckt in the 1920s, they acted as the guardians of conservative values, and successfully resisted the challenge of Liberalism and Socialism. In Otto Eduard Leopold von Bismarck-Schönhausen, Prussian Premier from 1862 and Chancellor of the Reich from 1871 to 1890, they found the most genial exponent of their traditions. In the later nineteenth century, their diminishing influence in Germany as a whole was shored up by the appearance of a group of industrial aristocrats — the 'smokestack barons', families such as the Donnersmarck, Hohenlohe, Lichnowski, or Schaffgotsch, whose vast wealth grew from industrial enterprise. In so far as the power-base of both groups was concentrated in the eastern provinces, in Pomerania, East Prussia, or Silesia, the influence of the loyalist aristocracy acted as a powerful brake on Polish aspirations.

Many features of life in Prussia, however, differed fundamentally from those in the neighbouring empires. For one thing, Prussia was a *Rechtstaat* — a political community which operated within the framework of law. Although the political institutions never amounted to more than a 'Façade Democracy', none the less the authoritarian system operated through regular procedures, and by legal means. It possessed a solid, well-oiled, and efficient bureaucratic machine, whose design and operation were publicly known and widely admired. But it was a machine which could be used equally effectively for the purposes of sound administration or for the suppression of minority or opposition elements. Thus, whereas in Russia the Poles recognized oppression in the irrational and arbitrary whims of the Tsarist authorities, in Prussia they encountered it in the all too predictable pedantry of petty officials supported by the letter and the majesty of the law.

Religious toleration was generally observed. Although it is not incorrect to talk of a Protestant Establishment, especially after the creation in 1817 of a National Church, religious conformity was not an essential criterion for social or political advancement. Ever since the influx of French Huguenots in the seventeenth century, Calvinism had prospered no less than Lutheranism. The Jews may have lost the communal autonomy which they had enjoyed under the Polish Republic; but many of them rose to prominence, and the rate of voluntary assimilation was high. Until the 1870s, the obstacles placed in the path of Roman Catholics were, at the most, informal. Bismarck's notorious *Kulturkampf* (Culture Struggle) was launched in 1873 in response to the advent of Rhineland and Bavarian Catholics to the Empire, and had no precedent in the Prussian past.

There was a long-standing tradition of social paternalism. The duty of improving and caring for the condition of the poorer and more vulnerable elements of society was ingrained in the Prussian ethic. It can be traced to the Protestant Pietism of the seventeenth and eighteenth centuries, when a precocious network of schools, orphanages, almshouses, and hospitals was created, and when men like August Herman Francke and his circle at the University of Halle taught the virtues of practical Christianity. It ensured that the emancipation of the serfs, undertaken between 1807 and 1823, was complete in Prussia before Russia had even commenced the process. Its influence can be observed in attitudes at both ends of the political spectrum, in the work of Ferdinand Lassalle (1825–64), a Breslau Jew and the founder of state socialism, and in that of Bismarck himself, whose social insurance scheme of 1878, to protect workers against sickness and accident, was far in advance of its time. Paternalism of this sort drew the sting of social ills and confined demands for national liberation to the political sphere.

Cultural life was highly developed. In the Revolutionary era, Berlin, the 'Sparta of the North' was enlivened by an unprecedented explosion of literary and philosophical excellence. The modest achievements of the Frederickian Enlightenment were far surpassed by those of Kant, Hamann, Schlegel, Fichte, Hegel, and Schopenhauer (who was born a Polish subject in Danzig, in 1788). Herder, Niebuhr, and Ranke founded a School of History which was admired and imitated throughout Europe. Humboldt, Chamisso, and Bunsen in the natural sciences, Savigny and Eichhorn in jurisprudence, are counted among the pioneers of their subjects. Kleist, Lessing, and Novalis raised German literature out of its doldrums. First Königsberg and then Berlin became intellectual centres of continental import. Men of talent and ambition were drawn from home and abroad, and not a few recruited into the Prussian service. In the intellectual salons of Henriette Herz or Rachel Levin, philosophers and poets mingled with politicians and aristocrats. The spirit of inquiry penetrated deep into educated society, and, coming at the very beginning of the Reform Era, made a profound impact on all spheres of life. Notwithstanding the authoritarian state, all political changes in Prussia were subjected to searching debate, and were thoroughly discussed at a high level. What is more, the excellence of intellectual life in Prussia was sustained. In the persons of Treitschke, Mommsen, or Max Planck, Berlin could boast no lesser status in 1900 than in 1800. In the absence of any comparable intellectual development in the Polish lands, many Poles were inevitably drawn into the world of German culture.

The Industrial Revolution came to Prussia early. The first steel-mill was erected in the Ruhr in the 1780s, and in Silesia in 1794. The first railway was built in 1847. Industrial enterprise and urban development were in German hands from the start, even in the Polish provinces. Political movements, deriving from economic and social change, were equally in German hands. Both Socialism as a whole, and Trade Unionism in particular, were all-German affairs, and were fundamentally opposed to any tampering with the Prussian state. Quite apart from official policy, therefore, many Poles in Prussia accepted that modernization went hand in hand with Germanization. This tendency was not offset until the very end of the century, when a new wave of unassimilated Polish proletarians flooded into the towns of Silesia and Poznania, and when, in the so-called *Ostflucht* or 'Flight from the East', a large number of Germans began to leave for central and western provinces. In this Age of Science and Industry, Prussia boasted one of the most modern societies of Europe and its Polish citizens were free to reap the benefits. Authoritarianism was bolstered by creature comforts.

Rapid social and economic change was generally contained by the established tradition of Reform. In the seminal work of Stein, Hardenberg, and Humboldt, programmes were launched to be developed and expanded throughout the century. In the decade, 1808–18, one can see the beginnings of social emancipation, municipal reform, and administrative reorganization: of a modern army, and of a modern education system with co-ordinated primary, secondary, and university sectors. Constitutional reform was delayed till 1847. This one delay gave rise in 1848–50 to the only serious crisis in modern Prussian history. In contrast to the absolutist systems, which for want of timely reform habitually lurched from one catastrophe to the next, the even tenor of Prussian government was rarely ruffled. In this respect, Prussian conservatism closely resembled enlightened British Toryism, which regularly defended the established order by stealing the thunder of its radical opponents. With the single exception of 1848, there was no general crisis in Prussia which might have been exploited by the Polish national movement to press separatist demands. In this context, the scope for active Polish politics was severely limited. It is not at all surprising that the separate structure of Polish life within Prussia rapidly declined during the nineteenth century. The remarkable revival of Polish national consciousness at the start of the twentieth century cannot be easily explained by reference to earlier events.

The right of the Poles to autonomy within the kingdom of Prussia was enshrined in the Treaty of Vienna. It was never applied to the Poles of Pomerania, West Prussia, or Silesia, and in the Grand Duchy of Posen was observed for barely thirty years. As constituted in 1815, the Grand Duchy had a territory of some 29,000 km² and a population of 850,000. Eight out of ten people spoke Polish as their native language. The oath of allegiance exacted from the nobility referred to 'the King of that part of Poland under Prussian rule'. The Viceroy, or *Staathalter*, Prince Antoni Radziwiłł was a Pole, and Polish was the official language, in schools, courts, and government. The local *Landrat* or Diet was elected by the nobles, and had the right of petitioning the King. After 1831, however, increasing restrictions were imposed. The Viceroyalty was abandoned. A new *Oberpräsident*, Edward Flotwell, proceeded with new rigorous policies. Noblemen who had assisted refugees and insurrectionists from the November Rising in Russian Poland were declared confiscate. The elective Diet was closed. German schools and societies were encouraged. In 1848, in the wake of the abortive Posnanian revolt, the Grand Duchy was abolished. Later demands for its reinstatement were never seriously considered.

Revolutionary Polish nationalism attracted few adherents, and scored no success. In the 1840s, a number of conspiratorial societies made their appearance in Posen, among them the Związek Plebejuszy (Plebeians' Union). In February 1846, some 254 people were arrested at the Prussian end of an intended all-Polish insurrection organized by the *émigré* Democratic Society. In the Berlin Trial of the following year, the eight leading defendants, including Ludwik Mierosławski, were condemned to death for treason, but not executed. They were released by the outbreak of Revolution in Berlin on 20 March 1848 amid popular demonstrations. Mierosławski rushed to Posen to head a National Committee, which was formed whilst the back of the Prussian authorities was turned. A local Polish militia was raised, and armed with scythes. Even so, the revolutionary nature of these events can be easily exaggerated. The political demands of the Committee were for effective autonomy, not for independence; the militia was intended for use not against Prussia but against the threat of Russian intervention. At the Pact of Jarosławiec on 11 April, the Committee was dissolved, when promises by General von Willisen about a Polish administration were

▼

accepted. Mierosławski, together with those of his militia who had refused to disband, were dispersed by the Prussian Army. As Frederick-William IV wrote to his sister, the Tsarina, 'I hope that lots of rebels will cross into the Kingdom of Poland, where Pashkievich can hang them.' The Tsarina replied, 'Hang them yourself.' Von Willisen's promises were ignored. The Grand Duchy became 'Provinz-Posen'; and the white eagle on its coat of arms was removed. It was the last and only revolutionary outbreak in Prussian Poland until December 1918.[3]

The integration of the Polish provinces into the unified governmental system of Prussia was part of a process which affected all parts of the Kingdom from the Rhine to the Niemen. As from 1850, a new constitution gave wide legislative powers to a revamped Prussian *Landtag* or 'Diet', which consisted of two chambers — the upper *Herrenhaus* or 'House of Lords', of some 240 hereditary and life peers appointed by the monarch, and the lower *Abgeordnetenhaus* or 'House of Commons', of some 350 to 450 elected deputies. The King retained firm control over the convocation and the dissolution of the Diet, as he did over the *Staatsrat* or 'Ministerial Council' and over the Army, the Judiciary, the Civil Service, and the organs of Local Government. A system of indirect suffrage was extended to all males over 25 years of age, divided by property qualifications into three distinct classes of voter. Each class returned its own College of Electors, whose task was then to elect the deputies. By this means, each deputy of the First Class was returned on average by 480 votes; in the Second Class by 1,920 votes; and in the Third Class by 9,600 votes. Indubitably, the franchise was weighted against the peasants and workers, which meant in the eastern provinces that the Polish element was put at a considerable disadvantage from the start. Only the Polish nobility could make its voice heard in both chambers. As from 1871, the government of Prussia was overlaid by the confederative machinery of the German Empire. Whilst the King and Ministers of Prussia assumed direction of the Empire's central institutions, additional electoral procedures had to be introduced for returning deputies to the *Reichstag* or 'Imperial Diet'. Between 1872 and 1888, local government too, was reconstructed. Henceforth, Prussia was to be divided into fourteen provinces, of which five – Pomerania, Posen, Silesia, West Prussia, and East Prussia – contained a native Polish element. Each province was subdivided into *Regierungsbezirke* (Governmental Regions), and each region into *Stadtkreise* (Urban Districts), and *Landkreise* (Rural Districts). Although democratic elective institutions functioned at all levels in the *Landtag,* the *Bezirksrat* (Regional Council), and the *Kreiserat* (District Council), all executive officers were appointed by, and were responsible to, the central government at all times. In such areas which were not ceded to Poland in 1918–21, these separate Prussian institutions continued to operate until the advent of the Nazis in 1933.

The temper and the possibilities of the Poles in Prussia were far better suited to conciliation than to revolution. In Posen, the conciliatory approach was strongly advocated by Dr Karol Marcinkowski (1800–46), a local physician and philanthropist, who in 1838 founded the Polish 'Bazaar' which housed a club, a shop selling folk crafts, and a bookstore. In 1841, he launched the Society for Educational Assistance (TNP) which granted scholarships to poor students. Marcinkowski's spiritual heirs can be said to include Karol Libelt (1807–75), a former revolutionary and defendant in the Berlin Trials who was converted by the failure of the 1848 adventure; August Cieszkowski, the philosopher, who initiated the short-lived Polish League; and above all, Hipolit Cegielski (1813–68), who, from humble beginnings behind the counter of the Bazaar, became a leading industrialist and the owner of the city's largest factory. Both Libelt and Cegielski were involved in the local press, and both were elected to the Prussian *Landtag.* Under their leadership, the Polish movement in Posnania developed marked characteristics. It was very staid and bourgeois, and in many ways was an avid imitator of German virtues. The Poles of Posen were consciously striving to outdo their German neighbours at their own game. 'If you are a Polish housewife', urged an article written in 1872, 'make your butter cleaner and better than the Germans do: have better vegetables, linen, fruit and poultry. In this way, you will save both yourself and Poland ... Learning, work, order, and thrift are our new weapons.'[4]

Education was a crucial issue. At the time of the Partitions, Prussia had nothing comparable to the schools of the National Education Commission in Poland (which Prussian sources none the less contemptuously dismissed as 'Potemkin's villages'). But after 1809, under Humboldt, a thorough, three-stage system of state education was constructed. The universities of Halle, Berlin, Königsberg, and Breslau were of formidable quality, and attracted some of the greatest minds of the age. At the secondary level they were supported by the state *Gymnazia* in every town and city. At the primary level, elementary schools or *Volkschule* appeared in every parish. By 1848, 82 per cent of children were attending school. Educational reforms, like most things in Prussia were inspired by a characteristic blend of liberal and authoritarian motives. The provision of universal education was furthered on the one hand by humanitarian progressives, who saw it as an essential ingredient of the campaign against child labour, and on the other hand by the Army's demand for literate recruits. Pedagogical methods were largely inspired by the theories of Jean-Henri Pestalozzi, whose treatise, *How Gertrude educates her children* (1801), remained a standard text in the training colleges, long after it had profoundly impressed Humboldt. In theory, Prussian children were to be taught self-reliance and self-fulfilment in an atmosphere designed to awake and nurture the natural talents of the individual, rather than to impose a code of external values. In practice, they were consigned to the mercies of a narrow-minded corps of state-trained schoolmasters, who all too often descended into the villages with the God-given air of cultural recruiting sergeants. Hence, somewhat ambiguously, they were expected to develop both the virtues of 'autonomous, inner-directed man' and the automatic reflexes of loyal, grateful subjects. Great emphasis was laid on technical education. Yet there was a clear distinction between the practical skills and vocational training in the *Volkschule* thought suitable for the masses and the scientific, investigatory spirit reserved for the élite of the *Gymnazium.* Polish anxieties, such as they were, centred on the language issue. Although little effort was made before the 1870s to suppress Polish schools, there was equally little attempt to support them, or to finance them from state funds. There

were no Polish institutions of higher learning; and outside
Posnania, the state *Gymnazium* at Kulm (Chełmno) in West
Prussia was the only one to use Polish as the language of
instruction. In the primary grades, Polish schools were established in all areas where the population was predominantly
Polish-speaking: yet instruction in Polish was largely viewed
as a preliminary aid to the teaching of German, and as a means
of preparing children for the higher, Germanized grades. The
situation resembled that in Wales or Western Scotland where
the British authorities gave exclusive preference to the teaching of English. After 1872, Germanization was systematically
enforced at all levels. In 1911, in Posnania alone, a network
of 2,992 schools served a population of two million – as
compared with barely four thousand in the Russian Congress
Kingdom serving a population almost five times greater. By
that time, illiteracy had been eliminated. But the Poles were
not completely Germanized. Polish literacy was encouraged
by voluntary associations such as the Society for Popular
Education (TOL) in Posen, and above all, by the Society for
Popular Reading-Rooms (TCL) which from 1880 onwards
created a system of two thousand Polish libraries from Bochum
to Bromberg.

The most unequivocal formulation of Prussian attitudes
towards the Poles was made, not surprisingly, by Bismarck
himself. At the time of the January Rising in Russian Poland,
a series of diplomatic canards was staged by people who
hoped that Bismarck might intervene against Russia and re-
establish a Polish state under Prussian protection. They should
have known better. The Chancellor had already made his
personal feelings about the Poles perfectly clear. 'Personally,
I sympathize with their position,' he wrote in 1862; 'but if
we want to exist, we cannot do other than extirpate them. A
wolf is not to blame that God made him as he is; which does
not mean that we shouldn't shoot him to death whenever
possible.' In reality, as the British ambassador in Berlin correctly reported to London, Bismarck was convinced that
Prussia would be 'seriously compromised' by the establishment of an independent Poland, and was likely to take the
field against the Poles if the Russians failed to suppress the
Rising unaided. Somewhat later, in 1869, he elaborated his

views at length. Faced in the *Landtag* by a Polish deputy, who had quoted Macaulay on the crime of the Partitions, and was demanding recognition of 'Polish rights', Bismarck launched into an inimitable tirade in defence of the Prussian government's conduct both in the past and at present:

The Polish Republic owed its destruction much less to foreigners than to the inconceivable worthlessness of those persons who represented the Polish nation when it was broken up . . . The participation of the Germans in the mutilation of Poland was a necessary compliance with the law of self-preservation . . . Gentlemen, if you contest the right of conquest, you cannot have read the history of your own country. It is thus that states are formed . . . The Poles themselves committed the crime of conquest a hundredfold . . . After the Battle of Tannenberg, Polish ravages in West Prussia left only three thousand of nineteen thousand German villages unscathed . . . Polonisation was pursued by fire and sword, Germanisation by culture . . . (Nowadays) Germanisation is making satisfactory progress . . . by which we do not mean the dissemination of the German language, but that of German morality and culture, the upright administration of justice, the elevation of the peasant, and the prosperity of the towns. The peasant from being a despised, ill-used vassal of some noble tyrant is become a free man, the owner of the soil he cultivates. Nobody plunders him now but the usurious Jew. German farmers, machines, and manufactories have promoted agriculture and husbandry. Railways and good roads have increased the general well-being . . . Schools organised after the German pattern impart elementary instruction to Polish children. Gymnazia teach the higher sciences, not by the hollow, mechanical methods of the Jesuit fathers, but in the solid German way which enables people to think for themselves. Army service completes whatever is left unachieved by the schools. In the Army, the young Polish peasant learns to speak and to read German. Through what he is taught in his company or squadron, and through intercourse with the German inhabitants of the garrison towns, he acquires ideas which enrich and emancipate his poor and fettered intelligence . . . Instead of grumbling perpetually, the Poles should look about them and gratefully acknowledge all that has been done for their country and its population under the Prussian regime . . . In the province of Posen, there are schools . . . gymnazia . . . seminaries, an asylum for the deaf and dumb, a madhouse, and a school for gardeners . . . I can proudly say that the portion of the whilom Polish Republic now under Prussian rule enjoys a degree of well-being, loyal security, and popular attachment as never existed, nor was ever even dreamed of within the limits of the Polish realm since the commence-

ment of Polish history . . . The Polish-speaking subjects of Prussia have
not been tempted to take part in demonstrations got up by a minority
composed of nobles, land-stewards, and labourers . . . On Danish and
Bohemian battlefields our Polish soldiers have testified their devotion
to the King with their blood, and with the valour peculiar to their race
. . . With all imaginable impartiality, and desire to be just, I can assure
you that Polish rule was an infamously bad one, and that is why it shall
never be revived . . .[5]

He returned to his theme on 1 April 1871. In the recent elections, Posen had returned a block of twenty 'stiff-necked
oppositionists', who dared to contest the impending incorporation of the Grand Duchy together with the rest of Prussia,
into the German Empire. After mocking the demagoguery of
Polish priests in the recent election campaign, the Chancellor
reminded the deputies that they had been elected to represent the interests of the Catholic Church, and that they had
'no mandate to represent the Polish people or nationality in
this House'. Then, with biting irony, he attacked their schemes
for collaborating with the Poles in Russia and for reviving a
Polish state within its historic frontiers:

The population of the West Russian provinces consists of ten percent of
Poles strewn about on their surface, either descendants of former conquerors or renegades of other races, and ninety percent who speak
nothing but Russian, pray in Russian, weep in Russian (especially when
under Polish domination), and stand by the Russian Government in
combating the Polish nobility . . . It is in the name of these six-and-a-half
million Poles that you claim rule over twenty-four millions, in a tone
indicating that it is a most profound and abominable tyranny and humiliation that you are no longer allowed to oppress and ride roughshod
over those people . . . Gentlemen, I would request you, therefore, to
unite with the majority of your Polish brethren in Prussia . . . in participating in the benefits of civilisation offered to you by the Prussian state
. . . Take your share honestly in our common work.[6]

The force of Bismarck's comments is undeniable. But his
tone was hardly designed to soothe. In the next two decades,
in the era of the *Kulturkampf* and the Colonization Commission, German—Polish relations were destined to deteriorate
sharply.

Although the *Kulturkampf* was not aimed exclusively at the
Polish provinces, its impact was soon felt there to maximum

effect. In 1872, a ministerial decree made the use of German compulsory in all state-schools, except for religious instruction. Polish was banned even as a foreign language, and could not be used as previously for teaching German to Polish children. Teachers were forbidden to join Polish and Catholic societies, and were offered financial inducements, the so-called *Ostmarkenzulagen,* for working in non-German districts. All graduates, including priests, were required to pass an exam in German culture. In 1876, German was made compulsory in all courts, and in all government offices from the Post Office to the ticket office of the railway station.[7] Regulations regarding immigration and residence permits were strengthened. In 1885, the Prussian Police expelled 30,000 Poles and Polish Jews who did not posses correct documents.[8] Although certain concessions were granted by Caprivi after 1890, the campaign was not abandoned. Nothing did more to strengthen Polish national consciousness.

The *Kulturkampf* also affected the Poles in that most of them were Roman Catholics.[9] The Primate of Prussian Poland, Archbishop Mieczysław Ledóchowski of Gnesen (Gniezno) (1822–1902), had compromised with the authorities so long as their demands were confined to trivialities. In 1872, he agreed that *Boże coś Polskę* should not be sung at Mass. But when government inspectors began to interfere with religious instruction in schools and with the running of theological seminars, he resisted. In 1873, together with his colleague in the Rhineland, the Archbishop of Cologne, he was arrested and imprisoned. After two years in gaol, he was exiled in Rome. Ninety Polish priests shared his fate, and many more were harassed. At a stroke, Bismarck ensured that Polishness and Catholicity in Prussia should be permanently identified. In Silesia, he channelled the Polish national movement into the hands of radical priests such as the Revd Kapica of Tychy, or the Revd Józef Szafranek (1807–74), and of Catholic journalists such as Karol Miarka (1825–82), editor of the *Katolik.* On the religious, as on the educational issue, repression proved counter-productive.

Polish nationality, in fact, revived under such ambiguous policies. Although Polish deputies complained in the *Landtag* about anti-Polish measures in the eastern provinces, German deputies were no less insistent on the growing threat to German supremacy. In the 1880s, the foreign visitor could have observed no Polish influence whatsoever in Stettin, and very little in Breslau or Danzig. But in Posen, as in many of the smaller towns of the east and south-east, the Polish element though secondary was very definitely still in evidence:

POSEN

Hotels (none of them quite first-class). HOTEL DE DRESDE Wilhelms-Str. 21, B & L 3, A ½, D 2½, B ¾m; DE ROME, Wilhelms-Platz I, with restaurant . . .; DE L'EUROPE, Wilhelms-Str. I; DE FRANCE, Wilhelms-Str. 15, frequented by Poles; . . .

Theatres. STADT-THEATER, Wilhelms, Platz, plays and operas; VICTORIA, Neustadter-Markt, in summer only; POLISH THEATRE, Berliner-Str. Summer only.

Pleasure Resorts. Schilling's on the Warthe, outside the Schillings-Thor; *Zoological and Feldschloss Garten,* beyond the Berliner-Thor; *Schweizerhof, Victoria-Park, Eichwald* (3M.) . . .

POSEN Polish POZNAN, the capital of the province of that name, the H.Q. of the 5th Corps d'Armée, and a fortress of the first rank, with 68,300 inhab. (More than ½ German, and ¼ Jews), and a garrison of 7000 men, lies at the confluence of the Cybina and Warthe. It is one of the most ancient Polish towns, having been the seat of a bishop from the end of the 10th Cent. and the residence of the Kings of Poland down to 1296. The immigration of Germans gave it importance as a great depot of trade . . . and it was a member of the Hanseatic League in the middle ages. The new part of the town, forming a striking contrast with the older and poorer quarters, has been erected since it came into the possession of Prussia in 1815, which rescued it from the low estate to which wars and other misfortunes had reduced it. On Sundays and holidays the streets are enlivened by the gay and quaint costumes of the peasantry, especially of the so-called *Bamberger,* distant descendants of Franconian immigrants though now genuine Poles to all intents and purposes.

In entering the town from the Central Station, we obtain a view of the imposing fortifications . . . Following either the Muhlen Strasse . . . or the St. Martin-Strasse, we reach the spacious and handsome Wilhelms-Platz, bounded on the E. by the *Stadt-Theater.* In front of the Theatre is a Monument to the soldiers of the 5th Corps d'Armée who fell at Nachod in 1866. At the corner of the Wilhelms-Strasse, is the *Raczynski Library,* a building adorned with 24 Corinthian columns, and containing 30,000 vols, presented to the town by Count Raczynski (open daily 5—8) . . . At right-angles to the Wilhelms-Platz, runs the Wilhelms-

Strasse one of the principal thoroughfares . . . On the N. it ends at the Kanonen-Platz, with the imposing new *Military Headquarters,* in front of which is the War Monument for 1870–1, with a statue of William I by Barwald . . . Farther to the S. is the Schlossberg, with the Royal Palace, now containing the Municipal Archives (open 9–1.), and the collections of the Historical Society of the province of Posen. At the S. end of Wilhelms-Str., in the churchyard of St. Martin's Church, is a monument to the Polish Poet, Mickiewicz, (d. 1855).

To the E. of the Wilhelm-Platz, is the ALTE MARKT . . . The *Rathaus* in the Alte Markt, was built in 1508 and restored in 1535 by Giovan Battista di Quadro, an Italian architect, who added the loggia. The tower, 214 ft high in the Baroque Style, commands an extensive view . . . The quarter to the N.E., is mainly inhabited by Jews, one of whose synagogues is in the Dominikan-Str . . .

The suburbs of Posen on the right bank of the Warthe are called the *Wallischei* (in Polish Chwaliszewo) and *Schrodka,* and are inhabited mainly by Poles of the poorer classes. Beyond it . . . the CATHEDRAL erected in its present form in 1775, is architecturally uninteresting but contains several treasures of art . . . the sumptuous Golden Chapel, erected in 1842 by a society of Polish nobles is in the Byzantine Style. Fine gilded bronze group of the first Polish kings, by Rauch, (their remains are in the sarcophagus opposite) . . .

The Museum of Count Melzynski, and the collections of the *Gesellschaft der Freunde der Wissenshafter,* a Polish Society, occupy the same building, Muhlen-Str. 35. They include paintings (of little value and doubtful authenticity), a library, coins, and prehistoric antiquities, (open daily 12–5, 1 M, Sun 10pf.; catalogue and inscriptions exclusively in Polish . . .)

The Protest. *Pauli-Kirche* close by, was built in 1867–9, – *Fort Winiary* affords the best survey of the environs, (tickets at the Commandent's Office, Wilhelms-Platz 16, 50 pf.)[10]

In the countryside, ruthless measures applied in the realm of land ownership met with little success. In 1886, Bismarck created the Prussian Colonization Commission, the *Ansiedlugskommission,* to encourage German settlers. In the government's eyes, this was a defensive measure designed to counteract the drastic *Ostflucht* or 'Flight from the East' which in twenty years before the First World War was to denude the eastern provinces of some three million German inhabitants. In Polish eyes, it was an aggressive measure designed to drive the Poles from their land. Furnished with an initial fund of 500 million marks, the Commission was empowered to purchase vacant estates and then to sell them to approved candidates. Even so, in the twenty-seven years of its existence to 1913, it could not prevent a decline both in the absolute number of German householders working the land and in the over-all area of their holdings. The Commission often found itself transferring property from one German owner to another. Yet by inflating the value of land from 587 to 1,821 marks per hectare, it encouraged landowners to sell to anyone who wanted to buy, whether German or Pole. Except in the valley of the River Notec, the *Netzedistrikt,* where some 22,000 German families were installed in a solid block, the Commission's gains were more than offset by its losses. Its activities were countered by those of the Polish Land Purchase Bank founded in 1897 and by Polish agricultural co-operatives. By 1913, the Polish 'Union of Credit Associations' under its patron, the Revd Piotr Wawrzyniak, had increased its membership to almost 150,000 peasants. A decree of 1908 empowering the Commission to expropriate 'unsuitable' landowners was never put into serious operation.[11]

The campaign against Polish landownership produced one of the folk heroes of Prussian Poland, Michał Drzymała (d. 1937). In 1904, Drzymała had succeeded in obtaining a plot of land in the district of Wollstein (Wolsztyn), but found that the rules of the Colonization Commission forbade him as a Pole to build a permanent dwelling-house on his land. In order to beat the rule, therefore, he set himself up in a gipsy caravan and for more than a decade tenaciously defied all attempts in the courts to remove him. The case attracted publicity all over Germany, and even found mention in the international press. It was highly typical of the national conflict in Prussia, where the Polish movement was dominated by peasants and where the state authorities confined themselves to legal methods of harassment.[12]

Paradoxically, therefore, the *Kulturkampf* and the Colonization Commission succeeded in stimulating the very feelings which they were designed to suppress. From the Polish point of view, they were the best things that could have happened. Without them, there might have been no Polish movement in Prussia at all. Until German officialdom chose to harass the Poles, Germanization was widely thought to be the natural destiny of all the Hohenzollerns' non-German subjects. After all, enlightened Englishmen and Americans of the same era largely assumed that all non-English speaking inhabitants of their countries would eventually be anglicized. Cultural homogeneity was accepted as a legitimate necessity of modern civilization. The English poet and pedagogue Matthew Arnold, for example, whose official memoranda as Inspector of Schools drew heavily on his knowledge of German education, fully condoned 'the swallowing up of separate provincial nationalities'. Although he took a close interest in Welsh affairs and wrote a study of Celtic Literature, he was also convinced that 'the sooner the Welsh language disappears . . . the better'. Ministers of Education who hammer English culture harder and harder into the elementary schools of Wales, he thought, were to be praised. So one cannot dismiss the Germanization policy in Prussian Poland as something uniquely barbaric. It was broadly conversant with similar programmes of social modernization all over Europe (or, *mutatis mutandis,* with the cultural programmes of Poloniza-tion undertaken in independent Poland after 1918). What was remarkable perhaps was the thoroughness and inflexibility of its application, and in consequence, the vehemence of the Polish response.

Henceforth, it was clear that the new German Reich was going to be far more inimical to Polish nationality than the old Prussian regime had ever been. In retrospect, 1871 can be seen as a decisive turning-point. The declaration of the German Empire in the Palace of Versailles, which proved so ominous for Western Europe, cast its shadow over the East as well. Henceforth, the good Prussian had not merely to show that he was a loyal servant of his King; he had to live up to his reputation as 'the best of Germans'. The imperial union of the German lands established Germanity as the touchstone of respectability, in a way that had never pertained before. In earlier decades, no one had ever considered that Prussia's Polish subjects were in any way less Prussian than its German, Danish, French, or Lithuanian subjects. In his famous address *An mein Volk* (To my People), delivered at Breslau on 17 March 1813, on the occasion of Prussia's re-entry into the war against Napoleon, Frederick-William III specifically

appealed to the separate peoples of his Kingdom – Branden-
burgers, Prussians, Silesians, Lithuanians – for a common
effort against the common oppressor. At this time the author
of the address, State-Councillor Theodor von Hippel, did not
judge the Polish-speaking element or the Germans as worthy
of separate notice. There is plenty of contemporary evidence
to show that the King's Polish-speaking subjects thought of
themselves, not as 'Prussian Poles', but as 'Polish Prussians' –
a phrase which in later times would have been considered a
contradiction in terms. The idea that the population of the
Kingdom could be categorized according to the language
which they spoke was entirely alien to the pre-nationalist era.
In 1835, in response to one of the earliest attempts to
conduct a linguistic survey, the squire of Langenau (Łęgowo)
in Mazuria, Samuel von Polenz, penned the following return:

On these properties, there are 52 persons of the male kind and 59 of
the female kind, who have command of both the Polish and the
German languages: 8 persons of the male kind and 11 of the female
kind, who can speak properly in Polish only, but who can mouth a few
broken words in German: 15 persons of the male kind and 12 of the
female kind who speak exclusively in German: one male who speaks
German, Polish, French, Latin, and a little Greek; another who speaks
German, Latin, French, and Hebrew, and another who speaks Russian:
and 16 persons of the male kind and 19 of the female kind who as yet
neither speak nor read any language at all, but merely shriek and
babble . . .[13]

It was quite inappropriate, of course, on the basis of this
return that the official charged with determining the number
of German-speakers should have recorded the population as
consisting of 175 'Germans', and 20 'Poles' (including the
one Russian). But it would be equally incorrect to imagine
that the majority were Poles. They were both Polish and
German at one and the same time, and all, irrespective of their
language, were first and foremost Prussians. Such distinctions,
which were understood by everyone in Frederick-William's
reign, were unthinkable in the Wilhelmian Era.

Thus, in the course of the nineteenth century, the relationship between Polish and German Nationalism was completely
reversed. In the pre-1848 era, both Poles and Germans had
seen each other as allies in the struggle against the dynastic

empires. In Prussian politics, German Unification had been a cause of the Left. It was espoused by the liberal opposition but dreaded by the conservative court and government, and it was taken to be entirely compatible with Polish Independence. Karl Marx was but one of many progressive Germans, moved by the tragedy of the 1831 Rising and by the Berlin Trial of 1847, who put Polish and German aspirations in the same programme:

The independence of the Polish nation is essential for no one more than for us Germans. What is it that has supported the power of Reaction in Europe ever since 1815, not to say from the first French Revolution? The Holy Alliance of Russia, Prussia, and Austria. And what is it that has held the Holy Alliance together? The Partitions of Poland, of which all three members of the Alliance have been beneficiaries.

Of course, it is not just a matter of creating some sort of sham Poland, but of creating a strong and viable state. At the least, Poland must occupy the territory of 1772, together with the catchment areas and the mouths of its great rivers, and must possess an extensive belt of the Baltic coastline.

Marx himself continued to hold these views for the rest of his life. Yet 1848 ushered in an era of uncertainty. In 1848, the German liberals did not fail to note that the Poles of Posen stood to obstruct full German unification. Friedrich Engels was one to react sharply. Writing to Marx on 23 May 1851 on the question of Posnania, he expressed opinions which would have been quite unacceptable only three years earlier.

The more I reflect upon history, the more clearly I see that the Poles are completely *foutu* as a nation and that they can only be useful as a means to an end up to the time when Russia herself is drawn into the agrarian revolution. From that moment, Poland will no longer have any *raison d'être* whatsoever. The Poles have never done anything in history except commit outrageous quarrelsome stupidities. It would be impossible to cite a single occasion when Poland, even as against Russia, had successfully represented progress or done anything whatever of historical significance . . .[14]

The contrast between Marx in 1848 and Engels in 1851 nicely illustrates the shift which even then was taking place in German opinion. Engels himself recanted his anti-Polish outburst in order to maintain solidarity with Marx. But for most

Germans, the change of heart was permanent. Under Bismarck, German Unification was adopted by the Prussian Right, and after 1871, the united and victorious Reich was welcomed by Left and Right alike. Any attempt to question the integrity of the Empire was seen as a treasonable threat to the general security and prosperity. In all nationalist debates, the Prussian establishment had been given to striking a lofty, neutral pose, judging any form of nationalism, whether Polish or German, as vulgar, unnecessary, and beneath one's dignity. But as Prussian views were gradually submerged into the newer enthusiasms of the Reich, so German hostility against Polish nationalism was able to grow. And the Poles responded in kind.

In the last decades before the First World War attitudes sharpened on both sides. On the German side, the hysterical chauvinism of Wilhelmian era made rapid strides. In 1894, the *Deutscher Ostmarkenverein* (German Society for the Eastern Borders) was formed in Posen to promote the welfare of German culture and German interests. Known to the Poles as the 'Hakata', from the initials of its three guiding spirits — F. Hansemann, H. Kennemann, and H. Tiedemann — it soon gained the reputation of a powerful, extremist lobby. Some of its slogans were reminiscent of later Nazi talk of German *Lebensraum*.[15] Petty anti-Polish measures were intensified. Street names, and official signs, even in cemeteries or public lavatories, were Germanized. Inowrocław was changed to Hohenzalza in line with many other places-names. Bonuses were paid not just to teachers, but to any German official who would serve in the east. Posen had the highest percentage of government employees in any city of the Empire. Schools, railroads, libraries, and museums were built on the strength of special grants. Every effort was made to exaggerate and inflame the German element's sense of insecurity. Even the socialists joined the chauvinist fashion. Max Weber, who joined the Pangerman League as proof of his loyalty, once remarked in public: 'Only we Germans could have made human beings out of these Poles.'[16]

On the Polish side, national feeling spread into classes and areas which hitherto had rarely considered themselves Polish. The Polish national movement, known to officialdom as the

Agitationspartei, put down grass roots in all the Polish provinces. In Posnania, it assumed the proportions of a veritable
mass movement. In May 1901, at Wreschen (Września), near
Posen, a school strike was launched against the imposition of
German into religious classes. Children who played truant
were flogged. Parents who supported their children were
gaoled. In 1906–7, school strikes affected almost half the
schools of the province. In Silesia, in the 1890s, a Polish press
appeared, and, in the persons of W. Korfanty (1873–1939)
and Adam Napieralski (1870–1928), the first Polish deputies
to the Reichstag. Among the Kashubs, the poet Hieronium
Dudowski coined the unheard-of slogan: 'No Kashubia without Poland – no Poland without Kashubia'. In Mazuria in
1890, the first Polish candidate ever was elected to the *Landtag*
at Allenstein. A national revival of such widespread proportions was inconceivable only one generation earlier.

To the outside observer at this stage, the exponents of
German and Polish nationalism displayed striking similarities.
Both cultivated myths about their own exclusive blood and
culture; both believed in their unique civilizing mission in
Eastern Europe; both regarded the other as a 'reactionary'
obstacle to the achievement of their 'rights', and as a usurper
of the 'ancient land of their forebears'. The Polish nobleman
who sold his estates to the Colonization Commission, like the
German who took a Polish bride, were both denounced as
renegades to their nation.

In *fin de siècle* Prussia, historical symbols enflamed growing Polish–German antagonism. In the feverish imaginations
of late Gothic-Romanticism, the Germans of the eastern provinces were tempted to see themselves as the sons of the
Teutonic Knights – an embattled minority of skilled and
dedicated warriors, gallantly holding the line against the
onslaughts of marauding pagans. It was no accident, when the
Emperor William II paid his official visits to Prussia, that he
was welcomed at the Marienburg by officials dressed in chain
mail, sallets, and crusaders' cloaks. His speeches, which stressed
the glorious past of the 'German East', were nicely calculated
to offend Polish sensitivities. The Poles accepted the challenge
with alacrity. For them, it was most uplifting to be reminded
of a medieval contest from which the Polish Kingdom had

eventually emerged triumphant. The wars of the fourteenth and fifteenth centuries were fought again by scholars and columnists in all the journals and popular magazines of the day. In 1900, Henryk Sienkiewicz published his best-selling novel, *Krzyżacy* (The Teutonic Knights), the Polish 'Ivanhoe', whose young Polish hero, Zbyszko, performs stirring deeds of derring-do to rescue his Danusia from the clutches of the dastardly Grand Master. In 1910, for the Five Hundredth Anniversary of the Battle of Grunwald, a public subscription was launched to raise a monument in commemoration of the Polish victory. Excluded from Prussia by official hostility, the organizers of the scheme were obliged to erect their monument in Austrian Galicia, in Cracow, where it was unveiled on 15 July by Ignacy Paderewski, to the strains of a rousing anthem specially composed for the occasion by Maria Konopnicka:

> We shall not yield our forebears' land,
> Nor see our language muted.
> Our nation is Polish, and Polish our folk,
> By Piasts constituted.
> By cruel oppression we'll not be swayed!
> May God so lend us aid.
>
> We'll not be spat on by Teutons
> Nor abandon our youth to the German!
> We'll follow the call of the Golden Horn,
> Under the Holy Spirit, our *Hetman*.
> Our armed battalions shall lead the crusade.
> May God so lend us aid.
>
> By the very last drop of blood in our veins
> Our souls will be secured,
> Until in dust and ashes falls
> The stormwind sown by the Prussian lord.
> Our every home will form a stockade.
> May God so lend us aid.[17]

Despite such displays of animosity, the political aspirations of the Poles in Germany remained modest to the very end. Loyalty to Prussia remained strong; recognition of the solid material benefits of German rule was widespread; and hatred of Russia was universal.[18] As conflict between the two great Empires grew increasingly probable, sporadic hopes for a united

Poland were largely subordinated to fears of the Russian invasion to which all the eastern provinces were obviously exposed. In the Reichstag, the Polish Circle remained socially conservative, and tactically cautious. In the administration of Caprivi, in return for the most nominal concessions, its members voted with the Government with such predictable monotony that its leader Józef Teodor Kościelski (1845–1911) was dubbed 'The German Admiral'. In 1914, it voted for the War Credits without a murmur. Its support for the war effort of the Central Powers received the blessing of Archbishop Likowski. During the War, there were occasional instances of Polish conscripts in the German Army writing home in fervent expectation of an independent Poland emerging from the bloodshed. Considerable excitement was caused by the German army's occupation of Warsaw in August 1915; and on 18 December that year a complacent *Reichstag* acceded to demands for the re-creation of the Congress Kingdom of Poland under German auspices. Yet there was no move to associate Prussia's other Polish provinces with the Kingdom, and no possibility of detaching them from Prussia. Throughout the Great War, hundreds of thousands of Poles marched to the strains of *Preussens Gloria* with never a thought but to keep in step. Pomeranian, Silesian, Prussian, and Posnanian regiments served on all fronts with distinction. There was never a hint of a mutiny, of a conspiracy, of an 'Easter Rising', until that marvellous German music suddenly stopped of its own accord.

* * * * *

In 1918, the vacuum left by the Revolution in Berlin and the abdication of the Kaiser was all the more painful for the sacrifices which had preceded them. On 26 December, Ignacy Paderewski passed through Posen on his way to Warsaw, having landed at Stettin in a Royal Navy destroyer, HMS *Concord.* He was welcomed by an outburst of popular feeling. The crowds took to the streets. The German garrison was expelled. After a brief skirmish, the province was freed. Two months of unpremeditated rebellion were sufficient to redeem 125 years of 'foreign occupation'. Posen became Poznań again, and joined the Polish Republic.[19]

Elsewhere, the Polish—German settlement was more protracted. The Treaty of Versailles awarded part of Pomerania, the so-called Corridor, to Poland, but left Danzig as a Free City, and subjected Upper Silesia, Allenstein, and Marienwerder to popular plebiscites. Three Silesian Risings failed to resolve the issue. The final suppression of the Prussian Partition was not complete until 1945. It was accompanied by the wholesale expulsion of millions of Germans. The old Prussian motto read *Suum Cuique* — 'To each, his own'; and so it came to pass. Law No. 46 of the Allied Control Council, of 25 February 1947, declared, 'The Prussian state with its central government and its agencies is hereby abolished.' It was rough justice, and strangely reminiscent of the Partition centuries before. The final partition of Prussia was even more final than the partitions of Poland.

CHAPTER FOUR
GALICIA:
The Austrian Partition (1773-1918)

As kingdoms go, the life of the Kingdom of Galicia and Lodomeria was short and sad. It was created in 1773 to accommodate the territories ceded to Austria by the First Partition of Poland, and was enlarged in 1795 by the addition of the westerly district of 'New Galicia' acquired at the Third Partition. In 1809, after the abortive campaign against the Duchy of Warsaw, it was obliged to abandon part of its recent acquisitions. But in 1815, at the Congress of Vienna, it recovered most of the former New Galicia, except for Cracow, and was compensated by the award of the easterly districts of Czortków (Chortkiv) and Tarnopol (Ternopil'). In 1846, it inherited the remaining effects of the late Republic of Cracow, thereby consolidating a territorial base which was to remain unaltered for the rest of its existence. (See Map 4.) The familiar distinction between Western Galicia, to the west of the River San, and Eastern Galicia to the east, coincided with a formal administrative division only briefly, in the years 1848–60 and 1861–7, but it continued in colloquial usage throughout the nineteenth century. According to the official historical fiction, the new kingdom was supposed to be a restoration of a long-forgotten medieval realm which had once been subject to the Hungarian Crown; and it derived its name from the ancient Ruthenian principalities of Halicz (Galicia) and Włodzimierz (Lodomeria). In fact, it possessed little natural coherence. Occupying a long, rambling swathe of territory to the north of the Carpathian mountains, from the Oder in the west to the Zbruch in the east, it covered over 20,000 square miles and was the largest single province of the Austrian Empire. Its absentee proprietors, the Habsburg Emperors, resided far away in Vienna. Its Governors and Viceroys, from Johann Count Pergen, appointed in 1773, to Karl Count Huyn, appointed in 1917, were loyal Habsburg servants. Its capital city of Lemberg (Lwów, Lviv) never aspired

Map 4.　　Austrian Galicia, (1773–1918)

beyond the bounds of solid provincial respectability. Its leading intellectual centre, Cracow, lived in the shadow of a more glorious, shattered past. Galicia, born from Maria Theresa's guilty pact with Russia and Prussia, was an unwanted child from the start, and never grew to full maturity. It passed away in October 1918, and few people mourned its passing.

The Habsburg home within which Galicia developed was unable to provide a secure or stable environment. In the century which followed the First Partition, Austria experienced a wide variety of political disasters and constitutional experiments. The pious absolutism of Maria Theresa (1740–80) gave way to the ambitious but impermanent reforms of her son, Joseph II (1780–90). The reigns of Leopold II (1790–2), and of Francis II (1792–1835) were disturbed by the upheavals of the Revolutionary Era, during which, in 1806, the old Holy Roman Empire was destroyed and superseded by the Austrian Empire. The reactionary and unbending rule of Metternich, whose supremacy continued for more than thirty years to the end of the reign of Ferdinand I (1835–48), was broken by the Revolution of 1848. The long reign of Francis-Joseph I (1848–1916) witnessed several profound changes. From the absolutist stance of his early years, he passed in 1860 into a period of timid experimentation, which started with the October Diploma of 1860 establishing a constitutional system, and which came to a head with the *Ausgleich* of 1867 initiating the Dual Monarchy of Austria–Hungary. In his later years, he made far-reaching concessions to demands for democracy and minority rights, and in 1907 admitted the principle of universal suffrage. He died in November 1916, when Austria was already on the point of collapse, leaving his great-nephew Charles I (1916–18) little hope of ruling effectively. Throughout the period, the imperial government in Vienna was so besieged by intractable problems of its own that it could spare but little attention for the special interests of Galicia.[1]

For almost a century after the First Partition, therefore, the Austrian Empire exhibited most of the negative features of the neighbouring regimes in Russia and Prussia. The state intervened in every sphere of social and political life. The labour services of the serfs were fixed by official *Robotpatente* or 'work certificates', just as the duties of the clergy were controlled by the Governor's *placetum* or 'statement of approval'. The jurisdiction of the nobles was replaced by that of the *mandatariusz* or 'state mandatary', who was paid by the landowner but was answerable to the state authorities. Taxation rose steeply above former Polish levels, bringing hardship to those least able to support it, especially to the peasants. The Army played a prominent role in public affairs, providing a privileged career for the sons of the nobility and demanding compulsory military service from the peasants. The imperial bureaucracy was numerous, powerful, hierarchical, and notoriously formal. In Galicia, it was staffed largely by immigrant Germans and Czechs. The police system was well developed. Surveillance and harassment of unreliable elements was accompanied by close liaison with the police forces of Russia and Prussia. The frontiers, whose most exposed sections ran across the Galician plain to the north of the Carpathians, were heavily garrisoned. The Censorship left little to the imagination. Although in this Catholic Empire, the traditional Marian cult was encouraged, the Emperor's Galician subjects were instructed to redirect their prayers from 'the Virgin Mary, Queen of Poland' to 'the Virgin Mary, Queen of Galicia and Lodomeria'.

In the latter part of the century, however, Austria lost all but the most residual pretensions to the style of a great power. There was little of the earnestness and dynamism of Prussia, and none of the ambition of Russia. In contrast to Berlin or St. Petersburg, Vienna was decidedly debonair. As Francis-Joseph was the first to admit, the work of Johann Strauss was to prove much more lasting than his own. Beset by the conflicting demands of seventeen recognized nationalities, the Imperial government had no major preoccupation but to survive. After the resounding military defeats in Italy in 1859, and at Königgrätz (Sadova) in 1866 at the hands of the Prussians, Austria fell rapidly into the German sphere of influence. By the turn of the century, she had lost almost all means of independent leverage in international affairs.

In these circumstances, as the outlying province of a declining Empire, Galicia always presented an easy target for mockery. In the nature of things, it did not possess the means or the will for resolving its manifold problems. Economically, it was one of the most backward areas of the Empire. It had few resources to satisfy the needs of a population, whose numbers rose from 4.8 million in 1822 to 7.3 million in 1910, in proportion to their impoverishment. The Imperial Salt Mines at Wieliczka brought little local benefit beyond the building of one of the Empire's first railways, the *Kaiser-ferdnandsnordbahn* from Vienna to Cracow, opened in 1848. The Galician oil-field at Borysław, discovered in the 1860s, was producing over 2 million tons of petroleum by 1908; but its short-lived wealth did not flow into the pockets of the slum-dwellers who crowded round the rigs. It was a standing joke among schoolboys that they lived in the land of 'Golicia and Glodomeria' – *Goły* meaning 'bare', and *głód* meaning 'hunger'.

Galician society was unbalanced in the extreme. A handful of aristocratic families, such as the Tarnowski, the Zamoyski, the Potocki, the Gołuchowski, the Lubomirski, and their like, who received patents of imperial nobility in the 1780s, lived in style from start to finish. Yet the vast majority of the population were indigent peasants. In 1887, the peasantry still composed 81 per cent of the population, and most of them were still illiterate. For them, it was almost academic whether serfdom existed, as it did to 1848, or whether it did not. In economic terms they saw no noticeable improvement in their condition. Yet the landowners themselves could hardly be described as a prosperous class. The total number of registered landowners did not exceed two thousand families – which marked a dramatic decrease from the state of affairs under the old Republic. Of these, some three hundred were foreigners: either immigrant Jews, like Lewis Namier's father, who were unable to buy land in Russia, or officials connected with the administration. Most of the non-registered land-owners, who did not participate in the rights of their estate, were so burdened with debts and mortgages that they could not live up to the style accustomed. It has been calculated that a mere four hundred families could rightly consider themselves to be independent country gentlefolk. This figure stands in glaring contrast to the 200,000 public officials, the 188,000 Jewish merchants, and the 220,000 Jewish innkeepers and licensees. The emergence of a viable class of landed small-holders and tenants was constantly delayed by the traditional division of family plots among children, and by the deleterious effects of chronic overpopulation. The development of a strong middle class was held back by the lack of commerce and industry, and distorted by the disproportionate number of undersized Jewish businesses in the wholesale trade and the professions. The Jewish community itself was severely inhibited by the sheer mass of its urban paupers, and by its incurable sense of insecurity. Except on the fringes of the Kingdom, in Borysław and in the Duchy of Teschen (Cieszyn) in Austrian Silesia, an industrial proletariat never existed.

The nationality pattern was hopelessly complicated. It is not completely accurate to maintain that the Germans (3 per cent in 1880) oppressed the Poles; that the Poles (45 per cent) oppressed the Ruthenians; that the Ruthenians (41 per cent) oppressed the Jews; or that the Jews (11 per cent), by virtue of their supposed economic stranglehold, oppressed everyone else. But misconceptions of this sort, which were common enough in Galicia, convey a real whiff of the endless arguments and conflicts which divided mutually exclusive and rival national groups. Every minority in this part of Europe felt oppressed in one way or another, and all complained bitterly of discrimination. In the early decades of Galicia's history, the Poles shared the embitterment of all their neighbours. After 1867, when for reasons of purely Viennese politics they were joined to the Magyars of Hungary and the Germans of Austria as one of the Dual Monarchy's three 'Master Races', they increasingly attracted the envy of the other minorities.

Cultural cohesion was wellnigh impossible. Under Maria Theresa, the official language of the Kingdom had been Latin. Under Joseph II, it became German. In 1869, Polish was put on an equal footing with German. Yet the Ruthenians continued to speak *ruski*; the Jews spoke Yiddish; and both of them demanded the right to education in their own language. Access to the world of high culture was denied to all except the Polish *literati*, and to the numerous intellectual *émigrés* who left for Vienna, Prague, or for Germany.

For most of the time, modern democracy was out of the question. For the first ninety-five years, Galicia was administered as an integral province of a centralized Empire. The aristocratic, provincial *Landesrat* (Diet) possessed an advisory role only, and failed to assemble for decades at a stretch. The autonomous government introduced in 1867 earned a reputation for gerrymandering and corruption. The era of modern party politics enjoyed only seven years of troubled existence before the onset of World War.

Economic, social, national, cultural, and political factors combined to aggravate the poverty in which most of the people lived. The *nędza galicyjska* or 'Galician misery' was proverbial. A well-informed analyst, writing in 1887, contrived to demonstrate that rural overpopulation in Galicia had outstripped that in all other parts of Europe, and was approaching levels prevalent in China and India. According to his study, the cumulative effects of inefficient agricultural techniques were compounded by rigid, conservative attitudes, by crippling taxation, and by the inordinate number of unproductive, petty officials; some 50,000 people were dying each year as a result of near-starvation conditions; and one-quarter of the total inhabitants could safely emigrate before any improvement might be expected. Of all the three Partitions, Galicia had the highest birth-rate and the highest death-rate, together with the lowest rate of demographic growth and the lowest level of life-expectancy. Galicia was in a worse predicament than Ireland at the start of the potato famine. As compared with the standard of living in England at that time, the average Galician produced only one-quarter of the quantity of basic foodstuffs, ate less than one-half of the standard English diet, possessed only one-ninth of the Englishman's propertied wealth, and received barely one-eleventh of the English farmer's return on his land; yet he paid twice as high a proportion of his income in taxes. One need not necessarily take Szczepański's figures as gospel to accept the obvious conclusions. All available statistics point in the same direction. Galicia could fairly claim to be the poorest province of Europe.[2] (See Table overleaf.)

Galicia's budget was not designed in Galicia's interest. The round figures for 1887 show a revenue from state and local taxes of 60 million złoties. From this, 34 millions had to be spent on the salaries of state employees; 10 millions went on

GALICIA, 1887: Collected Statistics
(after Szczepański)

	GALICIA	CONGRESS KINGDOM	GRAND DUCHY OF POSEN	GREAT BRITAIN	FRANCE	HUNGARY
1. *Territory* (in km² x 1000)	77.3	128.5	28.9	–	–	–
2. *Population*						
Total Population (millions)	6.4	7.8	1.7	–	–	–
Density (inhabitants per km²)	88	60	9	135	71	50
Rural Density	60	–	–	27	32	33
Death-rate (per 1,000)	32.8	25.9	27.5	–	–	–
Birth-rate (per 1,000)	44.1	40.3	43.8	–	–	–
Increase (per 1,000)	11.3	14.4	16.3	–	–	–
Life expectancy (years)						
3. *Agricultural Productivity* (per capita production of potatoes, corn, and meat expressed as metric centals of						
corn)	6.75	9.3	–	22	16	9.3
expressed as foodstuffs index	1	1.4	2	9	–	1.4
4. *Financial Resources* (per capita bank deposits, insurance and savings accounts, in zł)	13	–	–	200	115	34
5. *Annual Food Consumption*						
Meat (kg.)	10	–		50	34	24
Cereals (kg.)	114	–	–	200	284	182
Potatoes (kg.)	114	–	–	180	284	182
Milk (l.)	120	–	–	200	144	185
Beer (l.)	10	–	–	125	22	4
Wine (l.)	2	–	–	2	102	40
Total: as kg. of corn per capita	261	–	–	607	586	375
6. *Agricultural Returns* (in terms of zł. per morg, p.a.)	3.25	–	–	37	–	–
7. *Private Propertied Wealth* (real estate, land, immovables, as zł. per annum)	327	–	–	3000	–	–
8. *Taxation Rate* (as percentage of average earnings)	20	–	–	10	12.5	20
9. *Bureaucratic burden*						
Salaried state officials per 1,000	43,000					
percentage of population	3	–	–	–	–	–
percentage of private income	14.8					
10. *Railway Services* (kilometres per 100,000 population)	40	–	–	84	84	60

defence; and no less than 12 millions were sent in cash to the imperial Treasury in Vienna. After 6 millions were spent on the servicing of foreign loans, and 5 millions on the upkeep of the railways, the Kingdom was well into the red. The annual deficit was estimated at 21 millions. It is not difficult to imagine how little money was available for investment, for the public services, or for social and educational purposes.

For many peasant families, emigration offered the sole chance of survival. In the twenty-five years before the First World War, more than two million people left Galicia for good. No less than 400,000, or almost 5 per cent of the population, departed in 1913 alone. Some went to the adjoining industrial areas in Silesia, and in particular to the Duchy of Teschen where the Polish element in the expanding mining community at Karwina grew quickly into a strong majority. Others went to France or Germany. But most took the ship from Hamburg for America, joining the ceaseless tide of Europe's weary and oppressed who passed through Ellis Island on their way to the mines of Pennsylvania or to the frontier lands of the mid-West.

The most sensational event in Galicia's history occurred in 1846. In that year, the authorities received advance notice of the conspiracy which Mierosławski was planning to launch simultaneously in Prussia, Cracow, and Galicia on 21 February. In Posen, the Prussian police arrested the ringleaders without more ado. But in Austria the local officials seem to have panicked. Faced with small groups of armed Polish noblemen preparing to make their way to the rendezvous at Cracow, the District Officer of Tarnów, Johann Breindl von Wallerstein, enlisted the help of the local peasants. In particular, he sought the assistance of Jakub Szela (1787–1866), an irascible peasant from Smarzowy, famed for his successful litigations against wealthy landowners. Szela set to work to organize bands of serfs, who were promised an end to their feudal obligations if they would turn on their masters. In the ensuing mêlée, the estates of the noble conspirators were invaded. Noblemen, landlords, bailiffs, and protesting officials were butchered in cold blood. The innocent suffered with the guilty. Before long, the peasant bands were offering the severed heads of their noble victims to the authorities as proof of their zeal. In some cases, they appear to have been paid for their wares in salt. The situation was completely out of hand. A minor noble insurrection had turned into a major peasant *jacquerie*. In some districts, nine out of ten manors were razed to the ground. In the vicinity of Bochnia, Austrian officials were attacked indiscriminately. In the Tatra mountains, at Chołochów, a band led by the village priest and his organist raised the flag of Polish independence. It was nearly three weeks before the Austrian army, delayed by the Rising in Cracow, could arrive to restore order. By that time, more than two thousand Polish noblemen had been killed. The remaining merrymakers were dispersed. Szela was arrested as a matter of form, but was then rewarded with a large estate in the distant province of Bukovina. For the Austrian authorities, it was a sobering reminder of the excesses to which loyalty, no less than rebellion, could lead. For the Poles, it was a rude awakening to the fact that Polish-speaking peasants could not be relied on to support Polish noblemen in patriotic enterprises. But for the peasants, it was a liberating experience of the first importance. Having once shaken off their feudal dues, they could not easily resubmit. For Galicia as a whole, the *jacquerie* of 1846 exposed the shortcomings of the existing authoritarian regime, and prepared the ground for eventual autonomy.[3] (See pp. 336–8.)

Two years later, Galicia felt the shock-waves of the revolutionary disturbances in other parts of the Empire. In March, when news arrived from Vienna that Metternich had fled and that the Emperor Ferdinand had promised constitutional reforms, National Committees were formed in Cracow and Lemberg. In the 'Lemberg Address' of 19 March 1848, a group of prominent Galicians petitioned the Emperor for the emancipation of the peasants and for provincial Autonomy. In the heat of the moment, their loyalist sentiments were amended by the messengers entrusted with the petition's delivery; and, contrary to all common sense, a document was delivered in Vienna demanding Polish independence. A Galician Delegation, which attended the meetings of the insurrectionary Assembly in Vienna from July to October, contained a score of colourful and vocal peasants. They took an active part in the abolition of feudal services. Their leader, the

Lemberg liberal, Franciszek Smolka (1810–99), acted as President of the Lower Chamber. But the imperial army kept its nerve. In April, Cracow was bombarded by the Austrian garrison on Wawel Hill, and was the first of the Empire's rebellious cities to be reduced to obedience. Lemberg submitted in November, after similar treatment. By that time, General Windischgratz had already re-entered Vienna. In December, the discredited Emperor abdicated in favour of his nephew, Francis-Joseph, and Austria returned to its former absolutist ways. Assisted by the state of emergency required by the unfinished war against Hungary, Alexander Bach, the Minister of the Interior, was able to repress all political opposition. Plans for Galician autonomy had to be shelved once again. (See Chapter 15.)

Autonomy was not forgotten, however, and came to fruition by stages as a by-product of the Empire's military defeats and the continuing constitutional struggle between Austria and Hungary. The movement for autonomy was first revived by a group of conservative aristocrats headed by Count Agenor Gołuchowski (1812–75), who could press Vienna for concessions as their price for unwavering loyalty to the Crown, thereby ensuring that the Galician Poles could be used as a counterweight to the Magyar secessionists and the German radicals. Gołuchowski, who was Governor in Galicia in 1849, Viceroy in 1850–9, 1866–8, and 1871–5, and President of the Imperial Council of Ministers in 1860–1, acted as the link between the Habsburg Court and his fellow Polish grandees, the so-called 'Podolians'. In unison with the converted ex-radical, Florian Ziemiałkowski (1817–1900), he viewed autonomy from an essentially Whiggish position, seeing timely constitutional concessions as the best means of preserving the dominance of the landowning interest. At the same time, he hoped to parry the more militant Federalists, headed by Smolka, who aimed to create a 'Triple Monarchy' in which Galicia would enjoy the same equal and federal status as Austria and Hungary. The political struggle lasted for more than a decade, and ended with a compromise acceptable to both protagonists. The Emperor's initial concessions to the Autonomists' more limited demands in the institutional sphere were matched by further concessions to the Federalists'

more radical demands in the sphere of Polish culture and
education. The first step, in 1861, was taken in the wake of
the disastrous Italian war. Gołuchowski's own scheme for
'devolution' as embodied in the October Diploma was
amended by his successor as President of the Council of
Ministers, Antoni Schmerling; but the Emperor's February
Patent of 1861, which finally established a constitutional
system for Austria, also made provision for Galicia's separate
legal and administrative institutions. The second step was
taken during the crisis provoked by the defeat at Königgrätz.
In December 1866, a motion in the Galician assembly request-
ing implementation of the proposals for Autonomy was
accompanied by a loyal address to the Emperor: 'We stand
beside Thee, most Gracious Lord, and so we wish to stand'.
Loyalty was duly rewarded. In the Emperor's 'Fundamental
Law' of 21 December 1867, granting the governmental
changes which accompanied the Ausgleich, Galicia was not
forgotten. Both an elective legislature, the *Sejm Krajowy,* and
a provincial executive body, the *Wydział Krajowy,* were
created. But the Federalists were still not satisfied. Smarting
under the disappointment that Galicia had received fewer
powers than Hungary, they passed a resolution in 1868
demanding further reforms. Demonstrations occurred in
Lemberg, and the government felt obliged to give way. In
1869, the Polish language, which had recently been admitted
to schools and courts, was put on the same level as German
in all official business; in 1870, the Jagiellonian University
was empowered to reinstate Polish as the principal language
of instruction; in 1871, a Ministry of Galician Affairs was
created in Vienna to uphold the interests of the Kingdom
with the imperial government; in 1872, the *Akademia
Umiejętności* (Academy of Learning) was launched in Cracow
under the patronage of the imperial family; and in 1873, the
School Board was set up to provide a system of full-time
primary education in the local languages. By these measures,
Galicia was given the means whereby the cadres of the new,
autonomous administration could be staffed by well-educated
native candidates.

The government of Galicia, as organized between 1867 and
1918, showed a curious mixture of centralized, and devolved

bodies. The Viceroy, whose role superseded that of the former Governors, was appointed directly by the Emperor, and from his residence in Lemberg directed the work of the executive branch. Together with the Deputy Viceroy in Cracow, he controlled the Starostas of the 79 administrative districts (*Bezirke/powiat*) and beneath them, the village mandataries. His competence stopped short of the Army, the Posts and Telegraphs, the state railways, the Crown Domain, and the state forests, which were run directly from Vienna. The legislature, the *Sejm Krajowy*, was organized on the basis of an elaborate system of 'curias' or electoral colleges. Apart from thirteen *ex officio* deputies drawn from the Bishops, the university Rectors, and the President of the Academy, there were to be 44 deputies elected by the Landowners' Curia, representing some two thousand registered noble electors; 3 deputies returned by the Commerical Curia, representing the members of the Provincial Chamber of Commerce; 31 deputies returned by the Municipal Curia representing the incorporated cities; and 74 deputies returned by the 'Curia of the Remaining Commons', which was elected by representatives of the peasant communes. In the Landowners' Curia, each deputy was the direct representative on average of 52 voters; in the Commons' Curia, he was the indirect representative of 8,792! In all, less than 10 per cent of the population exercised a vote. The urban plebs were excluded from the suffrage altogether. True to the intentions of its original sponsors, the Sejm could not help but operate as a forum for the patronage and influence of the landowning class. Its legislative decisions were subject to the Emperor's veto, entrusted to the Viceroy; and its control over the Executive Department was purely perfunctory. Even so, in the realms of public works, justice, and education, it wielded effective powers. It was the only institution in the Polish lands at that time which gave an effective share in government to even part of the Polish population.

The achievement of Autonomy gave a signal boost to all forms of Polish national consciousness. Patriotic demonstrations came very much into vogue. In 1869, the accidental reopening of the tomb of Casimir the Great, by a workman digging in the crypt of the cathedral at Cracow, gave rise to extraordinary scenes of popular rejoicing. The solemn re-interment of the last remains of the great Piast was attended by tens of thousands of well-wishers. In that same year, the Third Centenary of the Union of Lublin provided a similar excuse for further festivities, and in Lemberg for the building of the huge Mound of the Union. The erection of patriotic monuments, such as Ryger's statue of Adam Mickiewicz in the Market Square in Cracow in 1898 or the Grunwald Monument in 1910, attracted masses of sightseers from all three Partitions.

A visitor to Galicia in this period would have been struck by the prevailing blend of local Slav and imperial Austrian influences. Karl Baedeker, describing Lemberg in 1905 for the readers of the English edition of his guidebook to Austria–Hungary, laid equal emphasis on the city's Polish and German connections:

Lemberg – Hotels. Hot. George, R. from 3K., B.90h; Hotel Imperial; Grand Hotel; Hotel Metropole; Hotel de l'Europe; Hotel de France.

Restaurants. At the Hot. George, Grand Hotel and Hotel de l'Europe; Stadtmuller, Krakowska-Str.; Rail – Restaurant at the chief station – *Cafes.* Theatre Cafe, Ferdinands-Platz; Vienna Cafe, Helige-Gheist-Platz.

Electric Tramway from the chief station to the Wały Hetmańskie and thence to the Kiliński Park, and to the Cemetery of Łyczaków – Horse Cars also traverse the town.

British Vice-Consul, Prof. R. Załoziecki.

Lemberg, (Polish Lwów, French Leopol) the capital of Galicia, with 160,000 inhab. (one-fourth Jews) is the seat of a Roman Catholic, an Armenian, and a Greek Catholic archbishop. There are fourteen Roman Catholic churches, a Greek, an Armenian and a Protestant church, two synagogues, and several Roman Catholic and Greek convents. The town itself is small, the finest buildings being in the four suburbs (those of Halicz, Łyczaków, Cracow, and Żółkiew).

The inner town is bounded on the E. side by the Wały Gubernartorskie,. and on the W. side by the Wały Hetmanskie, with statues of Hetman Jabłonowski, the defender of the town against the Turks in 1695, and of King John III, Sobieski, by Baracz. In the Ring, or principal Platz, which is embellished with four handsome monumental fountains, stands the Rathaus, built in 1828–37 with its tower 260 ft. high (good survey of the town from the top). – The Roman Catholic Cathedral, built in the 15th cent. in the late-Gothic style, was restored in the 18th cent. in the rococo style. The Armenian Cathedral is in the Armenian–Byzantine style (15th cent.). In front of it rises a statue of St. Christopher. The Dominican Church contains the monument of a Countess Dunin-

Borkowska by Thorvaldsen. The Greek Catholic Cathedral, in the basilica style, stands on a height in the Georgs-Platz.

The handsome Polytechnic Institution in the Georgs-Platz, completed in 1877, contains a large chemical–technical laboratory and is otherwise well equipped. In the Słowacki-Str., opposite the Park, is the Hall of the Estates, built in 1877–81 from Hochberger's design, with a painting by Matejko (the Lublin Union of 1567) in the session-room. In the Kleparowska-Strasse rises the Invalidenhaus, with its four towers. – At the Theatres (closed in summer), in the Skarbowska-Str, Polish plays and Polish–Italian operas are performed (the solos generally in Italian, the chorus in Polish). Near the theatre, to the S., is the Industrial Museum, open on week-days 9–2, 40h., Sun. 10–12 free; the library on week-days 11–2, Sun. 10–1, free.

The University (about 2000 stud.) was founded in 1784 by Emp. Joseph II. Adjacent, to the S., is the Botanic Garden. The Medical Faculty and the clinical institutions are in the Piekarska-Strasse.

Ossolinski's National Institute in the Halicz suburb, contains a library, relating chiefly to the literature and history of Poland, and collections of pictures, antiquities, coins etc. (adm. daily, except Mon. 10–1 and Tues. & Fri. 3–5, free). – The Dzieduszycki Museum contains important natural history collections and is always open to visitors on application to the keeper.

To the S. of the town is the extensive Kiliński Park (restaurant), the favourite promenade of the citizens, with a statue of Jan Kilinski (1760–1819), the Polish patriot, by Markowski. Fine views of the town may be enjoyed from the Unionshugel and from the top of the Franz-Josef-Berg (1310 ft.).[4]

After 1867, the political scene in Galicia enjoyed a period of relative stability. Agenor Gołuchowski continued as Viceroy until his death in 1875. Both Ziemiałkowski, who served as Minister of Galician Affairs in 1873–83, and Smolka, who served as Chairman of the imperial *Reichsrat* from 1881 to 1893, established themselves as politicians of the first rank. In view of the fact that both of them had been condemned to death in their youth for treasonable activities, their elevation may be seen as a sign of changing and more peaceable times. Their appearance in Vienna coincided with the careers of a younger generation of Galicians, who rose to prominence in the Empire. Professor Juljan Dunajewski (1822–1907) in the Ministry of Finance, Kazimierz Badeni (1846–1909) as President of the Council of Ministers, and Count Agenor Gołuchowski Jnr. (1849–1921), at the Ministry of Foreign

Affairs, were but three names among many men whose careers followed the line from Lemberg to Vienna. At the end of the century, the leadership of the conservatives in Galicia fell to Wojciech Dzieduszycki (1848–1909), Professor of Philosophy at Lemberg, and Minister of Galician Affairs in 1906–7. In a period when democratic parties were making their appearance, he widened the scope of the original 'Podolian' group, departing from its original exclusively aristocratic social base in a conscious manœuvre to defend the Polish establishment from the rising tides of Ukrainian and Jewish nationalism. In this, his outlook was very similar to that of Roman Dmowski in Russian Poland. It has been said with some force that the 'neo-conservatives' in Galicia were pursuing a policy which anticipated the programme of the National Democratic Movement in the Polish lands as a whole. It was entirely natural in the era of universal suffrage, in the last years before the World War, that the National Democrats should have made great headway amongst the Polish electorate, thereby reaping what the Podolians had sown.

Mass political parties were slow to develop, but when they did break surface, they sprouted forth in considerable profusion. Their leaders participated both in the *Sejm Krajowy* and in the imperial *Reichsrat*. As a result of prevailing conditions, almost all the new parties were anti-clerical and anti-aristocratic. Apart from the National Democrats, the most important of them was the *Polskie Stronnictwo Ludowe* (Polish People's Movement, PSL), founded in 1895. Its influential journal, *Przyjaciel Ludu* (The People's Friend), exercised an important influence of the peasantry and on their awareness of political and national issues. It cost its editor, Bolesław Wysłouch (1855–1937), the founding father of the movement, more than one spell behind bars.[5] In 1911, the party suffered a three-way split. Leadership passed away from the radical wing, the PSL-Lewica (Left) of Jan Stapiński (1867–1946), and into the hands of the more cautious PSL-Piast faction under Wincenty Witos (1874–1945) and Jan Dąbski (1880–1931).[6] In contrast to them, the *Polska Partia Socjalno-Demokratyczna* (Polish Social-Democratic Party) addressed its socialist programme to a necessarily restricted audience. Its leaders, Bolesław Drobner (1883–1968), Ignacy

Daszyński (1866–1936), and Jędrzej Moraczewski (1870–1944), like all socialists in Poland at this time, could not agree as to whether social revolution or national independence should command priority.[7] The impact of the new parties was considerably weakened by conflict on the national issue, and by the growth of parallel political parties formed by the German, Ukrainian, and Jewish communities. In a world of fragmented politics, most of the Polish parties were constrained to moderate their theoretical programmes in the interests of mutual assistance. In the *Reichsrat,* they formed a common front in the all-party Polish Circle of deputies. Nationalism and Populism were, in fact, the only two movements at this time with any chance of success. Socialism was of necessity a minority interest, as shown by the apochryphal story of the Polish socialist from Warsaw who was apprehended by the police on the Galician frontier. When asked by a police officer what he understood by Socialism, he said that it was 'the struggle of the workers against Capital'. To which, he received the inimitable reply: 'In that case you may enter Galicia, for here we have neither workers nor capital.'[8]

The cultural and educational achievements of the Poles in Galicia need no advertisement. The ancient Jagiellonian University enjoyed a new lease of life. Together with the University of Lemberg, and the Lemberg Polytechnic, re-endowed in 1877, it earned a worldwide reputation. The Jagiellonian's Faculty of History under Szujski and Bobrzyński; its Faculty of Medicine under Józef Dietl; and its Faculty of Physics under Z. F. Wróblewski and K. Olszewski, made distinguished contributions to their subjects. The Academy of Learning, with its five departments of scientific research, established important international connections, and was the predecessor of the modern Polish Academy of Sciences.[9] The learned societies, the libraries, the museums, the publishers, the bookshops, the theatres, the coffee-houses, and the journals and newspapers of Cracow and Lemberg supplied an intellectual market which transcended the frontiers of the three Empires. Lemberg was the home of the Ossolineum, an institute founded in 1827 by Józef Maksimilian Ossoliński (1748–1826) for the dissemination of Polish arts and sciences. It also saw the founding of the Polish Historical Society, and the senior Polish historical journal, the *Kwartalnik Historyczny* (Historical Quarterly), in 1884. Cracow was the home of the Czartoryski Museum, which opened its doors in 1878, thanks to the munificence of Prince Adam Jerzy's son, Prince Władysław Czartoryski (1828–94). It contained an art gallery, library, and archive. Among the theatres, the famous *Stary Teatr* in Cracow (Old Theatre) staged many of the *premières* of the classic Polish dramatic repertoire, and presided over the 'Golden Age' of Polish drama. Both Cracow and Lemberg had large municipal theatres modelled on the Paris Opera. Among the coffee houses, which fulfilled the function of intellectual clubs, it would be impossible to underestimate the debates and arguments resounding through the smoke-filled rooms of *Jan Michalik* in Cracow, or the *Szkocka* in Lemberg. In consequence of favourable political conditions, the number of books and newspapers published in Galicia exceeded those which appeared in the Russian and Prussian Partitions together. From the rich store of personalities who kept Polish cultural life at a peak of vigour, it would be hard to choose three or four which were typical of the whole. Galicia produced its share of splendid eccentrics, as well as its meritorious pedants. In some respects, the theatrical world, fed in the early period by the comedies of Aleksander Fredro (1793–1876) and later by Stanisław Wyspiański, was outstanding. Yet the most remarkable figures, perhaps, were those extraordinarily talented all-rounders, who could flit from genre to genre with equal brilliance. One such figure was Tadeusz Boy-Żeleński (1874–1941). A medical doctor by profession, he wrote the best-selling historical romance, *Marysieńka,* and was a regular performer in Cracow cabaret. Almost as a sideline, he completed single-handed one of the largest tasks in the annals of Polish culture, translating into Polish all the classics of French literature, in more than one hundred volumes.[10] Another was Professor Karol Estreicher (1827–1908), the Jagiellonian Librarian, who divided his time between dramatic criticism and the preparation of his epoch-making *Bibliografia Polska* (Polish Bibliography) in 22 volumes. A third was Wilhelm Feldman (1868–1919), who busied himself in political life as a socialist, a Jewish assimilationist, and in the World War as the envoy in Berlin of

Piłsudski's Legions. His popular survey, *Współczesna literatura polska* (Contemporary Polish Literature, 1902), and his scholarly *Dzieje polskiej myśli politycznej* (History of Polish Political Thought, 1914–20) quickly established themselves as standard works. He also found time for political propaganda, for writing novels, and for literary criticism, in which he led the opposition against the 'Young Poland' movement. Last but not least was the figure of Michał Bobrzyński, historian, educationalist, and Viceroy.

In many ways, the Ukrainian national movement was more advanced in Galicia than across the frontier in Russia, though for long it declined to accept the 'Ukrainian' label. The earlier emancipation of the peasantry, and the complacent attitude of the Austrian authorities, permitted the steady growth of nationalist activities throughout the second half of the century. The Uniate Church was free from the persecution which it had to endure in Russia, and was able to organize elementary education in the Ruthenian language. Ruthenian literature had its own 'Triad' of romantic writers, who published their first collection of folk verse in 1837. In Lemberg, a Ruthenian National House operated from 1848; a Ruthenian theatre from 1864; and the first Ruthenian high school from 1874. In organizational matters, the initiative lay for a time with the Old Ruthenians – a group which had a special interest in religious reforms, reviving among other things the study of Old Church Slavonic. After 1882, when an Austrian treason trial revealed that the Old Ruthenians had been receiving a secret subsidy from the Tsarist ambassador, the limelight passed to the younger group of *Narodovtsy* or 'Populists'. Henceforth, political activities intensified. Demands were made for social reform, for universal suffrage, for state-supported Ruthenian education, for closer contacts with the Ukrainians in Russia, and eventually for the creation of a 'Greater Ukraine from the San to the Don'. The Populists were the first group in Galicia to call themselves Ukrainians; but soon the name was to be applied to all sorts of groups and communities, from the intellectual activists in the towns to the peasant Hutsuls and Lemkos of the Carpathians, who had little prior sense of their common identity.

At the turn of the century a full range of Ukrainian political parties made their appearance in Galicia. Among many distinguished names, those of Ivan Franko (1856–1916), socialist and novelist, Mykhailo Hrushevsky (1866–1934), Professor of History at Lemberg; and Archbishop Sheptytsky, enjoyed special prestige. Yet tensions between the Ukrainians and the Poles were unavoidable. The situation before the First World War, when Ukrainians were calling for the incorporation of Galicia into their projected national state as the 'Western Ukraine', whilst the Poles called for its incorporation into an independent Poland as 'Eastern Małopolska', aptly illustrates the prevalence of crude prejudices and irreconcilable aspirations.[11] To many older citizens, nationalist politicking of that sort must have seemed distinctly 'un-Galician'.

The Viceroyalty of Michał Bobrzyński between 1908 and 1913 finds little space in present-day histories. A medieval historian who devoted himself to his studies and to the management of the School Board, and who as a politician remained staunchly *Kaisertreu,* has few modern admirers. As Viceroy, he succeeded Count Andrzej Potocki, who was assassinated in April 1908 by a Ukrainian terrorist. But instead of demanding retribution, he saw his task as one of reconciliation between the warring nationalities. At the provincial elections of 1911, he formed a 'Viceregal Block' for candidates who wished to support his programme for reforming the electoral system and for assisting Ukrainian education. When the Block won, he was denounced by the Catholic bishops, by the Galician conservatives, and most virulently of all, by the National Democrats. In their eyes, he had betrayed the Polish cause. Yet it was in his period of office that Piłsudski's Legions came into the open in Galicia, and began to hold manœuvres and train recruits. Bobrzyński turned a blind eye to their activities, deeming them a necessary part of Austrian foreign policy but an irrelevance to Galician domestic affairs. His style was tolerant, therefore, his aims limited, his intention of calming nationalist passions thankless. He resigned in May 1913, worn down by the attacks of his compatriots. He was the first and the last of the Viceroys to attempt to run Galicia in a truly democratic and even-handed manner. His resignation was followed the very next summer by the outbreak of war. It was Galicia's last chance. Apart from a brief tenure of

the Ministry for Galician Affairs in Vienna in 1917, Bobrzyński retired from active politics altogether. He advocated
loyalty to Austria to the end, not from any blind devotion to
the Habsburgs but from his fear of the destructive forces
which would take their place. Yet by any standard of political
integrity, his record was a worthy one. He looked beyond the
situation where one class and one nationality had lorded it
over the rest of society, and tried without much success to
initiate something better. He did not persecute the activists
and revolutionaries who congregated in his Kingdom, but
sought rather to make life sufficiently tolerable for rebellions
and conspiracies to become superfluous. Like many of the
Galicians whom he governed, he was not in sympathy with
Nationalism. But his contribution to the life of his nation,
and of its neighbours, was considerable.[12]

Galicia's fate was decided by men and forces far beyond
the control of anyone in Galicia. In August 1914, the Russian
Army rolled out of the east, and reached the outskirts of
Cracow. In 1915, the German counter-offensive pushed
forward from the west, and traversed the province in the
opposite direction. The retreating Russians adopted a scorched
earth policy. Villages were razed; railways, bridges, and factories were dismantled; the oil-wells at Borysław were fired;
over one million peasants, together with their livestock and
foodstores were deported. In 1916, General Brusilov reappeared on the eastern horizon, and smashed his way towards
the Carpathians. In 1917–18, as part of the Austrian Military
Zone, Galicia was plagued by starving refugees, by requisitioning, and by armies whose discipline was disintegrating. Its
distress exceeded that of the war-torn disaster areas of Belgium
and Northern France. At the end of the War, it was left
stranded by the collapse of the Austro-Hungarian authorities.
Together with the dynasty whose interests it had been
designed to serve, it sank without trace.

In later years, Polish commentators tended to look back
on Galicia with indulgence and even affection. For them
Galicia was the one place where Polish culture and ideals had
been kept alive, whilst the other partitions languished under
the hammers of Germanization and Russification. It was the
'Piedmont' of the resurgent nation. Despite the fact that

relatively few Galicians were actively interested in the cause of Polish independence, it is undeniable that the Galician experience played an important role in fitting the Poles for the independent status which was thrust upon them at the end of the War.

But Galicia must also be regarded as the Piedmont of Ukrainian nationalism. According to the last Austrian census of 1910, conducted in accordance with linguistic criteria, the Ruthenians made up 40 per cent of the total population, and in Eastern Galicia 59 per cent. In view of the fact that they possessed 2,460 primary schools and 61 gymnasia (as against 2,967 and 70 respectively in Polish hands), it could be argued that pro rata they had outstripped the Poles in promoting their national culture. In view of the poor prospects for separatist politics in Russia, they undoubtedly looked to Galicia as the base for all political developments in the future. Yet in the political sphere they still occupied a subordinate position. In the Landowners' Curia in 1914, they held only one seat out of 45; in the Commons' Curia, 48 out of 105; and in the Galician delegation to the *Reichsrat* only 25 out of 78. Poles might maintain that inferior Ruthenian representation was due to the inferior state of development of the Ukrainian community; the Ukrainians maintained that it was due to discrimination. All attempts to put Ukrainian language on an equal footing with Polish and German, except in the courts, met with determined resistance. Attempts to introduce it into the work of the University at Lemberg led to student riots. In such a situation, Austrian officialdom was sorely tempted to cultivate Ukrainian grievances as a convenient check on the stronger Polish movement. By so doing, they inflamed the Polish–Ukrainian antagonism which broke into open warfare as soon as the Habsburg regime collapsed.

Indubitably, in an age of national states, the Galician order must be viewed as something of an anachronism. Yet in a century in which Nationalism has been discredited no less than the Imperialism which it replaced, there are people still alive today who recall 'the good old days' of the Dual Monarchy with genuine nostalgia. There is at least one drawing-room in Cracow where the portrait of Francis-Joseph still hangs in its place of honour. There are Ukrainians from Lemberg (now Lviv′, the chief city of the Western Ukraine in the USSR), who wonder whether the changes of the last sixty years have all been for the better. From time to time, one can still meet an octogenarian, who can whistle the tune of *'O du meine liebe Oesterreich'* with gusto, or who can repeat what he used to recite every morning in school:

> O Lord preserve,
> O Lord support
> Our Emperor and our Land!
> Protect with Thy shield all those who serve,
> That by the power that Thou hast wrought
> The state may firmly stand . . .*

Intelligent people in Galicia did not need to be told that they lived in a poor and backward province, or that they were citizens of the feeblest of the partitioning powers. At the same time, they were free from the social and political pressures which dominated Polish life in the other Partitions. They were free from the cultural imperialism of Russia and Germany; they were free from the atmosphere of deprivation and harassment induced by Tsardom; and they were free from the rapid social changes, and the mania for self-improvement, which beset the Poles in Prussia. For this, they were truly grateful to the Habsburgs. As a result, they were less disposed to curse their fate, and more inclined to shrug or chuckle. An acute awareness of their limitations, and a proper appreciation of their blessings, gave them a sense of proportion and a sense of fun, which was lacking elsewhere. Galicia produced its share of romantics, of conspirators, of 'organic workers', of nationalist fanatics, and of Polish patriots; but it also produced an abundance of Loyalists, of conservatives, of sentimentalists, of sceptics, and of jokers. Although the differences may be hard to define, the world as seen from Warsaw or Posen did not look the same when viewed from Cracow. In Galicia, the Poles were used to looking at themselves, and to laughing. On the stage of *Jan Michalik*, nothing, not even Polish History, was sacred:

---

* *Boże wspieraj, Boże ochroń!* . . . was sung in Polish to Haydn's tune 'Austria', better known as the melody of Hoffmann's 'Deutschland, Deutschland über alles'.

For many long years, by Heaven aided,
Our nation preserved its mighty sway.
At whatever point they were not needed,
The Polish Hussars charged into the fray.
Then, when the nobles' ardour waned,
The flashing sabre was sheathed. Instead,
The blows of the nation's strong right hand
Were aimed to the peasant's defenceless head.
At last, even Heaven's patience was rattled.
Our conduct had Providence thoroughly riled.
The Almighty declared: 'I'll slaughter such cattle;
The merest sight of them drives me wild.' . . .
The fault is ours — a very great fault —
That the Lord has punished us all so cruelly.
For the internal enemy has launched his assault
On PROPERTY, on the FAITH and on the FAMILY.
Yet a knight in paper armour sounds the alarm,
As he rolls the stone from the door of the tomb:
'Arise, O Nation, gird your strong right arm;
At the third stroke, it's the crack of doom.'

Boy-Żeleński's impish doggerel was scandalous enough, even in Cracow, especially when he attacked more *risqué* subjects such as the clergy or the conventional sexual mores of the day. In political affairs, he remained a convinced sceptic, gently deriding the notion that national independence would somehow cure all the people's ills. His satirical temper, and his sceptical politics, were highly reminiscent of the Stańczyks, and represented the older Galician fashions which even then were giving way to the new, nationalist trends. It may have been inevitable that Austria–Hungary passed away. But everything that followed was not necessarily an improvement.

CHAPTER FIVE
FABRYKA
The Process of Industrialization

Until the middle decades of the twentieth century, no part of Eastern Europe could claim that Industry played a dominant role in economic or social life. In contrast to the countries of Western Europe, where the primary Industrial Revolution was often completed over one hundred years earlier, industrialization in the east was frequently postponed and frequently interrupted. In the Polish lands, where the first precocious factories appeared in the 1740s, it has proceeded intermittently over the last two centuries.

Any attempt to squeeze the history of Polish industrialization into a tidy theoretical model soon runs into serious difficulties. But that does not deter the theoreticians. In present-day Polish scholarship, three stages are usually distinguished. The earliest stage, from the 1740s to 1815, was characterized by the small-scale, local ventures undertaken mainly by feudal magnates for the improvement of their private estates. No fundamental economic change was involved, but advances in technology, science, trade, finance, and the organization of labour laid foundations for the future. The early factories represent a link between traditional craft and cottage activities, and later forms of mass production. The next stage, which began in 1815 and lasted until the Second World War, is referred to as Poland's 'First Industrialization'. In so far as its effects were incomplete, it is not deemed to qualify for the title of an industrial 'Revolution'. (Modern Polish historians prefer the term *przewrót* (changeover) to that of *rewolucja* (revolution).) The latest stage, since 1945, which coincides with the 'Second Industrialization' undertaken by the People's Republic, is still in progress.[1]

The focus of the First Industrialization was undoubtedly to be found in the Congress Kingdom. Here again, three phases are distinguished. In the first phase, from 1815 to 1864, attempts by the state to foster industrial enterprise, and in some instances, to own and direct it, met with only partial success. Polish experiments with 'the Prussian Road to Capitalism', if such indeed they were, lacked both capital resources and the support of a heavy industrial base. By 1850, the initiative was passing back into private hands, most typically into consortia formed from native landowning and manufacturing interests and from foreign concerns. The following decades saw a marked acceleration in the mining, textile, and metallurgical industries; but the delays in agrarian reform and the persistence of a semi-feudal society prevented any radical redirection of the mass of the population into the industrial sector.

In the second phase, from 1864 to 1918, many of the former inhibitions were removed, and Polish industry was drawn into the wider forum of European trade, finance, and labour. The years 1864 to 1883 saw a massive influx of western capital and machinery. At this time the Polish lands straddled the main divide of the European industrial map, separating the developed regions of Germany from the backward expanses of Russia and Austria. After 1880, the dividing line was artificially emphasized by Russia's protective tariff barrier, behind which the former Congress Kingdom prospered. For three decades before the First World War, Polish manufactures played a prominent role in the economy of the Russian Empire as a whole. The railway network expanded rapidly. Mechanization proliferated. Industrial concentrations transformed the landscape of specific geographical areas. Investment capital was made available through a decline in agricultural returns. Private enterprises were merged into public stock companies. Small-scale factories were linked into larger combines. Although peasant agriculture and small-scale, petty businesses continued to dominate the economy as a whole, the industrial sector reached a peak of performance in 1913.

In the third phase, from 1918 to 1939, the state authorities of the newly independent Republic fought against the odds to combine three separate industrial systems into an integrated whole, and, with manifestly inadequate resources, to construct an efficient infrastructure. Their tentative steps were rudely terminated by the Second World War, whose conclusion, as in most spheres of Polish life, necessitated a completely fresh start.

Poland's First Industrialization has inspired a great deal of economic theorizing, especially of the Marxist variety. Rosa Luxemburg's *Promyshlennoye Razvitie Pol'shi* (The Industrial Development of Poland) published in St. Petersburg in 1899 provided the theoretical arguments on which the Polish communist movement based its strategy for the first forty years of its existence. In her view, Polish industry formed an integral part of the Russian economy, and as such was essential to her hopes that Russia would share in the coming proletarian revolution of Germany and Western Europe. By the same token, she held that Polish Independence would be a retrograde step, which could only damage the prospects for Russian and European progress as a whole. (It was for this reason no doubt that the Tsarist censor approved her work for publication.[2]) Oskar Lange (1904—65), Poland's first delegate to the United Nations, whose *Ekonomia polityczna* (Political Economy) appeared in 1959, was more concerned with the typology of industrialization. According to his lights, Polish industry showed features characteristic of the 'capitalistic' and of the 'socialist' but not of the 'national-revolutionary' types.[3]

Yet non-Marxist models are no more helpful. Rostow's theory of economic growth, for example, can be applied to the history of the Congress Kingdom, and would suggest that the transformation of the 'Traditional Society' proceeded fitfully through the nineteenth century and that the crucial period of industrial 'take-off' occurred in the last three decades before the First World War. (See Map 5.)[4] But it does nothing to explain the artificial interruptions and sudden reversals of fortune which have characterized Polish economic history over long periods — in the Napoleonic Wars, in the mid-nineteenth century, and again in the years 1915—45. One suspects that international politics had more relevance than any purely domestic factors.

The fundamental objection to the suitability of all such theoretical models, however, lies in the doubtful assumption that the Polish economy has had a continuous history and can be studied and analysed as a coherent subject. The fact is, the Polish economy of today is not the end-product of a long process of organic development. It operates on a new territorial base, on a new infrastructure, and with a new population;

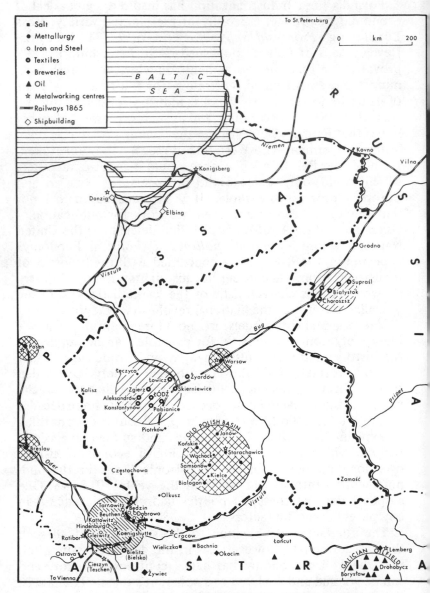

Map 5.   Industrialization, (c. 1900)

and its elements were thrown together by the political engineering of the Great Powers at the end of the Second World War. At earlier periods, its constituent parts were fully integrated into the economies of Germany, Austria, or Russia, from which they were torn in 1915, in 1918–21, or in 1945. To regard them as an economic entity at times when they were not associated with each other is, to say the least, anachronistic. This problem, which Polish scholars grace with the doubtful label of 'regionalization' cannot be dispelled. For any number of subjective reasons, one may regret, for example, that modern Poland's most important industrial region in Silesia was founded, expanded, and brought to maturity by German initiative within the framework of the Prussian economic system, and that its main connections throughout its Industrial Revolution were with other parts of Germany and not with the Polish lands. One may regret it; but one cannot deny it. The bulk of Silesian industry did not form part of Polish Economic History until 1945. As a result, the history of Polish industrialization, if such a subject exists at all can only be treated on an empirical and piecemeal basis.

Of all Polish industries, mining possesses the most venerable pedigree. At Rudy in the Holy Cross Mountains there are traces of a prehistoric mine, and of an underground gallery, dating from the second century of our era. At Wieliczka near Cracow, the salt mines have been worked for at least a thousand years, and in the reign of Kazimierz III became the first of many royal monopolies. At Olkusz, and at Sławków, lead and silver mines figure in princely charters from the thirteenth century. From 1500, Olkusz hosted the Royal Mint. In the early centuries, mining was organized on the basis of the *gwarectwo* system (co-operatives); the miners were freemen; finance was provided by the Cracovian bishops and patricians, notably by Jost Ludwig Dietz, alias Decius (1485–1545), historian, author, diplomat, economist, Master of the Mint, and *Żupnik krakowski,* 'Master of the Mines'; all the great magnates and courtiers of the time were tempted to invest. It was a slow and dangerous business. At Olkusz, the great Ponikowska gallery, started in 1548 was excavated at the rate of one yard every six weeks. At Wieliczka, fatal accidents eliminated up to 10 per cent of the work-force annually. But the pay and the food were good. In 1561, the Wieliczka canteen cooked 1,289 geese, 2,049 cocks, 1,969 hens, 498 capons, 9,453 carp, 380 pike, 43 deer, 53 hares, and 500 oxen: all for the nourishment of some 800 men earning up to 90 groszy per week (at a time when an entire ox cost less than 60 grozy). Free funerals were provided at the King's expense.[5]

In this same period, the iron industry was also well established. At Wąchock on the Kamienna River in 1179, the founding charter of the Cistercian abbey mentions the abbot's rights to all mineral deposits; and it was here that, under monastic management, the first medieval forges were constructed. By 1500, Wąchock could claim twenty-two of the 289 forges known in the Kingdom. The forges were built on the site of local iron ore deposits. The metal was smelted in furnaces fired with charcoal, and hardened by water-driven hammers. Annual production could not have exceeded twenty tons. In Danzig, Swedish ore and 'pigs' were processed, and re-exported as steel or 'Dantsick iron' to England. In 1612, an epic poem entitled 'Officina Ferraria . . .' (The Workshop of the Noble Iron Industry) was published in Cracow by Walenty Rozdzieński, the son of an industrial family, who described the techniques, and the dangers, of iron-making. 'Injuries often take half a year to heal', he wrote; 'There is no shortage of deafened and crippled invalids amongst us.'[6] Rozdzieński was writing at a moment when magnatial entrepreneurs had begun to construct furnaces of a more advanced type. In 1598, Cardinal Jerzy Radziwiłł (1556–1600), Bishop of Cracow, commissioned an Italian engineer, Giovanni Ieronimo Caccia of Bergamo, to construct a steel-furnace on his estate at Samsonów near Kielce. This laid the foundations of the Staropolskie Basin, and of the Republic's weapons industry. Similar enterprises were started at Krzepice and Panków near Częstochowa by the Crown Marshal Mikołaj Wolski (1550–1630), and in the eighteenth century at Janów and Konskie, by another Chancellor, Jan Małachowski (1698–1762). By 1781 the Republic possessed thirty-three 'great forges', each producing some 200 tons per year. Production had risen tenfold over two centuries. The metal, reheated twice in two separate processes, was of high quality. But perspectives were low compared with progress made in subsequent decades when iron was wedded to coal.

The Polish iron and coal industry developed in the shadow of Prussian enterprises in neighbouring Silesia, and was closely associated with the name of Stanisław Staszic. Staszic was almost the exact contemporary of Friedrich Wilhelm Reden, and shared his enthusiasms for geology and mining. In 1778, when Reden entered the Prussian Mining Board at Breslau, Staszic was beginning his career as administrator of the Zamoyski estates. For forty years, he watched as Reden installed all the latest acquisitions from his visits to England — in 1788, the first steam-pump in a coal-mine at Tarnowitz (Tarnowskie Góry); in 1796, the first blast-furnaces at Gleiwitz (Gliwice) and at Koenigshutte (Chorzów); in 1811, the mammoth coke-oven at the Koenigin Ludwika mine at Hindenburg (Zabrze). By this time, Silesia was producing over 100,000 tons of coal, and 20,000 tons of steel. 'To think', wrote Staszic from the other side of the frontier, 'that they take all their ore from us, but do not belong to us!' Staszic took his chance between 1816 and 1824, when he served as Director of the Department of Industry and Crafts of the Congress Kingdom. As author of a thorough geological survey of Poland, published in 1815 as *'O Ziemorodztwie gór dawnej Sarmacji'* (On the Fruits of the earth of the Mountains of former Sarmatia), he was able to proceed at once with a plan for the establishment of a co-ordinated Polish heavy industry. In the eight short years of his administration, all the existing furnaces of the Staropolskie Basin were modernized, and a new blast-furnace, named 'Józef' in honour of Viceroy Zajączek, built at Kaniów; the River Kamienna was channelled and given a powerful motive current; coal and coke was carried from mines at Będzin (Bendin) and Dąbrowa (Dombrova), in districts recently acquired from Prussia; copper and silver works were opened at Białogoń, to support the currency reform; a Polytechnical Institute was founded in Warsaw; numerous foreign engineers were invited to accept lucrative appointments, among them Philippe Girard, a French inventor, who was made technical consultant to the Mining Department at 5,300 roubles per annum, and the Department's German Director, Ludwig Hauke, at 1,000 roubles per annum. All these innovations occurred as part of Lubecki's transformation of the Congress Kingdom. It was Lubecki, if no one else, who said that 'coal and iron is for industry, what bread is for man.' Despite fluctuations of fortune, the future of Polish heavy industry was assured. In the 1830s, the *Bank Polski* invested heavily in steel. The huge *Huta Bankowa* (Bank Steelworks) at Dąbrowa, built in 1840, was one of the largest of its kind in Europe – so large in fact that it was unable to run at full capacity until the market improved twenty years later.[7]

In the course of the nineteenth century, heavy industry developed on all three sides of the conjunction of the Prussian, Russian, and Austrian frontiers in Silesia. Upper Silesia grew into Germany's second industrial region after the Ruhr. The Dąbrowa Basin became the principal industrial concentration in the Congress Kingdom, and, until the growth of Russian industry after 1880, in the whole Russian Empire. The district of Ostrawa (Ostrava) in the Duchy of Teschen was the richest industrial area of Austria–Hungary. In all three areas, predominantly German management combined with Polish labour. Yet, despite their geographical proximity, the connections between the industries of the neighbouring partitions were slight. From the Polish point of view, the economic pressures were centrifugal, and tended to keep developments within the bounds of the separate Empires. There was no point in taking coal from Kattowitz to Dąbrowa, or vice versa. So the lines of communication ran outwards from the three parts of Silesia, to Berlin, Warsaw, and Vienna, but not across the frontiers. Dąbrowa's iron was brought from the Donets in the distant steppes of Southern Russia rather than from nearby Silesia; its oil came from Baku, rather than from Galicia.

The development of the textile industry passed through similar stages. By the end of the eighteenth century, the old spinners' and weavers' guilds, handicapped by the proliferation of small merchants and middle men and by their own restrictive practices, were gradually outflanked by magnatial manufactories. The old centres of the cottage industry, at Brzeziny, Kościany, Biecz, and at dozens of small towns on either side of the Silesian frontier, had long since lost the prosperity that they once enjoyed after the Thirty Years War. They were now due to be overtaken by new locations further east. The old export trade to Germany was no longer viable. The realm of wool and linen was about to be invaded by King Cotton. The first textile mills in the Republic were built by the Radziwiłłs beside their palace at Nieśwież in Lithuania. Their example was followed by many magnates, most prominently in the 1770s at Grodno by Antoni Tyzenhaus (1733–85), Treasurer of the Grand Duchy, and in the 1780s at Łowicz and Skierniewice by the King's brother, Archbishop Michał Jerzy Poniatowski (1736–94). To the horror of his episcopal colleagues, the Archbishop converted his two primatial residences into weaving-sheds, and persuaded his royal brother to buy 34 of 225 shares in the venture. In 1807, at Ozorków near Łęczyca a new sort of experiment made its appearance. The ancient estate of the Szczawczyński family, consisting of a manor, a mill, and four hides of land supporting four families, was bought for the purpose of founding a textile settlement. It was chosen for the abundance of soft water suitable for bleaching, and for the availability of unemployed weavers. Within ten years of the land being leased to a consortium of ten clothiers and two tailors, it was supporting over two thousand people. In 1818, at nearby Zgierz, a similar settlement of wollen weavers was founded, and flourished. These two towns were the precursors of half a dozen more, which were to develop in the subsequent period into one of Europe's foremost textile regions.

Łódź's label as 'the Polish Manchester' is hardly justified, at least to anyone who is connected with the Lancastrian metropolis. Łódź never aspired to the political and cultural standing of Cobden and Bright's Manchester and was more a follower than a pioneer in the history of textile technology. Yet its extraordinary growth in the second half of the nineteenth century, after several false starts, serves to illustrate the complicated nature of Polish industrialization and the necessary coincidence of numerous contributory factors which made it possible. In 1793, when Manchester was already clothing half of Europe, the hamlet of 'Lodzia' sheltered only 191 souls. In 1840, after twenty years of state promotion, it had reached only 20,000. After that it never looked back. In 1900, it had 315,000 inhabitants; in 1939, 673,000; and in 1971, 765,000.

The successive experiments which marked the early, precarious beginnings of the textile industry in Łódź, were launched by Rajmund Rembieliński (1775–1841), the Prefect of Mazovia, who on a tour of inspection in July 1820 stopped near the hamlet, drew a line in the sand accross the old road from Łęczyca to Piotrków, and declared that the Government of the Congress Kingdom would found a new town on that very spot. Rembielinski, a veteran of Kościuszko's Rising, who in 1804 had published a drama entitled *Lord Salisbury* and who had served as the General-Intendant of Poniatowski's Army, was seeking the same benefits for the state which had accrued to private entrepreneurs at nearby Ozorków and Zgierz. His first scheme was for the production of woollen cloth. Large numbers of Silesian and Saxon weavers were known to be unemployed after the conclusion of the Napoleonic Wars, and a concerted effort was made to recruit them into Poland. On the model of a standard agreement originally drawn up in Zgierz, each weaver was offered 1.5 morgs of land, free materials for building a house, and six years' exemption from rent, taxation, and military service. The government was to construct a bleach-works and dye-works to be managed by the Weavers' Guild. In 1823, ten weavers had settled in, and in 1824 tenders were submitted for supplying uniform broadcloth to the Polish Army. By 1829 production had reached an annual value of 35 million zł. Unpredictably, these woollen pioneers were plagued by a constant scarcity of yarn. The local supplier, one Ludwig Mamroth of Kalisz, was causing trouble on the grounds that his former monopoly in the area was being threatened. More seriously, the November Rising eliminated the infant industry's main customer, and hopes of exporting to Russia were crushed by the reimposition of the tariff barrier. Rembieliński's second scheme, floated in 1824, was for linen. On this occasion, settlers were offered 3 morgs of land, half of which was to be planted with flax. Preference was given to immigrants, with proof of skills. An official Government concession, and a loan of 20,000 zł. was extended to an entrepreneur from Prussian Silesia, who laid plans for a settlement of forty-two houses in the suburb of Ślązaki (Silesians). Already in 1829, 133,000 yards of linen were produced. But this venture too was destroyed by the November Rising. Rembielinski's scheme for cotton manufacture was thus the third in line, and undoubtedly thrived from the failure of wool and linen. It was entrusted in the first instance to Christian-Friedrich Wendisch, an established Saxon manufacturer from Chemnitz, whose concession dated from October 1824, and then to Ludwig Geyer, another Saxon, who arrived in Łódź in 1828 with his family's entire fortune of 1,000 thalers. Wendisch took 87 morgs and a loan of 180,000 zł., with which he constructed two mills, and a water-wheel. By 1829, a mechanized spinning-mill with 192 power mules was supplying yarn for the hand looms of a hundred weavers. In this case, mechanization, supported by the credit of an established German company, enabled the crisis of 1831 to be weathered. Geyer took the point. Having survived for nine years on his original investment, aided only by a grant of 14 morgs and a tiny loan of 3,000 zł., he now approached the Russian directors of the *Bank Polski* in Warsaw for a loan of one million zł. With the loan secured, in 1837 he ordered a complete cotton combine from Belgium, with the mules driven by a 50 horse-power steam-engine. Thereafter, Łódź swung over to cotton almost completely, and became the servicing centre of a galaxy of satellite towns at Pabianice, Aleksandrów, Konstantynów, and Zduńska Wola. Its reorganization and mechanization were nicely timed to catch the full benefit of the arrival in 1845 of the first Polish railway from Warsaw to Skierniewice and Rogów. Another milestone was reached in 1854, when both the Geyer and the Scheibler factories in Łódź went over to mechanical weaving. Henceforth, Polish cotton could be delivered into the limitless Russian market, so long as the Russian Empire lasted. The elusive constellation of state and private enterprise, of technological advance, of foreign and native finance, of skilled and available labour, of favourable tariffs in a favourable market, and of expanding modern communications, occurred at the right moment in the right place to launch the most successful undertaking of Poland's First Industrialization.[8]

In due course, the woollen industry revived also. The ill wind of 1831 which had blasted the woollen companies of Łódź, blew to the good of the Grodno *gubernia,* whose location inside the new Russian tariff barrier exactly paralleled that of Łódź in relation to the Polish–Prussian frontier. Woollen weavers, who in the 1820s had migrated from Silesia to Łódź, in the 1830s moved on to Białystok. The old town of the Branickis became an important centre of cloth manufacture. By 1900, with its satellites of Choroszcz, Fasty, and Supraśl, it had grown into a conurbation numbering over 100,000 inhabitants.

The linen industry flourished at Żyrardów near Warsaw. The settlement, created in 1833 by the French engineer, Philippe Girard, from the Mining Department, obtained a monopoly of linen production in the Congress Kingdom from the Russian authorities. By 1885, it employed some 8,500 workers in the small town entirely dominated by the one great factory.

By the second half of the nineteenth century, the main textile manufactories of Russian Poland had outstripped the production of the Prussian and Austrian Partitions combined. Neither Leignitz (Legnica) and Neustadt (Prudnik) in Prussian Silesia, nor Bielitz (Bielsko) in Austrian Silesia, or adjacent Biała in Galicia, could compete with Łódź, Białystok, or Żyrardów. In the Congress Kingdom, new joint-stock companies absorbed the smaller private concerns to the point where in 1914 nine firms employed almost half of the workforce. Cheap female labour gradually drove male operatives from unskilled employment. Wages rose steadily but surely. Over-all production advanced in sporadic leaps and bounds which put Polish textiles near the top of the European producers.

In a country where the rural economy still predominated, the role of the mining, metallurgical, and manufacturing industries should not be exaggerated. The agricultural sector, still run by landowning interests, was equally important. Sawmills, flour-mills, sugar refineries, breweries, distilleries, tanneries, and paperworks were to be found in every Polish town and were far more common than mines and blast-furnaces. The machine industry was largely directed to the production of agricultural equipment. In many instances, food-processing factories, such as the sugar refineries of Lower Silesia and Kujawy, or the breweries of Żywiec and Okocim in Galicia, provided major sources of employment. Even in Warsaw, they were not overtaken by the metallurgical employers until the turn of the century.

The oil industry developed late, and was the sole industrial sector where Galicia led the field; but for a brief period its development was sensational. Oil was first discovered in the vicinity of Borysław in 1850, and the city hospital of Lemberg was lit by paraffin lamps as early as 1853. Further deposits of oil and gas were discovered right along the northern slope of the Carpathians. Deep-drilling techniques imported from Canada by a British engineer, W. H. MacGarvey, brought spectacular results. Production rose from 2,300 tons in 1884 to 2,053,000 tons in 1909. As the world's fourth producer at that time, Galicia's future prospects in Europe were judged second only to those of Baku and Rumania. By 1914, large international consortia were vying for concessions. The French Société Anonyme de Limanowa, the German Deutsche Erdoel AG, the 'Allgemeine Osterreichische Boden Credit Anstalt' of Vienna, and the British Premier Oil and Pipeline Co. Ltd. all made large investments. In the event, their money was wasted. In 1915, the retreating Russian army fired the wells. After the war, the French companies who by hook or by crook had ousted almost all their rivals, failed to raise the capital to recover the damage. Production did not reach the 1909 level until 1960, under Soviet management.[9]

Foreign enterprise played a vital part in the development of Polish industry. At the turn of the century, foreign capital has been estimated to account for 60 per cent of the Congress Kingdom's industrial production. Kronenburg's *Bank Handlowy* (Commercial Bank) disposed of French capital from the French Crédit Lyonnais; whilst the Warsaw *Bank Dyskontowy* (Discount Bank) had connections with the Deutsche Bank. The German contribution was paramount. Quite apart from their role in the industries of Prussia which were eventually joined to Poland, German entrepreneurs, technologists, and financiers were active throughout the Russian and Austrian Partitions. In the Congress Kingdom, a significant part was also played by British men, money, and machines. The name of 'Evans Brothers', founders in 1822 of the machine business which grew into the mammoth company of Lilpop, Rau, and Loewenstein, holds an honoured place in Polish industrial chronicles, as do those of John Macdonald, manager of the first ever machine factory in Poland at Zwierzyniec, near Zamość in 1805; of William Preacher, the first manager of the Bank Steelworks; and of John Pounds Pace, a fitter, who lost his life in 1830 at Białogoń when the tails of his frock-coat caught in the fly-wheel of a lathe. It is said on good authority that the lathes which Pace installed on behalf of Richard Sharpe and Co. of Manchester, were still in operation in 1956.[10]

The growth of industry was closely affected by the changing patterns of trade, and in particular in the Congress Kingdom by variations in the Russian tariff barrier. From 1819 to 1832, and again after 1850, the Congress Kingdom was included in the Russian customs area and Polish manufactures could pass freely into the Empire. The exclusion of the Congress Kingdom from the tariff customs area between 1832 and 1850, for purely political reasons, provided one of the principal causes for the marked deceleration of industrial growth in those years. Similar variations occurred on the Prussian frontier. From 1823 to 1825, the Congress Kingdom fought a tariff war with Prussia, which ended in an agreement which limited both the import of Prussian manufactures and the export of Polish grain. Restrictions on the import of German goods, introduced by the Tsarist government in 1877, further assisted Polish exploitation of the Russian market. In the 1880s, Russian textile manufacturers were so unnerved by Polish competition that they made repeated calls for the tariff barrier to be restored. By 1890, 70 per cent of the trade of the Congress Kingdom was with Russia.

Industry was also greatly stimulated by the railway boom, which reached the Polish lands in the sixth and seventh decades of the century. Earlier projects, such as the line between Warsaw and Dąbrowa proposed in 1834 by the *Bank Polski,* did not come to fruition. But in 1859, the Dąbrowa link was added to the Vienna line, and in the following years Warsaw was joined with St. Petersburg, Moscow, Kiev, and Danzig. By 1887, the Congress Kingdom had 1,302 miles of track. Thereafter, railway building in Prussian Poland far outstripped that in the other Partitions. By 1914, fifty lines led to the Russian frontier from Prussia and Austria; only ten of them continued on the Russian side. What is more, with two different gauges and three different braking systems, the rolling-stock from one part of the Polish lands could not pass over the frontier into the other parts. As a result, the Second Republic did not inherit a unified transport system.[11]

The First World War brought both encouragement and distress to Polish industry. On the one hand, the increased demands of the war economy boosted production, and provided added employment, especially in Upper Silesia. On the other hand, the scorched earth policy of the Russian army, which took the country's entire rolling-stock with them when they retreated in 1915, and the depredations of the German army, which dispatched complete Polish factories to Germany, especially from Łódź, caused untold damage. The post-war slump was catastrophically severe. In 1920, coal production was running at only 72 per cent of pre-war levels; cotton at 44 per cent; pig-iron at 36 per cent; oil at 69 per cent.[12]

In the era of independence from 1918 to 1939, Polish industry did not begin to solve its problems until the eve of the outbreak of war; and between 1939 and 1945, the economic catastrophes of 1914–18 were revisited on Poland with added interest. Almost every sphere of economic life was left in a state of helpless paralysis by the physical destruction of industrial plant, by the reduction and dispersal of the labour force, and by the dismantling and deportation of entire factories. Once the fighting stopped, however, it must be admitted that the post-war government possessed several advantages over its pre-war predecessors. The assets and resources of Poland's newly acquired Western Territories were far superior to those abandoned in the east. The destruction of antique equipment made room for modern re-equipment. The presence of millions of displaced persons, who could be settled wherever the planners wished, created a unique opportunity for enlarging the urban proletariat, and for curing rural overpopulation, at a stroke. Poland's 'Second Industrialization' could then be launched under new management and in entirely new conditions.

CHAPTER SIX

LUD:

The Rise of the Common People

Sceptics might well dispute whether modern Polish society is a valid subject for scientific study. In an era when, as often as not, Poland did not exist, when most Polish institutions had been destroyed; when the descendants of pre-Partition society were merged into the societies of the partitioning states; and when large sectors of the population denied any sense of Polish identity, it is difficult to isolate sociological phenomena relating exclusively to the Polish population. One can describe the condition of the Polish-speaking element within the social structures of Prussia, Russia, and Austria, but, not it seems, an organic social process which is specifically Polish. This does not mean that there is a shortage of Polish social historians. In this regard, one is reminded of Conan Doyle's famous Red-headed League, where, at the instigation of some unseen red-headed patron, droves of red-headed investigators gather at the British Museum to copy down facts about red-headedness from the *Encyclopaedia Britannica*. The exercise can be undertaken; but its findings are of limited value – except to red-heads.

Certainly, repeated and drastic alterations to the social base of the Polish lands between 1772 and 1945, are bound to fragment the subject to an unusual degree. The continual partitions, annexations, and frontier changes; the mass mortality, deportations, and population transfers; the ephemeral nature of states which appear and disappear, all ensure that 'Polish society' has never encompassed the same collection of people at any two successive moments in time. Even if the historian does accept that Polish society did exist as a coherent organism, he must concede that it was composed of numerous separate cells, which divide and coalesce, reunite, drift apart, and come together again in no simple pattern. The threads of discontinuity are no less evident than those of continuity. External interventions have exerted greater pressure for change than have the autonomous, internal forces of the native social process. In this part of the world, history has acted over the last two centuries like a vast social mincing-machine, grinding its hapless human contents into new assortments and combinations without regard to their inherent wishes or predilections. The Polish society which finally emerged in 1945 bore little resemblance to the five estates of the 'noble democracy' which had been fed into the mincer in the late eighteenth century. The essential changes which occurred during this period — the destruction of the old estates, the rise of new social classes, and most recently, the manufacture of the classless society — were achieved in a piecemeal, disconnected fashion. Yet the net result is clear. The multinational, multilingual, multistratified society of the old Republic, ruled by its noble Polish *naród,* or nation, has been transformed over five or six generations into a far more homogeneous society where the *lud,* the common people of workers and peasants, have risen to a position of apparent supremacy.[1]

*   *   *   *   *

Polish demography is blighted by the same weakness that confronts Polish social history in general. Statistics have to be collected from five or six different regional sources, and remarshalled into categories which are blatantly unhistorical. Territorial anachronisms are rampant. Modern Polish demographers often assume that the eastern lands beyond the Bug lie beyond their proper historical concern, whilst treating the population of the 'Western Territories' of the People's Republic as if they had always been part of Polish society. One can rarely be sure that like is being compared with like, nor, if it is, whether the findings have any historical validity. By constructing coherent, unified categories for their researches, without which admittedly all their statistical information would be valueless, the demographers belie the most important fact of modern Polish society, namely that for much of the time it did not form a unified whole. Scientific accuracy is in direct conflict with historical reality.

The growth of population in the Polish lands since the Partitions is not easily computed.[2] In 1772, at the First Partition, the Republic of Poland—Lithuania counted about

14 million inhabitants. In 1795, at the Third Partition, on much reduced territory, it counted barely 6 million. In the nineteenth century, the population of the three central partitions — the Congress Kingdom, the Grand Duchy of Posen, and Galicia — rose from 8.3 million in 1820 to 23.7 million in 1914. Calculations based on the territory of the Second Republic reveal a drop of 4.6 million, from 30.9 million to 26.3 million between 1914 and 1919; a rise of 9 million to 35 million in the course of the inter-war period; and another loss of over 6 million by 1945. In the People's Republic, the population has risen from 23.9 million in 1946 to 32.8 million in 1976. In so far as figures from different sources are compatible, some surprising conclusions can be made. Firstly, notwithstanding the Jewish Holocaust of 1941—4, losses among the native population during the First World War from death and deportations (14.9 per cent) were not far short of those inflicted during the Second World War (17.4 per cent). Secondly, war losses of almost 11 million during the twentieth century did not far exceed the natural increase of just twenty-one years between the wars. Thirdly, despite the losses, the natural increase of the Polish-speaking element of the population, which in the two centuries since the First Partition has grown from perhaps 8 million in 1772 to some 35 million at present has kept pace with the European average.

Population density presents equally tricky problems. In the old Republic in 1772, it stood at 19.1 km^2. In the nineteenth century, it rose in the Duchy of Posen from 30 km^2 in 1820 to 72 km^2 in 1910; in Galicia from 50 km^2 to 104 km^2; in the Congress Kingdom, from 27 km^2 to 93 km^2. In this same period, taking the three central Partitions together, it rose from 35.4 km^2 to 94.8 km^2. Before the First World War the Polish lands stood in a similar position to that of the German Empire (104.2 km^2), holding a mid-way position between the two extremes of 132 km^2 in the British Isles and 21 km^2 in European Russia. By 1939 in the Second Republic, density fell to 90 km^2 in consequence of the sparsely inhabited eastern provinces. By 1971, in the People's Republic on a more westerly base, it has risen to 105 km^2, slightly higher than that of France (94 km^2) but well below that of Italy (180 km^2), Great Britain (228 km^2), or West Germany (239 km^2).

As a predominantly Catholic country, Poland has sometimes enjoyed a reputation for exceptional feats of reproduc-
tion. In effect, the reputation is not entirely borne out by
available statistics, and one can well imagine the motives of
the Protestant Prussian sources which originally propagated
the myth. Rates in the natural increase have fluctuated wildly.
At the end of the nineteenth century, a high birth-rate of
43.5/00 was offset by an unusually high death rate of 26/00.
Average life expectancy did not exceed 40 years. Taking the
century as a whole, the estimated rate of increase of the
Polish lands at 0.75, was less than that of Germany (0.85),
Great Britain (0.93), or Russia (1.06). The increase of the
Catholic Poles was slower than that of the Jews or of the
Ukrainians. In the twentieth century, exceptional population
explosions in compensation for war losses have not been
sustained. The natural increase − 14.3/00 in 1921−38, 19/00
in 1946−56 − has doubled the European average on two
occasions. After the Second World War, the birth-rate soared
well beyond 30/00 and briefly approached levels current fifty
years before; but in the 1960s it was falling rapidly. Like
most European countries, the People's Republic was destined
to experience the familiar pattern of 'bulge' and 'trough'.

Throughout the modern period and right until the Second
World War, the Polish population was overwhelmingly rural
in character. The urban population, estimated at a maximum
of 10 per cent at the Third Partition, had reached only 18 per
cent by 1900, 27.4 per cent by the census of 1931, and
31.8 per cent by the first post-war census in 1946. In this
respect, Poland trailed not only the countries of Western
Europe but also neighbouring countries such as Czechoslovakia
(65 per cent in 1931) or even the USSR (33 per cent in 1939).

Ethnic statistics are particularly suspect. Where kinship,
religion, and language are inextricably confused, no reliable
definition of ethnicity exists. In areas of mixed settlement,
especially on the western and eastern peripheries, intermarriage was widespread; bilingual and bireligious families
were not uncommon. People subjected to official questionnaires notoriously gave different answers to different investigators. Even so, it can be safely asserted that the Polish element
has steadily expanded its place in the population at large ever

since the seventeenth century. From an estimated 40 per cent in 1650, the Poles moved on to over 50 per cent by 1791, to 65 per cent by language in 1900 and 68.9 per cent in 1931, to 88.6 per cent in 1946, and 98.7 per cent in 1951. The People's Republic of Poland, exceptionally, is overwhelmingly Polish.[3]

*   *   *   *   *

The elimination of the Szlachta, the noble estate, was achieved by the progressive annulment of their legal privileges. In Galicia, a limited number of Polish families of senatorial rank were admitted to the nobility of the Austrian Empire. The Lanckoroński, Gołuchowski, Tarnowski, Potocki, Czartoryski, and Lubomirski families, and others like them, maintained their privileged status throughout the nineteenth century. In Prussia, too, noblemen with land were able to register their title, and to adapt to changed conditions without much difficulty. Only in Russia did the authorities take active measures to repress an estate which they regarded as incurably hostile to the Tsarist order. Successive registrations, in 1800, in 1818 in Lithuania, and in 1856 in the Congress Kingdom, provided the occasion to eliminate thousands of Polish families from the noble list. Successive confiscations, impressments, and reprisals after each of the Risings, had the same effect. By 1864, at least 80 per cent of the szlachta were effectively *déclassé*. Only the wealthiest and best-connected noblemen were permitted to enter the ranks of the Russian *dvoryanstvo*. In the process, they often acquired a new Russian life-style, which demanded strict political conformity and service, and permitted at least till 1864 such practices as the sale of serfs. In each of the three Partitions, it was the numerous petty nobility which suffered most acutely. It has been estimated that in the last years of the Congress Kingdom one-quarter of the *zaścianki* enjoyed a lower standard of living than the average serf. Deprived of all legal standing, some of the remnants of an estate which had once dominated the life of the old Republic, clung to their way of life in the countryside with dogged persistence; others drifted to the towns to be recruited into the professions, into government service, into commerce, into the intelligentsia; many sank without trace into the peasantry, and the working class. In 1921, the March Constitution of the 'Second Republic' formally abolished the noble estate altogether. Noble families of 'immemorial' ancestry, like those who had obtained their titles of *'Graf'* or *'Baron'* from the partitioning powers, lost all claim to separate legal status. (See Diagram C.)

The abolition of the noble estate, and the suppression of their legal privileges, did not necessarily disperse the landed property, the political influence or the social status of the ex-noble families. It was the greatest fortunes which showed the strongest instinct for survival. In the egalitarian aura of the Second Republic it was amusing to address a Radziwiłł or a Zamoyski as *'Pan'* (Mr) or *'Porucznik'* (Lieutenant), or whatever; but there was little pretence that the magnates had really been reduced to the level of common citizens. In 1919, Józef Potocki, speaking to Sir Harold Nicolson at the Peace Conference in Paris, could still describe his Prime Minister, Ignacy Paderewski, in the most patronizing of terms: 'Yes, a remarkable man, a very remarkable man. Do you realise that he was born in one of my own villages? At Chepetówka, actually. And yet when I speak to him I have absolutely the impression of conversing with an equal . . .'[4] For the Radziwiłłs and Potockis and their ilk were still exceptional by any standards. The greater part of the szlachta were merging fast into the population at large. Parcellation was nibbling into their estates. Landowning was in decline as a profitable enterprise. The younger generation was taking off into business, into the professions, into politics or public employment, into the Army. The Second World War completed what was already far advanced. The eastern provinces, where the great estates were concentrated, were annexed by the USSR. In the People's Republic, the Land Reform of 1946 redistributed landed property among all and sundry. Nowadays, everyone, and no one, is a nobleman.

The old *mieszczaństwo* or 'burgher estate' was not so much destroyed as overwhelmed. The reforms of the Four Year Sejm had been directed to an estate of puny proportions, which had been declining for two centuries. After the Partitions, Danzig until 1815 and Cracow until 1846 were the only cities to enjoy a measure of their former privileges and thus

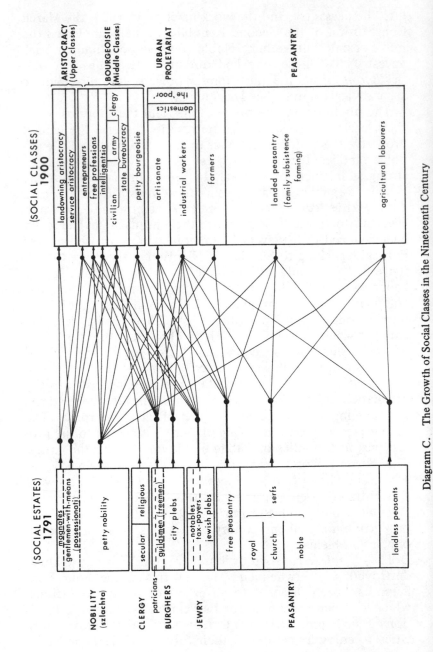

Diagram C. The Growth of Social Classes in the Nineteenth Century

to preserve the special legal status on which the fortunes of the burgher estate had been founded. Municipal charters were in force in the Congress Kingdom until 1869–70, when Russian practices were introduced and when large numbers of small towns lost their separate municipal rights completely. In the course of the nineteenth century, urban life was changed out of all recognition by the growth of new industrial towns and suburbs, whose inhabitants lived and worked without reference to the ancient order. Even so, several ancient institutions survived. The *Gildia* or 'merchant confraternity' was retained as a convenient means for organizing commercial taxation. The *Cech* or 'Guild' continued to function in the interests of those traditional trades and crafts which were not affected by the new habits of a mass labour-force, and was not abolished until 1948. The transition from the burgher estate, which had been defined by specific legal privileges to the ranks of the 'bourgeoisie' who were characterized by their social and economic function, was, for most families, imperceptible. Whether or not one described oneself or one's friends as *mieszczanin* (burgher), or *burżuj* or (bourgeois), depended largely on whether one intended to be polite.

The Jewish community, which to all intents and purposes under the old Republic had enjoyed the status of an autonomous estate, was subjected to the separate legislations of the partitioning powers, and was changed out of all recognition. By 1918, it had lost its exclusively religious identity and its legal privileges, and had been fragmented by a wide variety of social, economic, cultural, and political developments.

The emancipation of the serfs took place over some sixty years spanning the first half of the nineteenth century.[5] It was achieved piecemeal, by different authorities in different regions acting for different motives, and by different methods each with its particular virtues and vices. One method, first introduced in 1807 under French auspices in the Duchy of Warsaw and in Prussia, was simply to declare that all people were equal before the law. In theory, this put the serf on the same legal footing as his lord. In practice, by upholding the lord's title to possession of the land and by emphasizing the contractual basis of the new relationship between lord and tenant, it exposed the peasantry to new forms of exploitation.

Henceforth, if the peasant refused to accept the terms of employment or tenancy proposed by the landlord, he and his family faced eviction, homelessness, and destitution. As at subsequent stages of Emancipation, pretexts could be found to clear manorial land of peasants altogether. These *rugi* or 'clearances' were much feared, and discouraged the majority of peasants from insisting on their new-found liberties. Hence, most of the egalitarian ideals remained a dead letter. Personal legal freedom did not engender economic freedom. Another method, *oczynszowanie* or 'rentification', sought to transmute ancient labour services into money rents, thus bringing the feudal estates into line with land worked by the free peasantry. It was first practised in the late eighteenth century on the municipal estates of the city of Poznań, and on the great magnatial latifundia of the Zamoyskis, Myszkowskis, and Potockis: later in Prussia, in the Congress Kingdom, and in the Republic of Cracow. Unfortunately (from the peasant's point of view), it was usually attended by so-called *regulacje* or 'adjustments', whereby part of the peasants' holdings were ceded to the lord without compensation, together with their rights to free use of the forests, meadows, or mills of the village. In this way, the peasant was cast headlong into the cash economy with all its opportunities and dangers. At the same time, he did not gain full possession of the land. He could well find that the task of earning his rent and of supporting his family from a diminished holding was more burdensome than the tribulations of serfdom. Thus, by the early nineteenth century, it was widely recognized that the abolition of the feudal system could only succeed if the peasants were able to gain full possession of the land that they worked. Half-measures compounded existing problems. The economic efficiency, and the moral validity, of serfdom was called increasingly into question. One by one, inch by inch, the governments conceded the principle of *uwłaszczenie* or 'impropriation' whereby the serfs were granted the right to landed property.

Much, however, depended on the continuing political debate and on the conditions which landowners were able to insert into the various statutes of Emancipation in each of the three Partitions. In Prussia, the first step was taken in 1811 when a royal edict permitted the impropriation of state peasants in return for the cession of between one-third and one-half of their holdings. The reform of 1816 extended the process to the larger private estates. But only a small sector of richer peasants could hope to buy their land outright, and most had to think in terms of rentification. Land Purchase was confined to those peasants who already owned their own farm equipment, and it required the payment of a cash sum equivalent to 25 years' rent. It proceeded slowly over four decades. In the Grand Duchy of Posen, the local reform of 1823 furnished a solitary instance where territorial adjustments in favour of the landlord were accompanied by compensation payments for the peasant. Even so, mass clearances were so common that they had to be controlled by legislation. The class of landless agricultural labourers multiplied rapidly. The last group of serfs – the peasants of the smaller private estates under 25 morgs (6.4 hectares) – were released from their obligations in 1850. Overall, therefore, the process of Emancipation in Prussia was harsh but relatively swift. In some ways it resembled the contemporary campaign for Enclosures in England, but it telescoped the pains and stresses into four decades. In Austria, personal freedom and possession of the land were granted to the peasants outright at one stroke, by the Imperial Act of 7 September 1848. Within nine short years, over half a million Galician estates were transformed. In this case, the landlords were compensated by the government, which recouped its expenses through a new land tax levied on lord and peasant alike. Unfortunately, in the haste of the moment, the landlord's title to woods and meadows was upheld, and no attempt was made to resolve the confusion surrounding the *serwituty* (minor feudal services not involving labour) and the *propinacja* (the peasant's obligation to buy liquor in the lord's tavern). As a result, disputes dragged on for the rest of the century. In Russia, serfdom lasted longest of all. The *ukaz* of 1846, and its successor in 1858, made token attempts to encourage rentification, but did little to satisfy growing demands. It was left to Alexander II to realize that if measures were not taken by the government 'from above', then the peasants would take measures into their own hands 'from below'. In territories incorporated into the Russian Empire, full Emancipation was granted by the *ukaz* of 3 March 1861. In the Congress Kingdom, it became embroiled in the politics of the January Rising. Here, in face of a peasantry which had enjoyed personal freedom for half a century and which was being offered attractive terms by the land decrees of the secret Insurrectionary governments, the Tsar could not afford to hold back. The *ukaz* of 18 March 1864, was notably generous. Russian policy followed the Austrian example, seeking political advantage from social concessions and compensating the landlords from funds created by new taxation. (See p. 358.)

In the short term, the immediate, visible effects of Emancipation were slight. As a result of the 'adjustments', less than half of the farmland actually passed into peasant hands — 48.9 per cent in the Congress Kingdom in 1864; whilst 46 per cent remained in the hands of the hereditary landowning class. From the economic point of view, the peasant still lived at a distinct disadvantage *vis-à-vis* his former master. Only the wealthier element in the village benefited directly. If, over the next thirty years, some peasants were able to increase their holdings, purchasing lands from their indigent neighbours, both gentlemen and peasants, others could not prosper. The number of landless peasants quadrupled. Many of these had no option but to leave the village for ever. No clear solution was offered to the problem of the *serwituty*. Many villages lost all right to graze their cattle in the manorial pasture, or to cut timber in the manorial forest. Their chances of successfully prosecuting their squire in court were slim. Friction, disputes, and chicanery persisted. No clear advantage was gained by the replacement of manorial jurisdiction by the peasant commune (*gmina*). In Russian Poland, the peasant assembly (*gromada*) elected its chairman (*sołtys*) and its headman (*wójt*), whose activities were closely subordinated to the orders of the Tsarist police. In this way, the paternal rule of the local squire was replaced by that of foreign officialdom. In Prussia and in Galicia, the local squire was admitted into the workings of village administration, and his traditionally dominant role waned only slowly.

The material condition of the peasantry did not improve dramatically. Freedom did not necessarily engender prosperity.

Living standards barely kept pace with the pressures of the population explosion. Even in Prussia, the famine of 1863—6 spread sleeping-sickness in the countryside; whilst in Galicia emigration was widely accepted as the only alternative to a life of semi-starvation. The ancient three-field system maintained its hold in many regions until the turn of the century, perpetuating and ensuring periodic shortage of bread, especially in the spring. Scattered family strips were not consolidated. Potatoes, black bread, and cabbage formed the basis of the diet, supplemented by concoctions of turnips, beans, nettles, millet, buckwheat, couchgrass, origan, and even birch-bark, and sometimes by meat on Sundays. Dairy products were sent in preference to the market, whilst plain water was drunk more often than milk, grain, coffee, or vodka. Colourless, homespun clothes were the norm. The man wore a canvas shirt over loose trousers, his wife a linen shawl. The magnificently coloured regional costumes, which became the fashion after 1870, were reserved for Sundays and festivals. Shoes were doffed on leaving the church or the market, and in all but the harshest weather. The timber-built, thatched cottage, with its wood-burning stove and its single room sparsely furnished with primitive furniture, provided shelter but a minimum of comfort. Manufactured goods were expensive, and unobtainable by those sectors of the rural population who lived largely outside the money economy. Purchases concentrated on agricultural implements. Education was rare. The old ways changed very slowly. All convincing descriptions of the Polish village in the nineteenth century stress its traditional, eternal, human qualities:

. . . life burbled along with its usual deep stammer, splashing like running water, constantly overflowing in the same brisk exuberant stream. The village of Lipce lived its usual everyday existence. At the Wachników's there was a christening; at the Klebów's there was a betrothal, where they amused themselves well enough even without an orchestra, as it was Advent; elsewhere, there was a funeral . . . Jagustynka was taking her children to court over the division of her late husband's estate. Everywhere some affair or other was in progress. In almost every cottage, there was always something new to be discussed, to be derided or to be bemoaned. On those long winter evenings, the women would gather in various cottages, distaff in hand. My Jesus! What guffaws, what shrieks,

what gossip, what games were there, so much so that the merry ripples
spread into the roadway. On all sides, such quarrels, friendships, and
intrigues proliferated, such private schemes and public demonstrations,
such fussing brawls, and harangues as occur in swarms of ants or bees —
that the walls of the cottages shook from the uproar.

And each man lived in his own way, as he thought fit, as was most
convenient and sociable for him and for others, as the Lord God
ordained.

Whether people lived in want, in need or in troubles, whether they
lived roisterously, clanking their glasses with their friends, strutting
about and bullying their neighbours and chasing after the girls, or
whether in their feebleness they leaned against the warmth of the stove
waiting for the priest's last comfort — whether happy or depressed or
neither — they all lived lustily, with all their strength, with all their soul.[6]

As always, the peasants were distinguished by their profound attachment to the land, which was the source of their
security and the sole repository of their ambitions. According
to Leninist analysts, this link was weaker among the poorer
peasants, who, unable to compete with the *kulaks,* were
thought certain to increase in numbers and to provide sound
revolutionary material. In the view of other observers, the
distinction between rich, middle, and poor peasants was a
false one. Rich peasants did not aim to become large-scale,
gentlemen-farmers in imitation of the nobility; they clung to
the old ways, hired a few labourers to ease their old age, and
in the event of sickness, or a surplus of daughters, were resigned
to the inevitable decline of their family fortunes. The poor
peasants aimed for little more in life than to produce healthy
sons, to marry them well, to escape from debt, and to buy a
stronger horse. The 'middle peasant' was not a species condemned to extinction, but could be variously described as a
declining rich peasant or a rising poor one. Over three or four
generations, every peasant family expected to experience
alternating periods of prosperity and adversity. All accepted
the old routine of subsistence farming as a way of life. All
looked on the world, like the weather, with a fatalism born
from centuries of serfdom. All saw themselves as a race apart,
as different from the squire and the government inspector as
from the factory-slave or the landless agricultural labourer.
Nowadays, more than ten decades after Emancipation, they

THE RISE OF THE COMMON PEOPLE

THE RISE OF THE COMMON PEOPLE 191

can still be seen across the length and breadth of Poland.

All the indications are, therefore, that the Polish peasants were not just the members of a socio-economic class. Like their Russian counterparts, whom until the mid-nineteenth century they closely resembled, they were the bearers of a separate civilization, as distinct and as ancient as that of their noble masters. Their very name of *chłopi* was derived from that of the *Kholopy* — the slaves of old Slavonic society. Widely dispersed in isolated villages, they had little scope for concerted social action; but their powers of passive resistance were proverbial. Their imperviousness to the modern concepts of law and property: their inveterate addiction to pilfering, arson, and random violence; the inimitable rhythm of their work, where periods of back-breaking toil were interspersed with prolonged displays of idleness and drunkenness; their ambivalent relationships with their lord, the *pan*, whom they hated and loved by turns; their incurable beliefs in fairies, folk-magic, incantations, rituals, potions, faith-healing, and all manner of so-called superstitions; and above all their ineradicable conviction that the land was theirs, irrespective of the technical details of its legal ownership; all these things made for an ultra-conservative culture, whose values were obstinately preserved in spite of the dispositions of well-intentioned reformers. In the sixty or seventy years when Emancipation was in the air, the philanthropic master who cared to ask his peasants' opinion invariably received the same reply, in Poland as in Russia. *'My wasi',* the peasants said, *'a ziemia nasza'* (We are yours, but the land is ours). In other words, the peasants were not specially concerned about their personal freedom. As at any period in history, they had few objections to serfdom so long as it improved their security of tenure. In the nineteenth century, they only settled for Emancipation when they realized that it was the best way of reversing the encroachments of the demesne and hence of diminishing the lord's control of 'their' land. For the peasant who was happy enough to be tied to the soil and had no desire whatsoever to leave his village, Emancipation by itself was meaningless. Contemporary reformers, and modern social theorists, have ignored these factors at their peril. In later times, political innovators who advocate collectivization of the land have cast the communist state in the role of the feudal landlord, and have inevitably earned the peasants' undying hatred.[7]

None the less, in the long term, the effects of Emancipation were very important. Henceforth the peasants were free to move where they wished, to seek new employment, to make contracts, to buy and sell, to send their children to school, to organize themselves politically. Almost all the outstanding social developments of the last hundred years, from industrialization and scientific agriculture to mass education and mass politics, could not possibly have happened if a class, which in 1900 still included 82 per cent of the total population of the Polish lands, had not first been freed from the chains of serfdom. Emancipation spelled the end of the estate-based society and gave a major boost to social mobility. Seen in a wider perspective, it was the fundamental precondition for the full exploitation of new economic conditions and for the formation of new social classes.

The politicization of the peasantry began soon after Emancipation. Its characteristic manifestations appeared in the 1860s in the co-operative movement, principally in Prussia: and in the 1890s in the formation of peasant parties, principally in Austria.

The co-operative movement was originally concerned with popular Credit Banks, making short-term loans to the peasants for farm improvements or the purchase of machinery; but it soon spread into the realm of agricultural production and marketing. The peasant *rolniki* or 'farmers' circles' helped their members to make bulk purchases of fuel, grain-feed, and fertilizers, and to sell their meat, grain, or dairy products on favourable terms. They played a vital role in rural education and in improving farming methods. In the struggle with the Prussian Colonization Commission they entered the real estate business, buying land in competition with the government and selling it to Polish peasants. In that same era, especially in Silesia, they spread into food marketing. Under the influence of clerical pioneers such as the Revds A. Szamarzewski and P. Wawrzyniak, Polish workers were encouraged to form co-operative societies for buying food from the Polish peasantry, thus eliminating the German or Jewish middleman.

The stimulus given to the awakening national consciousness is obvious. The Prussian example was followed in Austria in the 1890s by the proliferation of the so-called *Kasy Stefczyka* or 'Stefczyk's Tills' — mutual credit societies organized on lines pioneered by F. Stefczyk (1861–1924) — and in Russia, with less success, by attempts after 1905 to found co-operative food stores. In the inter-war period, the co-operative movement, encouraged by the law of 1920, blossomed mightily. The Co-operative Union, *Społem* (Together), and its various successors opened branches in every region of the Republic, and was supported by every national minority. According to the figures for 1937, a total of 12,860 co-operatives represented 7,812 Polish, 3,516 Ukrainian and Byelorussian, 773 Jewish, and 759 German organizations: analysed by type, they counted 5,517 credit societies, 2,973 agricultural-food, 1,804 food consumer societies, and 1,498 dairies. Total membership topped three million. As shown by repeated attempts to bring it under central political control — in 1938 by the *Sanacja* regime, in 1939 by the Nazi and Soviet occupation authorities, and in 1948 by the People's Democracy — the co-operative movement represented a strong and independent feature of Polish social and economic life. Significantly enough Edward Abramowski (1868–1918), the leading theorist of Polish co-operativism and one of the pioneers of social psychology, advocated the concept of ethical anarchy, where the free will of autonomous social groups was given precedence over the claims of the sovereign state.[8]

The *Polskie Stronnictwo Ludowe* (The Polish Peasants' or People's Party, PSL) was founded in Rzeszów in July 1895, in prospect of the forthcoming Galician elections, by a group of politicians who had long been active in peasant circles. Jakub Bojko (1857–1943), Jan Stapiński (1867–1946), the long-serving editor of *Przyjaciel Ludu* (The People's Friend), Bolesław Wysłouch (1855–1937) and their associates, quickly rose to prominence both in Galicia and in Vienna. In the course of the next two decades they launched a party which was to remain a major factor in Polish politics for fifty years. For many reasons, however, they failed to mobilize the peasantry into a unified political force. Their influence in Prussia, and in Russia where a separate PSL *'Wyzwolenie'*

(Liberation) operated from 1915, was limited. Persistent differences over social priorities and political tactics, over attitudes to the landowners, the clergy, the national minorities, and the government of the day, led to constant schisms. The right-wing PSL-*Piast* under Wincenty Witos (1874–1945) parted company from Stapiński's radical PSL-*Lewica* (Left) as early as 1914. Further fragmentation occurred in 1926 with the secession of Dąbski's *Stronnictwo Chłopskie* (Peasant Movement). Brief appearances in Witos's coalition governments in 1920–1, 1923, and 1926, did no more to enhance the PSL's influence than did participation in the 'Centre-Left' Opposition in 1929, or the formation of the federated *Stronnictwo Ludowe* in 1931. The massive revival of the movement in 1944–7 served only to arouse the hostility of the USSR and the communists, who effectively organized its suppression.[9]

Among the new classes of the nineteenth century, the new middle stratum (meaning that part of society which lay between the old propertied class on the one hand and the peasants and workers on the other) was most unlike anything which had existed before. It coalesced round the core of the burgher estate, whose revival was envisaged by the Constitution of 1791 and realized in the life of the Duchy of Warsaw; and it drew heavily on the *déclassé* nobility and on the Jews. It included a numerous bureaucratic class, unknown in the old Republic: commercial, industrial, and financial entrepreneurs, the *burżuazja* (bourgeoisie) proper; a less prosperous grouping of professional and service families; and, as in all parts of Eastern Europe, an influential *inteligencja* (intelligentsia). Most characteristically, it contained a high proportion of Germans, Jews, Russians, and even Czechs and Hungarians: some assimilated, some not: some who were native born, and some who arrived from distant regions of the three partitioning Empires. Its activities were most in evidence in the towns of Russian Poland, less so in Prussia or in Galicia.

The prototypes of the *burżuazja* first appeared in the late eighteenth century. Two prominent figures, Antoni 'Prot' Potocki (1761–1801), one-time Palatine of Kiev, who combined a landed fortune with commercial business and who built a fleet of trading ships on the Black Sea, and Fergusson

Piotr Tepper (died 1794), one-time shopkeeper on Warsaw's Old Town Square, who lent over 11 million zł. to King Stanisław-August, were both bankrupted by the crisis of 1793. At that time, their individual fortunes were each estimated at 70 million zł., or approximately three times the entire annual expenditure of the Kingdom. Their successors included several banking and industrial dynasties. Jakub Epstein (1771–1843), one-time officer on Kościuszko's staff, made his fortune through French military contracts in the Duchy of Warsaw. His third son, Hermann E. Epstein (1806–67), farmed the Customs and Excise of the Congress Kingdom, was elected Chairman of the Warsaw–Vienna Railway Co., and ennobled by the Tsar. His grandson, Mieczysław Epstein (1833–1914), founded Warsaw's Discount Bank, owned the 'Zawiercie' firm, and served for thirty years as President of the Warsaw Stock Exchange. Leopold Kronenburg, a participant of the January Rising, was the proprietor of banking houses in both Warsaw and St. Petersburg, and was active in promoting railways and metallurgical industries. Hipolit Wawelburg (1843–1901), an international financier on the same scale, founded the influential Technical School in Warsaw in 1891. Jan Bloch (1836–1902), perhaps the king of Polish railwaymen, was remembered for his prophetic book, *Przyszła Wojna* (The Future War, 1898) which correctly predicted the economic consequences for Poland of war between Germany and Russia. In the world of industry, four English brothers, Thomas, Andrew, Alfred, and Douglas Evans, pioneered the machine industry. Stanisław Lilpop (1817–66), an engineer expanded their business into rolling-stock and machine tools. In Łódź, the Fraenkel, Poznański, and Geyer families of mill-owners presided over the growth of textile empires.[10]

The great bourgeois families were as rare, and as rich, as the ancient magnatial clans. The two often intermarried. Their success rested on the pullulating, ant-like activities of lesser businessmen — the merchants, brokers, restaurateurs, undertakers, insurance-agents, craftsmen — who serviced the life of the growing towns. In Poland, this *drobnomieszczaństwo* or 'petty-bourgeoisie' was marked by its strong Jewish element, by its inimitable 'jargon' and affectations, and by its fierce social ambitions. Except in those few areas where the industrial

proletariat appeared in force, it provided the only sizeable
barrier between the upper classes and the peasant masses.

The category of government employees covered a multitude
of sins. It ranged from several thousand Russian 'service
aristocrats' awarded land in Poland after the Risings, to professors, schoolteachers, inspectors, civil servants, army officers,
policemen, clerks, and woodsmen in the state forests. Here,
in view of the intensely political nature of government service
in the nineteenth century, sharp divisions of attitude developed. The schoolteachers in particular headed the movements
for national revival, and as such bore the recriminations of
their 'loyalist' colleagues.

In inverse proportion to the bureaucrats, the independent
professions were relatively sparse. Doctors, lawyers, journalists,
and technical consultants had frequently undergone a foreign
education in France or Germany. Here, rivalry between Jews
and Gentiles was at its most acute.

The prominence of the bureaucracy also gave special meaning to the intelligentsia. Unlike its counterparts in Western
Europe, the intelligentsia could never be equated, even broadly,
with the 'educated classes', and a degree of political disaffection was taken for granted. In Poland it developed after the
Partitions, and adopted the mantle of guardian of the national
heritage. The writers, critics, artists, and students at its core
were drawn from various social origins, but most typically
from ex-nobility. The dominant Polish element was joined by
imitators and rivals in each of the non-Polish communities.[11]

The role and status of the clergy also underwent important
transformations. In Russia and Austria the Catholic priest was
controlled by the secular as well as the ecclesiastical authorities.
The suppression of many monastic and teaching orders thrust
the parish clergy into the forefront of educational, and hence
of political, conflicts. Even so, the clergy were one of the
very few groups who could fairly claim to have retained the
substance of a separate estate.

Divergences among the middle stratum were considerable,
therefore, and all the component groups, defined on varying
criteria of wealth, function, and status, were bound to overlap.
They were united only by their common desire to be distinguished from the toiling masses. In so far as they flourished

mainly in the towns, they may be regarded as the urban partner of the landowning classes in the countryside.

Once peasant labour was free to move from the countryside into the industrial towns, the industrial proletariat grew rapidly. Although in numerical terms, it did not match its counterparts in the countries of Western Europe, it transformed the social scene in several well-defined localities. In Upper Silesia, in the Dąbrowa Basin, and above all in the Łódź area, entirely new proletarian concentrations sprouted where in 1800 there was nothing but green fields. All the main urban centres multiplied their population in the course of the century at least ten times over. By 1931, 12.7 per cent of the population of the Second Republic was dependent on industrial employment.

The condition of the Polish proletariat at the turn of the century however, did not invite superlatives. The squalor, the pressures, and the attitudes were reminiscent of scenes in England a century before. In Łódź, and in smaller towns like it, for people who still had their roots in the ageless routines of the countryside, life in a textile-mill was at once dark, satanic, and unavoidable. It was organized by a new race of entrepreneurs and managers, the so-called *Lodzermenschen,* who drove themselves and their employees with the same inhuman frenzy as their machines:

BOROWIECKI — But for us, in a factory where you are just one of a million cogs, it makes all the difference. We did not employ you in order to practise philanthropy, but in order to work: work, and nothing else. Here everything depends on perfect efficiency, on precision and harmony; and all that you're doing is to raise confusion . . .

HORN — I'm not a machine; I'm a man.

BOROWIECKI — At home perhaps. But in the mill, no one is asking you to pass an exam in the Humanities. In the mill, we want your muscles and your brain; and that's what we pay for. Here you're a machine like the rest of us. So just do what you're supposed to. There's no place here for bliss . . .

He was enveloped in stifling, super-heated air. The huge, sheet-iron frames were groaning like distant thunder, as they spewed out an endless stream of rigid, coloured cloth.

On the low tables, on the floor, on the trolleys, vast piles of material were stacked. In the dry clear air of the room, with its wide walls of window-glass, they shone with the dimmed colours of trench-gold, of purple with a glint of violet, of navy blue, of old-fashioned emerald-like sheets of metal with a dull, dead lustre.

Barefoot workmen, dressed in nothing but smocks, moved around silently and automatically, their eyes glutted by the orgy of colour, their bodies answering to the needs of the machines.

From time to time someone would look out from this fourth storey window on to Łódź which loomed through the smoke and fog. On one side, they looked out on to a thousand huddled chimneys, roofs, houses and leafless trees: on the other on to fields merging into the horizon, and on to a long line of low tenements strung out along a band of black mud between rows of bare poplars. The greyish, whitish, grimy expanse was covered with the remnants of the Spring thaw, and dotted here and there with red-brick factories which stood out from the fog with the dull tone of freshly skinned meat.

The machines howled incessantly; the transmission belts whined incessantly . . . Everything in the vast four-sided room full of sad colours, sad light, and sad people, moved in time with the gigantic metal driers − shrines of the despotical Power-God. Borowiecki felt on edge, and absent-mindedly inspected the goods . . .

'What a foolish lad!' he thought of Horn.

And then as he watched the droves of people working in silence − 'I was once like that myself . . .'[12]

Industrial wages in the era before the full expansion of the market economy form a subject of great complexity. In Polish history, with three Partitions to reckon with, it defies all generalizations (including this one). In view of the vast reservoir of manpower in the countryside, unskilled labour was cheap; and prior to Emancipation it had often to compete with that of unpaid serfs. Skills and services, in contrast, were at a premium. Differentials were bound to be large. Highly-qualified technicians possessed great earning power; labourers did not. Even so, in view of very low food prices, it is often surprising how much low wages could in fact buy. Statistics collected by Tadeusz Korzon from the last days of the old Republic show the Grand Secretary of the Crown earning 14,000 zł. per annum, a University Professor up to 10,000 zł., an architect 2,000 zł., a carpenter up to 1,095 zł., a common soldier, 262 zł. At the Małachowski's forge at Końskie in 1788, the forgemaster earned up to 8,000 zł. per annum, the lowest paid workman 4 zł. per week. At this same time, a pound of meat cost only 10 groszy; a pair of men's boots

15 zł.; a cow up to 50 zł., and a yard of the finest Tyzenhauz silk 18 zł.; the upkeep of a beggar cost the Warsaw Police Commission 280 zł. per year. From this, one might well conclude that it was better to be a Warsaw beggar than a royal soldier. Forty years later, at the Białogon Foundry, William Preacher, the English technical director, was paid 1,040 roubles (6,890 zł.) per annum; Jan Hurhaut, a mechanic, 600 roubles; and the factory carpenter, 110 roubles. At that time, a suit of clothes cost 200 zł.

The politicization of the proletariat took place at a slightly later date than that of the peasantry. The organization of proletarian political parties was preceded by the spontaneous formation of *związki zawodowe* or Trade Unions.

The Polish Trade Union movement sprang to life in Prussia and Austria in the 1890s, and in Russia after the Revolution of 1905−7. In the early decades, its constituent unions were extremely local in character. Being 'horizontal' in structure, with each union encompassing a wide variety of trades and interests, they could exert a strong influence in their particular factory or district, but defied any moves towards centralized amalgamation. They were subject to the most variegated political patronage. They were courted by nationalist organizations, by Catholic charitables, by Jewish, German, or Ukrainian societies, and in Russia by the Tsarist police. Socialist, and still less Marxist, inspiration was a relative rarity. Their first concern was for the pay and conditions of their members, not for political ideology or for national independence. Attempts to construct a common political front invariably failed. In the inter-war period, at least five separate Trade Union Federations came into existence, each claiming some measure of competence over the working class as a whole. The Union of Trade Associations (ZSZ), dominated by the left-wing of the PPS counting some 501,000 members in 1921, stood in constant rivalry with the Amalgamation of Polish Unions (ZZP), dominated by the National Democrats counting in 1919 some 570,000 members. Each spawned splinter organizations, but both contrived to avoid direct government control. The socialist Trade Unionists, headed by Jan Kwapiński (1885−1964), launched a successful drive to unionize agricultural labourers in the countryside. The communists, despite two decades of tireless effort, made little headway until they forcibly reorganized the Trade Unions on 'vertical' authoritarian lines after 1945.[13]

The parties which sought to champion the proletarian cause by more consciously political means were reft by the same divisions which beset Trade Unionism. The Polish Socialist Party (PPS) happened to be formed in 1892 at a moment when the revival of the national issue commanded more immediate interest than hopes for a classless society. As a result it was forced to compete for the attention of the new working class with less obviously proletarian organizations. In particular, it came into conflict with Dmowski's National Democracy, and with Dmowski's wayward child, the National Workers' Union (NZR), which from 1908 onwards acted quite independently. In the process, it was subjected to endless splits and schisms. The main schism of 1906 which propelled the PPS-*Lewica* (Left) on its road towards the anti-nationalist communist camp, and the PPS-*Rewolucja* (Revolution) on the road to its obsession with national independence, was never healed. Directing its attentions to Russian Poland, the PPS enjoyed little influence during the formative years over the Polish Social Democratic Party (PPSD) in Galicia, or over the tiny PPS of the Prussian Partition, with which in April 1919 it was eventually merged. Its rivalry with the communists, whose theoretical programme threatened to seduce its intellectuals, and whose tampering at the grass roots threatened to disrupt its mass organizations, rumbled on throughout the inter-war period. (See Chapter 22.) Its ambiguous relationship with Piłsudski, who had been one of its most militant activists, and with Piłsudski's Legions, caused endless complications. Its brief brush with power in the Moraczewski Government of 1918—19, was not repeated; and its experiments in opposition, with the peasants in the 'Centre-Left' block of 1929—30 and in the Popular Front with the communists in 1935—6, knew little success. None the less, whether in Sejm or Senate, in the Trade Unions or in youth organizations such as the 'Red Boy Scouts' or the 'Workers' Universities', it remained the leading force of the Polish Left; and, together with the PSL was one of the two mass political movements to survive the Second World War. Its leaders included Tomasz Arciszewski

(1877–1955), Adam Ciołkosz (died 1978), Ignacy Daszyński (1866–1936), Chairman in 1921–8 and 1931–4, Herman Diamand (1870–1941), and Mieczysław Niedziałkowski (1893–1940).[14]

Within the over-all growth of the Polish proletariat, the growth of Warsaw, the country's largest city with the largest concentration of urban workers, occupies a special place. In the nineteenth century, Warsaw's economic and social progress was hardly ruffled by the repeated political upheavals. The Risings of 1794, 1830–1, 1863–4, and 1905–6, though of enormous psychological importance, must be seen as minor interludes in the city's expansion. In the last decades of the old Republic, Warsaw had already become an important commercial centre, and was laying the foundations of future industrial enterprise. In 1784, in addition to the Royal Foundry by the Barbican, the gun-works at the Arsenal, the Porcelain Factory at Belweder (Belvedere), and the well-known Dangel coachworks on Elektoralna St., there were no less than 66 breweries, 27 flour-mills, and 31 brick-kilns. After the Napoleonic wars, the numbers of people seeking employment rose dramatically. The population leaped to 139,000 in 1840; 230,000 in 1861, 594,000 in 1900; and 764,000 in 1910. In the second half of the century, Warsaw attracted five main railway lines, and grew into one of the major junctions of Eastern Europe. Factories were built along the new lines of communication, especially in the western and eastern suburbs. The metallurgical industry gradually overhauled the older food-processing and textile sectors as the main employer. A full range of public services was duly installed, usually by foreign concessionaires. The German gasworks (1865) was followed by the Belgian, and later the Swedish, Telephones (1881), the English Waterworks and Sewerage (1882), and the French electrical Power Station (1903). The horse-tramway, which operated from 1865 to the First World War, was assisted by a network of narrow-gauge suburban trains.

Warsaw's city centre saw important architectural additions. Under the Congress Kingdom, the former Saxon Square was remodelled by Antoni Corazzi. Bankowa Square was adorned by the neo-classical façades of Lubecki's Palace, the Ministry of Finance, and the Bank Polski (1828). The Staszic Palace,

originally the home of the Society of the Friends of Science
and now the seat of the Polish Academy of Sciences, received
a Russian neo-byzantine facelift. Corazzi's Grand Theatre
was completed in 1834. After the January Rising, construction work was redirected to the roads, bridges, offices,
churches, and housing, which were required to service the
new suburbs. Broad modern boulevards, such as the Aleje
Jerozolimskie (Jerusalem Boulevard) and the Nowy Świat
(New World) were designed to provide rapid thoroughfares.
The Krakowskie Przedmieście (Cracow Faubourg) was
widened, and was linked to the newly paved riverfront. After
250 years of freedom, the Vistula was again spanned by three
permanent bridges – the Alexander Suspension Bridge (1865)
built by the engineer Stanisław Kierbedź (1810–99); the
strategic northern railway bridge (1876); and the lengthy
Poniatowski Viaduct (1912). Most of the city's twelve
boroughs received municipal halls, several of them, as at
Skaryszew or Praga, surrounded by squares and parks. The
thirteen city gates received formal arcaded pavilions. The
styles of the new churches were as eclectic as the religious
denominations which they served. The neo-gothic was
favoured by the Reformed Evangelical Church in Leszno and
by St. Florian's in Praga; the neo-romanesque by St. Peter-
and-Paul in Koszyce; the neo-baroque by St. Charles Borromeo
in Powązki; and the neo-byzantine by the numerous Russian
Orthodox churches. A start was made with municipal housing
schemes by the construction of workers' barrack blocks in
Czerniaków: in the organization of a municipal medical service
by the opening of 1866 of a hospital in Praga – an offshoot
of the ancient Child Jesus Hospital – and in the provision of
recreational facilities by the formation in 1889 of a 'Planting
Committee' devoted to parks and open spaces. None of these
developments were remarkable in the European context; but
they did turn Warsaw into one of the more modern cities of
the Russian Empire. Much of the initiative was due to the
long-serving Russian President of the City, General Sokrates
Starynkievitch (1820–92), who repeatedly intervened at
St. Petersburg with the Tsarist authorities on behalf of
Warsaw's welfare. Yet nothing could adequately conceal the
towering symbols of Warsaw's spiritual subjection. To the

north of the city, on the banks of the Vistula, the homes of 15,000 people were demolished to make way for the colossal Alexander Citadel (1831–65); in the city-centre, the architect Henri Marconi designed a splendid new Prison (1835) in Renaissance style — the infamous 'Pawiak'; on the Saxon Square, rose the intrusive silhouette of the Cathedral of St. Alexander Nevski (1912). The Citadel and the Prison were unmistakable reminders of Russian power; the Cathedral, with its five gilded domes and its detached Byzantine belfry, 240 feet high, the incarnation of Holy Russia, could be seen from almost every street corner.

In many ways, Warsaw was but ill equipped to deal with the tidal wave of urban immigrants. Most of the public services arrived very late, and proved quite inadequate to the demand. In 1890, only one house in three possessed running water, only one in fifteen any form of sanitation. The great majority of Varsovians were crowded into large multi-storied tenements, each built round an enclosed courtyard with its pump and well-head. Many streets were unpaved, or lined with open sewers. Electrical power was not generally available until the last years before the War. Typhus and tuberculosis claimed many victims. The death rate stood at 32 per thousand. Educational services were rudimentary. The one Russian University was fed by six boys', and four girls', secondary schools. Entry was largely confined to the 'protected' sons and daughters of Russian officials. At the primary grade, schooling in the Russian state system was less popular than private lessons in secret Polish or Jewish classes. In 1882, 46 per cent of the population had received no form of education whatsoever. The institutions of local government had never been allowed to develop. With the brief exception of Wielopolski's experiment in 1862–3, Warsaw had been directly subject to the Russian army authorities ever since the suppression of the November Rising. The City President, appointed by the Tsar, was checked by a Vice-president who traditionally acted as chief representative of the Third Department. All political activities were strictly controlled by the police. In this respect, Warsaw was deprived of the municipal liberties normal for all cities of comparable size elsewhere in Russia.

Varsovian society was transformed out of all recognition.

In the early part of the century, the urban plebs largely consisted of independent tradesmen and craftsmen, of whom in 1854 there were more than 15,000. In succeeding years, the growing labour force was rapidly drawn into dependence on larger firms managed by wealthy entrepreneurs. The number of industrial workers trebled and quadrupled, to reach more than 40,000 by the turn of the century. At the same time, a distinct class of blue-collar, or rather 'wing-tie', workers emerged, to staff the overblown bureaucracy. At the upper end of the social scale, the remnants of the city magnates were outpaced by the new German and Jewish bourgeoisie — by the Fraenkels, Epsteins, Rosens, Bergsons, Steinkellers, and Kronenburgs. Perhaps because poverty and despair were so common, Warsaw was marked by the struggling, grasping, ambitious men who were determined at all costs to exploit the opportunities which an expanding and overcrowded city afforded. Its streets were coloured no less by the beaux, the bohemians, and the businessmen than by the beggars, whores, soldiers, and Russian ice-cream sellers with whom they jostled. Its frenetic tensions and ambitions retailed in the popular literature of the day, were well satirized by Cyprian Norwid in his *Recipe for a Warsaw novel*:

> Three landlords, stupid ones: cut each in two;
> That makes six. Add stewards, Jews, and water,
> Enough to give full measure. Whip the brew
> With one pen; flagellate your puny jotter.
> Warm, if there's time, with kisses; that's the cue
> For putting in your blushing, gushing, daughter,
> Red as a radish. Tighten up, and add cash,
> A sack of cold roubles; mix well, and mash.[15]

Within the rapid growth of Warsaw's population as a whole, the growth of the Jewish community was particularly outstanding. From some 5,000 in 1781, Jewish numbers rose to 15,000 in 1810, 98,968 in 1876, and to 219,141 at the imperial Census of 1897. These figures represented respectively 4.5 per cent, 18.1 per cent, 23.8 per cent, and 33.9 per cent of the city's inhabitants. They can be explained partly by an extraordinary upsurge in the natural increase and partly by the influx of Jewish immigrants from the more easterly regions of the Pale. Overcrowding was intense. Unemployment, and underemployment, were rampant. Social tensions were unavoidable. Warsaw was steadily being judaized, and invaded by people unable to support themselves. Escape from the ghetto, though perfectly legal, was difficult. Conditions aroused widespread comment, especially among observers of the Left whose social conscience they affronted. Stefan Żeromski, for example, in the novel *Ludzie bezdomni* (Homeless People, 1900), painted the realities in compelling detail:

... Threading his way through the narrow alleys, and among the kiosks, stalls, and corner shops, Judym entered Krochmalna Street. This gutter, in the guise of a public thoroughfare, was flooded with stifling sunshine. A fetid smell, as from a graveyard, spread from the narrow gap between the street and the little square. Here, as always, the Jewish ant-hill seethed. An old Jewess was sitting on the pavement as she always did, selling beans, peas, and pumpkin seeds. Soda-water sellers were wandering about, with canisters at their sides and glasses in their hands. The mere sight of such a glass which that filthy pauper was clutching in his hand, smeared with congealed syrup, was enough to give one contortions. One of the sellers, a girl, was standing beneath the wall. She was dishevelled to the point of undress. Her face was jaundiced and lifeless. She waited in the sun, since passers-by on the sunny side were more likely to be thirsty. She was holding two bottles filled with some sort of red fluid. Her grey lips mumbled constantly, repeating perhaps some frightened curses on the sun and on life in general ...

To right and left stood a row of shallow shops, each of them like cupboards boarded over with paper, coming to a sudden end a couple of paces from the pavement. The wooden shelves carried a few cheap cigarettes, pickled eggs, smoked herrings, chocolate in tablets, sweets, slices of cheese, carrots, garlic, onion, cakes, turnips, dried peas, and redcurrant juice.

In each of these shops, a heap of black mud lay smouldering on the floor, and even in the heat preserved something of its natural humidity. Children, covered in dirty rags, were crawling all over it. Each such hole was the resort of several persons who passed their life there in gossip and idleness. At the rear, sat the father of the family, a greenish-faced melancholic, who never left his place from dawn to dusk, gazing out into the street in the hope of making his fortune.

One step further, one could look through an open window into a tailor's workshop, a dim cave with low ceilings, exuding a powerful odour, where men and women, bent and bowed, worked out their shortened lives. Right opposite, stood a hairdresser's salon, making wigs for devout Jewesses. It was one of several in a long row. Pale, sickly,

languid girls, dishevelled and unwashed, were setting the curls in position . . . From the courtyards, from the doorways, even from the rooftops, sick, lean, long-nosed, blotchy faces peered out with indifference
through patient, sorrowful, bloodshot eyes onto this world of misery,
dreaming of death . . . [16]

Time brought no relief. In the first two decades of the twentieth century, when the rate of increase of the non-Jewish
proletariat slowed down, the Jews of Warsaw stood fair to
attain the position of an absolute majority. By 1918, numbering some 319,000, they had reached 42.2 per cent of the
whole. It was a nice paradox; but at the moment of national
independence the capital of Poland contained virtually as
many 'non-Poles' as Poles. Warsaw not only sheltered more
Jews than any other city in Europe; it was only just losing to
New York the claim of being the principal Jewish sanctuary
in the world. Thereafter, Warsaw's Jews entered a period of
relative decline. In the 1920s, the renewed influx of peasants
into the city served to strengthen the Polish element; whilst
the Jewish community itself was reduced by the emigration
of many young people to the West. By 1939, the total Jewish
population had risen only modestly to 375,000. Their proportion to the population at large, at 29.1 per cent, had fallen to
levels current fifty years before.

In the Second Republic from 1918 to 1939, social reforms
in Poland achieved only limited success. But the social effects
of the Second World War overshadowed everything which had
happened in the century since Emancipation. All classes without exception were assaulted by the Nazi and Soviet Terror.
The educated and propertied classes suffered inordinately.
The national minorities were eliminated. The intelligentsia,
the landowners, the bourgeoisie, and the civil servants were
decimated. Almost all who survived lost either their property
or their previous source of income. By a sudden and terrible
process of elimination, only the peasantry and the proletariat
remained relatively intact.

In People's Poland, therefore, no social revolution was
necessary. The levelling of society had been largely accomplished by the War. Under the rule of a People's Democracy,
the common people were supposed to enter their inheritance.

CHAPTER SEVEN
KOŚCIÓŁ:
The Roman Catholic Church in Poland

The prime concern of the Roman Catholic Church in Poland, as in any other country, has always lain with the cure of souls. The first duty of the clergy has been to propagate the Faith, to administer the sacraments, and to tend the quick and the dead. Their main energies across the centuries have been directed more to the individual lives of the faithful than to the public life of the state and nation. Seen from the Catholic point of view, the Polish Millennium has witnessed an unrelenting struggle against ignorance and sin — a struggle in which the eternal values of religion had always to take precedence over the temporary considerations of the prevailing social order. To this way of thinking, where the salvation of one soul is thought to cause greater rejoicing in Heaven than the survival on this earth of the entire Polish nation, the Church has traditionally claimed to stand aloof from mere politics. It is a point of view that must be appreciated even by those historians who might claim to understand the Catholics' purposes more profoundly than the Catholics do themselves.

Yet it would be idle to suppose that the affairs of the Church could ever be satisfactorily abstracted from the secular world in which they exist. Even the most idealist Catholic would concede that the progress of the soul is achieved through the tribulations of the body; whilst materialist commentators find little difficulty in explaining the spiritual preoccupations of the Church in terms of its power, wealth, and status. The Roman Catholic Church has always been part of the world of Polish politics, whether it likes it or not. Not only in its corporate existence as a wealthy, ancient, and respected institution, but also through the actions and attitudes of its priests and people, it has exerted a powerful influence on all political developments. What is more, the history of the Roman Catholic Church provides one of the very few threads of continuity in Poland's past. Kingdoms, dynasties, republics, parties, and regimes have come and gone; but the Church seems to go on for ever.[1]

As a result of the Partitions, the ancient ecclesiastical Province of Poland was rent in pieces. The six dioceses of Galicia were subordinated to the Metropolitan Archbishop of Lwów. Six dioceses incorporated into Russia were subordinated to the Archbishop of Mogilev, who thereupon acted as Metropolitan to all Roman Catholics in the Empire. Five dioceses were transferred into Prussia. The metropolitan role of the See of Gniezno which in 1795 found itself in Prussia, in 1807 in the Duchy of Warsaw, and in 1815 back in Prussia, passed in 1818 to the newly created Archbishop of Warsaw who at the Tsar's request became head of the Church in the Congress Kingdom over seven recognized dioceses. These arrangements lasted for the next century, with only minor alterations. The Archbishop of Breslau, who administered the Church in Brandenburg as well as in Silesia, and the Bishop of Ermeland (Warmia), whose competence extended over the whole of Pomerania and West Prussia, were directly subordinated to the Roman Curia. The See of Cracow, which had declined to the status of a vacant vicarate, was promoted in 1875 to an Archbishopric, and was conferred in turn on three of the most powerful Polish churchmen of their day – Cardinal Albin Dunajewski (1817–94), Cardinal-Prince Jan Puzyna (1842–1911), and Cardinal-Prince Adam Stefan Sapieha (1867–1951). In 1925, the Concordat signed by the Vatican with the Polish Republic re-established a united Polish Province with five metropolitan sees, at Gniezno-Poznań, Warsaw, Wilno, Lwów, and Cracow.

The office of Primate underwent similar changes of status. Following the death by suspected suicide in April 1794 of Michał Jerzy Poniatowski, the King's brother and last Primate of the Republic, the vacancy was not filled. The primatial dignity was conferred between 1807 and 1818, on Count Ignacy Raczyński (1741–1823), Archbishop of Gniezno, who reigned over the Church in the Duchy of Warsaw and then in the Congress Kingdom. From 1818 to 1829, it was conferred on his successors in Warsaw, but thereafter never reconfirmed. In Galicia, it was conferred exceptionally on

Archbishop Andrzej Alojzy Ankwicz of Lwów (1774–1838). Since 1919 the office of Primate of Poland has returned to the See of Gniezno, and has been held in turn by only three men – by Cardinal Edmund Dalbor (1869–1926), by Cardinal Augustyn Hlond OJB (1881–1948), and since 1948 by the redoubtable Cardinal Stefan Wyszyński (b. 1901).

In the era of the Partitions, the governments of the three Empires did not hesitate to intervene in religious affairs in general, and in ecclesiastical matters in particular. In Austria, the Emperor Joseph II (1780–90) initiated a policy of subordinating Church to State. Appeals to Rome were forbidden. No papal or episcopal decrees could be published without imperial approval. Church schools and theological seminaries were turned into secular, state-run colleges. Some hundreds of monastic orders were abolished, and their property confiscated.

In Prussia, the Catholic clergy were supervised by the Protestant Consistory. The gradual dissolution of monastic property, begun in 1816, contributed to the upkeep of the secular clergy and to the state educational fund. An acrimonious dispute in 1839–40 over mixed marriages mirrored the events of the *Kulturkampf* of the 1870s.

In Russia, the gracious guarantee of religious liberty proclaimed by Catherine II at the time of the First Partition stood in marked contrast to the long and sorry history of persecutions to which the Roman Catholics, and especially the Uniates, were subjected. In the case of the Catholics, Tsarist policy was designed to subordinate all ecclesiastical affairs to the direct control of the secular authorities. The goal was to be attained by the strict supervision of all appointments; by the total denial of all access to Rome; by control of the Church's material resources; and from 1801, by the creation of a state-controlled supervisory body, the Sacred College in St. Petersburg. Once these provisions were instituted, the protests and demands of the Vatican could be safely disregarded. When it suited Russia's purposes, any Roman decree, including the dissolution of the Jesuit Order, could be ignored. The terms of the two Concordats, in 1847 and 1883, could be openly flouted. From an early date, the administration of the Roman Catholic Church in Russia was deliberately entrusted to a series of incompetents, and of imperial time-servers, who had no interest in defending their charge from the onslaughts of autocracy. As a result of the November Rising, almost half of the Latin convents of Russian Poland were closed, whilst payment of the stipends of the clergy was turned over to the state. Unauthorized correspondence with Rome was punishable with summary deportation. All sermons, pronouncements, and religious publications were to be approved by the Tsarist censorship. All seminaries were to be inspected by the Tsarist police. As a result of the January Rising, the great majority of Catholic orders were disbanded. The entire landed property of the Church was confiscated together with the estates of lay patrons of Catholic benefices. The conduct of the Sacred College was placed under the Ministry of the Interior, and all business between the College and the diocesan curias was handed over to lay police-approved delegates. In 1870, open conflict was provoked in the diocese of Wilno when steps were made to introduce a Russian-language liturgy. The most that can be said about religious toleration in Russia is that no attempt was ever launched to close the Roman Catholic churches wholesale.[2]

In the case of the Uniates, however, Tsarist policy aimed at total extirpation. The Uniates, whose forebears had abandoned Orthodoxy, were treated as renegades and traitors. The chosen method was that of forcible conversion to Orthodoxy. The campaign started in 1773, in the year of Catherine's proclamation of religious liberty.[3] In the following decades, an Orthodox 'mission' visited the former Polish provinces of Volhynia, Podolia, and Ukraine with fire and sword. Cossacks were billeted on recalcitrant villages, and given unlimited licence to plunder, carouse, and kill until the peasants submitted. Uniate priests were faced with the choice between submission or violence. Parents were threatened with the abduction or mutilation of their children. Resisters were tortured and killed. Apostates were given rich rewards. Along a trail strewn with blood and humiliation, with mass suicides and unrecorded martyrdoms, the missionaries of the Empress effected the confiscation of most of the Uniate churches, and the nominal conversion of some four-fifths of the Uniate population. Two further operations — one sponsored by

Nicholas I in the Russian Empire in 1827–39 and another by Alexander II in the former Congress Kingdom in 1873–5 – brought the campaign to its inevitable conclusion. On the first occasion, the Tsar formed a separate Uniate College in order to drive the Uniates from the protection of the Catholic hierarchy, and then ordered the merger of the remaining Uniate dioceses into their Orthodox counterparts. In celebration, Nicholas struck a medal with the inscription: 'Separated by hate 1595, reunited by love 1839'. On the second occasion, the destruction of the Uniate community in the Polish provinces served as a necessary prelude to the policy of Russification. As usual, it was undertaken at the point of Cossack lances:

At Pratulin in the district of Janów, the troops fired and killed thirteen persons. The expedition was led by Kutanin, the governor of the district and by a Colonel Stein. The survivors were cast into chains and sent to the prison at Biały, whither they walked to the singing of hymns . . . An old peasant called Pikuta, refused to submit, and his words were repeated by all the men of Pratulin in the Governor's presence: 'I swear on my white hairs, for the safety of my soul, and as I wish to see God at my death, that I shall not renounce one syllable of our faith, nor will my neighbours. The holy martyrs bore so many persecutions, and our brothers have spilled so much blood that we must imitate them.' When a woman was ordered to sign an Orthodox document on pain of exile to Siberia, she refused. 'Then we shall take your child'. 'Take it', she said, 'God will take care of it.' Having blessed the child, she put it into the hands of the thugs. She was called Kraiczikka . . .[4]

These scenes were re-enacted in village after village. Eventually, the Uniate Church was so wasted that it could take but little advantage of the brief interlude of toleration in 1906–14. Wherever possible, its adherents took refuge among their co-religionists across the frontier in Galicia. The Terror to which they were subjected, for reasons of undiluted bigotry, was the true spiritual ancestor of the ideological purges of the Soviet period.

The true temper of Russian policy can be gauged, among other things, from the legislation on relations between the Catholics and the Orthodox. Catholic priests were forbidden to administer the sacraments to anyone except to their registered parishioners, and by a clause of the Concordat of

1847 immediate exile in the Siberian *gubernias* of Tomsk or Tobolsk awaited Catholic converts from Orthodoxy. Mixed marriages were virtually impossible, not because of the Catholic rules governing the religious education of children, but because the Tsarist authorities claimed the right to take such children into state care. At the same time, every encouragement was given to Catholic apostates. On condition of their conversion to Orthodoxy, Catholic convicts were granted official absolution from their crimes, whilst their wives were permitted to divorce and remarry. Contrary to the usual practice of the Russian Church, ex-Catholic priests were given licence to take a wife after their Orthodox ordination.

The stance of the Vatican, was, to say the least, ambiguous. Although some controversy surrounds the motives of individual pontiffs, it is a simple fact that the Roman Curia failed to convince Polish Catholics of their good intentions. Throughout the period of the Partitions, the Vatican showed itself to be negligent, if not openly hostile, to Polish aspirations. Alienated by the strong link between national liberation and social radicalism, the Curia saw no reason why the Church should intervene too energetically with the Powers on the Poles' behalf. In an era when Tsardom was seen as the chief guarantor of the social order, *'Render unto Caesar'* was the recommended text in all political matters. Polish Catholics were constantly enjoined to turn their thoughts to things eternal, and to leave the affairs of this world to the legitimate, anointed authorities. In the 1790s, the agony of the old Republic was viewed in Rome as a fitting reward for the Jacobins and libertarians who had supposedly led their country to disaster. In the post-Napoleonic decades, the maintenance of the Holy Alliance, and by implication the perpetuation of the Partitions of Poland, was accepted as Rome's first diplomatic priority. At the end of the century, an encyclical of Pope Leo XIII openly commended the principle of Triloyalism to all the Polish bishops. Of course, it would be wrong to imagine that the Vatican enjoyed perfect relations with the partitioning powers. Constant difficulties arose not only with Orthodox Russia and Protestant Prussia, but also with Catholic Austria, where the Josephine spirit lingered on. None of the ruling Empires was prepared to grant

the Catholic Church unrestricted control over its appointments, over its property, or over the education of youth. For
this reason, the Vatican was not prepared to risk further
deterioration in Church—State relations. The Popes had no
direct means of exerting pressure on rulers who contravened
the declarations of religious toleration; but by failing to
speak out in public in defence of justice and compassion,
they lost a large measure of their moral standing.[6]

The Vatican's failure to support successive Polish Risings
gave deep offence in Poland. Despite the fact that the Confederates of Bar saw themselves as champions of the Catholic
faith, neither Clement XIII nor Clement XIV uttered a word
in their defence. The latter pontiff openly welcomed the
First Partition on the grounds that the 'Apostolic Empress',
Maria Theresa, could henceforth protect the Church more
effectively. In 1792, Pius VI blessed the efforts of the Confederation of Targowica, 'to bring calm and happiness to the
Republic'. In 1793, he rejected the Polish ambassador's
appeals for aid against Russia; and in 1795, horrified by the
confiscation of Church silver and the lynching of prelates by
the Warsaw mob, he ordered the hierarchy to co-operate in
full with the partitioners. In 1832, Gregory XVI condemned
the November Rising in terms which later he found hard to
retract. 'These terrible calamities', he wrote in an encyclical to
the Polish bishops, 'have no other source than the manœuvres
of certain purveyors of fraud and lies who use the pretext of
religion to raise their heads against the legitimate power of
princes.' During the January Rising, Pius IX delayed his criticisms of Russian conduct until the insurrectionaries were
virtually defeated. His encyclical of 24 April 1864, berating
'the potentate who oppresses his Catholic subjects' began
with the unhappy words *Vae mihi quia tacui* (Woe to me that
I kept silent . . .). At the end of the century, the association
of Polish nationalism with Socialism, especially in the programme of the PPS, caused the Church constant misgivings.
Not until August 1920, when the future Pius XII, then papal
Nuncio in Warsaw, stood on the ramparts of Radzymin and
cursed the advancing hordes of Antichrist in person, did the
Vatican express any obvious sympathy for the Polish cause.

The Vatican's apparent indifference could not be easily

explained to Polish Catholics, many of whom had clung to their faith as a last consolation against alien oppression. In intellectual and patriotic circles, it formed a subject for ribald satire. No one could deny the force of the famous conversation in Słowacki's drama *Kordian*, where the Polish hero is granted an audience with the Holy Father and begs his indulgence:

A tapestried room in the Vatican. The Pope, in golden slippers sits in an armchair. Beside him, on a golden three-legged tiara stands a parrot with a red neck. A Swiss Guard, opening the doors for Kordian to enter, announces him loudly:

SWISS GUARDSMAN: Count Kordian, a Pole.

POPE: Welcome, kinsman of Sobieski. (*He extends his foot. Kordian kneels and kisses it*). Poland is continually overwhelmed by benefactions from Heaven, is she not? Daily, I thank God in the name of this happy land. For the Russian Emperor, like a veritable angel bearing an olive branch, is ever most favourably disposed to the Catholic religion. We ought to sing Hosanna . . .

PARROT: (*raucously*) Miserere.

KORDIAN: Holy Father, I bring you a sacred relic. It is a handful of earth from a place where ten thousand men, women, children, and old folk were murdered . . . without the blessing of the sacraments. Treasure it where you treasure the presents of the Tsars, and give me in return a tear, only a tear.

PARROT: Lacrymae Christi.

POPE: Down, Luther, down! What, my son, have you not seen St. Peter's, the Circus, and the Pantheon? On Sunday you must hear our tenor in the choir of the Basilica, newly arrived from Africa . . . Tomorrow you shall see me in all my glory, dispensing blessings 'to the city and the world'. You shall see whole races on their knees before me. Let the Poles pray to God, reverence the Tsar, and hold fast to their religion.

KORDIAN: But this handful of bloody earth? Does no one bless that? What shall I tell my friends?

PARROT: De profundis clamavi, clamavi.

POPE: Down, Satan, down . . . My son! May God guide thy steps, and grant that thy people cast the seeds of Jacobinism from their bosom, henceforth devoting themselves entirely to the worship of God and the cultivation of the earth, holding nothing in their hands but litany, rake and hoe.

KORDIAN: (*throwing his handful of earth into the air*) I scatter the ashes of the martyrs to the four winds. I return to my native land with a sorrowful heart.

POPE: If the Poles be conquered, thow canst be sure I shall be the first to excommunicate them. May religion increase like an olive tree, and the people live in peace in its shade!
PARROT: Hallelujah.[7]

This scene, truly Dantean in its bitter irony, was written in 1828 as a piece of fiction, but it correctly anticipated Pope Gregory's attitude to the November Rising. No amount of apologies and corrections issued by the Vatican in subsequent years could atone. The damage had been done. Later, Gregory XVI claimed to have been deceived by the Russian ambassador, and eventually denounced 'the congenital duplicity of the Church's enemies' in a secret speech in Consistory. But few people in Poland ever heard of that.

Despite the Tsarist government's refusal to compromise over the treatment of Catholics and Uniates, political pressures drove the Vatican to regulate its relations with Russia wherever possible. Not surprisingly, the Concordat of 1847, signed on the initiative of the reforming Pius IX, soon proved to be an empty instrument. Remonstrations by the western powers at the Conference of Paris, where Russia was obliged to restate its adherence to religious liberty, actually provoked the Tsarist authorities to increase their harassment of Catholics. The suppression of the January Rising was followed by a wave of terror. On this occasion, the Pope's initial reticence was interpreted in St. Petersburg as a sign of weakness, whilst his belated protests inspired a vindictive response. In an audience in December 1865, the Tsarist chargé d'affaires in Rome insolently told the Pope that 'Catholicism is equivalent to Revolution'. A formal break in relations was unavoidable. In the ensuing period, the Catholic Church in Russia survived a concerted attack, which did not end until the signing in 1883 of a second Concordat as inconclusive and as unsatisfactory as the first. There was simply no means whereby an autocratic government could be constrained to honour its obligations. As a result, ordinary people in Poland were sorely tempted to think that the Holy Father had abandoned them, and hence to believe that their own brand of Catholicism was more Catholic than the Pope.

The traditional practices of the Church were defended with vigour against all the innovatory ideas of the Age. The torrent of speculative philosophy emanating from Germany was viewed in Catholic circles as a new Reformation, and when Polish Messianism began to assume religious as well as political overtones its propagators soon earned ecclesiastical condemnation. In this respect, both the writings of Bronisław Trentowski (1808–69) in Freiburg and the activities of the adventist sect founded among Polish émigrés in Paris by Andrzej Towiański (1799–1878) were roundly denounced. Among many writers who entered the list in defence of conservative Catholic values, Feliks Kozłowski (1803–82) published a critique of Trentowski entitled *Początki filozofii chrześcijańskiej* (The Beginnings of Christian philosophy, 1845). Michał Grabowski (1804–63), dubbed 'the Primate' of Catholic publicists, attempted to steal the thunder of the nationalist Romantics by writing historical novels of a distinctly sentimental and devotional flavour. In the company of Bishop Ignacy Hołowiński (1807–55) and of his fellow novelist, Henryk Rzewuski, he organized the so-called 'Côterie of Saint Petersburg' – a group of ultra-loyalist, ultra-Catholic Poles centred in the Russian capital around the weekly *Tygodnik petersburgski*. Favoured both by the Tsarist authorities and the Roman hierarchy, they nourished a distinct branch of Polish public opinion which lasted throughout the nineteenth century.

None the less, the Polish clergy frequently shared the radical ideals of national and social reformers. The low clergy in particular, who knew the privations of the common people and the impositions of officialdom at first hand, professed a far more fundamental brand of Catholicism than their superiors, and supplied a steady stream of activist recruits to the political movements of their day. No account of the Confederation of Bar would be complete without the jeremiads and political prophecies of the almost legendary 'Father Marek'.[8] Slightly later, the Revd Franciszek Ksawery Dmochowski (1762–1808) started life as a modest schoolteacher of the Piarist Order; but his career led him into active politics in Kołłątaj's 'Smithy' and Kościuszko's Rising; to immense literary achievements as translator among other works of *Paradise Lost* and the *Iliad;* and eventually to Protestantism, marriage, and the secretaryship of the Society of the Friends of Science. In a later generation, the Revd Piotr Ściegienny (1801–90), sometime Vicar of Wilkołąż near Bełz, founded a famous revolutionary conspiracy among the peasants of the Lublin area. The Revd Stanisław Stojałowski (1845–1911), a pioneer of rural education and of agricultural co-operatives, was the founder of the Christian-People's Movement (SCh-L) in Galicia. In the inter-war period, the Revd Eugeniusz Okoń (1882–1949), a fiery orator from the Lublin region, voiced the most urgent demands for agrarian reform in the Sejm of the Second Republic. These names form but the visible tip of a huge company of anonymous Catholic priests who spent their lives submerged in the service of their parishes, agonizing between needs of their flock and the reticence of the hierarchy. As might be expected, the great majority did not openly rebel, and held to the traditional discipline of their calling. But those who *did* break loose, attacked the ills of society with a fury that often surpassed that of their secular colleagues. Over one thousand Polish priests were exiled to Siberia in the period 1864–1914. Their temper was clearly reflected in Piotr Ściegienny's *Letter of the Holy Father to Peasants and Craftsmen,* written in 1842. This political tract, which was disguised as a supposed encyclical from the luckless Gregory XVI, contained a simple man's guide to the principles of Christian socialism, and detailed proposals for social revolution:

Go, and teach the nations — those are the words of Christ.

I, Pope Gregory, in the name of Jesus Christ, Son of the living God, hereby grant fifteen years' indulgence to anyone who reads this letter or listens to it attentively five times over. In the name of the Father, the Son, and the Holy Spirit, Amen . . .

I have already appealed to those who oppress you that they accept you as people and that they do not oppress you with labour services, rents and gifts in kind: I have even begged your Kings and Emperors that they should not burden you with taxes, nor send you to war and slaughter like cattle, nor waste your blood in their own interest . . . but their hearts are hardened . . .

My children, you know not what happiness is. Born in slavery, you think that God created you to suffer cold and hunger, to work not for yourselves but for the landlords, and to live in the grossest ignorance . . . But I tell you that God created all people, including you, so that all should use his divine gifts freely, labouring only for yourselves, for your wives and children, for the old and sick . . . God, my brothers, gave you the land, gave you will, understanding, and memory, gave you everything necessary for a comfortable and happy life . . . If, therefore, you are poor and miserable, it is not through God's will, but through your own will or that of evil people . . .

God commands that you love your neighbour as yourselves . . . And everyone is our neighbour, whether Catholic or Jew, Pole or Ruthene, Russian or German, soldier or craftsmen, peasant or lord; for all people are brothers and should love each other like friends . . . But whosoever desires your misfortune is your enemy . . .

Your enemies are not so many that you cannot prevail over them. Only the will is lacking. If each defends the other from attack, you will prevail. If not, if each looks aside at his neighbour's ills, you will all perish.

When you see and hear that your neighbour is being beaten on the demesne, do not assist his tormentors but help and defend him. What he suffers today, you will suffer tomorrow.

It is you who by your labour feed and clothe the lords; and in return they despise you, and call you Hams, hounds, dogcatchers, and thieves. This should not be . . . What should be is that every married man should have his own parcel of land . . . his own house, barn, cattle, and farm utensils . . . and that every person should read and write . . .

You say, if you fail to do your duties, that the soldiers will come and force you. But the soldiers, my brothers, should not coerce you. After all, who are these soldiers whom you fear so much? They are your own children, your relatives, your friends . . . The soldiers should depose the lords and kings as enemies of human kind, and should hold to the peasants . . .

Wars, my brothers, shall soon come to an end, and man shall no longer kill men. One last war alone must happen, a war of justice, in defence of your families, of your loved ones, of your Freedom, of your rights . . . This war will not be fought by peasant against peasant, by the poor against the poor, but by the peasant against the lord, by the poor against the rich, by the oppressed and unhappy against the oppressors and the affluent . . . by Poles and Russians together against the kings and lords . . .

You know how a lord holds to a lord, and a Jew to a Jew. So must the poor and hungry hold to the poor and hungry. Do not obey the lord or the priest who would persuade you to side with the monarchs . . . But good lords you should obey, and love, for they can help you mightily.

You must believe, dear children, that I Pope Gregory, heartily desire your happiness. For this reason I do enjoin you in God's name to do

what I tell you: firstly, that you forsake all liquor until you have overcome your enemies . . . secondly, that one man at least in every village
should learn to read and write . . . thirdly, since kings, officials, landlords, officers, and many priests do not wish for your freedom, that
you should not read this letter to any unknown person, to any drunkard,
to any publican, flunkey, secretary, bailiff, organist, elder, or mayor . . .

As I tell you, it is fitting that you all know and understand your own
Good, your own interest and your own happiness which you will only
achieve when you all act on it together . . .

My dear children, I expect that you will heed the advice that I have
given you, and that you will calmly and confidently prepare for the
great change which will soon occur to your advantage.[9]

For his pains, Ściegienny was condemned to an indefinite term
of hard labour in Siberia. Yet his reputation lived on. The
peasants of the Lublin area were still singing ballads about
him in the twentieth century.

Trapped between the ultra-conservative stance of the
Vatican on the one hand, and the radical tendencies of the
lower clergy on the other, the Polish bishops possessed little
room for political manœuvre. In conditions prevailing from
the mid-eighteenth century onwards, it was most unlikely
that any churchman of independent mind would ever have
been promoted to the episcopate. In the last decades of the
old Republic, most of the bishops were in the pay of Catherine
II. In the nineteenth century, the hierarchy was closely bound
by ties of class and family to the ruling élite of the Empires.
They were congenitally biased against radical politics of any
sort. In addition, they were well aware that open expressions of dissent could swiftly deprive them of all influence.
The fate of Bishops Załuski and Sołtyk, deported to Russia
by Repnin in 1767, stood as a constant reminder for would-be
martyrs; whilst the sight of their vacant sees, handed over to
civilian administrators, made anyone who valued his position
think twice. The See of Cracow was kept vacant in this way
by the Austrians for forty-eight years, in consequence of the
expulsion in 1831 of Bishop Karol Saryusz Skorkowski
(1766–1851). The See of Warsaw was occupied for only
eight years between 1829 and 1883, the See of Wilno for only
seventeen years between 1815 and 1918. Only one of fifteen
suffragan bishops envisaged by the Russian Concordat of 1847

was actually installed during its currency. Still more humiliating was the Tsarist practice of inserting blatantly disreputable political appointees, unapproved by Rome, into the highest positions on the episcopal Bench. Catherine II's imposition of Gabriel Podoski as Primate of Poland was matched by her elevation of Stanisław Bohusz-Siestreńcewicz (1731–1826), an ex-Lutheran chaplain of the Russian army, to the metropolitan Archbishopric of Mogilev, or by Nicholas I's installation of one Jozef Siemiaszko (died 1868), an unbridled careerist, as Uniate Bishop of Wilno and chief administrator of the Uniate College. Appointments of this sort were clearly designed to destroy the integrity of the Church. Most Polish bishops, therefore, lived in an atmosphere of thinly veiled intimidation. Many succumbed. Some, especially in Prussia, were able to reach a working compromise with their political masters. Ignacy Krasicki (1735–1801), Bishop of Warmia and eventually Primate of Poland, contrived to divide his time between the Court of Stanisław-August, where he was a prominent literary figure of the Polish Enlightenment, and the Court of Berlin, where he was a frequent house guest of the Prussian Kings. In a later age, Archbishop, and later Cardinal, Aleksander Kakowski (1862–1939), served during the First World War as a willing figure-head of the Germans' Regency Council. The number of Polish prelates who chose the path of defiance was not exorbitant.

Yet the episcopate did make its contributions to the roll of patriots and martyrs. In the repressions that accompanied the January Rising, the least expression of dissent could provoke the direst consequences. In 1863, Bishop Adam Krasiński (1810–91) of Wilno was summarily abducted to twenty years' exile in the depths of Russia for daring to make an offer of mediation between the Tsar and the insurrectionists. Archbishop Zygmunt Feliński (1822–95) of Warsaw, the personal nominee of Alexander II, suffered a similar fate for raising the question of Polish autonomy in a private letter to the Tsar that was leaked to the French press.[10] In 1868, Bishop Wincenty Popiel of Płock (1825–1913) was deported for resisting the imposition of lay delegates to the Sacred College. In 1869, Bishop Konstanty Łubieński (1825–69) of Augustów died from maltreatment during his transportation to Russia.

During the Russian Revolution, the Polish hierarchy in the eastern provinces suffered still more severely. Archbishop Jan Cieplak (1857–1926), the last Catholic metropolitan of Mogilev, was arrested by the Bolsheviks, and died soon after his return from a Soviet prison. Monsignor Konstanty Romuald Budkiewicz (1867–1923) of Wilno, like many anonymous victims among the lesser clergy, was shot.[11]

In the later nineteenth century, whilst upholding its conservative social philosophy, the Catholic Church was drawn increasingly into all manner of social and cultural enterprises, and eventually into party politics. Traditional charitable activities among the sick, the poor, and the young were extended into the factories, trade unions, publishing and intellectual circles. The *Chadecja* (Christian Democratic Movement) was founded in 1902 to counter the popularity of Socialism, and to moderate the influence of Dmowski's National Democracy. Originating in Poznania as a by-product of the conflict over the language issue in schools, it gave rise in 1905 to a similar movement in Russian Poland, the 'Association of Christian Workers' (SRC), and in 1908 in Galicia to the 'Christian Social Movement' (SCS). In terms of numbers, it soon gained a dominant position in the Polish working class, especially in Poznania and Silesia. Its leading figures included Władysław Korfanty, Karol Popiel, and Bishop Stanisław Adamski (1875–1926). Its main press organs included *Polonia, Rzeczpospolita,* and *Głos Narodu* (The Voice of the Nation). A veritable renaissance of Polish Catholicism ensued. Thrown into the thick of social conflict, young Catholic activists were obliged to rethink the intellectual foundations of their Faith, and to redefine their goals. In the population at large, the cult of St. Francis of Assisi whose *Fioretti* has appeared in a Polish translation by Leopold Staff, answered a strong need for simple, humble Christian virtues in a complicated, arrogant, pagan world. In the seminaries, especially of the Polish Dominicans, Thomist philosophy enjoyed a marked revival, which led in the first months of Independence in 1918 to the foundation of the Catholic University of Lublin (KUL).[12]

The assertion of specifically Catholic values added a new dimension to Polish intellectual life. Journals such as *Prąd*

(Trend) and the Jesuit *Przegląd Powszechny* (General Review) in Cracow, and writers and theologians such as Walery Gostomski (1854–1915) or Jacek Woroniecki (died 1949), dissociated themselves from clerical conservatism no less than from 'godless socialism' or 'loveless nationalism'. The new generation of Catholic intellectuals who first made their appearance before the First World War took a neutral position in the current debate between Socialists and Nationalists, between Piłsudski and Dmowski, between Left and Right. They were offended by the blasphemous messianic metaphors of the insurrectionaries with their visions of 'Poland – the Christ of Nations' and embarrassed by the xenophobic, and frequently anti-Jewish utterances of the chauvinists. Christian charity and loyalty to Rome both combined to raise them above the petty concerns of national politics, and yet to provide them with a distinct moral viewpoint on all the important issues. In the course of the twentieth century, as the stock of Polish Nationalism and Polish Socialism has been steadily discredited, they and their successors have gradually emerged as the strongest and most independent element of the Polish intelligentsia. Without them, the Roman Catholic Church could never have aspired to its present role as the bastion of non-communist culture, and the focus of the loyal opposition.

In some ways, however, extreme forms of Polish nationalism did impinge on religious life. There had always been a strong temptation to make Catholicism the exclusive touchstone of national identity, and there were many clerics, as well as popular demagogues, who gave way to it. The dangers were obvious. When a Catholic apologist proclaimed that 'there are only as many good Poles as there are good Catholics', he probably thought that he was making a contribution to public morality.[13] In effect, he was gratuitously insulting all the non-Catholic Poles, and all the non-Polish minorities of Poland. In a country where Roman Catholics formed only two-thirds of the population, it was quite unprofitable to talk in this way. Even so, there was always a section of public opinion for whom the Roman Catholic Church was not sufficiently patriotic. The use of the Latin mass, and the obedience of the Polish See to the Roman Curia, were both points which gave rise to demands for a breakaway erastian Church. In Poland, itself, these demands never generated widespread support. But it is curious to note how the schismatic Polish National Church, founded in 1875 in the USA (in reaction to the English language policies of the Irish clergy in America), has been adopted and encouraged by the political authorities of People's Poland. For a time after the Second World War, the communists hoped that official support for the Polish National Church might cause a serious rift in the ranks of Polish Catholics. But the split did not materialize on any significant scale, and the propagation of the vernacular liturgy by the Second Vatican Council has removed any chance of serious disruption.[14]

Another curious and persistent schism was instanced by an excess not of nationalism, but of traditional devotionalism. The Order of the Perpetual Adoration of the Virgin Mary, known as *Mariawici* (Mariavites), was founded secretly in Płock in 1893 by the followers, male and female, of Felicja Kozłowska (1862–1921), a former Clarissite nun. Curiosity about Mother Felicja's visions quickly turned to scandal when the Order unilaterally elected its own Bishop. Rumours of orgiastic practices, and of the Mother Superior's quasi-hypnotic control over her fanatical 'slaves of Mary', led to open conflict. In 1906, twelve people were killed at Leszno near Warsaw, when the local peasants recaptured a Mariavite church by storm. In Rome, the Mariavites' miracles were dismissed as hallucinations, and the Sect was formally excommunicated. But it survived. For most of the founder's lifetime, it was protected by the Tsarist authorities. Thereafter, it inherited a considerable fortune in property, and split into two distinct fractions – the 'Old Catholic Mariavites' at Płock, and the stricter 'Catholic Mariavites' at Felicjanów. Eighty years after its foundation, it still claims a nominal establishment of 63 parishes.[15]

In the twentieth century, the Roman Catholic Church in Poland has failed to reap the reward which many of its leaders believed to be its due. It has never achieved the status of a national Established Church. In the Second Republic between 1918 and 1939, it had to compete with a wide variety of religions and denominations, and its political influence was restricted by the markedly anticlerical temper of the ruling élite. In the Second World War, it was mutilated no less than other Polish institutions. Although no effort was made to close the churches completely, the Nazi and Soviet Terror fell indiscriminately on believers and on unbelievers, on the clergy and the laity alike. Several bishops, and over three thousand priests, lost their lives. Gestures of defiance, such as that of Cardinal Adam Sapieha, who pointedly served Governor Hans Frank a plate of cold porridge, or of the Blessed Maksymilian Kolbe (1894–1943), who voluntarily entered the starvation bunker of Auschwitz,[16] were not forgotten. By the time of the Liberation, most of the old suspicions about the Church's 'unpatriotic' or 'collaborationist' tendencies had been dispelled.

The outstanding qualities of Roman Catholicism in contemporary Poland display a complicated blend of the old and the new. On the one hand, traditional devotionalism is still very strong, especially among the peasant masses. Churchgoing is normal. The entire population of the villages, and of working-class districts in the towns, walks to Mass, and kneels submissively for long periods. The singing is rich and lusty. Religious processions are scrupulously observed. On Catholic feast days, fields and factories are deserted. Annual Pilgrimages, to Częstochowa or to Kalwaria Lanckorona, attract hundreds of thousands, if not millions. The Marian Cult flourishes as never before. In almost every home, the image of the Holy Mother, Queen of Poland, hangs above or beside the crucifix; the rosary is counted, and the *Pasterka* recited. Traditional authoritarianism is also strong. The parish priest, 'God's deputy', enjoys great social prestige. He both expects, and is expected, to make clear pronouncements on all issues of public concern. The Hierarchy demands absolute obedience, and is not free from a touch of theatricality. On the other hand, the clergy is well educated, and is fully conversant with modern conditions. Catholic intellectuals play a prominent part in all debates. Most innovatorily, the Church has found itself possessed of a monopoly in religious belief unparalleled in previous Polish history. According to Korzon, in 1791 Roman Catholics formed 54 per cent of the population of the old Republic. In 1931, in the Second Republic, they represented perhaps 65 per cent; in 1946, in the People's Republic, 96.6 per cent. This provided the Church with an unrivalled platform from which, in the absence of all political opposition, to assert itself as the chief moral arbiter of the nation, the principal popular counterweight to an unpopular communist regime. It is an odd state of affairs, but in People's Poland, in the heart of the Soviet bloc, the Roman Catholic Church emerged as prosperous, as confident, and as secure as never before.

*   *   *   *   *

The Church's path, therefore, is strewn with ambiguities. Sometimes, no doubt, the Church has failed the Nation. Sometimes, no doubt, it has closed its eyes to social ills and to political injustices. Sometimes, no doubt, it has proved itself unworthy of the Faith. But of the central fact, that the Roman Catholic Church embodies the most ancient and the most exalted ideals of traditional Polish life across the centuries, there can be no doubt whatsoever.

CHAPTER EIGHT
KULTURA:
Education and the Cultural Heritage

Culture, literally, is that which can be cultivated. In the biological world, it is concerned with plants that can be grown in the fields, or with enzymes and bacteria which can be grown in the laboratory. In human affairs, it refers to the sum total of attitudes, beliefs, principles, values, assumptions, reflexes, tastes, mental habits, skills, and achievements which distinguish one society from another, and which can be transmitted from one generation to the next. In the life of the Polish nation, and of others like it, it is the most precious part of the national heritage. It is the one thing which gives the promise of eternity.[1]

Historians rarely agree on the nature and springs of culture. Christian and post-Christian writers often imply that it is something akin to the soul of the individual — something innate, mysteriously endowed by God, inimitable, insubstantial, but unmistakable. Marxists hold that it is an emanation of socio-economic forces — the highest product of the particular stage of development which society has reached, believing that feudal, capitalist, or socialist cultures possess material and organizational attributes as well as artistic and intellectual ones. The pseudo-psychological and the sociological schools of history tend to suggest that culture can be measured, described in questionnaires, and reduced to 'models'. Everyone agrees, however, that it provides a prime area for social and political conflict. Every social group wishes to educate its children in its own image. Every nation seeks to preserve its values from outside intervention. Every government hopes to lead its subjects into the paths of loyalty and mutual concord. In the Polish lands, where the population was conscious of belonging simultaneously to different classes, nations, and states, it was sure to be subjected to a wide variety of competing cultural claims.

In the lives of those people who were conscious of their

separate Polish identity, the struggle to safeguard and expand the nation's culture was unrelenting. In a country whose political independence had already been undermined in the mid-eighteenth century, it often constituted the last line of defence. It was directed at two groups in particular – to the educated minority, whose national consciousness was well developed, and to the uneducated masses, whose awareness of national or political allegiances had still to be awakened. It concentrated on two interrelated campaigns – on the nurture of the Polish language, and on the education of children.

Unlike most of its counterparts in Eastern Europe, the Polish language was a fully competent all-purpose cultural instrument long before the Partitions. Unlike Czech or Slovak or Ukrainian, for example, whose vocabulary and syntax had to be fashioned by nineteenth-century grammarians, or Magyar, which could be used for some purposes but not for others, Polish possessed a rich literature, and was currently employed by all classes of society and in all the branches of the arts, sciences, and government. Its development had progressed further than Russian, and did not lag behind German. Until the growth of modern technology in the late nineteenth century, it must certainly be classed as one of the major European languages. An important landmark was reached in 1807–14 with the publication of the first large-scale Polish dictionary. The lexicographer, Samuel Bogumił Linde (1771–1847), the son of a polonized Swedish family from Thorn, had worked as a young man in the Załuski Library. His *Słownik języka polskiego* has aided everyone who has ever studied the Polish language.[2]

Education raised its head as an issue of public policy in the last decades of the old Republic, and occupied a prominent place in the minds of the political reformers of the Enlightenment. Earlier, in the seventeenth century, the Republic had possessed a network of 1,500 schools, fired by the healthy competition of the Catholic hierarchy and the Protestant sects. The older foundations, from the Jagiellonian University in Cracow to the Lubrański Academy (1517) in Poznań or the German Academic Gymnazium in Danzig (1550), were complemented by numerous, distinguished dissenting academies –

the Calvinists in Nieśwież, for example, and in most of the towns of Lithuania, the Czech Brethren in Leszno, the Arians in Pińczów and Raków, the Lutherans throughout Royal Prussia — and by the colleges of the Jesuit and Piarist Orders. By 1750, however, this network had fallen into decay. The old foundations were moribund. Most of the Protestant academies had closed their doors. Both the Jesuits and the Piarists had fallen into a mindless routine, mechanically instructing their pupils in meaningless, grammatical formalities. A key role in the revival of education was played by the Revd Stanisław Konarski (1700–73), sometime Provincial of the Piarist Order, who united many strands of the Enlightenment in his broad span of interests. As editor of the series of *Volumina Legum* (1732–9), he made a major contribution to legal and constitutional studies; as author of *O skutecznym rad sposobie* (On effective government, 1763), to the political debate; and as a disciple of the French physiocrats, to the promotion of economic enterprises. In 1740, he founded the Collegium Nobilium in Warsaw, for the improvement of young noblemen, and in the 1750s revised the entire curriculum and educational philosophy of his Order. His lifetime was spent in patient preparation for changes which he never saw. In 1773, the year of his death, the expulsion of the Jesuits, and the creation of the National Education Commission opened up educational vistas of a completely new sort.[3]

The National Education Commission, sometimes called 'Europe's First Ministry of Education', was created by order of the Sejm on 14 October 1773 and functioned until April 1794. It was funded from confiscated Jesuit property, and in twenty years under the Chairmanship of Ignacy Potocki (1750–1809) organized two universities, 74 secondary schools, and 1,600 parish schools. Its main aim was to replace the moribund and fragmented Catholic schools by a coherent state system inspired by secular and national ideals. It replaced Latin with Polish as the language of instruction in schools and universities, and promoted a wide range of subjects, from modern languages to natural sciences, where both the practical needs of the individual and the requirements of the state were kept in view. Girls were to be educated as well as boys. Hygiene and physical activity, art and midwifery were encouraged no less than book learning. National holidays and national occasions, were to be observed in addition to the old church festivals. Teachers were to be trained in state colleges, and paid in accordance with a national salary scale. The Society for Elementary Books set to work in 1775 to provide a full range of textbooks for all grades prepared by specialists at home and abroad. Its secretary, Grzegorz Piramowicz (1735–1801) an ex-Jesuit, himself composed the basic manual for elementary teachers, *Powinności nauczyciela w szkołach parafialnych* (The duties of the teacher in parish schools, 1787), and the first school anthology of Polish poetry – *Wymowa i poezja dla szkół narodowych* (Diction and Poetry for National Schools, 1792). Important textbooks were prepared in mathematics by Simon Lhuillier of Geneva, in logic by the Frenchman, Étienne Condillac, in physics by Jan Michał Hube (1737–1807), headmaster of the Collegium Nobilium, in botany by the Revd Krzysztof Kluk (1739–96), Vicar of Ciechanów, in Polish and Latin grammar by Onufry Kopczyński, in Ancient History by J. K. Skrzetuski (1743–1806), in ethics by Antoni Popławski (1739–86) . . . In the third part of his work, directed at pupils learning the essentials of 'respectable conduct', Popławski stated boldly: 'We are all without exception born equal . . . and all are united by our common needs, and by sharing in the fruits of mutual assistance.' This statement, published in 1787, is proof enough of the precociously progressive spirit of Polish education in the era of the country's darkest political tragedy. At that moment, some 15,000 pupils were registered in the Commission's secondary schools alone.[4]

The achievements of the National Education Commission were enhanced by royal patronage. The extraordinary energy of Stanisław-August and his circle in the cultural sphere was born of their impotence in promoting effective reform in other quarters. Their attack on the Church's monopoly in education was seen as the surest means of undermining the long-term prospects of the conservative party whose aim was to prevent change in the Republic at all cost. They were well aware of the odds, yet hoped that their cultural triumphs would transcend a long series of political disasters. In this regard the King's speech to the Commission in 1783 was marvellously prophetic:

Much of my work, and many of my ideas directed to the improvement of our condition, have already failed. But that does not extinguish in me the strong desire to strive in any way I can for the good of the nation. As long as I live, I shall not cease to devote my time and fortune to the Fatherland. It may be that Providence, which has sent us so much bitterness, will not allow us to enjoy the happy fruits of our labour in our own lifetime. It may well be that the Fatherland will not reap the benefits until our gravestones have been sealed long since. Yet if the Fatherland will be in the future what it is today, if our descendants will be its sons, if they will be Poles, then that is enough to arouse our efforts to ensure their good . . . Let us not say that 'God has abandoned us for ever'. Rather let us say that God is punishing us and tormenting us so that we may enjoy better times . . .[5]

Special attention was paid to the universities. At first the Commission adopted a hostile position towards the professional cadres of Cracow and Wilno who merely 'wrap young men's heads in Latin, as with cabbage leaves'. But in face of the King's reforming zeal the hostility soon waned. In 1776, Hugo Kołłątaj (1750–1812), a young canon of the cathedral in Cracow, presented a memorandum 'On the introduction of sound studies into the Cracow Academy'. The next year, he was appointed Rector. In 1780, the Commission reorganized and secularized both the Jagiellonian University and the Wilno Academy. Each university was composed of two colleges, the Collegium Fizicum and the Collegium Moralium, each of which in turn contained three schools — of Mathematics, Physics, and Medicine, and of Theology, Law, and Letters. At different times during the Partitions, each of these two reformed universities was to carry the torch of Polish culture alone amidst the tidal waves of state-sponsored Russian and German enterprises.[6]

The spirit of the National Education Commission lingered on long after its members had been dispersed. For several decades, the partitioning powers paid little attention to the schools in their Polish provinces. The Tsarist government was particularly lethargic. In Lithuania, Byelorrussia, and Ukraine, Polish schools founded before the Partitions continued to function. At Krzemieniec in Volhynia, the Polish Liceum founded in 1805, offered courses at university level. In the Wilno School District administered by A. J. Czartoryski, the

University of Wilno was served by seventy Polish secondary schools and over a thousand elementary ones. In the Duchy of Warsaw, and the Congress Kingdom, the development of Polish schools went forward without serious interruption. The Duchy's Board of Education made provision for universal primary education. By 1820, 1,222 elementary schools and 35 secondary schools, organized by *Départements* (from 1819 by *Województwa*) served the newly founded University of Warsaw (1816) together with a wide range of technical and professional colleges. At this time, Polish education was far in advance of anything in central Russia.[7] In Prussia, in contrast, the state educational system was orientated towards German culture from the start; and, except in the Grand Duchy of Posen between 1815 and 1831, no attempt was made to support separate Polish schools. There was never any Polish university in Prussia. Students seeking higher education automatically required a knowledge of German, and were obliged to study at a university in Germany. In Galicia, education remained firmly in the hands of the Church. The Piarist and Bazilian Orders were particularly active. With the exception of the first three grades of the elementary schools, lessons were conducted either in German or in Latin. The secularized University of Lemberg (1784), and in 1795–1815 and 1848–70, the Jagiellonian University in Cracow, were German institutions. The Republic of Cracow, in 1815–46, ran a Polish educational system modelled on that of the Congress Kingdom. (See Map 6.)

The middle decades of the nineteenth century saw several important developments, especially in Russia and Austria. As a result of political tensions, the Tsarist Government was shaken from its previous lethargy. There were alarming swings in policy. Periods of brutal state intervention, alternated with periods of half-hearted reconciliation. In 1850, as earlier in 1821, the temporary exemption of the peasants from compulsory school contributions threatened to destroy the entire fabric of elementary education at a stroke. In Lithuania in 1822, and in the Congress Kingdom in 1839, the autonomy of the Polish school districts was withdrawn, only to be briefly reinstated under Wielopolski's auspices in Warsaw in 1861–4. Yet from 1830 onwards, there was an unmistakable, intensify-

Map 6.   Polish Schools in the Russian Empire, (1822)

ing trend towards Russification. In Galicia, the opposite happened. Following the grant of autonomy in 1867, the entire school system, together with the two universities, was polonized. Thus, if at the start of the century Polish culture had flourished most openly in the Russian Partition, and in the Congress Kingdom, henceforth it was promoted exclusively by the Austrian authorities in Galicia.

The critical point was reached in the 1880s. Twenty years after the final Emancipation of the peasantry, the pressures of industrialization, urbanization, and the population explosion put mass education into the forefront of social policy. The absolute number of Polish schoolchildren was rising dramatically in Russia and Prussia, at a time when the campaigns to eradicate Polish culture were reaching their peak. In Galicia, conflicts arose with the Ukrainians who demanded equal rights with the Poles. At that same time, a new generation of educated Poles, among whom the pioneers of Women's Emancipation were most noticeable, were deprived of all meaningful participation in political life. They sensed a situation in which the traditional language and values of Polish society would soon be swamped by the brainwashed products of the state-backed mass education. Terrorism and political activism may have been for the few; but cultural activism was for the many. Thousands of young people of both sexes, who recoiled from illegal acts, found a mission in life by fighting for Polish culture. In Russia, the typical Polish 'patriot' of the turn of the century was not the revolutionary with a revolver in his pocket, but the young lady of good family with a textbook under her shawl. In Prussia and Austria, where political organizing was permitted, Polish schoolteachers formed the backbone of the national movements.

This generation of *révoltés* went forth as missionaries into their own land. They were as determined to manufacture 'true Poles' as the authorities were determined to train 'good Germans' or 'good Russians'. In this, from the same human material, they contended not only against the power of the state, but also in large measure against the Church, which suspected them of secular if not of libertarian attitudes, against the widespread indifference of the 'respectable' population, and against the rival missionaries of other national movements operating on the same ground. They had their own special view of reality, in which the existing Empires, with all their pomp, institutions, frontiers, and false loyalties, were little more than a superficial imposition on the eternal Polish land and people, waiting to be free. They drew their strength from secret Polish circles, which met in Minsk and Kiev no less than in Warsaw, Poznań, or Cracow. They drank deeply of all modern literature — Buckle, Spencer, Taine, J. S. Mill, Darwin, Lassalle, even Marx; and, without wishing to admit it, they were deeply influenced by the prophets of German nationalism — Fichte, Herder, Nietzsche — whose success they both admired and resented. They would have liked D'Azeglio's epigram of 1860: 'Now that we have made Italy we must make Italians'; although Poland, unlike Italy, did not yet exist.

It is not hard to show that the view of the nation as conceived by these missionaries was highly fanciful. The very fact that they had to battle against the entrenched attitudes of people whom they themselves regarded as 'Poles' is proof enough. On this score, one of their apostles Wacław Nałkowski (1851–1911) made a clear distinction between the *nerwowiec* or *mózgowiec*, (the 'worrying and thinking man') and the inert mass of the nation as a whole. He divided the latter into three types. The *ludzie-drewna* (Tree-people) were impervious to patriotic feelings, and lived mechanical, unthinking lives. The *ludzie-byki* (Ox-people) were capable of patriotic feelings, but having insufficient intelligence were unable to break away from the herd. The *ludzie-świnie* (Swine-people), although highly intelligent, sought only 'to roll in the mud' — (rolling in the 'mud' for the patriot being a metaphor for dabbling in cultures other than Polish). He even identified certain transitional types such as 'crypto-swine', 'ox-like swine', and 'tree-like swine'. The starting-point for all such convolutions was the assumption that the 'nation', as conceived by the missionaries, was the one and only Good. In this light, the cause of Polish culture was both idealistic and élitist.[8]

Even so, their achievements were enormous. In thirty years of ceaseless activity, the cultural patriots not only neutralized the efforts of the Germanizers and Russifiers; they actually began to overtake them. By the turn of the century, the state system of education in Prussian and Russian Poland was floundering amidst a tidal wave of private, informal or 'underground' Polish cultural enterprises.

Most famous perhaps was the Flying University, founded in Warsaw in 1882–3 by Jadwiga Szczawińska (1863–1910). Meeting every week in different locations to avoid detection, the groups attracted the support of radical professors, such as Władysław Smoleński, Adam Mahrburg (1855–1913), or Ludwig Krzywicki (1859–1941), and Jan Władysław David (1859–1914), the philosopher, Szczawińska's husband. In time, four separate faculties were organized, and diplomas were issued at the end of courses as rigorous as anything offered in the public sector. Maria Skłodowska-Curie was but the best-known of the graduates. After 1906, when the Flying University was legalized, it took the name of the 'Society for Scientific Courses', and in 1919 the 'Free Polish University'. It still has its imitators today.[9]

Sympathetic benefactors sought to bypass the state system by founding private schools. In 1897 the Higher Technical School opened its doors in Warsaw, on the initiative of two local industrialists, Hipolyt Hawelburg and S. Rotwand, and three years later, the Warsaw Polytechnic. In the absence of a Polish university, these two institutes attracted the highest quality of teachers and students. In the last decade of the century, the number of private schools in the Vistula provinces doubled, and, in the period of concessions following the Revolution of 1905–7, doubled again.

Self-education became a veritable craze. Its devotees were aided by the monthly *Poradnik dla samouków* (Guidebook for the Self-taught) to which all the luminaries of the day contributed. Amazingly, it has been estimated that one-third of the population of Russian Poland, young and old, was engaged in some form of home-study at the turn of the century.

Special emphasis was laid on Libraries. In an era when Polish literature was widely regarded as subversive, book collections had to be preserved in secrecy. In Kalisz, in 1873, it was known that the only full set of the unexpurgated Brockhaus Edition of *Collected Polish Authors,* published in Leipzig in 1858, was to be found in the study of the acting Russian Governor, Rybnikov, an ardent Slavophile. One night, Rybnikov's books were stolen by unknown burglars, and deposited in the Town Gaol, where the Chief Constable's son undertook to hide them from his father's mystified agents. Elsewhere, public libraries sprang up under the cover of religious or social organizations. By 1897, the Warsaw Charitable Society (WTD) was maintaining twenty-three branch libraries. An attempt to purge the shelves of such 'degrading authors' as Hugo, Zola, and Dumas led first to the expulsion of the Society's conservative Chairman, Prince Michał Radziwiłł, and then to the suppression of the libraries by the police.

A concerted effort was made to export Polish culture to the masses. Both the PPS and Dmowski's Polish League ran extensive educational programmes, which were greatly boosted by the school strikes of 1904–7. Campaigns to educate the peasants were disguised as 'Bee-keeping Societies' or 'Sports Associations'. In the towns, devoted teachers held lessons in private homes, addressing their labours to a mixture of truants, adult illiterates, and youthful volunteers. In 1911, a report submitted to the Russian Policemaster of Sosnowiec, revealed the alarming extent of the problem in the towns of that area:

I have the honour to report to Your Excellency the existence of the following illegal schools in the district entrusted to me:
  In the settlement of Modrzejów:
  1. In the house of Pergricht, the son-in-law of the foreman, Najer, a dangerous person by name of Rusek is teaching;
  2. Two secret Jewish schools are to be found in the house of Szczekacz, but it is hard to say who the teacher is. (Modrzejów lies in the Police District of Dąbrowa.)
  In the village of Niwka:
  3. Maria Góralska, the daughter of an official of the 'Jerzy' Mine, holds lessons in a house belonging to the Company on the other side of the street from the clinic;
  4. Janina Drozdowska and her sister hold lessons in another house of the same company on Wesoła Street;
  5. The aunt, or possibly the mother of the manageress of the 'Jutrzenka' store, name unknown, teaches in the flat ajoining the store;
  6. The mother of Stanisław Chrzanowski, an official of the 'Jerzy' Mine, teaches in her house on Wesoła Street;
  7. A certain Woźniczek, the son of a workman at the Sosnowiec Company's Machine Factory, teaches in a house belonging to the company;

8. The daughters of an official of the same company called Wieruszowski are holding lessons;
9. There's a Jewish School in the house of Szulim Lubelski — teacher unknown;
10. The daughter of a guard on the Warsaw—Vienna Railway called Filak teaches in Duda's house. (Niwka lies in the Police District of Ząbkowice.)

There are other schools which I have been unable to discover. In some of the schools, e.g. in Rusek's, Góralska's, or in that of the Drozdowska sisters, a considerable number of children, up to fifty at a time, are taught in two shifts . . .[10]

The First World War brought the cultural conflict to a sharp conclusion. Henceforth the Powers were driven to make cultural overtures to the Poles in the hope of winning their political support. In 1916, the Regency Council in Warsaw authorized its Ministry of Education to reorganize schools and university on Polish lines. This brought the former Congress Kingdom into line with Austrian practices in Galicia. This cultural triumph, at the end of half a century of struggle, did not in itself bring national independence; but it made a great difference to the temper of the new Polish Republic when independence was realized only two years later.

In the cultural field, the first experience of Independence between 1918 and 1939 brought many disappointments. The crushing rate of illiteracy, and the disaffection of many ethnic minorities unable or unwilling to communicate in Polish, meant that the work of the cultural missionaries was far from complete. Indeed, the state educators frequently viewed themselves as the heirs and successors of the patriotic pioneers of the Partition period. In the Second World War, cultural warfare was joined in its most intense form. Systematic attempts were made to eradicate Polish culture, not merely by proscribing it in public in the manner of former Prussian and Russian policies, but by killing and dispersing its leaders and teachers. The Polish reaction was instinctive. The printing of Polish books, the teaching of Polish children, the organization of Polish university courses, and the reading of Polish literature, was carried on in secret — in the underground, in all the occupied cities, in the forest refuges of the partisans, in *émigré* groups in London, Jerusalem, or Tashkent, even in the concentration camps. In 1945, as a prize for untold sacrifices, the attachment of the survivors to their native culture was stronger than ever before. The labours of two centuries have been vindicated. Stanisław-August, and all those devoted men and women who followed in his footsteps, would have had cause to rejoice.

*   *   *   *   *

By 1945, the corpus of Polish mass culture, as distinct from phenomena emanating from narrow social groups was composed of at least four main overlapping sub-cultures. The first of these was 'popular' or 'peasant' culture (*kultura ludowa*). A large part of the urban proletariat still maintained contact with their native villages. The elimination of the nobility and the decimation of the pre-war bourgeoisie, left only a small number of families which had no deep roots in the countryside. 'Folklore' — the ancient sayings, wisdom, stories, dances, and dress of the peasantry — have not yet become a collector's item.

The second was Catholic culture. The Church had not left the propagation of the Faith to chance. The vast majority of Polish children had been baptized and had passed through the course of preparation for First Communion. Even those who in later life abandoned their religious belief, were thoroughly familiar with the language, the teaching, and the practices of Catholicism.

The third might be described as 'imitation Western' culture. In direct reaction to the cultural fare supplied from official sources, Poles have traditionally looked to the West for inspiration. Whether in literature or political ideas, in music, arts, or in fashion, in artefacts, and in technology, the products of London, Paris, Rome, or New York are automatically considered superior to anything deriving from Central Europe or from the East. The Polish language itself, which has never been subjected to the axe of native purism, is filled with latinisms and westernisms of every sort.

The fourth, and perhaps the most important, was Polish literary culture. In the course of the nineteenth century, Polish literature had addressed itself to all the problems and genres of the age. In politics, Poland may have been of little consequence, but in literary matters, she remained an important force, only surpassed in Eastern Europe by the great age of German and Russian literature. What is more, as a result of mass education, the educated Pole could share his ideas and interests with a mass audience. In this regard, the achievement of the pre-war *Sanacja* regime in lowering illiteracy from 33 per cent in 1921 to 18 per cent in 1937 was of capital importance.

In so far as none of the dominant sub-cultures owed anything to the former partitioning powers, the success of the Polish educational crusade over two centuries may be taken as granted. The accretions of German and Russian elements, once so important in Polish culture, have been largely erased. From the purely national point of view, this represents a great triumph. At the same time, one cannot deny that in certain respects Polish culture has been impoverished. Much of the cosmopolitan, multi-lingual and international flavour of earlier generations has been lost. Exclusive reliance on the Polish language, which is no longer a means of international communication even in Eastern Europe, has served to isolate Polish society from the world at large. Whereas before the First World War the educated Pole moved in circles which used German, Russian, and French, as well as Polish, in their everyday lives, his successor after the Second World War has to be content with restricted sources of information filtered through censored translations, or has to burn the midnight oil over Eckersley's *English for Foreigners*. To this extent, the quantitative triumph of Polish culture has been attended by its qualitative limitations.

CHAPTER NINE
ŻYDZI

The Jewish Community

In the centuries preceding the Partitions, the Polish–Lithuanian Republic had progressively attracted to itself the largest Jewish community in Europe. The Jewish estate had multiplied faster than any other social group. The great catastrophes of Chmielnicki's Rebellion and of the Massacre of Human proved to be only temporary setbacks. From some 200,000 at the time of the Republic's formation in 1569, the total number of Jews had increased to almost 800,000 at the moment of the Republic's demise. During the nineteenth century, the lands of partitioned Poland harboured the main reservoir of Jewish manpower and intellectual dynamism in the world, and, until the great Exodus to America reached its height, contained four-fifths of world Jewry. In the words of Responsa No. 73, of the great Cracovian rabbi Moses Isserles 'Remuh' (1510–72): 'It is better to live on dry bread, but in peace, in Poland.' Similarly, in one of the puns so beloved of Hebrew scholars, *Polin* (Poland) stood for *'poh-lin*: Here, one rests'.[1]

As a result of changing political conditions, the term 'Polish Jew' possessed several different connotations. In its original sense, it simply referred to the Jewish population of the former Polish state, and included people who came to think of themselves not as 'Polish' but as 'Russian', 'Galician', or even 'German' Jews. In later times, it referred either to Jewish citizens of the reborn Polish Republics, or else to that sector of East European Jewry which was assimilated into Polish language and culture.

In the course of the nineteenth century, the Jewish community was subjected to the forces of radical change which beset all remnants of the defunct Republic. In many ways, its transformation followed a path parallel to that of the wider Polish community. At the outset, its fortunes centred on the system of separate estates of the realm, whose ancient legal

240

privileges were now set to be destroyed. At the end, it was a modern nation united only by the bonds of common origins and of common identity. As with many other social groups, the old order had to be dismantled before the new one could be assembled. In the process, many elements of the old order were lost forever. Confusion and insecurity were increased, not diminished. As the peasants, too, were to find, emancipation was not necessarily equivalent to liberation.

Jewish Emancipation proceeded at a different pace, and by different methods, in each of the three Partitions. In the immediate aftermath of 1773, both Frederick the Great and Maria Theresa began by expelling numerous poor Jews back into Poland in a move to 'protect' their new Christian subjects. In Galicia, important reforms were initiated in 1782 by Joseph II, who viewed Jewish autonomy as an anachronism. By introducing state education and military service, and by abolishing the *kahal*, he sought to bring the Jews into the mainstream of public life and German culture. In Russia, after some vacillation, Catherine II pursued the simpler aim of keeping the Jews apart from the population at large. In 1786, she restricted Jewish residence to the cities, and from 1791 to a Pale of Settlement which was gradually expanded over succeeding decades to cover twenty-five western *gubernias* of the Empire. With the exceptions of the Crimea and Bessarabia, the territory of the Pale as finally defined in 1835 coincided very largely with the lands annexed by Russia from Poland–Lithuania. In the Duchy of Warsaw, the decree of 1807 on personal liberty, which ended serfdom, was suspended in relation to the Jews, and was never fully implemented. In Prussia, where Frederick II had extended limited protection to wealthy Jews in certain specified professions, full civic equality was established in 1812. Thus, by the end of the Napoleonic period, many ambiguities and disabilities remained. In the Congress Kingdom, as in Prussia, the granting of civil equality in 1822 was attended by the abolition of the *kahal*. Other restrictions, such as the clauses *De non tolerandis Judaeis* in municipal charters, remained in force until 1862. In the Prussian provinces newly acquired by the Treaty of Vienna, the principle of Jewish Emancipation was not put into effect until 1846; in Austria, it had to wait until 1848, and in some minor respects, until 1867; in the realms of the Tsar, it was never permanently established. In the Russian Empire, the draconian measures of Nicholas I, briefly relaxed under Alexander II, were swiftly reinstated in the reign of Alexander III. According to the May Laws of 1882, the regulations of the Pale were to be strictly enforced; Jews were to be barred from the senior ranks of the army and bureaucracy, and from buying land; they were to be given only limited access to secondary and higher education, to the professions, or to posts in local government. Further relaxations introduced in 1905–6 had little time to take effect before the Empire itself was swept away. Thus, if in the old Republic, the children of Israel had sometimes felt that they were bondsmen in the Land of Egypt, in Russia, they knew for certain that they had been carried off into the Babylonian Captivity. (See Map 7.)

In all three Partitions, the imposition of the institutions of the authoritarian state affected every aspect of Jewish life. The gradual reduction in the jurisdiction of the *kahal,* and the growth of the powers of the state authorities, meant that the Jews for the first time became full citizens of the countries in which they lived. Whereas in Poland–Lithuania, they had managed their own affairs in their own way, they now had to assume a civilian identity similar to that of all other citizens. For one thing, they incurred the wrath of officialdom, and the resentment of other tax-payers and conscripts. For another thing, in order to be taxed and conscripted, they needed to appear on the official Registers; and in order to be registered, they needed to be given surnames. In Austria and Russia, registration proceeded from 1791; in Prussia, which at that time included Warsaw, it was carried out by the *Judenreglement* of 1797. In Galicia and in Prussia, the Jews were often awarded surnames according to the dictates of German officials, who used the occasion to exercise their limited sense of poetic invention. In this way, the world was given the Apfelbaums, Rosenblums, Weingartens, Goldfarbs, Silbersteins, Schwartzkopfs, and Weissmanns. In the Russian Pale, the Jews frequently adopted a surname based on their family's city of origin or, like the ex-slaves in America, on the name of the noble proprietor of the estate where they lived. Thus in addition to the Warschauers, Wieners, Posners,

Map 7. The Jewish Pale of Settlement in Russia

Minskers, and Pinskers, there appeared Jewish Potockis, Jewish Czartoryskis, and Jewish Wiśniowieckis.

Official hostility was expressed in a variety of ways. In Galicia, special taxes were imposed on religious practices. The candle-tax, and the levy assessed on the attendance roll of the synagogues, penalized the Jews' devotion to their religion. In the Congress Kingdom, a liquor-tax struck specially hard at Jewish licensees. In Russia from 1805, military conscription frequently took the form of the wholesale deportation of entire age-groups of Jewish youth to distant garrisons of the Empire. In this respect, the Jewish towns of the Pale suffered the same brutal treatment as the settlements of petty Polish nobility. Under Nicholas I, Jewish conscripts came under heavy pressure to submit to Christian baptism. Repeated attempts were made to suppress Jewish education. In 1835, the use of Hebrew in schools, and in official documents, was formally banned — though to little immediate effect. In the second half of the century, the Russification of public life affected the Jews no less than the Poles. The endemic pogroms which followed the May Laws were largely organized by official provocateurs. The appearance of the police-sponsored Jew-baiting gangs, the Black Hundreds, was but the latest expression of a rooted conviction in official circles that all Jews were potentially disloyal.

Social mobility greatly increased. No longer confined to their own ghettos, Jewish families could try to migrate to the suburbs, to the countryside, or even to foreign countries. In Galicia, it was often said in jest that the only successful expedition of 1848 was the Long March of the Jews on the two miles from Kazimierz to Cracow. In Russian Poland, in Warsaw and Łódź, wealthy Jewish families moved out from the city centres. In some cases, they moved over the frontier into Galicia where they were free to buy land. Economic constraints and severe overcrowding forced increasing numbers to emigrate abroad. Between 1800 and 1880, the natural increase of the Jews of the Pale was in the order of 500 per cent. Similar conditions prevailed in Galicia. At the end of the century, the threat of active persecution increased emigration and turned a steady stream into a stampede which continued until the First World War. Although statistics vary, there can be little doubt that more Jews left the Polish lands than stayed behind. They went in stages: first to Vienna or Berlin, then to England or France, and above all to America. Some were well prepared, and departed legally. Invited by their *Landmannschaft* or 'Regional Council' abroad, they were provided with tickets for the journey and with work when they arrived. Others departed illegally, especially from Russia, and could make no preparations. At the ports of embarkation, they sold themselves to redemption agents, who gave them a free passage to America in exchange for three, five, or seven years' bonded labour on arrival.[2]

Political and cultural disintegration proceeded apace. In a world where traditional structures were visibly crumbling, the attitudes of the Jewish community polarized on all the issues of the day. Conservative elements, unable to rule by authority, sought at all costs to preserve the purity of the Orthodox Jewish religion. The Chassidic challenge, first mounted in the eighteenth century, gained further strength in the nineteenth. Radical elements, reacting strongly against the authoritarian habits of the *kahal,* were pushed in the directions of Assimilation, of Socialism and Marxism, and eventually of Zionism. Modern Jewish leaders worked to reconcile the numberless antagonisms which arose not only within the bounds of the Jewish community itself, but equally between the Jews and each of the nationalist movements of the region. By 1918, when the collapse of the partitioning powers heralded a new era, the spectrum of Jewish politics revealed every conceivable permutation of social, religious, and ideological interests.

None the less, the traditional practices of Judaism maintained their hold on the Jewish masses throughout the nineteenth century. Whilst the schism between the Mitnaggedim and the Chassidim continued, the influence of Reformed Judaism, emanating from the rabbinical Conferences in Germany in the 1840s, made only a marginal impact in the Polish lands. Polish Jewry was noted both for its piety, and for its devotion to religious scholarship. Among the Orthodox, the ancient art of *Pilpul* (literally, Pepper) or 'theological hair-splitting', continued to find its practitioners. The older religious academies in Cracow and Vilna were joined by new foundations, such as the famous *Yeshivot* at Valozhin (Wołożyń) in Lithuania, which flourished from 1803 to 1893 or at Mir near Grodno which was active from 1815 to 1939. The principles of religious education were thoroughly revised, and from the so-called *Musar* movement received a strong injection of ethics. Among the new generation of educators, a distinct trend towards asceticism was apparent, notably at Nowogródek. Among the Chassidim, the impact of the Habad was strong both in Central Poland and in Lithuania, marking off the western and northern communities from the more popular, mystical trend in the east. From the example of Elimelech of Lizensk (Leżajsk, 1717–87), who first expounded the role of the *zaddik,* veritable dynasties of learned Chassidic leaders were founded at Przysucha, Koch, Bełz, Międzybóż, and above all, at Gur (Góra Kalwaria), near Warsaw. The Alter family of Gur were widely regarded as hereditary sages of the Sect, and their court became the object of popular Jewish pilgrimages as fervent and as uplifting as those which brought the Catholic peasants to the nearby Bernardine church and Calvary Way. In the course of time, the Orthodox rabbis abandoned their hopes of suppressing the Chassidim. Having lost all jurisdictional powers, they had no means of enforcing religious conformity. Although never reconciled to Chassidic practices, they were increasingly concerned to form a common religious front for the defence of Judaism against the numerous reform movements of the age.[3]

The first of these reform movements was that of the *Haskalah* or 'Jewish Enlightenment'. Founded in Berlin in the late eighteenth century in the circle of Moses Mendelssohn, it sought to modify the exclusively religious content of Jewish education and to integrate the Jews into the mainstream of European culture. Its disciples, known as *maskilim* or 'men of understanding' gained many adherents in the towns of Silesia, and at the turn of the century in Galicia, where over one hundred Jewish schools, using German as the language of instruction, were founded. In 1816, the Rabbi of Lemberg thought fit to place them under a ban. In the subsequent period, the movement spread into the Russian Pale, where the first Jewish school of the new type was opened at Human in 1822, and to a much smaller degree, into the Congress Kingdom.

For a time it gained the approval of the Tsarist authorities who recognized an instrument for disrupting the solidarity of the Jewish community and for setting the Jews on the road to political subservience. In this they were sadly mistaken, for in the long run the principal achievement of the *Haskalah*, whilst undermining religious Judaism, was to sow the seeds of modern Jewish nationalism.[4]

In due course, the *maskilim* were challenged by reformers who wanted to extend the ideals of the *Haskalah* into the political and social spheres. Not content with limited educational aims, the Assimilationists wanted the Jews to abandon their exclusive communities and to participate fully in all branches of public life. Throughout Jewish History, of course, Jews who wished to escape from the constrictions of the ghetto, had always possessed the option of accepting the dominant religion, language, and culture of the country in which they lived. In the Polish lands, isolated converts to Christianity had followed this course for longer than anyone could remember; and the Frankists of the 1760s had provided an instance where the phenomenon briefly assumed mass proportions. But at that stage, no one had advocated Assimilation as a policy for the Jewish community as a whole. In the early nineteenth century, however, with the influx of French Revolutionary ideas, new voices were heard. In 1816, when the Berlin scholar, D. Friedlander was asked for an opinion, his pamphlet on 'The Improvement of the Jews in the Kingdom of Poland' strongly supported the replacement of the Yiddish language by Polish, as a first step to the closer integration of the Jews into Polish life. In the 1820s, a group of Warsaw bankers and intellectuals calling themselves 'The Old Testament Believers' adopted Friedlander's programme as part of their campaign to abolish the local *kahal.* At this juncture, Joachim Lelewel was speaking of Poles and Jews as 'brothers walking hand in hand' towards a common future. In the November Rising of 1830–1, many Jews gave their lives for the Polish cause.[5] A Jewish Militia was formed to assist in the defence of Warsaw. In 1848 in Galicia, Rabbi Dov Beer Meisels (1798–1870) of Cracow openly urged his flock to support Polish political demands. In the following decade, this same leader, now Chief Rabbi of Warsaw, joined prominent members of the assimilated Jewish bourgeoisie, such as Leopold Kronenburg and Herman Epstein, in a concerted movement to reconcile Polish and Jewish interests in religious, cultural, and economic matters. Kronenburg's newspaper, *Gazeta Codzienna* (Daily Gazette), edited by the novelist Ignacy Kraszewski, was specifically launched for the purpose of promoting Polish–Jewish understanding. In the political crisis of 1861–2, vividly portrayed in Kraszewski's novels *Dziecię starego miasta* (A Child of the Old City, 1863) and *Żyd* (The Jew, 1865), Warsaw's Jews played a leading role in the patriotic demonstrations. Synagogues were closed in solidarity with the Catholic churches, in protest against police excesses; rabbis appeared in the company of priests and pastors at public services and funerals; Chief Rabbi Meisels was arrested, and imprisoned. Here was the high point of the assimilationist trend. In a mood of patriotic euphoria, it looked to many that the common humanity of Poles and Jews would overcome their mutual rivalries and suspicions. During the January Rising of 1863, a Jewish journal, *Jutrzenka* (The Morning Star), edited by Ludwik Gumplowicz (1838–1909), boldly called for the total integration of Jews into Polish life.[6] It was not to be. The collapse of the Rising bred widespread disillusionments. Many Jews, like many Poles, felt that their sacrifices had brought no concrete benefits; and each was tempted to blame the other for the resulting tribulations. Assimilation slowly faded from fashion, first in Russian Poland, and then in the other Partitions.[7] In many ways, it was a noble ideal, fuelled by the desire to surmount the ancient barriers which divided peoples who lived in the same land, breathed the same air, 'were subject to the same diseases', and might have been 'healed by the same means'. Unfortunately, from the viewpoint of most Jewish leaders, Assimilation was heading in the direction of the complete submergence of a separate Jewish identity. To both conservatives and radicals, it seemed that the Jews were being asked to solve their problems by going into voluntary liquidation. As the Jewish historian Dubnow commented, 'Polonisation of the Jews assumed *menacing* [*sic*] proportions'.[8] Henceforward, Jewish reformers increasingly execrated such assimilationist ideas as continued to circulate, turning instead to projects which sought not to transcend the Jewish heritage, but to reinforce and to expand it..

The Hebrew Revival sprung directly from the work of those earlier *maskilim* who, as part of their educational experimentation, had dared to use the sacred language of the Scriptures as a medium for secular literature. It displayed many of the features of other cultural revivals which all over Eastern Europe in that same era were rescuing moribund national languages from oblivion. In Galicia, the first pioneer of modern Hebrew was Józef Perl (1774–1839) of Tarnopol, whose satirical writings made fun of the obscurantist habits and attitudes of the Chassidim. On the Russian side of the frontier, the scholar and philologist, Izaac Ber Levinsohn (1788–1860) of Krzemieniec, undertook the task of reconstituting the vocabulary and syntax of Hebrew for contemporary usage. In the hands of their successors, the Hebrew language was adapted to a variety of literary genres, some purely artistic, others overtly political. The historian Nachman Krochmal (1785–1840) of Tarnopol, whose *Guide to the Perplexed of the Age* appeared in 1851, is sometimes seen as the first ideologist of Jewish Nationalism. His outlook was shared by Abraham Mapu (1808–67) of Slobodka near Odessa, who wrote historical novels, and by a long line of Hebrew *maskilim* poets. Prominent among them was Jehudeh Loeb Gordon (1830–92) of Vilna, whose poem *Hakitzah Ammi* (Awake, my people) came to be regarded as the credo of the *Haskalah* in the Pale. Secular attitudes and the cultivation of Hebrew went hand in hand, and from 1863 were systematically promoted by the Society for the Dissemination of Jewish Culture in Russia. By the end of the century, Hebrew was sufficiently well developed for its most enthusiastic promoters to think of turning it to everyday use in their homes. Unable to realize their ambitions in the conservative social atmosphere of the established Jewish communities, where their linguistic innovations were often thought to be downright sacrilegious, they began to contemplate emigration to Palestine. In this way, a direct intellectual link can be observed between the *Haskalah*, the Hebrew Revival, and cultural Zionism.[9]

The Yiddish Revival occurred at a slightly later date. Whereas

Yiddish — a branch of Middle High German exported to
Poland–Lithuania in the Middle Ages and commonly known
as *żargon* (jargon) — had been mainly preserved by the oral
tradition, it, too, in the hands of modern publicists and
grammarians, was converted into a literary and political
medium. In Poland especially, where opposition to the
secular use of Hebrew was strongest, Yiddish came to be
preferred in the Jewish press and in Jewish secular literature.
Written in the Hebrew alphabet, it was first used for popular
prose and poetry in the sixteenth century, and was later
developed by the Chassidim for disseminating the chronicles
and legends of their sect. Later it was adopted for modern
prose composition and for poetry and drama. Interestingly
enough, many of its practitioners, such as Isaac Leib Peretz
(1852–1915) of Zamość, began their careers as Polish and
Hebrew writers, moving into Yiddish at the turn of the
century. Owing to the Nazi Holocaust, however, the best
known of modern Yiddish writers, Isaac Bakvish Singer
(born 1904, in Radzymin), will probably be the last.[10]

The language issue was of crucial importance. In 1897, the
mother tongue of over 90 per cent of the Jews in the Pale
and in Galicia was still Yiddish; Hebrew, as the scriptural
language, was no more spoken in everyday life than Latin was
spoken by Catholic Poles or Old Church Slavonic by Russians.
At the same time, a certain proportion of Jews had always
possessed a working knowledge of German, Polish, or Russian
as a means for communicating with their Gentile neighbours.
Now, a distinct element among the educated classes could be
seen to be abandoning Yiddish altogether. An estimate of
1913 put the proportion of Jews in the Pale with Polish or
Russian as their mother tongue at 7 per cent. Hence the long-
term effects of secularization were divisive in some respects
and cohesive in others. The assimilatory trend had helped to
narrow the gulf between East European Jewry and the Gentile
population at large. In this, in Prussia and in western Galicia,
where Yiddish-speakers could adapt most readily to the
German environment, it was very successful. Simultaneously,
it served to erect new barriers, not only between the Jew of
German culture and the Jew of Polish or of Russian culture,
but also between the assimilated on the one hand and the

unassimilated on the other. The mid-century Hebrew trend was confined to a marginal intellectual élite; whereas the later educational and publishing ventures in Yiddish were directed at the masses. At the end of the century, the cultural patterns were far more complicated than at the beginning.

The principal catalyst in changing Jewish attitudes at the end of the century had undoubtedly been provided by the repressive legislation of the May Laws, and by the accompanying pogroms. The physical violence which erupted at this time in central Russia was largely avoided in the Vistula provinces. The anti-Jewish riot sparked off in 1881 in Warsaw by news of the Tsar's assassination seems to have been a spontaneous affair, and there was no instance in Warsaw or Łódź, as in Moscow or St. Petersburg, where unregistered Jews were expelled *en masse* from their homes. Yet the psychological trauma among all sections of Jewry was enormous. Limited acts of violence gave rise to unlimited rumours, and to fears of further violence to come. As a result, and in some cases overnight, moderate men and women became radicals, and radicals became extremists. The trend towards Assimilation received a setback from which it never recovered. The various cultural movements were seen to be inadequate to the needs of the day. Zionism — Jewish Nationalism — had reached the moment of take-off.[11]

The disturbances of 1882 aggravated the problems of Polish Jewry in a very specific manner, however. As a result of the pogroms, considerable numbers of Jews from the Russian areas of the Pale sought refuge in the Polish *gubernias,* or in Galicia. The newcomers, known in Poland somewhat inaccurately as *Litvaks* or 'Jews from Lithuania', differed from the native Jews in two important respects. In the first place, embittered by their humiliating experiences, they contained an unusually large element of political militants. In the second place, the educated people among them were largely Russian-speaking, and as such essentially indifferent to Polish interests. Their arrival proved unsettling in the extreme, and was resented no less by the leaders of Orthodox Polish Jewry than by the Polish Catholics. Their influx seriously damaged the Polish Orientation, hindered the process of assimilation into Polish culture, and accelerated a wide variety of radical political programmes. Many of them used their sojourn in the Polish provinces as a staging-post on their way to Western Europe, America, or Palestine. But many stayed behind to take a conspicuous part in the socialist, communist, and Zionist movements. In Polish eyes, these 'alien Jews' were largely responsible for disrupting the supposed harmony of earlier Polish—Jewish relations. Unwittingly, they certainly did much to launch the popular stereotype of the *'Żydo-komuna'*, associating Marxism and Communism with Russian Jewish intellectuals, which was destined to enjoy a long currency in Poland.

In the 1880s the fashion for emigrating to Palestine gained rapid momentum. An association calling itself *Hibbat Zion* (Love of Zion) spawned local branches throughout Galicia and the Pale, and staged the first of its federated Conferences at Kattowitz in Silesia in 1884. In the seventeen years before its merger into the World Zionist Organization (WZO), it provided a major stimulus to the concept of 'practical Zionism' and supplied many of the earliest recruits for the first Jewish colonies in Palestine. Very soon, however, a distinct difference of emphasis appeared between the movement's two main centres. The Russian Branch, in Odessa, headed by Dr Leo Pinsker, stressed the social, economic, and cultural advantages of emigration. For the Polish Branch in Warsaw, in contrast, the slogan 'To Palestine' possessed much more fundamental, religious overtones.[12]

The religious overtones of Polish Zionism were present from the start, therefore. Whereas in Galicia and in the Russian areas of the Pale, Zionism must be viewed as a culmination of the secular movements of the century, in the Polish provinces it was frequently embraced by people who still maintained their traditional religious beliefs. So-called 'Religious Zionism' sought to reconcile the claims of Jewish Nationalism with those of Orthodox Judaism; and it was no accident that its founding fathers were almost all distinguished Polish rabbis. One of the earliest tracts advocating Jewish agricultural colonies, the *Dervishat Zion* (Seeking Zion) of 1862, was written by the Talmudic scholar and Rabbi of Thorn, Zvi Hirsch Kalischer (1795—1874) who, in turn, was said to have taken his ideas from his colleague and neighbour, Rabbi Elijah

Guttmacher (1795–1874) of Grodzisk. Twenty years later, the better-known activities of Rabbi Samuel Mohilever (1824–98) pushed the same combination of interests to their logical conclusion. During his visit to Paris in 1882, Mohilever, who was Rabbi first of Radom and then of Białystok, had the distinction of persuading Baron Edmund de Rothschild to finance the original Colonization Scheme in Palestine. He was one of the guiding spirits behind the religious wing of *Hibbat Zion*. In 1897, his outspoken message to the founding Zionist Congress at Basle urged the delegates, in tones of thinly veiled suspicion, to remember the claims of religion:

Highly honoured brethren! Leaders of the Chosen People, beloved Sons of Zion, may you be granted eternal life! . . .
5. The basis of the Hibbat Zion is the Torah, as it has been handed down to us from generation to generation. I do not intend this statement as an admonition to any individual regarding his conduct, for as our sages have said, 'Verily, there are none in this generation fit to admonish.' Nevertheless, I am stating in a general way that the Torah, which is the source of our life, must be the foundation of our regeneration in the land of our fathers . . .
May the Eternal, the Blessed, the Exalted, the Keeper and Redeemer of Israel, bring to pass the saying of his prophet, (Zechariah: 7–8): 'Thus saith the Lord, Behold I shall bring my people from the East; from the lands of the setting sun, I shall bring them, and they shall dwell in Jerusalem. They shall be My People, and I shall be their God in truth and righteousness.'[13]

Rabbi Mohilever's message served to remind the Congress, if any such reminder were necessary, that the religious tradition was still uppermost among the Jewish masses of the Polish lands. As shown by another favourite Hebrew pun, 'Polonia' could also be read as *Poh-lan-ya* (God rests here).

It is all too common, in fact, to exaggerate the influence of new ideas on the ghetto communities of Eastern Europe. Unlike the Jews of Britain, France, and America, or even of Germany, the Jews of Galicia and of the Pale clung to the old ways with tenacious conservatism. They were as distinct from the world-wide Diaspora, as they were from their Christian neighbours. Life in the small Jewish towns of the East had a self-perpetuating quality which proved impervious to innovations. The practice of arranged adolescent marriages, the ritual importance of Sabbath observance, the obligatory dietary and hygienic rules, and the distinctive dress and hairstyles, the *kaftan,* and the side-curls: all served to make people dependent on traditional social norms from a very early age. Youngsters who defied the rules in thought or deed, risked outright rejection by their relations, and were often driven to extreme radicalism on the rebound. The maxim of the *Haskalah,* 'Be a Jew in your home, and a man outside', could be practised in Berlin, London, Paris, New York, and conceivably in the larger centres such as Warsaw, Vilna, or Odessa. But in the *shtetln,* in the typical rural backwaters, it could never be followed with any degree of comfort.[14]

Opposition to mainstream Zionism emerged from many sources. On the conservative side, orthodox religious elements sought to preserve the educational projects of the movement from godless progressives. Thus, only four years after Rabbi Mohilever's message to the Basle Congress, the *Mizrachi* or 'Spiritual Centre' was founded to protect the interests of the rabbinate within the WZO. This centre was the direct progenitor of the National Religious Party in present-day Israel. In 1912, the still more conservative *Agudat Israel* (Union of Israel) was launched with the aim of rejecting Zionism outright. Its sponsors included the Alter of Gur. In the First World War, it was patronized by the German authorities, and by a special team of Neo-orthodox German rabbis, imported to mount an anti-Zionist campaign among the Jews of the occupied Pale.

Socialist criticism, too, came in both limited and absolute varieties. The *Poalei Zion* Party (Workers of Zion), founded like the *Mizrachi* in 1901 and copying their tactics, kept within the Zionist fold whilst seeking to influence developments in line with their own particular principles. Its most influential ideologist, Dov Ber Borochov (1881–1917), used Marxist arguments to show that emigration offered the only sure escape from European Jewry's growing economic and social conflicts. Its most illustrious member, David Ben-Gurion (1886–1973), born at Płońsk near Warsaw, took an active part in the revolutionary strikes of 1905–6 before heading for Palestine and his eventual elevation as the first Prime Minister of Israel. The Jewish *Bund,* in contrast – The

Allgemeiner Yiddisher Arbeiterbund in Lite, Poilen, un Russland (United Jewish Workers' league in Lithuania, Poland, and Russia) — denounced the Zionist cause as a middle-class nationalist fantasy. Marxist and internationalist in complexion, it was founded in Vilna in 1897, and took the lead in forming the revolutionary Russian Social Democratic Party. Offended by Lenin's organizational chicaneries, its leaders sided mainly with the Mensheviks.[15] Polish Jews of the Litvak variety, such as Maxim Litvinov (1876–1951), the future Soviet Commissar of Foreign Affairs, who was born at Białystok, or Róża Luksemberg (Luxemburg) (1870–1919), born at Zamość, shared much of the *Bund*'s outlook, but tended to move directly into the all-Russian branches of the Social Democratic Movement.

For the historian, the growth of Jewish political parties in the Polish provinces offers striking parallels with contemporary developments in Polish politics. *Mutatis mutandis,* the aims and demands of the Zionist movement for an exclusive national homeland, not to mention their strident tone, closely matched those of the Polish National Democrats; whilst the Zionists' ambivalent relationship with Judaism ran parallel to that of the Polish nationalists with the Roman Catholic Church. The attempts of *Poale Zion* to reconcile their national and socialist interests reflected contemporary stresses within the PPS, and led to exactly the same sorts of schisms and factions. Both the name and the ideological stance of the *Bund* closely resembled those of the SDKPiL. None the less, the measure of mutual sympathy and collaboration between the Jewish parties and their local Polish counterparts varied enormously. The Zionists and the National Democrats were competing for influence on the same middle-class ground, and were offering diametrically opposed visions of the future — the one purely Jewish, the other purely Polish. In consequence they regarded each other with undisguised hatred, the former complaining about 'anti-Semitism' the latter about 'anti-Polonism'. The Jewish socialists enjoyed somewhat better relations with the PPS, especially when they chose to work for socialism at home in Poland rather than abroad in Palestine. Polish-speaking Jews of the socialist persuasion, of whom in Łódź, Warsaw, Grodno, and Białystok there were many, tended to join the PPS rather than the *Paole Zion* or the *Bund*. The Bundists, whose only point of sympathy with the Zionists lay in their common hostility to Polish nationalism, showed little concern for Polish affairs before the First World War. After the October Revolution, the majority joined the SDKPiL, and the PPS (Left) in the communist camp; but their violent suppression in Soviet Russia inspired a sudden change of heart. The Polish branch of the *Bund* continued to function in Warsaw till 1939, and moved much closer to the PPS. A small communist faction, the *Kombund*, existed in the political underworld from 1921, in collaboration with the KPRP.[16] (See Chapter 22.)

The currents and eddies of Assimilation in the Polish provinces were extremely complicated. They were determined not only by infinite gradations in the extent to which Jews were willing to merge themselves into the population at large, but also by the baffling variety of 'host communities' and by widely differing degrees of mutual antipathy. The problems arising from attempts to assimilate the Jews into Polish culture offer but one example of problems which arose in their varying relations with Germans, Russians, Ukrainians, Lithuanians, and Byelorussians, with Catholics, Protestants, Uniates, Orthodox, and Muslims; with the nobility, bureaucracy, intelligentsia, bourgeoisie, peasantry, and proletariat; and with every conceivable combination of each and every one. Within the Polish intelligentsia, Polonized Jews formed an important and prominent element. Yet in Polish-speaking society at large, assimilated Jews formed only a modest minority. For social reasons, many assimilated Jews shunned publicity of their Jewish origins, and merged imperceptibly into Polish Catholic circles. Those who preserved their religious beliefs tended to refer to themselves as 'Poles of the Mosaic Faith'. In Gentile society, it was usual to make the distinction between the predominant *Israelita*, who had preserved both his race and his religion, the *Żyd*, who had preserved his Jewish identity but not necessarily his religion, and that wide category of 'ex-Jews', or people of Jewish descent who had severed their ties with Jewry for good.

Over the years, the Jewish Question accumulated a considerable body of comment in Polish literature. The classical state-

ment on the subject was made by Mickiewicz in *Pan Tadeusz*
in the scene where Jankiel, the Jew, treated his Polish hosts
to an impromptu concert on the dulcimer in celebration of
their common liberation from Russian domination. 'The
honest Jew', Mickiewicz wrote; 'loved his country like a Pole'.
Later on, in the age of Positivism, there were numerous
attempts to dampen the fires of growing antagonism. Bolesław
Prus, the novelist, was one of many who felt that present
difficulties were not insuperable:

If I could believe, as some of my colleagues do, that the Jews constitute
a power, I would be willing to think of this Jewish question as a real
problem. Unfortunately, as far as I can see, the Jews in no wise constitute
a power, except possibly in so far as they are rather numerous and their
proletariat is multiplying rather rapidly.

There are some who think that the Jews are the sole capitalists
among us, hence a financial force. I, on the contrary, regard the vast
majority as the poorest of the poor. There are those who accuse them
of unusual solidarity, which again I find amusing because, as far as I
know, their faith is not only divided into classes, filled with mutual
hatred and scorn, but has also a reactionary and a progressive party, and
even, it would seem, religious sects. Finally, there are those who are
fearful of Jewish mental prowess, which, though it doubtless exists,
represents no danger for our race.

It may be that this view is erroneous. In any case, it would have to
be refuted by facts. Until this happens I shall continue to believe that
the Jews fill us with apprehension and aversion only because we know
nothing about them and because we make no effort to get to know
them. How ridiculous . . . that we . . . do not study the customs, religion
and life of almost a million of our fellow-citizens, who will sooner or
later be fused with us into a uniform society.

What then lies at the root on this 'minor problem'? Is it the nationality or the religion of the Jews? Certainly not. The Jews are not a
nationality, and no one has any intention of depriving them of their
religion. But there are other factors — ignorance and caste feeling. So
let me draw attention to the fact that ignorance and caste feeling are
not unique to Jewish separatism. We must sorrowfully admit that in our
beautiful country ignorance reigns supreme from the basements to the
rooftops . . . In this respect, the Chassidic Jews, with their superstitions
. . . and belief in miraculous rabbis, are no glaring exception.

As for the Jewish caste spirit — dear Lord! Where is there no caste
spirit? Is it so long ago that gentlemen were ashamed to learn a trade or
to engage in commerce? And how many officials are there today who

would give their daughter in marriage to a locksmith or a carpenter? . . .
    To these ingredients, let us add Yiddish, the long black coat, and
early marriages. Let us sugar it all over with poverty, which is responsible
for swindling and usury, and we shall have the whole cake . . . It is
unsavoury; but I cannot believe that it will not collapse one day under
the pressure of education and progressive ideas.[17]

Prus's arguments contain their share of liberal fallacies; and
most of his predictions were not realized; but they reveal the
main arguments and counter-arguments of his day. In the
decade before the First World War, when the growth of
Zionism invalidated all denials of a separate Jewish nationality,
the level of debate deteriorated. The 'Anti-Semites' and 'the
Pro-Semites' battled each other incessantly, in a barrage of
recriminations and of mutually exclusive claims.
    In the circumstances, a measure of intercommunal animo-
sity was perhaps inevitable. It was encouraged by the age-old
social and economic deformations of Polish and Jewish society,
by poverty and demographic pressures, and above all, by the
growing tendency in Eastern Europe for all national groups
to seek their own separate salvation in their own separate
way. Polish hostility towards the Jews was complemented by
Jewish hostility towards the Poles. In an age of rampant
Nationalism, inter-communal solidarity was badly hampered.
So long as the Empires of the partitioning powers remained
in place, the numerous renascent nations of the region were
trapped like rats in a cage, where it was easier to bite one's
neighbour than to break down the bars of the common
servitude.
    During the First World War and its aftermath the predica-
ment of the Jewish community entered a phase of acute
danger. Having no vested interest in the victory of one side or
the other, they were blamed for disloyalty by all sides at
once. Having no means of raising a force of their own, they
were one of the few national minorities of the area who could
not see to their own defence. For seven long years, from
August 1914 to October 1920, Galicia and the Pale were the
scene of innumerable military actions. They were trampled
incessantly by the combatants of the Eastern Front, of the
Russian Civil War, of the Polish–Ukrainian War, and of the
Polish–Soviet War. When the fighting finally stopped, the

Treaty of Riga left a million Jews on the Soviet side of the frontier, and over 2 million in the Polish Republic.

The rebirth of Poland seemed to many Jews to herald the crossing of Jordan. The destruction of the Russian Empire, the support of the western democracies, and the founding of the League of Nations with its guarantee of Minority Rights all pointed to an end of the chronic insecurity which had prevailed for almost half a century. With this in view, Jews volunteered for service both in Piłsudski's Legions and in the Polish Army during the Soviet War; and a substantial element openly voiced their sympathies for the new Republic right from the beginning. Notwithstanding the hostility of the Zionists, and of extreme Polish nationalists (who succeeded at the height of the Battle of Warsaw in persuading the authorities to intern all Jewish volunteers as potential Bolshevik subversionists), the majority of established Jewish leaders decided to co-operate with the government. In May 1919, the first Congress of Poles of the Jewish Confession, widely reported in the Polish press, recorded their aims and aspirations:

The First Congress of the Founders
of the Association of Poles of the Jewish Faith
RESOLUTIONS
. . .
1. The Poles of the Jewish Faith, penetrated with a sincere feeling of love for Poland will, in spite of the difficult conditions of their existence, serve their country as devoted sons, and will always be ready to sacrifice their lives and fortunes for its benefit and glory.
2. The Congress condemns with indignation the spreading of hatred among fellow-citizens and especially the 'pogroms' which are perfectly incompatible with the spirit of the Polish Nation. These savage outbreaks injure not only Jewish citizens . . . but cause detriment to the good name of the Polish Nation, and are not in harmony with the ancient traditions of Poland.
3. The Congress protests against every separatist tendency aiming at the creation of a distinct national organisation in Poland.
4. The Congress recognises that the Jewish Question in Poland is an internal question and expresses the conviction that it will be solved by the Polish Commonwealth according to the principles of justice.
5. The Congress addresses to the whole of Polish society . . . the request to declare their disapproval of the 'pogroms' . . . and to prevent in the future in the eyes of the democracies of the whole civilised world the

staining of Poland's flag with the blood of Jewish citizens . . .
6. The Congress asks the Government to use all the means in its power
for the firm establishment of friendly and harmonious relations among
all the citizens of Poland . . .[18]

This trend faded in due course, leaving many of its advocates
isolated from Polish and Jewish society alike. Jewish assimilationists, resentful of the lukewarm response to their demands,
sometimes reacted in violent language. A much quoted, and
long-remembered article 'On the oversensitivity of the Jews',
which appeared in 1925 in the influential journal *Wiadomości
Literackie* (Literary News), and which listed a number of
pejorative Jewish characteristics, was written by none other
than Antoni Słonimski, the poet, one of the leading Jewish
advocates of Polish culture in his generation.[19]

Regrettably, the condition of Polish Jewry in the inter-war
period is often described out of context. It has always lain in
the interests of the Zionist movement, which sought to
persuade the Jews to leave their homes in Poland, to paint
Polish life in the most unfavourable colours. Yet the Zionist
viewpoint, which was hardly representative of the Jewish
masses as a whole, has received much greater publicity abroad
than that of any other interested party. In view of the
Holocaust of the Second World War, it is all too easy to be
wise after the event, and to suggest that the tribulations
of 1918—39 were a preamble to the ensuing tragedy. Historians must tread with extreme caution in an area where dis-
interested sources are very scarce. It is undeniable, of course,
that the economic and social standing of the Jews deteriorated.
The growth of industry, of a Polish middle class, of state
enterprise, and of peasant co-operatives, all diminished the
opportunities for traditional Jewish business. Unassimilated
Jews were not welcome in state employment, and were
effectively barred from a wide range of occupations, from the
Army and Civil Service, even from the schools, the state
liquor monopoly, and the railways. In all the professions,
efforts, either covert or open, were made to keep the entry of
Jews to a level commensurate with their numbers in the
population as a whole. No state subsidies were forthcoming
for Jewish schools. In this way, economic pressures aggravated
psychological insecurity. It has to be remembered that most

Jewish families found themselves in the Polish Republic irrespective of their personal inclinations. Like the Palestinian Arabs after the Second World War, the Polish Jews in 1918–21 found that a new state had been created around them, and that they were hostages to political fortunes entirely beyond their control. Some were favourably inclined; others were not. The Polish authorities encouraged Jewish religious bodies but frowned on those which possessed a separatist or nationalist flavour. What is more, an unprecedented demographic explosion countermanded all attempts to alleviate social conditions. The Jewish population rose to 2.7 million in 1931, and to 3.35 million in 1939. As a result, no less than 400,000 Jews emigrated from Poland for good in two decades. Still more would have left if entry to Palestine and to the USA had not been restricted. These facts are incontestable. The difficulty is to put them into some sort of meaningful perspective. In a new, multi-national society, intercommunal antipathies were commonplace, and the Jews were not exempt from the irritations and antagonisms which divided every ethnic group from the others. Yet it must be stressed that the pressures and discriminations to which the Jews were exposed were nothing exceptional. In terms of wealth, education, and social position, the Jews occupied a middling position among the minorities, inferior no doubt to that of the Germans in the western districts, but superior to that of the Ukrainians and Byelorussians in the east. In a society where the Jews formed 10 per cent of the total population — in Warsaw and Wilno 40 per cent, and in towns such as Pinsk 90 per cent — it was difficult to raise the hysterical Jew-scares which flourished in neighbouring countries. Almost every Polish family possessed Jewish friends or relatives, traded in Jewish shops, consulted Jewish doctors or lawyers, or drank their beer in the local Jewish tavern. The smooth functioning of Polish society as a whole could not be divorced from the success of the Jewish concerns which were integrated into it. One might have deplored that dependence; but it was in no one's interest that radical measures be taken against it. Only one influential Polish party, the National Democrats and their successors, were openly hostile to 'the native foreigners in our midst'; and they were no more rabid in their views on Jewry than on Germans,

Ukrainians, socialists, or gipsies. If we are to believe a leader of the Jewish *Bund* in pre-war Warsaw, even the virulence of the National Democrats had its limits:

. . . the nationalists . . . had great psychological and other difficulties in accepting the ideas of Fascism and Nazism . . . They were not revolutionaries like the Nazis in Germany or the Fascists in Italy: they were old-fashioned reactionaries. They were active in organising economic boycotts, but they would not encourage physical pogroms. They were for a *numerus clausus* at the universities, but were not for closing them completely to non-Catholic, Polish citizens . . . They were in favour of establishing two classes of citizens with different political rights, but were not for taking these rights away completely from any group. They were ready . . . to inflict severe wounds . . . on any semblance of liberal parliamentary democracy, but they also accepted . . . the existence of political parties representing all shades of opinion (with the exception of the communist party). Their cultural chauvinism was mitigated by the traditional respect and admiration for . . . Europe's Latin culture . . . The Nationalist party could never really become monolithic and totalitarian in its philosophy. Loyalty to the Roman Catholic Church was a basic feature of the party image . . . [20]

The National Democrats' opponents on the Left — the socialists, communists, and the liberal intelligentsia as a whole, were overtly pro-Jewish. The one active Fascist formation, the *Falanga* of Bolesław Piasecki (1914—79), attracted little popular support, and was dispersed by the police on the two occasions, in 1934 and 1937, when it dared to take openly to the streets. The militant Jew-baiters, such as the Revd Stanisław Trzeciak, one-time Professor in the Catholic Academy at St. Petersburg, who participated in the Nazi 'Panaryan *Weltdienst*', or Edward Chowański, an editor from Katowice, who served a nine-month jail sentence for announcing the destruction of the world by the Jews, did not go unchallenged. Press reports in the West of 'Pogroms in Poland', though accepted by Jewish commentators, were repeatedly discredited by the investigations of independent British and American observers. The so-called pogrom in Lwów, in November 1918, turned out to be a military massacre where three times more Christians died than Jews. The so-called pogrom in Pinsk in March 1919 turned out to be work of a panicky lieutenant, whose order to execute thirty-five suspected Bolshevik infiltrators was

described by a US investigator as 'fully justified by the circumstances'; the pogroms in Wilno in April 1919 and again in
October 1920 were occasioned by the Red Army's hasty
retreats, and by military reprisals against suspected collaborators. Polish Jews in the 1930s were indeed subjected to a
number of ugly threats and denigrations, and to a mounting
wave of economic hardship and emotional insecurity. After
Piłsudski's death, the OZON leadership saw little place for
the Jews in their vision of Polish national unity. The law of
April 1936 limiting *shehitah* (ritual slaughter) to Jewish
localities caused needless inconvenience. Yet the crude campaign to discredit the 'Judaic—Masonic Circle' of the Republic's
President, Ignacy Mościcki, rebounded on its instigators. In
terms of real violence, the Polish Jews suffered nothing
compared to the *Sanacja* regime's brutal pacifications of rebellious peasants or of separatist Ukrainians; and they never
experienced the sort of assaults meted out to their compatriots
in neighbouring Hungary, Romania, Germany, or the Ukraine.
By 1939, no satisfactory solution to the deteriorating problem
had been found; and the future was indeed bleak. But historians who glibly state that 'the writing was on the wall', or
that the Polish Jews were standing 'on the edge of the
destruction', or who quote a Warsaw rabbi to the effect that
'We were waiting for death', are mouthing a very partial view
of Polish affairs. As Isaac Cohen, of the Anglo-Jewish Association pointed out, Jews who imagined they were maltreated in
Poland did not have long to wait for conditions which made
Poland look like paradise; and as Sir Horace Rumbold, British
ambassador in Poland was quick to stress: 'It is of very little
service to the Jews to single out for criticism and retribution
the one country where they have probably suffered least.'[21]

The destruction of Polish Jewry during the Second World
War, therefore, was in no way connected to their earlier
tribulations. The Nazis' 'Final Solution' differed from other
forms of inhumanity not just in degree, but in kind. It was no
mere pogrom on a grand scale; it was a calculated act of
genocide executed with the full authority of the German state,
a mass murder committed in full accordance with the dictates
of the Nazis' unique, and alien ideology. What is more, it was
not planned in advance. In the first eighteen months of the

German Occupation, more Jews died in campaigns directed against the Polish intelligentsia (which contained a high proportion of Jews) than in actions specifically directed against the Jewish community. At this stage of the war, the Nazi leaders were intent on herding the Jews into reservations, and subjected them to innumerable indignities and violences. In some instances, as in the deliberate burning of the ghetto at Będzin on 9 September 1939, they committed large-scale massacres; but they had no clear intention of killing the Jews outright. They still entertained fanciful schemes of settling them on an unspecified island of the British Empire, of auctioning them off to the highest bidder, or of deporting them to Central Asia. As they were still at peace with the USA, they were obliged to take some minimal account of American sensibilities. They were not faced with the problems of disposing of the inhabitants of the reservations until those earlier schemes were invalidated by the emergence of the British–Soviet–American Alliance of mid-1941. It was at that moment, and no earlier, that the Final Solution was finalized.[22]

One of the meanest of modern historical controversies surrounds the conduct of the non-Jewish population towards the Nazis' Final Solution. Some Jewish writers, whether scholars or novelists such as Leon Uris, have spread the view that the Poles actually rejoiced at the fate of the Jews or at best were indifferent 'bystanders'. Polish apologists have gone to great lengths to publicise the instances where Jews were helped, or even rescued from the Nazis, by courageous civilians. Both sides in the controversy overlook the realities of life under the Nazi Terror, which was so much fiercer and more protracted in Poland than anywhere in Europe. To ask why the Poles did little to help the Jews is rather like asking why the Jews did nothing to assist the Poles. Stories of individual gallantry, though real enough, vastly exaggerated the opportunities for chivalry which actually existed. In a world where immediate death awaited anyone who contravened Nazi regulations, the Nazis could always exact a measure of co-operation from the terrified populace. The Polish slave doctor in Auschwitz, the Polish partisan in the woods, the Polish peasant fearful of reprisals, cannot be judged by the morality of free men in normal times, any more than one can judge the Jewish informers who sought to ransom their lives by denouncing their fellows, or the Jewish prostitutes who worked in SS guardrooms. Both Poles and Jews were victims to the Terror, and were conditioned by it. It is perfectly true, of course, that some of the partisan bands murdered fugitive Jews out of hand. It is also true that the Home Army failed to oppose the construction of the Ghettos in 1939–40 or the mass deportations of 1941–3. Yet to turn such facts into evidence of wilful neglect would seem to perpetrate a libel as vicious as any which has been levelled against the Jews themselves. In the nature of things, the Underground was notoriously suspicious about all refugees, outsiders, and strangers, not only about Jews, and protected just as many as they turned away. The Polish Underground failed to oppose not only the actions against the Jews, but equally, until 1943, all the executions and mass deportations of Polish civilians. In the earlier years of the war, it was simply too weak and too disorganized to attempt anything other than local diversions. With the one exception of the Ghetto in Łódź, which survived till August 1944, the Final Solution was all but complete by the time the Underground was strong enough to take action. In the meantime, the Council of Help for the Jews (RPZ), organized by the Government-in-Exile's Delegate, arranged for tens of thousands of Jews to be hidden and cared for. The survivors were all too few, but in the circumstances, it is hard to see how it could have been otherwise.[23] (See Chapter 20.)

The effects of the Final Solution need no elaboration. Of the 3.35 million Jews in Poland in 1939, an estimated 369,000, or 11 per cent survived. The largest group of survivors were those who fled or were incorporated into the USSR in 1939. Over 40 per cent of Polish citizens reporting to the reopened Polish Consulate in Russia, at Kuibyshev in 1941, were Jews. Some of these, including Menahim Begin, born at Brześć in 1913, reached Palestine in the ranks of General Anders's Polish army. The rest survived in Poland by hiding in barns, cellars, and rafters, by assuming false identities or by the protection of peasants. In 1945–6 some 200,000 Polish Jews crossed into People's Poland from the USSR; but most of them passed through on their way to Israel and to destinations further afield. A significant number were recruited into the PPR, or were employed by the communist Security Forces — thereby reviving the old spectre of the *Żydokomuna*. But in the over-all view, the 40,000 resident Jews in a population of 24 million were numerically negligible. For the first time in half a millennium, Poland had ceased to be Europe's most important Jewish sanctuary.

CHAPTER TEN
WOJSKO:
The Military Tradition

Few nations in the last two hundred years have seen more military action than the Poles. In the eighteenth, as in the twentieth century, the Polish lands regularly provided an arena for Europe's wars. In the nineteenth century, they supplied the armies of three martial empires with numberless recruits and conscripts. Yet no European nation has reaped fewer rewards for the sweat, and blood expended. As often as not, the Polish soldier has followed foreign colours. When marching under the Polish flag, or in Poland's cause, he has met, almost invariably, with defeat. It is a sad fact, but Poland has been obliged by circumstances to act as one of Europe's principal nurseries of cannon-fodder.[1]

By the middle of the eighteenth century, the old Army of the Polish—Lithuanian Republic had fallen into almost total decay. It had not undertaken a foreign campaign since the wars of the Holy League in the 1690s, and then only as a mercenary force of the Habsburgs. Its operations in the Great Northern War had failed to deter the country's Russian and Swedish invaders, and had ended in 1717 with its legal limitation to a nominal establishment of 24,000 men. Thereafter, it proved both unwilling and incapable of challenging the numerous foreign and domestic military formations which marched around the Polish territories during the rest of the Saxon Era. It played only a marginal role in the War of the Polish Succession, and none at all in the Silesian Wars, the War of the Austrian Succession, or the Seven Years War. The natural reluctance of the nobility to support the growth of a modern standing army was reinforced by the obvious dangers of creating a force which would pose a threat to Russian, Austrian, and Prussian ambitions. Even so, Poland—Lithuania was not short of soldiers. Vast numbers of indigent petty noblemen filled the ranks of a military caste of proportions unequalled in Europe. But their contempt for state service, their preoccupation with private wars and vendettas, their perpetuation of the myth of the *Pospolite Ruszenie,* the 'Noble Host', their dislike of drill, their obsession with cavalry to the detriment of all other branches of warfare, and their opposition to the idea of raising an 'ignoble army' of peasant conscripts, put them at a marked disadvantage in relation to all their neighbours. Private armies abounded; and the great magnates like Karol Radziwiłł, Xavery Branicki, or Antoni Tyzenhaus, maintained military establishments which would have been the envy of many European principalities – replete with their own officer corps, professional acadamies, uniforms, regulations, and armament industries. But their divided counsels ignored the requirements of mutual defence. By 1781, the ratio of trained soldiers in the service of the state to the adult male population had reached 1:472. This derisory statistic compared with 1:153 in France, 1:90 in Austria, 1:49 in Russia, and 1:26 in Prussia. Here was a fine paradox indeed. Europe's most militarized society was incapable of defending itself. The individualist military traditions of the nobility may well have predisposed the Poles to the insurrections of the nineteenth century; but they could not save the noble Republic.[2] (See Vol. I, Chapters 17, 18.)

The military establishment of the state was revived in Poland by Stanisław-August, and continued intermittently for sixty-six years. From 1765 to 1831, constant attempts were made to develop Polish military potential to a level commensurate with that of the neighbouring countries. For most of this period, an independent Polish army was in existence. Defeats and disbandments were not sufficient to destroy a certain continuity in traditions and personnel. The revival began in 1765 with the founding of the *Korpus Kadetów* (Cadet Corps), a military college designed to raise a new generation of officers in the spirit of patriotism and enlightenment. It was continued after 1775 by the Military Department of the Permanent Council, which abolished the old 'national' and 'foreign' contingents and began to form the cadres of a centralized and consolidated Army of the Republic. The artillery corps was refounded; the cavalry was reorganized, a code of military regulations was introduced; theoretical works were published by J. Bakatowicz and J. Jakubowski.

By 1788, when the Great Sejm first voted for a standing army of 100,000 men, the capacity to realize this goal undoubtedly existed. Only four short years remained, however, before the Russian wars of 1792–3 and 1794. Individual brilliance could not compensate for deficiencies in training, weapons, and numbers. Kościuszko's plan to mobilize the peasantry on the basis of one infantryman for every 5 *dym* of land, swelled the ranks of his insurrectionary army to 150,000 men.[3] But it could not match the disciplined professional formations of Prussia and Russia. Even so, the experience gained was not entirely lost. Kościuszko himself was but one distinguished product of the *Korpus Kadetów*; and his own subordinates — Kniaziewicz, Dąbrowski, Zajączek, Niemcewicz — were to provide the backbone of the Polish Legions (1797–1802), the Army of the Duchy of Warsaw (1807–13), and the Polish Army of the Congress Kingdom (1815–31).

The Napoleonic episode initiated three decades of strong French influence. If the impact of the Legions was mainly psychological, the introduction of six-year conscription in 1807, affecting every man in the Duchy of Warsaw between 21 and 28 years of age, brought military experience and training to the broad mass of the population. Napoleonic strategy and tactics of surprise and attack were well matched to memories of the Szlachta's fighting habits and to legends of Tarnowski and Sobieski. In the three-year Elementary School, and the annual Application Course (*Szkoła Aplikacyjna*), systematic attention was paid to military and technical education. (See Chapter 12.)

The Army of the Congress Kingdom extended French ideas into formations remodelled in the Russian image. The imposition of Russian practices on to the conduct of the General Staff and in the merciless discipline of the ranks, undoubtedly supplied an important factor in the political crisis of 1830. At the same time, the thorough schooling of officers, and the extension of the conscription period to ten years, enabled the Polish Army to enter the lists against the Russians with some reasonable confidence. The Russo-Polish war of 1831 provided one of two occasions in modern history when the Poles have faced the Russians on an equal footing.[4] (See Chapter 13.)

From 1831 to 1914, no formal Polish army of consequence existed. Polish military enterprises, whether in the risings of 1846, 1848, and 1863; in Mickiewicz's Legion in Italy, or in the Polish Cavalry Division in the Crimea, lacked any potential for concerted and consolidated action. They belonged to that romantic world of amateur and partisan warfare, where it is more important to play the game, and to stay in the field, than to think of winning.[5]

Throughout this long period of over eighty years, the participation of the Poles in the armed services of the partitioning powers represented an experience of prime importance. The presence in the Polish provinces of huge Russian, Prussian, and Austrian garrisons, and the organization of permanent military districts dependent on St. Petersburg, Berlin, or Vienna, had important consequences for the social, economic, and cultural life of the entire region. Whole generations of young Poles were conscripted to the ranks. There they were instilled with the prevailing political loyalism of their regiments, and learned to follow their commands in Russian or German. In Prussia, the army's demand for literate recruits provided a major stimulus to state education, and hence to Germanization. By 1901, 99 per cent of recruits from the province of Posen, for example, could write and speak German. In Russia and Austria, where educational standards were lower, Polish identity was not submerged so easily. At the same time, large numbers of educated Poles were drawn into the various officer corps. Although Polish Catholics fared less well in the service of Protestant Prussia and Orthodox Russia, Polish names can be found on the staff lists, and on the rolls of honour of all three imperial armies. Marshal Konstanty Rokossowski (Konstantin Rokossovskiy, 1896–1967) born in Warsaw the son of a Polish engine-driver, who joined the Russian army during the First World War, was but the last of many Polish predecessors in the Tsarist service, including Władyslaw Anders (1892–1970), J. Dowbór-Muśnicki (1867–1937), Zygmunt Piłsudski, R. Łągwa (1891–1938), and Lucjan Żeligowski (1865–1947). In Prussia, Poles were less common among the officers than among the NCOs, the backbone of the German service; but in Austria men such as Tadeusz Rozwadowski (1866–1928), Stanisław

Szeptycki (1867–1946), and Stanisław Haller (1872–1940) who were awarded commands at the highest level, were by no means isolated examples. All these soldiers were strongly affected by the traditions of the armies in which they served, not least by the intensity of their experiences in the trenches of the First World War. When they were called on to form a new Polish army, it is not surprising that they found great difficulty in working together.

To a certain extent, the Polish Legions of the 1914–17 campaign re-enacted the scenario of their Napoleonic predecessors, after whom they were named. Their goals were not fully achieved, either in the military or in the political sphere. Piłsudski's idea of fighting for Polish Independence under Austrian orders proved no more practical than Dąbrowski's scheme of fighting for Napoleon in the hope of restoring the old Republic. The political conditions laid down in 1917 by the Germans within the command of the Central Powers proved quite unacceptable. (See Chapter 18.) Yet the psychological impact of the Legions was again great; and the sudden emergence of national independence only seventeen months after their forcible disbandment gave an unparalleled opportunity for the ex-legionnaires in the military dispositions of the Second Republic. Apart from Piłsudski himself, Generals Józef Haller (1873–1961), Marian Kukiel (1895–1976), Kazimierz Sosnkowski (1885–1963), and Władysław Sikorski (1881–1943) all gained early military experience in the Legions.[6]

The role of the army in the life of the Second Republic was of paramount importance. The army was largely responsible for guarding and preserving the manna of independence which so fortuitously dropped from heaven in 1918. The General Staff's confidence in Poland's military capacity proved illusory; but in 1939 the devotion and courage of the ranks in impossible conditions was often exemplary.[7] (See Chapter 19.)

In the Second World War, control of numerous Polish military formations did not lie in Polish hands. In 1940, the reconstituted army which fought under French orders at Narvik and in France numbered 80,000 men. After the fall of France, the remnants passed to Great Britain to be reformed as the First Polish Corps under British command. After 1941 two separate Polish armies were raised in the USSR. The first, the Polish army in the East, formed largely from released deportees and commanded by General Władysław Anders, left Soviet territory for the Middle East, where they were eventually incorporated into the Second Polish Corps of the British Eighth Army. Their extraordinary odyssey, from prison camps in Siberia and Central Asia to Buzuluk on the Volga, to Tashkent, to Pahlevi in Persia, to Baghdad, Jerusalem, Cairo, Tobruk, Anzio, Rome, to the Sangrio and the Gothic Line, has never been satisfactorily recounted to western readers. The second appeared in 1943 as the Kościuszko Infantry Division. Politically subordinated to the Polish communists in Moscow, it was entirely subject to the Soviet Command. In March 1944, under General Zygmunt Berling (1896–1980), it emerged as the First Polish Army and participated in the campaigns of the Eastern Front. At this stage, the Poles fighting in the British Army numbered some 195,000; those under Soviet orders, 78,000. In 1944–5 these figures were increased to 228,000 and 400,000 respectively – the latter by conscription in liberated Polish territories. All those men were called to make great sacrifices whose ultimate purpose was somewhat ambiguous. In the Battle of Britain in 1940, Polish pilots accounted for some 15 per cent of enemy losses, thus contributing significantly to the salvation of Great Britain. Yet no reciprocal gesture was ever made by the British, either in 1939–40 or in 1944–5, for the salvation of Poland. At Lenino on the Ukrainian Front in October 1943, at Monte Cassino in Italy in May 1944, and at Arnhem in September 1944, Polish units showed immense courage and suffered heavy casualties in the course of operations of doubtful value. At the end of the war in Europe on 9 May 1945, the First Polish Armoured Division stood at Wilhelmshaven, the Second Corps at Bologna, and in the east, the First Armoured Corps was on the Elbe in Czechoslovakia. The only Polish formation to enjoy a wide measure of autonomy, the partisan *Armia Krajowa,* received as little practical support from the Western Allies as it did from the Soviets. The considerable Polish effort in the war against Hitler was not matched by any corresponding benefits relating to Poland's future destiny.[8] (See Chapter 20.)

In the last two centuries, Polish arms have won only one unaided victory. The 'Miracle of the Vistula' in August 1920 is as exceptional in the modern history of Poland as in the career of the Soviet Army. Once, and once only, the Poles emerged victorious in single-handed combat with the forces of their great neighbour. How it happened is a matter for debate. It certainly cannot be attributed to careful planning or systematic preparation. Piłsudski himself called it 'a scrap', 'a brawl', 'a *bagarre*', an 'absurdity'. He talked of 'the nullity of forces available', 'the irrationality of feebleness', and 'the excessive risk contrary to all sound military principles'. His enemies pointed to the skill of the visiting General Weygand, to the folly of Tukhachevsky, or the machinations of Stalin, or even to divine Providence, to anything except the nerve and determination of Piłsudski. One does not know the full explanation; and if the present political censorship prevails, the Polish public will never know even the basic facts.[9] (See pp. 394–9.)

In the circumstances, no lasting corporate military tradition could develop in Poland. Repeated defeats have repeatedly slighted the competence of each generation in the eyes of the next. Momentary hopes have always been followed by bitter disillusionment. The officer corps, the regimental units, the military colleges have never enjoyed sufficient success or continuity to bequeath their outlook and experiences to their successors with any sense of confidence. What has developed, in contrast, is a strong belief in the private virtues of the individual Polish soldier. Stamina and fortitude in adversity, the ability to improvise, devotion to the cause, and carelessness for one's own safety, are traits which have won the admiration of comrades in all the armies where Poles have served. These qualities are celebrated in the vast repertoire of Polish military folklore:

Wojenko, Wojenko,	War, Sweet War,
Cóżeś ty za pani	What sort of mistress are you
Że za tobą idą	That you can be pursued
Chłopcy malowani?	By all those beautiful boys?[10]

They are to be found in songs from Bathory's campaigns in Muscovy, in the lively mazurkas of the uhlans, and above all in the words of the March of Piłsudski's legions — *My, Pierwsza Brygada* (We of the First Brigade):

Legiony to, żolnierska buta	The Legions stand for a soldier's slog,
Legiony to, ofiarny stos;	The Legions stand for a martyr's fate,
Legiony to, żebracka nuta;	The Legions stand for a beggar's song,
Legiony to, straceńców los;	The Legions stand for a convict's death.
My, Pierwsza Brygada,	We are the First Brigade;
Strzelecka Gromada,	A regiment of rapid fire.
Na stos,	Our fate,
Rzuciliśmy swój życia los,	Our very lives are at stake.
Na stos, na stos'.	We've cast ourselves on the pyre.[11]

Inevitably, legends abound. Deprived of their due share of military glory in modern times, the Poles are constantly drawn to tales of their nation's valour in the past. *Ogniem i mieczem* (By Fire and Sword), Henryk Sienkiewicz's fictional trilogy of stirring adventures in the Swedish Wars of the 1650s, retains its pre-eminence in the world of popular literature, and has headed the popularity charts in a recent vogue for historical films. Like all the heroes of real history, from Sobieski, to Kościuszko, Poniatowski, Sowiński, and Major Hubal, Pan Wołodyjowski gains added stature from the fact that his feats were performed in a setting of national catastrophe. Thus, to the Polish way of thinking, individual virtue can triumph over corporate disaster; the prowess of the Polish soldier redeems the failures of the Polish army; and self-respect is drawn from defeat.

Of all the analysts of Polish military affairs, none has proved more accurate, or more prophetic than Jean-Jacques Rousseau. Writing in 1771, on the eve of the Partitions, he predicted that Poland would never have an army to match those of her neighbours. 'You will never have an offensive force', he wrote, 'and for a long time you will never have a defensive one. But you already have . . . a preservative force which will protect you from destruction, even in bondage, and will protect your government and your freedom in their only true sanctuary — in the hearts of the Poles.'[12]

CHAPTER ELEVEN

EMIGRACJA:

The Polish Emigration

Together with Ireland, Sicily, and parts of Germany, the Polish lands have produced a disproportionate share of European emigrants. Almost one-third of all ethnic Poles live abroad. A surprisingly large part of them maintain some form of contact with the old country. As at any time during the last two centuries, they play an important, and by now a traditional role in the life of the state and the nation.[1]

The emigrants can be classified in two distinct categories — political and economic. (Those who fit into neither category, such as the beloved spouses of foreign nationals, have only marginal statistical significance.)

The political emigration began in the 1730s and has continued at regular intervals ever since. Stanisław Leszczyński in his Duchy of Lorraine was but the first and best known example of countless Poles who have been driven from their homeland by adverse political fortunes. Somewhat later, the Confederates of Bar maintained close links with France, many of them retiring to Paris after their defeat in 1772. In 1795, 1831, 1846–8, 1864, 1905, and 1944, the failure of successive Risings propelled generation after generation of patriot-rebels to the west. In the twentieth century, the re-establishment of an independent Polish state has occasionally served to reverse the flow. Yet after the upheavals and forcible deportations of 1939–45, Polish emigrants could be counted not in thousands but in millions. A few of these returned to the People's Republic; but virtually none whose homes lay in territories annexed by the Soviet Union, in Wilno or Lwów, could willingly be persuaded to return there. In the post-war era, strict controls on the free movement of the population have been abetted by relative political stability. But in 1956, and especially in 1968, significant groups of people have left Poland for political reasons.

In the nature of things, political *émigrés* include a high

proportion of educated, principled people; but of all the Polish exoduses none has ever matched the generation of 1831 for the quality of its adherents and for its outstanding intellectual achievements. This *Wielka Emigracja* (Great Emigration) embraced almost the entire political élite of the Congress Kingdom, and included a large part of the artistic talent of the day. Its record was far more distinguished than that of its contemporaries who stayed at home. Whether in the garrets of Paris or in the wastes of Siberia, their intensity of feeling, the sustained energy of their political organizations and debates, the brilliance of their literary and scientific enterprise command respect and admiration. Like all men in their condition, deprived of the comforts of home and kin, the Great Emigration was forced to drink the cup of bitterness amidst increasing disillusionment. How many of them in their outpourings echoed the words of that greatest of all politi al exiles, who wrote of *la crudeltà*, of 'the cruel fate which excludes me from that beautiful fold where I slept as a lamb'. Yet for three decades and more, in the darkest days between 'November' and 'January' in the interval before the establishment of national autonomy in Galicia, they led the nation from afar. Throughout this period, Prince Adam Czartoryski, 'the uncrowned King of Poland' presided from his Hotel Lambert in Paris over the main focus of independent Polish politics. He enjoyed greater personal authority than any contemporary figure, in Poland or abroad. His numerous opponents fired the feuds and debates which kept fundamental issues alive. His literary confrères — Mickiewicz, Słowacki, Krasiński, Norwid — forged, from Romanticism, the single most important School of modern Polish literature. These names, and their considerable works, have acted as an inspiration for all their successors until the present day.[2]

Economic emigration was confined to somewhat tighter chronological limits. It began in the 1840s, swelled into a flood in the later nineteenth century, and came to a sudden halt in 1939. It developed from the practice of seasonal migration and never lost some of the latter's characteristics. The demand for labour on the large-scale Prussian estates, and later in the mines and factories of Silesia, Saxony, or Westphalia, attracted a steady flow of Polish peasants from the east. At first they came just for the harvest, or for a spell of industrial employment in the winter, after completing the year's work on their own farms. Later, they travelled further afield, to Belgium and France, and from the 1860s, to North and South America; and they stayed for longer periods. But most typically, like the *Gastarbeitern* of present-day Europe, they stayed in contact with their families at home, remitted their savings, and looked to an early return as soon as circumstances allowed. Many returned after a lifetime's career abroad to retire at home. Even today, almost forty years after all economic emigration ceased, there are still Poles who return to the People's Republic from America, to spend their American pensions in comfort and to be buried, with characteristic fastidiousness, in their native soil.[3]

In the later nineteenth century, increasing rural overpopulation and grinding urban poverty forced large numbers of people to emigrate to America with no thought of return. Established emigrants wrote home with exaggerated stories of their success. Extravagant tales abounded:

Here in America you can take as much land as you need. You do what you like. Nobody watches you. Wheat and other grain is harvested twice a year. The land needn't be manured or tilled. Manure is burnt or thrown into water. Gold is dug like potatoes. The hares are huge, and they're not afraid of men. You can have as much meat as you like. Pigs, cattle, and horses breed in the woods. And the frogs are as big as cows. If you meet one on the road, you must drive round it so as not to upset the cart. Fruit grows on all trees, and everyone can pick their fill . . . All this is written on paper, and stamped. The organist has read it twice.[4]

Germans, Jews, and Ukrainians from the Polish lands jostled with the mainstream of Polish-speaking Catholic peasants who crowded the westbound railway platforms and the decks of packet boats out of Hamburg, Danzig, and Riga. Regular agencies ferried their clients to a new life beyond the sunset. Not uncommonly, peasants from neighbouring localities would form a group, put themselves in the charge of a priest, and depart *en masse*. In 1854, for example, one of the earliest Polish groups to leave Silesia founded the first Polish parish in Texas. Inspired by German colonists from the same Prussian province, who were already settling the rich lands of the south Texas plain, one hundred and fifty emigrants assembled at

Oppeln (Opole) under the orders of a Franciscan friar, the Revd Leopold Moczygęba (1824–91), took a ship at Bremerhaven, and sailed for New Orleans. They carried a few personal belongings, a few agricultural implements, and a large wooden cross for erection in their new homeland. In the following Spring, at Panna Maria, now in Karnes County fifty miles from San Antonio, Father Moczygęba made the first entry in the parish register:

'Pauline Bronder, AD MDCCCLV, die nona Februarii, nata et a me infrascripto eadem die baptizata est filla legitima Simon Bronder et Juliae Pilarczyk, conjugorum Catholicorum, cui nomen Paulina impositum est. Matrina Julia Kyrish. Ita testor, Fr. L. B. M. Moczygęba.'[5] *

The infant Paulina, lawful daughter of Simon and Julia Bronder, godchild of Julia Kyrish, could look forward to a life which her forebears had never imagined.

These economic emigrants differed markedly from their political counterparts. They were poor and they were largely illiterate, overwhelmingly peasants, small craftsmen, or miners. They left their Polish homes deliberately, wilfully turning their backs on a homeland which had offered them little but poverty and oppression. They possessed very little awareness of Polish cultural and political traditions. Most of them never set foot in Warsaw or Cracow, and had certainly never benefited from what was to be found there. They went straight from their Polish village to a factory in Essen or to a farm in Kansas. When they died, they could not leave their children much of their Polish heritage — just the memories of their village, their country dialect, their religion, a few peasant songs and dances, a crumpled wedding costume in the national style, and in the cupboard a naïve souvenir marked 'Kalwaria Zebrzydowska' or 'Jasna Góra'.

Statistical information on the Polish emigration is not easily available. Official records in the nineteenth century usually mention emigrants' citizenship, but not their nationality. Even if the historian so wishes, it is often impossible to distinguish

* 'AD 1855, on 9 February, a legitimate daughter was born to Simon Bronder and Julia Pilarczyk, Catholic man and wife, and on the same day was baptized by me the undersigned, and given the name of Paulina. The godmother was Julia Kyrish. Witness thereto, Brother L. B. M. Moczygęba.'

Prussian Poles from Prussian Germans, Galician Poles from Galician Ukrainians, or Russian Poles from Russian Jews. By 1939, however, tentative figures suggest that some 195,000 Poles had settled permanently in Brazil: some 450,000 in France, some 250,000 in Canada, some 1.5 million in the USA, and over 2 million in Germany. Taking into consideration the natural increase over the last century, and the constant re-injection of political refugees, an estimate of between 9 to 10 million people of Polish extraction living abroad becomes entirely credible. Even so, this total is not complete. There are still a million and a half Poles living in the USSR, some voluntarily, others by force of circumstances. It should also be remembered that large numbers of Jewish, Ukrainian, Lithuanian, and German emigrants, who since emigrating have rejected all sense of Polish identity, did none the less originate from the Polish lands, and not infrequently were educated in Polish schools, or travelled on Polish passports. Their exact numbers are incalculable, but any global estimate of emigrants 'of Polish origin' in its widest sense must surely be approaching the 15 million mark.

Nowadays, the American 'Polonia' takes pride of place. An estimated six and a half million Polish Americans constitute not only the largest single Polish community abroad but also one of the largest ethnic minorities of the USA. The pioneers are to be found on the earliest pages of American colonial history, and contain at least one doubtful candidate for the doubtful honour of having discovered the New World before Columbus. According to sources which claim no general acceptance, Jan z Kolna (John of Kolno) alias 'Scolnus', a sailing-captain in the Danish service, reached the coast of Labrador in 1476. More certainly, in October 1608, an emigrant ship, the *Mary and Margaret,* carried among its passengers the first Polish settlers into Jamestown, Virginia. Michał Łowicki, merchant; Zbigniew Stefański of Włocławek, glass-blower; Jan Mała of Cracow, soap-maker; Stanisław Sądowski of Radom, water-mill constructor; and Jan Bogdan of Kołomyja, shipwright, had presumably been recruited in Danzig by the Virginia Company, and belonged to a team of technicians specially ordered by Governor John Smith to establish the infant colony's economy. Ten years later the

Polish artisans of Jamestown were said to be responsible for the continent's first industrial strike and, in their game of *palant,* for the invention of Baseball. In New Amsterdam, in 1659, the city's Grammar School was run by a certain Dr Curtius from Poland, whilst in 1622 Al(brecht) or Al(exander) or Al(bin) Zaborowski (d. 1711), a noble Arian refugee from Royal Prussia, first set foot in the New World from the deck of the *De Vos.* His eldest son, Jakub, was seized as a boy by the Iroquois and lived henceforth with the Indians. Four younger sons fathered the far-flung 'Zabrisky' family. In the Midwest, in the eighteenth century, Antoni Sądowski, of Philadelphia, a fur-trader, opened up the valley of the Ohio. His sons, Jacob and Joseph 'Sandusky' figured prominently in the expeditions which founded the settlements of Cincinnati (Ohio) and Harrodsburgh (Kentucky). There were Polish participants in all the great events of American history. In the War of Independence, apart from Tadeusz Kościuszko and Kazimierz Pułaski, whose exploits are known to every schoolboy, there were Poles such as Karol Blaszkowicz, a naval cartographer, who fought for the Loyalists, and others such as the New England privateer, Feliks Miklaszewicz, who fought for the Revolution. On the western frontier, there were Poles such as Henry Lyons Brolarski of St. Louis, who worked as a leading entrepreneur on the overland trails to California and Oregon in the 1840s and 1850s. On the west coast, there were Poles among the Russians from Siberia who first developed Alaska, and who in 1811 built Fort Ross on San Francisco Bay. In 1848, a surgeon of the US Army Medical Corps, Dr Paul Wierzbicki, born at Czerniawka in Volynia, wrote a book which shook the continent. His *California as it is, or as it may be, or a Guide to the Gold Region* was the first volume printed west of the Rockies, and served as the standard guidebook for thousands of hopeful prospectors in the Gold Rush of 'Forty-nine. In the Civil War, there were Poles such as General Kacper Tochman of Virginia, a veteran of the November Rising and a noted racialist, who served on the Confederate staff, and others, like General Włodzimierz Krzyżanowski (1827–87), a Posnanian, who served the Union. Oddly enough, both Tochman's Polish Brigade and Krzyżanowski's Polish Legion, which distinguished itself at the second Bull Run and at Gettysburg, consisted largely of Germans. These early Polish names belonged, of course, to accidentals, and there were those among them whose Polishness was doubtful, if not downright spurious. Tochman's wife, for example, who called herself Apolonia Jagiello, turned out, in reality, to be a Ms Eisenfeld of Vienna. There were several supposedly Polish royals in circulation, including a Jan Sobieski (1842–1927), who was a ranking officer in both the Union and Mexican armies. What exactly were the Polish connections of Lorenzo Sobieski Young, whose name is recorded in Salt Lake City among the 143 founders of the Mormon colony, it is difficult to say.[6]

The main influx of Poles to the United States began after the Civil War. But then they came in force, and they kept coming until they penetrated every state of the Union. Their arrival coincided with the growth of the industrial towns of the Midwest and the north-east, and it is there, in Milwaukee, Chicago, Detroit, Cleveland, Buffalo, Pittsburgh, Philadelphia, and Baltimore, that the greatest concentrations still reside. Others headed straight for the countryside of New England or for the open prairies. Prosperous Polish farming communities can be encountered in Connecticut, Pennsylvania, and Massachusetts, no less than in Michigan, Minnesota, Wisconsin, and Illinois. The names of Warsaw (Alabama), Kosciuszko (Mississippi), and Pulaski (Tennessee), like hundreds of similar small towns, betray the provenance of their founders. As usual, statistics are controversial. But the records from the US Immigration and Naturalization Service would suggest that the over-all parameters for immigrants identified as Polish either by 'race' or 'people', or by 'country of birth' must lie between a minimum total of 1,486,490 and a maximum total of 1,823,540. (See Table overleaf.)

Despite their numbers, however, the Polish Americans have still to make a proportionate impact on American life. Isolated instances of individual success, such as Senator Edmund Muskie, John Krol, Archbishop of Philadelphia, or Professor Zbigniew Brzeziński, cannot conceal the fact that Polish Americans do not yet, as a community, enjoy great social prestige. As an organized group, they cannot compete with the influence, for instance, of the three million American Jews.

IMMIGRANTS TO USA

a) Giving Poland as their 'place or country of birth':

1820–1885	33,489
1885–1898	131,694
1933–1946	46,473
1947–1972	466,001
Total	677,657

b) Identified as Polish by 'race or people':

1899–1907	675,038
1908–1919	677,620
1920–1932	90,815
Total	1,443,473

TOTAL: Polish Immigrants		2,121,130
less	*Re-emigrants*	
1908–1932	294,824	
1947–1972	2,766	
Total	297,590	
TOTAL: Permanent Polish Immigrants		1,823,540[7]

Nor have their votes or their lobbying ever inspired US Foreign Policy to defend Poland's interests. In two World Wars, they made a disproportionate contribution to the US armed services. Drawn from only 4 per cent of the total population, in 1917–18 they supplied 12 per cent of America's war dead, and in 1941–5 17 per cent of America's enlisted men. In social terms, their educational and communal organizations are less effective than those of the Ukrainians, with whom they are often compared. In political terms, their problems command less notice than those of the Blacks, Chicanos, or Amerindians. In the vicious world of the American ethnic jungle, the 'stupid and ignorant Pole' has been widely accepted as a standard stereotype, and provides the butt for innumerable and (for the Poles) insulting 'Polish jokes'. How different from the popular stereotype of the 'noble Polish lord' still current in parts of Europe! Reasons no doubt exist. Like the Irish and the Sicilians, the greatest influx of Poles at the start of the century, especially from Galicia, contained a disproportionate number of 'the wretched refuse' of Europe's most 'teeming shore' – people so oppressed by poverty and near-starvation that they made for America from an instinct of mere survival. They accepted the most degrading forms of employment, withstood the most grinding labour, suffered the greatest exploitation, sweated and interbred in the dirtiest slums. They were the gangers of the great American Railway Age, and the 'industrial niggers' of the northern cities. As one Canadian textbook on the subject has phrased it: 'Poles and police courts seem to be invariably connected in this country. It is hard to think of the people of this nationality other than in that vague class of undesirable citizens.'[8] Even Woodrow Wilson, when a Professor at Princeton, had to be taken to task for referring to the Poles as 'inferior'.[9] Nowadays, perhaps, the situation is changing. The extraordinary social mobility of the USA is fast diluting the old ethnic ghettos. One hypothesis for the persistence of the Polish Americans' unfavourable image points to the resentment felt by more fortunate minorities at the advancement of former underdogs. Those underdogs may yet have their day.[10]

Even so, important divisions still divide the Polish American community. The 'old Poles' of the economic emigration do not mix easily with the 'new Poles' of the more recent political emigration. Among the politicals, a wall of suspicion divides the professional anti-communists of the pre-war generation from later refugees from People's Poland. The generation of 1939, which was deprived of its birthright by the communist victory, has nothing in common with the generation of 1968 which, as often as not, willingly served the Stalinist regime. Numerous organizations compete. The Roman Catholic community grouped in thousands of Polish parishes commands the greatest numerical following, which mainly supports the Polish Roman Catholic Union. The Polish Seminary of Saints Cyril and Methodius, with its associated Center for Polish Studies at Orchard Lake (Michigan), goes back to 1885. More recently, an 'American Częstochowa' has been developed round the Polish church and community centre at Doylestown (Pennsylvania). The dominance of the Irish and German priests in the Roman Catholic hierarchy of the USA, and the Americanization policy of replacing national parishes with territorial ones, led to constant troubles and eventually to a minor schism. The small, breakaway Polish National Church, founded in 1875, seeks to preserve the exclusively national character of its parishes, together with its Polish language liturgy. In the secular sphere, the Polish National Alliance was founded in Philadelphia in 1880, and in its turn founded Alliance College at Cambridge Springs (Pennsylvania). In Chicago, there is a Polish R.C. Union and Museum. In New York, the Kościuszko Foundation was created in 1925 to promote Polish cultural enterprises, and has taken the lead in maintaining links with Poland. From time to time, its neutral political position has been fiercely attacked, notably by militant bodies such as the National Committee of Americans of Polish Origin (KNAPP), which made a determined effort after the Second World War to turn the Polonia Congress against any form of contact with the communist regime. The Polish Institute of Arts and Sciences in America Inc. acts as a forum for academic and professional activities, and publishes *The Polish Review*. The Józef Piłsudski Institute of America Inc., under its veteran director, Wacław Jędrzejewicz, possesses a valuable library and historical archive.

Relatively speaking, the Poles of Canada include a larger proportion of politicals than is the case in the United States. In the post-war era, the presence of prominent figures such as General Sosnkowski, Ambassador Romer, or Consul Brzeziński made Montreal a natural centre for *émigré* politics. In Quebec, the Poles have to face the problem of multiculturalism – that is, the choice of assimilating into Francophone or Anglophone society. Important communities thrive in Ontario, Manitoba, and British Columbia.[11]

The Poles of Brazil are concentrated in the provinces of Parana, Santa Catarina, and Rio Grande do Sul. In both World Wars, they sent volunteer detachments to fight with the Polish army in Europe.[12]

In Europe, the 'old Poles' are concentrated in France, Belgium, and Germany, especially in the mining districts of Pas-de-Calais, Le Nord, Liège, and the Ruhr.[13] In many ways they resemble their counterparts in America, maintaining their identity in Catholic parishes and through cultural societies. Political circles, in contrast, traditionally gravitated to Paris, to Rome, or to Switzerland. The Bibliothèque Polonaise opposite Nôtre Dame, the Instituto Istorico Polacco by the Piazza Roma, and the National Polish Muzeum at Rapperswill on Lake Zürich attest to important Polish activities in the past. In recent times, however, the centre of Polish *émigré* politics has shifted permanently to London.

The Poles of Great Britain differ from their transatlantic compatriots in several important respects. Although the origins of the community can be traced to the early nineteenth century, their numbers were never very great until the Second World War. Although they have known their share of economic hardship, they must nearly all be classed as politicals. The vast majority came with the Polish Armed Forces, the Government-in-Exile or as wartime refugees and post-war DPs, who had fully expected to return home as soon as the War ended. They were invariably anti-communist; frequently with military connections, and usually from the eastern provinces. They stayed on because they refused to recognize the Soviet takeover in Poland, or because their homes had been incorporated into the USSR. Embittered by the failure of their aspirations for an independent Poland, and reluctant to put down roots in their involuntary exile, they lived in a spiritual ghetto of their own, and made few contacts with British society at large. Nearly forty years after their arrival, and in spite of considerable re-emigration to Canada and Australia, their numbers stand at about 150,000. They are the true successors of the Great Emigration of the previous century. Politicians of influence from pre-war and wartime days – General Anders, President August Zaleski, Edward Raczyński, Marian Kukiel, Adam Ciołkosz, Jędrzej Giertych – all took up residence in London, which remains the centre of publishing and politicking in the old style. The Polish Government-in-Exile, the legal continuator of the Second Republic, though unrecognized, continues to operate. The President convokes the *Rada Ministrów* (Council of Ministers) every fortnight in the *Zamek* (The Castle) at 43 Eaton Place. The most active body, however, is the amalgamated Association of Polish Combatants (SPK) which broke away from the 'legalists' in 1954. The Sikorski Muzeum, the Polish Library, the Polish Cultural and Social Centre (POSK), the Polish Research Centre, the Underground Research Centre and other institutions provide important community services. The *Dziennik Polski* (Polish Daily) and the fortnightly literary publication *Wiadomości* (News) complement the main *émigré* journal, *Kultura* (Culture) in Paris. The Polish-University-Abroad, though much diminished, still functions. The Church of Andrzej Bobola provides the focal point of Roman Catholic life. Elsewhere in the United Kingdom, there are large Polish communities in Glasgow, Manchester, Bradford, and Coventry. There are Polish boarding schools at Fawley Court (Oxon.), for boys, and at Pitsford (Leics.), for girls. In all major centres there are Polish parishes, Polish clubs, and Polish Saturday schools. The tone is gradually changing as the new British-born generation comes to the fore. But if the spirit of pre-war Warsaw, Wilno, or Lwów has survived anywhere it is in the rooms of the *Ognisko Polskie* (the Polish Hearth) in Kensington.[14]

The Poles of the USSR fit into two distinct categories. On the one hand, there are the remnants of the Polish and polonized population which has inhabited Lithuania, Byelorussia, and Ukraine since time immemorial. On the other hand, there are the political deportees. In both cases, it may seem odd that people whose homes were excluded from Poland by a change of state frontiers or whose ancestors were transported to Siberia in chains, should be classed as 'emigrants'. Yet the final result is much the same. For better or for worse, they have been physically separated from that main Polish community to which their forebears once belonged. They share most of the problems of those who departed to the west of their own free will. The political deportees have a very long history. Each generation of Poles which was dumped in the depths of the tundra or the steppe in 1832, 1864, 1906, 1940, or 1945 has talked of encountering Poles of an earlier generation who had shared the same fate. In each of the traditional areas of exile, the new arrivals were welcomed by ex-insurrectionists who in some cases were unable to speak Polish, but who were fiercely proud of their Polish origins. From time to time evidence emerges of the huge numbers involved in these terrible and obscure happenings, as in 1866 when the great Bajkal Mutiny occurred, or more recently in 1942–3 when the Polish Army in Russia succeeded in evacuating itself and its dependants. The population transfers of 1945–7, and the Amnesty of 1956 gave two rare opportunities for many thousands of Poles to leave the USSR. But many would not, or could not, leave. For families who had lived in Russia for centuries, the chance to 'return' to Poland did not always prove attractive. Others were not given the choice. The fate of hundreds of thousands of Polish civilians deported in 1939–40, and of tens of thousands of Home Army prisoners arrested in 1944–6, is still not exactly known.[15] (See pp. 447–52, 479–80.)

The Polish presence in Israel deserves special mention. The larger part of European Jewry, whose survivors fled to Palestine after the Second World War, once shared their destiny with the Poles in Poland. It is perhaps a natural prejudice that the modern generation should choose to forget their links with a country which, willy-nilly, hosted the Holocaust. Yet all do not forget so easily. The 'Street of the Just' in Tel-Aviv bears witness to more Polish names than to those of any other nation. And Jerusalem is one of the few cities in the world where a visitor with a sound knowledge of Polish need not fear losing his way.[16]

Internecine political divisions are an innate feature of life in exile, and can be traced in the history of the Polish Emigration from the very beginning. The émigrés customarily divided themselves into conservative 'whites' and radical 'reds'. Wybicki's conservative *Agencja* in Napoleonic France had its rivals in Dembowski's radical *Deputacja* and in the Society of Polish Republicans. Czartoyski's Hotel Lambert was flattered by a bevy of democratic oppositionist factions, from Lelewel's TDP (Polish Democratic Society, 1832–62) with its *'Centralizacja'* (Central Co-ordinating Committee), to the more socially-minded *Lud Polski* (Polish People 1832–46) in London, and the 'Young Poland' in Berne. In this period, Lelewel's mantle as prophet of the Left was gradually assumed by Stanisław Worcell (1799–1857). A freemason, *Carbonaro*, ex-deputy to the Insurrectionary Sejm and a friend of Herzen and Mazzini, Worcell was instrumental in keeping the Polish cause on the agenda of most progressive and international organizations in Europe during his lifetime, as he was in the rise of Polish socialism. With time, the split between the 'whites' and 'reds' deepened significantly, as moderate policies failed and demands for socialism and terrorism grew ever more insistent. In England, which sheltered the more extreme elements of the day, the *Gromada Rewolucyjna* (Revolutionary Assembly, 1856–61) was linked with international communist-utopian circles. Its successor, the *Ognisko Republikańskie Polskie* (Polish Republican Hearth, 1867–70) had Pan-slav overtones, whilst the *Związek Ludu Polskiego* (Union of the Polish People, 1872–9) was directly connected with Marx's First International. The ZSSP (Union of Polish Socialists Abroad) was the forerunner of the PPS. The ideas generated by these groups commanded greater respect than their puny membership suggests, and they hold a definite place in the history of Polish political thought. In the First World War, Dmowski's Polish National Committee was challenged by Piłsudski-ite 'activist' organizations. In the Second World War, the Government-in-Exile in London was attacked and later superseded by Soviet-sponsored organizations based in Moscow.

Attempts to harmonize the opposing factions rarely succeeded for long. From 1837 to 1846 Lelewel and the Hotel Lambert co-operated in forming the *Zjednoczenie Emigracji Polskiej* (United Polish Emigration) until the fiasco of the Cracow Revolution. From 1866 to 1871, a revived ZEP lasted until the collapse of the Paris Commune which its leaders had supported. Thereafter there were few signs of united action. The followers of Dmowski in the 'National Camp' and of Piłsudski in the 'Independence Camp' could never be persuaded to make common cause so long as each harboured hopes of dominating Polish politics. In the First World War, Dmowski's Polish National Committee fought in the Allied side whilst Piłsudski's Legions fought on the side of the Central Powers. In the Second World War, the official Government-in-Exile in London was systematically and deliberately discredited by the unofficial Polish communist organizations in Moscow. The only political compromises ever worked out between the two rival groupings — Sikorski's Treaty with the USSR in 1941, and Mikołajczyk's adherence to the TRJN in 1945 — soon proved to be empty bargains. In the post-war era, the Polish *émigrés* share little beyond a common loathing of the communist regime which in their eyes is an illegal usurper. The ancient feuds between the National Democrats and the Piłsudski-ites, between the pro-*Sanacja* element and the anti-*Sanacja* element, still preoccupy *émigré* circles forty years after they lost all relevance.

Ethnic and religious divisions have been no less evident than purely political ones. It is a notorious fact that ethnic and religious groups in emigration lose all sense of sympathy with regard to other communities with whom they were once closely associated in their countries of origin. Polish Jews abroad seek out their Jewish co-religionists and rarely seek contact with Polish organizations. Polish Catholics establish themselves in Catholic parishes, and rarely seek contact with Jewish organizations. Ukrainians, Germans, Lithuanians, Czechs each go their own way. People who in Central Europe were once neighbours and friends, have become strangers in London and New York. It is the source of much prejudice, and of much needless friction. For those who still take pride in the country of their ancestors, it is understandably hurtful to meet others who deny their origins, or who, whilst admitting to be 'from Poland' or having Polish as their mother tongue, none the less ostentatiously deny that they are Polish.

Social divisions persist, too. It is true that a certain camaraderie of misfortune sometimes helps to narrow the gulf between *émigrés* of differing social origin. Yet a small cosmopolitan coterie of wealthy and intermarried aristocratic clans, who used their fortunes to invest in property or to open Swiss bank accounts, have been able to involve themselves in the social, commercial, or intellectual life of all the European capitals with an air of complete confidence. They include all the magnatial names of pre-Partition Polish society. In the same way, professional people with exportable qualifications or with influential foreign contacts can rapidly establish themselves and prosper. Their lifestyle stands a world apart from that of the average proletarian emigrants who work as miners, labourers, seamstresses, or domestics, and who struggle for decades to feed their families and pay the rent.

In the popular view, however, the strongest Polish impact on the international scene was probably made not by *émigré* groups, but by individuals. Musical, scientific, and artistic talent is the most readily marketable commodity; and all the unpronounceable Polish names best known to the world at large belong to talented individuals who have made their way through their exceptional skills, personalities, or temperaments. As might be expected, wandering Poles have made disproportionate contribution to travel and exploration, and to related subjects such as cartography, ethnography, and geology. Sir Pawel Edmund Strzelecki (1796–1873) mapped the Australian interior and named its highest mountain; Aleksander Hołyński (1816–1893) explored Lower California and predicted the Panama Canal; and a whole series of Polish deportees in Russia, from the famous Maurycy Beniowski (1746–86) to Bronisław Piłsudski (1866–1918), who pioneered the scientific discovery of Siberia, Central Asia, and the northern Pacific. Their compatriots turn up unexpectedly in the most far-flung places, like Michał Czajkowski (1804–86) known as Sadik Pasha, in Turkey; like Karol Rolow-Miałowski (1842–1907) as a revolutionary in Cuba; like Ignacy Domeyko (1802–89), as a geologist and educationist in Chile, or like Ernest Malinowski (1818–99), as the railway pioneer of Peru, where he constructed the highest railway line in the world. At the turn of the century, Helena Modjeska (Modrzejewska, 1840–1909) the actress, was perhaps the first Polish exile to hit the main headlines. She was the forerunner of numerous others, including Jan de Reszke (1850–1925), the operatic tenor, and his brother Edward (1885–1917), a Wagnerian bass; Marie Curie-Skłodowska (1867–1934), physicist; Ignacy Jan Paderewski (1860–1941), pianist; and Wacław Nijinsky (Nidziński, c. 1889–1950), the dancer. Joseph Conrad (J. K. Korzeniowski, 1857–1924) made his name as an English novelist, just as Guillaume Apollinaire (Apolinaris Kostrowicki, 1880–1918) did as a French poet. In more recent times, these early exiles from Poland have had successors in Arthur Rubinstein (born 1888), pianist; Wanda Landowska (1877–1959), clavichordist; Leopold Stokowski (1882–1979), conductor; Sir Lewis Namier (1880–1960), historian; Henryk Szeryng (born 1918), violinist, and sometime Secretary to General Sikorski; Sir Casimir Gzowski (1813–98) and Ralph Modjeski (1861–1940), architects and designers respectively of the Niagara and Benjamin Franklin Bridges; Casimir Funk (1884—1967), biochemist; Bronisław Malinowski (1884—1942), social anthropologist; Stanisław Ulam (born 1909), mathematician; Jacob Bronowski (1908—76), philosopher of science; Pola Negri (Apolonia Chałupiec, born 1897), and Marion Davies, starlets; Samuel Goldwyn (1882—1974), film producer; and Joe Coral (born 1904), bookmaker.

The continuing existence of a large Emigration colours every aspect of Polish life. In the economic sphere, it has always provided the home country with one of its main sources of income. Remittances to relatives in Poland, tourist visits, and the enterprise of *émigré* businessmen make a significant contribution to the balance of payments. In the political sphere, the Emigration provides the major forum for free debate and for the critical analysis of all Poland's problems. With the persistence at home of a one-party, totalitarian regime, it fulfils the very necessary function of a committed, if absent, opposition. There is no reason to suppose that it holds the best interests of the nation to heart any less than the leaders of the Polish United Workers' Party. Most importantly, in the cultural sphere, the Emigration ensures that free expression can be given to the full variety of ideas and sentiments on which a living culture depends. It keeps the population in contact with the outside world, and reduces the effects of bureaucratic controls. In this respect, it complements and counterbalances the activities of the state-run cultural organizations in Poland. Quite apart from their political significance, which is difficult to assess, one cannot doubt that the cultural service rendered to Poland by journals like *Kultura* or *Wiadomości*, and by the Polish broadcasts of the BBC, CBC, Voice of America, or Radio Free Europe, is immense indeed. Above all, the Emigration serves to remind all Poles, in the best possible tradition, that the nation is not coterminous with the state, and that its needs do not necessarily coincide with the dictates of a political regime.

For their part, the authorities in Poland cannot remain indifferent to the issue. The Emigration is too large, and too influential to be ignored. Like the *Sanacja* leaders before the War, who launched the World Union of Poles Abroad, the leaders of the People's Republic make strenuous efforts to win over the *émigrés*. From modest beginnings in 1955, the Polonia Society in Warsaw has steadily expanded its activities, invites selected guests to Poland, tempts the younger generation with subsidized travel and summer courses, and indulges, through the Interpress Agency, in shameless propaganda. Its political line is to denigrate all memory of the Polish Independence Movement, especially of the leftist, anti-Russian, Piłsudski-ite variety, and, whilst preaching *ad nauseam* of the *émigrés'* duty to their adopted countries, to appeal to their simple patriotic instincts. Yet formidable obstacles remain. On the one side, the political *émigrés* cannot be expected to reconcile themselves easily to a regime which deprived them of a rightful place in the land of their birth. No amount of special pleading can hide the fact that the communist regime condoned the USSR's annexation of the eastern provinces, where many *émigrés* were born, and that for many years after the War People's Poland could not guarantee the safety, let alone the civil rights, of independent-minded people. Secure in the justice, if not the practicality of their cause, the political Emigration has made the traditional choice to live and die abroad in freedom rather than to surrender to manipulation at home. Their epitaph may be borrowed from lines addressed to another defeated nationality:

> Your name and your deeds were forgotten
> Before your bones were dry;
> And the Lie that slew you is buried
> Beneath a deeper lie.
>
> But the one thing that I saw in your face
> No power can disinherit.
> No bomb that ever burst
> Can shatter the crystal spirit.[17]

On the other side, political priorities prevail over moral scruples. A Party which adheres to Leninist principles cannot allow itself to put any trust in people whom it does not control.

Emigration, therefore, seems to be a permanent part of the Polish condition. For those who emigrated willingly or even gladly, the experience was quickly overcome, and in some cases, the homeland was soon forgotten. But for those who departed under the duress of economic or political misfortune, the step could never be easily taken. For them, Mickiewicz's moving translation of Childe Harold's Farewell holds far deeper meaning than for most of Byron's original English readers:

Adieu, adieu! My native shore	Bywaj zdrowy, kraju kochany
Fades o'er the waters blue;	Już w mglistej nikniesz pomroce
The night-winds sigh, the breakers roar	Świsnęły wiatry, szumią bałwany
And shrieks the wild sea-mew.	I morskie ptactwo świergoce!
Yon sun that sets upon the sea	Dalej za słońcem, gdzie jasno głowę
We follow in his flight.	W zachodzie pogrążą piany,
Farwell awhile to him and thee.	Tymczasem słońce bywaj mi zdrowe,
My native land – Good Night!	Bywaj zdrów, kraju kochany.[18]

For many, even today, the most fitting summary of their lot may be found in the sad little verse composed ten days before his death by the indefatigable Julian Niemcewicz:

O exiles, whose worldly wanderings are never complete
When may you rest your sore and weary feet?
The worm has its clod of earth. There's a nest for the wild dove.
Everyone has a homeland; but the Pole has only a grave.[19]

Niemcewicz's own tombstone, in the graveyard at Montmorency, bears an inscription composed by his friends. It ends with the line, which among the *émigrés* is equally famous:

I tam gdzie już łez niema, on łzę Polski złożył (And there, where tears are banished, he still shed Poland's tear.)[20]

CHAPTER TWELVE
VARSOVIE:
The Duchy of Warsaw (1807-1815)

Like many ephemeral states of the Revolutionary Era, from the Republic of Lombardy to the Kingdom of Westphalia, the Duchy of Warsaw was a child of war. It was conceived from the uneasy liaison between Napoleonic France and the stateless Polish nation, and born amidst the defeats of the three partitioning powers. Its character was marked by an inimitable mixture of revolutionary idealism, nationalist enthusiasm, and naked militarism. It shared in the brief glory of the French imperial system, and was crushed by the victorious resurgence of the Third Coalition.[1]

The Polish liaison with France could be traced back beyond Kościuszko's Rising to the Confederates of Bar and Le bon roi Stanislas. But after the Revolution, there was a direct bond of common interest between the governments in Paris challenging the *Ancien Régime* in the West, and the principal victim of the dynastic empires in the East. From 1793, when Prussia and Austria mounted the War of the First Coalition against France, to 1815, when the forces of the Third Coalition were finally triumphant, the French and the Poles were facing the same enemies. France became the main source of assistance for the Poles, and the scene of much Polish political activity. In 1794–7, Paris was the seat both of Józef Wybicki's Polish *Agencja* (Agency) and of Franciszek Dmochowski's rival republican *Deputacja* (Deputation). In December 1796, the Agency was responsible for persuading the leaders of the Directory to form the first auxiliary Polish Legion, which was to fight under General Henryk Dąbrowski (1755–1818) in the ranks of the army of Italy. The Deputation directed its efforts towards an underground resistance movement within Poland, and organized the abortive expedition of Joachim Denisko, whose band of hopefuls crossed the Dniester into Austrian Galicia in July 1797. In the following year, it merged into another *émigré* group with similar objectives, the Society of Polish Republicans.

Napoleon took a personal interest in the Polish Question, especially when it promised to supply him with new recruits. His entourage included a number of Poles, among them his Jacobin adjutant, Józef Sułkowski (1770–98), who was killed in the Egyptian campaign. For several years, he enjoyed the favours of a Polish mistress, Maria Walewska (1789–1817). At Napoleon's instigation, Dąbrowski's Legion was soon joined by two more: in Italy in 1798 by a second Polish Legion under General Józef Zajączck (1752–1826), and in Germany in 1800 by the Légion du Rhin under General Karol Kniaziewicz (1762–1842). The Polish legionnaries marched under the French tricolour, but wore distinctive Polish uniforms. On their shoulder flashes they displayed the Italian slogan, 'Gli uomini liberi sono fratelli' (Free men are brothers). Although the greater part of them were peasant conscripts captured by Napoleon from the Austrian army, they were encouraged to address each other as 'Citizen' and were not subject to corporal punishment. Some 25,000 men passed through their ranks in the five or six years of their existence.

From the start, however, Napoleon's callous handling of the Poles left little room for confidence. He never discussed his Polish plans except in the grandest of generalities, and conspicuously avoided any commitment which might have cramped his freedom of political action. It is significant that Kościuszko, who lived in Paris after his release from Russia in 1796, firmly refused to associate himself with any of Napoleon's schemes. 'Do not think', he said, 'that Bonaparte will restore Poland. He thinks only of himself. He hates every great nationality, and still more the spirit of independence. He is a tyrant whose only aim is to satisfy his own ambitions. I am sure that he will create nothing durable.' With the assistance of his secretary, Józef Pawlikowski (1767–1829), Kościuszko composed the famous pamphlet entitled *Czy Polacy mogą się wybić na niepodległość?* (Can the Poles win their Independence?). In it, he argued that the captive nation could not count on the support of France or of any other foreign power, but must rely exclusively on its own strength and resources.[2] Kościuszko's comments proved to be all too true. The Legions were never used for purposes related to

Polish independence. The First Legion was decimated by Suvorov at the battle of Trebbia in 1799; the second at Marengo in 1800; and the Légion du Rhin soon afterwards at Hohenlinden. The reserves were posted to pacification duties in occupied Italy, and in 1802–3 were drafted with the expedition sent to crush the rebellion of Negro slaves on Santo Domingo. Men who had volunteered for service in the Legions in the hope of liberating Poland found themselves fighting in the Caribbean as the instruments of colonial repression. They died in their thousands from swamp fever before a handful of survivors surrendered to the British. Disillusionment was general. In 1801 at Lunéville, Napoleon made peace with his enemies and all agitation on the Polish Question was abruptly terminated. After the first surge of enthusiasm, many Poles abandoned all thoughts of a Napoleonic rescue. In aristocratic circles, the prospect of a French alliance was clouded by the associated threat of social revolution. In Warsaw, an efficient Prussian administration was not unappreciated. In St. Petersburg, foreign policy fell into the control of a Polish nobleman, Prince Adam Jerzy Czartoryski (1770–1861), who was laying plans of his own for the restoration of a united Poland under the aegis of the new Tsar, Alexander I.[3]

In this situation, Polish affairs were completely subordinated to the rivalry between Napoleon and the Coalition. Any Polish state that was to be created would, of necessity, be an expression more of the Balance of Power than of the wishes of the people. In 1805, the balance tipped decisively in Napoleon's favour. The French occupied Vienna. The Russian army tramped across the Polish lands from end to end, only to be thoroughly beaten with their Austrian allies at Austerlitz on 5 December. On 14 October 1806, at Jena and Auerstadt, the Prussians were annihilated. Berlin was occupied. In November, Davout took Poznań, whilst Murat entered Warsaw. The three partitioning powers were prostrate. Dąbrowski and Wybicki, the old campaigners, were persuaded to issue an 'Appeal to the Polish Nation'. Zajączek set to forming yet another Northern Legion, Prince Józef Poniatowski, after much deliberation, was persuaded to accept command of the new Polish forces. Napoleon's first visit to

Warsaw on 19 December 1806 led to the formation of a Ruling Commission, headed by Stanisław Małachowski, one-time President of the 'Great Sejm'. Yet no hint was dropped as to the Emperor's ultimate intentions. The campaign of 1807 in Pomerania and East Prussia against the Russians and Prussians was fought without any indication of its political aims. After the indecisive battle of Eylau (Iława) in February, and Gneisenau's brilliant defence of Colberg, Napoleon was quite prepared to hand the whole of his Polish conquests back to Prussia. Even after his final repulsion of the Russians at Friedland in June, he entered negotiations with the Tsar with the clear intention of trading Poland in exchange for concessions elsewhere. But the Tsar refused to comply. The creation of the Duchy of Warsaw under French auspices, as envisaged by the Treaty of Tilsit in July 1807, resulted from the Tsar's refusal to undertake the administration of Prussian Poland for himself. On this occasion, as on many others, the fate of the Polish lands was imposed by foreign negotiators acting exclusively for reasons of their own. In Polish eyes, this was the fourth Partition.

The territory of the Duchy was carved from the lands of the Prussian Partition. It included South Prussia (Mazovia and Wielkopolska) but not Danzig, which was made into a Free City, nor New East Prussia (Białystok) which was ceded to Russia. In 1809, in consequence of the war with Austria, it was enlarged by the addition of Cracow, and of 'West Galicia' (Lublin, Zamość). At its greatest extent, it comprised some 154,000 km^2, with a population of 4.3 million people, of whom 79 per cent were Poles, and 7 per cent Jews. At best it could be described as a rump Polish state, with no access to the sea, and with no prospect of uniting the Polish lands as a whole. The name of 'Poland' was carefully avoided. (See Map 8.)

The Duchy's French Constitution was presented in Dresden by Napoleon on 22 July 1807. Frederick-August, King of Saxony, was appointed as hereditary duke. His powers were ambiguously described as 'absolute, under the Protector of the Rhine'. He was a conscientious man, who spoke Polish, but made only four visits to Warsaw. He, or his Viceroy, was to enjoy full executive powers through the five ministries of a

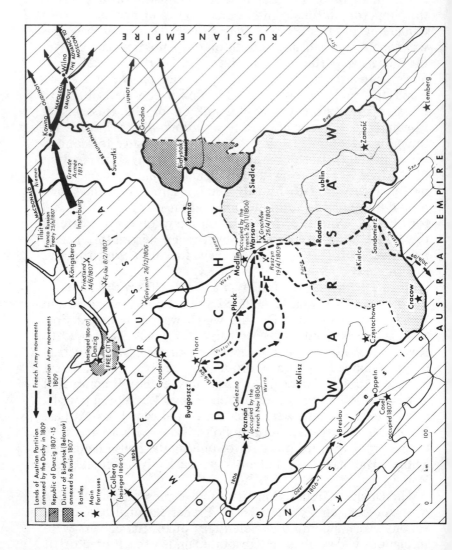

Council of State, and through the Prefects of the six, later ten, departments. There was to be a bicameral Assembly with an appointed Senate and an elected lower house, but no principle of ministerial accountability. Like the district councils in the provinces, the legislature was limited to an advisory role. An independent judiciary was to operate the Code Napoléon. Polish was to be the official language of government.

Under this system, with an absentee monarch, the President of the Council of State, the enlightened Stanisław Kostka Potocki (1755–1821), and his five nominated colleagues possessed considerable freedom of manœuvre. The policies of its dominant personalities – Poniatowski at the Department of War, Stanisław Breza (1752–1847), and above all Count Feliks Łubieński (1758–1848), the Director of Justice, were limited less by the formal constitution than by the continuing presence in Warsaw of Marshal Davout with 30,000 Saxons, and by the watchful care of the French Residents – Étienne Vincent, Jean Serra, Louis Bignon, and from 1809, the meddlesome Archbishop Dominique de Pradt.

In the social sphere, the Constitution introduced radical changes. Article 4, which made the statement that 'all citizens are equal before the law', overturned the ancient system of estates at a stroke. Four simple words – 'L'esclavage est aboli' – put an end to serfdom as a legal institution. Yet much confusion ensued. The legal privileges of the nobility were not specifically rescinded, and their social supremacy was not immediately affected. In the short term, the predicament of the peasantry actually deteriorated. Despite the Land Decrees of 12 December 1807, which regulated the relationship between landlord and tenant, the security of the ex-serf had been much diminished. It was small comfort to know that he could now sign a new contract with his former master, or even challenge his master in court, if by so doing he risked summary eviction with the loss of home, land, and employment. For the time being, the newly freed peasants had nowhere to go but the army.

Religious emancipation proved equally illusory. The Constitution retained Roman Catholicism as the religion of state. A decree of 1808 on Jewish Disabilities suspended full civil rights for the Jews pending greater assimilation.

The true purposes of the Duchy were best revealed in the military and financial spheres. Whatever gestures were made to 'Liberté', 'Egalité', or even 'Fraternité', there is little doubt that the Duchy was intended to raise the maximum of men and money for the benefit of the Napoleonic Empire as a whole. In 1808, general conscription was introduced. All men between 20 and 28 were called to arms for six years' service. The army, which was gradually expanded from 30,000 men in 1808 to over 100,000 in 1812, consumed over two-thirds of the state's revenue. Lavish gifts of land and property were distributed among the commanding generals, whilst gangs of forced labourers toiled to improve military installations. Twenty thousand peasants were mobilized to rebuild the fortress of Modlin. In 1812, the number of troops quartered in Poland at the Duchy's expense reached almost a million. In return for his Polish uniform, the citizen was taxed with Prussian thoroughness, treated with Russian indifference, and was expected to lay down his life for the French Emperor on the orders of a German King.

Nothing was more symptomatic of Napoleon's exploitation of the Duchy than the shocking fraud of the 'Bayonne Sums'. According to a convention signed in the French resort in 1807, the French government ceded possession of former Prussian state property to the Duchy of Warsaw by selling it for a sum of 25 million francs payable over only four years. In this way, the Polish tax-payer was required to devote almost 10 per cent of the budget to redeem mortgages, buildings, and equipment which had been taken from him by the Prussians only twelve years before, and which had come into French possession as a prize of war. Generosity was not of the essence.[4]

Meanwhile, the trumpets of glory called Poles to the colours. After a generation of unmitigated humiliation, there were plenty of young men determined to prove their prowess on the battlefield. From the brilliant Polish 'Chevaux Légers' of the Imperial Guard to the new regiments of Poniatowski's own army, from the heights of the Peninsula to the depths of Russia, Polish valour went on parade as never before since the days of Sobieski.

On 30 November 1808, Napoleon paused at the gates of Madrid. His advance was blocked by a single Spanish division which held the narrow defile of Somosierra, leading on to the lofty plateau where the Spanish capital stands. Sixteen guns were holding off fifty thousand men. After repeated attempts to force the position with infantry, the First Regiment of Chevaux Légers were given the order to charge. The three hundred Varsovians under Jan Kozietuski obeyed. Eight minutes later, the survivors emerged from the top of the ravine, a thousand feet and three miles above the admiring Emperor. All the guns were captured. The Spaniards' resistance was broken. Madrid was captured. In later years, talk of the charge of Somosierra evoked the same reactions in Warsaw as mention of the Charge of the Light Brigade in London. The flower of the nation's youth was thought to have perished in a distant land for the sake of a courageous gesture. In fact, the exemplary sacrifice of those few men ensured the passage of a whole army.[5]

In the campaign of 1809, the Poles had a more immediate interest. The Duchy of Warsaw sustained the full weight of the Austrian attack, and its army performed with distinction. Archduke Ferdinand d'Este crossed from Galicia at the head of 25,000 men, and in spite of a setback at the battle of Raszyn on 19 April, forced his way into Warsaw. But Poniatowski stayed in the field. A series of cavalry raids deep into Austrian territory, to Sandomierz, Zamość, and Lemberg, undermined the Archduke's position. When news arrived in July of Napoleon's victory at Wagram, Poniatowski was on the point of entering Cracow. Throughout these months, he outmanœuvred not only the superior numbers of the Austrians but also the extraordinary conduct of his Russian 'allies', who, alarmed by the nightmare of a resurgent Poland, took active measures to obstruct him. At the Treaty of Schönbrunn, the Duchy was rewarded with the annexation of Cracow and West Galicia, whilst Russia helped itself to the district of Tarnopol. For the first time since the Partitions, a Polish army had taken to the field under Polish command and had succeeded in reuniting two important pieces of the shattered Polish lands. National sentiment revived. Hopes were raised anew. Poles from Lithuania swam across the Niemen to escape from Russia and serve in the Duchy's army. Poles from the Prussian and Austrian Partitions came over to swell the ranks; and all were offered citizenship in the Duchy's service. For a brief moment, it looked as if the Polish nation might regain control of its destiny.

The year 1812 saw the climacteric of the Napoleonic adventure. For the French, the Russian Campaign was just another act of revolutionary imperialism. For the Russians, it presented the supreme test for the integrity and durability of their Empire. For the Poles alone, it was a war of liberation. When the Grande Armée crossed the Niemen on 24 June, most of its soldiers were aware only that they were crossing the frontier of the Russian Empire. But the thousands of Poles among them were more conscious that they were crossing the historic frontier of the Grand Duchy of Lithuania. As they tramped towards Wilno, they knew that they were destroying the barrier which had kept the two parts of the old Republic apart for the last twenty years. It is true that Napoleon had made no specific promises. Although he chose to refer to the campaign as 'the Second Polish War', his spokesman, the Duc de Bassano, was only prepared to say that 'a complete restoration of Poland was one possible way of terminating the conflict'. On the Lithuanian side, expectations rose feverishly. A number of magnates, fearful of social disorder, continued to support the Tsar. But the mass of the population fervently awaited their hour of deliverance. Adam Mickiewicz, who witnessed the events as a boy of fourteen, re-created the atmosphere in ringing tones:

O memorable year! Happy is he who beheld it in our land! The common people still call it 'the year of harvest'. But soldiers call it the 'year of War' . . .

Already the stork had returned to its native pine, and had spread its white wings, the early standard of Spring. And after it, the swallows gathered above the waters in noisy regiments . . . In the evening one could hear the call of the woodcocks as they rose from the thickets. Flocks of wild geese honked over the forest before alighting wearily to feed. In the depths of the sky, the cranes kept up a constant clamour. Hearing this, the watchmen asked each other what storm had driven the birds forth so early, and what was the cause of such disorder in the winged kingdom.

For now new swarms of plumes and pennons shone bright on the hills, like flocks of finches, plover, and starlings, and came down into the meadows. They were cavalrymen. In strange array, with arms never seen before, regiment followed regiment. The iron-shod ranks flowed along the roads, straight across the country, like melted snow. Black shakoes projected from the wood; bayonets glittered, row after row; and the infantry swarmed forth, countless as ants . . . Horses, men, cannon, eagles flowed on, day and night. Fires glowed in the sky. The earth trembled. Thunder rolled in the distance . . .

War! War! Its roar reached into every corner of the Lithuanian land. The strange glare in the sky was seen even in the darkest forest, by peasants whose ancestors had died without seeing beyond the boundary of the wood, who knew no other sounds in the sky than those of the wind, and who had met no other guests than their fellow woodsmen . . . The bison, hoary and bearded, shook in his mossy lair, and ruffling his mane . . . fled to deeper refuge . . .

O memorable Spring of war and harvest! Happy is he who watched as you blossomed with corn and grass, and glittered with men: How rich you were in history; how big with hope! I see you still, fair phantom of my dream. Born in slavery, and chained by my swaddling bands, I had but one such Spring in my whole life.[6]

These lines form the setting for one of the most celebrated scenes of Polish fiction — 'the last old-Polish banquet' at Soplicowo, where all the feuds and quarrels of the manor were reconciled, and everyone rose to the noble toast *Kochajmy Się* — 'Let us love one another!' The centrepiece of the banquet was the virtuoso recital on the dulcimer performed in honour of General Dąbrowski by the old Jew, Jankiel:

At last, when the old man turned his eyes on Dąbrowski he covered them with his hands, and he wept a flood of tears.
— 'General', he said, 'our Lithuania has waited for you a long time, as long as we Jews have awaited the Messiah . . .'
He wept as he spoke. The honest Jew loved his country like a Pole. Dąbrowski extended his hand, and thanked him; and Jankiel, doffing his cap, kissed the leader's hands.[7]

The Poles in the Grande Armée numbered almost 100,000 men. Thirty-five thousand of them were concentrated in the Fifth Polish Corps under General Poniatowski, the only national formation in the entire motley host. They marched in the vanguard, and entered Wilno on 28 June, where a Ruling Commission was installed under the Dutchman, General

Dirk Van Hogendorp. They reached Smolensk in August. They fought at Borodino. In September they entered Moscow. Exactly two hundred years after Gosiewski had put the Russian capital to the torch, they watched as it burned again. In Warsaw, at a meeting of the Society of Friends of Science, the poet Koźmian read an Ode to the destruction of Moscow:

> Where is it now, that Monster of Nature,
> That Giant, that terror of the peoples?

After the meeting, Koźmian was taken on one side by Stanisław Staszic, who advised him to delay publication of the Ode until the war was over. *Olbrzym walczy*, he said — 'the Giant is still fighting.'[8]

And so it proved. The Tsar did not sue for peace. In October, the terrible retreat began. Blizzards, marauding peasants, Cossacks, frostbite, and starvation pared the ranks inexorably. The 'Chevaux Légers' under the heroic Paweł Jerzmanowski were detailed to hold the rearguard. At Smolensk, and on the Berezina, thousands perished. In December, Napoleon drove through Warsaw *en route* for Paris, in total silence. He failed to call on Walewska, who was left to pursue him to Paris, and eventually to Elba. Two weeks later, the first survivors of the Fifth Corps arrived — one general, 12 officers, and 124 men. In all, 20,000 Poles survived from the 100,000 who had crossed the Niemen six months before. Warsaw could not be defended. In February 1813, the Russian Army appeared. A provisional Supreme Council was established under General Vasily Lanskoi, and his deputy, Nikolai Novosiltsov. For the next two years, the Duchy of Warsaw was ruled as a Tsarist protectorate, awaiting the pleasure of the victors.

The last act of independent will was carried out in the Duchy's behalf by Józef Poniatowski. Refusing offers of clemency from the Russians, he determined to fight to the last at Napoleon's side. He gathered the reserves of his army together, and retreated into Germany. His end came in the Battle of the Nations at Leipzig, on 19 October. Surrounded in a bend of the River Elster by Prussian and Russian forces, the Polish contingent was caught in the thick of the French defeat. Mortally wounded by three bullets, Poniatowski scorned all suggestions of surrender or retirement. Spurring his horse into the water, in a flurry of sniper fire, he sank from view.[9]

Poniatowski's death is often quoted as yet another example of suicidal Polish courage. In effect, it was an outcome consistent with an intolerable predicament. Like many of his countrymen, he had wavered long before throwing in his lot with the French. For him, Napoleonic service had demanded a painful change of direction and loyalties. It had involved years of devotion and blood-letting. To have changed his loyalties yet again, as his master the King of Saxony did, was all too worrying for an infinitely weary and honest man. Like the rest of his generation he hoped; he fought; he served, and only found rest in honourable defeat.

CHAPTER THIRTEEN
KONGRESÓWKA:

The Congress Kingdom (1815-1846)

The Congress of Vienna did not assemble in September 1814 for the main purpose of discussing the Polish Question. No Polish representative was invited. But, as on future occasions, dissension among the Powers turned the settlement of the Polish clauses into a major obstacle. Castlereagh, the British Foreign Secretary, raised the issue of Polish independence as a means of trimming the pretensions of his partners in the victorious Third Coalition. His *Memorial on Poland* of 23 October suggested three alternative solutions. The first envisaged a sovereign Polish state within the frontiers of 1772; the second, a return to the position in 1791, including the Constitution of 3 May; the third, a new partition of the Duchy of Warsaw along the line of the Vistula. To Alexander I, none of these alternatives looked as attractive as a plan prepared in conjuction with Berlin, whereby Russia would take the whole of the Duchy of Warsaw if Prussia were permitted to take the whole of Saxony. In January, deadlock was reached. Talleyrand proposed a new alliance between Britain, France, and Austria to resist the Russo-Prussian combination. For a moment, renewed war threatened, until news of Napoleon's flight from Elba brought the diplomats to their senses. The common front was restored. On the Polish Question, the Powers agreed on compromise. Prussia settled for Poznań and the western fringe of the Duchy of Warsaw, taking only half of Saxony, together with Danzig, Swedish Pomerania, and several Rhineland principalities into the bargain. Austria resigned her claim to West Galicia, but gained Tarnopol, and kept most of New Galicia. Cracow was to be a Free City under the joint protection of the Powers. The Russian Empire was to benefit from a minor frontier rectification near Białystok, whilst the Tsar assumed the crown of a new and independent 'Kingdom of Poland'. A Treaty incorporating these provisions was signed by the three partitioners on 3 May

1815. On 9 June, one week before Waterloo, the Treaty of Vienna itself was signed. In effect, if not in name, the fifth Partition of Poland had been accomplished.[1]

The Congress Kingdom of Poland, with its 127,000 km^2, was smaller than the Duchy of Warsaw in 1809. Its population of 3.3 millions was less than that of the old Prussian, or the Austrian, Partitions. It could not be compared to the old *Korona* prior to 1793, still less to a restoration of the old Republic as a whole. On the international scale, it was roughly equivalent in size, though not in resources, to the United Netherlands created at the same time. In Polish eyes, it was the result of a very unsatisfactory compromise:

> *Bez Krakowa, Poznania, i Wieliczki,*
> *Polska nie warta ani świeczki.*
> (Without Cracow, Poznań, and Wieliczka
> Poland is hardly worth a candle.)

In the Polish language, it was popularly referred to by the affectionate diminutive, the *Kongresówka*: 'the poor little creation of the Congress'. (See Map 9.)

At the same time, it had to be granted that the Kingdom's prospects were not entirely bleak. Its population was destined to multiply rapidly, reaching over 6 million by 1864, and over 13 million by 1910. It contained the largest single concentration of Poles of any state in Europe, and was the natural focus of Polish cultural life. In Warsaw, it possessed the historic capital of the Republic; and its title successfully revived the forbidden name of 'Poland'. As the eastern frontier with the Russian Empire had been declared open to future modifications, there were hopes that at some future date a benevolent Tsar might extend the Kingdom's territory eastwards and reunite it with the former Grand Duchy of Lithuania.

The Constitution of the Kingdom gave little room for complaint. Designed in haste by Prince Czartoryski, it none the less provided the widest possible freedoms within the framework laid down by the Treaty. It is true that the Tsar, in his dignity as King of Poland, reserved strong executive powers for himself. He was to nominate all officials, from the Viceroy and the Commander-in-Chief down. He was to appoint the

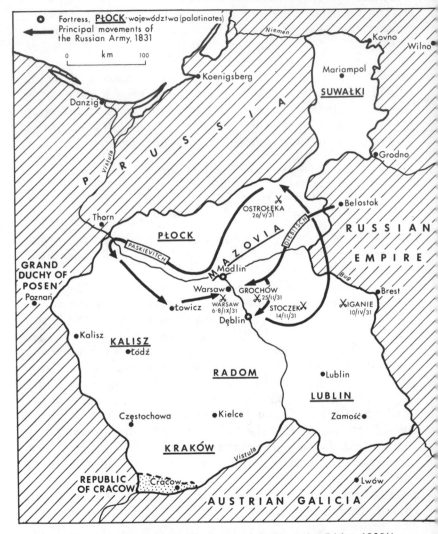

Map 9.   The Congress Kingdom, and the November Rising, 1830/1

Administrative Council. He had the prerogative of convoking and of proroguing or dissolving the Sejm. He had the right to veto and to amend legislation, and to insist that Foreign Policy was conducted in common with that of the Russian Empire. He was to act as the supreme court of appeal at law, and was to control the civilian police through the Ministry of the Interior in St. Petersburg. Even so, the Kingdom possessed many of the marks of a genuine constitutional monarchy. It had its own Government, its own judiciary, its own elected Assembly or Sejm, its own civil service, and its own army. The Napoleonic Code, the freedom of the press, the principle of religious toleration, the personal liberty of the subject, and the peasantry's right to acquire land, were all formally guaranteed. Polish was to be the language of all official business. In view of the fact that the Constitution was drafted with the approval of the reactionary Holy Alliance, it must be regarded as a surprisingly liberal document. On paper at least, it was one of the most progressive constitutions of Central Europe.[2]

The leading personalities of the Kingdom reflected the Whiggish liberalism of the day. The Viceroy, General Józef Zajączek, had mellowed considerably since his Jacobin days; but a veteran of Kościuszko's National Rising and of Dąbrowski's Legions was not the sort of man one might expect to encounter as the chief Polish lieutenant of the Russian autocrat. The Commander-in-Chief, Grand Duke Konstanty Pavlovitch (1779—1831), the Tsar's brother, was one of very few figures with independent influence in Russia. His morganatic marriage to a Polish woman, Joanna Grudzińska, had denied him the right of succession; and his sentimental attachment to all things Polish contrasted sharply with his delight in all forms of brutal military discipline. He was a man suspended between two worlds, and not infrequently in two minds. Most of his subordinate generals — Dąbrowski, Kniaziewicz, Chłopicki — had served Napoleon and the Duchy of Warsaw rather than in the Russian Army. Civilian circles were still dominated by the great figures of the Enlightenment, notably by Stanisław Kostka Potocki and by Stanisław Staszic. The Administrative Council could call on a number of Polish magnates already experienced in the Russian service, among them Prince Adam Jerzy Czartoryski and Prince Xavery Drucki-Lubecki. Although there were plenty of people, especially in the Catholic camp, who harboured reservations of one sort or another about the Constitution and its supporters, the only person to oppose it actively from the start was the Tsar's personal plenipotentiary, Nikolai Novosiltsov (1761–1836). It is significant that Novosiltsov's office, though of prime political importance, had no legal standing in the Constitution. Here, from the outset, was an agency which could be used as the channel for all manner of arbitrary and extra-constitutional assaults and stratagems.

Education proved a matter near to the liberals' hearts. For five years under its director, Stanisław Potocki, the Commission for Religious Denominations and Public Enlightenment strove to build on the achievements of the old National Education Commission and of the Duchy of Warsaw's Education Board. In 1816, Warsaw University opened its doors to five faculties. The Mining School at Kielce, the Agronomic Institute at Marymont, and the Preparatory Polytechnical School in Warsaw, were all designed to train a new scientific and professional elite. In 1821, over one thousand primary schools were in operation. Inevitably friction arose with the Church, which resented the growth of secular education under state patronage. Potocki was attacked from all sides. When, in retaliation, he dared to propose the dissolution of the Catholic teaching orders, he was forced to retract. Then in 1820, when he published an anticlerical satire entitled *Podróż do Ciemnogrodu* (A Journey to Ignoranceville), he was forced to resign. Thereafter, reaction set in. The next Director of the Commission, Stanisław Grabowski (1780–1845), closed two-thirds of the Kingdom's primary schools. Jewish schools were also discouraged. Priority was given to the secondary *Gymnazia* with their predominantly upper-class clientele. Potocki's history textbooks eulogizing the democracy of ancient Athens were replaced by more conservative volumes which extolled the virtues of imperial Rome. It was a sign of the times.[3]

Economic life experienced similarly acute swings of fortune. At first, an over-enthusiastic government so squandered its meagre resources that by 1821 it faced bankruptcy. The Tsar threatened to incorporate the Kingdom into the Empire if the budget were not balanced immediately. Thereupon a remarkable recovery was staged by Prince Lubecki, who served as Minister of the Treasury from 1821 to 1830. Tax evaders were promised the death sentence. The deficit was eliminated. Tax revenue trebled. Prosperous state monopolies were re-established in salt and tobacco. In 1828, the Polish Bank was founded to manage fiscal affairs, and to co-ordinate state-backed credit operations. Large sums were earmarked for investment in trade and industry. In this decade, Lubecki − 'Le Petit Prince' as Alexander called him − proved to be the most successful of Polish 'Conciliators'. Grimly determined to preserve the link with Russia, he brooked no opposition and laid the foundations of a modern and viable economy.[4]

The army remained the chief guarantee of the Kingdom's independence. With permanent cadres of 30,000 men, capable of rapid expansion in wartime, it was a force which no neighbouring power could easily ignore. Assigned 40 per cent of the state's expenditure, it was well armed and well trained. It wore Polish uniforms, marched behind Polish colours, and used Polish as the sole language of command. Replenished by conscripts engaged on ten-year service, it soon assumed an air of professional pride and competence. Special attention was paid to officer training. The three cadet schools in Warsaw, serving the Infantry, Cavalry, and Artillery, turned out a new generation of graduates buoyant with soldierly pride and *esprit de corps*. Russian influence was limited to the army's divisional structure, to facilitate prospective co-operation with Russian formations − and to the sensitive matter of military descipline. Corporal punishment had never been permitted in Poniatowski's day, and its introduction in 1815 on the Russian model caused great offence. The endless parades which the Grand Duke organized on the Saxon Square in Warsaw were attended by public displays of flogging and of running-the-gauntlet. They provided one of the rankling but avoidable irritants in an otherwise satisfied and highly competent fighting force.[5]

Within this context, political life developed without undue strain. Much of the fury of the early years was drawn by the battle between the clericals and the anticlericals over schools, civil marriages, divorce, and censorship. In this, the Tsar found himself lobbied from both sides. The first session of the Sejm in 1818 proceeded smoothly. It was opened by Alexander in person, whose speech in praise of the Constitution was widely but mistakenly construed as the harbinger of changes to come in Russia itself. A protest from the floor of the House against the government's failure to present the budget for approval was left unanswered.

Opposition began to coalesce in the 1820s on two separate fronts. In the Sejm, it centred on the activities of the two Niemoyowski brothers, Wincenty (1784–1834) and Bonawentura (1787–1835), whose 'Kalisz Group' held amendations of government policy to be an essential function of the legislature. In the second session of the Sejm, in 1820, when a bill to increase the powers of the Procurator-General was blocked, the Tsar could hardly contain his astonishment. The parliamentary election of the Niemoyowski brothers was administratively annulled. The Sejm was dissolved, and its reopening delayed until 1825. This was the first clear sign that praise for the Constitution even from a supposedly liberal Tsar should not be taken too literally. Other members of the Sejm caused offence by criticizing the government's dilatory attitude to agrarian reform.

In the country at large, opposition centred on the growing fashion for secret political clubs. In this, Freemasonry held an old and established position in Polish society. It traditionally attracted the harmless sort of benign noblemen, to whom both Alexander I and his father, Paul I, felt themselves to belong. In 1815, it had thirty-two lodges in the Kingdom, and could rightly claim to control a large sector of progressive and patriotic opinion. In 1819, Major Walerian Łukasiński (1789–1869) founded the *Wolnomularstwo Narodowe* (National Freemasonry), a more militant branch of the movement, which soon recruited a following in the Sejm, in the provinces, and in the army. In 1821, when the Tsar banned its activities throughout his realms, many of the more determined members passed into Łukasiński's conspiratorial National Patriotic Society. This latter organization, the predecessor of several others of the same name, spawned a network of local cells across the Polish lands. It was devoted to the goal of full national independence, and continued to exercise an influence long after its separate cells ceased to respond to the centre. Łukasiński's arrest and incarceration in 1822 marked the start of growing conflict with the authorities.[6] In student circles, a rash of amateur revolutionary clubs appeared, each with its own heroes, philosophy, and newspaper. The Varsovian *Panta Koina* (All Together) of 1817 had contacts both in Germany and in Russia. It was broken up by the flurry of international police enquiries inspired by the murder at Jena in Germany of the Tsar's resident Minister. The *Związek Wolnych Polaków* (League of Free Poles) of 1820 put out feelers to Wilno and Cracow; but it, too, was broken up by the police. In the army, firm connections were established with fellow-conspirators in Russia. The *Towarzystwo Zjednoczonych Słowian* (Society of United Slavs) kept in contact with the Russian 'Northern' and 'Southern' Societies, and with an 'Association of Military Friends', which operated among the officers of the Lithuanian Corps stationed at Belostok. Although one cannot doubt the integrity of men who undertook conspiratorial adventures against the Tsar, it is hard to believe that they presented any serious danger to the forces of law and order.[7]

The main troubles at this stage occurred not in Warsaw but in Wilno. The relatively benevolent regime in the Kingdom bore no resemblance to the repressive establishment across the frontier in Lithuania. When Czartoryski retired from his post in Wilno in 1814, his successors did all in their power to reverse his pro-Polish policies. The University of Wilno, which for a brief period had flourished as the premier centre of Polish literature and learning, came under direct assault from a company of ardent Russifiers. The *Towarzystwo Filomatów* (Philomatic Society), founded in 1817 by Adam Mickiewicz and Tomasz Zan (1796–1855) as a focus for their literary activities, was soon driven to adopt distinctly political overtones. It co-opted the support of faculty members, notably of Joachim Lelewel, the Professor of History. In 1821, two new organizations were formed. One, the *Towarzystwo Filodelfistów* (Philodelphist Society), was openly devoted to the idea of reuniting the two parts of the old Republic of Poland–Lithuania. The other, the *Związek Zielony* (Green League), was a precocious example of Populism, which took to the countryside to woo the peasantry. Ominously, the spread of these enterprises caught the attention of Novosiltsov, who travelled to Wilno to conduct investigations in person. In November 1823, the police struck. Mickiewicz and Zan, and eight of their colleagues were summarily exiled to the central Russian provinces. Lelewel was dismissed. The entire conspiracy, such as it was, was dispersed. The lesson for the people in Warsaw was clear. The mask of liberalism sported by the Tsarist authorities in the Kingdom was little more than skin-deep.[8]

With the accession of Nicholas I in 1825, the mask was cast aside. Shaken to the marrow by the Decembrist Revolt in the Russian Army, the new Tsar made no pretence of his contempt for constitutional government. An autocrat alike by temperament and by conviction, the 'Nebuchadnezzar of the North' regarded the Kingdom of Poland as a boil on the body of Holy Russia, ripe for cauterization. He did not overlook the Decembrists' Polish connections, and was specially incensed by reports of the supposedly seditious disposition of his Polish army. Having flooded the Kingdom with the agents of his newly formed Third Department, and finding an eager servant in a reinvigorated Novosiltsov, he promptly set a Commission of Inquiry to review the problem of the secret clubs. By so doing, he provoked the *cause célèbre* of the decade. In 1828, the ring-leaders of the Patriotic Society were brought before a tribunal of the Sejm, and charged with the capital offence of treason. The prosecution demanded a harsh verdict, and expected the Senators to comply. Surprisingly, perhaps, they did not. With the one dissenting voice of General Krasiński, the Senators ruled that membership of an unapproved society did not in itself constitute a treasonable act. The chief defendant, Lt.-Col. Seweryn Krzyżanowski (1787–1839), who was charged with conducting negotiations with the Decembrists, was awarded only three years detention. The Grand Duke Constantine exploded in anger. He interned the offending Senators of the tribunal in the Royal Castle, and forbade publication of their verdict. After the Tsar had intervened from St. Petersburg, the sentences were unceremoniously quashed. The competence of the tribunal was retrospectively revoked. The prisoners were transported in chains to Siberia.

When the Sejm reassembled in 1830 to review its legislative programme, its members were duly chastened. The conservative element was jubilant. In the prevailing atmosphere of fear and suspicion, there was little chance that the constitutional process could be resumed in a systematic way.

For the time being, however, any thoughts of active sedition were confined to the lower ranks of the officer corps. A series of timely military reforms, including the suspension of public floggings and the improvement of pay structures, had failed to stem the sense of injustice created by the repression of the associates of the Decembrists and by the constant harassments of the Third Department. At the time of the Sejm tribunal, all Polish officers had been required to renew their oath of allegiance to the Tsar. Their sharp sense of honour was touched to the quick. Already in 1829, a group of cadets at the Infantry School had discussed the possibility of assassinating the Tsar at his forthcoming Polish coronation. In 1830, an instructor at the same School, Second-Lieutenant Piotr Wysocki (1794–1857), began to conspire with a young Colonel, Józef Zaliwski (1797–1855). Together they hatched an armed rebellion. In the summer of that year, they met up with a band of civilian plotters who were devising a scheme for killing the Grand Duke Constantine.[9]

* * * * *

The year 1830 in Europe saw the first general outburst against the system blessed by the Congress of Vienna. By the Protocol of London, Greece was proclaimed an independent state. In Paris, in July, the Bourbon monarchy was overturned and replaced by the rule of the Citizen-King, Louis Philippe of Orleans. In Brussels, in August, the Dutch House of Orange-Nassau was expelled, and Belgian Independence declared. Paris assumed its former role as the flash-point of revolutionary tempers, and many appeals rang out for all the oppressed nations of Europe to shake off the rule of Reaction. The poet and dramatist, Casimir Delavigne, a fervent supporter of Louis Philippe, was one of many who remembered Poland. His verse, *La Varsovienne,* echoed the common struggles of the Poles and the French in the Napoleonic Era, and called them to arms:

Il s'est levé, voici le jour sanglant;
Qu'il soit pour nous le jour de délivrance!
Dans son essor, voyez notre aigle blanc,
Les yeux fixés sur l'arc-en-ciel de France.
Au Soleil de Juillet, dont l'éclat fût si beau,
Il a repris son vol; il fend les airs; il crie:
　　　'Pour ma noble patrie,
Liberté, ton soleil ou la nuit du tombeau.'
　　　Polonais, à la baïonette!
　　　C'est le cri par nous adopté,
　　　Qu'en roulant le tambour repète:
　　　A la baïonette!
　　　Vive la liberté!

Pour toi, Pologne, ils combattront, tes fils,
Plus fortunés qu'au temps où la victoire
Mêlait leur cendres aux sables de Memphis,
Où le Kremlin s'écroula sous leur gloire.
Des Alpes au Thabor, de l'Èbre au Pont-Euxin,
Ils sont tombés vingt ans, sur la rive étrangère.
　　　Cette fois, Ô ma mère,
Ceux qui mouriront pour toi, dormiront sur ton sein.
　　　Polonais, à la baïonette! . . .

Sonnez clairons! Polonais, à ton rang
Suis sous le feu ton aigle qui s'élance.
　La Liberté bat la charge en courant,
　Et la victoire est au bout de ta lance.
Victoire à l'étendard que l'exil obragea
Des lauriers d'Austerlitz, des palmes d'Idumée!
　　　Pologne, bien-aimée,
Qui vivra sera libre, et qui meurt l'est déjà!
　　　Polonais, à la baïonette! . . . [10]

At last the day of blood has dawned.
May it be the day of our deliverance!
See the white eagle in all its splendour,
Whose eyes were fixed on the rainbow of France
When it took to the wing in the sunshine of July.
Now, as it soars aloft, hear its cry:
'My noble country! For Thee, we pledge our doom:
Either the Sun of Freedom, or the night of the tomb!'

> Poles, to the bayonet!
> That is our chosen cry
> Relayed by the roll of the drum.
> To arms, to die!
> Long live Freedom!

Poland, for you, your sons will fight
In a happier time, than that when Victory
Mingled their ashes with the sands of Memphis,
Or when the Kremlin crumbled beneath their glory.
From the Alps to the Tabor, from the Euxine to the Ebro,
They perished for twenty years on the foreign shore.
But those that give their lives for the Motherland now
Shall sleep safe in her bosom for evermore.

> Poles, to the bayonet! (etc.)

Sound the trumpets! Poles, to your ranks!
Follow your eagles through the fire as you advance.
Liberty sounds the charge at the double,
And Victory stands at the point of your lance.
All hail to the standard that exiles crowned
With the laurels of Austerlitz, with the palms of Idumée!
O beloved Poland! The dead are free already;
And those who live shall win their liberty.

> Poles, to the bayonet! (etc.)

In Warsaw, an explosive political situation developed rapidly. Rumours that the Tsar might use his Polish army to suppress the revolutions in France and Belgium caused general consternation. Unrest in the Cadet Corps reached fever pitch. Wysocki's band of conspirators were joined by others outside the army, including Maurycy Mochnacki. Plans for an armed demonstration were accelerated. In October, a strike at the Fraenkel Factory over working conditions spread existing tensions to the civilian population. In November, the police launched a wave of preventive arrests. On 18 November, the press carried the first notices for General Mobilization, both of the Polish Army and of the Lithuanian Corps. In a situation where the authorities knew that mutiny was afoot, and where the conspirators expected to be seized at any moment, it was an open question who would strike first.

Violence and confusion erupted on the night of 29 November. An assassination squad of eighteen men headed by Ludwik Nabielak was to attack the Belweder Palace and kill or capture the Grand Duke Constantine, whilst a detachment of Cadets under Wysocki was to march into the city centre, disarm the Russian garrison, and seize the Arsenal. Everything went wrong from the start. The fire in a deserted brewery which was intended as the signal for co-ordinated action, was started half an hour early, before the conspirators were in position. Its flames alerted the garrison, and filled the streets with troops and firemen. At Belweder, the assassins burst into the palace, stabbed a uniformed figure standing before the Grand Duke's suite and shot another as he fled from the back door. Their first victim was the Governor of Warsaw, Lubovitsky, their second the Russian General Gendre. As they rushed into the city shouting 'The Grand Duke is dead', Constantine emerged from his wife's bedroom, where he had taken refuge, and tried to organize his staff. In the city, the cadets retreated from a vain attack on the cavalry barracks. Soon they were joined by a raging mob. General Potocki, a patriotic Pole, who declined to take command, was shot. General Trębicki, their own Commandant, suffered the same fate for the same reason, having cursed his pupils as 'ignorant murderers'. Another Pole, General Lewicki, mistaken in the dark for the Russian, General Novitsky, was killed in his carriage.

The Arsenal was rushed by the mob. The Grand Duke refused to commit his troops. 'The Poles have started this disturbance', he said, 'and it's Poles that must stop it.' A regiment of the Polish Light Horse advanced as far as the Castle Square, but lacking clear orders, held back. By midnight, stalemate was reached. The rebels were in control of the town, but the Russian garrison was still intact. Prince Lubecki was the only person to keep a cool head. Calling the Administrative Council together, and in consultation with Czartoryski, he agreed to take the lead in ending the rebellion and reaching an accommodation with the Tsar. This 'November Night' was a drama which most of its actors would have liked to forget.[11]

Owing to the ineptitude of the original conspirators, political leadership of the Rising passed immediately to people who had never favoured armed insurrection and who had every intention of avoiding a confrontation with Russia if at all possible. Hence the political aims of the Rising were only formulated after its outbreak, and at first were entirely conciliatory. The Provisional Government which appeared on 4 December was nothing other than a revamped version of the old Administrative Council. It was formed at Lubecki's instigation, and concealed its essentially conservative make-up by co-opting Julian Niemcewicz and Joachim Lelewel, together with Prince Czartoryski and General Józef Chłopicki (1771–1854). Within a week, it surrendered its formal authority to Chłopicki, whose personal dictatorship was considered to offer a more efficient means of pursuing its objectives. At this stage, full priority was given to the task of reaching an amicable settlement with the Tsar. Nothing was done to avoid further provocation. Grand Duke Constantine was allowed to leave Warsaw unmolested, taking his troops and his political prisoners with him. Chłopicki refused to put the army on a war footing. At the same time, Lubecki hoped that negotiations with the Tsar would lead to progress on the constitutional issue and on his scheme for closer ties between Poland and Lithuania. It was an odd situation. The loyalist leaders of a mutinous rebellion were hoping to exact constitutional concessions from the Autocrat in return for bringing the Rebellion to a close.

The Tsar, however, had other ideas. Nicholas had no desire

to negotiate with rebels, however loyal they professed to be. From the very beginning he determined to crush the Poles by force. In his first communication with Constantine, he had declared that 'Russia or Poland must now perish'. The 'November Night' had played straight into his hands. There is some doubt whether he had already decided to overturn the Constitution of the Kingdom before the outbreak occurred. But now all hesitation was cast aside. Nicholas had a perfect opportunity for teaching the Poles a lesson, and for installing the sort of government in which he believed. Polish negotiators who travelled to St. Petersburg were unable to get a hearing. As soon as Constantine had been safely extracted from Warsaw, preparations were laid for assembling a punitive force. General Diebitsch was given command of 120,000 men who throughout January were concentrated in the region of Belostok. When news arrived at the end of the month that the Polish Sejm had voted for the legal dethronement of the Tsar, Nicholas was able to order an immediate invasion of the Kingdom. Diebitsch crossed the frontier on 5 February 1831. By this act, a local rebellion was transformed into a national war.

In Warsaw, the moderate designs of the Government grew steadily more extreme, as all attempts to reach a settlement failed. Step by step, cautious men were replaced by 'activists'; the activists by radicals; the radicals by desperadoes, and the desperadoes by a military clique. Over the nine months of the Government's existence, control passed successively from Chłopicki and his 'Whites' to the liberal, centrist, leaders of the Sejm; from the Sejm to the largely extraparliamentary 'Reds'; from the 'Reds' to the Warsaw mob; and from the mob to General Krukowiecki. It was a political process of classic simplicity, driven on by the logic of a conflict where all remedies could be tried, but where none, given the nature of the protagonist, could possibly succeed. The first stage came to an end in January. Patient negotiation had yielded nothing. A restless Sejm appointed a fifteen-man commission to supervise General Chłopicki's decisions, and on 19 January eventually forced him to resign. At this point, Polish patience, already strained by the intransigence of the Tsar, suddenly snapped. After a memorial meeting on 24 January in honour of the Russian Decembrists, executed by the Tsar six years before, the restraint of the Sejm evaporated. On the next day, a Sejm decree announced that the throne of Poland was vacant. Nicholas was dethroned. It was the moment of no return. A new constitution declared that the government should be accountable to the 'Sovereign Sejm'. Pending the appointment of a new ministry, Chłopicki was reinstated. After three weeks, Czartoryski emerged as the President of a ruling Council. On 18 February, he took over from Chłopicki, and the second stage began. It was to last until May. Meanwhile, he had to fight the war.

The outcome of the Russo-Polish War of 1831 was not a foregone conclusion. The absolute numerical superiority of the Russian forces was dissipated by their need to occupy and garrison all the area they controlled, by long lines of communication, and by their necessarily offensive posture. The Poles, in contrast, were operating on their own ground, amidst a friendly population, from a central and well-defined base in Warsaw. The Polish Army was organized round professional cadres, whose equipment and training were superior in every branch except the artillery. On several occasions in the first three months, it inflicted terrible casualties on the Russians who were repeatedly frustrated in their attempts to advance. Its weaknesses lay principally in the high command and, by extension, in morale. There was a striking difference between the dash and courage of the troops and the extreme caution and indecision of the General Staff which, after Chłopicki fell in battle in February, was headed by General Jan Skrzynecki (1787–1860). Skrzynecki had little belief in victory, and made several approaches to Diebitsch to arrange a political settlement. He had even less faith in the politicians, in whose work he increasingly interfered. As a clerical and conservative, he could not abide the growing influence of the 'Reds' and lost his post in August amidst charges and countercharges of treason and conspiracy. In every field, he earned his name of *Kunktator* (the Delayer), exercising a negative influence on his subordinates – Henryk Dembiński, Józef Bem, Jan Krukowiecki, and in particular on his talented Chief-of-Staff, Ignacy Prądzyński (1792–1850). At first, the army performed well. The initial Russian offensive was brought to a halt by a series of fierce rearguard actions: at Stoczek on 14 February, at Dobre and Wawer and at the bloody struggle of Grochów near Warsaw on 25 February, where Diebitsch suffered almost ten thousand casualties. A Polish counter-offensive brought two major victories to Prądzyński, who annihilated one Russian corps at Dąby Wielkie on 31 March, taking ten thousand prisoners, and dispersing another at Iganie on 10 April. It was accompanied by two enterprising raids, one into Volhynia and the Ukraine by General Dwernicki and the other into Lithuania by General Gielgud. Inexcusably, the Polish successes were followed by a prolonged period of inactivity. Diebitsch was allowed to regroup to the north. On 26 May at Ostrołęka, he destroyed the cream of the Polish infantry. Bem's enterprising deployment of rocket forces could not prevent a decisive defeat. Thereafter, the initiative lay in Russian hands.[12]

The political crisis which developed in Warsaw in June is usually ascribed to the defeat at Ostrołęka. But it can equally be argued that the mistakes of the General Staff which precipitated Ostrołęka were themselves engendered by political divisions already far advanced. Political and military disintegration went hand in hand. For three months, Czartoryski patiently pursued a diplomatic policy in Vienna, Paris, and London, whilst holding off the clamours for a social revolution at home. He was hoping against hope for a military success which would force the Tsar to negotiate, encourage the Powers to intervene, and defuse criticism at home. When success was not forthcoming, his caution was discredited. His authority was prolonged by the fitful spread of the Rising to Lithuania. Deputies reached the Sejm in Warsaw from Belostok, Vilna, and Minsk. Peasants in Samogitia sang, *Dabar lenkai naprapula kol Zemaitiai gyui* (Poland has not perished, whilst Samogitia is still alive). But Gielgud failed to dislodge the Russians from their Lithuanian bases, and fierce repressions began. In the Sejm, the Kalisz Group held the ring for a time between the Whites and the Reds. Two of their leaders held seats in the Government. But attitudes polarized incessantly. When the conservative camp successfully blocked a bill for distributing state-owned land among soldiers and peasants, the radical Patriotic Society came to the fore. It exercised an influence far greater than its tiny membership might have indicated. Suppressed by Chłopicki in December, it now set the pace in political discussions. Its slogan, 'For your freedom and ours', was aimed at Czartoryski and at the Tsar alike. Its militant leaders — Tadeusz Krępowiecki (1798–1847), Jan Nepomucen Janowski (1803–86), Jan Czyński (1801–67), and the Revd Aleksander Pułaski (1800–38) — and their journal, *Nowa Polska* (New Poland), combined demands for an intensified war effort with calls for emancipation of the serfs and the Jews. They frightened as many people as they converted. In Łódź, mill owners raised units for service with the Russians. Elsewhere, in Lublin, Kielce, Kalisz, and above all, in Warsaw itself, the workers supported the Rising, and initiated a rudimentary armaments programme. Senior clerics urged restraint; radical priests urged resistance. Both landowners and peasants adopted contradictory positions. By June, Skrzynecki was threatening to discipline the Opposition. When a bill to reintroduce dictatorial powers failed by only seven votes, he struck of his own accord. Unsuccessful officers, political critics, and alleged spies and provocateurs were seized and put on trial. But the rot continued. No sooner had the Sejm resolved to replace Skrzynecki with General Dembiński, when the Warsaw mob took over. On the night of 15 August, the prisons were forced. Thirty-four prisoners, including four generals, were butchered in cold blood. The following day order was restored by the army. The barricades were destroyed. The mob leaders were shot. The Patriotic Society was disbanded. General Jan Krukowiecki (1772–1850), the governor of Warsaw, was declared Dictator. Czartoryski fled the capital, and took refuge with the army. The forces of the Rising were tearing themselves apart.

Meanwhile, the Russian army was building a position of unassailable superiority. Diebitsch, who fell victim to cholera, was replaced by General Ivan F. Paskievitch (1782–1856). The main force had taken to the valley of the Vistula to the north, and was receiving heavy reinforcements from Prussia. On 27 July, Paskievitch crossed the river unopposed in the vicinity of Thorn, and began his march on Warsaw from the west. By the time of the August 'coup', he had already captured the main Polish supply centre at Łowicz, and was preparing to lay siege to the capital. The defenders hurriedly threw up earthworks and fortifications. Forty thousand men, dispersed along a wide horseshoe, were to hold a line against almost twice their number. Some 95 horse-drawn cannon were matched against the Russians' 390. The key position, in Redoubt No. 54 and the churchyard at Wola, was commanded by General Jan Sowiński (1777—1831), a veteran of both the Prussian and Napoleonic armies, who had lost a leg in Russia in 1812. The assault was launched at 4 a.m. on 6 September, and lasted two full days. Paskievitch counted on the sheer weight of men and metal to overwhelm suicidal bravery. Redoubt No. 54 was blown to pieces, together with its defenders and attackers, when a desperate Polish hero put a match to the powder store. In the churchyard at Wola, Sowiński's corpse, shredded by bayonets, lolled against a gun-carriage, eerily erect on its wooden leg, long after the tide of battle had flowed into the city centre. Warsaw capitulated at midnight, 7—8 September, amidst the glare of burning suburbs, convoys of refugees, and the recriminations of the General Staff. Krukowiecki and Prądzyński were taken into captivity.[13]

In military terms, the Rising was far from defeated. Three separate army corps were still in the field, with a total of 60,000 men at their disposal. Ramorino to the east, Różycki to the south, and Rybiński entrenched in the great Napoleonic fortress of Modlin, might well have stretched Russian resources to the full. But the will to fight was broken. Once the heart of the Rising in Warsaw was pierced, the limbs ceased to function. The ranks of the army melted away. The surviving political leaders, like Czartoryski, fled to Galicia, or to Prussia. The last focus of resistance at Zamość surrendered on 21 October. From beginning to end, the most tragic of Polish Risings had lasted just 325 days.

The tragedy of the November Rising lay in the fact that it was largely unnecessary. Unlike 1794 or 1863 or 1905, which were provoked by systematic oppression, the events of 1830—1 were preceded by a period in which the main part of the Polish nation had enjoyed greater freedoms than at any point during the Partitions. The original conspirators acted without the approval of anyone beyond their immediate circle, and without any conception of further developments. Given the slightest grain of understanding from the Tsarist government, they would have been rounded up like any other band of amateur adventurers, and their grievances attended to. Unfortunately, the total obduracy of the Tsar, the absolute refusal to negotiate or compromise, the brutish insistence on unconditional surrender from the start, turned a minor conspiracy into a major conflict. In 1830, the Polish nation did not possess an unusual proportion of 'hotheads', 'troublemakers', or 'revolutionaries'. It did not display any innate tendency to commit communal suicide. The extreme attitudes which came to the surface in the course of the Rising were manufactured by a situation in which reasonable men were denied the chance of behaving reasonably. It was Nicholas I who turned even pro-Russian conservatives like Adam Czartoryski into active rebels. It was the Russian government which provoked the very reactions it supposedly sought to avoid. It was Tsarism which fostered the negative qualities of Polish nationalism.

As a result of the Rising, attitudes hardened on all sides. In Russia, where nothing was known of Polish attempts at conciliation, the Poles were cursed by reactionaries and dissidents alike. From his official position in the Russian Legation at Munich, Feodor Tyutchev wrote a celebratory ode:

> Как дочь родную на закланье
> Агамемнон богам принес,
> Прося попутных бурь дыханья
> У негодующих небес, —
> 5 Так мы над горестной Варшавой
> Удар свершили роковой,
> Да купим сей ценой кровавой
> России целость и покой!
>
> . . .
>
> 25 Сие-то высшее сознанье
> Вело наш доблестный народ —
> Путей небесных оправданье
> Он смело на себя берет.
> Он чует над своей главою
> 30 Звезду в незримой высоте
> И неуклонно за звездою
> Спешит к таинственной мете!

Ты ж, братскою стрелой пронзенный,
Судеб свершая приговор,
35 Ты пал, орел одноплеменный,
На очистительный костер!
Верь слову русского народа:
Твой пепл мы свято сбережем,
И наша общая свобода,
40 Как феникс, зародится в нем.*[14]

Indignation was general. The feelings of loyal Russian subjects were no less aggrieved than those of the intellectuals, who considered that the Poles had given Nicholas a perfect pretext for crushing all Reform in Russia. Everyone was incensed by the torrent of criticism unleashed in Western Europe. Alexander Pushkin composed a violent retort *To the Slanderers of Russia*:

Клеветникам России
Vox et praeterea nihil.
О чем шумите вы, народные витии?
Зачем анафемой грозите вы России?
Что возмутило вас? Волнения Литвы?
Оставьте: это — спор славян между собою,
Домашний, старый спор, уж взвешенный судьбою, —
Вопрос, которого не разрешите вы.
Уже давно между собою
Враждуют эти племена;
Не раз клонилась под грозою
То их, то наша сторона.
Кто устоит в неравном споре:
Кичливый лях иль верный росс?
Славянские ль ручьи сольются в русском море?
Оно ль иссякнет? — Вот вопрос.
Оставьте нас: вы не читали

---

* As Agamemnon brought his own daughter to the sacrificial altar, imploring the angry heavens to grant a breath of favourable breezes, so we have struck a blow on sorrowing Warsaw. Indeed, it is the integrity and peace of Russia that we buy at this bloody price . . .

Our valiant nation is led by a higher conscience, and boldly takes the path of divine justice. It senses a star above its head in the invisible reaches of the sky, and follows that star to its mysterious goal.

And you, who have been pierced by the arrows of brothers are fulfilling a prophecy of Fate. You have fallen, like a pure-blooded eagle on the cleansing pyre. Trust in the word of the Russian people. We shall gather your ashes with reverence. In them, like a phoenix, our general freedom will be reborn.

Сии кровавые скрижали;
Вам непонятна, вам чужда
Сия семейная вражда;
Для вас безмолвны Кремль и Прага;
Бессмысленно прельщает вас
Борьбы отчаянной отвага —
И ненавидите вы нас. . .
       За что ж? Ответствуйте: за то ли,
Что на развалинах пылающей Москвы
Мы не признали нагой воли
Того, под кем дрожали вы?
     За то ль, что в бездну повалили
Мы тяготеющий над царствами кумир,
И нашей кровью искупили
Европы вольность, честь и мир? *

Among the Poles, the defeat of the Rising caused the greatest single outburst of national feeling, and of literary activity in the nation's history. Here was a catastrophe well matched to the talents of the Romantic generation. Ordinary people simply wept in frustration and rage. Frederyk Chopin had left Warsaw only three weeks before the outbreak. He ate his Christmas dinner in a restaurant in Vienna, fuming at the

* What's all this uproar, pundits of the nations?
  Why do you threaten Russia with anathema?
  Is it the riots in Lithuania that have given you such offence?
  Lay off! This is a quarrel of Slavs among themselves,
  An old, domestic quarrel already weighed by Fate,
  An issue which won't be solved by you.

  These tribes have engaged in hostilities for centuries.
  First their side, then ours, would often bow before the storm.
  Who will stand firm in this unequal contest,
  The conceited Pole, or the faithful Russian?
  Shall the Slav rivers merge into the Russian sea,
  Or shall the sea itself run dry? That's the question.

  Leave us alone. You have not read the bloody reckoning.
  For you, these family antagonisms are strange and meaningless.
  Neither the Kremlin, nor Praga, means anything to you.
  You are thoughtlessly seduced by the courage of this desperate struggle;
  And you hate us!
  And for what? Answer! Is it because
  In the ruins of blazing Moscow we did not heed the arbitrary will
  Of him under whom you all trembled?
  Is it because we hurled that towering idol into the abyss,
  And with our blood redeemed the freedom, honour and peace of Europe? . . .[15]

conversation of the diners at the next table. One said: 'God
made a mistake when he created the Poles.' The other replied:
Ja! In Polen ist nichts zu holen' (Yes, nothing good comes
out of Poland). Chopin's correspondence to his parents was
filled with uncontrolled rage. He was in Stuttgart in August
when he heard that Warsaw had fallen:

. . . the enemy must have reached our home. The suburbs must have
been stormed, and burned. Johnny, where are you? Willem has certainly
perished on the barricades. Oh God, dost Thou exist? Thou Art, but
revengest not. Hast Thou not seen enough of these Muscovite crimes, or
art Thou Thyself a Muscovite? My poor, kind father! Perhaps you are
hungry and cannot buy bread for Mother. Perhaps my sisters have fallen
victim to the fury of the Muscovite scum . . . The Muscovite is lord of
the world . . . Oh, why could I not slay a single Muscovite? . . .[16]

Elsewhere in Europe, similar powerlessness reigned. Those
who had taken no interest in Poland's fate maintained their
silence. Those few who had urged action, were stricken with
remorse. In France, Casimir Delavigne, for one, was quickly
forced to change his tune:

La Pologne ainsi partagée,	What human hand could have avenged
Quel bras humain l'aurait vengée?	Poland, so divided.
Dieu seul pouvait la secourir.	God alone could have helped her.[17]

In Germany, widespread sympathy for the Poles and fear of
Russia, was reflected in a wave of popular *Polenlieder* (Songs
of Poland):

> Schlaf ein, du weisst ja nicht, o Herz,
> Warum du weinst.
> Schlaf ein, ich will den wahren Schmerz
> Dich lehren einst.
>
> Schlaf ein, o Herz, was kummert dich
> Der Feinde Sieg?
> Dein Vater feil fur dich und mich
> Im Heldenkrieg.
>
> Dich wird erziehn dereinst der Zar
> Zur Sklaverei
> Doch als ich dich, O Kind, gebar
> War Polen frei.

Sleep, my little one, You cannot say
What makes you cry.
Sleep on. Despite the pain, some day
I'll tell you why.

Sleep on, dear Heart. Why such misery
At the triumph of our foes?
Your father died for you and for me
In a war of heroes.

Soon you'll be taught and enslaved in the ways
of Russian Tsardom.
Yet you were borne and delivered in the days
Of Poland's Freedom.[18]

In Great Britain, as in the United States, liberal opinion
was outraged. The November Rising in Poland triggered the
first of many waves of Russophobia which were to break over
the Anglo-Saxon public on repeated occasions during the
century. A Literary Association of the Friends of Poland was
launched in Scotland by the poet, Thomas Campbell, and by
Lord Dudley Stuart. In the House of Commons, in July 1833,
J. Cutler Fergusson MP, armed with information supplied by
the Hotel Lambert, introduced the most important of several
debates on the Polish situation. Lord Morpeth elucidated
Poland's historic role. The Nonconformist, Spurgeon, and
the Jewish member, Goldsmith, both paid tribute to Poland's
tradition of religious toleration. Daniel O'Connell denounced
the Tsar as a 'scoundrel'. Thomas Attwood denounced the
passivity of the British government. The House unanimously
passed a vote of censure on Russia's conduct. But nothing
more was done. Thomas Campbell revived his poem, of which
only one line is generally remembered: 'And Freedom shrieked
as Kosciuszko fell.'[19]

Another bad poet called Antrobus, apologizing for the
weakness of his 'poetic effusions', composed a lengthy ode
on *The Wrongs of Poland*, whose well-meaning lines aptly
recorded the inarticulate rage of Poland's many sympathizers:

In sable weeds Britannia mourning stands
O'er fallen Sarmatia's bier; bathing with dew
Of truthful pity, the unfading wreaths
That thickly cluster round her trophied urn . . .
O land of heroes, could the Muse portray

A tithe of what thy children have endured,
Each face would wear the mourning of the heart;
All voices join in execration loud.
No pen can picture true thy mighty wrongs;
No tongue reveal the many springs of woe;
Oppression, murder, rapine, torture, lust,
All cruelty, in each appalling form:
Most deadly fruit of blind despotic rage,
That like the feigned Promethean bird of hell
By gorging human flesh more ravenous grows . . .
But Russia, thou! in guilt and might supreme
To deal with Thee, how shall the Muse essay?
What spell, what power invoke? For words are vain.
Yet wouldst thou list awhile, thou mightst perchance
Some new-found truth like hidden treasures find
And gain the knowledge that was never thine
To know thyself, and all thou call'st thine own;
As in a mirror, thou thyself might'st view,
And learn to loathe what others loathing see . . .[20]

Dissenting opinions were voiced from only two sources. Several MPs protested against the pointless expression of inflammatory sentiments by people who had no intention of matching their words with deeds. Richard Cobden was alone in protesting against the prevailing Russophobia on the grounds that Poland's fate represented 'the triumph of justice'. In a study of Russia, published in 1835, Cobden argued that the kind of catastrophes which had happened to Poland 'only befall neglected, decayed, disorganised, ignorant, and ir-religious societies, and their anarchic governments'. Whilst praising the prosperity of Prussia and the prospects of ex-panded Anglo-Russian trade, he maintained that the Polish Rising was caused by the desperate attempts of a licentious nobility to recover their former privileges. Like many of his heirs and successors on the radical Left, the apostle of Manchester Liberalism was so eager to demonstrate his brilliant powers of social analysis that he was tempted to score a cheap success by attacking a defenceless target abroad. In so doing, he uttered some of the harshest words ever directed against Poland. Like many western liberals today, in his haste to discredit the prevailing attitudes of the Establishment of his own country, he was led into the ridiculous position of absolving the despotic practices of a foreign Autocracy which were the very antithesis of what he really stood for.[21]

* * * * *

Russian retribution fell hard on the prostrate Polish provinces. In the Kingdom, Paskievitch, now 'Prince of Warsaw', richly earned his more popular title, the 'Hound of Mogilev'. In Lithuania, the practised cruelty of General Mikhail Muraviev (1794–1866) amply justified his sobriquet of 'the Hangman'. Since his own brother had been exccuted during the Decembrist Revolt, the General was at some pains to point out that he was 'not one of the Muravievs that get themselves hanged, but one that does the hanging'.

Punishments were inflicted in a harsh and methodical manner. All Polish officers who had served during the Rising were automatically cashiered and, in spite of an official amnesty, transported. The rankers were drafted into Russian regiments serving in the Caucasus. These military measures affected up to 100,000 men. To examine the conduct of the civilian population, field tribunals were set up in every district. Nobles implicated in the Rising were declared confiscate. Some 2,540 manors were sequestrated in the Kingdom – almost 1 in 10 – and some 2,890 in Lithuania. Civil servants were dismissed from their posts. Active rebels were sentenced, together with their families and associates, to penal servitude in Russia. The so-called 'cantonists', who were the dependants of rebels sentenced *in absentia*, were obliged to pay the penalty by proxy. By these means, a further 80,000 Poles were condemned to deportation. Some 254 political and military leaders were condemned to death. It took years before the endless lines of convict wagons, with their clanking chains and groaning inmates, wended their way to their final destinations four and five thousand miles away in distant Siberia. In the case of Prince Roman Sanguszko, a prince of the blood, the Tsar personally insisted that he should make the whole of the terrible journey on foot. The lands, possessions, and offices of the convicts were distributed among loyalists, or more usually among Russian newcomers. Some 10,000 Poles left the country of their own accord, forming the core of 'The Great Emigration'. The remaining population was subjected to punitive taxation, and to reparation payments totalling 2 million roubles. A huge army of occupation was settled on the Kingdom at the Kingdom's expense, and put to work to construct a complex of impregnable fortresses.

The spirit of the Tsar's dispositions was evident in the meticulous detail of his every behest:

Order a search to be made in Warsaw for all the flags and standards of our former Polish Army and send them to me. Find also all those captured from us and dispatch them to the commissary. All revolutionary objects, such as the sword and sash of Kościuszko, should be confiscated and sent here to the Cathedral of the Transfiguration. Similarly, all the banners should be taken out of the churches. Find me all the uniforms of the late Emperor, together with all the things which belonged to him personally. Take away thrones and all related items and send them to Brest. After a period of time, order General Berg to detail some competent person to seize, pack, and dispatch to Brest the University Library, and the collection of medals, as well as the library of the *Société des Belles Lettres*. In a word, gradually remove everything that has historical or national value, and deliver it here; also the flag from the Royal Castle. Order the Archives and the Bank to be sealed . . .[22]

The defeat of the Rising spelt an end to the Constitution. The provisions of the Treaty of Vienna in this regard were flouted. In theory, the Constitution of 1815 was superseded by an Organic Statute of government published on 14 February 1832. But even this was ignored. In practice, the Kingdom was ruled by military decree. All civil rights were suspended, except by grace of the Tsar. The Army, the Sejm, the Universities, all the higher institutes of learning, were abolished. There were no more political events to record.

By virtue of the Rising, the Holy Alliance was given the opportunity of tightening its grip on the international scene. The papal encyclical *Cum primum* of 1832 explicitly condemned the Rising, and praised the Tsar for its suppression. In 1833, an abortive incursion into the Kingdom of Galicia by the indefatigable Zaliwski encouraged the partitioning powers to synchronize their plans. At a conference at Münchengrätz in Bohemia, Russian and Austrian negotiators made provision for the common suppression of any future Polish troubles. The Prussians were not slow to join them.[23]

For nearly thirty years, the Congress Kingdom lingered on

in name only. So long as Nicholas and Paskievitch were alive, there was no chance of relief. One by one, the surviving Polish institutions were dismantled. In 1837, the Polish *wójewodztwa* (palatinates) were replaced by ten Russian *gubernias*. In 1839, the Education Commission was abolished. All its schools were placed under the direct control of the Ministry of Enlightenment in St. Petersburg. In 1841, the Polish Bank lost its emissary rights; the Polish *złoty* was withdrawn from circulation in favour of the rouble. In 1847, the Napoleonic Code was curtailed, and the Russian Criminal Code introduced. In 1849, to the vast consternation of the ordinary people, the Russian imperial system of Weights and Measures replaced the 'New Poland' system of 1818; the *mila* (mile), the *łokieć* (yard), the *włóka* (hide) of 16.8 hectares, the *korzec* (bushel) and *cetnar* (quintal of 100 kilograms) gave way to the *versta* (two-thirds of a mile), the *arshin* (28 inches), the *diesyatina* (2.7 acres), the *chetvert'* (209.9 litres), and the *pud* (16.8 kg). To all intents and purposes, the *Kongresówka* was dead. The attempt to revive it in 1861–4 produced another round of violent, and, as it proved, fatal convulsions.

Meanwhile, the prisoners and exiles bore their fate as best they could. Many did not live to see the amnesty proclaimed at the start of the new reign of 1855. Wincenty Niemoyowski died in 1834 on the road to the Urals. Krzyżanowski died in Siberia in 1839. Łukasiński survived, but was not granted an amnesty. Blinded and chained, he was one of the convicts whom the Grand Duke Constantine had evacuated from Warsaw in December 1830. He eventually died in the Schlüsselburg prison in 1868, after forty-six years in total darkness — the last pathetic symbol of the departed Polish Kingdom.

CHAPTER FOURTEEN
CRACOVIA:
The Republic of Cracow (1815-1846)

At the end of the Napoleonic Era, the only city of the former Republic of Poland–Lithuania to demand independent status was Danzig. Before 1793, Danzig had enjoyed extensive municipal liberties, and from 1807 to 1815 under French auspices, had become an independent Republic. Its solidly German inhabitants feared and hated the traditional impositions of Prussian rule, against which in 1797 they had revolted. At the Congress of Vienna, the statesmen weighed these considerations, and in their wisdom gave the status of a Free City not to Danzig but to Cracow. Contrary to the fervent petitions of its citizens, Danzig was re-annexed to Prussia.

As far as it is known, the only desire of the Cracovians at this time was to be reunited with that main Polish community of which their ancestors had once been the undisputed leaders. But any such simple solution was frustrated by the rivalry of the Powers. Austria, which had held Cracow from the Third Partition in 1795 to its annexation by the Duchy of Warsaw in 1809, was not prepared to see it pass into the Russian sphere in the Congress Kingdom. The Russians were not prepared to see it return to Austria. The Prussians were happy enough to preserve a bone of contention between their two rivals. Hence, by the Treaty of 3 May 1815, Cracow was established as a Free City. Ambiguously enough, it was to be 'free, independent, and neutral' and yet 'under the protection' of the three Powers. To the Poles, it was universally known as the *Rzeczpospolita Krakowska,* the Cracovian Republic.' Its Constitution, like that of the Congress Kingdom, was the work of Adam Czartoryski. Put into effect in 1818, it provided all the forms of a liberal parliamentary system. The Lower House of the Sejm, the *Zgromadzenie Reprezentantów* (Assembly of Representatives), was to meet annually, and, elected by male suffrage, was to be responsible for legislation. The Upper House, the *Senat Rządzący* (Ruling Senate), consisted of thirteen elected members, including two from the Jagiellonian University and two from the episcopal Curia, and was to control executive business. Its chairman, the City President, was to hold office for a term of three years. His appointment and his executive decisions required the approval of the three Residents of Austria, Prussia, and Russia. The city's territory, which measured 1,164 km^2 (455 square miles) and included three small towns — Chrzanów, Jaworzno, and Krzeszowice — and 244 villages, stretched for 30 miles along the northern bank of the Vistula. Its population, numbering 140,000, was made up of 123,000 Catholics and 18,000 Jews. Its Militia, commanded by 11 officers, could muster 500 infantrymen and 50 cavalrymen. Its frontiers on the west bordered on Prussian Silesia, in the north near Miechów on the Congress Kingdom, and, on the south bank of the river from the suburb of Podgórze to the Abbey of Tyniec, on Austrian Galicia. Its citizens were protected by explicit guarantees of civic and personal liberty, and its economy by the principle of Free Trade and by the absence of external tariffs.[1]

For ten years, Cracow prospered. So long as Warsaw remained the centre of Polish political life, the older capital could devote itself to trade, and to smuggling. It soon established itself as a major entrepôt of Central Europe, a clearing-house for all the forbidden goods and wanted men of the neighbouring states. The Jagiellonian University reclaimed its autonomy, and reintroduced Polish as the language of instruction. The *Towarzystwo Nauk* (Society of Sciences) expanded the system of local schools. The local landowners took to coalmining. Nothing untoward occurred until 1827. But in that year, the three Residents refused to confirm the Senate's choice of a new President, reinstating instead Count Stanisław Wodzicki (1759–1843) for a fifth term. Wodzicki, a distinguished botanist, was the entrenched opponent of radical trends emanating from the University, and by grace of Russian patronage had been serving simultaneously as a Senator in the Congress Kingdom. His reinstatement was contrary to the spirit if not to the letter of the Constitution, and clearly indicated that the Free City's freedom was less than complete.

The outbreak of the November Rising in the Congress

Kingdom shattered Cracow's short-lived idyll. The Free City became the first refuge of Poles fleeing from the Russian army, and in this way attracted the attention and the wrath of the Powers. In September 1831, when the remnants of Różycki's Corps, together with Prince Czartoryski fled to Cracow, they were closely pursued by a Russian force under General Rudiger. For two years, the Constitution was suspended. The Presidency was kept vacant. Secret ballots and open debates were terminated. The represenatatives of the University were rusticated from the Sejm. The City was ruled by a Conference of Residents.

In the 1830s, revolutionary activities mounted inexorably. Smuggling gave way to political conspiracy. For the next fifteen years, Cracow acted as the main link between the Polish lands and the headquarters of the Emigration in Paris. The *émigré* conspirators were in close touch with the radicals in the University, and felt that they could count on the city mob and on the local miners. The Polish 'Carbonari', 'Young Poland', and the *Stowarzyszenie Ludu Polskiego* (Association of the Polish People) were all at work in Cracow. So were the police and the spies of the Powers. Both the Russians and the Austrians kept armies close at hand. In 1836, the death of a police agent provided the pretext for a joint occupation of the Free City. The Austrian, General Kaufmann, deported five hundred people to Trieste for shipment to the USA. New repressions followed a further incident in 1838. When the Austrians formally withdrew in 1841, they kept their forces at the far end of the frontier bridge in Podgórze. Whilst a loyal Opposition sought to re-establish the Constitution, the revolutionaries planned a new rising. The servile President, the Revd Jan Schindler, sought only to curry the favour of his Austrian patrons.

The long-awaited Rising went off in February 1846, at half-cock. Misplanned by Mierosławski, it proved to be a nine-day wonder. Co-ordination with the other partitions was obstructed by preventative arrests. Co-operation with the nobility of Galicia was interrupted by the outbreak of the Jacquerie. Concerted action was hampered by divided counsels and by the entry of the Austrian Army under General Collin. Even so, on 20 February 1846, riots and demonstrations in the City quickly led to the erection of barricades. General Collin beat a hasty retreat, taking the Bishop, and the three Residents with him. On the 22nd, a manifesto, 'To the Polish Nation', announced the formation of a National Government headed by a revolutionary triumvirate:

Poles!
The hour of revolt has arrived. Poland, rent asunder, is rising again and uniting. Our brothers have risen in revolt in the Duchy of Poznań and in Congress Poland. They are fighting with the enemy in Lithuania and in Ruthenia. They are fighting for holy rights taken away either by fraud or by force. You know what has happened already, and is happening even now. The flower of our youth rots in the prisons; the elders who gave us their advice have been dishonoured . . . Brothers! One more step, and Poland and the Poles will be no more. Our grandchildren will curse our memory, for leaving a beautiful country in ruins, for allowing valiant people to be put in chains, and for the fact that they must profess a foreign religion, speak a foreign language, and be the slaves of those who infringed our laws . . . All free nations of the world are calling on us not to let the great principle of nationality fail. God himself, who someday will demand an account, is calling us.

Our number is twenty million. Let us rise up in arms as one man, and no one can destroy our strength. This will bring such freedom as has never been known on this earth. We will construct a social system in which every individual will enjoy material goods according to his merits and his talents; in which no privilege of any sort will have a place; in which every Pole will find security for himself and his family; in which everyone not blessed by nature will find without humiliation the unfailing help of the whole of society; where the peasant will become the owner of the land which today is his only conditionally; where tenant dues and labour services will cease to exist; where service for one's country will be rewarded with grants of land from the national estates.

Poles! There is no class distinction among us. From now on, we are all brothers, sons of one Mother, our native land, and of one Father on high . . . Let us call on him for aid, and he will give us victory.

J. Tyssowski
L. Gorzkowski
A. Grzegorzewski. [2]

Two days later, in view of irreconcilable differences of opinion, Jan Tyssowski (1811–57), an *Adjunkt* (Reader) of the University, declared himself Dictator. On the 26th, the National Guard, which sallied forth into Galicia with six thousand enthusiastic but untrained volunteers, was dispersed at the battle of Gdów by the Austrian Colonel Benedek and his peasant allies. On the 27th, there was an abortive right-wing counter-coup staged by Professor Michał Wiszniewski; whilst the left-wing leader, the twenty-four-year-old Edward Dembowski (1822—46), led a religious procession over the bridge into Podgórze to win the support of the peasants. Dembowski, cross in hand, was slain by the first Austrian volley. All resistance collapsed. On 3 March, Tyssowski fled to Prussia, and his remaining forces capitulated. On 4 March, the advancing Russians joined the Austrians in Cracow's ancient Market Square. If it had not been for the deaths and punishments which ensued, this Cracovian 'Revolution' would have had all the spirit and banality of an unruly student Rag. (See pp. 147—8.)

As a direct result of the Rising, the Free City was suppressed. An Austro-Russian Treaty of 16 November 1846 awarded Cracow to Galicia. The Austrian Emperor added the 'Duke of Krakau' to his already excessive list of titles. Twelve hundred men were arrested, some hundred of them were incarcerated in the Kufstein fortress. Tyssowski, interned by the Prussians, was eventually allowed to emigrate to the USA. As on similar occasions elsewhere, France and Great Britain lodged diplomatic protests against the violence done to the Treaty of Vienna.

*   *   *   *   *

On the second anniversary of the Cracovian Rising, on 22 February 1848, Karl Marx was addressing a meeting in Brussels, in the company of Joachim Lelewel. 'Once again,' he declared, 'the initiative was taken by Poland, not this time by feudal Poland, but by democratic Poland. Hence Poland's liberation has become the point of honour of all Europe's democrats.'[3] It was a fine thought destined to remain unfulfilled. Although in the fateful year of 1848, the barricades were due to reappear in the streets of Cracow, they caused the Austrian authorities little embarrassment. When, on 26 April, an order to clear the city of all non-residents was ignored, General Castiglione simply cleared the Market Square, and bombarded the city into submission. On this occasion, the National Committee lasted only two days. These events, the afterbirth of the abortive Rising of 1846, underlined the pathetic weakness of the Polish national movement at that time. Despite Marx's hopes, Poland did not take the initiative in the Springtime of Nations. For the Poles, 1846 proved to be the false harbinger of a blighted Spring.

As usual, one of the few lasting monuments to the tragedies of 1846 was carved in words. Appalled by the fiasco of the Rising in Cracow and of the attendant *Jacquerie*, Kornel Ujejski (1823–97) composed one of the most intense of all Polish hymns. In Galicia at least, *Z dymem pożarów* was adopted as the national anthem of the Poles, and was sung on all patriotic occasions with a fervour which matched the words:

> Through fiery smoke, through brothers' blood and ashes
> To Thee, O Lord, our fearful prayers ring out
> In terrible lamentation, like the Last Shout.
> Our hair grows grey from such entreaties.
> Our songs are filled with sorrow's invocation;
> Our brows are pierced by crowns of rooted thorn;
> Our outstretched hands are raised to Thee in supplication
> Like monuments to Thy wrath, eternally forlorn. [4]

CHAPTER FIFTEEN

WIOSNA:

The Springtime of Other Nations (1848)

The year's happenings began in Sicily on 12 January, when the citizens of Palermo rose in revolt against King Bomba. Later that month the Germans of Schleswig-Holstein shook off the rule of Denmark. On 24 February, the barricades reappeared on the streets of Paris and Louis-Philippe was driven to abdication and exile. In March, revolutions occurred in Budapest, Vienna, Milan, Rome, Munich, and Berlin. Prince Metternich himself joined the long list of princes and premiers who were obliged to abandon their thrones or their capitals. In Dublin, the Young Ireland movement of John Mitchel and Thomas Maegher openly incited the Irish to shake off British rule. In April, the Hungarian crisis moved into open warfare — the first of many to do so. In London, Feargus O'Connor organized the last Monster Petition of the Chartists. In May, at Frankfurt-am-Main, a German parliament assembled to discuss the political unification of Germany. In one country after another the authority of legitimate monarchs was swept aside by the upsurge of popular animosity. Outbreak followed outbreak, with no obvious prospect of relief. As a speaker at the funeral of the Irish 'Liberator' Daniel O'Connell had forecast in the previous year, Europe seemed to be in the grip of a 'general Revolution which threatens to encompass the world'. It looked an admirable moment for a Polish rising.

The ideas which burst bud during this 'Springtime of Nations' could be classified under three main headings — constitutional, social, and national. All three were relevant to the Polish condition. Constitutional demands sought to overthrow the arbitrary practices of the hereditary monarchs. In France, they were largely directed towards the campaign for universal suffrage; in most central European and Italian states to the formation of a responsible legislature. In the Papal States and in Prussia, they had already been anticipated by the reforms which Pope Pius IX and King Frederick William IV

340

had variously instituted in 1846–7. In most other places, they were conceded unwillingly, by force of popular pressure. As King Wilhelm of Wurtemberg complained, 'I cannot take the field on horseback against ideas.' Social demands, in contrast, sought to break the bonds of feudalism and of class privilege. In France they centred on the full enfranchisement of the proletariat and on the right to work; in Central Europe on the abolition of serfdom. Here was the occasion for the publication of Marx's *Communist Manifesto*: 'Workers of the world unite! You have nothing to lose but your chains.' Nationalists demanded the redrawing of the entire map of Europe, and to replace the old dynastic empires with new democratic republics based on the principle of the self-determination of peoples. This was a signal moment in the history of Marxism, of the Italian *Risorgimento,* in the German *Vormarz,* and in the reassertion of Hungary. The Polish cause appeared to have numerous active allies, all inspired by cognate aims. Thomas Meagher, invoking 'the sword of Poland sheathed in the shroud of Kościuszko', was but one of many orators to pay his respects to the Polish cause.[1]

Yet the Poles lay low. In Russia, Nicholas I was one of the very few monarchs whose realms were not seriously disturbed. In Warsaw and Vilna, memories of the November Rising were still too painful to permit a new adventure. Peasant emancipation could not be publicly discussed. In Galicia, memories of the Jacquerie were still more recent, and inhibited nationalist activities on any large scale. The National Committee in Lemberg framed its demands for local autonomy in the text of a loyal address to the Emperor. In Cracow, the National Committee lasted less than a month. In Prussia, in March and April, when the King momentarily lost control in Berlin, the Duchy of Posen was left to its own devices, and a National Committee was formed there also. But the extent of the revolutionary intentions of the Posnanians at this juncture has been much exaggerated. The German liberals proved no more intolerant of the Polish element in their midst than the Hohenzollerns had ever been. The Rising in Posen, launched on 20 March, had been dispersed by the end of April. It could not be compared to the much more radical and far more determined resistance of the German proletariat of Breslau, whose barricades were not demolished until May 1849. Elsewhere in Silesia and in Pomerania, the embryonic Polish movement confined itself to the language and educational issues, and to successful demands for the abolition of residual feudal services.[2] (See pp. 120–1, 148–9.)

The Polish contribution to 1848 was less in evidence at home than abroad. In Italy, Adam Mickiewicz formed a Legion under the slogan: *Ubi Patria, ubi male* (Wherever there is evil, there is our homeland). It was a generous gesture which antagonized all the governments, and brought the Polish cause no known benefits. The Legion never exceeded five hundred men. It fought in August 1848 against the Austrians in Lombardy; in April 1849 in Genoa against the Royalists; and in June in the vain defence of the Roman Republic. Having failed thereafter to break through from Italy to Hungary, it was disbanded in Greece.[3] Elsewhere in Italy, unemployed Polish generals offered their services to all and sundry. Mierosławski briefly appeared at the head of the rebel forces in Sicily. General Wojciech Chrzanowski (1793–1861) left his refuge in Paris to take command of the Piedmontese Army fighting the Austrians. General Władysław Zamoyski (1803–63), sometime adjutant to the Grand Duke Constantine, travelled from London to help with the reorganization of the army in Sardinia.

By far the most celebrated Poles of 1848 were those who served in Hungary. Józef Bem, who had made his reputation as an artillery officer in the Russo-Polish War of 1831, arrived from Paris to organize the insurrectionary forces in Vienna. Later, he took charge of the Hungarian Army of Transylvania. For several months in 1849, until defeated by the overwhelming forces of the intervening Russians, his brilliant improvisations kept the Habsburg forces at bay and enabled Kossuth's infant Republic to survive. His colleague, General Henryk Dembiński (1791–1864), also served as Hungarian Commander-in-Chief, and led the Magyar Corps in Slovakia. Ironically enough, the task of curbing these two Polish heroes fell to their old adversary, Ivan Paskievitch, Prince of Warsaw.[4]

In the war of words, as distinct from the wars of deeds, a prominent role was played by the short-lived Slav Congress.

Convened in Prague in June 1848 under Czech auspices, it was largely concerned with the problems of the Slavs of Austria and Hungary. Only two Russian representatives attended — Bakunin, the anarchist, and Miloradov, an Old Believer. Neither was really representative. The Polish delegates, together with the Ukrainians, were assigned to a 'Mazurian-Ruthenian Section'; and one of their number, Karol Libelt, newly released from prison in Berlin, was elected President of the Congress. Yet it soon became clear that the Polish cause enjoyed very little support. Although Libelt succeeded in inserting a clause on Polish independence into the 'Manifesto to the Nations of Europe', the Czechs were not prepared to contemplate the creation of a unitary Polish state; and the Ukrainians were openly hostile. The Russians, too, if consulted, would undoubtedly have taken a negative attitude. The Poles, whose strongest antipathies were directed against the Tsarist regime, effectively discredited the great Russian brother to whom most of their fellow-Slavs were looking for salvation. By so doing, they made themselves highly unpopular, especially amongst the Czechs. It was not insignificant that the Whitsun riots which broke out in Prague only ten days after the Congress opened, were blamed by the local press on unspecified Polish provocateurs. The bombardment of the city by Windsichgrätz spelled an end both to the Slav Congress and to all future thought of Austro-Slav harmony.[5]

The debates of 1848 revealed fundamental differences of opinion among the Poles themselves. The Manifesto of the Polish Democratic Society (TDP), which had been published in France in 1836 and had inspired most of the revolutionary activities of the Poles in the intervening period, had described a Poland which stretched from the Oder to the Dnieper and from the Baltic to the Black Sea. Joachim Lelewel was still propagating the idea that the Polish nation included 'all the sons of all the lands of the old Republic'. Karol Libelt, however, observing the distaste which these traditional Polish concepts aroused at the Slav Congress, was obliged to take a new tack. In Libelt's opinion, Poland could not be restored 'as a unitary state with a national government ruling as in the past over Lithuanians, Ruthenians, and Prussians', but would have to be revived 'as a federation of all these racially distinct lands'. Here was the germ of a schism in Polish political thinking which was to persist for the next hundred years. Polish disappointments in Prague were reflected in France and Germany. In Paris, the socialist opposition was the only French party to pay anything more than lip-service to the Polish cause. On 15 May, Blanqui's attempt to seize control of the National Assembly was attended by shouts of 'Vive la Pologne'. But Blanqui was arrested, and his supporters dispersed by the National Guard. The wordy declarations of the French liberals were devoid of any serious commitment to Poland. Like Guizot eighteen years before, Lamartine made suitable gestures in the direction of the Poles so long as he held no responsible position. But from the moment that his own regime was recognized, he categorically refused to raise the Polish Question. 'The Poles are the ferment of Europe,' he said; 'they want a crusade for the conquest of a sepulchre.' 'We love Poland,' he declared; 'we love Italy . . . but most of all we love France.' There can be no doubt that in Lamartine's view French and Polish interests did not necessarily coincide.[6]

In the German Parliament in Frankfurt, the Polish Question received a thorough airing. Yet here again, only the extreme Left, in the speeches of Leisler, Blum, and Ruge, was prepared to pay any serious consideration to Polish arguments. As soon as a conflict of interest between the Germans and Poles in Posnania was identified, the great majority of the German delegates adopted extreme chauvinist positions. Wilhelm Jordan, an East Prussian, asked whether it was right that in the Grand Duchy of Posen 'half a million Germans should live as naturalized foreigners under people of lesser cultural content'. Junghan and Schelka raised the ominous concept of German *Lebensraum* in the East. A Historical Committee advocated that the Polish area of Posnania should be restricted to a rump 'Duchy of Gnesen' containing scarcely one-quarter of the population. On 2 May, the Parliament voted 342 to 41 for the full incorporation of the existing Duchy of Posen into Germany. The lines of antagonism were clearly drawn. The Polish reaction was understandably bitter. Jan Chryzostom Janiszewski (1818—91), a delegate from Upper Silesia, was moved to utter some of the classic pronouncements on

German—Polish relations. 'Culture which withholds freedom', he said, 'is more despicable than barbarism'; or again, echoing Rousseau, 'The Poles have been swallowed, but by God you won't digest them.'[7]

As the summer advanced, the revolutionary fervour of the previous months burned itself out. The forces of Reaction revived. In June, General Cavaignac initiated a military dictatorship in Paris after a bloody confrontation with the radicals. In Britain, Mitchel, Meagher, and O'Brien were convicted of high treason, and were transported to Australia. The Chartist Petition collapsed. The King of Prussia was already back in Berlin. Radetzky's victory at Custozza in July prepared the way for the recovery of Austria, and in October the Emperor Francis Joseph returned to Vienna. By the end of the year, the Austrian army was beginning to eliminate the pockets of resistance in the Italian states, and was bracing itself for the final assaults on Lombardy and Hungary. The Prussian army was undertaking a similar campaign in Germany on behalf of those princes who were unable to fend for themselves. The Russian army was restoring order in the Danubian principalities on behalf of the Turks, whilst Louis Napoleon, newly elected President of the French Republic, was mounting an expedition to reinstate the Pope in Rome. The King of Prussia, having refused 'to grovel in the gutter' for the crown of Germany offered him by a chastened German Parliament, proceeded to chase the Parliament from the scene altogether. By the middle of 1849 it was all over. The Poles, like everyone else, were returned to their several obediences, and had less to show than most for the year of excitements.

Thus the Poles had found themselves on the defensive in 1848. For reasons which were hard to comprehend at the time, the most indefatigable of Europe's oppressed nations was somehow unable to participate fully in Nationalism's Rites of Spring. Although the Poles of Austria and Prussia were to benefit from the social and constitutional reforms conceded by the governments, they did so through no special merit of their own. They made no appreciable progress on the national issue itself. Both in Cracow and Poznań, they lost such remnants of national autonomy that they had hitherto enjoyed. The Poles in Russia were silent. There was no advance whatsoever in reuniting the three Partitions. For Germany and Italy, 1848 was indeed the year of promise. For Hungary, it spelt first success and then disaster. But for Poland, it brought forth only two or three tiny leaves which promptly withered on the bough.

CHAPTER SIXTEEN
RÊVERIES:
The Thaw and the January Rising (1855-1864)

The last years of the reign of Nicholas I brought no relief either to the Congress Kingdom or to the Poles of Lithuania. The political life of Warsaw and Vilna was frozen solid. The repressions which followed the November Rising were more than sufficient to keep the Tsar's Polish subjects quiet throughout the alarms of the 1830s and 1840s. The reconstruction of absolutism in Austria after 1848, and the dominance of the conservative party in Prussia, suited his purposes well. The outbreak of the Crimean War against Britain and France in 1854 revived hopes that the Polish Question might once again be adopted by the Western Powers. But the Tsar was perfectly well aware of this contingency, and redoubled his precautions against any Polish adventure that might have ensued. The Polish Emigration was roused to yet another effort on behalf of the homeland. Prince Czartoryski engaged in the last great diplomatic campaign of his life. At first, it seemed that Palmerston might moderate the scepticism which had marked his reactions to Czartoryski's earlier representations in 1832, 1838, and 1848; and there were signs that he might share the enthusiasm of Napoleon III's Foreign Minister, Count Walewski for a military diversion against Russia in the Baltic. But the moment soon passed. In order to ensure the neutrality of Austria and Prussia in the war, the British and French were obliged to drop all thoughts of playing the Polish card. At the Conference of Vienna in April 1854, they abandoned their original intention of adding the independence of Poland to their list of war aims. At the Peace Conference in Paris in March 1856, the Russian minister was pleased to report that he had never heard the word 'Poland' so much as mentioned. Meanwhile, three Polish military formations were raised to fight in the Balkans against Russia. The Cossack Legion of Sadyk Pasha (Michał Czajkowski) participated in the recovery of Bucharest in 1854 by the Turks. A Polish Eastern Division

under General Władysław Zamoyski was supported by the
Hotel Lambert. Finally at the start of 1855, Adam Mickiewicz
left Paris on his last journey to Constantinople, to explore
the possibility of forming yet another Polish Legion to fight
alongside the Turks. Tired and sick, he died on 26 November
1855 before anything could be arranged, and was buried in
the Christian cemetery beside the Sea of Marmara. His one
last satisfaction came with the news that Nicholas I was
already dead.[1]

The accession of Alexander II (1818–81), the Tsar-Liberator,
had an important effect on the whole Empire. This was the
occasion when 'the Thaw' was coined to describe the relaxations which followed the thirty-year ice age of his father's
reign. Alexander was no liberal, and was firmly opposed to
all separatist national movements. But in the humiliating
circumstances of the Crimean defeat, he was convinced that
limited concessions must be made in order to avoid a general
explosion. In St. Petersburg, his government was headed by
Prince Alexander Gorchakov, and in Warsaw by Gorchakov's
brother, Paskievitch's successor as Viceroy. On his first visit
to Poland in 1856, the Tsar made a point of warning against
exaggerated expectations. 'Pas de rêveries, messieurs', he
warned (No daydreaming, gentlemen!). Yet his words were
not taken at their face value. By declaring an amnesty for
Poles still lingering in Siberia from 1831, by reopening the
Polish Medical Academy, and above all by inviting Polish landowners to contribute to the topical debate on Peasant
Emancipation, the Tsar inevitably created the impression that
limited change was at last possible. He gave an inch, and his
Polish subjects immediately thought of taking a mile. With
the approval of the new Viceroy, the right of assembly was
restored. A host of new organizations and institutions whose
real function was not immediately apparent sprang up. In
1858, the Agricultural Society was formed for the improvement of land management, and presided over by Count
Andrzej Zamoyski (1800–74), whose own estates at Klemen-
sów were a model of progressive management. In February
1861, in Warsaw, a City Delegation was formed by the
industrialist Leopold Kronenburg (1812–78), ostensibly as a
body for transmitting the opinions of the leading citizens to

the Viceroy. In effect, both these societies were active political organs in disguise. The Agricultural Society, with 4,000 country members, and seventy-seven branches scattered through Poland and Lithuania, bore a remarkable resemblance to the noble Sejm of the old Republic. The Delegation soon produced a City Guard capable of assuming the duties of police and Cossacks. Among the more radical elements of society, secret conspiratorial circles were re-created. There appeared Polish variations on the Russian populist Narodniki, like the *Związek Trójnicki* (League of the Yoke), formed by Polish and Ruthenian students in Kiev intent on evangelizing the peasant masses. There were groups of dissident officers in the army, working closely with Russian counterparts. There were political discussion groups, like the *Millenerzy* (Millennarians) of Edward Jurgens (1827–63), who began to speculate on the political strategy of national movements. All these served to swell an unmistakable change of mood, which came to be called 'the moral revolution'. Forbidden subjects were openly discussed. Pulpits resounded to appeals for fraternal reconciliations. Catholics and Jews, Poles and non-Poles, joined in declarations of mutual reconciliation. Following the example of Kronenburg, and the encouragement of the Chief Warsaw Rabbi, Dov Beer Meisels (1798–1870), Jewish assimilation came into vogue. A steep rise in patriotic fervour was clearly observable. Demonstrations were organized on the flimsiest pretext. *Boże coś Polskę* was openly sung in the streets. There was a rally organized on the occasion of Prince Napoleon's visit, and another for that of Francis Joseph. On 11 June, the funeral of General Sowiński's widow turned into a giant religious procession. So did a demonstration on the thirtieth anniversary of the November Rising. On 25 and 27 February 1861, huge crowds gathered to welcome the Annual General Meeting of the Agricultural Society. After less than five years, the thaw was turning into an uncontrollable flood.[2]

To contain the situation in Warsaw, the Tsar turned to a man whose advice had been persistently rejected over the previous months. Count Alexander Wielopolski, Margrave Gonzaga-Myszkowski (1803–77), was an aristocrat of the old school. He combined the Whiggish politics of Prince Czartoryski, with the temper of a sergeant-major. As he once said: 'You can't do much *with* the Poles, but with luck you might do something *for* them.' Impervious to the promptings of public opinion, and entirely sanguine about the futility of diplomatic action, he felt confident that he was the one person in the world who, by timely reforms and forceful action, could redeem the shortcomings of his countrymen. His aims were strictly limited. In the constitutional sphere, he proposed to give effect to the Organic Statute of 1832, and to appoint a State Council with advisory functions. He proposed to introduce loyal Polish officials into the civil bureaucracy, and to open a *Szkoła Główna* or 'Main School' of university status in which to train them. He proposed to form Commissions to inquire into Land Reform and Jewish Emancipation. These proposals were first aired in February 1861 in the crisis which preceded Wielopolski's appointment as Commissioner for Education and Religious Cult, although they were not definitively approved by the Tsar until 1862. In the meantime, Wielopolski pressed forward. In April 1861, he became Commissioner for Justice and eventually in June 1862 the formal Head of the Civil Administration of the Kingdom. Never had one man possessed so much power and influence in the Kingdom's affairs. From the start, the Tsar's one condition was that 'discipline' should be restored.[3]

The restoration of discipline was no simple matter, however, in spite of Wielopolski's ruthless determination. The use of coercion multiplied the troubles it was supposed to quell. On 27 February 1861, when five demonstrators were killed by a police salvo, Wielopolski fiercely reprimanded General Heidenreich for the pointless brutality. On 8 April 1861, when one hundred civilians were killed on the Castle Square, he stopped the massacre in person by rushing in front of the Cossacks at great peril to himself. Yet, in a sense, he was directly responsible. It was on his orders that the Agricultural Society and the City Delegation had been forcibly disbanded; and he could not complain too loudly when the popular outcry caused the forces of order to panic. Viceroy Gorchakov died of a heart-attack. In the summer of 1861, when the conspiracies and demonstrations continued, Wielopolski was obliged to authorize a campaign of more rigorous repression.

The funeral of Archbishop Fijałkowski prompted another vast procession, and the risk of further bloodshed. On 14 October, a state of emergency was declared. Cossacks broke into the churches to disperse the worshippers. Patriotic hymns were banned. Catholic and Jewish clergymen were deported. The Citadel was packed with thousands of arrested persons. Inevitably, almost all the political groups formed in recent times took counter-measures, and began to consider concerted resistance. In October, a secret City Committee was organized by the radical 'Reds'. Its purpose was to prepare an armed struggle in support of national independence and social revolution. Its leading figures at this stage were Apollo Korzeniowski (1820–69), the father of Joseph Conrad, Ignacy Chmieleński (1830–70), an advocate of random terrorism, and Jarosław Dąbrowski (1836–71), an army Captain recently transferred from St. Petersburg. In December, a rival Directory was organized by the 'Whites' under Kronenburg and Zamoyski. At the end of the year, Wielopolski was curtly ordered to proceed to St. Petersburg under guard, and to explain himself to the Tsar.

The Marquis's inimitable formula was nicely contradictory, but could not be bettered. Reform could not be abandoned for fear of popular disillusionment. Repression could not be relaxed for fear of renewed disorder. So Reform and Repression must proceed in concert. After five months of hesitation, the Tsar suddenly gave formal approval to Wielopolski's proposals. In June, Wielopolski returned to Warsaw and took office as the Head of the Civil Administration. In accordance with a decree provisionally published in the previous year, the peasants were to commute labour dues into money payments. The year 1862 saw the first harvest in central Poland where no serf need have provided labour for his lord without remuneration. In the autumn term, the Main School admitted the first intake of students into its Medical, Mathematical, and Philosophical Faculties. At the same time, the police undertook a wave of preventive arrests. In August, Jarosław Dąbrowski was arrested and sent to Russia for trial. In September, Zamoyski was summoned to St. Petersburg, and after a brief interview with the Tsar, was given a passport and placed on a ship leaving for France. Wielopolski could

smell a rebellion, but was unable to trace its source. He decided
to force it into the open. His chosen instrument was the
Branka, or 'forced conscription'. After saturating the Kingdom
with 100,000 troops, he prepared to draft 30,000 young men
into military service. He did not know who the conspirators
were, but could be sure that most of their able-bodied supporters would be caught among the draftees. The *Branka* was
timed for 14 January 1863. It was the immediate cause of
open hostilities.

Owing to the activities of Wielopolski and to the prolonged
tension, the outbreak of the January Rising took a very different course to the events of 1830. Wielopolski was very
conscious of the precedent, and intent on avoiding a repeat
performance. As it happened, he provoked a conflict of a
different nature but of no less gravity. He knew that the conspirators would have to flee the *Branka* in order to survive;
and he knew that they could not possibly hope to have an
army or civil service at their command. What he did not realize
was that they did have a fully fledged political programme,
an extensive financial organization which was already raising
funds, and the cadres of an underground state. In military
terms, the Polish insurrectionists of 1863 were of necessity
worse equipped than their predecessors of 1830–1. But in
conspiratorial and political terms, they were far more professional. Indeed, the 'Reds' of the National Central Committee
(KCN), the successor to the old City Committee in Warsaw,
were well able to provoke the provocateur. At the beginning
of January thousands of young men crept out of Warsaw into
the Kampinos Forest. When the *Branka* was sprung, only
1,400 conscripts were actually caught in the trap. Two days
later the Russian garrisons were attacked simultaneously in
scores of places all over the Kingdom. Wielopolski was not
faced with an amateur plot of the sort hatched in the
November fog by Wysocki and Zaliwski. He was faced from
the start by a guerrilla war, which was master-minded by
unseen hands from within his own capital, and which kept
Europe's largest army at bay for sixteen months.[4]

Political divisions among the leaders of the Rising were unavoidable in the circumstances. The failure to capture the
town of Płock, which had been chosen for the Rising's head-

quarters, meant that the leadership was forced either to ramble round the countryside or to operate under the noses of the Russians in Warsaw itself. Contact between the centre and the provinces was intermittent. The commanders of individual guerrilla bands enjoyed considerable autonomy. Strict political conformity could not be expected. Most of the societies and factions maintained their separate identities, and pursued their own particular policies. The Reds were constantly at odds with the Whites; and both the two main camps were divided by rightist, centrist, and leftist splinter groups. A welter of ideological positions were publicized. The leadership was in constant contention. In the initial phase, the initiative lay exclusively with the Reds. The Rising depended largely on the KCN, and its energetic, youthful chairman Stefan Bobrowski (1841–63), a populist student from Kiev. In March, the Whites reacted to the threat that Mierosławski might gain general recognition by choosing a supreme commander of their own. For nine days, Marian Langiewicz (1827–87), a soldier trained in the *émigré* academy at Cuneo, enjoyed the doubtful title of 'Dictator', before being forced to withdraw into Galicia. Bobrowski, who was not informed of the move in advance, took umbrage and was killed in a duel. Thereafter, on the proclamation of a secret National Government on 21 March, the two camps lived in uneasy alliance. The Whites generally controlled policy and, in the person of Karol Majewski (1833–97), the over-all command. There were two attempts to seize control by the terrorist wing of the Reds. One attempt in May failed, but another in September succeeded. The latter Coup preceded an abortive assassination attempt on the life of General Berg which released a wave of police reprisals. Finally in October 1863, when the ranks were already decimated by death and defeat, a new Dictatorship was formed, to heal the rift between Whites and Reds, and to provide co-ordinated military leadership. Romuald Traugutt (1825–64) served as the political leader and military commander of the Rising until his arrest in the night of 10/11 August 1864.

In spite of political differences, the underground state showed remarkable resilience. It organized one of the world's earliest campaigns of urban guerrilla warfare, and was the prototype of similarly successful enterprises which the Poles were to operate in similarly harsh conditions in 1905–7 and again during the Second World War. It operated on the same ground as the Russian authorities, and in many cases doubled their functions. It was run by officials, who to all outward appearances were ordinary citizens, officially employed as bank clerks, postmen, or merchants, but who in reality were ministers, secretaries, agents, or couriers of the National Government. It had five permanent Ministries, each with its separate staff, their seals of office, and their secretariats in cellars and boxrooms. Its own great Seal bore the inscription: 'RZĄD NARODOWY – WOLNOŚĆ, RÓWNOŚĆ, NIEPODLEGŁOŚĆ' (National Government – Liberty, Equality, Independence). It possessed an efficient Treasury, which collected taxes from volunteers by request and from recalcitrants by force, and which received both loans, and protection money from industrialists, landowners, and shopkeepers. It had a security corps of 'stiletto men' who kept order in Warsaw, and an intelligence network which penetrated all the civilian departments and military garrisons of the enemy. Its couriers travelled by road and rail to all ends of the Empire. Its diplomatic agents circulated in all the capitals of Europe. Yet apparently, it did not exist. As the new military Governor, Field Marshal Feodor Berg (1798–1874), who took over from Wielopolski, told the new Viceroy, the Grand Duke Constantine: 'I have reached the conclusion that I do not belong to it myself; and nor does your Imperial Highness.' (See Map 10.)

In April 1863, the Rising spread eastwards into Russia. Emissaries were sent to all parts of the old Polish–Lithuanian Republic. The response was mixed. In the Ukraine, there was a major outbreak at Miropol on the Slucz. But the bearers of a Golden Letter written in Ukrainian and calling the locals to action, met the same fate as the Russian *Narodniki* and were massacred by the peasants. In Byelorussia, there was considerable activity both among the Jews at Pinsk and in the countryside. Konstanty Kalinowski (1838–64), a Polish nobleman, who operated in the region of Grodno and Białystok, published a rebel journal, *Muzhytskaia Pravda* (Peasants' Truth), and is regarded as one of the founding fathers of Byelorussian Nationalism. In Lithuania, the Rising briefly assumed the same

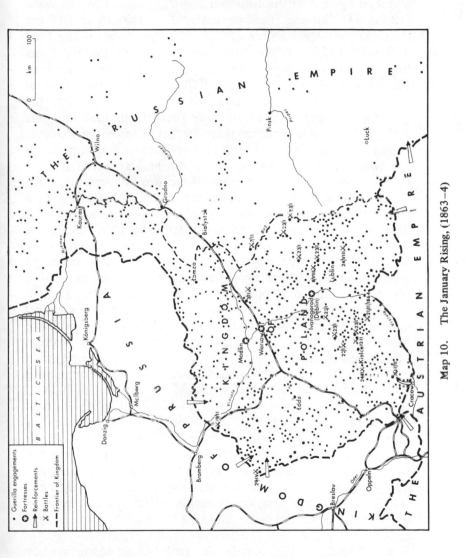

Map 10.   The January Rising, (1863—4)

proportions as in the Kingdom. The work of the White leader Jakub Gieysztor (1827–97), a lawyer from Wilno, was matched by that of the Red lieutenant, Zygmunt Sierakowski (1826–63), among the peasants. The radical priest, the Revd Antoni Mackiewicz (1827–63), remained in the field well into 1864. To the immense chagrin of the Russians, there is no doubt that Lithuania opted for Poland at this time. The original Manifesto of the KCN had been addressed to 'the nation of Poland, Lithuania, and Ruthenia'. In the summer of 1863, they showed by their deeds that this 'one nation' was no less a reality than the 'one Empire' of Russia.

In the nature of things, military action was fragmented. Of the two hundred thousand Poles who are estimated to have carried arms during the Rising, there were never more than thirty thousand in the field at any one time. Most of them were scattered among hundreds of partisan bands operating in all the woods and wildernesses of the land. In the sixteen months that the Rising lasted, 1,229 engagements were fought — 956 in the Kingdom, 237 in Lithuania, the rest in Byelorussia and the Ukraine. Typically they took the form of hit-and-run raids on isolated Russian garrisons, or of fleeting skirmishes on the flanks of army concentrations. The largest number of actions were fought in the Holy Cross Mountains south of Kielce, in the Lublin *Gubernia,* and in regions bordering on the Galician and Prussian frontiers. The typical partisan band or *'partia'* would coalesce round a man with army experience who tried to knock his student or peasant volunteers into shape. In general, they sought to avoid direct confrontations with the superior forces of the enemy. The only action which assumed the scale of a pitched battle occurred at Małogoszcz near Kielce on 24 February 1863 when Langiewicz led three thousand peasant scythemen and noble swordsmen against the Russian guns. The only commander to enjoy a position resembling that of a regular GOC was col. Józef Hauke, alias 'Bosak' (1834–71), who emerged in September 1863 and later served under Traugutt.

The 'Battle' at Zyrzyn in the Holy Cross Mountains on 8 August 1863, was representative of countless others. A guerrilla band commanded by one Heidenreich, 'the Crow', and by an Irish volunteer named O'Brien de Lacey laid ambush to

PLATE I
DIPLOMACY AND
DEFIANCE

(Left) P. Delaroche, *Prince Adam Jerzy Czartoryski, 1770–1861*

(Below) F. Paderewski, *Prince Józef Poniatowski, 1763–1813*

PLATE II. TIMELESS TRADITIONS

W. Wodzinowski, *The Harvesters' Rest*

Anon., *Peasant Devotions at Easter*

PLATE III. WAR AND PEACE

S. Witkiewicz, *The Wounded Insurrectionary, 1863*

A. Gierymski, *Feast of the Trumpets* — Jewish New Year, 1884

PLATE IV
ROMANTIC VISIONS

(Right) W. Wankowicz, *Adam Mickiewicz*

(Below) A. Lesser, *The Death of Wanda*

PLATE V. JESTER AND PROPHET

K. Sichulski, *Józef Piłsudski*

PLATE VI. DOCTRINE OF THE TWO ENEMIES

L. Wintorowski, *Gun-carriages ahead!* The Polish–Soviet War, 1920

E. Mesjasz, *The Battle of Mokra,* 1 September 1939

PLATE VII. FORCE AND FRAUD

W. Siwek, *Entry to Block 11,* Auschwitz, 1943

Long Live the Government of National Unity, June 1945 (photo)

PLATE VIII. WORKERS AND PEASANTS

A. Kobzdej, *Pass the brick* (1952)

V. Hofman, *Confession*

a Russian column on a lonely stretch of the road to Dęblin. They had seven hundred men with which to overpower two companies of Russian infantry and a squadron of Cossacks. After five hours of firing, almost all the Russians were left for dead whilst 'the Crow' retreated with the treasure chest of 200,000 roubles which they had been guarding. In a war in which no major fortress or city was ever obliged to surrender, the rebels counted Zyrzyn a great victory.[5]

The diplomacy of the Rising was equally desultory. In February 1863, the Western Powers took fright when Bismarck sent General Alvensleben to St. Petersburg to sign a Military Convention providing for common action. But Bismarck was prudent enough to let the Tsar suppress the Rising himself, and the Powers were never faced by the reality of an active Prusso-Russian combination. One Tripartite Note from Britain, France, and Austria on 17 April, which protested against violations of the Treaty of Vienna, and another on 17 June, which called on the Tsar to make concessions, represent the sum total of the diplomats' achievement. The first Note gave rise to an Amnesty whose conditions were certain to prove unacceptable. The second was rejected outright, on the grounds that too many concessions had already been made without response. In a century where the Polish Question never inspired the Powers to actual intervention, diplomatic historians are tempted to record these gestures as major incidents.

The Rising had a greater impact on public opinion than on governments. In the western democracies, the Russophobia of the 1830s, and of the Crimean War was given a further stimulus. *The Times* puffed and wheezed against the iniquities of Russian autocracy. Foreign correspondents wrote moving accounts of the Polish martyrdom. Herzen, Marx, Garibaldi applauded Poland's courage. Foreign volunteers queued up to join the Polish service (though many did not arrive). The ill-fated voyage of the SS *Ward Jackson* which carried two hundred volunteers from Gravesend to their final destination on a sand-bank in Prussia amply illustrates the limited means and mixed motives of foreign sympathizers.[6] In Russia, a wave of nationalist outrage swept the rostra. Despite a small number of Russians and Ukrainians who came over to the

Polish side, the vast majority of Russian commentators denounced the Polish plot to discredit the Tsar. All the charges and recriminations which had been levelled at the Poles after 1831 were revived in a still more virulent form. Tyutchev repeated what he said thirty years before. Dostoevsky echoed Pushkin's comments in still more mystical tones. Herzen, whose journal *Kolokol* lost half of its readership overnight, was forced to retract his views. The gulf between Russia and Poland, and between Russia and Europe as a whole, was opened still wider.[7]

The peasant question ran through the politics of the Rising from start to finish. It lay at the root of Alexander's original conviction that relaxations were necessary, and took a prominent place in his way of bringing the conflict to a close. All the parties involved were forced to compete intensely. Some people thought that the peasants should be emancipated as a matter of principle; some thought so in order to win their support. None could afford to let the issue go by default. Stage by stage, the stakes were raised. Step by step, each side offered the peasants more than the other. In 1858, the Tsar's first bid had invited the Polish nobility to submit their proposals. The response of the Agricultural Society was to propose that the labour dues of the serfs should be commuted into money rents. In 1861, Wielopolski went ahead with the Land Decree of 16 May which offered less than the Tsar's reforms in Russia. In 1863, the KCN's Manifesto talked of peasant 'ownership' of the land. In the end the Tsar was obliged to outbid even this. The *ukaz* of 18 March 1864 initiated a scheme for giving the peasants full freehold of the land they worked, and for compensating the landowners with state bonds. The response of the peasants to these blatantly political moves was sceptical. In general, they were no less suspicious of plausible young Polish gentlemen than they were of a liberal Tsar. The canny ones realized that they would get what they wanted in any case, without having to fight for it. The districts in the Kingdom where the peasants stood aloof from the Rising were less numerous than those in which they participated. In the Ukraine, the peasants were plainly hostile.[8]

At the time of the Tsar's decree on Land Reform in March 1864 the last Dictatorship of the Rising was still in full operation. The Dictator, Romuald Traugutt, was quite unlike any of the popular stereotypes of a Polish revolutionary. Lean, silent, cool, disciplined, efficient, he possessed most of the qualities so signally lacking in his immediate predecessors. He came from a small noble family in Podlasie and was married to Antonina Kościuszkówna, a relative of the 'Commander' of 1794. Until 1862 he had been a Lt. Col. in the Russian Army, and had served in Hungary and in the Crimea. He continued to farm his estate in obscurity for five months after the outbreak of the Rising, but in May was finally persuaded to take command of a guerrilla band of 160 men in the Dziadkowicki Forst near Kobryn. In July, he made his own way to Warsaw and impressed himself into Majewski's entourage. His rise thereafter was swift. In August and September, he visited Western Europe on behalf of the National Government, gaining personal interviews in Paris with Napoleon III and with the French Foreign Minister, Drouyn de Lhuys, and in Brussels arranging for the purchase of arms. He returned convinced that the western governments looked on Russia principally as 'a goldmine for capitalists', and that no early intervention could be expected. He slipped back into Poland with a passport made out in the name of a Galician merchant called Michał Czarniecki, took up residence in the Saski Hotel in Warsaw *vis-à-vis* the Viceroy, and calmly told the National Government of the Reds of his intention of forming a secret dictatorship. All opposition collapsed. The Reds either withdrew or submitted. On 17 October 1863, the National Government ceased to function. Henceforth, all business was co-ordinated, and all decisions of policy were taken by Traugutt alone. From his lodging at 3 Smolno Street with Mrs Kirkor, he attended to all correspondence, and personally supervised the activities of the Ministries. Together with his close confidants – Marian Dubecki, Józef Gałęzowski, J. K. Janowski, the Chief Executive and keeper of the seals, and Aleksander Waszkowski, the rough and ready 'City Commander' – he led a team of extraordinary skill and forcefulness. He purged the movement of all 'private firebrands', threatening to release the names of all recalcitrants to the police. He contrived to impose a tax on Polish citizens abroad, and floated a National Loan. He completely reformed the military organization, abolishing all separate commands and autonomous formations, and introducing the cadres of a regular army with corps, divisions, regiments, and battalions. He revived the idea of a *pospolite ruszenie,* the *levée-en-masse* of the entire population. He called for the implementation of the KCN's Emancipation decree, and ruled that each village should elect one man who could manage the changes. He even issued a decree providing the death sentence for landowners who continued to exact payment in lieu of labour dues. As a devout Catholic, he paid special attention to religious affairs and conducted a long correspondence with the Vatican, castigating the Pope's ambiguous posture towards Russian 'barbarism'. The last dispatch, to his agent in Rome, Józef Ordega, concerned an alliance recently signed with a Hungarian Committee professing similar aims. At 1 a.m. on 10 April 1864, he was seized in his bed by a squad of armed police, and incarcerated in the Pawiak Prison.[9]

The full exposure of the conspiratorial government proved no easy matter. Whereas the Police were successfully penetrated by sympathizers of the Rising, they themselves had not succeeded in penetrating the conspiracy. The cover which the leaders used was most convincing. Less than twenty people knew the Dictator's real identity. Only six persons were empowered to visit his lodging. The system of pseudonyms acted as a barrier between all officials and their agents, and against would-be informers. The Government's number code, based on selected editions of *Pan Tadeusz* and *Imitatio Christi,* was never broken. The flow of correspondence, of orders, and of arms, was never halted. Conferences between leaders took place in churches before dawn, or in pavement cafés. The work of the secretariats was carried on in the Biology Laboratory of the Main School, or in church halls under the guise of study circles or hobby groups. The State of Emergency did not limit their activities, and the mass arrests of the autumn had produced no prominent suspects. The break only came on 8 April when a Jewish student of the Main School, Artur Goldman, submitted under police interrogation, and agreed to talk. His deposition contained the following information:

. . . I once heard that the leader of a rebel detachment in Lithuania, Traugutt, a former army officer, was due to arrive in Warsaw as the commercial traveller of a firm in Lwów, and that he would take over the leadership of the National Government . . . The above-mentioned Traugutt did indeed arrive, under the name of Michał Czarniecki, but where he stayed, I don't know. His description was as follows: medium height, large head, swarthy complexion, dark hair, large black sideburns and small beard, ordinary white spectacles, age 33–35 . . .[10]

Even then, Czarniecki steadfastly denied his true identity. Nothing was found in his room to incriminate him. The statements of interrogated prisoners were vague and contradictory. Not until Traugutt was officially identified by a former colleague from his old battalion, did he admit to anything, and then only to having organized the Rising single-handed and without accomplices. The case was tried on 18 July:

A Court Martial held in the Alexander Citadel in Warsaw reviewed the military-judicial case of the following persons of various rank:

1) Romuald TRAUGUTT, arrested under the name of Michał Czarniecki, retired Lt.-Col. of 3 Battalion of Sappers, Catholic, aged 38, married with two daughters, nobleman . . . Dictator in the National Government . . .

2) Rafał KRAJEWSKI, 29, Catholic, bachelor, freelance architect . . . Director of the Department of the Interior . . .

3) Józef TOCZYSKI, 37, Catholic, bachelor, book-keeper in the Public Highways Administration, formerly exiled to Siberia in 1848, returning in accordance with the Gracious Manifesto of 1857 . . . Director of the Treasury . . .

4) Roman ŻULIŃSKI, 30, Catholic, bachelor, teacher of Gymnazium No. 1, . . . Director of Revolutionary Supply . . .

5) Jan JEZIORAŃSKI, 30, Catholic, married with two children, controller at the Tobacco Board . . . Commissar for Foreign Relations . . .

6) Tomasz BURZYŃSKI, 29, Catholic, married, Under-Secretary at the Warsaw Criminal Court . . . representative for Płock and Augustow . . .

7) Marian DUBECKI, 26, Catholic, bachelor, teacher at the District School, formerly exiled from Volhynia to Vyatka . . . Commissioner for Ruthenian Affairs.

8) Tomasz ILNICKI, 50, Catholic, married, childless, an official of the Polish Bank . . . chief teller of the revolutionary Treasury . . .

9) August KRĘCKI, 21 Catholic, bachelor, trainee at the Treasury . . . secretary . . .

10) Roman FRANKOWSKI, 22, Catholic, student at the Main School . . . secretary . . .
11) Gustaw PAPROCKI, 19, Jew, student at the Main School . . . secretary . . .
12) Zygmunt SUMIŃSKI, 19 Catholic, student at the 'Main School' . . . secretary . . .
13) Edward TRZEBIECKI, 23, Catholic, non-registered nobleman, trainee at the Police Reformatory Court . . . secretary.
14) Kazimierz HANUSZ, 20, Catholic, archivist . . . secretary.
15) Władysław BOGUSŁAWSKI, 25, Catholic, student at St. Petersburg University . . . press secretary . . .
16) Benedykt DYBOWSKI, 29, Catholic, bachelor, teacher at the 'Main School', who permitted the revolutionary secretaries to meet in the School's auditorium . . .
17) Jan MUKLANOWICZ, 30, Catholic, pharmacist . . . who permitted the conspirators' correspondence to be delivered at his shop . . .
18) Helena KIRKOR, 32, noblewoman, who permitted the chief conspirators to meet in her house . . . and disposed of their papers after the arrest . . .
19) Emilia and Barbara GUZOWSKA, 30, 27, spinsters, who harboured the revolutionary Supply Department in their lodging . . . and frequently changed their address in order to confuse the police . . .
20) Alexandra WRÓBLEWSKA, 18, spinster, daughter of a gingerbread manufacturer who received and distributed the conspirators' correspondence . . .

All these persons were brought before the Court on the order of the Viceroy and Commander-in-Chief of the Kingdom of Poland in that they all took a particular and prominent part in the late rebellion.

The circumstances of the case are subject to the following:
— Articles 83, 96, 175, 196, 605, of the Code of Military Discipline, Vol. I:
— Articles 285, 360, 364, of the Code of Capital and Penitentiary Punishments:
— Circular of 24 May 1863 to directors of military departments.

Result: Having taken all circumstances into consideration, the Hearing finds that the following are guilty: 1) TRAUGUTT, in that a) he killed one Kwiatkowski by a revolver shot, for the purpose of maintaining discipline in the rebel ranks, b) commanded a rebel unit in the Grodno area, c) left the country without permission, d) . . . took the chief and independent command of the secret union known as the National Government . . .; 2) KRAJEWSKI . . . to 20) WRÓBLEWSKA. All are members of the secret conspiracy . . . and in that capacity belonged to the main branch of the Polish Rising.

Guided by the Circular of 23 May 1863, the Hearing recommends: *A.* that the defendants 1) TRAUGUTT. . . to 15) BOGUSŁAWSKI, having committed offences relating to the above Circular in the first degree, should be condemned to death by hanging; *B.* . . . to *F.* that the remaining defendants be sentenced to other punishments.

This judgement is hereby presented for the gracious confirmation of the Viceroy and Commander-in-Chief of the Polish Kingdom.

Presiding Lt.-Gen.	(–) HAGMAN
Member, Maj.-Gen.	(–) KOZNAKOV
Member, Maj.-Gen.	(–) DOKUDOVSKII
Deputy Member, Maj.-Gen.	(–) OPPERMAN
Member, Maj.-Gen.	(–) LEVSHYN
General-Auditor	(–) POLTORANOV
Ober-auditor	(–) AFANSEYEV [11]

It was an odd situation. A handful of clerks, students, and teachers led by one junior officer were exposed as the ringleaders of a movement which had challenged the entire Russian Empire. They were presented to the world as a gang of criminal drop-outs and misguided youth. Those prisoners who showed repentance and assisted the authorities escaped further trial, and were given minor punishments by administrative decree. The deserving cases among them were given financial aid. All but five of the fifteen condemned to death had their sentences commuted to hard labour or exile. The rest of the two hundred thousand rebels simply melted away.

The final act was performed on 5 August 1864. At 9 a.m., the gates of the Alexander Citadel opened, and the official hangman walked out at the head of a procession. A wide common gallows with five nooses waited on the nearby ramparts. A mounted escort of helmeted gendarmes lined the five horse-drawn muck-carts which carried the prisoners. Each man was manacled to the arm of a brown-cowled Capuchin friar. Traugutt, still dressed in the blue trenchcoat in which he had been arrested, was absorbed in his last confession. The sentence was read aloud. The prisoners were blindfolded, dressed in the death smock, and brought to the gallows. A woman's voice called 'Courage, brother!' Then, one by one, Traugutt, Krajewski, Toczyski, Żuliński, and Jeziorański were hanged by the neck until they were dead.

*   *   *   *   *

As in 1831, Russian retribution was not long delayed. On this occasion, the Tsarist authorities were determined not merely to eradicate all trace of the late insurrection but also to suppress all public manifestations of Polish nationality. At least one guerrilla 'party' was still in the field. Its leader, the Revd Stanisław Brzoska (1834–65), had served as the Chaplain-General of the Rising, and had first joined the movement in 1862 after being imprisoned for preaching patriotic sermons. Now he was the last surviving Staff Officer. He held his own in the countryside of Podlasie until December 1864, when he was captured. He was executed at Sokołów on 23 May 1865. By that time, the main civilian dispositions of the government were painfully clear. In Warsaw, General Berg was in the process of closing down all the separate institutions of the Congress Kingdom. In his three years as the last Viceroy of the Kingdom, from 1863 to 1866, he rescinded all Wielopolski's reforms and all concessions made to Polish language and culture. In 1864, he formed an Administrative Committee whose first task was to supervise the policy of peasant emancipation, but which soon took charge of the entire programme of Russification. The Committee's Director, Nikolai Milyutin, had served as Secretary of State for the Kingdom in St. Petersburg, and was the author of the plan to use the supposedly loyalist peasantry against the patriotic nobles and intellectuals. In seven years of ceaseless attention to detail, the Committee transformed the Polish Kingdom into a Russian province. All branches of the administration were subordinated to the relevant ministries in St. Petersburg, and were staffed by Russians. In 1864, both the Kingdom and the name of Poland were formally abolished. The Tsar relinquished his duties as King of Poland, and Warsaw became the capital of the *Privislinskiy kray* (Vistulaland). In 1866, the 10 Polish *gubernias* were divided into 85 *powiats* or 'districts'; and most of the district towns lost their separate municipal rights. In 1867, the Polish Education Commission was closed down for the second time. In 1869, the Main School was replaced by a new Russian University. By 1871, when the Administrative Committee concluded its business, the only item which distinguished the conduct of affairs in Vistulaland from that pertaining in other parts of the Russian

Empire was the continuing use of the Napoleonic Code in the civil courts.

In Lithuania, where there were no official Polish institutions to be disbanded, repression of the Polish element took cruder forms. In the summer of 1863, General Muravyev, the 'Hangman', returned to his stamping-grounds of thirty years before, and as Governor-General of Vilna harried the Poles with merciless determination. In the preceding period, as Minister for State Lands in St. Petersburg, he had opposed the policy of Emancipation, and had suffered politically as a result. He now vented his spleen on the participants, real or imagined, of the January Rising. Not content with the prosecution of offenders by legal means, he launched a reign of terror, where people were killed, tortured, and exiled, villages were razed, and estates confiscated, with no thought of, or recourse to, the law.[12]

In both Poland and Lithuania, the repression of the January Rising left permanent scars. A whole generation of Poles were deprived of their careers, and of their normal expectations of advancement. Thousands of Poles took once more to the cruel road to Siberia, packed into cattle trucks or shackled together in long lines, slowly trudging across the tundra to camps and prisons in the most distant fastnesses of the Empire. These were the cream of the Polish nation – the most active, the most courageous, the most idealistic men and women in society. Most of them never returned. This time there was no general amnesty, not even after twenty-five years. At the end of the century, when the revolutionaries, socialists, and convicts of the next generation were sent to Siberia, in much better conditions and in lesser numbers, they found that their places of exile were still inhabited by deported Polish families. Lenin himself, who spent three years in southern Siberia in 1897–1900, recalled the warm welcome which he found in the house of a former Polish partisan. But in due course, Lenin was released; the Poles of 1864–5, were not.[13]

* * * * *

The dissolution of the Congress Kingdom prompts an interesting comparative question of Russian policy. The Congress Kingdom had not been unique within the realms of the Tsar in its enjoyment of self-government, but had shared the privilege with the Grand Duchy of Finland. Annexed in 1809 from Sweden, Finland was ruled until 1917 as a separate constitutional monarchy of which the Tsar was the hereditary Grand Duke. Hence the question is posed as to why the Grand Duchy of Finland should have survived and prospered whilst the Kingdom of Poland should have been so regularly harried and in the end destroyed. Surely, it might be argued, if the Russian government was so completely opposed in principle to all forms of independence and national liberty, it would certainly have found some pretext for treating the Finns to the same display of imperial will that was exercised against the Poles. The usual answer, implied if not always explicit, is that the Poles brought their misfortunes on themselves. According to current stereotypes, the Poles were troublemakers, whilst the Finns were jovial, law-abiding citizens; the Finns were responsible members of the great Russian family whilst the Poles were not. Unfortunately, this simple answer avoids the crux of the matter. It is undeniable that Poland had produced more than its share of troublemakers. Both the November and the January Risings were sparked off by men who were intent on causing as much trouble for the Russians as they could. Similar bloodymindedness was to make itself apparent on numerous occasions in the future. But it must still be decided whether these Polish 'hooligans' behaved as they did from a combination of original sin and national character, or whether they were reacting to intolerable provocations. Before concluding that the Poles were more irresponsible than the Finns by nature, it is necessary to show firstly that the Polish troublemakers were somehow representative of the nation as a whole, and secondly that they were subjected to the same experiences as the Finns. On this last score, it is not difficult to enumerate several important differences. For one thing, the Congress Kingdom occupied the most important strategic location of the entire Russian lands. It lay astride Russia's landbridge to Europe and to Germany in particular; Finland lay on the fringe of Scandinavia, with no direct link except with the Norwegian Arctic and with Swedish Lapland. For strategic reasons, if for nothing else, the Russian government was bound to respond much more sharply to political insubordination in Poland than to similar disturbances in Finland. Strategic considerations occasioned the presence in Poland of massive Russian armies, and the armies in their turn to a wide range of frictions with the civilian population. For another thing, the Poles of the Congress Kingdom formed part of a nation whose members in Austria, Prussia, and Lithuania shared their sense of a common identity. They constantly posed the Russian government with the potential threat of irredentism, which could not have been removed unless all the Poles had been coralled into one state. The Grand Duchy of Finland, in contrast, contained practically the whole of the much smaller Finnish nation, which looked to Russia for protection against its former Swedish masters. What is more, the Poles were Slavs. According to the ancient Muscovite canon, all Slavs were brothers; all were the natural subjects of the Tsar; and all could be treated as his chattels, his little 'Christian souls'. The Finns, who were not Slavs, were seen as foreigners living under Russian protection, and as such belonged to a different category of humanity. In the Russian view, together with the Germans of the Baltic provinces, it was entirely proper that the Finns should be awarded a wide measure of autonomy. Lastly, and perhaps most importantly, the Poles were seen as the dominant élite of the old Polish Lithuanian Republic. They were the living descendants of a society which had been overturned by force but whose values none the less continued to persist throughout western and southern Russia. Despite their Slav origins, they were Europeans who looked to Paris and Berlin for their passions and their fashions. Above all in the tradition of the noble democracy, they were individualists who stubbornly looked to their own consciences for their ideas of right and wrong. They were a living rebuke to all the myths and legends on which the Russian Empire had been built. Together with the Jews, in whose company they had been incorporated into Russia, they were the advocates of a vibrant democratic culture, and as such were the natural opponents of Autocracy. For all these reasons, Tsarist officialdom was never able to treat the Poles in the same way as it treated the Finns. Poles who at various times have advocated 'Finlandization' in the belief that their relationship with Russia might be modelled on that enjoyed by the Finns, have ignored the most fundamental political realities. The Russians looked askance at the autonomy of the Congress Kingdom from the start. Fearing the consequences of indecision, they repeatedly attacked minor troubles with hostile outbursts of needless severity, thereby generating the vicious circle of repression, insurrection, and renewed repression. As masters of the political situation, the Russians were free to act as they chose. The Poles could only react to the lead that they were given. Thus, if the troubles of the Congress Kingdom stood in stark contrast to the relative serenity of Finland, the explanation must be sought no less in Russian attitudes than in Polish ones.

Meanwhile, Polish resistance was crushed. For forty years, the Poles of the Congress Kingdom were submerged into the general stream of life in the Russian Empire. Thoughts of revenge were confined to the peripheries of national opinion. Public politics did not resurface in any significant way until 1904. In the interval, 'Poland' descended once more 'into the abyss'.

CHAPTER SEVENTEEN
REWOLUCJA:
Revolution and Reaction (1904-1914)

The last decade before the World War saw tension rising throughout Eastern Europe. In 1904–5 Russia was plunged into the first military conflict since the Congress of Berlin. In 1907, the Anglo-Russian Convention completed a diplomatic system which openly pitted France, Russia, and Great Britain against the Central Powers – Germany and Austria–Hungary. The Bosnian Crisis of 1908 heralded a protracted confrontation which led to the Balkan Wars of 1912–13 and the assassination at Sarajevo in 1914. Throughout these years, political loyalties were put to a severe test. Under the threat of war, patriotic fervour mounted. Dissident elements seized the chance to press for concessions. Loyalists grew more loyal, critics grew more critical, militants more militant, the Poles more Polish. Among a welter of social and economic problems and demands, the Polish Question was salvaged from obscurity. It all started on 6 February 1904 when the Japanese attacked the Russian fleet in the harbour of Port Arthur in Manchuria.

In Russian Poland, the outbreak of the Japanese War caused a ripple of excitement. In recent years, the growth of new social classes had engendered embryonic political formations which were now emerging as fully-fledged parties. Although the era of constitutional politics was not officially proclaimed until October 1905, a number of Polish parties did not delay in issuing their manifestos. Conferences were held, and policies were planned, in foreign sanctuaries. Meeting in Vienna, the right-wing Realist Party called for the introduction of equal rights into the Polish provinces. Its wealthy, propertied members equipped a Catholic Hospital Train for service on the Manchurian front. Dmowski's National League, soon to transform itself into the National Democratic Party, demanded the polonization of education and administration. The liberal Polish Progressive-Democratic Union, headed by

Alexander Lednicki (1866–1934) and Aleksander Świętochowski, declared in favour of a measure of Polish autonomy which would be compatible with the continuing integrity of Russia. On the Left, Piłsudski's illegal Polish Socialist Party (PPS) envisaged an armed struggle to force the abolition of military conscription and to further its hopes of social revolution and national independence. Its first *bojówki,* or 'battle squads' were formed in May 1904. In Paris its representatives discussed joint action with a number of potential allies including the Russian Social Revolutionaries, and Georgian and Latvian nationalists. The leaders of the less influential Social Democratic Party (SDKPiL), subordinated their plans to those of their Bolshevik and Menshevik mentors. The SRs and the Jewish *Bund* increased their activities in the western provinces. A deteriorating economic situation encouraged political militancy. The Japanese War closed Far Eastern markets to Polish industry. One hundred thousand Polish workers were laid off work. Most people in employment were obliged to take a cut in pay. Demonstrations and protests were broken up by the police with increasing violence. Twenty people were wounded when a salvo was fired into the crowd at Białystok on 28 September. The gravity of the crisis was underlined on 13 November 1904 when a gun battle erupted on the Grzybowski Square in Warsaw. A company of gendarmes had charged into a crowd of singing Sunday demonstrators, aiming to confiscate a red banner which read: 'PPS: *Precz z wojną i caratem! Niech żyje wolny, polski lud'* (PPS: Down with the war and with Tsardom, Long live the free Polish people). They were met by a hail of bullets from a squad of gunmen. Six men were killed, scores injured, and hundreds arrested. This was the first open challenge to Russian authority in Poland for forty years. It preceded the 'Bloody Sunday' outbreak in St. Petersburg by three months.[1]

The extent of Polish ambitions was evidenced by visits to Japan undertaken by rival political leaders. Early in 1904, Piłsudski had been in contact with the Japanese ambassador in London. In June–July he travelled via New York and San Francisco to Tokyo, only to find that Dmowski was already installed there in the Hotel Metropole. Each man proffered mutually contradictory advice. Dmowski was strongly opposed to a Japanese foray into Polish affairs, fearing that foreign intervention would force the Tsarist government to abandon all ideas of constitutional reform. He intimated that the National Democrats would use all the means at their disposal to prevent anti-Russian disturbances in Poland. Piłsudski, in contrast, urged the creation of a Polish Legion, to be recruited from Polish prisoners in Japan and from Polish–American volunteers and to be commanded by officers provided by the PPS. He maintained that one-third of the Russian troops in Manchuria were of Polish origin, and that they would be very willing to desert. 'The common interest of Japan and Poland', he declared, 'lies in the weakening and breaking of Russian power'.[2] In the event, the Japanese government took no decisive action. Their military attachés in London and Paris were authorized to supply the PPS with arms and explosives in exchange for intelligence on the dispositions of the Russian Army in Poland. In the autumn, both Dmowski and Piłsudski returned to Europe to apply themselves to an uncertain future. The one continued to count on political methods; the other on armed confrontation. In the next few months they would both enjoy moments of elation and of disillusionment, but neither would claim any definitive success.

The 'Bloody Sunday' massacre in St. Petersburg on 22 January 1905 unleashed passions in Poland which at first favoured the activists. The immediate reaction took the form of a school strike which lasted for nearly three years. Thousands of teachers and pupils responded to appeals to boycott classes until instruction in Polish was restored. The Russian University in Warsaw was half-deserted. On 28 January 1905, the PPS and SDKPiL called for a General Strike which occupied four hundred thousand workers for the next four weeks. It was the prelude to thousands of spontaneous strikes all over the country. In 1905–6, a total of 6,991 stoppages occurred, involving 1.3 million people. Industrial workers in the towns were joined by agricultural labourers in the countryside. After several false starts, the 'Battle Organization' of the PPS went into action. The first bombs that they threw failed to explode. One of them was picked up and pocketed by a casual Cossack. Intended attacks on Oberpolitzmaistr Nolken, and on General Novosiltsov at the Warsaw Railway Station, failed to materialize. But on 21 March an explosive device effectively halted a twelve-man police patrol on Chłodna Street in Warsaw. Henceforth, a murderous underground war was waged between the terrorists and the immense network of police agents, spies, and informers. On May Day, mass rallies were organized in defiance of the authorities in almost every town and city. In Warsaw, thirty-seven people were killed. There were fatalities in Łódź and Częstochowa. Public order gradually disintegrated. Minor provocations in the Jewish quarters were overshadowed by an extraordinary spontaneous campaign against criminal elements suspected of collaboration. On 24 May, hundreds of workers from the metal factories of Praga poured across the Vistula bridges and attacked the 'red light' district of Warsaw. Brothels were ransacked; gang-leaders were lynched; in the Old Town, a posse of slaughterers' mates armed with meat axes demolished a house where 150 ponces had taken refuge. A stream of assorted hacks and whores fled into the suburban woods. In this period, the Warsaw police issued more than forty thousand passports for foreign travel. In June, attention reverted to Łódź. A renewal of the General Strike degenerated into open hostilities. When barricades were thrown up, the Tsar declared a State of War. For three days, between 22 and 24 June, General Shuttleworth used all the forces at his disposal to clear the streets. In one week, 55 Poles, 79 Jews, and 17 Germans lost their lives. In all, Łódź suffered more than a thousand casualties. On 21 July, Warsaw was again shaken by the execution of 19-year-old Stefan Okrzeja, a prominent member of the PPS 'Battle Organization' and hero of the battle of Grzybowski Square. In August, the *bojówki* filled their coffers with a series of bank raids. On the 15th, the police organized a diversionary pogrom in Białystok. The pace was quickening. The troubles in Poland were joined by still more widespread disturbances in Russia as a whole. Soviets of Workers' Deputies were formed in factories; the troops mutinied; peasants went on the rampage. In September, a humiliating treaty was signed with Japan at Portsmouth (New Hampshire). The revolutionaries took heart. In St. Petersburg, Trotsky proclaimed 'All Power to the Soviets', and an all-Russian strike. The revolt was turning into a revolution.

Under the pressure of war, rebellion, and defeat, the Tsar was gradually obliged to make concessions. In April 1905, a patent on religious toleration released the residual Uniate communities from active persecution. Trade Unions were legalized. In Poland, the Polish language was reinstated in private schools, but not in state institutions. The Polish *Macierz Szkolna* (School Board) was given official approval. Poles were to be permitted to buy lands in the western provinces. Finally on 30 October an Imperial Manifesto promised the introduction of a written constitution, and the establishment of a parliamentary assembly. In accordance with the Manifesto, elections for seats in the first *Duma* were called in April 1906. In this way, the work of the terrorists and revolutionaries created an opening for the constitutionalists. In Polish terms, Piłsudski and the PPS had fostered a situation which Dmowski could now exploit. As the terror diminished, conciliatory politics intensified.

In retrospect, it is easy to see that the Constitution of 1906 was little better than a confidence trick. It introduced universal suffrage, with a view to keeping Autocracy intact. Russia was to remain 'one and indivisible'. The Tsar retained the right to approve all legislation. The Ministers were to be free of parliamentary control. The *Duma* was to debate, but not demand. The electors were divided into four curias which gave a preponderant influence to property-owners and state officials. The new institutions graciously established at the Tsar's command could be abolished in the same manner. Those observers who felt that the Reform might plant the seed of later liberalization were soon disabused. The *Duma* produced little by way of liberalization or regional autonomy. It acted as a screen behind which autocratic power could convalesce. The constitutional manœuvres of 1906–7 took place to a background of terror, police raids, lock-outs, and reprisals. The strikers were inexorably starved and bullied into submission. Starting on 29 December 1906, all the factories of Łódź were closed indefinitely until all the manufacturers' conditions were accepted by all the workers. Thousands of people were deported to their villages of origin. Hundreds were arrested. The official executioner of Łódź, Ryszard Fremel, brother of an *Ochrana* agent killed by the

PPS, personally supervised the deaths of 104 prisoners. The adventures of the *bojówki* grew increasingly desperate. The simultaneous attack on one hundred targets on 'Bloody Wednesday' on 15 August 1906; the abortive attempt on the life of Governor Georgii Skalon on 18 August; the raids at Rogów on 8 November 1906 and at Bezdany near Wilno on 26 September 1908, could not hide the obvious fact that the tide had turned against them.[3]

For practical purposes, Polish participation in the *Duma* was confined from the start to the National Democrats. The left-wing parties boycotted the elections; the right-wing Realists and Progressives were heavily defeated at the polls. In the first *Duma,* the Polish Circle consisted of some 32 National Democrats from the Vistula provinces, in addition to 23 additional members elected in Lithuania, Byelorussia, and the Ukraine. It stayed close to the Kadets, and refused to join the active Opposition. In the second *Duma,* which was called in October 1906, the Polish Circle was reduced to 46, and was led by Dmowski in person. A Project for Polish Autonomy presented in 1907 was one of many departures which incensed the Tsar, and led to the dissolution. The third *Duma* assembled later that year under the shadow of reaction. The new Premier, Pyotr Stolypin, combined a talent for administrative reform with a heavy hand for dissidents. He arbitrarily changed the suffrage to the disadvantage of all mino- rity groups, and vigorously attacked the disloyalty of separatist movements. The joint Polish—Lithuanian—Byelorussian Circle possessed only 11 members. Dmowski was driven to rethink his strategy. He supported the Anglo-Russian Entente, and started out on a 'Neo-Slavic' tack, which presupposed the common interest of Poles and Russians in the coming struggle with Germany. Yet his immediate plans were constantly frustrated. His tone grew markedly more strident. His defeat at the elec- tion of 1912 for the fourth *Duma* was engineered by the Jews and socialists of his Warsaw constituency. It marked the bank- ruptcy of a programme which had linked extreme nationalist rhetoric to tactics that brought no visible progress towards autonomy. Long before the dissolution of the fourth *Duma* at the outbreak of war, Dmowski's conciliatory policy was no less discredited than Piłsudski's revolutionary one.[4]

In the course of the crisis, all strands of the Polish national movement were rent by feuds and schisms. In almost all those areas where the National Democrats gained mass support, the non-Polish elements of the population were antagonized. The National Workers' League (NZR) came to control one-third of the working class. Its leaders formed *bojówki* on the PPS model, and used them to contest the influence of left-wing parties in factories and unions. In Łódź, the National Democrats' *Gazeta Polska* openly urged the use of force to suppress 'socialist anarchy'. Dmowski's enemies believed that he had reached an agreement with the Tsarist government, in which the future autonomy of Poland would be traded for present co-operation in suppressing the PPS. Political, sectarian murders were running at forty or fifty per week. The National Democrats were specially responsible for the new antipathies which developed between Poles and Jews. Dmowski's virulent intolerance was brought to the surface. The socialists were left to make despairing appeals for inter-communal fraternity:

Comrades!
The understanding and the solidarity of the workers, without regard to the divisions among them or to the differences of origin and religion, are the best instruments for ensuring the victory of our cause and for liberating the working masses from all forms of coercion.

The Tsarist government is well aware of this, and tries to dissipate our unity by inciting racial and religious hatreds. Wherever it has succeeded, as in Kishinev or in Baku, where Christians have attacked Jews, and Tartars have massacred Armenians, it is excited by the smell of blood, and feels stronger . . . This same frightful tactic has been applied in Poland for a long time. But our proletariat is too experienced to fall for such a trick, and is strong enough to prevent assaults on its various social components.

However, the government's policy is also supported by all those for whom the class struggle is a permanent affront . . . Catholic priests, Jesuits, and National Democrats are all spreading hatred of the Jews. It is perfectly understandable, of course, that they should be furious at the part which the Jews are playing in all revolutionary movements. But it is both naïve and stupid of them to imagine that we also might share their hatred . . . Jewish blood, shed on the streets of Łódź, mingling in the gutters with the blood of Poles and Germans, has formed a cement which binds the various elements of our proletariat into one powerful

whole . . . In the ranks of our warriors, we recognize neither Jew nor German nor Russian, but workers grappling with the Tsarist monster for freedom and human happiness.
Long live international workers' solidarity!
Shame on the dark forces of reaction!
By unity, we shall overcome Tsarism!
July 1905.   Workers Committee in Łódź,
                                           Polish Socialist Party (PPS)[5]

The socialists had troubles enough of their own. The 'young men' of the PPS leadership constantly pressed for intensified terrorism, defying the more cautious counsels of the 'elders'. The Leftists clamoured for social revolution at the expense of national independence. The 8th PPS Congress in Lemberg in 1906 patched up a compromise. But the 9th Congress in Vienna in November revealed a permanent split. The PPS (Lewica) under Feliks Kon and Henryk Walecki broke away on the first stage of its journey towards the SDKPiL and eventual communism. The PPS (Rewolucja) under Piłsudski kept control of the Battle Organization and set off in a direction where nationalism was more clearly in view than socialism. Each of the factions was destined for still more splitting. By 1908, Piłsudski had abandoned all intimate ties with the PPS, and took his immediate followers into Galicia to prepare a regular military force. In 1911–14 the PPS (Rewolucja) spawned two sub-factions – the 'new PPS' and the PPS (Opozycja) of Feliks Perl and Tomasz Arciszewski. In this state of advanced fragmentation the PPS reflected the fratricidal condition of the Polish national movement as a whole.[6]

Events in Russian Poland inevitably influenced developments in the other partitions. The period of the *Duma* coincided with the introduction of universal suffrage in Austria. In Galicia, as in Russia, nationalists of Dmowski's persuasion made rapid progress, attacking Ukrainians as well as Jews. Their crude sneers against Governor Bobrzyński explain in ample measure why the latter was willing to turn a blind eye to Piłsudski's paramilitary activities. In Prussia, many Poles were attracted by Dmowski's denunciations of Germany. The school strikes of 1906–7 were directly inspired by the precedent in Russia. In all three Partitions, there was a distinct acceleration of the nation's pulse. It belied a feverish condition attended by excessive internal stress which brought no improvement to the nation's body politic as a whole.

The crisis of 1904–8 was the nearest that Polish society ever came to an organic Revolution. Later, in 1917–18, the Polish lands were buffered from the effects of the Revolution in Russia by German occupation. In the Second World War, the revolutionary social changes were to be engineered by foreign enemies, not by native forces. Meanwhile, after 1908 reactionary policies were reasserted in almost every sphere. The assassination of Stolypin in 1911 brought Reform to an end. The Polish *Macierz Szkolna* was disbanded. The expansion of the *zemstva* into the western provinces was bedevilled by conflicts between peasantry and landowners. The implementation of municipal reform in the cities was obstructed by Polish–Jewish rivalries. In 1912 the nationalization of the Warsaw–Vienna Railway resulted in the dismissal of thousands of Polish employees. The secession of the district of Kholm (Chełm) to the *Gubernia* of Kiev was clearly intended to facilitate Russification and to prepare the way for the wholesale reconversion of Uniates. In a darkening international scene, fears of a German invasion could be easily excited. On 3 August 1914, when War was declared and the first Cossack regiment passed through Warsaw on its way to the front, the Polish population lined the streets and cheered.

CHAPTER EIGHTEEN
FENIKS:
The Rebirth of the Polish state (1914-1918)

In its origins the First World War had nothing to do with Polish problems. It was born of German rivalry with France, Britain, and Russia, and from Austria's troubles with Serbia. But the outbreak of hostilities in August 1914 automatically breathed fresh life into the Polish Question. For the first time since 1762, Berlin was at war with St. Petersburg. The solidarity of the partitioning powers, scarcely ruffled during the nineteenth century, was broken at last. For the first time since the Napoleonic period, the Polish lands were to be turned into an international battleground. In Silesia and Galicia, and later on in Byelorussia and Polesie, the Eastern Front was to bring the Polish people into direct contact with the conflict, and with all the ideas and horrors of the day. For the first time in history, mass conscript armies were to be raised by each of the three Empires. Unprecedented demands were to be made on the civilian population, straining their loyalties to the utmost. The Polish lands were not merely the theatre of operations. They were the area where Russia and the Central Powers were forced to compete for the minds and bodies of their Polish subjects.[1] (See Map 11.)

As the prospect of an early verdict receded, each of the contestants felt obliged to outdo its rivals in the lavishness of the promises which each hoped would win Polish support. In 1914–16, the Tsar, the Kaiser, and the Emperor-King proposed mounting degrees of autonomy. By 1917, the President of the United States, the Provisional government in Petrograd, and even the leader of the Bolsheviks declared themselves in favour of Polish independence. In 1918, they were copied by France, Italy, Japan, and, last of all, Great Britain. Most of these declarations were pious invocations, with no chance of implementation by the men who made them. The Germans alone were in a position to turn their words into deeds but failed to do so very effectively.[2]

378

Map 11.   The Eastern Front, (1914—18)

Yet the spectre of independence, once raised, could not be laid. Over the four years of the war, the political atmosphere was transformed. The habitual disillusionment of previous decades was gradually replaced by a vague, but fervent expectancy. Among the Poles themselves, optimists felt elation at the tempting prospects which the fickle fortunes of battle presented. Pessimists felt appalled at the certainty that fratricidal slaughter was unavoidable. There were tens of thousands of young Poles in each of the armies. In this situation, in September 1914, Edward Słoński wrote perhaps the best-known verse of the war years:

> We're kept apart, my brother,
> By a fate that we can't deny.
> From our two opposing dug-outs
> We're staring death in the eye.
>
> In the trenches filled with groaning,
> Alert to the shellfire's whine,
> We stand and confront each other.
> I'm your enemy: and you are mine.
>
> So when you catch me in your sights
> I beg you, play your part,
> And sink your Muscovite bullet
> Deep in my Polish heart.
>
> Now I see the vision clearly,
> Caring not that we'll both be dead;
> For *that which has not perished*
> Shall rise from the blood that we shed.[3]

In every centre where political activity was possible, Polish organizations appeared from nowhere. In Cracow, a conference on 16 August 1914 brought to life a Supreme National Committee (NKN), which aimed to unite all Polish independence movements under the Austrian aegis.[4] Its first President was Professor Juliusz Leo (1862–1918), the long-time Mayor of Cracow. Its military department was headed by Władysław Sikorski (1881–1943). It was supported by all the leading party leaders of Galicia, and operated for three years. It maintained links with Piłsudski's Polish National Organization (PON), the political wing of the Legions, but the relationship was anything but easy. In Warsaw, on 10 September 1914, the National Democrats formed a Central Citizens' Committee (CKO), ostensibly to provide social assistance to war victims, in effect also to support Dmowski's Polish National Committee (KNP), which at this stage was still devoted to the goal of autonomy under Russia. The KNP soon moved in 1915 to Petrograd, and thereafter to Lausanne in Switzerland.[5] In London, a Polish Information Committee (PKI) was created to help Poles affected by the Aliens' Registration Order and to publicize the Polish cause. It was patronized by R. W. Seton-Watson, the leading British advocate of the East European national movements, and counted August Zaleski among its most energetic members [6] In Switzerland, a Central Polish Relief Committee (CAP) was established at Vevey by I. J. Paderewski, the pianist. Both the British and the Swiss centres strove to co-ordinate aid to areas of Poland devastated by war. The CAP opened branches in London, Paris, Rome, and Washington, which were destined to fall under the influence of Dmowski's KNP. The two main tendencies in Polish politics at this time were represented on the one hand by the so-called 'activists', proclaiming the call for an active struggle against Russia at the side of the Central Powers, and on the other hand the so called 'passivists', who put their faith in Russia and later in the western Allies.

The number of Polish military formations multiplied likewise. On 16 August 1914, Piłsudski merged his Riflemen with other paramilitary groups of the same persuasion, and formed the Polish Legions.[7] He took command of the First Brigade of the Legions himself: hence the origin of his familiar nickname, *Komendant* (The Commandant), and the Legion's marching song, *My, Pierwsza Brygada*. The Second Brigade was commanded by Col. Hüttner, and from July 1916 by Col. Józef Haller (1873–1960). The Third Brigade, formed in 1916, was commanded by Col. Stanisław Szeptycki (1867–1950) and then by B. Roja (1879–1940). After their first, disastrous independent adventure in August 1914, the Legions were subordinated to Austrian orders. Associated with the Legions was Piłsudski's élite formation, the Polish Military Organization (POW), a secret conspiratorial body, designed for diversionary and intelligence operations. This survived when the Legions were eventually disbanded.[8] On the Russian side, the National Democrats recruited a volunteer Puławy Legion, directly intended to challenge Piłsudski's influence. In later stages of the war the Germans formed the *Polnische Wehrmacht,* an auxiliary corps for garrisoning the Polish lands conquered from Russia; the Russians formed a Polish Rifle Brigade within their own army; the French formed a 'Polish Army' from captured prisoners-of-war. The Americans and Canadians facilitated recruiting to Polish formations in one or other of the Allied armies.[9]

By 1916, the total number of Poles serving in the war reached 1.9 million. This included 4 per cent of the population in the Vistula provinces; 14.8 per cent of the Polish population of Prussian Poland, and 16.3 per cent of Galician Poles. In the course of the fighting they were destined to suffer over one million casualties including 450,000 dead.[10]

The campaign on the Eastern Front was launched by Piłsudski before any of the professional armies had moved. Following the proclamation of a fictitious National Government, on 6 August 1914, a group of Riflemen crossed the Russian frontier from Galicia and marched on Kielce. They made an extraordinary sight. The cavalrymen were carrying saddles on their heads in the hope of capturing horses from the enemy. On the outskirts of Kielce they were welcomed by their own women who presented them with bouquets of flowers. The townspeople as a whole, fearing Russian retribution, stayed indoors A short street skirmish with a Russian patrol drove the 'liberation army' out. In less than a fortnight, they were back in Galicia. This was the fiasco which persuaded Piłsudski to submit to Austrian orders, and to leave the fighting for the moment to the regular armies.[11]

The Russian offensive prepared to roll eastwards in two sectors, in East Prussia and in Galicia. To this end, the Commander-in-Chief, the Grand Duke Nicholas, distributed a Manifesto to the Polish Nation:

Poles!
The hour has struck when the dreams of your fathers and forefathers can come true.
A century and a half ago, the living body of Poland was torn in pieces; but her soul did not die. It was kept alive by a hope for the resurrection of the Polish nation and for its fraternal union with Great Russia.
The Russian Army brings you the blessed news of that union. May

the frontiers that cut across the Polish nation be erased.

May the Polish nation be joined in one under the sceptre of the Russian Emperor. Under that sceptre Poland will be reborn, free in her own faith, language, and self-rule.

Russia expects only one thing of you, namely, that you show respect for all those other people whose fate has been bound to yours by History.

Great Russia steps forward to meet you with an open heart and with a brotherly hand extended in friendship. She firmly believes that the sword which slew the common enemy at Grunwald has not tarnished.

The Russian battalions stretch from the shores of the Pacific Ocean to the Northern Seas. The dawn of your new life is breaking.

May the banner of the Cross shine forth as a symbol of the Passion and the Resurrection of the nations.

(Signed) Supreme Commander-in-Chief,
General-Adjutant, Mikołaj [12]

The sickly, religious tone of the Manifesto fell awkwardly from the lips of a Romanov, whose predecessors had been responsible for the political and religious persecutions of the past. Although written in Polish, not Russian, it fell completely flat when published on posters bearing the Polish flag in an upside-down position. It was typical of many such manifestos issued by all sides as the war wore on.

On the southern sector, against the Austrians, fortune smiled on the Russians. By Christmas, the Cossacks were at Wieliczka, in sight of Cracow. But on the northern sector, they were overwhelmed. Drawing the oncoming hordes into the woods and backwaters of the Mazurian lakeland, Hindenburg contrived to surround and annihilate two Russian armies. This great victory, in which almost two million Russians were taken prisoner, was named by the Germans after the nearby town of Tannenberg. It was proclaimed to be the final Teutonic revenge for the defeat of Grunwald on a nearby site 504 years earlier.

The German counter offensive was mounted in August 1915 and continued through the year. From their first breakthrough at Gorlice in Galicia, the *Wehrmacht* tramped relentlessly eastwards. On 5 August they entered Warsaw, on 25 August, Brest, on 18 September, Vilna. In 1916, Mackensen crossed the Carpathians and invaded Romania. These victories won territorial gains which were not reversed for the rest of the war. Except in Polesie and Eastern Galicia, which were the scene of Brusilov's advance in 1916, German and Austrian control of the Polish lands was unchallenged for the duration. In 1917, the *Wehrmacht* pressed on into the Baltic States, Byelorussia, and the Ukraine. At the beginning of 1918, they were threatening Moscow itself.

German political dispositions were sensibly delayed until the military situation was stabilized.[13] At first, the conquered territories were run by the Military. A German Zone of Occupation was created, with a Governor-General, Hans von Besseler (1850–1921) resident in Warsaw. An Austrian Zone of Occupation was centred on Lublin. Beyond the Bug, the *Oberkommando-Ost* was created with its headquarters at Vilna. Political debates lasted for nearly two years. German leaders were unprepared for the new developments. 'It was not our intention to reopen the Polish Question,' declared the Chancellor, Bethmann-Hollweg, in the Reichstag: 'it was the fate of battles'. One project called for the creation of a permanent buffer zone or *Grenzstreifen* from which 16 million Poles could be deported into Russia to make way for reliable German settlers.[14] Another idea, put forward by Frederick Naumann, envisaged a formal union of Austria–Hungary and Germany. In this '*Mitteleuropa*', Poland was to enjoy autonomy under German auspices. The Austrians were scandalized. In August 1916, the Germans announced their intention of reincarnating the defunct Congress Kingdom, and in the autumn, the Kaiser discussed the outlines with Francis Joseph at Pless (Pszczyna) in Silesia. According to the 'Two Emperors' Declaration' published on 5 November, Poland was to be 'independent', within so far undefined territorial and constitutional limits. A Provisional Council of State (TRS), convoked in Warsaw by the joint action of the German and Austrian Governors-General, drew exclusively on Activist support, and resigned after eight months' operation. It was replaced by a Regency Council, consisting of Archbishop Kakowski (1862–1938), Prince Zdzisław Lubomirski (1865–1941), and Count Józef Ostrowski (1850–1924). This body acted in the name of a Kingdom without a King, and of a Regency without a Regent. It was entirely subordinated to the German military authorities. It made some progress in February 1918, when it appointed an executive Council of State, responsible for twelve 'Ministries' and intended to polonize the administration. But its credibility was soon undermined by the Treaty of Brest–Litovsk, signed by the Germans with the Bolsheviks on 3 March. Polish opinion condemned the Treaty, to which no Polish representatives were invited, as an insolent assault on Polish interests in the lands beyond the Bug. In Polish eyes, the Treaty of Brest–Litovsk accomplished the Sixth Partition.[15]

The part played by the Polish Legions in the campaign of the Eastern Front was not undistinguished. Their baptism of fire under Austrian orders took place on 21 October 1914 at Laski near Dęblin. Their moment of glory came in the triumphal Uhlan charge at Rokitna on 13 June 1915. In the next two years, they saw action in Subcarpathian Ruthenia, in Podolia, in Volhynia, and in the great battle of the Stochód valley in Polesie. In 1917, however, their purpose began to waver on account of a proposal to transfer them to the *Polnische Wehrmacht.* The extent of the German success, and the imminent collapse of Russia, undermined Piłsudski's original motives. He no more wanted a complete German victory than a Russian one. So on 21 July 1917 he refused to transfer his allegiance from Austria to Germany. Piłsudski's interview with von Besseler, the German Governor of Warsaw, was entirely uncompromising:

PIŁSUDSKI:	Your Excellency, do you imagine for one moment that you will win the nation's confidence by hanging Polish insignia on each of the fingers of the hand which is throttling Poland? The Poles know the Prussian stranglehold for what it is.
von BESSELER:	Herr von Piłsudski, you know that in these stirring times Poland needs a leader of vision, and you are the only one whom I have been able to find. If you go along with us, we will give you everything – power, fame, money . . .
PIŁSUDSKI:	Your Excellency does not understand me, and does not wish to understand. If I were to go along with you, Germany would gain one man, whilst I would lose a nation.[16]

Most of the legionnaries refused to swear the oath to the Kaiser. Piłsudski was arrested and imprisoned in Germany. His men

were interned in German camps. Józef Haller escaped into
the Russian lines, and made his way via Murmansk to France.

German control of the Polish lands destroyed Dmowski's
chances of raising the Polish Question effectively in Russia.
At the end of 1915 he sailed from Petrograd for the West. In
London he missed no opportunity of besmirching Piłsudski as
'pro-German' and 'anti-Ally', and added to the scare which
equated Yiddish-speaking Jews with German agents. He
handed a list of Polish activists and Jews including August
Zaleski and Lewis Namier to Scotland Yard, and persuaded
the Home Office to transfer the work of the PKI to trusties
of his own. At the same time, he flattered the Foreign Office
with exaggerated visions of 'half-a-million or even a million
Polish soldiers' who would lay down their lives for the Allied
Cause, if only the Allied governments would recognize the
brand of Polish Independence which he was now advocating.
For his pains, he was awarded an honorary doctorate at
Cambridge University.[17] In Paris, he made contact with
sympathetic politicians, but was inhibited by the strong
French ties with the Tsarist authorities. In Lausanne, he joined
forces with the leaders of the CAP, and prepared for the re-
establishment of the KNP. The whole burden of Dmowski's
campaign at this stage was to win official recognition for his
own movement as the sole and exclusive representative of a
future Polish government. He nearly succeeded. But, for the
moment, nothing could change so long as the western governments continued to regard the Polish Question as an internal
matter for their great Russian ally.

The February Revolution in Russia changed the scene
overnight. The emergence in Petrograd of Russian liberals
who had been associated with the Polish Circle of the *Duma*
for over a decade put a declaration on Poland high on the
Provisional Government's agenda. The Proclamation was made
on 30 March 1917. It proclaimed an 'independent Poland'
but deferred the details to a future Constituent Assembly.[18]
It was followed on 9 April by a general Declaration of the
Principle of National Self-Determination. At the end of the
month, it appointed a Polish Liquidation Commission under
Alexander Lednicki, an associate of the Cadets, and Chairman
of the 'United Polish Associations'. Lednicki's task was to

prepare for the transfer of Russian state property to Polish control. This was quite impossible owing to the continuing German occupation of all the Polish provinces.

It is true that the Provisional Government's Proclamation on Poland was preceded on 21 March 1917 by a similar declaration made by the Petrograd Soviet of Workers and Peasant Deputies.[19] But this Bolshevik initiative cannot be considered as anything more than a private statement of intent. At this stage, the Bolsheviks had no authority in Russia; and their pronunciations on Poland carried no more weight than the resolutions of workers' committees in Warsaw, Berlin, or Tokyo on the future of Russia. Their earliest authoritative statement on the Polish Question came in the third clause of the Decree of 29 August 1918 denouncing the former secret Treaties, including the Partitions. Even then, they had no means of enforcing their views, and no intention of making specific commitments. No one knew what the Bolsheviks understood by 'Poland'.

The February Revolution in Russia coincided with the rapidly intensifying American interest in the problems of the war. At a meeting with Paderewski in November 1916, President-elect Woodrow Wilson recorded his first known expression of sympathy for the idea of an independent Poland. On 21 January 1917, in his first State of the Union Address to the Senate, he made mention of a 'united Poland' and its right of 'access to the sea'. One year later, on 8 January 1918, the thirteenth of Wilson's 'Fourteen Points' on peace aims spoke of a 'united, independent and autonomous Poland with free, unrestricted access to the sea'. This generous statement of American views on Poland was the only such statement by a leader of the Powers which was not extracted by the force of events.[20]

In 1917–18, the policy of all the Western Powers towards Poland changed out of all recognition. Partly as a result of the American entry in the war on their side, partly as a result of the Russian collapse, but largely as a result of their desperate search for any means possible of embarrassing Germany, they abandoned their former rigid opposition to Polish Independence. But they did so grudgingly. As late as 11 March 1917, the French government signed an undertaking with Russia not to interfere in Russian frontier arrangements. On 22 March, Lord Hugh Cecil reminded Parliament that British recognition of Polish Independence was equivalent to the Russians proposing Home Rule for Ireland. One month later on 26 April, in line with the Provisional government's Declaration, Bonar Law, the Chancellor of the Exchequer, welcomed Poland on behalf of HMG. In June, in France, Poincaré's decree formalizing arrangements for the Polish Army pushed matters still further. In September, the French government's unilateral recognition of the KNP as the official body for political liaison with the Polish army caused general consternation. There was much confusion over the exact terms of the recognition agreement, and the British feared that the French had stolen a march on them. British recognition of the KNP in October was phrased in deliberately vague language and exclusively in the interest of Anglo-French solidarity. Even so, it was soon regretted. Dmowski could not now be prevented from behaving as if he were the Crown Prince of the future Polish State. General pronouncements on Polish Independence were by now fairly common. But the first specific joint guarantee by all the Allies for the 'restoration of Poland in its historical and geographic limits' was not made until 2 March 1918, and then only in curiously obscure circumstances. It was made at Jassy in Romania where Allied negotiators were trying to persuade Poles from the mutinous 9th Russian Army in Bessarabia, together with fugitive elements of Haller's 2nd Legionary Brigade, that they should continue the fight against Germany. It was not repeated in public form until the joint British—French—Italian—American Note of 3 June 1918.

In themselves, the Allied Declarations achieved little. Few of Dmowski's half-million recruits materialized. The five divisions of the Polish Army in France never exceeded 100,000 men, and only one division was ready to join the fighting on the Western Front. Their Command was entrusted to French generals and, after his arrival from Murmansk, to Józef Haller. In Russia, the nominally pro-Allied Polish Corps of General Dowbór-Muśnicki spent more time fighting the Red Guards than the Germans. Based on Minsk in Byelorussia, it drew its strength from Polish units of the disintegrating Russian Army, and used them for the protection of local landowning interests.

Its efforts were more than balanced by thousands of Poles who joined the Reds, and fraternized with the German garrisons of the *Ober-Ost*.[21] In such a situation, it was difficult to see how the Allied governments could ever turn their declarations on Poland into effect.

In Warsaw, the fluctuating fortunes of the Eastern Front provoked alternating moods of despondency and of high expectation. At the outset, the citizenry was strongly Loyalist, and supported the Russian mobilization with exemplary vigour. The socialist and nationalist opposition, crushed in the wake of 1905–6, was hardly in evidence. News of the German bombardment of Kalisz aroused general indignation, reinforcing the contention of the dominant National Democrats that Poland's future lay with Russia. But events soon passed beyond the Loyalists' control. Unrest amongst the working class was aroused by rising food prices, by forced conscriptions for fortress repair, and by unemployment resulting from the evacuation of industrial plant to Russia. A Citizens' Committee, headed by Prince Lubomirski, was originally intended to supervise welfare work; but it soon formed a core round which local, and then national politics, could crystallize. In March 1915, when the Tsar granted the city its municipal autonomy, denied since 1863, Warsaw was already turning its back on the old order. In the summer, when the retreating Russians wilfully destroyed all the city's bridges, stations, and metalworks, sympathy for the Tsarist connection evaporated overnight. The German Occupation, which lasted from 6 August 1915 to 13 November 1918, was established in an extremely volatile situation. The spontaneous celebration of the Polish National Day on 3 May 1916, for the first time in fifty years, betrayed the nationalist feelings which were now about to surface. In that same year, the repolonization of the University of Warsaw, the formal declaration of the restored Kingdom of Poland with its advisory Council of State in the Royal Castle, and the ceremonial entry of the Polish Legions, underlined the readiness of the Germans to make far-reaching concessions. Yet 1917 saw the limit of those concessions. Repeated strikes revealed the persistence of economic distress; whilst the arrest of Piłsudski gave a glimpse of the iron fist beneath the German glove. The grip of the German military regime over the Regency Council never wavered until the autumn of 1918.

When it finally occurred, the collapse of the Central Powers took place with startling rapidity. The first crack in the monolith appeared on the Western Front on 'Black Friday', 18 July 1918, when the French, British, and Americans broke through the German lines and started an advance which gradually gained momentum. But no irremediable breach appeared until October, when on the Eastern Front the soldiers of the Austro-Hungarian army simply packed their bags and made for home. In three weeks, the Austrian Zone of Occupation was denuded of its garrisons. The Czech regiments made for Bohemia; the Magyars for Hungary; the Tyroleans. for Tyrol; and the Galicians for their towns and villages. The officers lost all semblance of order, and disappeared in the general mêlée. State officials handed over the keys of their offices to the caretakers, and departed. The astonished population which had lived under military law for four years, was left to their own devices. They had been abandoned. The first Polish territory to find its freedom in this way was Cieszyn. On 28 October 1918, the National Council of the Duchy of Cieszyn Silesia declared its independence, announced its intention of joining the Polish Republic (which did not then exist), and signed a treaty ceding the western part of the Duchy to the local Czech council.[22] Cracow found its freedom on the same day. Lwów, freed on 1 November, was seized simultaneously by Polish and Ukrainian elements.[23]

The politics of the Austrian collapse were exceedingly confused. In Cracow, the leaders of the 'Polish Circle' of the *Reichsrat* formed a *Polish Liquidation Commission* (PKL) to administer Galicia in the absence of orders from Vienna. Its chairman was Wincenty Witos. Some of its more conservative members were still calling in 1919 for loyalty to the Austrian Empire, even when the Austrian Empire had ceased to exist. In Lublin on 7 November, in the former headquarters of the Austrian Zone, socialist leaders formed a 'Provisional People's Government of the Polish Republic', with Daszyński as Premier. As the only party to have consistently favoured independence in previous years, they could not fairly claim to be representative of the nation as a whole. But their association with the Legions, and their radical National Manifesto won them a measure of popular support.[24]

At this point, the crack spread to the German Zone. Kiel was in mutiny. The revolution had broken out in Berlin. The German Command in Warsaw, as elsewhere, lacked orders. The soldiers of the garrison began to form 'Soviets' on the model that they had learned in the *Ober-Ost*. The workers joined them, and formed Workers' Committees. The Regency Council was powerless. Its attempt to form a 'Government' under J. Świeżyński in place of the late Council of State, found no support. Anarchy threatened. Then, the unexpected happened. Piłsudski, released from Magdenburg Castle on 10 November, arrived at Warsaw Station. He was the one man whose reputation was big enough to save the situation. His Socialist past promised a measure of influence over the leftist workers; his military experience gave a chance that he could deal with the German Command. On 11 November, the day of the Western Armistice, he took office as Commander-in-Chief, on the plea of the Regency Council. He proposed to the German Command that they should simply lay down their arms and take the first train out, before civil commotion erupted. The Germans readily agreed. Hardened stormtroopers handed over their rifles to schoolboys. The Citadel was abandoned to a gang of youths. Besseler fled, leaving his copious wine cellar intact. Within a few hours, the Germans had gone. Warsaw too was free. Within three days, the entire Kingdom up to the Bug was clear of German troops. On 14 November, the Regency Council surrendered all its functions to Piłsudski, to whom it gave the title of Chief-of-State. On that same day, he accepted Daszyński's demission of the Provisional Government in Lublin, and took charge of all political affairs. Thus began the attempt, in Lewis Namier's words, 'to build Poland while Russia and Germany slept'.

From the legal point of view, it is difficult to know exactly what state it was that Piłsudski was now controlling. It was hard to say whether he had merely succeeded to the Polish Kingdom as revived by the Germans in 1916 or whether he was already in command of the Polish Republic whose legitimate existence was not certainly confirmed, by democratic elections and by international recognition, until the following

January. For practical purposes however, the key to the situation lay in the fact that Piłsudski was in sole control, and that neither the KNP nor the Allied governments had played any part in his appointment. This was enough for Dmowski to claim that the appointment was 'illegal' and for the Allied governments to look with great suspicion on the ex-Austrian Brigadier and German prisoner who had 'seized control' of a country which they had hoped to control themselves. In truth, Piłsudski's appointment was neither 'legal' nor 'illegal'. He had arrived in Warsaw from prison and exile with no precise knowledge of what he would find. Like Lenin in Petrograd in the previous year, he had 'found power lying in the street'. As he stooped to pick it up, the Polish phoenix fluttered from the ashes of war which lay at his feet.

In subsequent years, many Polish historians have assumed that the rebirth of the Polish state was the natural conclusion of the nation's struggles during the period of Partition. In their view, it formed the only proper, not to say the inevitable, destination of 'the Road to Independence'. Certainly, the recent publication of popular memoirs from the First World War, such as that of a Polish soldier fighting in the ranks of the German army, reveals the extent to which ordinary Polish people were fervently yearning for the restoration of their long-lost homeland.[25] Yet one cannot assume that the wish was necessarily the father of the deed. In actual fact, the Poles were given very little opportunity to fight for their independence. All the enterprises which they undertook in this direction, including the Legions, were defeated. All the plans which were laid for the creation of a Polish state in conjunction with the Central Powers, with Russia, or with the Western allies, came to nothing. The outcome of the War in the Polish lands was exactly foreseen by nobody, and in the event involved virtually no fighting. If the historian is to distinguish the achievement of national independence in November 1918 from the subsequent campaigns fought to preserve and defend that independence, he can only conclude that the wishes and actions of the Polish population were, to the very last moment, largely irrelevant. To at least one sceptical commentator, the creation of an independent Poland in 1918 was the result of 'a fluke'. To people of a religious turn of mind, it looked like a miracle.

CHAPTER NINETEEN
NIEPODLEGŁOŚĆ:
Twenty Years of Independence (1918-1939)

Molotov called it 'the monstrous bastard of the Peace of Versailles'. Stalin called it 'pardon the expression, a state'. J. M. Keynes, the theorist of modern capitalism, called it 'an economic impossibility whose only industry is Jew-baiting'. Lewis Namier called it 'pathological'. E. H. Carr called it 'a farce'. David Lloyd George talked of 'a historic failure', which had 'won her freedom not by her own exertions but by the blood of others', and of a country which 'imposed on other nations the very tyranny' which it had endured itself for years. 'Poland', he said, 'was drunk with the new wine of liberty supplied to her by the Allies', and 'fancied herself as the resistless mistress of Central Europe'. In 1919, Lloyd George was reported as saying that he would no more give Upper Silesia to Poland 'than he would give a clock to a monkey'. In 1939, he announced that Poland had 'deserved its fate'. Adolf Hitler called it 'a state which arose from the blood of countless German regiments', 'a state built on force and governed by the truncheons of the police and the military', 'a ridiculous state where . . . sadistic beasts give vent to their perverse instincts', 'an artificially begotten state', 'the pet lap-dog of Western democracies which cannot be considered a cultured nation at all', 'a so-called state lacking every national, historical, cultural and moral foundation'. The coincidence of these sentiments, and of their phraseology, is unmistakable. Rarely, if ever, has a newly independent country been subjected to such eloquent and gratuitous abuse. Rarely, if ever, have British liberals been so careless of their opinions or their company.[1]

The Polish Republic came into being in November 1918 by a process which theologians might call parthenogenesis. It created itself in the void left by the collapse of three partitioning powers. Despite Molotov's assertion, it was not created by the Peace of Versailles, which merely confirmed what already existed and whose territorial provisions were limited to defining the frontier with Germany alone. It was not the client state which the Allied governments had been preparing to construct in 1917—18 in collaboration with Dmowski's National Committee in Paris. It was not the state which the Bolsheviks hoped to construct as their Red Bridge with revolutionary Germany. And it was not the puppet Poland which Russia, Germany, and Austria had variously proposed in the course of the Great War. It owed its procreation to no one, not even to the Poles themselves, who, fighting with distinction in all the combatant armies, had been constrained to neutralize each other as a political force.[2]

The collapse of all established order in Central and Eastern Europe condemned the infant Republic to a series of nursery brawls. In 1918—21, six wars were fought concurrently.[3] The Ukrainian War, which started in Lwów in November 1918 and ended with the collapse of the West Ukrainian Republic in July 1919, established Polish control over East Galicia as far as the River Zbrucz. The Posnanian War with Germany which erupted on 27 December 1918 was settled by the Treaty of Versailles on 28 June 1919; but the Silesian War, prosecuted intermittently through the three Risings — 16—24 August 1919, 19—25 August 1920, and 2 May—5 July 1921 — was not settled until the Silesian Convention, signed in Geneva in 1922. The Lithuanian War, which disputed possession of the city of Wilno (Vilnius), began in July 1919 and continued in practice to the truce of October 1920; in theory, in the absence of a formal peace treaty, it continued throughout the inter-war period. The Czechoslovak War, launched on 26 January 1919 by the Czechoslovak invasion of Cieszyn (Tešin) in abrogation of a local agreement, was terminated by Allied arbitration on 28 July 1920. Minor conflicts in Spisz (Spiš) and elsewhere in the Carpathians persisted till 1925. Gravest of all was the Soviet War, which alone threatened the Republic's existence. This was an ordeal by fire, which left an enduring mark. (See Map 12.)

The Polish—Soviet War had implications far beyond those which most text-books allow. It was not related to the Russian Civil War which proceeded concurrently on other fronts; it was not waged by the Poles as part of Allied Intervention in

1. DUCHY OF CIESZYN SILESIA, declared for Poland 28/10/1918; the eastern area awarded to Poland by Council of Ambassadors 28/7/1920. (from AUSTRIA). N.B. the western area, the Zaolzia (Transolzia), annexed by Poland from Czechoslovakia, 1/10/1938.

2. WESTERN GALICIA, taken over by the Polish Liquidation Commission (PKL), 28/10/1918 to 10/1/19 (from AUSTRIA).

3. AUSTRIAN ZONE OF OCCUPATION OF KINGDOM OF POLAND, subject to Polish Provisional Government at Lublin, from 4/11/1918. (from RUSSIA).

4. GERMAN ZONE OF OCCUPATION OF KINGDOM OF POLAND, evacuated by German Army, 11/11/1918, handed to the government of J. Piłsudski by the Regency Council 14/11/1918. (from RUSSIA).

5. EASTERN GALICIA, disputed with the West Ukrainian Republic, Nov. 1918 – July 1919; occupied by Polish Army; awarded to Poland by League of Nations, 1923.

6. GRAND DUCHY OF POSEN, seceded from Prussia following the Poznań Revolt, 26/12/1918 - 16/2/1919. (from GERMANY).

7. TREATY OF VERSAILLES, 28/6/1918. Territory in addition to the G.D. of Posen awarded to Poland, incorporated 20/1/1920. (from GERMANY)

8. JANOWO, NAPROMEK, GRUNWALD: villages awarded to Poland following the East Prussian Plebiscite, 23/7/1920. (from GERMANY)

9. ORAWA)   awarded in part to Poland by the Council of Ambassadors, 28/7/1920
10. SPISZ)   from HUNGARY)

11. MIDDLE LITHUANIA: occupied by Polish Army, 9/10/1920, incorporated into Poland by referendum March 1922. (from RUSSIA).

12. EASTERN BORDERLANDS, occupied by German Army to February 1919; contested with Soviet Russia during the Polish-Soviet War, 1919-20; awarded to Poland by Treaty of Riga, 18/3/1921. (from RUSSIA).

13. UPPER SILESIA: south-eastern part of the Plebiscite Area, awarded to Poland by the Council of Ambassadors, 20/10/1921

Map 12.   The Formation of the Polish Republic, (1918–21)

Russia, and cannot be described as 'The Third Campaign of the Entente'. For the government of Piłsudski, who preferred the Bolsheviks to the Whites in Russia, it was fought to maintain the independence of non-Russian areas of the former Tsarist Empire. For the government of Lenin, it was fought to re-create that Empire in socialist guise, and to spread the Revolution to the advanced capitalist countries of Western Europe. It was caused in the first place by the Germans' withdrawal from the intervening zone of occupation, the *Ober-Ost,* in February 1919, and continued without a break until 12 October 1920.[4]

The Soviet War grew out of the first unplanned skirmish which occurred at Bereza Kartuska in Byelorussia on 14 February 1919. In the first phase, in 1919, the initiative lay with the Poles. Piłsudski's home city, Wilno, was recaptured in April and Minsk was taken in August. Yet in the autumn, in spite of urgent pleas from the Entente, Polish support for the advance of Denikin's Whites against Moscow was expressly withheld. Peace talks miscarried owing to mutual suspicions over the future of the Ukraine. In 1920, the action expanded dramatically. Over one million men were deployed on a swiftly moving front stretching from Latvia in the north to Romania in the south. From January onwards, the Red Army was constructing a huge strike force of 700,000 men on the Berezina. On 10 March the Soviet Command gave orders for a major offensive to the west under the 27-year-old General, Mikhail Tukhachevsky. But Piłsudski nipped these preparations in the bud. A sharp attack at Mozyrz in March, the daring march on Kiev launched on 24 April, and the fiercely contested Battle of the Berezina in May, all served to delay the Soviet advance. Then in the summer, fortunes changed. Budyonny's First Cavalry Army smashed its way through the Polish lines in Galicia in June, and on 4 July Tukachevsky broke out from the Berezina. 'To the West!' ran his order of the day. 'Over the corpse of White Poland lies the road to world-wide conflagration.' By the beginning of August, five Soviet armies were approaching the suburbs of Warsaw. The situation was critical. Allied diplomatic intervention had failed to produce an armistice. The frontier line proposed by the British government, the so-called 'Curzon Line', was rejected by Poles and

Soviets alike. The British refused to give Poland military assistance despite their clear obligation to do so. The French declined to reinforce their small Military Mission. French military credits for Poland were terminated. A vociferous propaganda campaign, under the slogan 'Hands off Russia', led world opinion astray at a time when Soviet Russia was laying violent hands on its Polish neighbour. Lenin's diplomats preached peace, while his generals practised war. German dockers in Danzig and Czech railwaymen in Brno contrived to delay the few foreign supplies for which Poland had paid in hard cash. On 10 August, the 'Red Cossacks' of Ghai crossed the Vistula west of Warsaw. The scene in the capital was strangely calm. Although the police made a number of preventive arrests, suspecting that sections of the working class or of the Jews might harbour communist sympathies, the inhabitants showed no inclination to welcome the Russians. The old military section of the PPS was revived, and took the lead in the activities of the all-party Council for the Defence of the Capital (ROS). In face of the common enemy, class divisions were forgotten. The Workers' Battalions, brandishing staffs and scythes, marched off to join the army in the company of the middle-class Citizens' Watch, which had paraded beforehand in boaters and wing-collars. Lord D'Abernon, the British Ambassador at Berlin, who witnessed the preparations at first hand, was amazed by the nonchalance of a city about to be stormed:

26 July. I continue to marvel at the absence of panic, at the apparent absence indeed of all anxiety. Were a methodical system of defence being organized, the confidence of the public might be understood, but all the best troops are being sent to Lwów, leaving Warsaw unprotected.
27 July. The Prime Minister, a peasant proprietor, has gone off today to get his harvest in. Nobody thinks this extraordinary.
2 August. The insouciance of the people here is beyond belief. One would imagine the Bolsheviks a thousand miles away and the country in no danger.
3 August. Made an expedition up the Ostrów Road...Curiously enough, most of the people whom I saw putting up barbed wire were Jews . . .
7 August. I visited this afternoon the proposed new front in the direction of Minsk Mazowiecki. A treble entanglement of barbed wire is being put round Warsaw at a radius of 20 kilometres, and a certain number of trenches have been dug . . .

13 August. There is singularly little alarm. The upper classes have already left town, in many cases having placed their pictures and other valuables in charge of the muzeum authorities. Warsaw has been so often occupied by foreign troops that the event in itself causes neither the excitement nor the alarm which would be produced in a less experienced city.[5]

As it happened, D'Abernon's worst fears were not realized. At the very moment when the enemy was pausing to deliver the final blow, the Polish Army re-formed in a manœuvre of daring complexity. Exhausted divisions were pulled from the line, and were transferred to new positions, one, two, or even three hundred miles distant. An assault force was hurriedly assembled to the south on the River Wieprz. Providentially for the Poles, the overconfident Tukhachevsky did not press his advantage until 13 August. Then, to his surprise, Warsaw's fragile defences held firm. Although the wire encirclement was pierced by the first rush of enthusiasm at Radzymin, the initial attack on the Vistula bridgehead was repulsed. The main Soviet force was contained to the north by the skilful operations of Sikorski's Fifth Army on the Wkra. On 16 August, to Tukhachevsky's dismay, the Polish assault force sliced through his rear, severing all lines of communication. To his total confusion, on 18 August he realized that his entire army was encircled. The Soviet rout was complete. A hundred thousand Russians were taken prisoner. Forty thousand fled into East Prussia. Three Soviet armies were annihilated. The rest struggled eastwards in total disarray. This was the 'Miracle of the Vistula'. In the following weeks, Piłsudski scored success after success. At Komarów near Zamość on 31 August, Budyonny's Cavalry Army was caught in a pocket, and nearly trapped. The charges and counter-charges of the Polish and Soviet cavalry on that day have been claimed as the last great cavalry battle of European history. Izaak Babel' served in the rear of Budyonny's Red Cossacks, and related how they were chased back out of Poland in the direction from which they had come:

We reached Sitanets in the morning. I was with Volkov, the quartermaster. He found us a hut on the edge of the village. 'Wine,' I said to the old woman, 'wine, meat, and bread'. 'There ain't none here', she said, 'and I don't remember the time when there was.' With that, I took

some matches from my pocket and set fire to the rushes on the floor.
The flames blazed up. The old woman rolled on the fire and put it out.
'What are you doing, sir,' she cried, recoiling in horror. 'I'll burn you,
old hag,' I growled, 'together with that calf of yours which you have
obviously stolen.' 'Wait,' she said. She ran into the passage and brought
a jug of milk and some bread. We had not eaten half of it when bullets
began to fly outside. Volkov went to see what was happening. 'I've
saddled your horse,' he said; 'mine has been shot. The Poles are setting
up a machine-gun post only one hundred paces away.' There remained
only one horse for the two of us. I mounted in the saddle, and Volkov
clung on behind. 'We've lost the campaign', Volkov muttered. 'Yes,' I
replied.[6]

Budyonny was obliged to retire altogether. On the Niemen in
the north, Tukhachevsky was treated to another lesson in
mobile tactics. By the end of September, the Red Army
began to disintegrate; mutinies broke out in the garrison
towns of Byelorussia; disorderly troops and deserters were
running amok among the Jews and peasants of the countryside; the Poles looked set to march on Moscow unopposed.
Suddenly, Lenin sued for peace. All former machinations
were dropped. The Poles were offered as much territory in
the borderlands as they cared to take, on the one condition
that a halt to the fighting was called within ten days. In a
compromise which Piłsudski was to denounce as 'an act of
cowardice', the Polish negotiator at the peace talks, Jan
Dąbski (1880–1931), struck the historic bargain with his
Soviet counterpart, Adolf Ioffe. The Armistice was signed on
12 October, and took effect on the 18th. After much wrangling,
final terms were agreed and confirmed by the Treaty of Riga,
18 March 1921.[7] (See Map 13.)

The significance of Polish victory in 1920 was not lost on
contemporaries. In Western Europe, the feelings of many
people who heaved a sigh of relief at that time, were summed
up by the British Ambassador in Berlin, Lord D'Abernon, in
Gibbonian tones:

If Charles Martel had not checked the Saracen conquest at the Battle of
Tours, the interpretation of the Koran would now be taught at the
schools of Oxford, and her pupils might demonstrate to a circumcised
people the sanctity and truth of the revelation of Mahomet. Had Piłsudski
and Weygand failed to arrest the triumphant advance of the Soviet Army

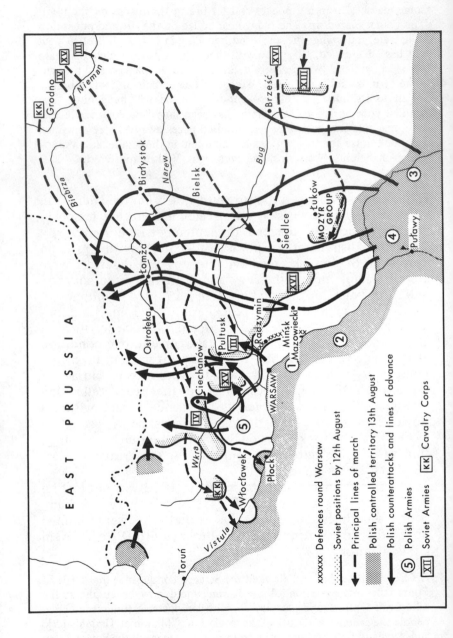

at the Battle of Warsaw, not only would Christianity have experienced a dangerous reverse, but the very existence of western civilisation would have been imperilled. The Battle of Tours saved our ancestors from the Yoke of the Koran; it is probable that the Battle of Warsaw saved Central, and parts of Western Europe from a more subversive danger — the fanatical tyranny of the Soviet.[8]

On the Soviet side, Lenin soon recognized the magnitude of the defeat; and in conversation with the German communist, Clara Zetkin, openly admitted his mistakes:

The early frost of the Red Army's retreat from Poland blighted the growth of the revolutionary flower . . . I described to Lenin how it had affected the revolutionary vanguard of the German working class . . . when the comrades with the Soviet star on their caps, in impossibly old scraps of uniform and civilian clothes, in bast shoes and torn boots, spurred their small brisk horses right up to the German frontier . . . Lenin sat silently for a few minutes, sunk in reflection. 'Yes,' he said at last, 'so it happened in Poland as perhaps it had to happen . . . In the Red Army, the Poles saw not brothers and liberators, but enemies. The Poles thought and acted not as in a social, revolutionary way but as nationalists, as imperialists. The revolution which we counted on in Poland did not take place. The workers and peasants defended their class enemy, and let our brave Red Army soldiers starve, ambushed them, and beat them to death . . . Radek predicted how it would turn out. He warned us. I was very angry and accused him of defeatism . . . But he was right in his main contention . . . No, the thought of the agonies of another winter war were unbearable. We had to make peace.'[9]

In none of these early conflicts did the Allied Powers exert the authority which they claimed to be theirs. Their efforts to arbitrate by distant preaching were despised by all the parties concerned. Their numerous Commissions and token military contingents were powerless to impose their preferred solutions. Of the three plebiscites which they tried to organize, in East Prussia, Silesia, and Cieszyn, the first two were disputed, and the last one abandoned. During the Polish—Soviet War, their offices were rejected by both sides, despite continuous negotiating. General Weygand, when he arrived in Warsaw in the crisis of August 1920 without invitation, was pointedly ignored, and played no significant part in the victory.[10]

The fundamental problem facing the Republic was the problem of integration. The population, institutions, and traditions of the three Partitions had to be welded into one new entity. At first, six currencies were in circulation; five regions — Posnania, Silesia, Cieszyn, East Galicia, and Central Lithuania (Wilno) — maintained separate administrations; there were four languages of command in the army; three legal codes; and two different railway gauges; eighteen registered political parties competed for power. In the nature of things, political life could not have closely resembled that of the established states of Western Europe. (See Map 14.)

In the formal sense, the Republic was designed as a liberal democracy. The Constitution of 17 March 1921 was modelled, at the instigation of conservative elements, on that of France's Third Republic, but at the insistence of the Peasant and Socialist parties, paid special attention to social welfare. It began with a historical invocation:

In the Name of Almighty God!

We, the people of Poland, thanking Providence for freeing us from one and a half centuries of servitude, remembering with gratitude the bravery, endurance, and selfless struggles of past generations, which unceasingly devoted all their best energies to the cause of Independence, adhering to the glorious tradition of the immortal Constitution of 3 May, striving for the welfare of the whole, united, and independent mother-country, and for her sovereign existence, might, security, and social order, and desiring to ensure the development of all moral and material powers for the good of the whole of regenerated mankind and to ensure the equality of all citizens, respect for labour, all due rights, and particularly the security of State protection, we hereby proclaim and vote this Constitutional Statute in the Legislative Assembly of the Republic of Poland.[11]

Later clauses, after subordinating the executive government to a bicameral Sejm elected by universal suffrage, guaranteed the legal equality and protection by the State of all citizens irrespective of 'origin, nationality, language, race, or religion'; the abolition of hereditary and class privileges and titles; the rights of property, whether private or collective; the regulation of land-owning with a view to creating 'private farming units capable of adequate productivity'; the rights of free expression, freedom of the press, freedom of assembly, freedom of conscience, and religious practice; the right to

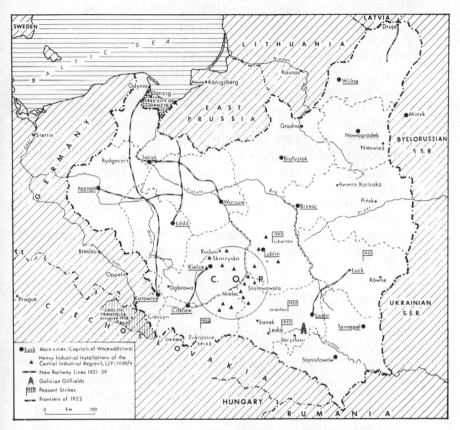

Map 14.   The Second Republic, (1921–39)

unemployment and sickness benefit, to protection against the abuses of child, female, and injurious employment, to education at the expense of the state; and the retention by Minorities of their specific nationality, language, and character.

The political stance of the leading circles was unashamedly nationalist. 'Polishness' became the touchstone of respectability. The dominant parties of the constitutional period – the PPS (Polish Socialist Party), the PSL (Polish Peasant Movement), and the National Democrats all shared the concern for national unity which under the later *Sanacja* regime assumed overriding priority. In practice, this left very little scope for minority interests or for those political groups, whether conservative or revolutionary, which were not impressed by the nationalist fashion. The Catholic Church was pushed on to the fringes of political life, whilst the Communist Party (KPRP), by boycotting the first elections, expressly prefer-ed an underground existence. The army, in contrast, which had played such a prominent role in the formation of the Republic, represented a political instrument of the first importance. In the era of the 'Colonels', which followed Piłsudski's death in 1935, it assumed a dominant position.[12]

The fires of Polish nationalism were fuelled by the fact that the ethnic minorities were so large. According to the linguistic criteria of the 1931 census, the Poles formed only 68.9 per cent of the total population. The Ukrainians with 13.9 per cent, the Yiddish-speaking Jews with 8.7 per cent, the Byelorussians with 3.1 per cent, and the Germans with 2.3 per cent, made up nearly one-third of the whole. In specific areas, they constituted a dominant majority. Their cultural sensitivities were sharpened by marked economic discrepancies. For the historical reasons far beyond the ken of the new Republic, the Ukrainian community of the south-east consisted overwhelmingly of poor, illiterate peasants. The Jews, crowded into their small town ghettos, provided a disproportionate section both of the pauperized proletariat and of the rich professional and entrepreneurial classes. The Germans in the western towns constituted a small but relatively wealthy bourgeoisie. Although the civil equality and cultural autonomy of the minorities were formally guaranteed by articles 95, 101, and 110 of the March Constitution, their separate aspirations were fundamentally incompatible with the aims of national unity as conceived by government Polish circles. From the start, the Poles were thrown into competition with the equally uncompromising nationalisms of their fellow citizens. None the less at the 1922 Elections, the Block of Nationalities returned 81 out of 444 deputies from about 16 per cent of the vote, and to the end of the decade strove to work within the system. From 1930, it transferred its support to the official BBWR (Block for Co-operation with the Government), seeking protection, as its leaders saw it, from the still greater danger to its freedoms from the rampant National Democrats. By that time, however, Polish officialdom had lost its initial willingness to meet the special demands of the national minorities. For the rest of the life of the Second Republic, intercommunal tensions steadily intensified.[13] (See Diagram D.)

Close on five million Ukrainians formed the largest single minority, compactly settled along the length of the Carpathian mountains as far west as the River Poprad, and distributed more unevenly in the south-eastern districts of Przemyśl, Rawa Ruska, Kowel, Łuck, Równe, Krzemieniec, Drohobycz, and Kołomyja (see Map OO). After the failure of the West Ukrainian Republic and of Piłsudski's alliance with Petliura, the Ukrainian population was obliged to postpone all aspirations towards autonomy. But they retained the social and cultural organizations founded in Galician days; and a number of national parties, both radical and liberal, were free to operate. The old Ukrainian Social Democratic Party (USDP), continued to function intermittently in the Polish Republic, but its efforts were minimized by the schism that drove half of its members into the illegal pro-soviet communist underground, and the other half into close co-operation with the PPS. A similar fate overtook the *Sel-Rob* (Ukrainian Socialist Peasant-Workers' Union). The Ukrainian Socialist-Radical Party (USRP) with its journal *Hromadskiy Holos* (Communal Voice) recruited significant support among the peasantry in Volhynia and in the Stanisławów district. In the company of the liberal Ukrainian National-Democratic Union (UNDO), which had inherited many of the older social, cultural, and co-operative organizations together with the newspaper *Dilo* (The Cause) in Lwów, it participated in Polish parliamentary

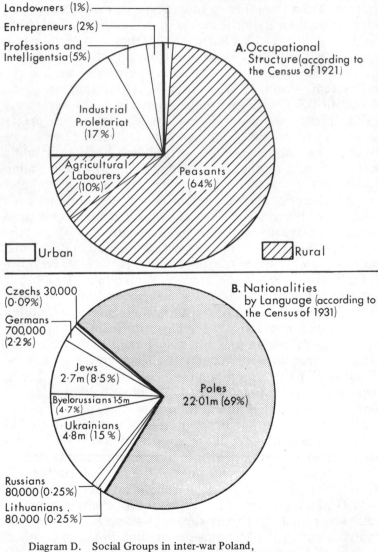

Landowners (1%)
Entrepreneurs (2%)
Professions and Intelligentsia (5%)

A. Occupational Structure (according to the Census of 1921)

Industrial Proletariat (17%)

Agricultural Labourers (10%)

Peasants (64%)

☐ Urban   ▨ Rural

Czechs 30,000 (0·09%)
Germans 700,000 (2·2%)

B. Nationalities by Language (according to the Census of 1931)

Jews 2·7m (8·5%)
Byelorussians 1·5m (4·7%)
Ukrainians 4·8m (15%)

Poles 22·01m (69%)

Russians 80,000 (0·25%)
Lithuanians 80,000 (0·25%)

Diagram D.   Social Groups in inter-war Poland,
a) by occupation (1921)   b) by nationality (1931)

life. Yet none of these parties could stem the rising hostility
of the Polish community at large against Ukrainian separatism.
Bit by bit, conciliatory politics gave way to terrorism. The
illegal Ukrainian Military Organization (UOV) and its successor from 1929, the Organization of Ukrainian Nationalists
(OUN) operating from sanctuaries in Germany and Austria,
launched the campaign of sabotage and murder which in the
1930s undermined all foreseeable hopes of reconciliation. The
assassination in 1931 of Tadeusz Hołowko (1889—1931), a
prominent socialist theoretician and associate of Piłsudski,
and in 1934 of the Minister of the Interior, Col. Bronisław
Pieracki (1895–1934), provoked the *Sanacja* regime into
vicious reprisals. Minor partisan campaigns in 1932–3 in
Volhynia, Polesie, and in the Lesko area, were answered by
the advance of the Polish army and police in strength, and
by the razing of villages suspected of harbouring the rebels.
The internment camp at Bereza Kartuska was first constructed
in 1934 to accommodate the prisoners of this emergency.
Many Ukrainian schools were closed; Ukrainian peasants
unable to read or write in Polish were struck from the electoral
register by over-zealous officials. Polish military colonists
were settled in frontier areas. The Ukrainian national movement, alienated in Poland and horrified by the stories of
forced collectivization and mass starvation across the border
in the USSR, looked increasingly towards Germany for
comfort and support.[14]

Three million Jews suffered from other difficulties – from
economic regression, from a demographic explosion, from
growing racial discrimination, and not least from excessive
publicity. At the same time, for the twenty years of the
Second Republic, many spheres of Jewish life in Poland
experienced a last brief period of relative well-being. Jewish
schools, both primary and secondary, educated a whole new
generation of youngsters. Several private Jewish school
systems – the *Khorev* system run by Agudat Israel, the secular
Hebrew *Tarbut* system of the Zionists, the Yiddish CYSHO,
and the bilingual, Polish–Hebrew *Yavne* system of the
Mizrachi – competed both with each other and with the
Polish state schools. The Jewish press flourished, both in the
Polish and Yiddish languages. *Nasz Przegląd* (Our Review) in

Warsaw, *Chwila* (The Moment) in Lwów, and *Nowy Dziennik* (New Daily) in Cracow, enjoyed wide circulation. The Jewish theatre, especially in Warsaw and Wilno, reached the peak of its achievement. Jewish film-makers produced scores of Yiddish movies. Jewish scholars earned wide reputations. Jewish writers of the Yiddish 'New Wave' issued their first rebellious manifestos. The *Yidischer Visnshaftlekher Institut* (Jewish Scientific Institute, YIVO), founded in Wilno in 1925, the central agency of Yiddish activities, could fairly claim to be one of the foremost centres of Jewish culture in the world. Jewish politicians of the most variegated persuasions operated freely, both in municipal and in parliamentary politics. In the first Sejm of 1922, the Jewish caucus claimed 35 members, surpassing the representation of the socialists. In the Piłsudski era, the Agudat Israel threw its weight behind the BBWR. Even in the 1935–9 period, when all democratic parties were curtailed, a few Jewish deputies and senators continued to sit. Figures such as Rabbi Moshe Elihu Halpern or Yitzhak Gruenbaum, the Zionist leader, were men of national standing. In the 1930s, the ascendancy of the conservative parties was overtaken by the Zionists, whose influence, however, was fragmented into at least seven main groupings – the Revisionists, the Mizrachi, the General and Galician Zionists, the *Hitahadut* (United Zionist Labour Party), and the two factions of Paole Zion. Outside the Sejm, especially in the Jewish Trade Unions, the *Bund* carried considerable weight. Jewish members featured prominently both in the PPS and the KPP. At the local level, the Jewish communal organizations, the *kehillot,* functioned under the supervision of the government *Starosta.* By the law of 1927, they were elected by Jewish male suffrage and were empowered to raise their own finances. Jewish social bodies, from hospitals and orphanages, to sports clubs, musical societies, and insurance and co-operative associations, proliferated in all areas. Jewish middle-class life, in particular, moved along in an aura of confidence and affluence. In 1919, Roza Pomerantz-Meltzer, a Zionist, gained the distinction of being Poland's first woman deputy. In 1938, Lazar Rundsztejn, a Jewish flyweight, won his class in the national boxing championship. Anyone who has seen the remarkable records which these people left behind them, and which have been collected in YIVO's post-war headquarters in New York, cannot fail to note the essential dynamism of Polish Jewry at this juncture. All was not well; but neither was it unrelieved gloom.[15] (See also pp. 260–3.)

Two million Byelorussians shared the experience of their fellow Ruthenians, the Ukrainians. Together with 'Western Ukraine', 'Western Byelorussia' formed the heart of Poland's most backward region, the so-called 'Polska-B' (Second Class Poland), and had no separate political or administrative status. After an initial period when far-reaching concessions were made in the realm of a free press, democratic elections, national education, and political organizations, 1924 saw the onset of an official reaction against incipient Byelorussian separatism. The Byelorussian language, now wedded to the Latin alphabet, was given little support; and three hundred Byelorussian schools were turned over to Polish teachers. The Byelorussian *Hramada* (Commune), a socialist peasant movement, was broken up by police action in 1928, and its leaders imprisoned. In the 1930s the Byelorussian countryside took its share of punishment from the *Sanacja*'s pacification campaigns. Polish officialdom tended to favour Byelorussian Catholics, whom they classified as *Białopolaki* (White Poles), whilst suspecting the Orthodox Byelorussian *Rusini* (Ruthenes) of potential irredentism. A new wave of oppression began in 1935 when more schools, Orthodox churches, and cultural societies were closed down. By 1939, the Byelorussians were still largely unpoliticized. The few that were politically active showed little enthusiasm for the Polish connection. They were due for a rude awakening.[16]

Close to one million Germans were served by a plethora of political, cultural, and social organizations, many of which were amalgamated in 1931 in the central *Rat der Deutschen in Polen* (Council of Germans in Poland). The German Socialist Workers Party in Poland (DSAP) was formed in 1925 from older German socialist groups working separately in Upper Silesia, Łódź, and Poznań. It ran its own trade unions and youth movement, whilst co-operating closely with the PPS. Both these organizations were opposed by a nationalist *Jungdeutsche Partei* (Young German Party) operating from Bielsko (Bielitz). In the 1930s, the entire German community felt the shock-waves of Hitler's rise to power, and from 1935 was courted by the local *Landesgruppe-Polen* (Regional Group-Poland) of the Nazi Party and its press organ, *Idee and Wille* (Idea and Will).[17]

Other national minorities, including the Russians and Lithuanians of the north-east, and the Czechs of the extreme south-west, had insufficient numbers to influence anything but the local scene.

The temper of political life was unremittingly radical. All the leading personalities of the 1920s from Wincenty Witos the Peasant leader and three times Premier, to Ignacy Daszyński, the Socialist, and to Piłsudski himself, professed distinctly radical ideas. Even the National Democrats, who formed the main opposition both to the early coalition governments and to the later *Sanacja* regime, must be described as 'Right-Radicals' whose stance on most issues of the day was anything but conservative. The traditional conservative movements, such as those which had once operated in Galicia or were centred on the clerical and landowning interests, were relegated to sulky subordination. A society in which two-thirds of the population was engaged in subsistence agriculture and where one-third consisted of national minorities, could hardly afford the gradualist, liberal climate of prosperous and well-established western countries.

The task of reintegrating Polish society into a coherent whole began as soon as the Second Republic was created. The task was formidable. The material resources, and as it proved the time available, were extremely limited. According to the Census of 1921, the geographical distribution of the population put 25 per cent in the towns and 75 per cent in the countryside; the occupational structure was made up of manual workers (27 per cent, of which almost half were agricultural labourers); peasants (65 per cent); intelligentsia and professions (5 per cent); entrepreneurs (2 per cent) and landowners (under 1 per cent). Yet statistical analysis does little to describe the full extent of social problems. Old loyalties and old patterns of behaviour died hard. The impact of new all-Polish institutions — Schools, Civil Service, Taxation, Army — was bound to be slow. Little could be done by way of financial initiatives to subsidize significant common enterprises.

Industrialization continued modestly in channels forged before independence. Inevitably perhaps, tensions increased. Indeed, in the 1930s, serious polarization was observable both between the state authorities and the masses, and between the dominant Polish majority and the other national minorities. One of the few factors militating for social cohesion was to be found abroad, where the repellent prospect of incorporation into Nazi Germany or Stalinist Russia gave all Polish citizens, irrespective of their differences, a strong sense of common interest. (See Diagram D.)

In a rural society, agrarian problems automatically took priority. At first, great hopes were placed in Land Reform, as demanded by the PSL. On 10 July 1919, the Sejm declared in favour of breaking up estates of more than 400 hectares; and on 15 July 1920, at the height of the Red Army's offensive, a law was passed providing for the purchase of surplus land at half its market value. Neither action brought results. Finally on 20 July 1925, at the third attempt, the Sejm set a minimum target of 200,000 hectares per annum to be parcelled out among the peasants at full market value. Altogether, between 1919 and 1938, 2,655,000 hectares passed into peasant hands; over one-fifth of the landed estates of Church, State, and private landowners were diminished, and 734,000 new holdings were created. In itself, this was a considerable achievement. But in the event, it did little to relieve the pressure on the land or the poverty of the multiplying peasant masses. By virtue of hard experience, it was found that the conditions in the countryside were actually deteriorating. After a brief revival in 1928–9, the rural economy fell into a decline from which it never fully recovered. In the next decade, farm prices were halved; the cash income of peasant families dropped to almost one-third; government subsidies to agriculture were quartered. As borrowers defaulted on loans, credit was suspended. Investment in machinery virtually stopped. The rate of parcellation slowed to a crawl. In so far as the crisis in Poland was caused by the world recession, it was not exceptional. But the lack of finance, both state and private, which might have ameliorated the most acute effects, led to far greater suffering than in Western Europe. Social ills multiplied. Peasant families could not feed their children, or, for want of the obligatory pair of shoes, could not send them to school. Usury flourished, together with drunkenness. The Jewish money-lender and tavern-keeper for no fault of his own, attracted general disgust. Sequestrations of debtors' property, violently executed, were violently resisted. Political militancy increased. The *Związek Rolników* (Farmers' Union) founded in 1929 by members of the PSL 'Wyzwolenie' opposed the lethargy of the government-sponsored Central Society of Agricultural Circles (CTKR). The reunited *Stronnictwo Ludowe* attracted growing support, and was held responsible for the disturbances which occurred with mounting frequency. The first strike broke out at Limanowa near Cracow, in February 1932, and quickly spread to the Warsaw area. Peasants refused to pay the tax levied on goods taken to market, and demanded a reduction of prices in the products of the state monopolies. Hundreds of protesters and SL activists were arrested. At Lubla near Krosno, and at Apanów near Cracow, the police opened fire when the peasants insisted on holding their traditional Whitsun festival in defiance of a ban on public meetings. The first four victims of the troubles were killed. In June, a more serious incident occurred at Berehy Dolne, near Sanok. Here the peasants were protesting against Count Potocki's voluntary 'Festival of Labour', where they had all been invited to give a day's free work reconstructing the local highway. They feared the return of serfdom. Five hundred police, a battalion of infantry, and a squadron of war-planes arrived to restore order. Here, 6 persons were killed; 278 held, and 3 condemned to death for incitement. In 1933, the confrontations between peasants and police assumed the proportions of a minor guerrilla war, especially in the districts of Łańcut, Rzeszów, Leżajsk, and Przeworsk. There were scores of deaths, hundreds of police casualties, and thousands of arrests. For three years, a breathing-space was enforced by the Government's proscription of the SL, and by the appointment of Juliusz Poniatowski, a former member of the PSL (Wyzwolenie), to the Ministry of Agriculture. Unfortunately, there were no quick solutions. Poniatowski's long-term answer to rural overpopulation was to support industrialization, and to invest in the development of 'Polska B'.

In 1936–7, rural disturbances recurred. As a result of earlier disillusionments, the policies of the Peasant Movement (SL) were undergoing marked radicalization, and the movement's militant youth sections – the Union of Rural Youth's *'Beacon Fires'* (ZMW – *Wici*) – were calling the peasants to a campaign of active struggle. This was the most important manifestation of *Agrarism* (Peasant Power) in modern Poland, and a prelude to the formation of the Peasant Battalions in the Resistance of the Second World War. Despite the closure of its branches, and the arrest of its most prominent supporters, such as Professor Stanisław Kot, the historian, the SL continued to expand its membership and influence. In August 1937, the extraordinary solidarity of peasant strikers in the districts of Cracow and Kielce led to more brutal repressions, and to some forty deaths. Because the strikes were so widely scattered, however, the authorities had no easy means of dealing with them:

When the strike started, the roads leading to Brzesko Nowe were closed. Numerous peasants joined in, some from conviction, others from curiosity. A small number of blacklegs heading for the market were left to the care of our SL members from Grobla, who, in the best of humour, broke a few of the eggs concealed in their pockets and bosoms. There were no loaded carts at all, except for that of a certain Piorów, a cattle dealer, whose shaft was smashed.

At 8 o'clock the police arrived with five men. They fixed bayonets, loaded their weapons, and ordered the strikers to disperse. They arrested me, together with my colleague, Zygmunt Mackiewicz, the local secretary of the *Wici*. . . . When one of the gendarmes tried to prod comrade Siudak with his bayonet, Siudak pulled a sabre from under his overcoat and parried the attack with professional skill. Overawed by the strikers' resolution, the police retreated, taking us with them. But on the way to Brzesko we met with a gang of peasants working on the Vistula dykes, and they released us from arrest. In this last incident, the initiative was taken by a non-unionized peasant, Antoni Zakrzewski, who started to belabour the policemen with a shovel . . .

The epilogue to the story took place in the District Court at Proszowice . . . where on the basis of charges laid against me, I was given concurrent sentences of two months' imprisonment.[19]

Clearly, tensions in the countryside were running high. No one could have dreamed that within a couple of years these same rural backwaters would offer the only tenuous refuge from disturbances of a far more catastrophic kind.

The problems of the industrial proletariat, though real enough, were less fundamental than those of the peasantry. In a stage of limited industrialization, the Polish worker often regarded the chance of employment in industry as an extra bonus, as a stroke of good fortune; and he could usually return to his village in hard times. Industrial wages, which to modern eyes look derisory, ensured an income that was twice as high as that of the average peasant family. Official unemployment figures which reached a maximum of 446,000 or 10 per cent of the industrial labour-force in 1936, ignore the far more serious unemployment concealed in the over-populated rural areas, usually estimated at between 5 and 6 million, or up to 45 per cent overall. In this situation, the workers' tolerance of harsh conditions was much higher than it has since become. The problems which arose were of a different order than those encountered in Western Europe, where an over-all unemployment rate in Great Britain of 10 per cent in the 1930s was regarded as a unique national catastrophe. It is amazing how little trouble there was. Within the limitations imposed by the economic crisis, much was done. The eight-hour day was introduced by the Sejm in 1919; safety precautions were governed by the statutory legislation; living conditions were improved by the Society of Workers' Estates (TOR). Yet the direct intervention of the government in welfare was largely confined to state-owned enterprises. Less than 20 per cent of the registered unemployed qualified for relief payments of any sort. The task of ameliorating working-class life was largely left to overburdened charities, or to self-help organizations run by the PPS and the NZR. The abuses of private employers were not easily controlled, and disruptive action against state enterprises carried heavy criminal penalties. Industrial strikes occurred on a large scale in 1922–3 during the Hyperflation, and in 1933–7 at the height of the Slump. On the former occasion, the trouble began with a general strike of railwaymen in February 1921, which was answered by the militarization of the railways. In November the following year, the miners of Dąbrowa launched another general strike against reductions in pay; and courts-martial were established to deal with troublemakers. This was the prelude to the 'Cracow Rising' of 6 November 1923,

which flared from a general strike called by the PPS. Street
demonstrations turned suddenly into pitched battles with the
police. Soldiers summoned to restore order came to the aid
of the workers, who for a couple of hours found themselves
in control of the city. By which time, thirty-two workers and
policemen were dead, and the organizers had called an end to
the proceedings. On this occasion, more protracted but less
violent disturbances occurred in Łódź, and Dąbrowa. The
industrial 'sit-in', known as the 'Polish Strike', provoked legal
sanctions against state employees, and inspired a stricter
definition in the Criminal Code of the right to strike. Polish
workers had little to be pleased about, except for the fact
that they were not peasants.[20]

In economic policy, the necessary priorities were perfectly
clear. In the first years of the Republic's existence, the entire
economic system had to be constructed from scratch. There
was no integrated infrastructure, no common currency, no
established financial institutions or government agencies.
There was no direct rail link between Warsaw and several
provincial cities. Until the opening of Gdynia in 1927, there
was no Polish seaport. In 1918–20, the German *OstMark,* the
Austrian crown, and the Polish mark, were all in circulation
and all inflating wildly. In November 1918, the rate of the
Polish mark against the US dollar stood at 1:9; by January
1923 it reached 1:15,000,000. Stop-gap taxation barely
covered 10 per cent of expenditure. The budget could not be
balanced until 1926. From the start, the priorities were first
stability, and then investment. The problems were of the
same magnitude as those facing Russia. Yet the chosen
methods excluded coercion. In the 1920s a series of reforms
largely associated with the name of Władysław Grabski,
brought matters under control. The introduction of the
'Złoty' currency, the establishment of the Bank Polski in
1924, the diversion of taxation from wealth on to income
and turnover, the raising of foreign loans in America, France,
and Italy, and the growth of investment funds for Public Works
and rural improvements, all contributed to the emergence of
a viable system. Thereafter, external factors, including the
German Tariff War of 1926–30, the Great Slump of 1931–4,
and finally the diplomatic crisis of the 1930s which put defence

costs to 27.5 per cent of government expenditure, all strained Poland's modest economy to the utmost. Polish industry encountered unsurmountable difficulties. According to some present-day observers, it was passing through the 'inevitable symbiosis of late, imperialist capitalism'. In other people's eyes, it was suffering from the obvious effects of Independence, which had destroyed the old infrastructure and had disrupted former markets, without providing adequate resources for adjusting to new conditions. Its managers were attempting to develop along western capitalist lines, without the full support of western capital. The population of the Second Republic was less industrialized in 1929 (13.2 per cent) than that of the former Congress Kingdom in 1900 (17.6 per cent). The accession of the eastern Borderlands with their very primitive rural society in no way compensated for the loss of the vast Russian market, which under hostile Soviet management was permanently closed. The windfall of Upper Silesia was blighted by its severance from traditional services and customers in Germany. Poland's low credit rating deterred foreign investment, which, far from putting the country at the mercy of predatory speculators, was sadly missed. Fundamental shortcomings in the railway network and in power supplies demanded investment beyond the state's capacity. The main railway line between Silesia and the newly constructed port of Gdynia, designed to facilitate coal exports, was not completed until 1929; the main line from Warsaw to Cracow via the Kielce Tunnel was built in 1933; the electrification campaign of 1936–9 increased power supplies by 600 per cent over former levels, but even so did not achieve the same results as in Germany or Russia. Government investments were concentrated in the armaments sector, notably in the azote factory at Mościce, and the weapons establishments. As a result, in relation to other European countries, Poland remained industrially very underdeveloped. It was particularly vulnerable to the pressures of the Slump, and in most of the main sectors failed to regain the production levels of 1913. In those few sectors where production made significant increases, as in the food-processing industries, prices were so low that little impact was made on the over-all situation:[21]

	1913	1923	1929	1932	1935	1938
Gross Industrial Production	(100)	71.2	85	–	70	98.7
Coal Production (million tons)	41 (100)	36 87	46 112	–	–	38 92
Iron Ore (million tons)	0.493 (100)	0.449 91	0.660 133	–	–	0.879 178
Steel (million tons)	1.677 (100)	1.129 67	1.377 82	0.570 34	–	1.441 93
Oil (million tons)	1.114 (100)	–	–	–	–	0.507 45
Finished cotton	(100)	–	–	54.2	–	84.7
Salt (million tons)	0.193 (100)	–	–	–	–	0.647 (335)
Sugar (thousands of tons)	57 (100)	–	822	–	309	491 (861)

The generally bleak picture of inter-war industry was lightened by a determined government initiative launched in March 1936. Having maintained a stable currency throughout the Depression, albeit at great social cost, and anticipating a balanced budget for the first time since 1929, the *Sanacja* authorities ventured precociously into state planning. The Chief planner was Vice-Premier and Minister of Finance, Eugeniusz Kwiatkowski (born 1888). The Plan, which sought to match Poland's economic needs with her strategic requirements, was to be mainly funded from internal sources. It was assisted by one important loan from France of 2,600 million francs. It gave priority to war industry, and then to improvements in the industrial base – especially to railways, electricity, and gas. Its principal achievement was the construction of the Central Industrial Region (COP) in the so-called 'Security Triangle' on the confines of the palatinates of Cracow, Kielce, and Lwów. Two major installations, the hydroelectric station at Roznow and the steel combine at Stalowa Wola were well advanced by the time that War intervened. In this same short period, all branches of industry showed clear signs of rapid recovery from the Slump. In terms of the Industrial Index of 1928 (=100), the Polish performance by 1938–9, at 119, was superior to that of either Belgium at 81 or France at 82. For post-war analysts, who for political reasons have often painted the unplanned pre-war capitalist economy in unflattering colours, the very existence of the State Plan of 1936–9 with its accompanying industrial record represents a unique embarrassment. To uncommitted observers, it is less surprising that broadly similar dictatorial regimes, pre-war and post-war, faced with broadly similar problems, should have followed broadly similar policies.[22]

In the educational sphere, daunting problems faced the new authorities. When Polish-speakers formed barely two-thirds of the population, and when barely two-thirds of the Polish speakers were officially literate, one arrives at the stark conclusion that literate Poles formed only 44 per cent of society as a whole. Despite immense progress in a short time, conflicts soon arose. A 'Teachers' Sejm' assembled in 1919, to prepare programmes for the unified state system of compulsory, free education which began to function three years later. By the school-year of 1928/9, 96 per cent of children of school age between 7 and 14 years were attending school. By the end of the inter-war period, global illiteracy had been substantially reduced. In the 1930s reforms initiated by Minister Janusz Jędrzejewicz (1889–1951), and by his successor and brother Wacław Jędrzejewicz, encouraged the development of secondary education. Inevitably, in a developing society where resources were scarce, educational supply lagged far behind popular demand. Only the most exceptional peasant children could hope to obtain higher education. The national minorities were largely left to their own devices. Although few active attempts were made to suppress minority schools, the authorities made no secret of the fact that state funds would be used to favour the Polish sector. In the late 1930s an official *numerus clausus* sought to restrict Jewish pupils in selected schools and faculties to numbers proportionate to their position in the population at large. Humiliating 'Jew-benches' made their appearance. At the same time, the number of Ukrainian schools fell dramatically, from 2,500 in 1911 in Austrian Galicia, to 461 in 1938. In this respect, the Polish Republic proved less tolerant, and less successful than Galicia, and laid itself open to charges of cultural chauvinism.[23]

The role of the Polish Army extended far beyond the military sphere. It was a principal instrument for forging social and national unity. It rose above class and minority interests, and enjoyed great social prestige. In the 1920s it resisted close parliamentary control, and from 1926 was used by Piłsudski to manipulate the constitutional system. After Piłsudski's death in 1935, its activities in connection with the OZoN movement became overtly political. The personalities of Marshal Śmigły-Rydz and Col. Józef Beck dominated the so-called 'Goverment of the Colonels'. Throughout the interwar period, compulsory male conscription was in force. In the war years, in 1919—21 and again in 1939, well over one million men were mobilized. The peacetime establishment rose from 266,000 in 1923, to 350,000 in 1935 with 30 Infantry Divisions and 10 Cavalry Brigades. Under Piłsudski's personal management, a General Inspectorate of the Armed Forces (GISZ) assumed control of the *Tor wojenny* (War Track), whilst the Ministry of Military Affairs was left to supervise the ten military regions together with the normal running of the army's peacetime duties, the *Tor pokojowy* (Peace Track). By the outbreak of war in 1939, one of two motorized Armoured Brigades was still in the process of formation. Both the Air Force and the Navy were small by contemporary European standards.[24]

Unlike the army, the Roman Catholic Church did not possess any formal link with the State. In the March Constitution, it was awarded no more than 'the leading place among other religious denominations enjoying equal rights'. The ruling class, both before and after 1926, was decidedly anticlerical in tone. The *Chadecja* (Christian Democratic Party) enjoyed only one doubtful moment of power, when in 1923 it entered a brief coalition government together with Witos's PSL Party. Its right-wing rival, Dmowski's National Democratic movement, with whom in their mutual distress a tactical alliance might have been possible, never gained power. In 1925, the Concordat signed by the government with the Vatican gave the Church in Poland wide-ranging autonomy. The Latin, Uniate, and Armenian Rites were officially recognized. The clergy were freed from military service, from prosecution in the courts, and from personal income tax. They were given a large measure of control over the teaching of compulsory religious education in state-schools. Former church property, confiscated by the partitioning powers and now in the state possession, was to be used for the upkeep of ecclesiastical salaries. No agreement was reached over the conflicting claims of Church and State over the marriage law. Regulations deriving from before 1918 remained in force. Divorce was possible in districts of the former Prussian Partition, but not elsewhere. In the 1930s in conditions of growing political and social tension, the Church hierarchy moved into the attack. The 'Catholic Action' organization, introduced into Poland in 1930 under the Presidency of Count A. Bniński, was established in every parish in the country. Its subsidiary organizations – the Catholic Men's League, Catholic Women's League, Catholic Youth League – counted more members than any political party. A Plenary Synod, called at Częstochowa in 1936 for the first time in three centuries, and the 'International Congress of Christ the King' held in Poznań in 1937, were both manifestations of the Church's offensive against atheism. The growing *rapprochement* between the Church and the post-Piłsudski Camp of National Unity, inspired by their common fear of disaffected non-Catholic minorities, was interrupted by the outbreak of war.[25]

In foreign policy, the leaders of the Polish Republic put their trust in genuine independence, and in non-alignment. At Piłsudski's prompting, no more credence was given to the blandishments of the western allied governments, than in Germany or Russia. Poland's bitter experience in 1919–20 when she was left to fight the Red Army alone, permanently damaged French and British prestige. The French Military Convention of May 1921 was pointedly signed after the likelihood of further fighting was removed. Poland did not join the Little Entente. In the 1930s, the Treaty of Non-aggression signed with the Soviet Union on 25 January 1932 was matched on 26 January 1934 by a similar Ten-Year Pact with Germany. It is probably true that the Polish government was more impressed by the known monstrosities of Stalinist Russia than by the as yet potential horrors of the Nazi Reich. But there is plenty of evidence to suggest that Piłsudski seriously considered a preventive war against Hitler, if only the western powers had shown willing. 'Strict mutuality' was the basis for relations with both great neighbours, and the Doctrine of the Two Enemies was never abandoned.[26]

The watershed of political life was reached on 12–14 May 1926 when Marshal Józef Piłsudski mounted a *coup d'état* against the system which he himself had initiated. He had spent the four previous years in retirement, having refused to accept the Presidency under the restricted conditions of the March Constitution, and having protested against civilian interference in the running of the army. He had watched the powerlessness and instability of successive coalition governments with increasing disgust. He had taken particular offence at the way in which necessary reforms were constantly delayed and obstructed by the growing influence of his right-wing opponents, and by the sordid deals of party politicians. In May 1926, Wincenty Witos was preparing to form the third Right-Centre Coalition in three years. A right-wing coup was widely expected, to break the parliamentary impasse. The Left feared for its future. Piłsudski was persuaded to stage an armed demonstration. His aims were far from clear, and his mood anything but magisterial. He wanted to warn the Right against any adventures of their own, and would probably have been satisfied with the resignation of Witos's Coalition. He left his home in Sulejówek to the east of Warsaw on the morning of 12 May and, in the company of several mutinous Legionary Regiments, marched to Praga, and occupied the approaches to the Vistula bridges. But there he met with unexpected resistance. The President of the Republic, Stanisław Wojciechowski (1869–1953), an old socialist and associate of Piłsudski, drove down from the Belweder Palace and confronted the Marshal in the middle of the Kierbedź Bridge. It was a poignant moment. The President made it clear that any resort to force would be opposed by the government, and by those units of the army which remained loyal. The Marshal would be obliged either to accept political defeat and humiliation, or to turn his guns on to his former friends and subjects. But, having gone so far, there was no turning back. Fighting began in the afternoon, and continued for three days. A legionary regiment slipped across the river into the northern suburbs. The airport and railway station were captured early on, but control of the city centre was fiercely contested. Rival machine-gun posts were firing from all the main intersections. Some three hundred soldiers were killed, a thousand and more wounded. Taking the country as a whole, the government undoubtedly enjoyed the greater support and commanded the larger force. But the issue was settled by the socialist railwaymen whose strike paralysed communications and prevented government reinforcements from reaching the capital. On the morning of 14 May, Wojciechowski and Witos capitulated in the Belweder, and resigned from office. For the remaining nine years of his life, Piłsudski was to be the effective ruler of Poland. The Piłsudski camp was destined to dominate the Republic for the rest of its existence.[27]

The effects of the May Coup were profound, but not unduly sensational. Piłsudski refused to take formal control of political affairs, preferring to prolong a pseudo-parliamentary charade than to rule by personal dictatorship. Kazimierz Bartel (1882–1941), sometime Professor of Mathematics at Lwów Polytechnic, was appointed as Premier to the first of many short-lived governments which Piłsudski inspired. Ignacy Mościcki (1867–1946), sometime Professor of Chemistry at Lwów Polytechnic, was appointed President. The regime which emerged in 1926 kept power until the collapse of the Republic in 1939. It took its name from the slogan of *Sanacja,* which may be translated as a 'Return to (political) health', or, in view of its military overtones, as 'Ablutionism'. At all events, it was guided by a forceful, but very imprecise ideology, akin to Moral Rearmament, and born in a barrack-room of the contention that the sin in men's souls could be scrubbed clean by spit and polish. (According to its opponents, it blended the philosophies of Nietzsche and Kant – *nietzsche* in Varsovian slang meaning 'rubbish', and *kant* meaning a 'swindle'.) Its main instrument at the outset was the so-called Non-Party Block for Co-operation with the Government (BBWR) organized in 1927 by Col. Walery Sławek (1879–1939) with a view to managing the forthcoming elections. In 1928, having obtained the support of only one-quarter of the electorate in open voting, it lost confidence in proper methods, and in 1930 ensured a majority vote by arresting its leading opponents or cancelling their candidacies. Thereafter, it could not be easily challenged by legal means, especially when in April 1935 a new Constitution was introduced, giving wide powers of discretion to the President over the executive government and the Sejm. In the period after Piłsudski's death on the ninth anniversary of the May Coup, it inspired the formation by Col. Adam Koc (1891–1969) of the so-called Camp of Nation Unification (OZoN) with a much more disciplined and exclusive organization on the military model. The strident, and increasingly chauvinistic accents of OZoN, and its leading personalities such as General S. Skwarczyński and Marshal Edward Śmigły-Rydz (1886–1941), reflected the tensions which were growing in the internal no less than in the external sphere.[28]

Throughout the *Sanacja* era, the effectiveness of the democratic Opposition was gradually whittled away. In the first years, the main political parties of the Sejm — the Christian Democrats (ChD), the National Workers (NPR), the Peasant Movements (PSL), and the Socialists (PPS) — joined together to challenge the activities of the government-sponsored BBWR, and in 1929 to form the inter-party alliance of the Centre-Left (Centrolew). In June 1930, fearing that Piłsudski might face them with a further *fait accompli,* they called a Convention of People's Rights whose aims were no longer confined to parliamentary manœuvres:

The representations of Polish democracy, assembled on 29 June 1930 in Cracow, declare the following:
WHEREAS Poland has been living for more than four years under the power of the actual dictatorship of Józef Piłsudski: the will of the Dictator is carried out by changing governments: the President of the Republic is subject to the will of the Dictator: the nation's confidence in the law of its own State has been undermined . . . and the people have been deprived of any influence whatsoever over the Republic's domestic and foreign policy . . .
WE RESOLVE:
1. To struggle for the rights and freedom of the people is not merely the struggle of the Sejm and Senate, but the struggle of the whole nation.
2. Without the abolition of dictatorship, it is impossible to control the economic depression or to solve Poland's great domestic problems . . .
3. The abolition of dictatorship is the indispensable condition for preserving the independence, and assuming the integrity of the Republic . . .

AND WE DECLARE:

1. That the struggle for the abolition of Józef Piłsudski's dictatorship has been undertaken jointly by us all, and will be pursued jointly to victory;
2. that only a government possessing the confidence of the Sejm and of the nation will meet with our support . . .
3. that any attempt at a *coup d'état* will be met with determined resistance;
4. that the nation will acknowledge no obligations to a government which seizes power by such a coup . . .
5. that every attempt at terrorism will be met with physical force.

We further declare that the President of the Republic, Ignacy Moscicki, unmindful of his oath, having openly taken his stand with the dictatorship . . . should resign.*

The Convention states that it is the will of the broad masses of the Polish people to maintain peaceful relations with all neighbours . . . but also states that any attempts on the part of imperialists . . . to change the frontiers of the Republic will meet with determined resistance . . .

Long Live the Independent Polish People's Republic! Down with Dictatorship! Long live the Government of the Workers and Peasants' Convention![29]

Piłsudski's response was harsh. In the night of 9/10 September, the leaders of the Centre-Left were arrested, and confined in the military prison at Brześć-nad-Bugiem. In October, at the opening session of the Sejm, the Chamber of Deputies was packed with military officers carrying revolvers and drawn swords. To his lasting credit, Daszyński, the Marshal of the Sejm, refused to proceed under the threat of coercion. But in December, the gerrymandering of the BBWR finally produced the desired result at the elections. The leaders of the Centre-Left were put on trial. The final sentence on 15 June 1933 condemned A. Ciołkosz, S. Dubois, M. Mastek, and J. Putek, among others, to three years' imprisonment. The principal defendants, Wincenty Witos, Kazimierz Bagiński, Władysław Kiernik, Herman Liberman, and Adam Pragier, were sentenced in their absence, having been permitted to escape abroad. Their portraits appeared in every police station and town hall throughout the land on the lists of wanted men. Meanwhile, the right-wing opposition, in the form of Dmowski's Camp of Great Poland (OWP) was suffering its own eclipse. Formed in 1926 in response to Piłsudski's resurgence, it had drifted deeper and deeper into nationalist xenophobia. Disbanded by the police in March 1933 on the grounds of public security, it spawned several gangs of political mobsters, including Bolesław Piasecki's 'Falanga' (Phalanx) and the 'ABC Group'. Towards the end of the decade, many of its less hysterical members moved into the OZoN camp, thus ending for a time at least the ancient feud between the disciples of the dead Piłsudski and those of the retired Dmowski. Rivalry between the leftist and rightist wings of the opposition ensured a smooth path for the regime, and made further oppressive measures unnecessary. Abroad, opposition was focused on Paderewski's home at Morges in Switzerland. Despite his formal retirement from politics, the former Premier kept in close touch with his old associates, and his correspondence from this period reveals his growing unease at the conduct of the *Sanacja* regime. In 1932, news of the peasant strikes was sufficiently convincing for General Sikorski to hint at the possibility of the *Sanacja*'s impending collapse:

. . . There are many signs that the *Sanacja* camp, burdened with the consequences of the violence of 1926 and devoid of any legitimizing idea, is beginning to tremble and to fall apart. Today, the so-called ruling 'élite' of the state is drawn from a clique of colonels, who head one of the most stupid and harmful dictatorships imaginable, but who now see that the masses are not there simply to obey and to carry out orders . . . The demonstration in Zamość, impressive by virtue both of its mood and of its numbers (15,000) . . . shows that 'the strong government' is no longer in control of the situation . . .[30]

However, the *Sanacja* regime did not collapse, even after Piłsudski's death. In 1937–8, when the Morges Front was formally organized with the participation of Paderewski, Sikorski, Witos, Korfanty, and Józef Haller, it was more concerned with foreign policy than with domestic affairs; and it decisively influenced neither.

No one can claim that the policies of the Second Republic were an unbounded success. Parliamentary democracy collapsed after only eight years, and was never replaced by any consistent system. The arbitrary acts of the *Sanacja* regime were no more edifying than the political squabbles which preceded them. The May Coup, in the words of one bold spirit, must be likened to 'an attack by bandits on a lunatic asylum'.[31]

Violence was never far from the surface. The assassination in December 1922 of the first constitutional President, Gabriel Narutowicz (1865–1922) was followed by a series of notorious political murders, including that of the Soviet ambassador, Volkov, in 1927. In the 1930s, conditions were clearly deteriorating. The minorities were increasingly pressurized. The repression of Ukrainians in the countryside coincided with the growing threat to Jewish security in the towns. Antagonisms could be calmed neither by police action nor by publicity campaigns favouring official 'anti-anti-Semitism'. Agrarian reform gradually lost momentum. The peasant's lot was barely improved. Economic and industrial reform produced far too little, and much too late. Financial stability was achieved at the cost of low investment and high unemployment. State planning pointed the way to a future which had no time to develop. The mood of the working class was sullen, and its earning power derisory. Foreign confidence in Poland was low, and foreign capital notably lacking. All in all, social resources were strained to the utmost merely to keep pace with the soaring birth-rate, which pushed the Republic's population from 26.3 millions in 1919 to 34.8 millions in 1939. The one point of success, in education, proved a mixed blessing. Ignorant people had been docile. People who learned to read, also learned to be discontented. By the end of the 1930s, the radicalization of the Polish masses was already well advanced. If the Second Republic had not been foully murdered in 1939 by external agents, there is little doubt that it would soon have sickened from internal causes.

At the same time, one needs to keep these failures in proportion. It is essential to realize the enormities of the problems, and to judge Poland in the context of contemporary Europe. If there was hardship and injustice in Poland, there was no mass starvation or mass killing as in Russia, no resort to the bestial methods of Fascism or Stalinism. For example, to compare the rigours on the Polish internment camp at Bereza Kartuska (where seventeen persons are thought to have died) with the Stalinist purges which killed tens of millions, or to hint that the discomforts of the Jews under Polish rule were in some way related to the horrors of Auschwitz, is absurd. It is obviously true that Polish foreign policy under Col. Beck did not save the Republic. But it is doubtful whether anything that the Polish government might have done could have made much difference. The conditions of life in inter-war Poland were often very harsh; but they could not have been improved by recourse to Poland's neighbours.

Polish intellectual life, in particular, experienced a veritable explosion of creativity. In the pure sciences, the Warsaw School of Analytical Philosophy headed by Jan Łukasiewicz (1878–1956), the inventor of 'Polish notation', vied in the headlines of world learning with the Lwów School of Mathematics headed by Stefan Banach (1892–1945), the pioneer of Functional Analysis. The anthropologists, Edward Loth (1884–1944) and Jan Czekanowski (1882–1965); the linguisticians, Jan Baudouin De Courtenay (1845–1929) and Jerzy Kuryłowicz (1895–1978); and the economist Michał Kalecki (1899–1970), who is credited with expounding Keynesian economics before Keynes, figure among the founding fathers of their subjects. In all branches of the arts — but especially in graphic art, in drama, in poetry, and in music — established forms were challenged by a rash of experimentation. A mere catalogue of names serves little purpose; but the men whose sensational talents perhaps best express the vitality of their day are those of the two artist-philosophers, Leon Chwistek (1884–1944) and Stanisław Ignacy Witkiewicz, also known as 'Witkacy' (1885–1939). Chwistek first appeared as a painter, in the so-called Formist movement; but then he made his name as a logician. According to Bertrand Russell, Chwistek, together with Łukasiewicz and Leśniewski, was one of the six people in the world who had actually read and understood the technical sections of Russell's own *Principia Mathematica*. Later on, he expanded a hypothesis about aesthetics into a general philosophical theory of 'the plurality of reality'. His extravagant Bohemian lifestyle, no less than his ideas, scandalized the traditionalists. Witkiewicz, too, first emerged as a painter, and his psychological portrait studies remained very much in vogue. His novels, in contrast, and his forays into drama, which are now generally accepted as masterpieces of the Absurd, remained largely unknown until long after his tragic death. Eventually, his professional interest in theoretical aesthetics led him, like Chwistek, into speculative philosophy. In 1935, in his *Pojęcia i twierdzenia implikowane przez pojęcie istnienia* (Concepts and statements implied by the concept of existence), he expounded his theory of 'biological monism' and launched himself into a profound critique of 'sexless' contemporary thought. Appalled by the sterility of European culture, Witkiewicz resolutely prophesied its impending doom. With an exact appreciation of Poland's fate, he committed suicide in the night of 17 September 1939.

Although official encouragement played its part in fostering an environment that was sensitive to intellectual innovation, the main sources of inspiration obviously lay elsewhere. Polish culture has never thrived on state sponsorship. The lifting of the cultural Dark Age, formerly imposed by foreign, imperial regimes, is explanation enough for the cultural renaissance which accompanied the restoration of the Polish state. By the same token, the independent spirit which was given its head in the 1920s and 1930s does much to explain the extraordinary resilience of non-official culture in the face of philistine communist rule in the post-war period.[32]

Inter-war Warsaw possessed an unmistakable, bitter-sweet quality. It was characterized on the one hand by the pride and optimism generated by national independence, and on the other hand by the sad realization that the appalling problems of poverty, politics, and prejudice could not be alleviated by existing resources. The new government élite was jubilant. The Polish bourgeoisie relished the city's profitable metropolitan role. But the working class were restless; the Jews were apprehensive; and the intellectuals were openly critical. Existing tensions were aggravated by the renewed demographic explosion. In less than two decades, Warsaw's population almost doubled once more: from 758,000 in 1918 to 1,289,000 in 1939. Employment in the city was dominated by state enterprises — by the mushrooming bureaucracy, by the state railways, and by industries taken over from the German administration. Unemployment, which stood at 100,000 in 1918, was returning to similar levels in the 1930s. But still the immigrants came. The outer suburbs spread far and wide to accommodate the newcomers. Żolibórz was extended by one model housing settlement for army officers, and by another for civil servants. Nearby Marymont was submerged by one of the capital's reeking shanty towns. The city centre was adorned by a rash of modern, monumental architecture, and by the restoration of the choicest aristocratic palaces for official use. Intrusive reminders of the recent Russian past were replaced by patriotic monuments to Józef Poniatowski (1923), to the Unknown Soldier (1925), and to Frederyk Chopin (1926). The Jewish quarter, and many of the working-class districts, deteriorated into undisguised slums. Warsaw was a city of blatant contrasts, and of growing social polarization. The growth of the Civil Service, which employed some 113,000 people in 1938, was matched by the growing empires of the ponces, who employed some 30,000. Local elections were dominated by the NZR and by the Jewish *Folkspartei* – both of them entrenched in sectional interests, but neither representative of wider values. The politics of the capital had little in common with that of the Republic as a whole. Even so, from the cultural point of view, Warsaw was able to exert a dominant influence. The University of Warsaw, which in professors such as Jan Łukasiewicz, the logician, possessed men of international distinction, quickly overtook the prestige of the Jagiellonian University in Cracow. Warsaw's writers, from the established names of the older generation, such as Staff, Żeromski, or Kaden-Bandrowski to the rising poets of the Skamander Group – Jan Lechoń (1899–1956), Julian Tuwim (1894–1953), Jarosław Iwaszkiewicz (1894–1980), Bolesław Leśmian (1877–1938), and Antoni Słonimski (1895–1976) – outshone all competitors. Warsaw's press, from the National Democrat *Kurjer Warszawski* (Warsaw Courier) to the Piłsudski-ite *Kurjer Poranny* (Morning Courier), set the tone for national debates. Warsaw's theatres attracted the leading directors and producers, such as Leon Schiller (1887–1954) or Stefan Jaracz (1883–1945). Warsaw's star-studded musical world, led by the Contemporary Music Society of Karol Szymanowski (1882–1937), attempted to marry traditional and national tastes to modern techniques. What is more, all the established arts and media as patronized by respectable society were kept on their toes by a vibrant avant-garde culture, which flourished in the literary coffee-houses and the satirical reviews. On all these counts, Warsaw sought to transcend its terrible problems. For all its vices, it was a city full of life. When the testing time came, it was defended with heroism.[33]

In apportioning the blame for the final denouement of the pre-war crisis, the sins of Colonel Józef Beck (1894–1944), Foreign Minister from 1932 to 1939, have been specially exaggerated. To say that he was guilty of 'insane obstinacy' or of 'megalomania' at once misrepresents the man and his motives and inflates the role of Polish diplomacy. Attempts to cast him as the villain of the pre-war tragedy serve no purpose but to hide the culpability of much more prominent actors. Beck's cardinal sin, like that of Piłsudski before him, was to march out of step with his would-be Allied patrons. In 1934, he considered the merits of a preventive war against Hitler at a time when any such fighting talk was anathema in Paris and London. In 1937–8, he was thinking of protecting Poland's national and strategic interests in face of Nazi aggression at a time when Chamberlain and Daladier were seeking to appease Hitler at other people's expense. In 1939, he refused to make concessions to the Soviet Union, at a time when the appeasers were hoping that they might be rescued from Hitler by the Red Army. Beck's reluctance to trade Poland's freedom of action for doubtful advantages may have been inflexible, but was certainly even-handed. He resisted the advances of Goering and Ribbentrop no less than those of Litvinov and Molotov. The fate of neighbouring Czecho-slovakia, whose government had followed the àdvice of the Allies, did not inspire confidence. If Beck was at fault as a diplomat, the fault lay not in his very appropriate suspicions of Hitler and Stalin, but in his naïve belief in the sincerity of Allied guarantees and assurances.[34]

The viewpoint, much favoured by western commentators, that the Polish government was purposefully dallying with the Nazis is very wide of the mark. As early as March 1936, the General Inspectorate of the Armed Forces had commissioned a study of the strategic implications of German rearmament; and General Kutrzeba's critical assessment of the situation, underlining serious deficiencies in Poland's air defence, naval, and armoured forces, formed the background to subsequent diplomatic decisions.[35] The Polish Armed

Services were not capable of playing an effective defensive role unless supported by a powerful ally, and had no offensive capacity in the foreseeable future. For this reason, if for no other, the Polish leaders could not afford to become involved in Germany's aggressive ambitions in the east. Despite the suspicions of Allied statesmen, all attempts by Berlin to draw Poland into closer collaboration with Germany were resolutely resisted. It is in this context that two of Beck's more inglorious enterprises — the occupation of the Zaolzie in October 1938 and the ultimatum to Lithuania in March 1938 — must be judged. On both occasions, the Polish government took advantage of its neighbours' misfortunes to settle old scores and to indulge in a bit of bombastic self-congratulation; but the main preoccupation was to parry the threat of Poland's encirclement by Germany on both the southern and the northern flanks.

In the course of 1939 Poland's condition deteriorated from the chronic to the terminal. As soon as the Nazi propaganda machine turned its attentions to German claims on Danzig, and to what Germans called 'the Polish Corridor', it was clear that the Polish Republic was to be subjected to the same pressure tactics which had destroyed Czechoslovakia. By this time, it was also clear, even to Neville Chamberlain, that all further negotiations with Hitler on the Munich model were pointless. Instead, on 31 March, Chamberlain proffered an unconditional Guarantee, that Great Britain would do 'everything possible' to resist an attack by Germany on Poland's independence. The British Prime Minister must surely have known that in terms of practical assistance to Poland nothing was in fact possible. His purpose in making this gesture, unparalleled in the whole course of British History, was to deter Hitler, not to assist the Poles. He knew perfectly well that the British forces did not have the means available, either in men, ships, or planes, to intervene in Central Europe, and that he could not count automatically on the French Army to march on his behalf.[36] Hitler smelt the phoney nature of the Guarantee, and on 28 April responded by renouncing the Polish–German Pact of Non-aggression. The ensuing war of nerves was full of surprises. Both Gamelin and Ironside, the French and British Chiefs-of-Staff, gave precise, and as it proved, fraudulent assurances of their proposed action in the event of German aggression. Gamelin formally undertook to throw 'the bulk of the French army' across the Maginot Line; Ironside said that the RAF would match any German air raids on Poland with similar raids on Germany. Both Western governments began extended talks to found a common 'Peace Front' with the USSR, on the mistaken assumption that they could strike a bargain with Stalin and still dictate the terms. Stalin, like Hitler, was soon convinced that Allied policy was frivolous. In May, he dismissed the long-suffering Maxim Litvinov, with his Western connections, and installed in his place as Foreign Commissar the crude and impatient Vyecheslav Molotov. No significant agreement breakthrough was reached in the Allied—Soviet talks, which dragged on through the summer in Moscow.

Oddly enough, the coolest and clearest assessment of Poland's predicament was made neither in London nor in Warsaw, but from within the Axis camp by Mussolini's Foreign Minister and son-in-law, Count Ciano:

16 April (1939). Two long conversations with Goering . . . I was most struck by the tone in which he described relations with Poland. It was strangely reminiscent of the tone which not so long ago was used in Germany with regard to Austria and Czechoslovakia. Yet the Germans are mistaken if they think that they can carry on in the same manner. The Poles will be beaten; but they will not lay down their arms without a fierce and bloody struggle.

17 April (1939). I accompanied Goering to the station . . . On the whole, I got the impression that peaceful intentions still prevail even in Germany. Poland is the only danger that exists. I was less impressed by the substance of the comments directed against Warsaw, than by their contemptuous tone. The Germans should not imagine that they are simply going to hold a victory parade in Poland. If the Poles are attacked, they will fight. The Duce is of the same opinion.

15 May (1939). Conversation with Wieniawa [the retiring Polish ambassador in Rome] . . . I urged him to show the greatest moderation. Whatever will happen, Poland will pay the cost of the conflict. No Franco-British assistance will be forthcoming, at least, not in the first phase of the war; and Poland would quickly be turned into a heap of ruins. Wieniawa admits that I am right on many points, but believes in some eventual success that might give Poland greater strength. Alas, I fear that many, too many, Poles share his illusions.[37]

Meanwhile, the Nazis were awaiting their chance to exploit the fears and prejudices of the USSR. They knew that the Russians' hatred and contempt for Poland was no less than their own. Hitler repeatedly postponed his military plans, uneasy about the unresolved diplomatic situation. Then, in July, the break came. Under the cover of German–Soviet trade talks, Ribbentrop intimated that there was 'no problem' that could not be amicably resolved. Molotov responded the next morning. Amidst great secrecy, the terms were prepared. A public Pact of Non-Aggression between Germany and the USSR would bring the era of uncertainty in Eastern Europe to an end. At the same time, a Secret Protocol, designed to facilitate Germany's military preparations, envisaged the partition of Poland and the Baltic States between the two contracting parties. This Protocol spelled out Poland's death warrant:

Moscow, 23 August 1939

On the occasion of the Non-Aggression Pact between the German Reich and the USSR, the undersigned plenipotentiaries . . . discussed the boundaries of their respective spheres of influence in Eastern Europe. These conversations led to the following conclusions:

1. . . .

2. In the event of a territorial and political rearrangement of the areas belonging to the Polish state the spheres of influence of Germany and the USSR shall be bounded approximately by the line of the rivers Narew, Vistula, and San.

   The question of whether the interests of both parties make desirable the maintenance of an independent Polish State, and how such a state should be bounded can only be definitely determined in the course of further political developments.

   In any event, both Governments will resolve this question by means of a friendly agreement.

3. . . .

4. This protocol shall be treated by both parties as strictly secret.

For the Govt. of the	Plenipotentiary of the
German Reich.	Govt. of the USSR.
V. RIBBENTROP	V. MOLOTOV. [38]

In Polish eyes, the Nazi–Soviet Pact enshrined the Seventh Partition. As soon as Ribbentrop returned to Berlin, Hitler order the *Wehrmacht* to march.

None of which explains why, from beginning to end, the Polish Republic should have provoked such torrents of abuse from all sides. If Hitler and Stalin had reason enough to hate it, as an obstacle to their respective designs, the likes of Keynes, Namier, Carr, and Lloyd George did not. One cannot help speculating about their dubious motives. But such speculations belong more properly to the flights and fantasies of the liberal conscience than to the facts of Poland's unhappy history.

The Second Republic was indeed destined for destruction. But if in 1945, it was unimaginable that the European order could be reconstituted without a Polish state, this fact was largely due to the achievements of the Second Republic in those two unique decades of genuine independence between the first Great War and the Second.[39]

CHAPTER TWENTY
GOLGOTA:
Poland in the Second World War (1939-1945)

The Second World War was started by *Sturmbanfuehrer* Alfred Helmut Naujocks of the Nazi Security Service (SD). At 8 p.m. on 31 August 1939, he led an attack on the German radio station at Gleiwitz (Gliwice) in Upper Silesia. His men included a dozen convicted criminals referred to in his orders by the code-word *Konserwen* (Tin Cans), who had been promised a reprieve in return for their co-operation. After a brief encounter with the station guards, they burst into one of the studios, broadcast a patriotic announcement in Polish, sang a rousing chorus, fired a few pistol shots, and left. Once outside, the 'Tin Cans' were mown down by the machine-guns of the SS. Their bodies, carefully dressed in blood-soaked Polish uniforms, were abandoned where they fell, to be found in due course by the local police. Before the night was out, the world was awakening to the astonishing news that the Polish Army had launched an unprovoked attack on the Third Reich.[1] (See Map 15.)

The fighting began at 4.40 a.m. on 1 September, when the old German battleship *Schleswig-Holstein,* moored in the port of Danzig on a friendship visit, opened fire with its 15-inch guns on the Polish fort at Westerplatte. One hour later, the *Wehrmacht* tore down the barriers on the frontier roads at a score of points, and raced to the attack. General Heinz Guderian commanding the armoured force which roared across the Corridor in the direction of Chełmno, his birthplace, recalled those hours with special poignancy:

The first serious fighting took place north of Zempelburg (Sępolno) in and around Gross-Klonia, where the mist suddenly lifted and the leading tanks found themselves face to face with Polish defensive positions. The Polish anti-tank gunners scored many direct hits. One officer, one cadet, and eight other ranks were killed.

Gross-Klonia had once belonged to my great grandfather, Freiherr Hiller von Gartringen. Here, too, was buried my grandfather, Guderian.

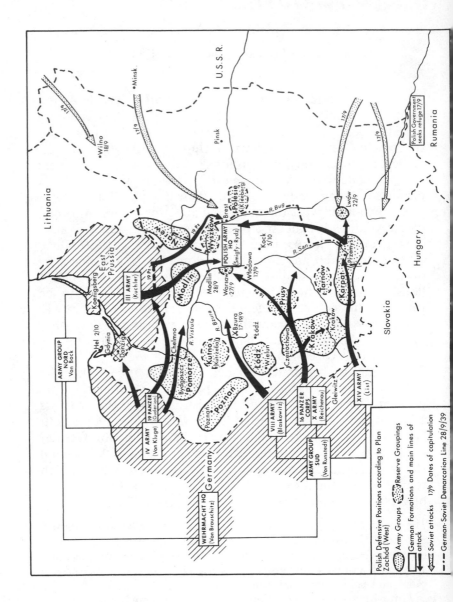

My father had been born in this place. This was the first time I had ever set eyes on the estate, once so beloved of my family.[2]

Air raids were launched on Warsaw, Łódź, Częstochowa, Cracow, and Poznań. Dive-bombers raided airfields in a determined attempt to destroy the Polish Air Force on the ground. Bridges were bombed, trains derailed, columns of refugees were strafed on the roads. Nazi *Einsatzgruppen* (Action Groups) roamed the rear areas, terrorizing the population and shooting hostages and prisoners. By 6 September, the Polish Command had abandoned its plan to defend the frontiers. Guderian's force had already crossed the Corridor, and was poised for an attack out of East Prussia in the direction of Brest-Litowsk. For three days, a Polish counter-offensive on the River Bzura organized by General Tadeusz Kutrzeba inflicted heavy losses on the advancing Germans; but outflanked to the north and to the south, it was soon overtaken by events elsewhere. By the end of the second week, Warsaw was surrounded. On 17 September, uninvited and unannounced, the Soviet army crossed the eastern frontier. The Polish ambassador in Moscow was summoned by Molotov, and was curtly told that, 'since the Polish Republic was no longer in existence', measures were being taken to protect the inhabitants of western Byelorussia and western Ukraine. In some places, the Soviet troops were welcomed in the mistaken belief that they were moving into action against the Germans. In other places, they were fired on. But the Poles continued to resist. Warsaw, abandoned by the government and the General Staff and burning out of control, was defended until 27 September. The peninsula of Hel held out till 2 October. At Lwów, General Sosnkowski improvised a line of defence against the Germans and the Soviets alike. But the inexorable effects of Nazi—Soviet collusion were clear for all to see. The Polish forces were caught in a trap, with no wall against which they could lean their backs and fight. Their President and Commander-in-Chief both crossed into Romanian internment. Army formations were ordered to disperse, to bury their weapons, and to fend for themselves. In the last few hours before the Soviet forces sealed the southern and eastern frontier, tens of thousands of soldiers and civilians escaped into Romania and Hungary. The last Polish unit in the field capitulated at Kock on 5 October.[3] After that, Poles could only fight abroad (see pp. 271–2), or in the Underground.

The legends of the September Campaign are better known than the facts. It is true that the Polish Army was fighting at a disadvantage from the strategic, technical, and political point of view. The sixty *Wehrmacht* divisions of von Brauchitsch were free to launch attacks from four directions at once: from East Prussia in the north, from Slovakia and Cieszyn in the south, from Pomerania in the north-west, and from Silesia in the south-west. They could choose the moment and the location. They were equipped with 2,600 tanks as against the Poles' 150; and by 2,000 modern war-planes as against 400. Their supply services were largely mechanized and motorized. They could wage the first Blitzkrieg in history at leisure, against an enemy which could not reply in kind. The Polish Army, commanded by Marshal Śmigły-Rydz, possessed some 40 divisions, but was overwhelmed in many sectors before the reserves could be mobilized. It was hampered by severed communications, by inferior weapons and organization, and by roads blocked with innumerable panic-stricken refugees. Even so, it should be remembered that the task of the Poles was not to defeat the Germans. In accordance with military discussions held in the summer, the Polish Army was only expected to hold the *Wehrmacht* for the two weeks required for its Western Allies to launch a major offensive with seventy battle-ready French divisions across the Rhine. In the event, the Poles fulfilled their task; the French and the British did not. What is more the Polish Army sold itself dearly. In four weeks of fighting, it inflicted over 50,000 casualties on the *Wehrmacht*. It was still fighting hard against the odds when the issue was settled by the entry of the Red Army on the German side in the second half of the month. In this light, its performance can be seen to be more creditable than that of the combined British and French armies when they, too, faced their baptism of fire in May 1940.

Every popular history of the campaign paints the picture of 'brave but foolish' Polish uhlans charging the German Panzers on horseback. It even happens to contain a grain of truth. In one or two places, isolated squadrons of Polish cavalry found themselves surprised by tanks and, despite their orders to the contrary, did try to fight their way out in the traditional fashion. Short of surrender, it was the only thing that cavalrymen could do. Yet it is quite unreasonable to accept such incidents as evidence for the mad courage, or for the technical incompetence, of the Polish Army as a whole. As the Germans learned to their cost in the later campaign in Russia, cavalry units were far from obsolete in the conditions of the Eastern Front. Red Army cavalry provided vital support to armoured and infantry divisions throughout the war. The Poles were indeed courageous; but they were not necessarily foolish. They were faced with an enemy whom they had never expected to face alone, and they were deserted by their allies. In the bitterness and humiliation of defeat, it was entirely natural that they themselves should propagate a legend which showed how they lost with a gesture of glamo rous defiance. It is entirely natural that people in the West and in Russia, unwilling to recognize the unworthy parts played by their own governments in 1939, should also want to believe it.[4]

The Polish forces lost some 60,000 men killed, and 140,000 wounded. The civilian casualties numbered many more. The Western Allies, who declared war against Germany on 3 September, had not fired a shot in Poland's defence. At the end of the month, the acting head of the British Military Mission in Warsaw, General Adrian Carton de Wiart arrived in London via Romania, and was received in Whitehall. General Ironside, the Chief of Imperial General Staff, commented: 'Your Poles haven't put up much of a show, have they?' Neville Chamberlain, the British Prime Minister inquired, 'Tell me, General, what effect have our leaflet raids had?'[5]

The entry of the Red Army into Poland on 17 September has never been properly explained. It prompted Churchill's famous remark that 'Russia is a riddle wrapped in a mystery inside an enigma.' Unknown to Churchill, of course, the invasion had been envisaged by the secret protocol of 23 August. Even so, its timing was highly peculiar. The German Command called on Stalin to join them as soon as they attacked; but Stalin had declined. In accordance with the 'hyena principle' for which Soviet policy was justly famed, it would have made better sense to delay the advance until the *Wehrmacht* had completed the actual fighting. Yet Stalin did not do that either. Instead, he ordered his forces to march when the campaign was only half complete. As far as one could tell, he was guided by a German forecast on 9 September that Warsaw would fall within the week, and by another communiqué on the 16th, which announced that Warsaw was already in German hands. This sequence of events would neatly explain Molotov's curious rationalization of Soviet actions. One need only imagine the mortification of the Soviet leaders on the following day, when they realized that the communiqué was false, and that they had committed their precious army to sacrifices that were strictly unnecessary. This was not the last time that Stalin was punished for taking the Nazis at their word. As a result, he created 993 Soviet heroes, who would otherwise have lived to fight another day.

The division of the spoils was arranged by a German–Soviet convention signed on 28 September. A demarcation line was fixed along the rivers Bug and San, to which the *Wehrmacht* now withdrew. For practical purposes, this line was regarded as a permanent frontier. Both zones of occupation were subjected to the unrestrained political engineering of their respective conquerors.

For Warsaw, the outbreak of the Second World War bore little resemblance to the outbreak of the First. The Germans of 1939 showed none of the circumspection of their predecessors in 1914–15, and the Varsovians showed none of their previous inclination to collaborate. The defence of the city in September 1939 set the tone for later defiance. Abandoned by the General Staff on the 6th and by the Government on the 7th, the capital's defenders, headed by General Walerian Czuma (1890–1962) and the city President, Stefan Starzyński (1893–1943), battled on against the odds, and under incessant aerial bombardment. The act of capitulation of 27 September was imposed by the German General Johannes Blaskowitz on a mutilated city whose victims already numbered scores of thousands and whose most ancient monuments – the Royal Castle, the Cathedral of St. John, and the Old City Square – had already been reduced to rubble. The immediate separation of the Jewish population governed by its *Judenrat* (Jewish Council) from the Aryan population governed by the *Urząd Miejski* (Municipal Office), enabled the Nazi administrators to obstruct all thoughts of mutual assistance from the start. The Terror, which began with the shooting of 106 hostages in Wawer on 27 December 1939, steadily mounted in intensity. The Ghetto, whose gates were finally closed in November 1940, was used as a collecting centre for Jews from all over Poland. For two years, disciplined by its own Jewish police force headed by the ill-starred Adam Czerniaków (1880–1942), it was forced to toil for the *Wehrmacht* in concentration camp conditions. The main deportations to Treblinka and Auschwitz took place in July 1942, and following the Ghetto Rising, in April 1943. Thereafter, it was used as the Gestapo's principal place of execution. By 1943, mass killings were commonplace amongst the population at large. Price inflation of over 300 per cent nullified the value of wages, while food rationing and food shortages reduced the average diet to starvation levels. Resistance was offered most typically by economic sabotage, by deliberate underproduction, by administrative devices such as the printing of bogus ration cards by the *Urząd Miejski*, by an elaborate black market, and, increasingly, by violence. On 14 December 1943, Governor Frank roundly blamed Warsaw for the ills of his *General-Gouvernement*. 'Warsaw', he said, 'is the source of all our misfortunes . . . the focus of all disturbances, the place from which discontent is spread through the whole country.'[6]

On the German side of the demarcation line, former Polish territory was divided into two distinct parts. The northern and western areas were directly annexed to the Reich. In the language of the day, they were referred to as lands of the 'New Reich' as distinct from those of the pre-1937 'Old Reich'. The more extensive central and southern areas were formed into a separate *General-Gouvernement*. (See Map 16.) In neither case, whether inside the Reich or outside it, did the population enjoy the protection of the civil law. All the occupied territories were designated as lawless *Arbeitsbereich* (Work Areas) where martial law was in force and where 'death' or 'concentration camp' were the only two forms of stipulated punishment for any type of offence. The Gauleiter

Map 16.   The German Occupation, (1939–45)

of the new Warthegau at Posen, Artur Greiser, curtly ex-
cluded all officials of the Berlin Ministries from his realm.
Albert Forster, Gauleiter of West Preussen-Danzig, and
Wagner at Breslau in Silesia were similarly high-handed. Hans
Frank, Hitler's one-time lawyer, took up residence in Wawel
Castle, and as Governor-General prepared to turn 'the ancient
German city of Krakau' into a model capital for his kingdom.
To all intents and purposes, Poland had become 'Gestapoland'.[7]

On the Soviet side of the line, administrative provisions
were staged with a greater show of democratic procedure.
The northerly area, including Wilno, was granted to the
Republic of Lithuania. This specious act of generosity masked
the further intention of the Soviet government, whose determination to annex Lithuania and the other Baltic States was
already implicit in the secret clauses of the Nazi–Soviet Pact.
The central area up to the Pripet was attached to the Byelorussian SSR, and the southern area with Lwów was attached
as 'Western Ukraine' to the Ukrainian SSR. In each of these
areas, plebiscites were organized by the NKVD to express
popular consent. Closed lists of handpicked candidates were
prepared. All citizens were obliged to vote. All abstentions,
spoiled papers, and protests were counted as votes in favour.
To nobody's surprise, the official list was declared to have
received the support of 92 per cent of the electorate. Packed
assemblies resolved unanimously to implore the Soviet government to admit the occupied lands to the Union. Even by
Soviet standards, this process represented a *coup de théâtre*
of impressive effect.

The conduct of the Soviet officials who led this operation
lacked any sensitivity to the interests or feelings of their new
charges. The First Secretary of the Ukrainian Communist
Party, Nikita Krushchev, recalled the episode with no qualms
whatsoever:

My main job was to set up organisations to represent the people of the
Western Ukraine and to give them a chance to declare themselves: did
they want to join the Soviet state or not? Delegations were elected to
an assembly at Lvov to decide this question . . .
    The assembly continued for a number of days amid great jubilation
and political fervour. I didn't hear a single speech expressing even the
slightest doubt that Soviet power should be established. One by one,

movingly and joyfully, the speakers all said that it was their fondest
dream to be accepted into the Ukrainian Soviet Republic. It was gratify-
ing for me to see that the working-class, peasantry and labouring intelligentsia were beginning to understand Marxist—Leninist teachings . . .
Despite all the efforts of the Polish rulers to distort our doctrine and to
intimidate the people, Lenin's ideas were alive and thriving in the
Western Ukraine.

At the same time, we were still conducting arrests. It was our view
that these arrests served to strengthen the Soviet state and clear the
road for the building of Socialism on Marxist—Leninist principles; but
our bourgeois enemies had their own interpretation of the arrests,
which they tried to use to discredit us throughout Poland.[8]

For Krushchev and his like, the aggrandizement of Soviet
power was all that mattered. The end justified the means.

For the entire currency of the Nazi—Soviet Pact, which
lasted from August 1939 to June 1941, Poland provided the
common ground where German and Soviet policy could
merge most closely. At the time of the fall of France and of
the Battle of Britain, Soviet oil flowed westwards to fuel the
engines of the Panzers and the Luftwaffe. German machinery
and arms flowed eastwards to replenish the ailing Soviet
economy. The new German cruiser, the *Lützow,* was sold to
the Soviet Navy, and renamed the *Pietrov Pavlov.* In January
1941, the USSR bought the District of Suwałki for 7,500,000
dollars in gold.[9] The Soviet press praised the victories of the
German army 'over the decadent forces of capitalism and
imperialism'. Nazi propaganda praised the achievements of
the great Stalin. *Pravda* explained that the Red Army had
moved into Western Byelorussia and Western Ukraine 'to
liberate our brothers of the same blood'. *Der Voelkischer
Beobachter* rejoiced that the German army was realizing
Hitler's dream of greater *Lebensraum* for the German race in
the East. The NKVD and the Gestapo worked in close collaboration. German communists from Russia were handed
over to the Gestapo in exchange for Russian *émigrés* and
Ukrainians from Germany. Both sides looked on Poles and
Jews with undisguised contempt. The 'racial enemy' of the
one was virtually indistinguishable from the 'class enemy' of
the other.[10]

In the first two years of the war, the Nazis prepared their

ground in Poland with methodical precision. No sooner had Hitler held his victory parade in Warsaw on 5 October 1939 than *Reichsfuehrer-SS* Heinrich Himmler saw the opportunity to put his racial theories into practice, and gave vent to his deeper thoughts on this subject:

The removal of foreign races from the incorporated eastern territories is one of the most essential goals to be accomplished in the German East . . . In dealing with members of some Slav nationality, we must not endow these people with decent German thoughts and logical conclu- sions of which they are not capable, but we must take them as they really are . . . I think it is our duty to take their children with us . . . We either win over the good blood we can use for ourselves . . . or else we destroy that blood. For us, the end of this war will mean an open road to the East . . . It means that we shall push the borders of our German race 500 kilometres to the east.[11]

Travelling round the country in his 'Special Train *Heinrich*', Himmler drove his minions forward in their tireless efforts to classify and segregate all sections of the population. District by district, town by town, village by village, all citizens were obliged to register with the Nazi authorities. They were allocated to one of four categories: *Reichsdeutsch*, for Germans born within the old frontiers of the Reich; *Volks- deutsch* (German Nationals) who could claim German ancestry in their family within three generations; *Nichtdeutsch* (non-Germans) who could prove themselves free of all Jewish connections; and *Juden* (Jews). These racial categories were further subdivided according to people's work capacity, and political loyalties, and each was issued with identity passes and ration cards. A first-class *Reichsdeutscher* in Poland received coupons for 4,000 calories per day; a Polish worker had to survive off 900; a non-productive Jew very often had nothing. Once classification was complete, segregation could begin. Enclosed ghettos or *Judenreservaten* were established in the towns. Those in Warsaw, Cracow, and Łódź (renamed Litmannstadt) were enlarged to accommodate Jewish deportees from the countryside and from abroad. At the same time huge numbers of non-Germans were subject to forcible deportation. Poles occupying desirable residences in the middle-class suburbs were expropriated without redress to make way for the influx of German officials and their families.

Many Poles from the Warthegau were expelled *en masse* to the *General-Gouvernement*. In the Polish Corridor, during the so-called *Aktion Tannenberg*, some 750,000 Polish peasants were driven from the land to facilitate the transfer of Baltic Germans from Soviet Latvia and Estonia. The first conscriptions of men and women for slave-labour in the Reich were organized. The first blond-haired children, whom Himmler noticed were closer to the 'Teutonic ideal' than his own, were kidnapped from Polish orphanages by agents of the Nazi bloodstock organization, the *SS Lebensborn* (Fountain of Life). In all public places, strict racial apartheid was enforced. Tram-cars, park benches, and the better shops and hotels were marked with the ominous sign 'NÜR FÜR DEUTSCHE' (Germans only). All non-Germans were confined to their own quarters. Detailed regulations governed every move. Poles were forbidden to possess wireless sets or to congregate in groups of more than three persons, except in church. Jews were forbidden to leave the Ghetto on pain of death.[12]

The impossibility of executing Himmler's schemes in any reasonable manner gave rise to widespread confusion, corruption, and brutality. Families with one parent qualifying for *Reichsdeutsch* status and another of Polish or Jewish extraction might try to bribe the registration officers for a lenient decision. Families who qualified for *Volksdeutsch* status might ask one relative to volunteer for the German list and another relative to refuse. In that way, they sought to get the best of both uncertain worlds. False papers, stolen ration cards, and spurious genealogies sprouted on all sides. Before long, the Nazi officials began to compete among themselves. Gauleiter Forster registered all the Poles in Danzig as Germans, just to spite the SS. The distribution of appointments brought the SS into conflict with the Political Organization of the NSDAP, then with the Führer's Personal Office and with the Governor-General. The *Gestapo* (State Police) and its dependent the *Sipo* (Security Police) fought over their victims with the *Kripo* (Criminal Police). The fate of individuals was settled by a palmful of jewellery, and, increasingly, by a bullet. In this situation, few self-respecting or intelligent German officials would seek employment in Poland, which quickly deteriorated into a hunting-ground for desperadoes and sadists.

In these first years of German Occupation, the death-toll did not compare with that of the following period. The concentration camps at Auschwitz (Oświęcim) and Maidaneck (Majdanek) were still being built, and had not yet assumed the character of extermination centres. It is true that Himmler and Frank agreed at an early date that the Jews of Poland must 'disappear'; but the technical facilities and the political will did not yet exist. It was not until the beginning of 1941 that a pilot plant at Kulm (Chełmno-nad-Nerem) proved the killing potential of *Cyclon B* gas cylinders over the cruder experiments with carbon monoxide and 'Gas Vans'.[13] For the time being, the only two actions which hinted at the Holocaust to come were the so-called *Ausserordentliche Befriedungsaktion* (Extraordinary Pacification Campaign) of May–August 1940 and the Euthanasia Campaign of 1939 40. The former consigned some ten thousand Polish intellectuals – professors, teachers, civil servants, and priests – to Dachau, Buchenwald, and Sachsenhausen, and in the Palmiry Forest near Warsaw led to the mass execution of 3,500 political or municipal leaders.[14] The latter eliminated all cripples and imbeciles from the country's hospitals. Apart from that, the violence was confined to localized reprisals, and to the sporadic war in the countryside against the partisans. The worst incidents occurred at Bydgoszcz (Bromberg) and elsewhere in Pomerania in October 1939 where some 20,000 Poles were killed in reprisal for the fighting between the Polish Army and the local German 'fifth column' in the town in September.[15]

In many ways, the work of the Soviet NKVD in eastern Poland proved far more destructive than that of the Gestapo at this stage. Having longer experience in political terror than their German counterparts, the Soviets had no need for wasteful experimentation. Their expertise had been refined, and their personnel thoroughly trained and replenished in the recent Purges; and they went into action with speed. As in the German Zone, the population was screened, classified, and segregated. But, in this case, all unfavourable elements were physically removed from the scene as soon as they were identified. An NKVD decree, issued in Wilno (Vilnius) in 1940 lists the categories of people subject to deportation:

1. Members of Russian pre-revolutionary parties — Mensheviks, followers of Trotsky, and anarchists;
2. Members of contemporary (national) political parties, including students belonging to student organizations;
3. Members of the state police, gendarmerie, and prison staffs;
4. Officers of the former Tsarist Army, and of other anti-Bolshevik armies of the period 1918—21;
5. Officers and military judges of the contemporary Polish and Lithuanian Armies;
6. Volunteers of all other armies other than the Bolshevik;
7. Persons removed from the Communist Party;
8. Refugees, political *émigrés,* and contraband runners;
9. Citizens of foreign states, representatives of foreign firms, etc.;
10. Persons who have travelled abroad. Persons who are in contact with representatives of foreign states. Persons who are esperantists or philatelists;
11. Officials of the Lithuanian Ministries;
12. The staff of the Red Cross;
13. Persons active in parishes; clergymen, secretaries, and active members of religious communities;
14. Aristocrats, landowners, wealthy merchants, bankers, industrialists, hotel and restaurant proprietors.[16]

Similar measures were applied in Byelorussia and the Ukraine.

The history of the Soviet deportations of 1939—40 from the occupied territories has been obscured by the passions which attended later events. It can be seen as the culmination of the Stalinist terror which started to snowball during the collectivization campaign and the Purges, and which did not cease until the German attack on the USSR in 1941. Its horrors were known and published long before Solzhenitsyn wrote his *Gulag Archipelago* but were largely ignored by a western public as yet unconditioned to receive them. The Poles were among the foremost victims. They were deported in four vast railway convoys which left for the east in February, April, and June 1940, and June 1941. They had all been processed by the NKVD and sentenced either to *lagier* (concentration camps), to hard labour, or to penal exile. The vast majority were convicted for no known offence, but simply because the Polish nation was seen as the inveterate enemy of its Russian masters. The conditions in those trains defy coherent language. The passengers had been told to pack emergency rations for one month, but to take a minimum of personal belongings. They were packed in a standing position in sealed, windowless, and unheated cattle-wagons, for a winter journey of three, four, five, or even six thousand miles. Their only view of the outside world was through a small opening under the roof which could be used for passing out excreta and corpses. Instances of derangement, frostbite, starvation, infanticide, even cannibalism occurred. Those who survived the trains often faced further journeys in the holds of river-boats, or on the backs of open lorries, to the farthest recesses of the Soviet wilderness. One man who lived to tell the tale was a trade unionist and a miner who was strong enough to withstand the rigours of a camp near the Cold Pole of the earth in north-eastern Siberia:

On 27 September 1939 I received an order from the political authorities of the Soviet administration . . . to call a meeting of all the workers' organisations . . . and to dissolve them. At this meeting, the NKVD representatives present handed me the text of a resolution to be submitted to the delegates of the workers' organisation and to be passed by them. By this resolution, the workers were to express their satisfaction at the incorporation of our eastern provinces into the USSR. Having refused to submit the resolution, I was immediately arrested, and confined in the jail at Drohobycz. In the course of the investigation which followed, I was accused of betraying the interest of the workers, of action inimical to Stalin, of support of Trotsky and other Soviet traitors, and so on. I was sentenced on 15 December 1939 to ten years' hard labour in a camp, by a military tribunal. Until 10 January I was kept in the Drohobycz prison, and then transferred to another prison in Lwów, and later from Lwów to Odessa.

In Odessa, I was kept in prison from 1 February until 7 March of the same year. The prison at Odessa was full of Poles. I was with thirteen other persons in a cell intended to accommodate two. From 7 March until 17 April I was one of a convoy being taken to Vladivostok. During the journey, the prisoners now and again received a little bread, but as a general rule nothing but tinned herrings with some boiling water in very small quantities. In Vladivostok, there was an enormous clearing-house from which prisoners were distributed among camps in the province of Khabarovsk . . . There were some 25,000 prisoners camping here in the open . . . On 20 May, together with a large transport of my fellow-prisoners, I was taken across the Sea of Japan to Magadan, and from there by lorry to another distributing centre. From this centre we proceeded to Maldiak, 1,700 kilometres away on the River Kolyma.

We arrived in Maldiak on 26 June 1940. There were four camps there, each containing 2,500 persons, and we lived in huts covered by tenting, one hundred prisoners to each hut. We slept on bare bunks made not of planks but of logs . . .

By the end of September, the snow was up to our knees. At Magadan, we had been given winter jackets, and in the camp a few received felt leg coverings and another type of warm jacket called *bushlaki.*

The whole region around the camp was utterly deserted . . . At each advance of the Soviets into the interior of their country, the native inhabitants moved further and further into the taiga . . .

Reveille was at 5 a.m. Before going to work, the prisoners got a piece of bread each and a portion of gruel. After this, and in a column four across, we were marched to our places in the mines. The mining was for gold. On our way to work, an orchestra sometimes played. The work on the surface consisted of digging earth, often mixed with gravel. We dug with picks, crowbars, and shovels, and in winter when the ground was frozen, with chisels. It was indeed convict's work. The daily norm was 125 barrels of earth dug, which then had to be pushed a distance of between three and four hundred metres. Below the surface these mines were 120–50 feet deep, and accidents were frequent . . . The unfortunate victims of accidents were hauled to the surface, their hands cut off as proof of death to be shown to the authorities, and the bodies thrust beneath the brushwood. At 12.30 there was half-an-hour break, and we got our dinner, consisting of 150 grammes of bread and a portion of thin skilly; and occasionally a piece of fish. After that we kept on uninterruptedly until 8 p.m. The prisoners who had not finished their norm by then had to work for two hours more . . .

The prisoners were of all classes . . . and of all nationalities of the Soviet Union and of the states who are her neighbours.

The orchestra very often played while the prisoners were at work. To the accompaniment of this music, the guards would call out prisoners whose work was especially feeble and shoot them there and then. The shots rang out one after another . . . A Jew from Lwów working alongside me was so exhausted that he repeatedly fainted at work. The guard ordered him to fall out, took him to a nearby shed, and there he was shot. I heard the shot, and saw his body a few minutes later. The same fate overtook prisoners for the slightest breach of regulations, especially for moving even a few steps from the spot where they were working, or for not keeping in line when they were marching. Everybody was pitilessly robbed the moment they arrived and all the prisoners were utterly demoralized . . .

As a result of the twelve- to fourteen-hour day, with no day of rest in the week, the prisoners suffer from exhaustion after a very short period, and are easily attacked by disease. Yet a prisoner only gets sick leave when he has at least 40 degrees of fever, and then only if the quota of sick leave for that day is not filled . . . Out of a camp of some 10,000 men, some 2,000 die every year . . . Every morning there are some prisoners who cannot be roused, having died during the night. In the first two and a half months of my time at Kolyma out of the total of twenty Poles in my group, sixteen died. Four, including myself, survived.

In winter, one has to work even in -65°C of frost. Clothes get worn very quickly in the mines. We went about wrapped in rags which we almost never took off . . . The prisoners' one dream is to get to hospital . . . Self-inflicted wounds were universal. A prisoner willingly chopped off his finger in the hope of getting admitted. I myself, with another Pole shortly before our release, decided to cut off our fingers and toes. We had come to the end of our endurance.

At the end of some months I was transferred from Maldiak to Berliach, where I worked as a welder in a motor-car dump. In this place for a whole three and a half months we never saw bread. We lived entirely off herrings. My wages were thirty-two roubles a month, and to earn this I was doing 100 per cent of the norm.

After the outbreak of war, the Poles were moved to the forests and used for felling trees . . . While at this forest work, I learned entirely by chance about the Polish–Soviet Pact and the 'amnesty' affecting all Polish prisoners. I saw the commandant to ask him about this. By way of reply, I was severely punished, having to stand for twenty-four hours in the open without food.

On 20 September 1941 we were moved back to Magadan. During the four-day journey we were not given any food. At Magadan I met some 1,200 Poles. From what they said, I learned that 60 per cent of the Poles deported to the camps along the Kolyma had died. Conditions at Magadan did not change much in practice after the amnesty. The same regulations remained in force as before.[17]

Many did not survive. By the time that the Amnesty was granted in 1941, (for crimes that had not been committed), almost half of the one-and-a-half million Poles deported in the previous years were already dead. The victims included 100,000 Polish Jews, headed by the Chief Rabbi of Warsaw, Moses Shore. The exact numbers will never be known.

In relation to sufferings on this scale, the death or disappearance of 15,000 Polish army officers might not cause much surprise. The officers had been taken into Soviet detention in September 1939, separated from the rank and file, and sent to three separate camps in western Russia. Most of them were not professional soldiers, but reserve officers mobilized during the German offensive. They were well-trained graduates — teachers, civil servants, businessmen, doctors, scientists. From the Soviet point of view, they were the cream of the class enemy. For eight months, until May 1940, they were able to correspond with their families at home. And then the correspondence suddenly ceased. From that time on, only one man from the 15,000 was ever seen alive again. He was sent for interrogation to Moscow at the time that the original camps were being disbanded. In April 1943, 4,321 corpses were disinterred by the Germans in the Katyn Forest, on the bank of the Dnieper near Smolensk. Most had their hands tied behind their backs, and each had a German bullet in the base of his skull. Many had decipherable documents in their pockets. There is no doubt who they were. The Nazis claimed that they had been killed by the Soviets in April 1940. The Soviets claimed that they had been killed by the Nazis in the winter of 1941. This explanation was dropped when someone pointed out that the victims were wearing summer uniform. One International Commission assembled by the Germans supported the German claim; another, assembled by the Soviets, supported the Soviet claim. To people who need final, documentary proof, the matter is still open. Yet to the satisfaction of most neutral observers, Soviet guilt is established beyond reasonable doubt. The Katyn massacre is the only 'Nazi War Crime' on Soviet territory which the Soviets never mention. The fate of the remaining 11,000 officers can only be imagined. In Polish eyes, this one crime has become the symbol for countless other, unrecorded atrocities committed by the Soviet Union against the Polish nation.[18]

It would be wrong, however, to suppose that the NKVD confined their attentions to the class enemy. They were equally merciless with those few Polish communists who had survived the recent Purge. Władysław Gomułka was one, who, finding himself in 1940 in the Soviet Zone in Lwów, preferred to take his chance with the Germans in the *General-Gouvernement*. The conclusion is unavoidable. At this stage, the USSR was seeking to prevent the resurrection of an independent Poland in any form whatsoever. Stalin was outpacing Hitler in his desire to reduce the Poles to the condition of a slave-nation incapable of ruling itself.

There is little doubt that if the Nazi—Soviet Pact had lasted much longer, the goal of the two participants with regard to Poland would have been achieved. By 1941, the Nazi extermination machine was moving into top gear. The Soviet needed no encouragement. Isolated from all outside help, the Polish nation could not conceivably have survived in any recognizable form. Fortunately for them, the vagaries of war turned in their favour. The Poles were saved by the German attack on Russia. Although four long years of horror remained, the Germans were to prove incapable of annihilating Poland single-handed. The Soviets, who for two years had acted as Hitler's chief accomplices, turned for Polish assistance. The Poles were spared total annihilation.

*   *   *   *   *

In the early summer of 1941, it was obvious that something was afoot. In May, the entire German assault force from Yugoslavia rumbled through southern Poland, and moved to new stations on the Bug and the San. In June, German units followed each other eastwards by road and rail towards the Soviet frontier. The movement of hundreds of divisions could not be concealed. Everyone except Stalin was convinced that the Nazi—Soviet Pact was drawing to a close. On 22 June, the *Wehrmacht* launched Operation Barbarossa, and invaded the USSR. For the next four years, the Polish lands formed first the rear area of the German—Russian War, and then one of the principal battlegrounds. Until the very end of those four years, German supremacy could not be seriously challenged.

In the shadow of its military success, the German administration in occupied Poland dropped all previous restraints. The *General-Gouvernement* was extended to include the District of Galicia. In the east, new zones of occupation were created in territories wrested from the Red Army. In Berlin, the Nazi leaders began to sketch out the details of their *Generalplan-Ost,* whereby, in the coming decades, the whole Slav population from the Oder to the Dnieper was to be replaced by German settlers. Within the over-all scheme, they imagined that some twenty million Poles could be resettled in Western

Siberia; some three to four million were suitable for re-Germanization; the rest were to be eliminated. In the first stage, all human and material resources were to be devoted to the war effort; all resistance was to be ruthlessly suppressed; all inferior and useless human beings — Jews, gipsies, Soviet prisoners-of-war, people unfit to work — were to be exterminated.[19]

Nazi economic activity deteriorated under the pressure of war from simple exploitation to frenzied destruction. In the territories annexed to the Reich, most sequestered industrial property passed into the hands of the *Reichswerke Herman Goering AG,* and was turned over to munitions. In the *General-Gouvernement,* official policies vacillated wildly. In 1939–41, a start was made with schemes to dismantle industrial plant for removal to Germany. But after 1941, it was more convenient to keep the factories nearer to the Eastern Front. From 1943, Allied bombing in western Germany encouraged industrial concerns to take refuge in the east. For a time, production levels exceeded those of 1938. Increasingly, economic life fell under the control of the WVHA (Main Department for Economy and Administration) of the SS, who tried, with no great success, to integrate it with their policies of racial and population control. In 1944–5, as the point of total dislocation approached, hundreds of thousands of underfed slave-labourers of both sexes and of every conceivable nationality were marched back and forth, from project to abandoned project, amidst the endless retreating convoys and demolition squads of the defeated *Wehrmacht.*[20]

To finance these operations, an *Emissionsbank in Polen* had been opened in Cracow in April 1940, as a filial of the central *Reichsbank.* Its paper money and wage-coupons provided a limited basis for trade and commerce in the *General-Gouvernement* but failed to check the rampant price inflation or the widespread 'official' and 'unofficial' black market. It stayed in business till January 1945.

The Nazi Terror intensified inexorably. From 1941, Poland became the home of humanity's Holocaust, an 'archipelago' of death-factories and camps, the scene of executions, pacifications, and exterminations which surpassed anything so far documented in the history of mankind.

Arbitrary executions by order of the police or military became an everyday occurrence. The selective executions of 1939–40 gave way to indiscriminate shootings and hangings. In the towns, prisoners and suspects were shot out of hand. In Warsaw, hardly a street corner did not witness the death of groups of citizens by the score and the hundred. Following an order on 16 October 1943 'to combat attacks against German reconstruction in the *General-Gouvernement*', the *łapanka,* or 'seizure of hostages in the street', became a commonplace. Hostages were killed or tormented publicly, in the full view of the populace forcibly assembled for the purpose.

Rural pacification proceeded apace. The well-known fate of the one Bohemian hamlet of Lidice, whose 143 men were killed in retaliation for the assassination of *SS-General* Reinhard Heydrich, was repeated in hundreds of Polish villages. An incomplete post-war count put their number at 299: Rajsk, 16 April 1942 (142 deaths); Krassowo-Częstki, 17 July 1943 (259); Skłoby, 11 April 1940 (215); Michniów, 13 July 1943 (203); Józefów, 14 April 1940 (169); Kitów, 11 December 1942 (174); Sumin, 29 January 1943 (118); Sochy, 1 June 1943 (181); Borów, 2 February 1944 (232); Łążek, 2 February 1944 (187); Szczecyn, 2 February 1944 (368); Jamy, 3 March 1944 (147); Milejów, 6 September 1939 (150); Kaszyce, 7 March 1943 (117); Krusze, 31 August 1944 (148); Lipniak-Majorat, 2 September 1944 (370) . . . The largest single pacification campaign took place between November 1942 and August 1943 in the region of Zamość, which had been designated for recolonization by German and Ukrainian settlers. Over 100,000 Polish peasants were forcibly evicted from some 300 villages. Those capable of work were transported to the Reich. The children were deported for Germanization. The troublemakers were sent for extermination to Auschwitz and Maidaneck. The rest were distributed throughout the *General-Gouvernement.* The scale of German ambitions in this regard can be judged by the fact that a further 400 villages embraced by this pilot project remained untouched, simply because the SS lacked the manpower to deal with them.[21]

The proliferation of Nazi camps exceeded anything which

existed elsewhere in Europe. They included six main categories. The Prisoner-of-War Camps – *Oflagen* for officers, and *Stalagen* for other ranks – were administered by the German military. In Poland they were mainly used for prisoners from the Eastern Front, and quickly shed all pretence of humane standards. A strict policy of starvation for all prisoners who refused to serve in German formations produced conditions unheard-of elsewhere in Germany. Some 500,000 Soviet prisoners, and some 50,000 Italians interned after the collapse of Mussolini in 1943, are thought to have died in *Stalag VIIIB* at Lambinowice, *Stalag VIIIC* at Żagań, *Frontstalag 307* at Deldin, or *Stalag 325* at Zamość. Other camps were administered by the SS or the Gestapo. Special Camps catered for various categories of prisoner, such as orphans, juvenile delinquents, or children selected for Germanization. The Labour Camps – *Judenlager* for Jews, *Polenlager* for Poles – were sited near major military work-sites, and were usually classified as 'labour reformatories'. The Penal-Investigation Camps such as that at Żabików near Poznań were created by the Gestapo to facilitate criminal and political enquiries. The Transit Camps were designed to accommodate deportees, people awaiting to be processed, and slave-labourers *en route* for the Reich. The Concentration Camps were the special concern of the SS, and were reserved for the political and racial enemies of the Nazi order. The main installations in Poland at Auschwitz-Birkenau (1940–5), Maidaneck (1941–5), Dora (1943–5), Treblinka (1942–4), and Plaschau (1944–5) near Cracow were supported by two thousand collecting centres and command posts. They were staffed by permanent cadres of German personnel. Their size and blatantly public activities prevented any realization of Himmler's policy of official secrecy. From their original detailment as places of internment or punishment, they soon developed into centres of systematic genocide: among other things as the sites of the Nazis' Final Solution of the Jews.[22]

Of all the camps, none achieved the proportions or the notoriety of Auschwitz-Birkenau, conveniently stationed on the lawless bank of the old Silesian frontier in the marshland at the junction of the Vistula and Soła rivers. It started its career in June 1940 as an internment centre for 10,000 political prisoners drawn from neighbouring Polish and Silesian prisons. In March 1941 it was extended to accommodate 30,000 inmates. At this stage, Auschwitz did not differ significantly from its predecessors at Dachau (1933), Buchenwald (1937), or Sachsenhausen (1936). The new arrivals were marched in to the strains of the camp orchestra, through the iron gateway with its slogan '*Arbeit Macht Frei*' (Work makes you free), past the double line of electrified wire-fencing, past the concealed machine-gun nests. Once inside, a camp number was tattooed onto their forearms; they were given a striped prison uniform, assigned a billet in one of the rows of grim prefabricated huts, and put to work. Their life expectancy was three months. In October 1941, further enlargements were begun. Owing to the war on the Eastern Front, and the Final Solution, several thousand acres of adjoining land was obtained at Brzezinka (Birkenau), to provide for 100,000 extra inmates. The SS-Guard was raised to 6,000 men, not counting the thousands of *Kapos* (trusties) and special detachments drawn from the prisoners themselves. A female section was built, together with railway facilities, fortified guard posts, and modern floodlighting. On 4 May 1942, the first of the four gas-chambers and crematoria consumed their first victims from the camp hospital. Thereafter, their average capacity rose to 20,000 bodies per day. At the height of the Final Solution in 1942–3, a train would arrive approximately every hour and unload its human cargo, living and dead, on to the long concrete platform. The able-bodied would be marched off to work. The old, the infirm, the young, and mothers with children were told they were to be deloused, were ordered to strip and were driven directly to the gas-chambers. Twenty minutes later, the special detachments would be shearing off the hair from the corpses, looking for jewellery concealed in body orifices, tearing out gold dental fillings with hooks, and carrying the mutilated remains on biers to the ovens. At the other end of the crematoria, further groups of workers would be dealing with the remains of the previous transport, draining off fat for the manufacture of soap, or shovelling the ashes into bags of fertilizer. This was the *Anus Mundi* whose motions were regulated with Prussian precision. Those of its countless victims who died swiftly were fortunate. Those who were spared the gas-chamber suffered far greater torments and degradation, whose details can only be imagined: mass-starvation; cannibalism; the roll-call; the *scheissmeister*; Bogers' swing; the wall of death; pseudo-medical operations on 'experimental persons'; sterilization; amputation; injected diseases; mock masses; theatrical executions; sexual perversions; human lampshades; headshrinking; 'parachuting'; *Aktion-'Kugel'* . . . The science of thanatology was brought to a pitch of theory and practice never equalled. Its brutalized subjects were given a brief reprieve for informing, bullying, and preying on their fellows; and then, as often as not, were destroyed themselves. At the moment of Liberation on 27 January 1945 by the Soviet Army, only 7,500 live inmates could be found, including 90 pairs of identical twins. By that time, according to evidence submitted at the Nuremberg Trials, Auschwitz-Birkenau had consumed over four million human beings.[23]

The human emotions which festered in Auschwitz defy description. Solid citizens were driven to perform the most unnatural acts:

Here comes a woman walking briskly, hurrying almost imperceptibly yet feverishly. A small child with the plump, rosy face of a cherub runs after her, fails to catch up, stretches out its hands crying 'Mama, Mama'.
— Woman, take this child in your arms!
— Sir, it isn't mine, it isn't my child! The woman shouts hysterically, and runs away covering her face with her hands. She wants to hide. She wants to reach those who will leave on foot, who won't leave by truck, who will live. She is young, healthy, pretty; she wants to live.
But the child runs after her, pleading at the top of its voice, 'Mama, Mama, don't run away'.
— It's not mine, not mine, not . . .
At that point, André, the sailor from Sevastopol overtook her. His eyes were troubled by vodka and the heat. He reached her, knocked her off her feet with a single powerful blow and, as she fell, caught her by the hair and dragged her up again. His face was distorted with fury.
— Why you lousy, fucking Jew-bitch. *Yebit 'tvoyu mat'.* So you'd run away from your own child! I'll show you, you whore! He grabbed her in the middle, one paw throttling her throat which wanted to shout, and flung her into the truck like a heavy sack of grain.
— Here, take this with you, you slut! And he threw her child at her feet.

— *Gut gemacht.* That's how one treats unnatural mothers! said an SS-man standing near the van . . .

A pair of people fall to the ground entangled in a desperate embrace. He digs his fingers into her flesh convulsively, tears at her clothes with his teeth. She curses hysterically, curses, blasphemes, until stifled by a boot, she chokes and falls silent. They split them apart, like a tree; and herd them into the car like animals . . .

Others are carrying a girl with a missing leg. They hold her by her arms, and by her one remaining leg. Tears are streaming down her face as she whispers sadly, 'Please, please, it hurts, it hurts . . .' They heave her into a truck, among the corpses. She will be burned alive, together with them.[24]

Conditions in the other concentration camps were no better. Treblinka, on the banks of the Bug 51 miles to the north-east of Warsaw, was a smaller camp than Auschwitz, custom-built for the purposes of the Final Solution:

MR. COUNSELLOR SMIRNOV: I beg you to describe this camp to the Tribunal.
RAJZMAN: Transports arrived there every day; their number depended on the number of trains arriving; sometimes three, four, or five trains filled exclusively with Jews — from Czechoslovakia, Germany, Greece, and Poland. Immediately after their arrival, the people had to leave the trains in 5 minutes and line up on the platform. All those who were driven from the cars were divided into groups — men, women, and children, all separate. They were all forced to strip immediately, and this procedure continued under the lashes of the German guards' whips. Workers who were employed in this operation immediately picked up all the clothes and carried them away to the barracks. Then the people were obliged to walk naked through the street to the gas chambers.
MR. COUNSELLOR SMIRNOV: I would like you to tell the Tribunal what the Germans called the street to the gas chambers.
RAJZMAN: It was called Himmelfahrt Street.
MR. COUNSELLOR SMIRNOV: That is to say, the 'street to heaven'?
RAJZMAN: Yes. . . .
MR. COUNSELLOR SMIRNOV: Please tell us, how long did a person live after he had arrived in the Treblinka Camp?
RAJZMAN: The whole process of undressing and the walk down to the gas chambers lasted for the men 8 or 10 minutes, and for the women some 15 minutes. The women took 15 minutes because they had to have their hair shaved off before they went to the gas chambers.
MR. COUNSELLOR SMIRNOV: Why was their hair cut off?

RAJZMAN: According to the ideas of the masters, this hair was to be used in the manufacture of mattresses for German women. . . .

MR. COUNSELLOR SMIRNOV: Please tell us, Witness, were the people brought to Treblinka in trucks or trains?

RAJZMAN: They were brought nearly always in trains, and only the Jews from neighbouring villages and hamlets were brought in trucks. . . .

MR. COUNSELLOR SMIRNOV: Please tell us what was the subsequent aspect of the station at Treblinka?

RAJZMAN: At first there were no signboards whatsoever at the station, but a few months later the commander of the camp, one Kurt Franz, built a first-class railroad station with signboards. The barracks where the clothing was stored had signs reading 'Restaurant', 'Ticket Office', 'Telephone', 'Telegraph' and so forth. There were even train schedules for the departure and arrival of trains to and from Grodno, Suwalki, Vienna, and Berlin.

MR. COUNSELLOR SMIRNOV: Did I rightly understand you, Witness, that a kind of make-believe station was built . . . ?

RAJZMAN: When the people descended from the trains, they really had the impression that they were at a very good station . . .

MR. COUNSELLOR SMIRNOV: And what happened later on to these people?

RAJZMAN: These people were taken directly along the Himmelfahrt-strasse to the gas chambers.

MR. COUNSELLOR SMIRNOV: And tell us, please, how did the Germans behave while killing their victims in Treblinka?

RAJZMAN: If you mean the actual executions, every German guard had his special job. I shall cite only one example. We had a Scharfuehrer Menz, whose special job was to guard the so-called 'Lazarett'. . . . This was part of a square that which was closed in with a wooden fence. All women, aged persons, and sick children were driven there. At the gates of the 'Lazarett' there was a large Red Cross flag. Menz, who specialised in the murder of all persons brought to this 'Lazarett', would not let anybody else do this job. . . . A 10-year-old girl was brought to this building from the train with her 2-year-old sister. When the elder girl saw that Menz had taken out a revolver to shoot her sister, she threw herself upon him, crying out, and asking why he wanted to kill her. He did not kill the little sister; he threw her alive into the oven and then killed the elder sister . . . They brought an aged woman with her daughter to this building. The latter was in the last stage of pregnancy. She was . . . put on a grass plot, and several Germans came to watch the delivery. This spectacle lasted 2 hours. When the child was born, Menz asked the grandmother . . . whom she preferred to see killed first. The grandmother begged to be killed. But, of course, they did the opposite.

The newborn baby was killed first, then the child's mother, and finally the grandmother. . . .

MR. COUNSELLOR SMIRNOV: Tell us, Witness, how many persons were brought daily to the Treblinka Camp?

RAJZMAN: Between July and December 1942 an average of 3 transports of 60 cars each arrived every day. In 1943 the transports arrived more rarely.

MR. COUNSELLOR SMIRNOV: Tell us, Witness, how many persons were exterminated in the camp, on an average, daily?

RAJZMAN: On an average, I believe they killed in Treblinka from ten to twelve thousand persons daily . . .[25]

The guards, especially those who wished to lend an air of order and decency to the proceedings, were brutalized beyond all human recognition. Rudolf Hoess, the Camp Commandant at Auschwitz from 1940 to 1944, penned in his autobiography, perhaps the most damning self-condemnation of human nature ever invented:

I had to appear cold and indifferent to events which must have wrung the heart of anyone possessed of human feelings . . . I had to watch coldly while the mothers with laughing or crying children went to the gas-chambers. On one occasion two small children were so absorbed in some game that they quite refused to let their mother tear them away from it. Even the Jews of the Special Department were reluctant to pick them up. The imploring look in the eyes of the mother, who certainly knew what was happening, is something I shall never forgot . . . Everyone was looking at me. I nodded to the junior non-commissioned officer on duty, and he picked up the struggling, screaming children in his arms and carried them into the gas-chamber . I had to see everything. I had to watch hour by hour, by night and by day, the burning and the removal of the bodies, the extraction of the teeth, the cutting off of the hair, the whole grisly business. I had to stand for hours on end in the ghastly stench, while the mass graves were being opened and the bodies dragged out and burned. I had to look through the peep-holes of the gas-chambers and watch the process of death itself . . . I had to do all this, because I was the one to whom everyone looked, because I had to show them all that I did not merely issue the orders and make the regulations but was also prepared to be present at whatever task I had assigned to my subordinates . . . In the face of such grim considerations I was forced to bury all human considerations as deeply as possible . . . I had to observe everything with a cold indifference . . . In Auschwitz, I truly had no reason to complain that I was bored . . . I had only one end in view, to drive everyone and everything forward, so that I could accomplish the measures laid down . . . Every German had to commit himself heart and soul, so that we might win the war . . . By the will of the *Reichsfuehrer SS,* Auschwitz became the greatest human extermination centre of all time . . .

When I saw my children playing happily, or observed my wife's delight over our youngest, the thought would often come over me, how long will our happiness last? My wife could never understand these gloomy moods of mine, and ascribed them to some annoyance connected with my work . . . I had become dissatisfied with myself. To this must be added that I was worried because of anxiety about the never-ending work, and untrustworthiness of my colleagues . . . My family, for sure, were well provided for at Auschwitz. Every wish that my wife or children expressed was granted them. The children could live a free and untrammelled life. My wife's garden was a paradise of flowers . . . The children were perpetually asking me for cigarettes for the prisoners. They were particularly fond of those who worked in the garden. My whole family displayed an intense love of agriculture and particularly of animals of all sorts. Every Sunday I had to walk them across the fields, and visit the stables, and we might never miss out the kennels where the dogs were kept. Our two horses and the foal were especially beloved. The children always kept animals in the garden, creatures which the prisoners were forever bringing them — tortoises, martens, cats, lizards. There was always something new and interesting to be seen there. In the summer they splashed in the paddling pool, or in the River Soła. But their greatest joy was when Daddy bathed with them. He had, however, so little time for such childish pleasures . . .[26]

These paragraphs were composed in a Polish cell in Cracow in 1947, a few days before their author, after due process of law, was himself executed on the site of his former duties.

The cold economic considerations are equally hard to comprehend. Auschwitz-Birkenau was designed by supposedly respectable architects and consultants, and the camp worked for the greatest firms in Germany. Its operations were subject to precise calculations of cost-accounting and quality control. Hoess's office was adorned by a huge mural diagram which detailed the end-products to be expected from any given input. Apart from the synthetic petrol produced in the camp's chemical factory, there was gold for the *Reichsbank,* and tons of bone fertilizer, soap, hair carpet, optical lenses from spectacles, and scrap wood and metal from crutches and artificial limbs. The WVHA had carefully estimated its profits in advance:

The hiring of concentration camp inmates to industrial enterprises yields an average daily return of 6 to 8 RM, from which 70 pf. must be deducted for food and clothing. Assuming an inmate's life expectancy to be 9 months, we must multiply this sum by 270. The total, is 1,431 RM. This profit can be increased by rational utilization of the corpse, i.e. by means of gold fillings, clothing, valuables etc., but on the other hand every corpse represents a loss of 2 RM, which is the cost of cremation.[27]

Inexplicably, production did not match expectations. By the end of 1942, even the SS began to realize that the extermination of one's labour force does not make good economic sense. One of their enterprises, the *Ostindustrie GmbH* was forced into liquidation when all of its employees were found to be dead. The Gestapo was ordered to poach workers from civilian industry on trumped-up charges in order to keep its own manpower reserves up to strength. In December 1942, Oswald Pohl, the head of WVHA, ordered that all 'maltreatment' of concentration camp inmates should end, as it was damaging efficiency; and in April 1943, he conceded that lack of fuel would eventually cause the Final Solution to be suspended indefinitely. These orders brought no relief. They condemned the remaining inmates to a slow death instead of a swift one, and burdened the SS with a 'work-force' of living skeletons who were not actually dead but could not work.

The brute statistics speak for themselves. In six years of the war, the population of the former Polish Republic was reduced by 6,028,000. Of these, some 2.9 million were Polish Jews. Some 644,000 Polish citizens (10.7 per cent) lost their lives as the direct result of war operations. A total of 5,384,000 citizens (89.3 per cent) were killed in executions, in pacifications, and above all in the camps. Of an estimated 18 million Nazi victims of all nationalities, over 11 million died in the occupied Polish lands. Of these, over 5 million were Jews. Sadly enough, the statistical breakdown of these terrible totals continues to be a subject to dispute.[28] Jewish investigators tend to count Jewish victims. Polish investigators tend to count Polish victims. Neither side wishes to stress the fact that the largest single category of victims was both Polish and Jewish. Not everyone, it seems, is content to count human beings.

The Resistance Movement flourished from the start. For the Poles, there was no question of collaboration. There was never any Polish Quisling, for the simple reason that in Poland the Nazis never really tried to recruit one. The Poles were given the stark choice: to submit completely, or to resist. When it was seen that no advantages were gained by submission, increasing numbers turned to resistance. In the early months of the war, scores of separate partisan bands took to the woods; hundreds of conspiratorial cells were formed spontaneously in the towns. They took their orders from no one: but they knew their task without telling; to harry and distract the enemy, both Nazi and Soviet, at every opportunity. One such 'lone ranger' was Major Henryk Dobrzański (1896–1940), known as 'Hubal', who met his death on 30 April 1940 in a village near Kielce, after a winter of stirring adventures. He was the first of many.[29]

The foundations of an organized Resistance were laid before the end of the September Campaign. On 27 September 1939, a group of army officers under General Karasiewicz-Tokarzewski formed the 'Polish Victory Service' (SZP) to continue the fight under cover. Somewhat later, in November, the 'Union of Armed Struggle' (ZWZ) was created by the new Government-in-Exile, to subordinate Resistance activities to the plans of the Western Allies. These two organizations gave rise in due course to the *Armia Krajowa* (Home Army), the AK, which could fairly claim to be the largest of European resistance formations. They were joined in 1941–2 by the numerous *Bataliony Chłopskie* (Peasant Battalions), the *'Be-Cha'*, formed to oppose the German deportation and pacification programmes, and by various right-wing groups such as the 'National Armed Forces' (NSZ) and 'National Military Organization' (NOW), and more loosely, by the diminutive, communist-led *Gwardia Ludowa* (People's Guard, GL). The disbanded Polish Boy Scouts Association (ZHP) put its members at the disposal of the AK, and formed its own clandestine storm troops known as the *Szare Szeregi* (the Grey Ranks).[30]

For a long time, the achievements of the Resistance were of necessity rather modest. With illegal assembly or the possession of arms punishable by instant death, the utmost caution was required. Even so, trains were derailed. Enemy convoys were ambushed. Prisoners were rescued from their Nazi guards. National art treasures were spirited to safety. A tablet commemorating the 'great German astronomer', Nikolaus Koppernick, was unscrewed from his statue in Warsaw. Patriotic Polish music found its way on to the German radio. Polish workers in German factories were persuaded to work even more slowly than usual. The underground press flourished, both in Polish and, for propaganda purposes, in German. All the main Polish universities, in Warsaw, Cracow, Lwów, and Wilno, officially closed by the authorities, restarted on a private, conspiratorial basis. The 'Secret Teaching Organization' (TON) built up an amazing network of clandestine classes, which eventually undertook the education of a million children. Valuable military intelligence, including details of the V1 and V2 rockets, was passed to the Western Allies.[31] Even in the camps, resistance cells circulated banned information and planned escapes and incidents. By the end of 1942, the Resistance felt able to answer terror with terror. On 8 October 1942, AK sappers destroyed the main marshalling yards in Warsaw. On 24 October, the GL bombed the *Wehrmacht's* 'Café Club' in Warsaw, in response to the public execution of fifty of their members. On 30 December, at Wojda near Zamość, a BCh company led the first armed challenge to the pacification programme. In January 1943, the AK formed the Diversionary Directorate (*Kedyw*) which in the following months sprung four Gestapo prisoners, and on 8 August conducted a colossal bank-raid in Warsaw. By the autumn of that year, open confrontations with German units were common in the countryside. Huge areas in the hills and forests, such as the 'Republic of Pińczów' near Cracow, were entirely cleared of enemy troops. With news of the German defeat at Stalingrad, preparations were made for a decisive showdown in conjunction with the advancing Red Army.

The Jewish Resistance Movement had still less room for manœuvre. Confined in the reservations from the earliest days of the war, the Jews had little chance to collect weapons or to collude with their non-Jewish colleagues. The Polish 'Council of Assistance for Jews' (RPZ), created by the AK in September 1942, had equally restricted opportunities. It assisted some 100,000 people to escape the Final Solution.[32] Even so, a 'Jewish Battle Organization' did exist, and did resist. Its hour of martyrdom started on 19 April 1943 when the final attempt to liquidate the remaining inhabitants of the Warsaw Ghetto was met by force. The SS-infantrymen commanded by *Brigadenfuehrer* Jurgen Stroop were driven back by gunfire from windows and barricades. The uneven battle lasted for three weeks. In that time, seven thousand Jewish fighters were killed; some six thousand were deliberately burned to death in their hideouts; fifty-six thousand Jewish prisoners were transported to the death-camp at Treblinka. This was the largest single act of Resistance until the outbreak of the Warsaw Rising in the next summer.[33]

Political co-ordination among the various resistance groups never achieved the desired results. (See Diagram E.) The AK and the BCh with their 400,000 men held an overwhelming superiority over their communist-led rivals, who in the GL and its successor, the *Armia Ludowa* (People's Army, AL) never controlled more than 10,000 supporters. Yet the mere 'mathematical majority' could not easily be translated into political terms. Co-operation between the two camps was limited to practical matters, and did not include an agreement on a common political programme once the war was over. On the one side, the AK was directly linked to the Government-in-Exile in London, whose *Delegatura* (Home Delegation) headed the administrative structures of an entire underground state, functioning both in the *General-Gouvernement* and in the Polish parts of the Reich. Policy decisions were taken in a Consultative Political Committee (PKP) supported by the four parties connected with the Government-in-Exile, and from 1942 were put into effect by the seven executive ministries. In 1944–5, they were referred to a political Council of National Unity (RJN) and an executive Council of Ministers. The office of chief Delegate was held successively by A. Bniński (1884–1942) in Poznań, Cyril Ratajski (1875–1942) in Warsaw, Professor Jan Piekałkiewicz (1892–1943), and J. S. Jankowski (1882–1953). On the other side, the GL and AL were directly subordinated to the communist Polish Workers' Party (PPR), which in turn had somewhat ambiguous connections with Moscow. The communist organizations, which had no measurable popular support at this time, avoided all thoughts of merger or patronage. On 1 January 1944, they formed their own National Home Council (KRN), which can be seen as the first seed of the future People's Republic. Meanwhile, they awaited the victorious Soviet Army, whose arrival in Poland was bound to transform political conditions beyond all recognition. (See Map 17.)

Any description of the Soviet Liberation of Poland must depend to some extent on one's definition of Poland. At its greatest extent, the Liberation can be said to have lasted from 4 January 1944, when the Soviet Army first crossed the pre-war frontier in Volhynia, to September 1945, when the Soviet authorities finally handed over the Western Territories to Polish management. In terms of the fighting on the present territory of the People's Republic, the Liberation lasted from the crossing of the River Bug on 19 July 1944 to the capitulation of Breslau on 6 May 1945. In the first critical period, in the absence of a binding international agreement on the future of the Polish lands, the Soviets were free to treat them as they thought fit. For practical purposes, they always treated districts east of the Bug as part of the USSR, and districts to the west of the old German frontier as part of the defeated Reich. Inevitably, there was a great deal of confusion. And there was a great deal of destruction. As the Front lurched unsteadily westwards, district after district was subjected to the same succession of events. When the *Wehrmacht* prepared to hold its chosen line of defence, it would be harried in the rear and on the flanks by partisans of all sorts — by one or all of the various Polish formations, by local peasant guerrillas, by Ukrainians and Byelorussians, or by Soviet groups parachuted behind the lines. Then the Soviet Army would attack, and an overwhelming surge of tanks and battle-hardened troops would drive the Germans from their positions. Immediately behind the receding front line marched a tidal wave of assorted human flotsam — exhausted German soldiers separated from their units, stranded partisans who wished to submit neither to the Germans nor to the Soviets, deserters, camp-followers of both sexes, escaped prisoners and criminals living off the land, and civilian refugees who did not know which way to turn. Finally, driving the stragglers before them,

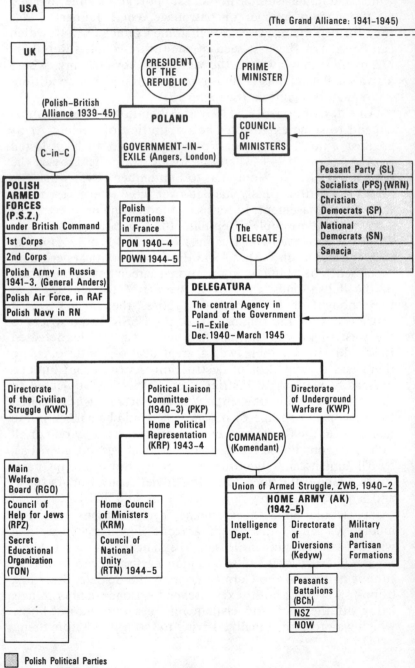

Diagram E. Polish Military ar

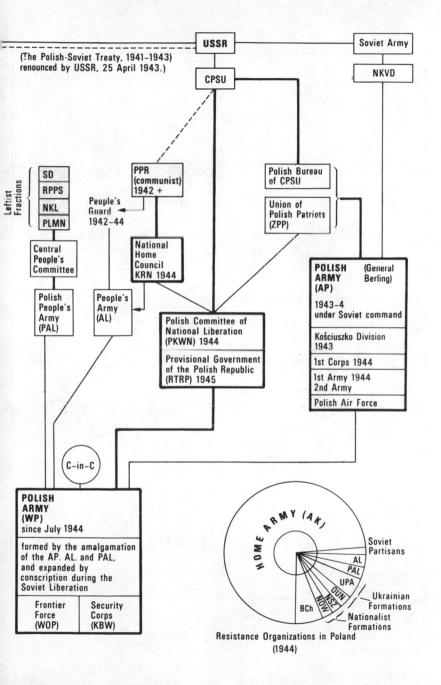

(The Polish-Soviet Treaty, 1941–1943)
renounced by USSR, 25 April 1943.)

USSR

Soviet Army

NKVD

CPSU

Leftist Fractions

SD
RPPS
NKL
PLMN

Central People's Committee

Polish People's Army (PAL)

PPR (communist) 1942 +

People's Guard 1942–44

People's Army (AL)

National Home Council KRN 1944

Polish Bureau of CPSU

Union of Polish Patriots (ZPP)

Polish Committee of National Liberation (PKWN) 1944

Provisional Government of the Polish Republic (RTRP) 1945

POLISH ARMY (AP)   (General Berling)

1943–4 under Soviet command

Kościuszko Division 1943

1st Corps 1944

1st Army 1944
2nd Army

Polish Air Force

C-in-C

POLISH ARMY (WP) since July 1944

formed by the amalgamation of the AP. AL. and PAL, and expanded by conscription during the Soviet Liberation

Frontier Force (WOP)

Security Corps (KBW)

HOME ARMY (AK)

Soviet Partisans

AL
PAL
UPA

Ukrainian Formations

OUN
NSZ
NOW

BCh

Nationalist Formations

Resistance Organizations in Poland (1944)

olitical Organizations, (1939–45)

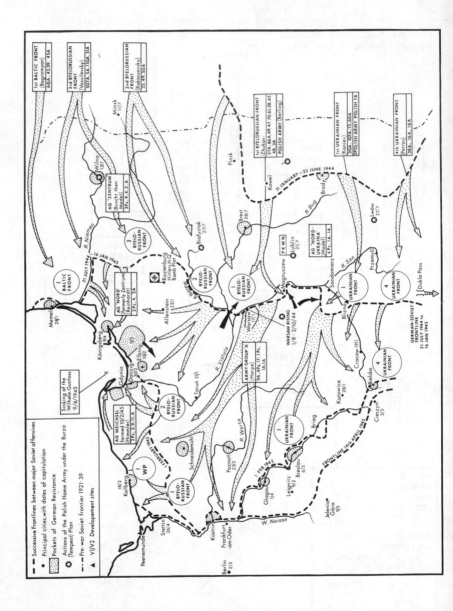

came the disciplined ranks of the Soviet Special Forces – the
reparation squads, the requisitioning brigades, the military
police, the political services, and proudest of all, in their
American jeeps, the NKGB.* These Special Forces were of a
size and nature unseen on the Western Front. Their task was
to impose the Soviet order on the occupied territories without fear or favour. According to Article 9 of the Treaty
signed on 26 July 1944 by the PKWN, the Soviet authorities
were granted full control over civilian security in the Soviet
army's rear. This gave them an open licence to subject the
population to the political exercise so bitterly remembered
from 1939–40. All existing local officials, from the mayor to
the municipal caretaker, were unceremoniously replaced, often
under the threat of charges of having collaborated with the
Nazis. Peasants were invited at gunpoint to surrender their
livestock and their foodstores. Members of the Polish Resi
stance were given the choice between instant arrest, and service
in one of the Soviet-sponsored formations. Anyone who
showed the slightest disinclination to obey immediately was
written off as a war casualty. Once a liberated area had been
processed in this manner, it was highly unlikely that anyone
would be left who might undertake political enterprises of
an independent character.

The political situation was extremely unpleasant. On the
one hand, the Soviet leaders openly declared themselves to
be the loyal allies of the Western Powers, and subscribed in
theory to the principles of the common, democratic, and
anti-Nazi alliance. On the other hand, they had denounced
the Polish Government-in-Exile, which was the accepted
authority on Polish matters in everyone else's eyes, and they
confined their dealings in Poland to persons and institutions
appointed by themselves in their own image. They began by
attacking all non-communist Resistance groups, especially
those who had assisted the Soviet advance, and by appointing
local administrators subservient to themselves, in every town

---

* The *National Commissariat of State Security* (NKGB), which grew out of the
National Commissariat of Internal Affairs (NKVD) in 1943, had special
responsibility for all areas liberated from German Occupation. It was superseded
in 1946 by agencies of the *Ministry of State Security* (MGB), the forerunner
of the present *Commissariat of State Security* (KGB).

and village throughout Poland. Figures of course, are not
available; but the victims must certainly be counted in tens of
thousands. Perhaps the saddest scene of the entire Liberation
occurred at Majdanek near Lublin in the late summer of 1944,
when the Soviet authorities made use of the former Nazi extermination camp to house detainees of the Polish Home
Army. The culmination of the process came in March 1945
when the remaining leaders of the Resistance were arrested
and deported for trial. Sixteen such leaders, including the
former Vice-Premier and Delegate of the Government-in-Exile,
Jan Stanisław Jankowski, and the last Commander of the
Home Army, General L. Okulicki, were sentenced in Moscow
in June 1945 as 'saboteurs and subversionist bandits', at the
very time when their ostensible patrons, the Western Powers,
were pressing Poles of all persuasions to settle their differences.[34] Nor did the Soviet Army depart once the Liberation
was complete. On the grounds that Soviet lines of communication to Germany had to be protected, the Soviet Army
was able to stay in Poland, and thus to guarantee that political
developments proceeded in accordance with the Kremlin's
wishes. It has been there ever since.

The critical moment had arrived in July 1944 when the
Soviet Army crossed the River Bug, and entered territory
which Moscow was prepared to recognize as belonging to the
future Polish state. On 22 July, with no prior consultation
with the other interested parties, they created at Lublin the
Polish Committee of National Liberation (PKWN) and invested
it with the powers of a temporary administration. The leaders
of the AK were placed in a quandary of the most acute
nature. As an arm of the legally constituted Polish government, and in command of the largest single element of the
Resistance Movement, they had every right to expect a share
in the political dispositions of the liberation. Absurdly, they
were being urged by their Western patrons to co-operate with
the Soviets, even when the Soviets refused to recognize their
existence. Co-operation on these terms was simply impossible.
What is more, their position deteriorated as the Soviet advance
continued. Their long-cherished strategic plan, code-named
'Burza' (Tempest), whereby units in the field were to restrict
operations against the Germans until they could act in concert

with the Soviet Army, was proving disastrous. At Wilno, at Lwów, and at Białystok, the AK, having emerged from the underground, had engaged the retreating *Wehrmacht,* and had fought alongside the Soviet Army, only to end up under Soviet arrest. In Volhynia, the 27 Infantry Division of the AK suffered a similar fate, after carving a blood-strewn path through the German lines in order to link up with Polish units serving in the Soviet ranks. At Lublin, AK units patrolling the captured city in advance of the Soviet Army, found that they themselves were to be interned, whilst their prize was to be handed over to the communist PKWN, newly delivered by air from Moscow. With the fate of the capital, Warsaw, in the balance, the situation was desperate. If the AK failed to throw its reserves into the fray, the likelihood was that Warsaw would fall under communist control and that the AK would be suppressed by the Soviets, without a word or a shot of defiance. If, on the other hand, the AK tried to wrest control of Warsaw from the Germans on their own, they were bound to be condemned for disrupting the Grand Alliance and for acting from motives of private political advantage. In Moscow, any operation which was not subject to direct Soviet supervision was sure to be denounced as an anti-Soviet adventure. In Warsaw, in the clandestine councils of the AK leadership, the alternatives were weighed and sifted. Ever since the third week of July, the AK Commander, General Tadeusz Bór-Komorowski was convinced that an armed rising in Warsaw would have to take place in the very near future. His objectives and priorities were expressed in a dispatch to London on 22 July:

1. Not to stop our struggle against the Germans even for one moment . . .
2. To mobilise the entire population spiritually for the struggle against Russia . . .
3. To crush the irresponsible activity of the ONR [extreme right-wing nationalists].
4. To detach from the Soviets as many as possible of the Polish elements already standing at their disposal . . .
5. In the event of a Soviet attempt to violate Poland, to undertake an open struggle against them.[35]

On that same day, the creation of the PKWN in Lublin showed that the Soviets were pushing ahead regardless with their own political dispositions; whilst the Bomb Plot on Hitler's life at nearby Rastenburg (Kętrzyn) in East Prussia hinted that the German collapse might be imminent. The *Wehrmacht's* partial evacuation of stores and administrative units from Warsaw seemed to signal the start of their retreat. But the AK still hesitated. Their supply of ammunition was only estimated to last for three or four days, and they still had no clear picture of the German–Soviet tank battle which was shaping up to the east of the Vistula. July 29 was a day of alarms. The pro-communist *P.A.L.* issued a proclamation, announcing quite shamelessly that the AK had abandoned Warsaw. Then in the evening at 8.15 p.m. Moscow Radio broadcast an appeal in Polish urging the Varsovians to rise: FOR WARSAW, WHICH DID NOT YIELD BUT FOUGHT ON, THE HOUR OF ACTION HAS ARRIVED. Yet an emissary from London ruled out large-scale assistance from the West. As the first Soviet units began to cross the Vistula on to their bridgehead at Magnuszew forty miles to the south, five armoured divisions of the German Ninth Army under the personal command of Field Marshal Model moved to the counter-attack to the east of Praga. At noon on 31 July, a full meeting of Polish military and civilian leaders again postponed their decision. But at 5.30 p.m., the local commander for Warsaw, Col. Antoni 'Monter' Chruściel (1896–1970), arrived with a report that Soviet tanks were entering Praga. Bór-Komorowski called in the Chief Government Delegate, Jankowski, who said 'Very well, then, begin.' Turning to Monter, he then gave him a brief but decisive order: 'Tomorrow at 1700 hours you will start Operation Tempest in Warsaw.' The die was cast.

There can be little doubt that the decision to launch the Warsaw Rising represents for the Poles the most tragic mistake in their recent history. It was taken for the most honourable motives, by men who had fought selflessly for their country's independence against all comers from the beginning of the war. Yet it had the most baleful consequences for the very cause which it was intended to serve. On the practical plane, it was precipitated by treacherous Soviet conduct in the libe-rated areas, and in the military sphere, by the overwhelming desire to strike a blow at the Nazi oppressors before they withdrew. For obvious reasons, however, it stood little

chance of ultimate success. Its timing, and its underlying
tactical considerations, were woefully misguided. Its political
goals were fundamentally unrealistic. The plan to seize Warsaw
in the brief interval between the German withdrawal and the
arrival of the Soviet Army, was entirely dependent on military
intelligence which only the Soviet Command could have
supplied. The idea that Warsaw could have been held by the AK
in the name of the Government-in-Exile without a subsequent
showdown with the Soviets was belied by all previous experience. The notion that the Western Powers could have
afforded to take the part of the Poles in any major dispute
with their Soviet Allies was, to say the least, unfounded.
Thus a fine ideal, and human emotions straining at the leash,
paved the way for catastrophe. When Bór-Komorowski gave
the order to launch the Rising in the hope that the Soviet
Army would enter Warsaw in the first days of August, he was
grasping at a straw in the wind. Only half an hour later, when
he learned that the T34 tanks sighted in Praga belonged not
to the main body of Rokossowski's army, but only to the
isolated patrol of an encircled Soviet unit, he knew that the
Rising was doomed. But it was too late to think again. The
couriers carrying the order had already disappeared into the
cellars and byways of the occupied capital, and could not be
recalled at short notice. The stage for tragedy was set. Those
historians who can bear to judge a man of unblemished
courage and devotion have said that Bór was guilty of 'gross
irresponsibility'.[36]

The Rising followed its course through sixty-three days of
savagery. In the first four days, the insurgents occupied the
city's central suburbs, but failed to take the airport, the main
station, the Vistula bridges, or the vital right-bank district of
Praga. Thereafter they were on the defensive. Some 150,000
ill-armed amateurs faced the professional retribution of the
Nazi war-machine. General Erich von dem Bach-Zelewski
picked his men with gruesome attention to detail. The regular
Wehrmacht formations were supported by the Posnanian
Military Police; by the *SS-Herman Goering* Regiment; by the
SS Viking Panzer Division; by three battalions of starved
Soviet prisoners; by Oskar Dirlanger's 'Anti-partisan' Brigade,
composed entirely of reprieved criminals; and by the infamous

'RONA Brigade'.* Their energies were directed no less against the defenceless civilian population than against the youthful insurgents. Their military task was assisted by low-level aerial dive-bombing and by long-range heavy artillery. Day by day, street by street, the Polish capital and its inhabitants were reduced to ashes. The pattern of operations was first witnessed in the main street of the Wola suburb, where the withdrawal of the AK under fire preceded the wholesale execution of 8,000 citizens. The capture of Ochota on 11 August was attended by the murder of 40,000 people. Hospitals were set alight together with their nurses and patients. Mass shootings were commonplace. Women and children were commonly roped to the hulls of Germans tanks as a precaution against ambushes. Rows of civilian hostages were driven in front of the German infantry as protection against snipers.[37] On 2 September the AK evacuated the Old City. One thousand five hundred survivors, carrying 500 casualties on stretchers, found their way down a single manhole into the sewers, and through four miles of waste-deep sewage to safety. On 6 September, Powiśle fell. Then, in the middle of the month, hope revived. Praga on the right bank was taken by Polish divisions under Soviet command, and attempts were made to cross the river. On 18 September, a daylight air-raid by British and American Liberators from Italy dropped 1,800 containers of arms and supplies. But there hope ended. Nine out of ten containers fell into German hands. The Western Allies could not afford regular assistance. The Polish Parachute Brigade under British orders was sent to Arnhem and not to Warsaw. Berling's Polish army suffered heavy casualties on the Praga bridgehead, and was forcibly withdrawn when it tried to persist after one briefly successful river-crossing. The fate of the city was sealed. Czerniaków fell on 23 September, Mokotów on the 26th, Żolibórz on the 30th. Isolated, and surrounded in an enclave of the city centre, the AK was forced to surrender. Although its own losses did not exceed

* RONA was the acronym of *Russkaya Osvoboditelnaya Narodnaya Armiya* (Russian National Liberation Army). The Brigade was formed from Soviet deserters in Russia in 1942, and was commanded by a former Soviet officer of Polish origin, Mieczysław Kamiński, who was later shot by the Germans for indiscipline.

20,000, some 225,000 civilians had already been killed. To continue the struggle was to invite a 'Final Solution' as complete as that which had already destroyed the city's Ghetto. General Bór signed an act of capitulation on 2 October. The AK was awarded combatant rights, and its men passed into *Wehrmacht* custody as prisoners-of-war. Thereon, the entire city was evacuated. Some 550,000 people were taken to a concentration camp at Pruszków. Another 150,000 were dispatched for forced labour to the Reich. In accordance with Hitler's order that Warsaw should be 'razed without trace', German demolition squads began to dynamite those buildings which remained standing. When the Soviet Army finally advanced into the ruins on 17 January 1945, a city which six years before had housed 1,289,000 inhabitants, did not contain a single living soul; 93 per cent of the dwellings were destroyed or damaged beyond repair. Such totality can hardly be matched by the horrors of Leningrad, Hiroshima, or Dresden.[38]

The exact role of the Soviet government cannot be ascertained without reference to documents that have not been published. It was widely believed that Stalin deliberately urged Warsaw to rise in the sure knowledge that his political rivals in Poland would thereby be destroyed by the Germans. Certainly, the USSR made no effort to assist the Rising for at least five whole weeks, and thereafter in only the most halfhearted and grudging fashion. At the time, Churchill described the Russians' behaviour as 'strange and sinister'. On 16 August, in Moscow, the US Ambassador was told that 'the Soviet Government do not wish to associate themselves directly or indirectly with the adventure in Warsaw.' On 22 August, in a letter to Churchill and Roosevelt, Stalin denounced the leaders of the Rising as 'a group of criminals'. Everything pointed to calculated treachery. Yet other factors must also be borne in mind. Rokossowski's failure to advance against Warsaw can be partly explained by the fierce counter-attack of two Panzer divisions launched on 2 August, and by Soviet military priorities dictated by their invasion of the Balkans in the middle of the month. The misleading broadcasts of Moscow Radio, which first called on the Varsovians to rise, and then condemned them for doing so, can conceivably be explained in

terms of the time-lag before routine propaganda adjusted to
the changing military situation. The Soviets' change of tactic
in the second week of September inspired little confidence.
After protracted intransigence, Stalin only granted permission to the Western Allies to land their aircraft behind the
Soviet lines beyond Warsaw, 'because we can hardly prohibit
it'. Co-ordination remained perfunctory. The quantity of
Soviet assistance was minimal. Churchill was convinced that
the Russians 'wished to have the non-Communist Poles
destroyed to the full, but also to keep alive the idea that they
were going to their rescue'. Undoubtedly, Stalin comes out
of the episode with no credit. At the same time, there was
little reason to expect that in the middle of the 'Great Patriotic
War' the Soviet Dictator should have made a generous gesture
to people who were fundamentally opposed to everything he
stood for.

Western observers were mesmerized by a conflict of a sort
which they themselves had not experienced. To the British
and Americans, at a point when the Western Front in
Normandy had only just been established, it was unthinkable
that the Soviet alliance should be upset for the sake of the
Poles. By 1944, no one wanted to be reminded of the fact
that the Soviet Union, hardly less than the Nazi enemy, had
been involved in the outbreak of war. Even today, western public opinion finds difficulty in grasping the paradox that their
salvation from Nazi Germany was largely undertaken by the
sacrifices of a Soviet ally whose practices were hardly less
abhorrent than those of the common Nazi enemy. It is still
separated by a world of incomprehension from those Poles
in Warsaw in 1944 who faced the paradox in the most immediate form. Churchill was alive to the agonies of the situation, and did his best to impress them on Roosevelt. In his
private letters to the American President, he regularly enclosed
detailed descriptions of the fighting in Warsaw, and on one
occasion the text of an appeal by Polish women to the Pope:

Most Holy Father, we Polish women in Warsaw are inspired with sentiments of profound patriotism and devotion to our country. For three
weeks, while defending our fortress, we have lacked food and medicine.
Warsaw is in ruins. The Germans are killing the wounded in hospitals.
They are making women and children march in front of them in order

to protect their tanks. There is no exaggeration in reports of children who are fighting and destroying tanks with bottles of petrol. We mothers see our sons dying for freedom and the Fatherland. Our husbands, our sons, and our brothers are not considered by the enemy to be comba-tants. Holy Father, no-one is helping us. The Russian armies which have been for three weeks at the gates of Warsaw have not advanced a step. The aid coming to us from Great Britain is insufficient. The world is ignorant of our fight. God alone is with us. Holy Father, Vicar of Christ, if you can hear us, bless us Polish women who are fighting for the Church and for freedom.

Roosevelt's reply was to say that 'there now seems to be nothing we can do to help them.' Yet the Rising had almost a month still to run. At the beginning of October, one of the last broadcasts from Warsaw was picked up in London:

This is the stark truth. We were treated worse than Hitler's satellites, worse than Italy, Roumania, Finland. May God, who is just, pass judge-ment on the terrible injustice suffered by the Polish nation, and may He punish accordingly all those who are guilty.

Your heroes are the soldiers whose only weapons against tanks, planes and guns were their revolvers and bottles filled with petrol. Your heroes are the women who tended the wounded, and carried messages under fire, who cooked in bombed and ruined cellars to feed children and adults, and who soothed and comforted the dying. Your heroes are the children who went on quietly playing among the smouldering ruins. These are the people of Warsaw.

Immortal is the nation that can muster such universal heroism. For those who have died have conquered, and those who live on will fight on, will conquer and again bear witness that Poland lives when the Poles live.[39]

In Churchill's considered opinion, these words were 'indelible'.

The suppression of the Warsaw Rising marked the end of the old order in Poland. For the remaining months of the War, the dispositions of the Soviet authorities were not seriously challenged. The Government-in-Exile in London lost its remaining influence on the course of events. Co-ordinated action against the Germans was left entirely to the Soviet Army. In January 1945, in the month when the USSR uni-laterally recognized the transmogrification of the PKWN into the Provisional Government of the Polish Republic (RTRP), the Home Army was formally disbanded. Its leaders were being arrested by the Soviet security forces. Some of the AK men turned their conspiratorial experience into anti-communist enterprises; some of them joined the communists; most of them, thoroughly confused and disillusioned, went home and awaited developments. It was a privilege to be still alive.

In those remaining months of the German Occupation, following the total evacuation of Warsaw's surviving inhabitants, the Germans systematically attacked the empty shell of the capital. Hitler had ordered that Warsaw be razed to the ground. *Verbrennungskommando* units tore at the ruins with dynamite, flame-throwers, and bulldozers. Their task was virtually complete when in January 1945 they were interrupted by the sudden advance of the Soviet Army. In three days' fighting, the troops of the First Byelorussian Front drove the German Ninth Army from the Vistula, and on 17 January entered the smouldering moonscape. On the 18th, they were joined by units of the First Polish Army in an improvised march-past along the line of the Aleje Jerozolimskie. Two weeks later the communist RTRP moved to Warsaw from Lublin, and the ministries of the Provisional Government began to function. An unknown communist, Marian Spychalski (born 1906), unannounced and unelected, made his appearance as the first post-war President of the city. The horrors of the German Occupation gave way to the mysteries of the Soviet Liberation.

When the Soviet Army crossed the frontiers of the Greater Reich, into Silesia, Prussia, and Pomerania, all caution was thrown to the winds. It is matter of common fact that Danzig was gutted long after the German withdrawal, and that many towns in Prussia and Silesia were destroyed in acts of apparently wanton vandalism. Scenes of unrestrained rejoicing were marred by a campaign of unrestrained savagery against German civilians. The distinction between friend and foe were often overlooked. The laughing Soviet trooper of the propaganda films, with a Polish child on his knee, was no more typical than the drunken looter with stolen watches on his arm and blood on his hands. German soldiers were hunted down like vermin. Members of the *Volkssturm,* young and old, were denied combatant status, and were killed out of hand. German graves, no less than German womenfolk and farm animals, were indiscriminately assaulted. The significance of the invaders' limited vocabulary, of *Davay* and *Frau, komm,* was known to everyone. Arson, battery, murder, group rapes, and family suicides marked the passage of the liberating armies on a scale unparalleled elsewhere in Europe. The well-documented devastation of Silesia, which was so much more severe than comparable events in the provinces of central Germany, has led some historians to suspect a calculated policy of driving the German population from their homes in anticipation of the Potsdam Agreement.[40] Everywhere, Soviet reparation squads set to work to collect industrial and economic hardware. They were interested in anything from factories to foodstores. Operating on an autonomous basis, they took no care to distinguish hostile from friendly territory. One of their many spectacular operations was to dismantle and to carry off to Russia the entire electrification system of the Silesian railways.

The most brilliant and candid evocation of the final advance through Poland was written by one of the Russian liberators, at that time an artillery officer of the Second Byelorussian Front. As the Soviet Army's last winter offensive took off from fortified positions on the River Narew in the vicinity of Warsaw, the observer was duly impressed by the tide of T34 tanks, mounted Cossacks, self-propelled guns and rocket batteries, and the long lines of motorized infantry in their Dodge, Chevrolet, and Studebaker trucks, which poured westwards across Mazovia and northwards into East Prussia. On 20 January 1945, he reached Neidenburg (now Nidzica in the district of Olsztyn):

> The conquerors of Europe swarm,
> Russians scurrying everywhere.
> In their trucks they stuff their loot:
> Vacuum cleaners, wine, and candles,
> Skirts, and picture frames, and pipes,
> Brooches, and medallions, blouses, buckles,
> Typewriters (not with Russian type),
> Rings of sausages and cheeses,
> Small domestic ware and veils,
> Combs, and forks, and wineglasses,
> Samplers, and shoes, and scales . . .

Zweiundzwanzig, Höringstrasse.
It's not been burned, just looted, rifled.
A moaning by the walls, half-muffled,
The mother's wounded, still alive.
The little daughter's on the mattress
Dead. How many have been on it?
A platoon, a company perhaps?
A girl's been turned into a woman,
A woman into a corpse.
It's all come down to simple phrases:
Do not forget. Do not forgive.
Blood for blood. A tooth for a tooth.
The mother begs, 'Tote mich, Soldat' . . .

Once there lived in days now past
A Comrade, a Parteigenosse,
Not the first and not the last
To lie prostrate, each in turn,
In that log-road beneath the wheels,
The wheels of Comintern.
Russia advances, a great power,
Hail to the advance's thunder.
Some schnapps would do me good, I feel,
But what would cheer me even more —
Is to go looking for some plunder. . . .

Allenstein has just been taken.
An hour ago, a sudden strike
Of tanks and cavalry overwhelmed it . . .
Now the night flares. Burning sugar.
It flames with violet-coloured fire
Over the earth. It seems to simmer,
A trembling blaze, a lilac shimmer . . .
Knocks. Rings. A tumult. Then we hear
A moment later, the cry of a girl,
Somewhere from behind a wall,
'I'm not a German. I'm not a German.
No. I'm — Polish. I'm a Pole.'
Grabbing what comes handy, those
Like-minded lads get in and start —
          And oh, what heart
          Could well oppose? . . .[41]

Two weeks later, the Soviet Army reached the Baltic shore
near Elbing (Elbląg). At which point, having questioned the

geniality of Joseph Stalin in one of his private letters, Solzhenitsyn was arrested and sentenced to ten years' penal servitude; and his vision of the Soviet liberation came to a sudden halt.

The Soviet advance was accompanied by the widespread flight of German civilians. Certain settlements were cleared by the *Wehrmacht* for military purposes; but many were spontaneously abandoned by their panic-stricken inhabitants. Rumours of the grisly massacre committed by the Soviet Army at Nemmersdorf in East Prussia, the first village of the Reich to be occupied, precipitated a general exodus. The winter roads were jammed with lines of 'trekkers' in horse-drawn waggons. Hundreds perished in attempts to cross the frozen sea of the Frisches Haff. Tens of thousands took refuge on the peninsula of Hel. The Baltic sealanes were criss-crossed with convoys of overladen and floundering evacuation ships, which frequently fell victim to Soviet submarines. The loss of the *Wilhelm Gustloff*, torpedoed off Gdynia on 30 January 1945, and of the *Goya* on 16 April, accounted for the death by drowning of some fifteen thousand passengers. These two tragedies, largely unnoticed amidst the general *sauve qui peut*, represent the two greatest maritime disasters in history.

By that time, however, the German defences were smashed beyond repair. Although local resistance would sometimes be mounted, on the Pomeranian Wall in January and February, and above all in the German 'fortresses' such as Bielsko, Glogau, and Breslau, which were ordered to fight to the last man, nothing could stop the flood of Soviet armies as they swept over or around all obstacles. When peace was declared on 9 May 1945, 2,078 days after the outbreak of war against Poland, the whole expanse of the Polish lands lay under complete Soviet control.

*   *   *   *   *

To anyone who lived through the War in Poland, the diplomatic negotiations concerning the country's future possess an air of distinct unreality. They did little to relieve the agonies of the Occupation, and modified the Soviets' chosen solution of the Polish Question in only the least essential details. It is odd that historians should pay them such unwarranted attention.[42]

In the era of the Nazi–Soviet Pact, the political isolation and the vulnerability of the Polish Government-in-Exile was amply demonstrated. Created in France in November 1939 under the Premiership of General Władysław Sikorski, and transferred in June 1940 to London, it enjoyed the full official recognition of the Western Powers. Yet it could not impress its interests on them. In particular, it could not persuade them to take cognizance of the fact that the USSR, no less than Nazi Germany, was responsible for the destruction of Polish independence and for the outbreak of war. It was welcomed as a partner in the war against Hitler, but resented for its constant hostility against the USSR, with whom all the Western governments were at peace. This situation could not improve until the *Wehrmacht* invaded Russia on 22 June 1941, and then only temporarily.[43]

For two years, from 1941 to 1943, the Polish Government-in-Exile was able to enter relations with its erstwhile Soviet enemies. The Soviet leaders, in their hour of need, were willing to treat with their former Polish victims. On 30 July 1941, diplomatic relations were established. The USSR stated its readiness to form a Polish army in Russia, to grant an Amnesty to all Polish internees, and to annul the provisions of the Nazi–Soviet Pact regarding Poland. On 4 August *Pravda* announced that the Polish–Soviet frontier was open to future settlement. A military convention was signed on 12 August. The suspension of blatant injustices was presented to the world as a magnanimous Soviet 'concession'.

The tensions persisting in this alliance between enemies were obvious from the start. The Poles, conscious of their weak position, were determined to concede not an inch in territorial or political matters. The Soviets resorted to all forms of pressure, provocation, and prevarication. Polish prisoners in the USSR were not promptly released. Polish and Jewish leaders were rearrested, imprisoned, and, in some cases, shot. The Polish Army did not receive promised support or supplies. Polish communist organizations, hostile to the Government-in-Exile, were revived. No satisfactory explanation was offered as to the fate of the 15,000 missing Polish officers. The Soviet press and propaganda agencies attacked Polish claims unceasingly. Soviet officials insisted on treating all Polish citizens of Ukrainian, Byelorussian, Lithuanian, or Jewish nationality as if they were Soviet subjects; and Soviet diplomats launched a campaign for the recognition of the Curzon Line frontier. The difficulty of getting a simple answer to simple questions was evident in every approach which the Poles made:

Conversation with Stalin. In the Kremlin. 14 November 1941

Ambassador KOT: You are the author of an amnesty for Polish citizens in the USSR. You made that gesture, and I should be grateful if you would bring influence to bear to ensure that it could be carried out completely.

STALIN: Are there Poles still not released?

KOT: We have still not seen one officer from the camp in Staro-bielsk which was dissolved in the spring of 1940.

STALIN: I shall go into that . . .

KOT: We have names and lists; for instance General Stanisław Haller has not been found. We lack the officers from Staro-bielsk, Kozielsk, and Ostashkov, who were transferred from those camps in April and May 1940.

STALIN: We have released everybody, even people whom General Sikorski sent to us to blow up bridges and kill Soviet people . . .

KOT: All the names are registered with the Russian camp commanders, who summon all the prisoners to roll-call every day. In addition, the *Narkomvnudziel* interviewed each man separately. Not one officer on the staff of General Anders' army which he commanded in Poland has been handed over.

(Stalin for a minute or two has been pacing slowly up and down by the table, smoking a cigarette, but listening closely and answering questions. Suddenly he goes swiftly to the telephone on Molotov's desk and connects with the *Narkomvnudziel.* Molotov gets up and also goes to the telephone.)

MOLOTOV: This is the way.

STALIN: NKVD? This is Stalin. Have all the Poles been released from the prisons? (He listens to the answer.) Because I have the Polish Ambassador with me and he tells me they haven't all been released. (He listens again then replaces the receiver and returns to the table.) I would like to ask you, Mr. Ambassador, when and where the Polish forces wish to go into action against the Germans . . .

KOT: I venture to emphasize that every Polish division formed . . . is of great importance in developing friendly feelings among the people at home towards the Polish—Soviet *rapprochement*.

STALIN: Of course. I realize that. (The telephone rings, and he goes to it and listens. He replaces the receiver and returns, saying in an undertone as though to himself, 'They say they've all been released.')

KOT: I wish to thank you for your promise concerning the further formations for our army and for the release of our citizens . . .

STALIN: As for myself, I personally am anxious to contribute to the restoration of an independent Polish state without regard to its internal regime.
. . .

Conversation between General Sikorski and Stalin in the Kremlin,
. . .

SIKORSKI: But I return to our question. I have to tell you, Mr. President, that your declaration of an amnesty is not being put into effect. Many, and those some of our most valuable people, are still in labour camps and prisons.

STALIN: (making notes) That is impossible, since the amnesty concerned everybody, and all the Poles have been released. (These words are addressed to Molotov, who nods.)

ANDERS: (at Sikorski's request handing over the details) That is not in accordance with the true state of affairs . . .

SIKORSKI: It's not our business to supply the Soviet Government with detailed lists of our people . . . but I have with me a list of some 4,000 officers who were carried off by force . . . Those men are here. Not one has come back.

STALIN: That's impossible. They've fled.

SIKORSKI: But where could they flee to?

STALIN: Well to Manchuria, for instance.

ANDERS: It isn't possible that they have all fled . . . These people are perishing and dying there in terrible conditions.

STALIN: They must have been released, and haven't arrived yet . . . Please understand that the Soviet Government has no reason for detaining even a single Pole.

ANDERS: Nonetheless, information is coming in concerning people exactly known to us, together with the names of the prisons and even the numbers of the cells in which they are locked up . . .

MOLOTOV: We've detained only those who after the war began com-
           mitted crimes, provoked diversions, set up radio stations
           etc. . . .
SIKORSKI: Don't let's discuss cases arising in wartime. It would be a
           good thing now, Mr. President, if you were to give public
           explanations of this question . . . After all, these people
           are not tourists, but were carried off from their homes by
           force. They didn't come here of their own choice; they
           were deported, and endured tremendous suffering.
STALIN: The people of the Soviet Union are well disposed towards
           the Poles. But officials can make mistakes.[44]

Despite the currency of the Declaration of Friendship and
Mutual Assistance, signed by Stalin and Sikorski on 5 December 1941, no chance was missed by the Soviets to hamper
the activities of the Government-in-Exile. The evacuation of
Anders's army from the USSR was only achieved after the
Soviets had withheld its food rations. The talks for post-war
Polish—Czechoslovak co-operation were torpedoed by Soviet
protests.[45] The signing of an Anglo-Soviet Treaty in May 1942
was attended by conditions designed to split the British from
their Polish allies. Polish—Soviet hostility was already rising
when on 12 April 1943 the Germans announced their discovery
of the Katyn graves. When the Government-in-Exile demanded
an investigation by the International Red Cross, the Soviets
used this demand as a pretext for severing diplomatic relations.
Henceforth, the Government-in-Exile had no communication
with the one power which exercised control over Polish
territory. All future discussion of Polish matters took place
between the representatives of the Powers without Polish
participation. The Soviet solution of Poland's future was
gradually confirmed by three great Allied Conferences at
Tehran, Yalta, and Potsdam.

Given the relentless character of Soviet diplomacy over the
Polish problem, it must be recognized however that Stalin's
views had changed fundamentally over the years. In 1939—41,
the Soviet dictator had showed a willingness to trample on
every vestige of Polish nationality or independence. From
1941 onwards, he constantly reiterated his desire to restore
'a strong and independent Poland'. His understanding of
'strength' and 'independence' differed considerably from that

which was held in Britain and America, or indeed in Poland; but was no less substantive for that. Anyone who has any doubts concerning the genuineness of Stalin's commitment should compare the post-war history of Poland with that of the Baltic States or the Ukraine. Stalin was the author not only of post-war Polish independence, but also of the peculiarly stunted interpretation of that concept which has prevailed in the post-war era.[46]

At the first meeting of 'The Big Three' at Tehran, from 28 November to 1 December 1943, discussions on the common front against Germany touched on the Polish issue. The division of Europe into zones of potential post-war influence implied that Poland would fall under Soviet control. It was agreed that the Curzon Line, rejected in 1920, was to form the basis for Poland's eastern frontier.[47] The western frontier between Poland and Germany was not thoroughly discussed. No information was made available to Polish representatives at this stage.

At Yalta, between 4 and 11 February 1945, Churchill and Roosevelt made token efforts to reassert their influence on Eastern Europe. Despite the unilateral recognition of the RTRP by the USSR, they insisted that representatives of the parties supporting the Government-in-Exile should be admitted to the Warsaw Government. They recognized Poland's right to lands annexed from eastern Germany, without defining their extent.

At Potsdam, between 17 July and 2 August 1945, the Powers briskly settled most of the problems still outstanding. Having briefly consulted with a Polish communist delegation, expertly rehearsed by the Soviets, they fixed the Polish–German frontier on the Oder and Western Neisse, approved the expulsion of Germans from Poland, Czechoslovakia, and Hungary, and insisted that free and democratic elections be held at the nearest opportunity to confirm the composition of the established government.

With that, the Western Powers left Poland to its fate.

*   *   *   *   *

The changes brought about by the War were deep and permanent. Seven years of slaughter refashioned the state, nation, and society more radically than a century of endeavour beforehand or three decades of communist rule afterwards.

In 1944—5, Polish sovereignty was revived on a new territorial base. As Churchill himself had proposed, Poland was moved bodily 150 miles to the west, like a company of soldiers taking 'two steps to the left, close ranks'. The eastern Borders, including Wilno and Lwów, had to be abandoned to the Soviet Union. The Western Territories, including Breslau (Wrocław), Stettin (Szczecin), and Danzig (Gdańsk) — described in official jargon as 'the Recovered Lands' — were acquired from Germany. Barely half (54 per cent) of the territory of the pre-war Republic passed into the People's Republic, which compromised only four-fifths the area of its predecessor (312,677 km² as opposed to 389,720 km²). The territory lost (178,220 km²) greatly exceeded the territory gained (101,200 km²). (See Maps 18, 21, 22, 23.)

Yet the resources of the Western Territories more than compensated for the Republic's diminished area. The territory lost to the USSR included the primitive undeveloped rural districts of 'Polska B'. The territory gained from Germany included rich coal and iron deposits, complex industrial installations, a modern network of roads and railways, and a large number of cities and seaports. The acquisition of Silesia and Pomerania, despite the fact that these provinces were denuded of their skilled German labour force, was sure to increase Poland's prospects of economic modernization and industrialization.

When post-war repatriation and expulsions were nearing completion the census of February 1946 showed that the population had fallen by almost one-third from the 1939 figure, to a mere 23.9 millions. The manpower of the Polish state had receded to the position of 1918. Over-all density had also fallen from 89.8 to 76.4 inhabitants per km². In other words, Poland had lost still more people than land. Only a small proportion of the population inhabitated the places where they had lived before the war. Most of the towns and the entire Western Territories had to be repopulated by refugees or families transferred from the Soviet Union. In all those localities where uprooted newcomers outnumbered the indigenous inhabitants, former social traditions survived with difficulty.

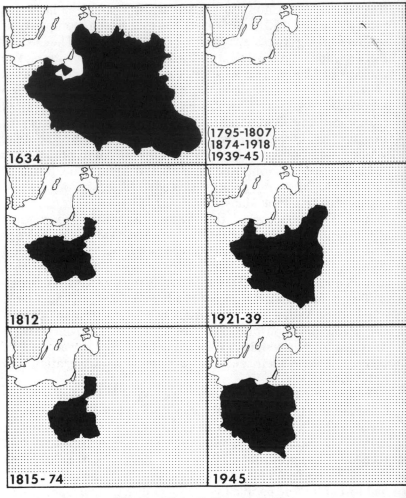

1634

(1795-1807)
(1874-1918)
(1939-45)

1812

1921-39

1815-74

1945

Map 18.   Poland's Changing Territory

Social structures had been transformed out of all recognition. Although no class had been inviolate from the ravages of occupiers, two groups had suffered out of all proportion to the others. The intelligentsia had been decimated. Polish Jewry had virtually ceased to exist. As a result, political, cultural, and economic life could never be the same.

The national minorities had almost disappeared. The loss of the Jews, the expulsion of the Germans, the incorporation of Byelorussians and Ukrainians into the USSR, and the influx of Poles from the east, left the Polish-speaking Roman Catholic population in an overwhelming majority. This fundamental change could not but affect the temper of public life. The People's Republic was to be the first truly national state in Polish history.

Thus when Poland reopened for business in 1944—5, under communist auspices, it was not merely the regime that was new. It was a new Poland.

CHAPTER TWENTY-ONE

GRANICE:

The Modern Polish Frontiers

People who live on islands, or on half-continents of their own, find difficulty in comprehending the territorial obsessions of landlocked nations. Never having faced the prospect of ceding Kent to Germany, or California to the USSR, they tend to look with quizzical unconcern, if not with contempt, on those who would lay down their lives for an inch of ground or for a dotted line on a map. In this respect, the passions concerning the history of modern Polish frontiers are far removed indeed from the main concerns of the Anglo-Saxon world. They are all the greater, since, with one signal exception, the Poles have not been permitted to fix their frontiers for themselves. One hundred years ago Poland possessed no territory at all. 'Oh Poland,' wrote Cyprian Norwid, 'how poor you are. I cannot discern the line of your frontiers. You have nothing left but your voice.' Nowadays all is changed. Poland's soul has been reclothed with a new body. But the process of reincarnation was not an easy one. It troubled European statesmen throughout the first half of the twentieth century, and provided one of the most intractable problems in the territorial settlements after both World Wars.[1]

The international debate on Poland's modern frontiers was initiated on 29 January 1919, at the Paris Peace Conference, in a memorable *tour de force* by the Chief Polish Delegate, Roman Dmowski. Speaking first in idiomatic French, and then in flawless English, he shocked his audience no less by the contents of his speech than by its technical brilliance. From this very first moment, however, it was clear that two very different and incompatible concepts were involved. Whereas Dmowski was talking of a territory based on the historic pre-Partition frontiers and containing all the peoples of that vast area, most of his listeners were thinking in terms of a small mono-national Poland confined to areas inhabited by ethnic Poles. Whereas the Poles assumed themselves to be masters of their own destiny, free to determine their frontiers on a basis of equality with the Great Powers, most foreign observers assumed that Poland was a client state whose demands must be trimmed to accommodate the interests of its superiors. On both points, everyone was thoroughly mistaken. As the result of changes which had occurred during the nineteenth century, it proved quite impossible to restore an updated version of the old *Rzeczpospolita*. Equally, as a result of the intermingling of ethnic groups, it was quite impossible to draw a simple ethnographic frontier. In the political sphere, it was as unrealistic for Polish leaders to model their conduct on that of the established powers, as it was for the powers to imagine that the Poles would simply do as they were told.[2] For twenty-five years, the rights and wrongs of the subject were debated *ad nauseam*, and to little avail. The injustices of the settlement following the First World War were used to fan the flames of the Second. The unreadable reports of innumerable Commissions, and the contentious arguments of Polish, Czech, German, and Russian apologists filled the shelves of libraries and the pages of the press. The names of obscure provincial localities, from Allenstein to the Zbrucz, became household words. Relief arrived only occasionally, when a British Prime Minister confessed to never having heard of Teschen, or to thinking that Silesia was somewhere in Asia Minor.[3] In the very nature of the problem, no single principle could be followed consistently. All decisions regarding the Polish frontiers were taken *ad hoc*, in conditions of thinly disguised international horse-trading. No attempt to trim the frontiers to the wishes of the population ever succeeded, until, at Soviet instigation, it was decided in 1944–5 to trim the population to the requirements of arbitrary frontiers.

In this quarter century of conflict, Polish territorial claims found little sympathy in the West, least of all in Britain or the USA. Changes made at Germany's expense in the Treaty of Versailles were soon regretted. The establishment of the 'Polish Corridor', the exclusion of Danzig from the Reich, and the division of Silesia, were widely regarded as the source of legitimate German grievances. Changes demanded by Poland at Russia's expense were countered with equal derision. Polish

demands for the restoration of 'historic Poland' were denounced as 'small power imperialism' (unlike those for the
restoration of the historic lands of St. Wenceslas, which were
somehow judged acceptable). As Gaythorne-Hardy remarked,
in a tone most characteristic of his generation, 'The new
Poland . . . seemed more distinguished by a reckless and
almost fanatical patriotism than by the diplomatic prudence
which her precarious position demanded.'[4] In hindsight, the
explanation of this attitude is not hard to locate. Anglo-Saxon
viewpoints in general, and British viewpoints in particular,
were dictated not only by the traditional concern for the
Balance of Power, but even more by the logic of traditional
alliances. In two World Wars, Great Britain was allied first
with Russia, and then with the USSR, and counted on Russian
manpower and on Russian sacrifices for the defeat of the
German armies. As a result, the British saw nothing derisory
about the establishment of Czechoslovakia within its medieval
limits. Czechoslovakia, after all, was only drawing on the territory of the defeated Central Powers. The British had little
objection in 1918—19 to the inclusion in Czechoslovakia of
numerous German or Hungarian minorities. At the same
time, they could never afford to countenance similar Polish
pretensions which brought them into conflict with the great
Russian ally on whom, in the last resort, their own salvation
was known to depend.

Poland's southern frontier is the only one to bear any resemblance to a natural barrier. For a thousand years the crest
of the central Carpathians had divided the Polish lands from
the Danube Basin and from the Hungarian domain. It had
formed the frontier both of the *Rzeczpospolita* and of
Austrian Galicia. In 1918—19, it was immediately accepted
as the natural frontier between Poland and Czechoslovakia.
In more than four hundred miles, there were only three gaps
in the watershed — at Spisz, at Orawa, and at Cieszyn. Each
of these teacups gave rise to protracted storms.[5]

The district of Spisz — in Czech, *Spiš*; in Slovak, *Spišsko*;
in Magyar, *Szepesseg*; in German, *Zips*; in Latin, *Scepusium*
— lay in the valley of the upper Poprad, a tributary of the
Vistula which cuts a deep defile through the main Carpathian
chain to the east of Podhale. Its medieval history can be traced

to 1108, when it passed into Hungarian possession as the dowry of Krzywousty's daughter, Judith. In 1412, thirteen towns in the northern part of the district — Nowa Wieś, Włochy, Podegrodzie, Poprad, Wielka, Sobota, Straże, Maciejowice, Biała, Wierzbów, Lubica, Ruskinowice, Twarożna — were returned to the Polish Crown as security for a loan that was never repaid; and for the next three centuries they were ruled by a Polish *Starosta* as an enclave within the Kingdom of Hungary. In modern history, Spisz figured as the first territory to be seized by the Habsburgs in 1769 in anticipation of the First Partition. It was on these grounds, to right the ancient wrong, that it was claimed by the Polish Delegation to the Peace Conference in Paris. From the ethnic point of view, the local population was extremely mixed. The *Górale* (Highlanders) of the mountain villages regarded themselves as a race apart, and cared little for the lowland politicians whether they came from Warsaw, Budapest, Bratislava, or Prague. The towns contained a strong contingent of German-speaking Saxons, and an important residue of ex-Hungarian soldiers and officials. From the practical point of view, the problem had been pre-empted by the uninvited presence of the Czechoslovak Army. After several fruitless attempts to arbitrate in this and other disputes, the Allied Powers decided on 28 July 1920 to impose a settlement on Poland and Czechoslovakia. As part of their judgement, five-sixths of the district of Spisz was awarded to Czechoslovakia, and only one-sixth to Poland. The Poles were loath to submit; and refused to release the village of Jaworzyna until a further ruling by the League of Nations in December 1923 went against them. The division of Spisz, as ordained by the Allied Powers, was effective from March 1924 to October 1938, and was revived in 1945.

The district of Orawa — in Czech, *Orava*; in Slovak, *Oravsko*; in Magyar, *Árva* — lay some forty miles to the west astride a river of the same name flowing into the southern watershed. The settlement of 28 July 1920 left only one village, Jabłonka, on the Polish side.

The Duchy of Cieszyn (in Czech *Tešin*, in German *Teschen*) sat in the centre of the Moravian Gate. It controlled the only low-level route across the mountains between the Black Sea and Bavaria. In the era before 1918, it formed the eastern half of the Duchy of Troppau and Teschen, commonly known as the province of 'Austrian Silesia'. At Bogumin (in Czech *Bohumín*, in German *Oderberg*), it commanded a key junction on the transcontinental Berlin to Baghdad Railway. At Karwina (Karvinná), there was a valuable coalfield, and at Witkowice (Vitkovice) and Trzyniec (Třynec) important steel-mills, recently acquired by a French company. In the valley of Jabłunków, in the south, the Austrian census of 1910 had recorded the purest concentration of Polish inhabitants in the Empire. In November 1918, when Austrian officialdom withdrew, local representatives of the Polish and Czech communities reached an amicable agreement, and a demarcation line divided the Duchy along ethnographic lines. Regrettably, this agreement proved unacceptable both in Prague and in Warsaw. The Czechoslovak Government laid claim to the Duchy on economic grounds, and on 25 January 1919 ordered its army to occupy the whole of the industrial area by force. For 18 months, confusion reigned supreme. A project for the independence of Cieszyn, supported by the local Germans, whom no one was considering, was rejected by the Peace Conference. Preparations for a plebiscite had to be abandoned in face of riots, strikes, terror, and counter-terror. The Inter-allied Plebiscite Commission under Comte de Manneville of France bore the insults and recriminations of Czechs and Poles alike, and, after surviving a siege in its headquarters in the ancient 'Brown Stag Hotel', quickly retired. Impasse at the Spa Conference passed the matter to the Council of Ambassadors whose verdict was given at 5.25 p.m. on 28 July 1920. The larger, western part of the Duchy, including the whole of the industrial area and far more Poles than Czechs, was awarded to Czechoslovakia. The town of Cieszyn was cleft down the centre, in the middle of the River Olža. The Market Square and the evangelical Jesus Church were to be in Poland: the railway station was to be in Czechoslovakia. Polish opinion was outraged. Paderewski signed the treaty only after three days' delay, and under protest. To him, and to most of his compatriots, it seemed that the Czechoslovak *coup de force* had paid off: that Beneš had impressed his policy on the Allies by exploiting Poland's weakness at the height of the

Red Army's advance on Warsaw; and that the Polish miners of Cieszyn had been sacrificed to the designs of Allied capitalists. The injury was nursed throughout the inter-war period, and, in the course of the Munich Crisis, revenged. From 1935, Beck constantly pressed his demands for the relief of Poles at the Zaolzie (Transolzia). On 2 October 1938, determined to deny strategic control of the Moravian Gate to the *Wehrmacht*, and unable to resist the temptation, he crossed his river at the head of the Polish Army. Spisz and Orawa were occupied at the same time. Eleven months later, the *Wehrmacht*'s magisterial advance through Cieszyn provided one of the two claws of the pincer whereby the fated Polish Republic was destroyed. Polish—Czechoslovak recriminations were revived among the Governments-in-Exile in London during the war, and were only settled by Stalin who treated the pleas of his rival clients with impartial contempt. It is a sad comment on this most symptomatic of East European disputes that the Soviet dictator could think of no better solution than that devised on the orders of the Council of Ambassadors twenty-five years earlier. In 1945, Cieszyn was again brutally divided down the middle. The frontier line was repainted across the central arch of the town bridge, and has remained in place to this day.[6]

Poland's northern frontier might seem to coincide quite naturally with the Baltic shore. In fact, in modern times, the sole stretch of the sea coast which maintained a close relationship with the Polish interior was to be found at the mouth of the Vistula. From the early Middle Ages Western Pomerania's connections lay firmly with the German lands; whilst eastern Prussia, conquered by the Teutonic Knights from its indigenous Balts, had never been subject to Polish settlement. The configuration of the Polish Corridor as described in the Treaty of Versailles corresponded in the main to the frontiers of the *Rzeczpospolita* in 1772, and satisfied Polish claims in large measure. Although German opinion strongly resented the Corridor, the Polish Delegation saw fit to challenge the Conference's decision in only three limited localities – at Danzig, and at Allenstein and Marienwerder in East Prussia. The 130 kilometres of Baltic coastline awarded to Poland at Versailles passed under Polish control

by the activation of the Treaty of 20 January 1920. On that
day, the ceremony of the *Zaślubiny z morzem* was performed
for the first time. Soldiers and civilians waded into the icy
waves of the Baltic, and with upraised hands saluted the
renewal of Poland's ancient 'Betrothal to the Sea'.[7]

Poland's claim to Danzig was based chiefly on economic
arguments. In the period of Prussian rule, the city's German
population had lost all trace of former Polish loyalties, and
in the 1930s was to provide many ardent recruits to the Nazi
cause. There was no serious doubt that any free plebiscite in
Danzig would have resulted in an overwhelming vote for reunion with the Reich. In this light, Lloyd George's insistence
at the Peace Conference on the formation of a Free City
must be seen as a concession to Polish pressure. In practice, it
gave equal offence to both Poles and Germans, and presented
Hitler with the specific pretext by which his invasion of
Poland in September 1939 was justified. The problem was
solved once and for all by the flight or expulsion of the
German Danzigers in the last days of the Second World War.[8]

The districts of Allenstein (Olsztyn) and Marienwerder
(Kwidzyn) both lay on the southern confines of East Prussia.
Both were subjected to popular plebiscites held under Allied
auspices in the summer of 1920. Polish charges against German
skulduggery, in particular against the fraudulent manufacture
of outvoters, could not conceal the overwhelming desire of
the population, including part of the Polish-speaking Protestants, to remain German citizens. The result, declared on
11 July 1920, showed a crushing majority of 460,000 votes
(96.52 per cent) for Germany to 16,000 (3.47 per cent) for
Poland. The Allied garrison, consisting of Italians and of
Irishmen of the Inniskillen Fusiliers, were sharply withdrawn
for fear of being politically contaminated by the Red Army,
which happened at that very moment to be bearing down on
them from the East. In those few neighbouring towns such
as Soldau (Działdowo) which the Red Army occupied before
its precipitate retreat in August, the Soviet commanders expressed their government's belief that this 'ancient German
land' should be returned to its rightful owners. German order
reigned supreme until 1945.[9]

Poland's western frontier raised problems of a much greater

magnitude. At the beginning of the twentieth century, the Oder River, the only recognizable dividing line between the Vistula and the Elbe, lay in the middle of solidly German areas. The German element was heavily preponderant in all the cities, from Stettin to Breslau; it dominated almost all the towns, and many of the country districts. Yet throughout these areas the proximity of an independent Polish Republic created tensions which reverberated for thirty years. It inspired one armed Rising in Posnania, and three in Upper Silesia. At the end of the Second World War Poland's western frontier was the last to be settled, and in the most arbitrary and controversial manner.

The Poznań Rising was followed by a minor civil war. It was sparked off on 26 December 1918 by the arrival of Ignacy Paderewski, on his way to Warsaw, thus breaking an uneasy division of power in the city between the local German *Soldatenrat* and a Polish 'Citizens Committee'. Demonstrations and counter-demonstrations soon led to pitched battles in the streets, and to the rapid polarization of the two communities. Within a week, the Polish 'Supreme People's Council' (NRL) took control of the city and the surrounding countryside, but failed in its attempts to reach an understanding with the government in Berlin. Its activities caused a rapid closing of the German ranks and the advance of *Grentzschutz* units. On 8 January 1919, it declared its independence. The fighting, which at Chodzież (Kolmar) on 8 January and at Szubin (Schubin) on the 11th caused several hundred fatalities, continued for four weeks until the NRL was recognized by the Interallied Control Commission in Germany as an 'Allied force'. The German *Reichswehr* operating from Colberg did not abandon its offensive designs until the Treaty of Versailles, which awarded the whole of the former Duchy of Posen to Poland, was signed. The NRL finally transferred its duties to the 'Ministry of the Former German Partition' in Warsaw in September 1919.[10]

The Silesian Risings were launched in protest against the terms of the Treaty requiring a plebiscite in the three most southerly regencies. The first Rising, lasting for eight days, from 16 to 24 August 1919, was centred on Rybnik and was brutally suppressed by the *Reichswehr*. It was followed by the arrival of an Interallied garrison drawn from British, French and Italian regiments. The Second Rising, from 19 to 25 August 1920, coincided with the zenith of the Soviet War. German demonstrators, prematurely celebrating the capture of Warsaw by Tukhachevsky, were forced on to the defensive by a wave of strikes and reprisals which soon engulfed the entire mining area. The Third Rising, and by far the most serious, was launched by Polish elements who refused to accept the result of the plebiscite. In the voting, which had taken place on 20 March 1921, 702,000 (59.4 per cent) voters opted for Germany and 479,000 (40.5 per cent) for Poland. Taken as a whole, the result was a resounding success for the elaborate German campaign. But in detail, especially in the industrial areas, it left several German enclaves stranded in the midst of a Polish sea. Wojciech Korfanty (1873–1939), long-serving deputy in the Prussian *Reichstag* and now Plebiscite Commissioner of the Polish Republic, was determined to resist. His speeches provided the inspiration for some 40,000 workers and partisans, many of them belonging to Piłsudski's POW, who took to arms. From 3 May to 5 July, they confronted the German forces on an equal footing, and succeeded in defending the industrial area against all assaults. Pitched battles, long since legendary, were fought at Góra Św. Anny (Annenberg) from 21 to 25 May and along the Kłodnik Canal, from 4 to 5 June. Although the insurrectionary leaders failed to recruit all Polish parties in Upper Silesia to their cause — the communists and socialists argued that the separation of Silesian industry from its traditional German market would have disastrous consequences — they convinced the Allied Powers that the plebiscite result could not be allowed to stand. On 20 October 1921, the Council of Ambassadors ruled that Upper Silesia was to be divided along new lines. Sixty-one per cent of the total plebiscite area was to remain in Germany, whilst the greater part of the coalfield, including Kattowitz (Katowice) and Koenigshutte (Chorzów), was to pass into Poland. This decision, which was widely denounced in Poland as a betrayal, was seen by its authors as a concession to Polish interests.[11]

The Polish—German frontier continued to rankle throughout the inter-war period. Its revision was pursued no less by

German democratic leaders in the 1920s, like Stresemann, than by Adolf Hitler in the 1930s. The glaring omission from the Locarno Treaty of 1925 of any guarantee of the status quo on Germany's border with Poland, parallel to that on her borders with France and Belgium, drove a lasting wedge of suspicion between Poland and the Western Powers. The problem of exporting Silesian coal across the new frontier to Germany lay at the root of the Polish–German Tariff War of 1925 9. Although the Silesian Convention, drafted by the League of Nations for problems of common concern, worked quite smoothly, there was little doubt that Germany was seeking a radical revision of the settlement. This was done, in no uncertain manner in 1939, when all former Prussian territory, was reincorporated into the Reich.

In 1945, the scheme to establish the Polish–German frontier on the Oder and Lusatian Neisse, and to compensate Polish territorial losses in the East by equal grants of territories in the North and West entirely denuded of their native German inhabitants, must be largely attributed to Soviet policy. Although British and American negotiators had long accepted the Oder line in the region of Frankfurt, they did not accept its extension to the western, Lusatian Neisse, as distinct from the eastern or Glatzer Neisse, until a very late stage. Although all Polish parties were eager to obtain Danzig, few had hoped for Breslau, and none had thought of Stettin. Mikołajczyk in particular was conscious of the burden of annexations which might revive German revisionism and which would tie Poland to the Soviet Union indefinitely. But he, and all who shared his reservations, were overruled by official representatives of the PKWN and TRJN, loyally mouthing the demands of their Soviet patrons. The last settlement, which was not intended to be necessarily final, was embodied in a communiqué of the Potsdam Conference of 2 August 1945:

The three heads of Government agree that, pending the final determination of Poland's western frontier, the former German territories east of a line running from the Baltic Sea immediately west of Swinemunde, and thence along the Oder River to the confluence of the western Neisse River and along the western Neisse River to the Czechoslovak frontier, including that portion of East Prussia not placed under the administration of the USSR . . . and including the area of the former free city of Danzig, shall be under the administration of the Polish State and for such purposes should not be considered as part of the Soviet Zone of Occupation of Germany.[12]

In practical terms, it has mattered little that the intended Peace Conference was never held. The Oder—Neisse frontier was recognized on 6 July 1950 by the German Democratic Republic, which had been established in the former Soviet Zone of Occupation. Thus the 'Recovered Territories' became an integral part of Poland long before international recognition of the fact was granted; Danzig became 'Gdańsk'; Breslau, 'Wrocław'; and Stettin, 'Szczecin'.[13]

Poland's eastern frontier has generated the greatest controversies of all. Its fortunes were bound up with the internecine history of the Polish—Russian borders, whose inhabitants contained relatively few Poles and no Russians, but whose ground had been disputed between Poland and Russia for centuries. In the twentieth century, the furthest Polish claim was made by Dmowski at the Peace Conference when he demanded the line of 1772. (Even Dmowski displayed a certain moderation, and avoided any mention of the *Rzeczpospolita*'s eastern frontier at its greatest extent in 1634.) The traditional Russian claim, preferred by Tsarist and Soviet regimes alike, coincided with the frontier of 'the Russian Vistula Provinces prior to 1912 on the Bug. In between these two extremes lay the vast expanse of the so-called 'ULB Area' (Ukraine, Lithuania, Byelorussia), and a whole graveyard of short-lived compromises. Leaving aside proposals of minor importance, there have been at least eight major proposals put forward between 1919 and 1945 (see Map 19):

1. *The revised Provisional Demarcation Line* proposed on 8 December by the Polish Commission of the Peace Conference in Paris. As this line referred exclusively to the proposals for the territories of the former Russian Empire, it stopped short on the old Russo-Austrian frontier, and did not extend into Eastern Galicia. It was never adopted by the Supreme Allied Council, and never formally presented to either the Poles or the Soviets.
2. *The Dryssa—Bar line* described in the Soviet Peace Note of 28 January 1920. This was more generous to Poland in

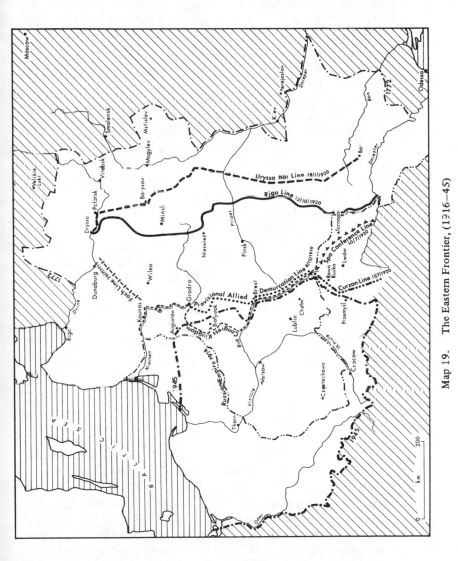

Map 19.   The Eastern Frontier, (1916–45)

territorial terms than the Allied Demarcation Line, and was recommended for acceptance by the Foreign Relations Committee of the Sejm in their report to the Chief-of-State. Owing to the breakdown of relations between the two parties in April 1920, it was never officially discussed.[14]

3. *The Spa Conference Line* was agreed in discussions between the British and Polish Prime Ministers, Lloyd George and Władysław Grabski on 10 July 1920. According to this agreement, the Polish–Russian frontier was to follow the Provisional Demarcation Line in the northern sector and the battlefront of the Polish and Soviet armies on the southern sector in East Galicia. It left Lwów (Lemberg) on the Polish side.

4. *The Curzon Line,* approved by the British Foreign Secretary, Lord Curzon, on instructions drawn up at Spa, was described in a telegram sent from the Foreign Office in London to Moscow on 11 July 1920. It was rejected by the Soviet Government one week later. Very curiously, it contained a serious discrepancy. Contrary to the intentions of its sponsors, its description of the proposed frontier in the southern, Galician sector, 'west of Rawa Ruska, and east of Przemysl to the Carpathians' did not coincide with the terms of the Spa agreement, and would have left Lwów on the Soviet side. This discrepancy, deriving most probably from a clerical error committed in London by diplomatic staff using maps and notes prepared earlier by Lewis Namier, caused great confusion in Allied counsels when it was discovered in changed circumstances in 1943.[15]

5. The line proposed by the Soviet representative, Adolf Joffe, at the outset of *Polish–Soviet negotiations at Riga* on 24 September 1920. At this moment of military defeat, the Soviet Government was prepared to make concessions to the Poles not far short of the 1772 frontier, on condition only that a ceasefire was arranged within ten days. On the advice of Stanisław Grabski, the National Democratic member, the Polish Delegation declined Joffe's overgenerous offer, choosing to fix a line 'more conducive to good neighbourly relations'.[16]

6. The final *Riga Armistice Line,* agreed between Joffe and Dąbski was signed on 12 October 1920. It formed the basis

of the territorial clauses of the Treaty of Riga of 18 March 1921, and acted as the formal frontier between the Polish Republic and the USSR until 1939.

7. *The Nazi—Soviet Demarcation line* of 28 September 1939 coincided very closely with the limits of the old Congress Kingdom.

8. The Polish—Soviet frontier of 1945.

Of all these lines, the Riga Line alone possessed moral validity. Freely agreed by the two contracting parties, it was free from all external sanctions. Its violation by the Red Army on 17 September 1939 represented a clear case of international aggression. However, it should not be forgotten that the Treaty of Riga effectively partitioned Lithuania, Byelorussia, and Ukraine without reference to the wishes of the population. By so doing, it obliged the Polish Government to abandon all thoughts of sponsoring a federation of independent nations on its eastern border.[17]

Frontier negotiations between Poland and the USSR have frequently been diverted by the presence in the border area of separatist movements whose wishes coincided neither with those of the Poles, nor with those of the Russians. In that twilight era between the retreat of the Tsarist Empire in 1915 and the creation of the USSR in 1922, several nationalities seized the opportunity, as the Poles did, to establish independent states of their own. Of these, the Lithuanian Republic survived for twenty-three years, from 1917 to 1940, the West Ukrainian People's Republic for only nine months, from November 1918 to July 1919. Both came into direct conflict with the Polish Republic.

The conflict with Lithuania centred on the future of Wilno — in Lithuanian, *Vilnius*; in Russian, *Vilna*; in German, *Wilna.* Although there were strong sentimental ties with Lithuania among all sections of Polish opinion, and hope in some quarters for a federal union, there was no serious objection to the creation of the Lithuanian national state. The trouble arose when the Lithuanian government in Kaunas (Kowno) not only laid claim to Wilno, but also declared it to be the capital of their Republic. As the Lithuanian-speaking element in the city did not exceed 5 per cent, the Polish majority there was not slow to protest. (The situation was analogous to that in the Celtic fringe of Great Britain, where a Welsh-speaking separatist movement might some day lay claim to Cardiff, or a Gaelic-speaking Republic of Scotland might have pretensions to the ancient capital of Edinburgh.) Furthermore, whilst the German army was supporting the Lithuanian nationalists, the Soviets were supporting the Lithuanian communists and the Polish Army was fighting them all. After the first occupation of Wilno by the Poles, the Supreme Allied Council proposed the so-called Foch Line, to keep the Polish and Lithuanian forces apart pending negotiations. But their intervention proved vain. In the course of the local Civil War and the Polish–Soviet War, Wilno was successively occupied by the German *Oberkommando Ost*; by the nationalist Taryba (1917–18); by the Polish *Samoobrona* (Self-defence) from December 1918 to January 1919; by the communist Lithuanian–Byelorussian SSR, from January to April 1919; by the Polish Army, from April 1919 to July 1920; and by the Russian Red Army, who on 14 July 1920 promptly handed it over to the Lithuanians. Its fate was sealed for the duration on 9 October 1920, when Piłsudski organized a fictional mutiny in his Polish Army in order to recover the city for Poland without offending openly against an Allied warning not to do so. After two years of nominal independence, the resultant state of Central Lithuania held elections to determine its future. Its request to be incorporated into the Polish Republic was granted by the Sejm in Warsaw in March 1922, and was eventually recognized by the Supreme Allied Council; but it was never accepted by the Lithuanian government in Kaunas.[18] Twenty years later, the Soviet authorities played the same sort of game, but in a much cruder manner. Having occupied Lithuania by force, and deported almost one-quarter of the electorate, they staged a fictional election to confirm the Lithuanians' request to be incorporated into the USSR. (See Map 20a.)

Poland's dispute with the Ukrainians involved a similarly complicated local conflict, and was ultimately settled in exactly the same way – by Soviet coercion. Here again, although Polish opinion looked on the creation of an independent Ukraine with favour, there were strong reservations

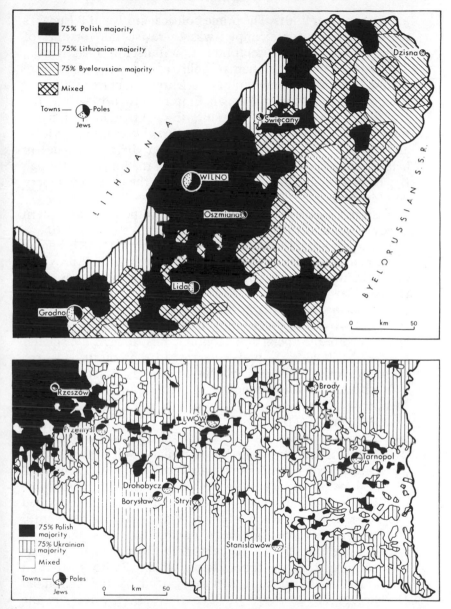

Map 20.   The Distribution of Nationalities, (1921)
a) The Region of Wilno   b) The Region of Lwów

about its proper limits. The prime political motive of Piłsudski's march on Kiev, for example, was to revive the fortunes of Petlura's Ukrainian Directorate as a buffer against Russia. Tragically, from the Ukrainian point of view, the Poles were willing to support the erection of a Ukrainian state within the bounds of the former Russian Empire, but not within the frontiers of Galicia. As a result, the Ukrainian nationalist movement was suppressed in Russia, first by Denikin's Whites and then by the Bolshevik Reds; whilst their colleagues in Galicia were suppressed by the Poles. In the long run, though the Poles gained a temporary advantage, the only beneficiary was Moscow.

Eastern Galicia — which was known to the Poles as eastern Małopolska, and to the Ukrainians as the Western Ukraine — was unquestionably an area of predominantly Ruthenian settlement. In the last years of Austrian rule, it had provided the Ukrainian national movement with its main base and refuge. (See Map 20b.) Yet the pattern of settlement, when examined in detail, was infernally complex. In the cities, including Lwów, the Poles enjoyed both numerical superiority and a favourable social and economic position. In the smaller towns, the Jews were preponderant. In the countryside, exclusively Polish, Catholic villages frequently existed side by side with exclusively Ruthenian, Uniate or Orthodox villages. In this situation, no simple line on a map could possibly have traced a meaningful divide between a Polish zone and a Ukrainian one. What was worse, by taking the law into their own hands from the start, the Ukrainian leadership wrecked all chances of co-operation or compromise. By their unilateral declaration of the People's Republic of Western Ukraine (ZURL) in Lemberg on 1 November 1918, they provoked the Poles into massive retaliation which did not relax until the whole province had been conquered. This campaign, which lasted until July 1919, absorbed the principal effort of the Polish Army at the time. Thereafter, the Polish frontier on the Zbrucz held firm. It was recognized by the Ukrainian Directorate on 24 April 1920 as Piłsudski's price for the march on Kiev, and on 18 March 1921 by the representatives of the Ukrainian SSR at the Peace of Riga. In 1923, its reluctant ratification by the Council of Ambassadors permitted the formal transfer of East Galicia into the Polish Republic.[19] Less than twenty years later, of course, this settlement, too, was overturned. In October 1939 in their agreement with the Nazis, as in 1944–5 in their dealings with Churchill and Roosevelt, the Soviet leaders successfully contrived to take the whole of East Galicia into the USSR.

In 1945, Poland's eastern frontier was imposed by Soviet policy. Its Polish advocates were confined to officials of the PKWN, the TPRP, and TJRN, who had been obliged by their Soviet patrons to accept its validity as a prior condition of their appointment. Its acceptance by Mikołajczyk was only effected by the most intense diplomatic pressure. 'You are on the verge of annihilation,' Churchill told him. 'Unless you accept the frontier you are out of business forever. The Russians will sweep through your country and your people will be liquidated.'[20] Its recognition by the Western Powers was confirmed at Yalta on the basis of the Curzon Line. A significant area more to the west round Grodno, was annexed by the Soviet Union. By that time, however, the matter was purely academic. It had already been decided to resettle all Poles from the east of the new frontier into the Polish People's Republic, and to deport all non-Poles from the west to the USSR. Inimitably, frontiers were to have priority over mere people.

In general, the history of modern Polish frontiers makes sad reading for anyone who may have imagined that the map of modern Europe had been drawn with regard either to magnanimity or to precision. The principle of national self-determination has been overruled with cynical monotony. As a result of the two wartime alliances between the Anglo-Saxon powers and the Russians, the Poles have never been granted the luxury of paying host to national minorities within their state in the way that was judged perfectly fitting for the British, or the Russians, or for that matter, for the Czechs. Danzig was denied them in 1919 on ethnic grounds, just as Cieszyn was denied them on economic grounds. The industrial area of Upper Silesia was granted to Poland in spite of a clear-cut German victory in the plebiscite. The wishes of the population of Lwów or Wilno were no more consulted in 1945, than they had been in 1939 or in 1919. At no point,

seemingly, was simple justice intended to prevail. The sole
strand of consistency is to be found in the aims of Russian
and of Soviet policy. In 1914, the Tsarist Foreign Minister,
Sazonov, published his vision of Eastern Europe in the future.
He called for the restoration of the old frontier of the
Congress Kingdom on the Bug; for the partition of East
Prussia; for the conquest of East Galicia; for the cession of
Danzig to a new Polish state united with Russia; and for the
expansion of Poland to the Oder. In the short-term, his plan
was frustrated. In the longer term, in Stalin's hands, it was
carried out with uncanny attention to detail.[21]

Much can be said for the present frontiers of the Polish
People's Republic. They are compact, well adapted for military defence, and based in the main on the line of the
mountains, the sea, and the major rivers. For the first time in
history, they enclose a Polish state which is inhabited almost
entirely by Poles, and which leaves no important Polish
minorities abroad. It is a fine state of affairs, and entirely
praiseworthy, were it not for the torrents of blood, suffering,
and specious arguments which have been expended in its
achievement.

*   *   *   *   *

Poland's fluctuating frontiers have caused fascinating complications in the realm of onomastics. Indeed, the profusion
of Polish place-names is often taken as a good reason for
studying some other part of the continent. Faced from the
start with rather unfamiliar and apparently unpronounceable
names, the bemused Anglo-Saxon is apt to despair completely
when confronted in every instance with two, three, four, or
even five variations. 'Wrocław', it seems, is the same place as
'Breslau'; 'Wilno', it appears, is sometimes disguised as 'Vilna',
or nowadays as 'Vilnius'; 'Lwów', unaccountably, can also be
described as 'Leopolis', 'Léopol', 'Lemberg', 'Lvov', and
'L'viv'. Different authorities prefer different versions for
reasons that are not always clear. Students in search of the
'correct version' are lost in a fog of conflicting advice until
someone eventually tells them that in the right context all
variations are equally correct.[22]

The problem is not unique to Eastern Europe, of course.

Anglo-Saxons tend to take fright, simply because they are usually unaware of similar manifestations on their own doorstep and because they normally insist on all information from foreign parts being translated into English. Very few Englishmen, for example, know that London is known to certain inhabitants of the British Isles as 'Llundain': or that Oxford is 'Rhydychen', and that Cambridge is 'Caergrawnt'. Very few bother to ask themselves why Ulster Protestants talk of 'Londonderry' and Ulster Catholics of 'Derry', or why 'Kingstown' was changed to 'Dun Laoghaire'. Not all Americans would know that their largest metropolis started life as 'Nieue Amsterdam', or that the capital of Texas is known to half the inhabitants of the Lone-star State as 'Agostino'. Given these examples, however, it does not need any profound grasp of foreign languages to realize that variations in usage depend partly on the viewpoint of the people who use them, and partly on the passage of time. Thus, the capital of Great Britain which once was 'Londinium' is now 'London'; to the Welsh, it is 'Llundain', to the French and Spanish 'Londres', to the Italians, 'Londra', to the Poles, 'Londyn'. By the same token, the capital of Silesia, which once was 'Vratislav', under Bohemian control became 'Vraclav'; under Habsburg and Hohenzollern rule 'Breslau'; and under Polish rule since the War, 'Wrocław'. To Latin scholars, it is still 'Vratislavia'. In German eyes, it is always 'Breslau', and for the Poles, forever 'Wrocław'.

Much of the trouble with respect to Polish names has arisen from the fact that many of the changes have taken place quite recently, and also because rival national movements have insisted on their own nomenclature as a point of honour. When the lid of the subject was lifted at the Peace Conference in 1919, a Pandora's treasure of towns and provinces flew out, never to be properly recovered. The Polish Delegation, as others like it, mesmerized its audience with lists of names of which no one else had ever heard. Not content with denouncing the rule of the partitioning powers, they objected to the use of established and familiar place-names, believing that their claims to former German or Russian territories would somehow be discredited by the use of German or Russian terminology. In several instances, the Allied arbitrators were constrained to coin neutral versions such as 'Teshen', or to revive archaic anglicisms such as 'Dantsick', in order to calm the distressed petitioners. At the end of the Second World War, however, the subject was hardly discussed. The Soviets were allowed to impose whatever terminology suited themselves and their protégés best. In Poland's Recovered Territories, every opportunity was taken to consign German names to oblivion, not merely as a symbol of victory over the Nazis, but in a spurious attempt to prove the Germans' falsification of history. In the former Polish territories annexed by the USSR, all existing Polish names were officially suppressed.

In this situation, the historian's duty undoubtedly lies in drawing his readers' attention to the ways in which the present differs from the past. The most cursory perusal of a nineteenth-century text will show how very different many 'Polish' places were at that period, from what they have since become. Having read Baedeker's description of Breslau, for example, it is pertinent to ask whether the author's evident emphasis on the city's Prussian and German connections does not derive from his own native German prejudice.[23] One should also ask whether the scarcity of Polish references derives from the absence in the city at that date of any substantive Polish influence. Unless Baedeker was a total charlatan, which in view of his international reputation is unlikely, the open-minded reader gets the distinct impression that Breslau may well have been a thoroughly German city. In which case, it is not unreasonable to refer to it at that period as 'Breslau' rather than as 'Wrocław'.

Turning to a comparable Polish text published in 1970, one is forced to admit that the picture is almost unrecognizable. Having read one's 'Travel-Guide Poland', it is pertinent to ask whether the evident emphasis on the city's Polish connections does not derive from the fact that the book was edited and published by an official agency of the Polish People's Republic.[24] One should also ask whether the scarcity of references to the city's German connections is due to the authors' prejudices or perhaps to the absence at that date of any substantive German influence. Unless the authors were total charlatans, which is unlikely, one gets the distinct impression that Wrocław in 1970 may well have been a thoroughly Polish city. In which case, it is not unreasonable to refer to it, in the post-war period, as 'Wrocław' rather than as 'Breslau'.

The guidebooks only hint at the catastrophic events which changed Breslau into Wrocław. In January 1945, at the advance of the Soviet Army, Hitler ordered *Festung-Breslau* to be defended to the last man. The resident civilians, almost entirely German, were ordered to abandon their homes, and to make their way in the depth of winter into the heart of Germany. Many of them, as helpless refugees, were incinerated by the RAF's fire-bomb raid on Dresden. Three months later, when the beleaguered survivors of Breslau's garrison capitulated, much of the Silesian capital had been razed to the ground. Its native inhabitants had gone. Its ruins were occupied by units of the Soviet and Polish armies, and then handed over to the administration of the Recovered Territories. In discussing the matter with Stalin in 1944, Mikołajczyk had remarked that Wrocław was 'a purely German town'. Stalin replied that in olden times it was a Slav city and 'nothing prevents it from returning to its former historical tradition'. (In this conversation, Stalin actually talked of 'Borysław'.[25]) In 1945–7, the city was completely repopulated by Polish refugees. Many of them came from Lwów, having suffered a fate at Soviet hands not too dissimilar to that suffered by the Germans of Breslau from the Nazis. The University, the Library, the Ossolineum Institute, together with thousands of their employees and their chattels, were transported from Lwów *en bloc*. Later on, other Poles drifted in from other devastated regions of the country. In this light, 'Wrocław' may better be regarded as a partial reincarnation of Lwów than as a continuation of Breslau. Nowadays, the city is thriving, and is vibrantly Polish. The older inhabitants often speak with the lilting accent of the East, thus betraying their distant origins. But the youngsters, over 50 per cent of the citizens, were all born here. As Polish Vratislavians, they feel themselves to be the direct descendants of those ancient Slavs who lived on this same ground over seven centuries ago. Their feelings, if understandable, are surely mistaken. Like their ageing German predecessors, now coming to the end of a bitter exile in the Federal Republic, they are the victims and the products of the Second World War.[26]

Similar exercises could be undertaken for almost all the cities of the Recovered Territories and for all the former Polish cities incorporated into the USSR. Szczecin, Koszalin, Gdańsk, Olsztyn, Zielona Góra, Jelenia Góra, Kłodzko, Opole, are essentially new communities whose new Polish names correctly suggest the essential discontinuity with their previous German past. 'Vilnius', capital of the Lithuanian SSR contains only a fraction of the families who lived there in pre-war days. Its present-day rulers try to dismiss the five centuries of its union with Poland as an irregular interruption in the city's natural progress. L'viv, capital of the Ukrainian SSR, contains only a fraction of the families who inhabited inter-war 'Lwów', or Austrian 'Lemberg'. Yet modern Ukrainians often talk as if it had always been 'their city' since time began.

In reality, Soviet L'viv had been manufactured in the same artificial manner, and for exactly the same reasons, as Polish Wrocław. Baedeker, writing in the 1890s in the era of Galician autonomy, presented the picture of a city of essentially Polish character overlain with official Austro-German overtones. Thirty years later, in 1927, the Director of the Polish government's Tourist Office stressed the Polish connections rather more strongly.[27] In his description of the main landmarks, Dr Orłowicz drew his readers' attention to the Plac Marjacki (St. Mary's Square) with Popiel's statue of Mickiewicz (1905); to the Sobieski Museum in the Royal House on the Market Square, formerly the 'Ring'; to the Wallachian Church (1580); and to the Cemetery of Łyczaków, with its special section dedicated to the Orlęta (the Young Eagles), the youthful defenders of Lwów in 1918–19. In addition to detailed descriptions of Polish art and monuments, he makes careful mention of Uniate–Ukrainian masterpieces in the Dzieduszycki Collection, in the Ukrainian Muzeum founded in 1912, in the Uniate Cathedral of St. George (1746) and in the church of 'St. Piatnyci' (1643). Thirty-five years on, in 1962, a present-day Soviet guidebook combines the Ukrainian and the Soviet versions of the city's history:

On the northern confines of the eastern Carpathians, on the River Polta, a tributary of the Bug, lies one of the most beautiful, Ukrainian cities — ancient, 700-year-old L'viv.

Its history is rich and famous. It was founded in the middle of the thirteenth century by Prince Danil Romanovitch, and named after his son, Lev. Together with the fortress on the top of the hill, the city served as a point of resistance against the waves of Tartar-Mongols attacking Europe.

In the fourteenth century, the lands of Galich—Volhynia sustained the invasion of Polish, Hungarian, and Lithuanian feudaries. Undermined by the struggle with the Tartars, the Principality was unable to withstand the oppression of neighbouring warlords.

In the mid-fourteenth century, the west Russian lands, together with L'viv, were seized by Polish feudaries supported by the Roman Pope, as a base for spreading the Catholic Faith to the east. Until 1772, noble Poland ruled over the Galich—Volhynian lands, until 'Galichinia' (Galicia) was taken by Austria. L'viv continued under Austrian rule until 1918. After the Great October Socialist Revolution the red banner of freedom was unfurled; but as a result of prevailing historical circumstances, L'viv was cast into slavery by the Polish Lords, who proceeded to suspend such laws as the working people of Western Ukraine had founded under Austria. L'viv became the centre of the struggle for the liberation of the workers of Western Ukraine and for their reunion with Soviet Ukraine. The ideas of Great October, and the successes of Soviet rule, inspired the West Ukrainian workers in their struggle for social and national liberation.

The unforgettable year of 1939 arrived. The Soviet peoples extended a helping hand to the workers of West Ukraine, L'viv became a Soviet city . . .[28]

Such is the modern destiny of Lemberg-Lwów-L'viv. Nowhere is it made clear that the one country to which the city never belonged prior to 1939 was Russia. Nowhere is there any explanation for the city's more usual listing in official Soviet literature in its Russian form of 'Lvov'. Nowhere is there any hint of the city's former Polish or Jewish associations. Nowhere, even in jest, is there any suggestion that the name ought really to be spelt as W-R-O-C-Ł-A-W. The violence to the historical record is hardly less evident than that of the 'unforgettable year' when the city's most abrupt transmogrification was achieved.[29]

Professional scholars may well believe that popular guidebooks lie beneath their dignity. If so, they are mistaken. The work of Baedeker and his successors of all ilks provides the basic information on which public knowledge of Eastern Europe is based. The prejudices, the mistakes, the selectivity, and the downright fantasies, may be more obvious, but are no less damaging than those which abound in academic accounts.

Yet for the student and historian with no axe for grinding, and with no preference for one East European language over another, the practical problem remains. With such a wealth of onomastic variations to choose from, people are bound to ask what name should be used in which circumstances. There is no simple answer, although a few simple guidelines can be suggested. Firstly, it is essential to recognize that nothing in this subject is absolute or eternal. Place-names should be reviewed constantly to take cognizance of changes which are constantly occurring. Ideally, the 'name' should always reflect the dominant cultural and political connections of the 'place' at the moment in question. If this involves talking in Chapter Three of 'Vratislav', in Chapter Twenty of 'Breslau', and in Chapter Twenty-three of 'Wrocław', the searcher after precision should not be deterred. Secondly, it is necessary to accept that linguistic conventions change less easily than political ones. When speaking German, it is far simpler to talk of 'Breslau' than of 'Wrocław', if only because the established corpus of literature on the subject in the German language has always used that particular form. When speaking Polish it is always simpler for purely linguistic reasons to talk of Wrocław. A German who prefers the German form no more implies that modern Wrocław is a German city, than the Poles who talk of 'Lipsk' and 'Dresna' imply that Leipzig or Dresden are Polish. Thirdly, it is important to remember that neutral versions, in English or Latin, themselves contain a distortion of reality, and may well carry serious implications. 'Warsaw' is clearly preferable to the native 'Warszawa' for scholars writing in English. But fully anglicized items of this sort are extremely rare. Most English forms were in fact taken from German or Russian usage, and became familiar to the Anglo-Saxon reader in the past in specific conditions which no longer apply — 'Cracow', for example, was borrowed from the German 'Krakau' in the distant days when the inhabitants of the city were mainly German-speaking. Finally, it must not be forgotten that all place-names take their validity from the purposes for which they were invented. Within their own terms of reference, they are all equally appropriate. Their propriety in any given situation can only be tested when the historian inquires for what purposes they are to be used, and in whose interest. All variations must always be kept in mind. Of one thing everyone can be certain. The cultural savages who have toured the records and the cemeteries of the Polish lands, erasing Polish, German, Jewish, Russian, or Ukrainian names in the hope of forcing many-splendoured reality to conform with their own monotonous fantasies, are to be pitied. Censors, who eliminate offending place-names from maps and records, in the pretence that the mode of the moment is somehow the eternal verdict of history, are deceiving both themselves and their charges. As in matters of more excitement, the reasonable man must always conclude: *Vive la différence!*

*　*　*　*　*

Whatever may be said about the settlement of 1945, it cannot be doubted that it is as final as any such political arrangement can be. Its finality does not derive from the wisdom of its perpetrators, but from their ruthlessness. Frontier problems were not so much solved as destroyed. Throughout Eastern Europe, national minorities who may or may not have been responsible for intercommunal tensions, were physically removed. From the point of view of modern governments, and of the superpower which now presides over the whole region, the result is extremely tidy. But the human cost was terrible.

For the historian, the 1945 Settlement presents a curious paradox. In reality, it constituted a radical break with the past, a giant leap away from conditions prevailing before the war, an arbitrary diversion of the historical stream. It was a colossal feat of political engineering. However, in almost every East European country, it is interpreted as the culmination of a natural historical process, and is constantly rationalized by reference to distant historical events, real or imagined. Everybody knows that History can be used to justify anything;

but in this case, the elaborate historical ceremonial, which the ideologists have laid on to sanctifying the decision of 1945, is almost as breathtaking as the great Settlement itself. It is as if the builders of the Suez Canal or of the Grand Coulee Dam felt obliged to explain their handiwork as nothing more than that which sun, tides, and geology would have achieved in the normal course of events. In Poland since the War, a whole generation has been instructed to assume that the present frontiers of the People's Republic surround the territory on which the Polish nation has evolved since time immemorial. They are encouraged to believe that the Polish *macierz* or 'Motherland' has always occupied this same fixed location, even when large parts of it happened to be inhabited for centuries by large numbers of 'aliens', or when political boundaries happened to run in completely different directions. According to the official view, the Poles always possessed the inalienable and exclusive right to inhabit the Recovered Territories of the west and north, even when *force majeure* prevented them from exercising it. By the same token, their own presence at any time on any plot or patch beyond the eastern bounds laid down by the Potsdam Conference must be regretted as a dastardly infringement of other nations' rights (even if some of those nations did not then exist). In brief, the People's Republic is to be seen as the natural product of History. It was delineated by men, whose deliberations under Soviet guidance were inspired by a correct appraisal of scientific principles, enabling them not merely to create a new Poland, but rather to recover the old one. In many ways, this is an extremely romantic picture, where the skill of the statesmen of 1945 is seen to have restored a classical masterpiece, cleaning the canvas of the accumulated grime and the clumsy retouching of the centuries, in order to reveal the ancient map of Poland in all its pristine splendour. For all the pretence of scientific method, the arguing is purely teleological. Its appeal, to a nation that has known such protracted insecurity, is not rational but emotional.

All Poland's eastern neighbours have now been incorporated into the USSR. From the purely territorial point of view, they have attained much. The Lithuanians have their Lithuanian SSR and, since 1940, their capital of Vilnius. The Byelorussians have their Byelorussian SSR, which stretches from beyond the Dvina to beyond the Pripet, and from Brest on the Bug to Vitebsk, Mogilev, and Gomel. The Ukrainians have their Ukrainian SSR which embodies the 'Great Ukraine from the San to the Don'. From other points of view, however, these Soviet nationalities have little to celebrate. Their incorporation into the USSR was accompanied by the physical liquidation of all independent national leaders, and by the mass deportation of whole segments of the population. Whilst receiving the nominal control of their language, culture, and national territory, they have been subordinated to the monopoly rule of the all-Union Communist Party, which acts as the instrument of a centralized, autocratic, Russian-dominated empire. Their constitutional rights are a sham. Their subjection is all too real. With the exception of the members of the ruling *apparat,* they tend to look on their former Polish connections with a mixture of regret and envy. (See Map 21.)

The Lithuanians, in particular, must often shake their heads in dismay. In the inter-war period, their sorry obsession with the question of Wilno (in which hardly any Lithuanians were then living) precipitated not merely the breach with the Polish government, but more seriously the rupture of plans to establish a defensive block of border nations.[30] Furthermore, it drove them into their dubious political alignment with the Soviets. The promise of Wilno was the bait which drew the Lithuanians into the Soviet trap. The sad results were seen in 1939–40. Soviet approval for the transfer of Wilno to Lithuania served merely as a prelude to the entry of the Red Army in June 1940, and the violent death of Lithuanian independence. To a certain extent, all the East European nations were guilty of pursuing narrow selfish aims at the cost of good neighbourliness and common security; but the Lithuanians are a classic case. They escaped from the sizzling Polish frying-pan only to jump with both feet into the raging Soviet fire.[31]

The Byelorussians had less chance than the Lithuanians to influence their fate. Their independent national republic (BNR) in Minsk lasted a mere nine months, from March to December 1918. Overrun first by the Red Army and then by the Polish Army, it was partitioned between the Soviets and

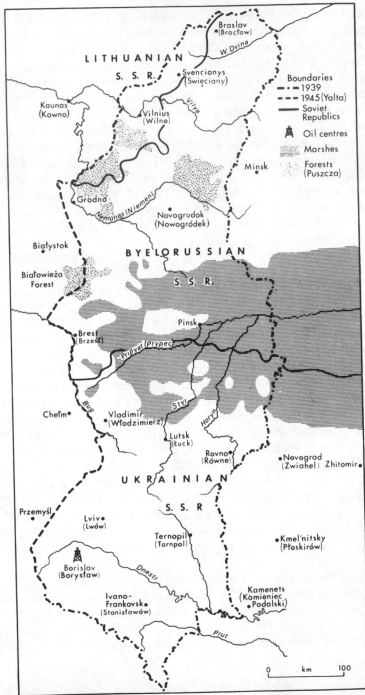

Map 21.   The USSR's Recovered Territories, since 1945

the Poles at the Treaty of Riga. In 1939, the reunion of the western and eastern partitions in a reconstituted Byelo-russian SSR was accompanied by the descent of the Red Army 'like a plague of locusts' and by massive purges. In the opinion of one of Byelorussia's few independent historians, any comparison between Polish and Soviet policies towards Byelorussia must be clearly unfavourable to the Soviet regime.[32]

The Ukrainians, who once stood to gain most from a proper understanding with the Poles, have most to regret. Like the Lithuanians, they demanded all their national rights in full and at once, and ended up with virtually nothing. The Ukrainian national movement with its slogan of 'Ukraine for the Ukrainians', took an inflexible and uncompromising stand on the territorial issue. In this, it closely resembled the equivalent position within the Polish camp of Dmowski's National Democrats, whom it was bound to meet in head-on collision. In the brief era of Ukrainian independence from 1918 to 1921, there was no significant group to match Piłsudski's Polish federalists, or even the milder Polish con-servatives. The Ukrainians could not agree with the Polish nationalists because of conflicting and mutually exclusive ter-ritorial claims; nor with the Polish federalists, because of ancient resentments deriving from the feudal regime of the old *Rzeczpospolita*; nor with the Polish conservatives, because of their recent experiences in Galicia. As a result, they were left to fight against their principal Russian adversaries, both Reds and Whites, in isolation.[33] Their unilateral seizure of Lemberg, in November 1918, at a time when only a small Ukrainian minority was living in the city, led to a nine-month war with the Polish Army, and to the loss of Western Ukraine to Poland.[34] Their recovery of Kiev in May 1920, in conse-quence of Ataman Petlura's improvised treaty with Piłsudski, was undertaken too late to prevent the counter-mobilization of irresistible Bolshevik forces.[35] In any case, Petlura's neces-sary recognition of Polish claims to the western Ukraine as Piłsudski's price for the assistance of the Polish army, dis-credited the Ataman in the eyes of his unbending compatriots. In this way, divided within and assailed from without, the Ukrainian National state (UNR) was ground into the dust. It

has never had the opportunity to resurrect. At the Treaty of
Riga, Ukraine like Byelorussia, was partitioned between the
Poles and the Soviets. In the inter-war period, Ukrainian
frustration was vented with special fury on the Poles. Since
a measure of nationalist politics was tolerated in Poland but
not in the USSR, the West Ukraine became the focus for
such Ukrainian organizations that were able to operate. But
nothing was gained. In the years which preceded the Nazi–
Soviet Pact of 1939–41, and the Nazi–Soviet War of 1941–5,
both the Poles and the Ukrainians lost all hope of common
action against their mutual enemies. By 1939, the Ukrainian
national movement was left with only one potential ally –
the Nazis: and when Hitler revealed his hand by the bloody
suppression of all independent organizations in occupied
Ukraine, it was totally isolated. Those Ukrainians who joined
the Germans in the *SS Galizien* Division were decimated on
the Eastern Front. One of the last secrets of the 'Last Secret'
is that the survivors of the *SS Galizien* were saved from
deportation to the USSR and from certain death, by virtue
of their claim to be Polish citizens.[36] Those who joined
the Ukrainian Insurrectionary Army (UPA) of Stefan Bandera
spent the rest of the Second World War fighting a three-sided
battle for survival in the underground against the Red Army,
the German *Wehrmacht,* and the Polish AK. For all their gallantry, their hopeless predicament was dictated by unreal
political attitudes and by an excessive mistrust of all their
neighbours. They were finally driven to earth in 1947, and
annihilated in the Bieszczady Mountains by a joint exercise
of the Soviet, Czechoslovak, and Polish People's armies. In
the sorrowful wake of so many disasters, Ukrainian attitudes
towards Poland are inevitably rather mixed. In the Soviet
Union, the question cannot be openly discussed, and in
People's Poland it is rarely raised in public. In the west,
among *émigré* circles it often provokes violent reactions
conditioned by pre-war, or wartime animosities. The majority
of Ukrainians abroad have been raised in the old nationalist
tradition, where exclusive possession of the national territory
in its maximal limits is regarded as the sole and ultimate
Good. For this reason, they still publish their maps of a
'Greater Ukraine', whose boundaries exceed those even of the

Ukrainian SSR. They still complain of the 'Polish occupation' of Peremishl (Przemyśl) and Khilm (Chełm). Little do they seem to realize how closely their position resembles that of their hated Stalinist and Polish nationalist enemies. Their historians still cling in the main to the old nationalist ideology which views the nation and its homeland as a constant reality throughout recorded history. It is an ideology which necessarily breeds resentment against those people who are seen to have offended against the impossible, sterile, unhistorical ideal. Little do they realize how closely they echo the official communist propagandists. In the schools of the Ukrainian SSR, as in the classrooms of the Ukrainian Emigration, children are still told that the Poles who once ruled in Kiev, and who once formed the single largest community in the population of the districts of L'viv, Ivanofrankivsk (Stanisławów), and Ternopil, were 'foreign oppressors', 'alien intruders', or 'imperialist landlords'. *Mutatis mutandis,* they are given exactly the same picture which old-fashioned Polish nationalists, (and their successors among Polish communist ideologues) have painted of the German presence in points west. It is nicely calculated to keep all the old antagonisms alive.[37]

Slowly, however, new opinions are beginning to emerge. Scholars are now appearing who write more of the ancient and common heritage of the Poles and the Ukrainians, and less of their modern divergences. The millennium of Polish—Ukrainian relations is fast approaching; and someone at least in the coming celebrations can be expected to recount the pros as well as the cons of the thousand years since Prince Volodymir (Vladimir) of Kiev launched his expedition against the 'Liakhs' in 981. Two invidious myths need to be laid — the first, that Poland's role in the east was entirely positive, and secondly that it was entirely negative. There are now historians who are prepared to debate whether the old Polish—Lithuanian state was not a stepmother if not a Mother, to Ukrainians and Poles alike. There are historians who regret the failure of the Union of Hadziacz as much as others rejoice in the success of Khmyelhytsky's Rebellion. There are historians who compare the striking similarity between the Russian Empire's successful absorption of Ukraine between 1654 and

1787, through the successive phases of protective association, limited autonomy, and full integration, with Russia's parallel but so far unfinished policy towards Poland since 1717. All these studies promise to moderate the tone of Polish–Ukrainian attitudes. Above all, they challenge both Poles and Ukrainians to examine the underlying assumptions of the Nationalism which has reigned for so long not only in their History, but also in their Historiography. They may serve to show that neither the Nation nor the Nation-State possesses moral validity in its own right, but only when it is promoted in conjunction with the basic ethical values of charity, humanity, and respect for the individual. 'Gentlemen, in the name of what do you want a national, independent, sovereign state?' Here perhaps is the central issue in the modern history and politics of Eastern Europe. In the hands of intolerant militants, Nationalism can be as oppressive, as cruel, and as repulsive as the Imperialism and the Absolutism whose iniquities originally brought it into being. In the process of re-evaluation, the historian's contribution must be to present the realities of the past in all their manifold variety. For too long, one-sided pessimistic prejudices have prevailed. Among the Poles, the best-known quotation on the history of Polish–Ukrainian relations comes from Sienkiewicz's magnificent but notorious concluding sentence of *Ogniem i Mieczem* (By Fire and Sword): *'Nienawiść wzrosła w sercach, i zatruła krew probratymcze'* (And Hatred swelled in people's hearts and poisoned the blood of brothers).[38] It now appears that other, more reconciliatory quotations can be found. Even in the era when Polish–Ukrainian antagonism was being fuelled by rival ambitions in Galicia, Pantaleimon Kulish was writing of the 'abominable duel and the bedevilled frenzy' of 'the headstrong Ruthenian and his implacable enemy of the past thousand years' — a duel of which 'not one of their descendants will be proud'. Even earlier, Taras Shevchenko was warning his compatriots against the temptation to rejoice in Poland's misfortunes:

> You boast, because we once
> Brought Poland to calamity . . .
> And so it was; Poland fell;
> But you were crushed by her fall as well.[39]

In the intervening years, such magnanimous words have all too often been ignored.

By removing the ancient territorial feud, the settlement of 1945 achieved by force what Poles and Ukrainians had proved incapable of achieving by mutual consent. The two related families which had lived for centuries under the same roof were roughly torn apart, and forced to move into separate quarters. Some have condemned the forcible separation out of hand: others have compared it to 'an inevitable divorce' — unpleasant in itself but preferable to the perpetual discord of an incompatible marriage. All must conclude that it has provided both parties with a period of respite, a time for sober reflection on the failures of the past and the opportunities of the future.

Of all Poland's neighbours, however, the Germans have the most reason to query the official version of Polish History as propagated in Warsaw. Whatever they may feel about the irrevocable loss of their eastern provinces — and they seem to feel a mixture of guilt, resentment, and indifference — they cannot consign a substantial slice of their heritage to oblivion. According to German historians of the old school, the permanent link of Pomerania and Silesia with the German lands was forged in 1138, and that of Prussia by the arrival of the Teutonic Order in 1226. Today, although the more extreme German claims have been proved false, no amount of sophistry can dismiss the fact the German element was dominant in those parts for the last six or seven hundred years. No one can deny that the population of Prussia's 'Polish provinces' played an integral role in modern German History at its most brilliant epoch. No one possessing even the most elementary knowledge of German culture can overlook the contribution to its development made by its 'easterners', from those cities and provinces recently incorporated into Poland. (See Map 22.)

If the propensity of the Polish authorities to build memorials to famous battles fought on their territory were to be applied in anything like an equitable manner, the present monuments at Legnica and Grunwald would be joined by a long list of others: by a monument to Wallenstein's engagement at Steinau-am-Oder (Ścinawa) in 1627; to Charles XII's victories over the Saxons at Ostenberg (Pułtusk), Punitz (Punice), and

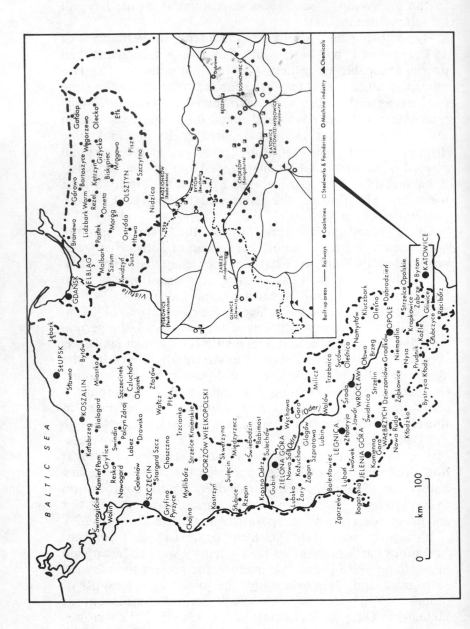

Chief Cities of Wojewodztwa (1975)

Allenstein	OLSZTYN
Breslau	WROCŁAW
Danzig	GDAŃSK
Elbing	ELBLĄG
Grünberg	ZIELONA GÓRA
Hirschberg	JELENIA GÓRA
Köslin	KOSZALIN
Landsberg	GORZÓW WIELKOPOLSKI
Liegnitz	LEGNICA
Oppeln	OPOLE
Schniedemühl	PIŁA
Stettin	SZCZECIN
Stolp	SŁUPSK
Waldenburg	WAŁBRZYCH

OTHER TOWNS

Bad Polzin	Połczyn Zdrój	Neusalz	Nowa Sól
Bischofsburg	Biskupiec	Ratzebuhr	Okonek
Bomst	Babimost	Reichenau	Bogatynia
Crossen	Krosno Odrzańskie	Reppen	Rzepin
Frankfurt-Ost	Słubice	Rosenberg	Olesno
Görlitz	Zgorzelec	Sagan	Żagań
Goldberg	Złotoryja	Schivelbein	Świdwin
Gollnow	Goleniów	Schönlanke	Trzcianka
Jauer	Jawór	Schweibus	Świebodzin
Krappitz	Krapkowice	Sommerfeld	Lubsko
Küstrin	Kostrzyn	Swinemünde	Świnoujście
Labez	Łobez	Zielinzig	Sulęcin
Landeshut	Kamienna Góra	Lublinitz	Lubliniec
Lübben	Lubin	Guhrau	Góra
Neurode	Nowa Ruda		

FORMER GERMAN COUNTY (KREIS) TOWNS

UPPER SILESIA

Beuthen	Bytom
Cosel	Koźle
Falkenberg	Niemodlin
Gross-Strehlitz	Strzelce
Grottkau	Grodków
Guttentag	Dobrodzień
Hindenburg	Zabrze
Kreuzberg	Kluczbork
Leobschütz	Głubczyce
Neustadt	Prudnik
Niesse	Nysa
Oppeln	Opole
Ratibor	Racibórz
Tost-Gleiwitz	Gliwice

LOWER SILESIA

Breslau	Wrocław
Brieg	Brzeg
Bunzlau	Bolesławiec
Frankenstein	Ząbkowice Śląskie
Fraustadt	Wschowa
Freystadt	Kożuchów
Glatz	Kłodzko
Glogau	Głogów
Gross-Wartenberg	Syców
Grünberg	Zielona Góra
Habelschwerdt	Bystrzyca Kłodzka
Hirschberg	Jelenia Góra
Lauban	Lubań
Löwenberg	Lwówek Śląski
Militsch	Milicz
Namslau	Namysłów
Neumarkt	Środa Śląska
Oels	Oleśnica
Ohlau	Oława
Reichenbach	Dzierżoniów
Schweidnitz	Świdnica
Sprottau	Szprotawa
Strehlen	Strzelin
Trebnitz	Trzebnica
Waldenburg	Wałbrzych
Wohlau	Wołów

POMMERN

Belgard	Białogard
Bütow	Bytów
Cammin	Kamień Pomorski
Greifenberg	Gryfice
Greiffenhagen	Gryfino
Kolberg	Kołobrzeg
Köslin	Koszalin
Lauenberg	Lębork
Neugard	Nowogard
Pyritz	Pyrzyce
Regenwalde	Resko
Rummelsberg	Miastko
Saatzig	Stargard
Schlawe	Sławno
Stettin	Szczecin
Stolp	Słupsk
Wollin	Wolin

EAST BRANDENBURG

Crossen	Krosno Odrzańskie
Guben	Gubin
Königsberg	Chojna
Landsberg	Gorzów Wielkopolski
Meseritz	Międzyrzecz
Schwerin	Skwierzyna
Soldin	Myślibórz
Sorau	Żary
Züllichau-Schweibus	Sulechów

EAST PRUSSIA

Allenstein	Olsztyn
Angerburg	Węgorzewo
Bartenstein	Bartoszyce
Braunsberg	Braniewo
Deutsch-Eylau	Iława
Elbing	Elbląg
Goldap	Gołdap
Heilsberg	Lidzbark
Johannisburg	Pisz
Landsberg	Gorowo
Lötzen	Giżycko
Lyck	Ełk
Marienburg	Malbork
Marienwerder	Kwidzyń
Mohrungen	Morąg
Neidenburg	Nidzica
Ortelsburg	Szczytno
Osterode	Ostróda
Preussisch-Holland	Pasłęk
Rastenburg	Kętrzyn
Rössel	Reszel
Rosenberg	Susz
Sensburg	Mrągowo
Stuhm	Sztum
Treuburg	Olecko
Wormditt	Orneta

GRENZMARK W. PREUSSEN

Arnswalde	Choszczno
Deutsch Krone	Wałcz
Dramburg	Drawsko
Flatow	Złotów
Friedeberg	Strzelce Krajeńskie
Kreuz	Krzyż
Neustettin	Szczecinek
Schlochau	Człuchów
Schneidemühl	Piła

Fraustadt (Wschowa); to Frederick the Great's victories at
Mollwitz (Małujowice, 1741), where he fled the field in needless panic, at Hohenfriedburg (Dobromierz, 1745), at Zorn-
dorf (Sarbinowo, 1758), and Leuthen (Lutynia, 1757); and
above all, to Frederick's great defeats at Gross Jagersdorf
(1757) and at Künersdorf (Kunowice, 1759). All these
engagements, however, are seen in Poland to be part of
'foreign' rather than of 'local' history, and as such are not
judged worthy of attention, even where the modern Polish
tourist might take comfort from the result. In educated
German minds, for instance, the name of Künersdorf conjures
up the same sort of noble reflections which the British associate with Kipling's *Recessional* and the French with Hugo's
lines on Waterloo in *L'Expiation*. Künersdorf was the site of
Prussia's greatest disaster, the cause of a situation where the
Russians threatened to destroy the Hohenzollerns for good,
the scene of untold carnage, and the subject of Christian
Tiegde's celebrated *Elegy* to 'Humanity butchered by Delusion
on the Altar of Blood'. Appropriately enough, as Kunowice,
it is now the Polish frontier station on the main railway line
between Berlin and Warsaw. Other monuments to past glory
might also be raised to Gneisenau's defence of Colberg
(Kołobrzeg) in 1806; to Napoleon's victory at Eylau (Iława)
in 1807; to Hindenburg's destruction of two Russian armies
in the Battle of the Masurian Lakes in September 1914, or
even to Piłsudski's repulse of the Red Army from their
intended advance into Germany in August 1920. A colossal
statue of Hindenburg, erected at Hohenstein (Pszczółki) in
memory of his success against the Russians was demolished
by the Nazis in 1944 to prevent its desecration by the advancing Soviet Army; whilst a diminutive memorial at Radzymin,
with the curious inscription 'KOŚCIUSZKO–RODACY–1920r'
(To Kościuszko, from his compatriots, AD 1920) is the only
mark of Piłsudski's success at the Battle of Warsaw.

Similarly, if the post-war Polish authorities were now to
commemorate all the famous sons and daughters of the 'Recovered Territories', commemorative plaques would have to
be fixed to the birthplace in Szczecin of Katherina von
Anhalt-Zerbst (1729–96) later Empress of Russia; to the
birthplaces in Gdańsk of Johann Hevelius (1611–87), the

beer-brewing astronomer, of Gabriel Fahrenheit (1686–1736), the physicist, of Artur Schopenhauer (1788–1860), the philosopher, and of the Von Schellendorf brothers, successive German War Ministers under Bismarck; to those in Poznań of Heinrich Graetz (1817–91), the historian, of Edward Lasker (1829–94), the National Liberal leader, of Field Marshal-President Paul von Beneckendorff und Hindenburg (1847–1934), and of Field Marshal Hans von Kluge (1882–1944); and to those in Wrocław of Friedrich von Gentz (1764–1832), Metternich's secretary and theoretician of the Balance of Power, of Friedrich Schleiermacher (1768–1834), the theologian, of Karl Lessing (1808–90) and Adolf Menzel (1815–1905), historical painters, of Ferdinand Lassalle (1825–64), the socialist, of Field Marshal Hermann von Eichhorn (1848–1918), of Sir George Henschel (1850–1934), singer, conductor, and founder of the Boston Symphony Orchestra, and of Max Born (1888–1970), the British scientist and Nobel Prize winner. By the same token, Morąg (Mohrungen) can claim J. G. Herder (1744–1803), the historical philosopher, mythologist, and collector of folk-songs; Zęblin near Koszalin (Cöslin) can claim Christian von Kleist (1715–59), the Prussian soldier and poet, killed at Künersdorf; Metschkau (Mieczków) in Silesia can claim Adalbert Falk (1827–1900), Prussian Minister of Education and author of the *Kulturkampf*; Kostrzyn (Küstrin), the scene of Frederick II's juvenile incarceration, can claim Admiral Alfred von Tirpitz (1849–1930) and Field Marshal Feodor von Bock (1880–1945); Belchau near Toruń can claim General Erich von Falkenhayn (1861–1922); Pokój (Carlsruhe) near Opole can claim both Ferdinand von Richthofen (1833–1905), the geographer and Chinese explorer, and his equally adventurous grandson, Manfred von Richthofen (1892–1918), the 'Red Baron', the leading air-ace of the First World War; Wąbrzeźno (Briesen) near Grudziądz can claim Walter Herman Nernst (1864–1941), formulator of the Third Law of Thermodynamics. Krzyżowa (Creisau) near Świdnica was given to Field Marshal Helmuth von Moltke (1800–91) in recognition of his services in the Austro-Prussian War of 1866. In later times, as the home of the Field Marshal's great grandson, Helmuth von Moltke (1907–45), who was hanged by the

Nazis for treason, it gave shelter to the 'Kreisau Circle' of German resisters.[40] Skyren, near Krosno (Crossen) on the Oder, was the home of Leon Count von Caprivi (1831–99), and Haynau (Chojonów) of Georg Michaelis (1857–1936). Both men in their day served as German Chancellors. Racibórz (Ratibor) was the centre of the Hohenlohe estates – the largest landed fortune in Central Europe: and Tarnowskie Góry (Tarnowitz) of the Donnersmarck fortune. Among the personalities of the Second World War, Panzer General Heinz Guderian (1888–1954) was born at Chełmno (Kulm) on the Vistula: *SS-Obergruppenfuehrer* Erich von dem Bach-Zelewsky (1899–1972), victor of the Warsaw Rising, at Lembork (Lauenberg) in Pomerania; and *SS*-General Kurt Daluege (1897–1946), Head of the Nazi *Ordnungspolizei*, at Kluczbork (Kreuzberg) in Silesia. The list is endless, and fills more entries in any general encyclopaedia than those of entire nations. Who is to say that so many distinguished names, and the ancient German communities which produced them, are now to be dissociated from the land of their birth? How, if they are simply struck from the record, can their evil deeds, as well as their noble ones, be remembered?

Yet encyclopaedic entries prove little. The really striking feature of German life in the East is to be found in the intensity with which the population's Germanity was associated with its homeland. For exactly the same feelings of insecurity which nowadays inspire their Polish successors, the patriotism and cultural zeal of the eastern Germans was all the more fervent for its exposure to the tensions of disputed border territory. In many ways, the Germans of Breslau or Posen were more staunchly loyal to German culture and to the German state than were many of their compatriots elsewhere in Germany (just as the 'Loyalists' of Belfast cultivate their Britishness far more demonstratively than most people elsewhere in the United Kingdom). None the less, if this patriotism sometimes possessed a truculent edge of which the Poles are all too well aware, it also inspired extraordinary achievements in all fields of human endeavour. In the realm of learning, the scholars and scientists of Breslau, whose German university took second place only to Berlin, produced name after name of international distinction. In the realm of the arts, too, the prominence of Germany's former eastern provinces is self-evident. From the Teutonic castles of Marienburg (Malbork) and Neidenburg (Nidizica), and the Gothic spires of Stettin's *Pieterkirche* and Danzig's *Marienkirche,* to the Renaissance curiosities of Hirschberg (Jelenia Góra), Bad Landeck (Lądek Zdój), or Neisse (Nysa), the florid Baroque of Grussau (Krzeszów) and Lubin (Łubiąż), and the tasteless ostentation of countless Wilhelmian public buildings, Poland's Recovered Territories are filled with architectural items which belong to the corpus of German, not of Polish, expression. The older theatres, concert halls, and galleries of Breslau, Posen, Stettin, and Danzig belong to the world of German, not Polish, culture.

Above all, in the realm of German literature, the contribution of the easterners was of paramount importance. As early as the thirteenth century, the court of Heinrich V, Prince of Silesia (1266—90), flourished as a resort of the Minnesingers. In the era of the Reformation and Counter-Reformation, the Protestant Johann Hesse (1490—1547) of Breslau, and the Catholic convert, Johannes Scheffler (1624—77), known as 'Angelus Silesius' (The Silesian Angel), wrote hymns and devotional works learned by German Christians of every denomination. The literary reforms of the seventeenth century were initiated by Martin Opitz von Boberfeld (1597—1639) of Bunzlau (Bolesławiec), developed by Friedrich von Logau (1604—55) and Christian Hoffmann (1618—79), both officials of the Silesian court, and perfected by Andreas Gryphius (1616—64), of Fraustadt (Wschowa). The Revival of the eighteenth century was finely represented by the work of von Kleist, whose poem *Der Frühling* (Spring) must appear in almost every volume of collected German verse. The growth of the Romantic Movement was greatly enhanced by E. T. A. Hoffmann (1776—1822), whose fantastic Tales were first conceived during the boredom of his duties as an official of South Prussia in Płock and Warsaw. The earnest realities of middle-class life in Breslau were exactly reconstructed by Gustav Freytag (1816—95), whose *Soll und Haben* (Debit and Credit, 1855) has been rated the archetypal German novel of the century. Similar acclaim was to be won at a later date by Arnold Zweig (1887—1968) of Glogau (Głogów) for *Der Streit um den Sergeanten Grischa* (The Dispute about Sergeant

Grischa, 1927). But the real prowess of the Silesian school was to be found in the lyric poetry of Joseph Freiherr von Eichendorff (1788–1857), who was born at Lubowitz (Lubomia) and died at Neisse, and of Gerhart Hauptmann (1862–1946) who lived at Agnetendorf (Jagniątków) in the Reisengebirge. Eichendorff's simple melodic lines, evoking gaunt hills, dark forests, and moonlit nights, frequently provided the inspiration for songs by Schubert, Schumann, and Wolf. His chosen themes of *Lust* (Nostalgia), *Heimat* (The Homeland), and *Waldeinsamkeit* (Loneliness-in-the-Forest) excite the same poignant sentiments for German expellees of the post-war generation as for his contemporaries. Here, if anywhere, is the banished soul of German Silesia:

> In a cool and gentle valley
> The mill-wheel still is turning.
> But my sweetheart has departed,
> And will not be returning.
>
> O valleys broad! O soaring crags,
> And fair green woods below!
> My refuge for reflecting
> On all life's joy and sorrow. . . .
> Deep in the forest stands engraved
> The quiet, telling truth
> Of how aright to live and love,
> Of where lies man's real wealth. . . .
> Yet I, too, soon must leave you.
> A stranger in a stranger's land,
> I'll watch on some packed avenue
> The world's immodest pageant.
>
> Misfortune and pain, like familiar thieves
> So stealthily overtake us;
> For everything that we hold most dear
> Must surely be parted from us.[41]

Indeed, from today's viewpoint, Eichendorff's exquisite nostalgia presaged the impending doom of German life in the east no less forcefully than the apocalyptic scenes of 'War' in the poetic premonitions of yet another Silesian, Georg Heym (1887–1912):

Hugely he towers above the glowing ruins,
And thrice thrusts his torch into the wild heavens. . . .
Through the storm-rent billows' fiery reflection
Into the deathly darkness of cold desolation,
Shrivelling the night with distant flames of horror
As fire and brimstone consume and engulf Gomorrah.[42]

Both Germans and Poles have still to come to terms with the changes of 1945. As in the Polish–Ukrainian case, the forcible separation of the nationalities has given an opportunity for respite and reflection. But in Polish–German relations, the wounds, if not older, are deeper, and may take longer to heal. Historians on both sides have begun to correct the grosser distortions which have fed nationalist prejudices in the past. On this score, scholars in West Germany do not have to operate within the ideological constraints prevailing in People's Poland or in the German Democratic Republic, and have undertaken the most far-reaching revisions. Nor has the West German literary scene lacked interest in Polish themes. In the work of Gunther Grass (born 1927 in Danzig), whose 'Danzig Trilogy' — *Die Blechtrommel* (The Tin Drum, 1959), *Katz und Maus* (Cat and Mouse, 1961), and *Hundejahre* (A Dog's Life, 1963) — must be counted among the masterpieces of contemporary literature, there are signs that the old *Polenlyrik* is not yet dead. As a witness to eastern Germany's catastrophe, Grass cannot write about Poland in the sentimental tones of his nineteenth-century predecessors. But his words are full of irony and ambiguity, and serve to discredit the hostile stereotypes which were prevalent in the Germany of his youth:

I have always said that Poles are gifted,
Perhaps too gifted. But gifted for what?
They are masterly kissers of hand and cheek,
And, what is more, past masters of Melancholy and Cavalry.
Don Quixote himself, you know, was a highly gifted Pole,
Who took his stand on a hillock near Kutno
With the rays of the sunset carefully at his back.
Lowering his lance, with its red-and-white pennants,
He mounted his highly ungifted charger,
And quite dependent on such beastly horse-power
Rode straight at the flank of the Field Grey ranks . . .

Whether it was done in a masterly fashion or otherwise,
And whether they were sheep, or windmills, or Panzers
Which kissed Pan Quixote's hands, I cannot tell.
At all events, he was embarrassed, and blushed in masterly fashion,
So I cannot say exactly; — but Poles *are* gifted.[43]

Even so, old prejudices die hard. National antipathies are
still strong. The myth of the thousand-year struggle between
Teuton and Slav, and the idea that it may yet bring final
victory to one side or the other, has not been completely
abandoned.[44] Yet common humanity demands that Germans
and Poles alike should be taught to think of themselves as the
common victims of their common enmity and to realize in
whose interests that enmity is kept alive. In reality, Polish—
German relations have been neither so consistently hostile
nor so simple as the events of the Second World War, and the
post-war propagandists, might lead one to believe. With this
thought in mind, it is interesting to note how closely Tiegde's
Elegy corresponds with the mood of the best-loved of English
elegies. Christopher Tiegde, wandering round the battlefield
of Künersdorf, was moved to thoughts uncannily reminiscent
of those of Thomas Gray in the churchyard of Stoke Poges.
In 1945, the pomp of Prussian power met its inevitable end,
and few Germans can now ignore whither the paths of glory
lead. Every traveller who crosses the new Polish frontier at
Kunowice might profitably read Tiegde's lines, composed
over a hundred years ago on that self-same spot. The poet's
obituary to the great 'World-Stormer', inspired by a temporary
defeat of the House of Hohenzollern can be applied with still
greater poignancy to the total collapse of the world of Adolf
Hitler:

> They can no more revile each other,
> Those who lie here, hand in hand.
> Their departed souls have gone together
> To a beautiful country, a friendly land,
> Where love in love's exchange is earned.
> Whenever fraternal peace is spurned,
> It's nothing but the minds of men,
> That keeps the World apart from Heaven.
> . . .
> To scorn a laurel wreath is surely noble.

Human contentment surpasses all fame.
The garlanded head becomes a skull
Whose withered garland the earth will reclaim.
As a storm-tossed leaf from the treetop flies,
So Caesar fell, one day of gloom.
Alexander of Macedon, a dust-pile, lies;
And Frederick is stretched in his narrow tomb.
Puny now is the great World-Stormer.
Fire and worms consumed his corporeal wreck.
All came to an end, like a thunder-clap in summer,
Whilst the satraps partitioned his Reich.[45]

PART TWO
Contemporary Poland
since 1944

CHAPTER TWENTY-TWO
PARTIA:
The Communist Movement

It is often said that the Polish communist movement has few native roots. It can be regarded as a plant grown mainly in a foreign frame and transplanted into the post-war Polish garden by Soviet political gardeners. In this light, it need not occupy too prominent a position in pre-war Polish history. At the same time, one should not underestimate the chances of the transplant, nor the degree to which it has adapted itself to the inimitable conditions of the Polish political soil.[1]

In its origins, the pedigree of the present-day Polish communist movement is usually traced to the beginnings of Polish Socialism as a whole, from which for sixty or seventy years it was not clearly distinguished. In the early nineteenth century, Polish socialists belonged to a tiny utopian élite, which had more influence in the Emigration than at home. Most characteristically their very earliest organization is thought to have been formed in 1832 in a disused naval barracks in Portsmouth, by a group of refugees from the November Rising.[2] They appeared in the persons of Lelewel, Worcell, and the Revd Aleksander Pułaski (1800–38) in the ranks of the Democratic Society, and of the *Zemsta Ludu* (People's Revenge), and formed a distinct branch of radical opinion amongst the 'Reds' of the two Risings. In the absence of an industrial society, their interests were focused on agrarian problems. Nothing in the nature of a mass organization can be observed until after the January Rising. The very first Polish Trade Union was established in Lwów in Galicia, by Polish printers in 1870. The first socialist strikes were organized in Poznań in Prussia in 1871 and 1872. In Warsaw, the first consciously socialist groups were organized in the form of private debating societies in this same period.

Already in the 1870s, however, two distinct trends were observable. The majority trend, inspired by Bolesław Limanowski (1835–1935), continued an earlier tradition where

Polish national demands were seen as a natural part of the socialist programme. It was patriotic, empirical, and practical in its approach to social problems. Its first organization, a revived *Lud Polski* (Polish People), was formed in Geneva and took Limanowski's pamphlet *Patriotism and Socialism* (1881), as its guiding text.[3] The minority trend, inspired by Ludwik Waryński (1856–89) specifically rejected Polish national demands. It was cosmopolitan, ideological, élitist, and not averse to terrorism, having close ties with the Russian 'People's Will'. One of its earliest public meetings, held in Warsaw on 29 November 1880 on the fiftieth anniversary of the November Rising, made a point of emphasizing its anti-patriotic stand. In a letter circulated to socialist leaders abroad, its organizers stated that 'the old motto – Vive La Pologne – has now disappeared completely from the class struggle between labour and capital'. This won them a rebuke from Marx and Engels.

Waryński's admirers often take him to be Poland's first Marxist, thereby implying that he had a firmer grasp of Marxism than Marx himself. At all events, he was a remarkable organizer, and one of the movement's most venerated martyrs. Born in the Ukraine, he operated in all three Partitions, and also abroad. In 1880, he figured as the principal defendant in the Cracow Trial of thirty-five socialists, but was absolved from all charges. Two years later in Warsaw, he founded the First Proletariat, a group which saw itself as the avant-garde of an imminent revolution. His establishment of a fighting fund among industrial workers enabled the group to survive for some four years, and in April 1884, at the textile town of Żyrardów, to sustain a successful strike for improved wages and conditions. Captured by the Tsarist police in the resultant wave of preventive arrests, he was put on trial in Warsaw in November 1885 on a charge of 'conspiring at the violent extirpation of the present political, economic, and social order.' Four associates – Kunicki, Bardowski, Ossowski, Pietrusiński – were condemned to death, and were hanged before the Alexander Citadel. Waryński himself, together with Ludwik Janowicz (1858–1902), was imprisoned in the Schlüsselberg, where he died.[4]

In the 1890s, Polish socialism matured to the point where mass parties could be formed with a real prospect of permanent existence. The largest group, the Polish Socialist Party (PPS) was founded in Paris in 1892, under the chairmanship of Limanowski. Its manifesto proclaimed the twin goals of proletarian dictatorship and national independence, to be achieved by non-violent methods. Its journal, *Robotnik* (The Worker), first edited by Józef Piłsudski was printed at Beaumont Square on the Mile End Road in London, for later clandestine shipment to Russia. Parallel, though entirely separate organizations were created in the shape of Ignacy Daszyński's Polish Social–Democratic Party (PPSD) in Galicia, and the diminutive 'PPS of the Prussian Partition' in Kattowitz. At the same time, but in direct opposition to the main-line socialist formations, a rival movement was created by a group of anti-patriotic militants who had been expelled from the All-Polish Delegation to the International Socialist Congress in Zurich in August 1893. Their 'Social Democracy of the Kingdom of Poland' (SDKP) was launched by Julian Marchlewski (1866–1925), and the brilliant young Róża Luksemburg (1870–1919). It was mirrored in Wilno by Feliks Dzierżyński's 'Social Democracy of Lithuania' (SDL). In 1900 the two organizations were joined together as the 'Social Democracy of the Kingdom of Poland and Lithuania' (SDKPiL). In this way, the fundamental and bitter schism between the patriotic socialists or 'social patriots' and the anti-patriotic 'social democrats' assumed lasting, institutional form.

It is interesting to note that the Jewish socialist movement in Poland displayed similar tendencies. The internationalist *Bund* (Jewish Workers' League), founded in Wilno in 1897, was closely aligned with the Russian Social Democrats, and opposed by the more nationalist *Paole Sion*.

Róża Luksemburg (Luxemburg), (1870–1919) deserves special mention. Born in Zamość, the daughter of an immigrant Litvak family from the east, she had few sentimental ties with her homeland. As such, she was very typical of the cosmopolitan, intellectual Jewish element which formed the backbone of the socialist, and later of the communist movements. As an associate of the Bolsheviks in Russia and as a co-founder of the Spartakusbund in Germany, she was destined to play a central role in the development of Marxist internationalism. An exceptional woman in a man's world, she was the single most influential theorist in the history of Polish communism.[5]

In the first two decades of the twentieth century, Polish socialism was beset by failures, and riddled with factions. In Austria, the PPSD acquired legal status, and from 1897 sent a vocal team of deputies to the Vienna parliament. But in Russia, the years of struggle and hope were brusquely terminated by the collapse of the Revolution of 1905–6. In 1908, the PPS (*Lewica*) or 'Left', insistent on maintaining the traditional trade-union structures and the traditional tactics of industrial action, departed from the Party's leadership, which as the PPS (*Rewolucja*), or 'Revolutionary Faction', prepared henceforth for organized military action. In 1911–16, a further faction, the PPS (*Opozycja*) or 'Opposition' of Feliks Perl and Tomasz Arciszewski peeled off in protest against the military obsessions of the leadership, which in any case was losing control of Piłsudski's more successful and by now independent formations. At this same time, the SDKPiL was rent by a schism of its own. In the course of the World War, the PPS recovered its momentum with the expectation of national independence, united on the need for a concerted effort to break the grip of the partitioning powers. The SDKPiL and the PPS (*Lewica*), in contrast, condemned 'the imperialist war' out of hand, believing that no advantage for the working class could be gained from it.[6]

By 1918, the way was open for a merger of the SDKPiL and the PPS (*Lewica*). Warsaw's leftist wits talked of a *mariage de raison* between a poor young man of good family with a rich girl of doubtful reputation. The Social Democrats could offer a consistent ideological line: the *Lewica* boasted a mass following. The founding congress of the new party was held in Cracow in December. It took the name of the Polish Communist Workers' Party (KPRP). Hostile to the 'bourgeois Republic' from the start, it chose to boycott the parliamentary elections of January 1919, and for that reason rejected the opportunity of legal activity. Despite its tireless propaganda, it could not conceal the plain fact that in the Workers' Councils, formed in 1918–19 on the model of German *arbeiterrat* and the Russian Soviets, its influence was far inferior to that of the

PPS, the *Bund,* or even of the right-wing NZR. Its following in the working class was minimal, and was confined to one or two districts in Warsaw, to Zamość, and to 'Red' Dąbrowa. In the last two areas, armed demonstrations by a self-styled Red Guard were suppressed by the Polish Army. The KPRPs peak trade union membership of 77,000 in 1919, compared to the 93,000 of the PPS at that time. In the following years, a number of obscure but congenial communist fragments were either integrated into or associated with the Party. These included the Polish-orientated 'CP of Upper Silesia'; the *Kombund,* an offshoot of the Warsaw *Bund;* the 'CP of Western Ukraine', a pro-Soviet reincarnation of the 'CP of Eastern Galicia'; and the 'CP of Western Byelorussia'.[7]

The Party's history in the inter-war period makes sorry reading. A series of catastrophic, strategic blunders paved the road to annihilation. The Polish communists were as unsuccessful in attracting the support of the Polish people as they were in winning the confidence of their Soviet patrons.

The years 1918–21 were filled with bitter disillusionment. From their refuge in Minsk, the Party leaders had daily awaited news of the Revolution in Warsaw. Six regiments of Polish Riflemen were formed in the Red Army's 'Western Division'. Yet the spontaneous revolution, and the Red Army's victory, both failed to materialize. Lenin spurned the KPRP's advice in matters of diplomacy and of social policy alike. In the summer of 1920, in the brief months of the Red Army's advance into Poland, he entrusted his political plans to Dzierżyński's *Cheka* (Political Police), and kept control of the Provisional Revolutionary Committee at Białystok in the hands of his own Bolshevik Poles.[8] His desperate instructions to Dzierżyński to shoot one hundred Poles for every communist executed by the Polish Army, and 'to destroy the landowners and kulaks ruthlessly and a bit more quickly and energetically', and to turn the land over to the poor peasants, were as offensive to the KPRP, which at that juncture was demanding instant collectivization, as they were to the population at large.[9] The Treaty of Riga, whereby the Bolshevik government formally recognized the Polish Republic, overturned the declared policy not only of the KPRP but also of the Comintern. Shock after shock eventually convinced the

Party's Second Congress (1923) that their original analysis of the internal and external situation had been woefully mistaken. In recognition of this fact, they had agreed to participate in parliamentary elections in 1922, and in 1925 changed their title to that of 'The Communist Party of Poland' (KPP).

In May 1926, the KPP gave open support to Piłsudski's *coup d'état.* In so far as the Coup was intended to forestall a right-wing Coalition, the decision was entirely logical. Yet in Warsaw it was rewarded by the prompt action of Piłsudski's gendarmes, who brutally dispersed the communist demonstrations of support. In Moscow, it was savagely denounced as an act of betrayal of the socialist camp. This 'May Error' remains an embarrassment to communist historians to this day.[10]

In the 1930s, the predicament of the KPP rapidly grew critical. In Poland, its members were popularly regarded as traitors to the national cause. Their two parliamentary deputies elected in 1922 had long since lost their seats. The intransigent hostility of the PPS effectively excluded them from practical working-class politics, and they failed to make any real progress towards a united Popular Front against the *Sanacja* regime. In the USSR, where many of the leaders resided, their failures were greeted with derision. Although the specifically Trotskyite line, together with the unrepentantly schismatic Isaac Deutscher (1907–67), was purged at the final Sixth Congress in 1932, the Party's Luxemburgist past, its largely Jewish leadership, and its strong advocacy of Comintern, as opposed to Soviet, interests, inevitably aroused Stalin's suspicions. Ignoring the simple fact that Soviet-style communism was repugnant to the vast mass of the Polish people, Stalin chose to explain the KPP's distress by its supposed infiltration by Polish counter-intelligence agents. In the middle of the Soviet Union's own Great Purge, a series of political trials of alleged 'Polish spies, provocateurs, and diversionists' led inexorably to the official liquidation in 1938 of the Party as a whole. At the XVIII Congress of the CPSU in 1939 a Soviet spokesman made a rare and oblique reference to the fateful decision which was already being put into effect:

In order to split the Communist movement, the Fascist and Trotskyite spies attempted to form artificial 'factions' and 'groups' in some of the Communist parties and stir up a factional struggle . . . The party that was most contaminated by hostile elements was the Communist Party of Poland, where agents of Polish fascism managed to gain positions of leadership. These scoundrels tried to get the Party to support Piłsudski's Fascist Coup in May 1926. When this failed, they feigned repentance for their 'May Error', made a show of self-criticism, and deceived the Comintern just as Lovestone and the police 'factionalists' of the Hungarian and Yugoslav parties had once done. It was the fault of the Comintern workers that they allowed themselves to be deceived by the class enemy, and failed to detect these maneuvers in time . . . The Communist Parties have investigated their leading workers, and have removed those whose honesty was questionable. They have dissolved illegal organisations which were particularly contaminated, and have begun to form new ones in their place . . .[11]

The KPP disappeared from the list of Comintern's affiliated parties. First the leaders, then the rank and file, were summoned by the Soviet GPU. They too disappeared. Adolf Warszawski (pseudonym, Warski), Józef Unszlicht, Maria Koszutska (pseudonym, Kostrzewa), Maksymilian Horwitz (pseudonym, Walecki), Juliusz Leszczyński (pseudonym, Leński), Stanisław Bobiński, Jerzy Heryng (pseudonym, 'Ryng'), Władysław Krajewski-Stein, all of them veterans of the SDKPiL or the PPS (*Lewica*) and lifelong devotees of communism, were shot out of hand or otherwise done to death in the Gulags. In all, some five thousand Polish communists, practically the entire active membership of the Party, were killed. The only ones to survive were those fortunate enough to find themselves in Polish gaols, or those who had been recruited into the Soviet security service. This Soviet game-bag must be compared to the two or three dozen communist victims of the *Sanacja* regime, and to the hundreds of Polish communists who died during the War at the hands of the Nazis. Trotsky, from his Mexican exile, saw the tragic episode, like the Nazi—Soviet Pact which it preceded, as a death-blow to internationalist communism. 'Poland will resurrect', he wrote, 'but Comintern never'. On this point, he was exactly right.[12]

The trauma of the Polish communists between 1938 and 1942 must surely arouse the compassion of their bitterest enemies. Their fate has been likened to that of some imaginary Jewish Nazi Party, which, having failed to recruit a significant number of Jews to the *Hitlerjugend*, was then condemned to the ovens of Auschwitz. Rejected from the start by their Polish homeland, the surviving members of the KPP had to come to terms with the fact that they were equally unwelcome in the great Soviet Homeland of Socialism. The agonizing paradox was nicely recorded by the communist poet, Władysław Broniewski (1897–1962), from his Soviet cell in the Zamarstynów Prison in Lwów:

'A Word with History' (1940)

Old Mother History, Queen of Them All,
how you do love raising a stink!
Orion peeps through the bars in the wall,
as we crouch on the bucket, in clink.

You sing me the same old patter-song
with the same half-derisive leer.
So, side by side, we go clanking along –
you since Time was, I since last year.

Immortal madam, why and whence
This passion for paradox that you display?
Do you really think that it makes good sense
to poison the world's bloodstream in this way?

For in the whole wide world I see
nothing but conflict, crisis and war.
It's hardly the moment, would you agree,
for us both to be doing 'stir'?

Why should a revolutionary poet
rot to death in this Soviet hole?
Dear History, it strikes a jarring note.
Surely, one of us is playing the fool.

Shame on you, madam, Queen of Them All!
Let me out of Zamarstynov! (Then,
on the other side of the wall,
we can both be arrested again).[13]

For the time being there was no possibility of relief. So long as the Nazi–Soviet Pact was in operation, Stalin had no care for Polish prisoners or for Polish organizations of any kind. Only at the very end of 1941, after Hitler's attack on Russia, and Stalin's subsequent change of heart towards Poland, could there be any question of restoring the Polish communist movement to a place in the over-all scheme of world communism.

The task of reconstructing the shattered remains of the movement fell to a courageous band of Poles in Moscow — the so-called Initiative Group headed by Marceli Nowotko (1893–1942), Pawel Finder (1904–44), and Bolesław Molojec. In view of the terrors of the recent past, and the horrors of the present, it was no mean feat of nerves and dedication to persuade the Soviet comrades that an independent Polish party should be reformed, and then to organize it under the noses of the Gestapo in Nazi-occupied Warsaw. Yet the feat was performed. On 5 January 1942, the central core of the new Party was conspiratorially assembled for the first time. The name of 'Polish Workers' Party' (PPR) was adopted. By the end of 1943, after Nowotko's mysterious assassination and Finder's arrest by the Gestapo, Władysław Gomułka (born 1905) emerged as First Secretary. The 'People's Guard' took the field alongside the Home Army in the battle against the Nazi occupation.[14]

The personality of Władysław Gomułka, or 'Comrade Wiesław' as he was known, reflected many of the fundamental characteristics of resurrected Polish communism. His official biography omits to mention the most formative events in his career; but reliable unofficial sources have revealed that an unwavering commitment to communist ideals and a lifelong revulsion to Soviet practices have provided the mainsprings of his political action. As a young man in the 1930s, sent for training at a Party School in the USSR, he saw the collectivization campaign in the Ukraine at first hand, and decided at an early stage that the same inhuman methods were never to be applied in Poland. In 1938–9, as an official of the Union of Chemical Workers, he had the good fortune to be arrested by the Polish police for illegal political activity, and thereby survived the Soviet purge of the KPP which carried off most of his comrades. At the outbreak of war, when the prisons were opened, he found himself in the Soviet zone of occupation, in Lwów, but characteristically declined the chance of an interview with the GPU, and fled to his own home town of

Krosno in the Nazi-controlled *General-gouvernement*. From there, in complete isolation from the Soviet authorities, he renewed his conspiratorial life. Moving to Warsaw at the height of the German Terror, he was at hand to step into the vacant post of General-Secretary of the PPR in November 1943. His appointment coincided with the publication of the full text of the Party's Manifesto *O co walczymy?* (What are we fighting for?), which gave equal prominence to the twin goals of national independence and social revolution. Despite its Marxist—Leninist language, this shift of emphasis brought the broad strategy of the communist movement closer to the old PPS than to the KPP, and promised to give the Party a reasonable chance of popular recruitment. In most other matters, Gomułka remained an orthodox, disciplined, and philistine communist. He had little time for intellectual theorists, or for artistic pursuits, and no interest whatsoever in liberal ideas. The stubbornness of his nature, forged in prison and in the underground, was to prove a stumbling-block not only to Soviet designs for manipulating Poland to their own uses but also at a later date to misguided hopes for 'liberalization'. Gomułka headed a group of men who believed that hard-line Polish communism offered the one sure guarantee for Poland against Soviet imperialism. For the next twenty-seven years, his outlook stamped itself on the basic aspirations of a movement which did not gain control of its own destiny until 1956.[15]

The rise of PPR from its obscure wartime origins to a dominant position in Polish politics by the end of 1948 was fraught with anxiety and alarms. No less than the KPP before it, the Party had to steer a perilous course between the hostility of the popular opinion in Poland and the suspicions of its Soviet patrons. A negligible membership, which by the time of Liberation had barely reached four figures, ruled out any possibility of free competition with the established democratic parties. Dependence on the USSR was unavoidable. At the same time, the leadership had to contend with the fact that Stalin simply did not trust foreign communists, and that the Soviet agencies preferred to work through people and organizations more directly under their control. For most of 1943—4, there was no effective communication between

Warsaw and Moscow. Political control of the Polish army in Russia was exercised through Wanda Wasilewska's Union of Polish Patriots (ZPP). The purging of local government in Poland during the liberation was conducted under the direct supervision of the NKVD. Most of the key positions in the Lublin Committee, and its successors, fell to non-Party Soviet employees, such as Edward Osóbka-Morawski and Michał Rola-Żymierski. At its first Congress in December 1945, the Party itself had to bear the influx of numerous appointees of the NKVD, who proceeded to arrogate the key ministries of state for themselves. Gomułka was surrounded by comrades fresh from Russia — Berman, Bierut, Minc, Radkiewicz, Zambrowski, Zawadzki — whose function was no less to keep him in line, than to follow his lead. Under these conditions, the Party's progress was remarkable. Whilst the elimination of the democratic Opposition was lamely left to the Soviet-run security organs, the organizations of all potential rivals and allies were effectively destroyed by the Leninist tactic of 'splitting from above and below' (see p. 569). In the process, the PRR's own membership rose dramatically to over one million in 1948. The moment was ripe for cementing the victory. On 15 December 1948, the PPR signed an agreement with the rump PPS whereby both parties would merge their separate identities in a new 'Polish United Workers' Party' (PZPR); the communists' other allies in the Government Bloc, the SL and the SD, were permitted to survive on strictly limited conditions. On paper, the process of manufacturing a dominant communist party could boast almost complete success. In theory, the internationalist tradition of the communists had been married to the national tradition of the socialists, with a view to procreating a synthetic 'People's Democracy'. In reality, the PZPR had a long way to go before it might be regarded as truly Polish or truly united. Its position in Poland was unchallengeable; but its formal unity was quite artificial. The formal victory had been achieved in a year when the Soviet stooges had forcibly suppressed the native communists and had prized the General-Secretary, Władysław Gomułka, out of office. The PZPR began its career in circumstances of agonizing humiliation.[16]

The structure of the party system as formed by 1948 is

officially described as a 'hegemony' (*partia hegemoniczna*). This term correctly describes the party's position in the politics of the so-called 'National Front', where several separate parties and allied formations have been allowed to exist so long as they admit to the leading role of the communists. It also hints at the persistence within the PZPR of several informal but well-defined factions. In the first decade after the war, observers were often content to distinguish between those comrades who were thought to answer directly to Soviet commands, the so-called 'POPy' (Acting Poles), and those who were not. But this distinction, though important, soon proved inadequate. The 'old communists', survivors of the KPP, provided a tiny band of idealist elders, a living reminder of the Party's sad history. The 'Warsaw Core', centred on Gomułka, was drawn from people who had re-created the PPR in Poland during the Nazi Occupation. The 'Partisans' headed by Mieczysław Moczar, veterans of the Party's wartime military organizations, were noted for their intolerant and philistine attitudes. The 'Patriots', veterans of the ZPP, were led in the post-war era by General Alexander Zawadzki (1899–1964). The 'People of the Oka', who came together in the Political Department of Berling's army, had the reputation for a revolutionary Bonapartist temper. On the ideological front, the Party could be divided between the 'Stalinists' and their opponents who favoured more brands of flexible 'national Communism'. The 'Stalinists' were themselves divided between those who sought to turn Poland into a pale, Russified, imitation of the USSR and those who wished to use Stalinist methods to create a fiercely independent, but uncompromisingly dictatorial, Polish regime. Each of these factions and opinion-groups were to reappear in the crises of the next thirty years.

To the impartial observer, many of the characteristic features of the communist regime can be seen to have some precedents in earlier stages of Polish history. The leftist dictatorship of a narrow political élite, which manipulates pseudo-democratic institutions in its own interest, is vaguely reminiscent of the pre-war *Sanacja*. So, too, are the Party's token gestures to social radicalism, and to anticlericalism. The authoritarian stance of the Party, no less than its sanctimonious rhetoric, resembles attitudes traditionally adopted by the Church hierarchy. In a deeply Catholic country, the similarity between the conduct of the Party, and that of the militant Catholic Orders, such as the Jesuits, cannot be overlooked. In historical terms, the 'dictatorship of the proletariat' can be seen as the latest in a long series of dictatorships, which through all the insurrections of the nineteenth century pursued avowedly democratic goals by manifestly undemocratic means. The exclusive, intolerant approach to the problem of national identity, which among other things had distinguished the PPR and the PZPR from the pre-war KPP, marks the ultimate victory of the basic ideas of Dmowski's National Democracy. The penchant for constructing institutions of national unity, irrespective of whether such unity really exists or not, is shared by the communist authors of the 'National Front' and its successor, the 'Front of National Unity' (FJN) with the designers of the pre-war BBWR and OZoN. The Party's fundamental strategy of linking a defensive alliance with one of Poland's stronger neighbours to economic and cultural autonomy at home conforms exactly to the long 'conciliatory' or 'realist' trend in Polish politics since the early eighteenth century. On all these points, the new comrade is but the old patriot writ large. The one thing that is new is the Party's Marxist—Leninist ideology, a vulgarized Russian version of nineteenth-century scientific philosophy, imported direct from Moscow.

* * * * *

By the time of its adoption in 1948 as the official state ideology, Marxism—Leninism had attracted very few native exponents. Indeed, Polish Marxism as a whole could only look back to one recognized pioneer, Stanisław Brzozowski (1872–1911), and in thirty years of post-war development has only produced two thinkers of stature. One of these, Adam Schaff (born 1913), was a member of the pre-war KPP and, after postgraduate training in Moscow, obtained the first Chair of Marxism—Leninism at Warsaw University in 1946. His works are perhaps less noted for their depth of penetration than for the wide variety of subjects, such as Semantics and Existentialism, to which their author's Marxist methods have been directed.[17] Schaff's

junior colleague, Leszek Kołakowski (b. 1927), has passed
through the successive stages of Marxist recruit, revisionist,
and rebel. Significantly, both Schaff and Kołakowski have
been purged from the Party whose ideology they had so
fervently proselytized in their early careers.

Kołakowski is the only philospher who has ever made a
serious attempt to marry Marxism to the established traditions
of the Polish intellectual heritage. In this, he was strongly
influenced both by the rigorous academic environment of the
Warsaw Philosophical Faculty, where he rose from student to
professor, and also by traditional Catholicism. Exceptionally
amongst post-war ideologists, he was prepared to respect the
principles of his opponents, to rely on rational argument
rather than on bluster and vilification, and to interest himself
in fundamental issues of ethics and religion. Before long,
he found himself at the head of a lone crusade to give Polish
Marxism a human face. Kołakowski's exposition of 'Non-
religious Christianity' promised to build the much-needed
bridge between official ideology and the religious beliefs of
the masses,[18] whilst his celebrated essay on 'The Priest and
the Jester' struck a doughty blow against the rhetorical
bombast and authoritarian dogma of Party propaganda. 'The
priest is the watchdog of the Absolute,' he wrote, 'the guardian of the cult of recognised and obvious truths. The
jester may circulate in good society, but he doesn't belong to
it and is impertinent to it, and throws doubt on everything
that is obvious.'[19] The overt comparison between communist
and Catholic dogmatism caused immense delight in intellectual
circles; and the role of court jester fitted Kołakowski's temper
exactly. But his triumph was short-lived. In 1966 he was
expelled from the Party, and in 1968 from the country.
Oxford's gain is Warsaw's loss.

The rise and fall of Kołakowski over the two decades after
1948 mark the brief period when Polish Marxism showed
signs of life. At first, during the infancy of the communist
regime, a measure of confrontation was only to be expected.
It says much for the maturity of Polish philosophy that the
debate was conducted in a much more civilized fashion than
elsewhere in Eastern Europe. Although political conditions
clearly favoured the outbursts of ambitious Marxist fire-

brands like Schaff, non-Marxists were allowed to express their opinions, and to voice their protests, in public. Established figures such as Tadeusz Kotarbiński, Kazimierz Ajdukiewicz, and Stanisław Ossowski published withering attacks on the cruder forms of official ideology.[20] Later on, indeed, there was reason to suppose that the combination of a relatively stable communist regime and of a staunchly Catholic population would have provided ideal conditions for a Marxist—Christian dialogue. In effect, attempts to establish this dialogue in Poland have proved peculiarly unfruitful. Recent experience would suggest that 'Polish Marxism' is a circle that cannot be squared. The guardians of Party truth have never felt sufficiently certain about their principles, or about the reactions of their Soviet masters, for a sustained debate to take place. Increasingly, they place their trust in policemen rather than in philosophers.[21]

* * * * *

In the context of the communist world as a whole, it is a sad irony that a Party which sees itself as the culmination of Poland's anti-authoritarian, anti-conformist, and therefore anti-Russian revolutionary traditions, should find itself obliged to advocate the Soviet brand of communism. Inevitably, there is a wide discrepancy between the Polish Party's theoretical pronouncements, which have to pay lip-service to the Leninist and Stalinist phraseology of the Soviet model, and its practical policies. As Gomułka and other determined spirits knew from the start, the Polish Road to Socialism could not possibly follow the Russian signposts. They would have concurred wholeheartedly with Stalin's dictum that communism in Poland resembled 'a saddle on a cow'. Unlike Stalin, however, they would have preferred to trim the saddle to fit the cow, instead of hacking the cow to fit the saddle. Unfortunately for them, their subordinate position within the Soviet alliance has always inhibited them from any active expression of their ideological preferences. Left to itself, the Polish Party would probably have adopted a position closer to that of the communist parties of Western Europe than to that of the CPSU. Such a course would be guided by a number of objective circumstances. The transformation of an industrializing society dominated by traditional Catholic values would seem to demand priorities more akin to those developed beyond the Soviet pale by communists in Italy or Spain than to those dictated by Lenin's Revolution in pre-industrial, autocratic Russia. The instinctive hostility of Polish society to the organs of state power, irrespective of the regime of the day, would seem to indicate that the prime Leninist concepts of Democratic Centralism (i.e. centralized Party Autocracy) or of the Dictatorship of the Proletariat (i.e. the Dictatorship of the Party over the People) are not well suited to Polish conditions. In foreign affairs, the Poles' extended experience of Partition, and their inside knowledge of the mechanisms of imperialist *realpolitik,* must necessarily arouse their suspicions about an international system where the world is increasingly divided into the rival, but interdependent spheres of the superpowers. The Poles have seen it all before, from the receiving end, and no amount of Soviet pressure can persuade a thinking Polish communist to admire what he sees. For all these reasons, a sovereign Polish Communist Party, freed from its Soviet chains, would be the first of the parties of the Soviet Bloc to give serious examination to the views of Tito, Togliatti, Dubček, Berlinguer, Carillo, and Mao. It would probably favour some limited concessions to parliamentary democracy. It would probably favour some form of European integration, and of European disarmament, as a means of ending the present partition of Europe. It would cultivate its contacts with China and the Third World, as its contribution to the struggle against the eventual partition of the world. Undoubtedly, ideas of this sort have always been discussed in private, in the innermost recesses of the Party's sancta; but they can never be publicly aired. The Polish comrades can still draw on their recollections of the anti-Tsarist, revolutionary underground; of Róża Luksemburg; of the international brigades in the Spanish Civil War; and of their brief experience of Popular Front tactics in the wartime Resistance. But ever since August 1944, when they joined the Lublin Committee, they have been firmly hung on the Soviet hook. They have always sensed that any open debate of divergent Marxist opinions would be regarded in Moscow as treasonable heresy, and would provoke the brutal retribution of the superpower on whom, in the last analysis, they ultimately depend. They have to choose between holding their tongues, or being silenced by force. The dictates of ideological honesty must take second place to the instinct of political survival. Theoretical argument must yield to practical requirements. Polish communism has always differed in important ways from the Russian variety. But so long as it cannot express its own words, it is bound to be viewed by the average Polish citizen, and by the world at large, as the creature of foreign masters and bureaucratic opportunists. The PZPR may well contain its share of patriots and of idealists. But their face is not seen, and their voice is not heard. In this way, the ruling Party of post-war Poland has relived the pains and the humiliations of every Polish regime except one in more than two and a half centuries.

As always, it remains an open question whether the younger generation of Polish leaders will respect the circumspection of their fathers. The Polish communist movement has more reason than most elements in modern Polish society to hate its past, and to resent the continuing Soviet oppressions of the present. When the latest generation of communists in Western Europe begin to denounce their predecessors as 'ideological corpses preserved in the Soviet freezer', there must be an overpowering urge among their counterparts in Poland to cast caution to the winds and to follow suit. Contrary to prevailing views, the PZPR is one of the few possible sources of effective political dissent, or even in suitable circumstances, of a future insurrection. Only then, when its leaders are seen to assert Poland's separate interest against that of the USSR, will the Polish communist movement be judged to have taken proper root.

CHAPTER TWENTY-THREE
POLSKA LUDOWA:
The People's Republic (since 1944)

In its essentials, the political history of post-war Poland is extremely simple. It tells how the USSR handed power to its chosen protégés, and how it has kept them in place ever since. In detail, however, it is extremely complicated, and largely hidden from public view. The relationship between Moscow and Moscow's men in Warsaw, both communist and non-communist, has seen several abrupt changes of fortune. What is more, the degree of leeway of the Polish regime, though always subject to ultimate Soviet sanctions, has usually been underrated by outside observers. There are three distinct phases. The first, from 1944 to 1948, witnessed the gradual construction of the communist People's Democracy; the second, from 1948 to 1956, saw the imposition of Stalinism; the third, since 1956, has seen Poland ruled by a native, 'national Communist' regime.

Yet politics are not the whole story. Any sympathetic description must surely match Poland's atrophied political development against the advances in social and cultural life and the real achievements of reconstruction from the ruins of the War.[1]

* * * * *

The origins of the present political order in Poland can be traced to 22 July 1944. On that day — whose anniversary has since replaced 3 May as Poland's official National Day — the first post-war government, the Polish Committee of National Liberation (PKWN) was formed under Soviet auspices in Lublin. Known in the West as the 'Lublin Committee', it assisted its Soviet masters in administering the lands liberated from German Occupation, and in due course formed the core both of the Provisional Government of the Polish Republic (RTRP) from January to June 1945, and of the Provisional Government of National Unity (TRJN) from June 1945 onwards. In this way, its activities spanned the transitional period which separated the collapse of the German Occupation from the full emergence of the communist-led regime in 1947.

The formation of the PKWN reflected at the central level what was happening on the local level throughout the length and breadth of Poland. Despite later legends, the Lublin Committee was created in Moscow and was imposed by the Soviet authorities. In the politics of the communist camp, it was the Kremlin's 'tit' for Gomułka's 'tat' when in January 1944 he had formed the National Homeland Council (KRN) without Moscow's prior approval. It contained a mixture of communist and non-communist members, the former drawn from both the Moscow-based Union of Polish Patriots (ZPP) and Central Bureau of Polish Communists (CBKP), and from the Warsaw-based Polish Workers Party (PPR). The Warsaw group, which included Gomułka and Bierut, did not arrive in Lublin until 31 July, that is, not until nine days after their signatures were supposedly placed on the Committee's Manifesto. They had been reluctant to leave the capital, where the outbreak of the Rising was daily expected, and then had to follow a tortuous route across the Front and into the Soviet lines. They did not reach full agreement with their colleagues from Moscow until 15 August. This means that all the documents relating to their agreement, though drawn up in August, had to be carefully antedated to 21 July to create an appropriate appearance of spontaneous unanimity.[2] Here was modern Poland's Targowica.

The Manifesto of the Committee, distributed in Chełm and Lublin and described in advance by Moscow Radio, cannot possibly have been properly endorsed by the leadership of the PPR in Warsaw. It must have been prepared and printed in Moscow, and as such reflected Soviet rather than Polish communist wishes.[3] The key appointments to the Committee were made with Stalin's express approval. They included Edward Osóbka-Morawski (Chairman), Stanisław Radkiewicz (Security), and Michał Rola-Żymierski (Defence). These men, whose adherence to Soviet policy was a prior condition of their nomination, were essentially Soviet employees. They were destined to keep their jobs throughout the governmental changes of the next three years. At this stage, they were completely dependent on Moscow's support. As Stalin himself told Rola-Żymierski, 'When the Soviet Army has gone, they will shoot you like partridges.'[4]

The doubtful legality of the PKWN was of less significance than its practical subordination to the Soviet authorities. On 31 December 1944, it claimed the status of a provisional government (RTRP), and on the next morning adjusted its name accordingly. This step, which was formally recognized only by the USSR, marks the moment when Stalin finally cast the prevailing ambiguities in Soviet policy aside. Preparing to meet with Churchill and Roosevelt at Yalta, he made it abundantly clear for the first time, that the future regime in Poland would principally lie in the hands of his own appointees. Henceforth, the chances that the Polish Government-in-Exile in London might play an equal role in post-war Warsaw were very slim indeed. Yet the blessings of unqualified Soviet support were not unmixed. Unqualified Soviet support implied unqualified Soviet control. The PPR, in particular, keenly resented its lot. At a meeting of the Plenum of the Central Committee on 21–2 May 1945, First-Secretary Gomułka complained that 'the masses do not regard us as Polish communists at all, but just as the most despicable agents of the NKVD' (*enkawudowska najgorsza agentura*). Zawadzki feared that the raping and looting of the Soviet Army would provoke a civil war. Ochab declared that the main problems facing the Party were those of the withdrawal of the Soviet Army and of 'Polish sovereignty'.[5]

The position of the RTRP was greatly strengthened on 21 April 1945 by the signing of a Polish–Soviet Treaty of Friendship, Mutual Aid, and Co-operation. This Treaty, which confirmed the Soviet view of Poland's frontiers and the Soviet hold over political security in Poland, was drawn up in Moscow without any reference either to the Western Powers or to the Government-in-Exile, or indeed to any democratically elected body. Yet it committed Poland to the Soviet camp for no less than twenty years ahead. It was prompted by the impending deliberations of the first Conference of the United Nations at San Francisco, whose prospective decisions regarding Poland it effectively pre-empted. It was, in fact, a very timely *fait accompli*, whose one-sided terms, renewed for a further twenty years in 1965, have determined Poland's domination by the USSR ever since. Once it was signed and sealed, the leaders of the RTRP could look forward with equanimity to their intended merger with more representative Polish politicians from London.

The Provisional Government of National Unity (TRJN) resulted from the declaration of the Yalta Conference for the union in Poland of 'all democratic and anti-Nazi elements'. Its details were decided during negotiations held in Moscow between on the one side Stanisław Mikołajczyk, the leader of the Peasant Party and the only former member of the Government-in-Exile in London willing to participate, and on the other Bolesław Bierut, as the spokesman of the RTRP, the KRN, and the PPR. They decided that Osóbka-Morawski should continue as Premier, with Mikołajczyk as First Deputy Premier and Minister of Agriculture, and with Gomułka as Second Deputy Premier and Minister for the Recovered Territories. Of twenty-four Ministries, only seven were directly in the hands of the PPR. The task of the new government, approved by the Potsdam Conference, was to govern the country until free elections could be held and a permanent constitutional system established. It took office on 28 June 1945, and lasted until February 1947. During these two years, its activities attracted little attention in the West. In Britain and America, wartime sentiments of gratitude and admiration for the Soviet Union were still strong. Only at the very end of the period, in 1947, when the TJRN had already fallen, did Western observers take stock of what had actually happened in Poland; and then they reacted in a fit of fierce, but impotent frustration.[6]

Economic and social policy in the immediate wake of Liberation was necessarily limited. The communists were concerned firstly that the vast amount of property accumulated by the German Occupation regime should be retained as a base for future nationalization, and secondly, that the larger landed estates should be parcelled out among the poor peasants. A decree to this effect was registered by the PKWN on 6 September 1944. In many cases, the peasants were taking the land without being invited to do so. Forced requisitioning was less welcome. In the summer of 1944, and again in 1945, the Soviet Army organized squads of workers from the towns to collect food in the countryside at the point of the bayonet. The peasants objected strongly. The PKWN decree tied their land grants to annual deliveries to the state at the rate of 15 quintals of wheat per hectare. These coercive methods were hardly conducive to increased production, and were abandoned in 1946.[7]

Meanwhile, elementary reconstruction was the order of the day. In Warsaw, lines of men, women, and children attacked the ocean of rubble with their bare hands; gangs of volunteers buried the thousands of corpses, and somehow public services were restored. The arrival of the capital's first post-war electric tramcar provoked scenes of wild rejoicing.

Yet the vast tides of human movement, both military and civilian, which had washed over Poland during the War, the Occupation, and the Liberation, continued to flow for at least two more years. In the era of the TJRN, they were swelled by the outbreak of civil war, by colossal programmes of Resettlement, and by agrarian reform.

The civil war had been provoked by the activities of the Soviet security forces during the Liberation. By demanding total submission, they provoked armed resistance from thousands of Poles who might otherwise have contemplated some form of practical co-operation. By branding their opponents indiscriminately as 'terrorists', 'bandits', or 'fascists', they gave rise to the impossible situation in which communist leaders were calling for a consolidated 'democratic front', whilst the security forces were killing, arresting, and deporting the very people who were supposed to co-operate. As always, violence bred violence. The Terror launched by the Soviets was answered in kind. Village mayors, local electoral officers, and police agents installed by the NKGB were murdered, or harassed and subjected to reprisals. Entire districts, especially in the Carpathians, fell into the hands of bandit kings, like the terrible 'Kapitan Ogień' (Captain Fire) of Zakopane. From the Soviet point of view, these developments proved most convenient, providing the best possible excuse for perpetuating their hold on the security services. A special Security Corps (*Korpus Bezpieczeństwa*) was raised for military operations in the field. The Ministry of Security in Warsaw continued to be run almost entirely by Russian, or by Soviet-trained, personnel.

Armed resistance centred on three distinct, and uncoordinated groupings. The first, the National Armed Forces (NSZ), had started life during the War as a brotherhood of right-wing, anti-communist partisans most active in the Holy Cross Mountains. They actively feared the advance of the Soviet Army, but had ceased to offer serious resistance by the end of 1945.[8] The second, the Association of Freedom and Independence (WiN), was founded in September 1945 from the ranks of the disbanded Home Army. As shown by the title of its political predecessor, the NIE (No) Organization, its simple aim was to prevent a communist takeover. It continued to operate throughout 1946, especially in the Lublin and Białystok regions. Its end came in February 1947, when 40,000 men took advantage of the proffered Amnesty, and laid down their arms in public.[9] The third, the Ukrainian Insurrectionary Army (UPA), was forced to fight on. Formed in 1943 with the aim of founding an independent Ukrainian state, free from all forms of oppression and patronage, it had fought with equal ferocity against Hitler and Stalin. In Volhynia, where it had commanded wide stretches of countryside, it came into conflict with both Polish and Soviet partisans. Its vicious reprisals against uncooperative Polish villagers at this time were subsequently to deprive it of sympathy in Poland. By 1945, the remnants of the UPA were politically isolated, and physically surrounded. Hemmed in on three sides by the armies of the USSR, Poland, and Czechoslovakia, they took refuge in the remote fastnesses of the Bieszczady Mountains. After numerous inconclusive encounters with the Polish forces, they scored a sensational success on 4 April 1947 by ambushing and killing the Vice-Minister of Defence, General Karol Świerczewski (1897–1947). Thereafter, their days were numbered. Świerczewski, a veteran communist and former commander of the 14th International Brigade of the Spanish Republican Army, was one of the few experienced soldiers which the Polish communist movement possessed; and his death spurred the Party to a final reckoning. In the summer of 1947, the Ukrainian villages of the Bieszczady region were systematically razed to the ground.

The entire population of the highland Lemko and Bojko clans was dispersed. Those who possessed Polish relatives were scattered through the 'Recovered Territories'; the rest were deported to the USSR. Deprived of all support, the remaining fighters were starved and strafed into submission. Their bunkers were bombed; their shelters and stores dynamited. A solitary band of survivors fought their way over the Carpathian ridge into Czechoslovakia, and thence, across five hundred miles of hostile territory to refuge in West Germany. Thus ended what official sources are pleased to call 'the struggle with the reactionary underground'.[10]

Post-war Resettlement programmes affected millions of people. For three years, Polish roads and railways were crammed with endless processions of refugees, deportees, repatriates, transients, expellees, and internal migrants. The refugees consisted of numberless families who had left their homes in Poland during the war, and who now took to the road to regain them of their own accord. The deportees were made up of people forcibly removed from Poland by the occupying powers, and now permitted to return. They included over 520,000 returning from forced labour in Germany, and a smaller number returning from the Soviet Union. (The Soviet Union held the greater part of its Polish deportees until 1956.) The repatriates consisted largely of Poles from the Eastern territories of the former Second Republic who were given the option of moving westwards within the new frontiers, and of those who voluntarily returned from Western Europe. The transients consisted largely of displaced persons, passing through Poland in transit, either from west to east, or from east to west. They included, in the one direction, the pathetic columns of Soviet deserters and prisoners-of-war on their way towards Soviet justice, and in the other, some tens of thousands of Polish Jews, who, having survived the War in Russia, were now making for the West and for Israel. The expellees (who in official Polish jargon were referred to as 'transferees') were made up of members of national minorities, mainly German and Ukrainian, who were removed from Poland in accordance with the Potsdam agreements. The internal migrants consisted of Poles redirected by the authorities from their former homes to new destinations in the

Recovered Territories of the north and west. Statistics vary sharply, but there can be little doubt that the customers of the resettlement programmes took part in one of the greatest demographic upheavals in European History. They were marshalled by the State Repatriation Bureau (PUR), which functioned from its creation by the PKWN in October 1944 until its abolition in 1950.[11] (See Diagram F.)

The largest single operation involved the expulsion of Poland's German population. Clause XIII of the Report of the Potsdam Conference had stated that 'the transfer to Germany of German populations or elements thereof remaining in Poland, Czechoslovakia and Hungary will have to be undertaken . . . in an orderly and humane manner.' These transfers, which were in no sense voluntary except for families with dual nationality, involved a total of some 16.5 million people. The Polish part of the operation, affecting 5,057,000 Germans from the former provinces of East Pomerania, East Brandenburg, Silesia, Danzig, and East Prussia, and from Central Poland was mounted in accordance with an agreement reached at Berlin between Polish and British representatives of the Combined Repatriation Executive of 14 February 1946:

1. *General Conditions* It is agreed by both sides that the transfer and movement of Germans from their homes in Poland and their resettlement in the British Zone will be carried out in a humane and orderly manner.

2. *TRANSPORTATION*
   Means of transport will be by rail using Polish and/or Soviet rolling stock, and by sea. The routes in the North will be:—
   Route A — From STETTIN to LUBECK by sea at rate of approximately 1,000 per day . . .
   Route B — From STETTIN to BAD SEGEBERG, via Lubeck, by rail at rate of 1,500 per day.
   The routes in the South will be:
   Route C — From KALAWSK (Kohlfurt) to MARIENTAL and ALVERSDORF via HELMSTEDT, by rail at rate of 3,000 per day (2 trains).
   Route D — It is later hoped to route a further 2,500 per day from KALAWSK (Kohlfurt) to FRIEDLAND . . .
   Soviet and Polish rolling stock and locomotives will run through to the above points.

3. *DATES OF COMMENCEMENT*

Route A —	Stettin—Lubeck	Date to be decided
Route B —	Stettin—Bad Segeberg	20 February 1946
Route C —	Kalawsk—Mariental/Alversdorf	20 February 1946
Route D —	Kalawsk—Friedland	Date to be decided

4. *ACCEPTANCE ARRANGEMENTS*
Expellees will be accepted by the British authorities on the border of Poland and the Soviet Zone, and for this purpose British Repatriation teams will be stationed at Stettin and at Kalawsk . . . to ensure that trainloads will not be turned back into the Soviet Zone . . .

5. *DISINFESTATION:* All expellees will be dusted with DDT Powder . . . British Authorities will immediately make available to Polish authorities at Berlin 3 tons of DDT . . .

6. *TRAIN GUARDS:* Polish authorities will supply guards, approximately 10 per train.

7. *SCHEDULES:* It would greatly facilitate dispersal arrangements . . . if all trains could arrive at reception points in the British Zone before noon daily . . .

8. *BAGGAGE:* Expellees will be permitted to take as much as they can carry . . .

9. *CURRENCY:* Expellees will be permitted to take a maximum of 500 RM per head . . .

10. *RATIONS:* Polish authorities will supply two days' rations, plus one day's reserve . . . on the rail route from KALAWSK, each train will leave with 3 days' rations, plus one day's reserve . . .

11. *MEDICAL*
    (a) The first shipments will be confined to expellees in good health . . .
    (b) Pregnant women will not be shipped 6 weeks before and after confinement.
    (c) . . . In the event of sickness, families will not be moved until all members are fit to travel.

12. *DOCUMENTATION:* Expellees will be in possession of individual papers. A nominal roll will accompany each train, together with a Movement Order suitably endorsed to the effect that all on board are free from communicable diseases.

T. KONARSKI	F. L. CARROLL
Commander	Lt.-Colonel,
Polish Representative, C.R.X.	British Representative, C.R.X.[12]

German sources describe this 'barbarous exodus' in the darkest possible tones. In West Germany, the *Bund der Vertriebener* (League of Expellees) has documented their sufferings in the minutest detail. They see the expulsions as a simple act of revenge, inspired by the same sort of racist and chauvinist motives that drove the Nazis to behave in like manner. They claim to be the victims of acts of atrocity and genocide, and count their martyrs in millions. Yet something in these arguments is seriously wrong. The number of the victims of 'Polish Revenge' as claimed in the 1950s exceeded the total figure of expellees as admitted by official Polish sources. On the German side, statistics were systematically exaggerated as a means of boosting the campaign for the recovery of the 'Potsdam territories'. On the Polish side, basic facts were regularly overlooked by people who pretended that Germans born in Silesia, Pomerania, or Prussia were bound 'as of right' to cede their homes to imported Polish 'autochtones'. The fact is that the Western Territories were taken from Germany and awarded to Poland as a prize of war. Yet their German inhabitants were expelled not by Polish 'revenge' but by a joint decision of the victorious allies. The management of the expulsions left much to be desired, if only because the Polish authorities did not possess the facilities to organize such a vast operation in comfort. Men, women, and children of all ages were taken from their homes and concentrated in collecting centres in the most primitive conditions. In some instances, as at Łambinowice (Lansdorf) in Upper Silesia, the site of Stalag VIII, they were obliged to assemble in facilities recently vacated by the Nazis. On the short journey to Germany, they were herded into accommodation reminiscent of other people's more extended travels into Russia. Some were beaten up; others were robbed or raped; many fell ill, or died; all were subjected to a violent experience they will never forget. For the first time in their lives, a great mass of ordinary and decent Germans were reduced to the sort of predicament which most ordinary and decent citizens of Central and Eastern Europe had come to regard as normal.[13]

Agrarian reform affected every village in Poland. As the natural sequence of earlier declarations of intent issued by its

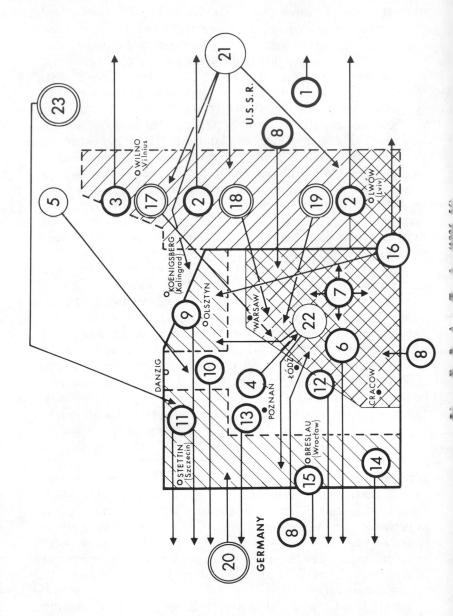

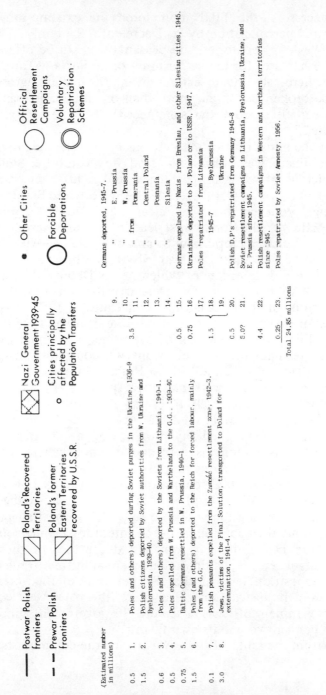

Postwar Polish frontiers

Prewar Polish frontiers

Poland's Recovered Territories

Poland's former Eastern Territories recovered by U.S.S.R.

Nazi General Gouvernment 1939-45

o Cities principally affected by the Population Transfers

• Other Cities

Forcible Deportations

Official Resettlement Campaigns

Voluntary Repatriation Schemes

(Estimated number in millions)

0.5	1.	Poles (and others) deported during Soviet purges in the Ukraine, 1936-9
1.5	2.	Polish citizens deported by Soviet authorities from W. Ukraine and Byelorussia, 1939-40.
0.6	3.	Poles (and others) deported by the Soviets from Lithuania, 1940-1.
0.5	4.	Poles expelled from W. Prussia and Wartheland to the G.G., 1939-40.
0.75	5.	Baltic Germans resettled in W. Prussia, 1940-1
1.5	6.	Poles (and others) deported to the Reich for forced labour, mainly from the G.G.
0.1	7.	Polish peasants expelled from the Zamość resettlement zone, 1942-3.
3.0	8.	Jews, victims of the Final Solution, transported to Poland for extermination, 1941-4.

3.5	9.	Germans deported, 1945-7.
	10.	" " E. Prussia
	11.	" " W. Prussia
	12.	" from Pomerania
	13.	" " Central Poland
	14.	" " Posnania
		" " Silesia
0.5	15.	Germans expelled by Nazis from Breslau, and other Silesian cities, 1945.
0.75	16.	Ukrainians deported to N. Poland or to USSR, 1947.
1.5	17.	Poles 'repatriated' from Lithuania
	18.	1945-7 Byelorussia
	19.	Ukraine
0.5	20.	Polish D.P.'s repatriated from Germany 1945-8
5.0?	21.	Soviet resettlement campaigns in Lithuania, Byelorussia, Ukraine, and E. Prussia since 1945.
4.4	22.	Polish resettlement campaigns in Western and Northern territories since 1945.
0.25	23.	Poles repatriated by Soviet Amnesty, 1956.

Total 24.85 millions

predecessors, the TRJN completed the existing movement towards parcellization by its Decree of 6 September 1946. In the Western Territories, the peasants were to be offered lots of 15 hectares for arable farming, or 20 hectares for pasture. Elsewhere, all private estates over 100 hectares gross were to be broken up. In all, more than one million peasant families benefited from the scheme; 814,000 new farms were created.[14]

In the midst of such momentous upheavals, the Provisional Government was obliged to tread very carefully. Stalin was suspicious of his Polish protégés, and held them on a tight leash. As early as October 1944, he had ordered Bierut, 'either change your methods or clear out.' Now, according to Mikołajczyk, the communist leaders of the government met every Thursday morning with an anonymous Soviet Colonel (whom he believed to be Ivan Serov, the head of 'Smyersh') to receive their orders of which he, as Deputy Premier, was kept blissfully ignorant. The non-party Ministers were intensely suspicious of their communist colleagues; the PPR was suspicious of their rivals; and the electorate, if it had time to think of politics, was suspicious of everyone. The undertaking to stage 'free and unfettered elections' was constantly postponed. In its place, on 30 June 1946, a Referendum was held, whose terms of reference were blatantly spurious. By inviting the electorate to vote 'THREE TIMES YES' to questions lifted bodily from the established platform of the Opposition, the government abandoned any pretence of moral integrity. But it forced its opponents into the dilemma where they had either to give unanimous support to the 'Government Bloc' or else to renege on their commitments. In the trial of strength that ensued, Mikołajczyk's Peasant Party chose the latter course. By asking the voters to say 'NO' to the first proposition about the abolition of the Senate, they merely sought to give the lie to the government's deception. In those few districts where opposition tellers were admitted to the count, the opposition learned that 81 per cent of the voters had followed its instructions. Elsewhere, the votes were counted by government officials in secret. The government announced a 68 per cent vote in its own favour.[15]

Within the ranks of the government, the communists of the

PPR were preoccupied with deep calculations of ideological strategy and tactics. Their broad strategy in this period preceding the open assumption of power was based on their concept of a Democratic Bloc. In this, they proposed a specific variant of the front technique, which differed in several crucial respects both from the 'Popular Front' of the pre-war years, and from the so-called 'National Front' in neighbouring Czechoslovakia. In Poland, the communist movement was so weak that it could never have contemplated open competition with the 'bourgeois' parties. Their only possibility was to conceal their weakness, and to concentrate on the destruction of their rivals. Their Democratic Bloc did not envisage any genuine concessions to their partners in the government, and was mainly designed as an instrument of delay and control. Ideological tactics relied heavily on camouflage. Words such as 'communist' were carefully avoided, even in the Party's name. *Kulak* was one of the few words of abuse which were not applied. In the internal jargon of the Party, the Russian-sounding *samokrytyka* (self-criticism) was replaced by the Romish *autokrytyka*. Political tactics concentrated on the splitting of rival formations in the classic Leninist manner 'from above and from below'. Rivals who refused to play found themselves faced with bogus parties bearing the same name as their own, and led by former colleagues who had been successfully suborned. Such was the fate of Mikołajczyk's Peasant Movement, and of the old anticommunist PPS. Administrative tactics sought to monopolize the levers of power. Positions of nominal authority in each of the ministries could safely be left in the hands of an opponent so long as a couple of communist deputies were there to hold their chief in check. Slowly but surely, by fair means and foul, the PPR was working its way towards its goal of acting, as Gomułka put it, as 'the hegemon of the nation'.[16] After two years of preparation, it finally agreed to hold the long-delayed Elections on 19 January 1947.

Economic and social policies were inevitably obstructed by the political struggle in progress. The PPR could not launch fully-fledged communist policies of its own until it held a more secure position in the government and in the country as a whole. The two major developments of these years − the

Nationalization Law of January 1946, and the launching of the Three Year Plan for 1947–9 — were inspired not by the communists but by the socialists. The former nationalized all enterprises capable of employing more than 50 workers per shift, and put nine out of ten enterprises under state control by the end of the year. The latter was based on western rather than Soviet economic methods. On the agrarian front, Mikołajczyk limited himself to attempts at obtaining legal title deeds for peasants who had received land from parcellized estates. This was an obvious safeguard against future collectivization.

The January Election of 1947 gave the communist-led Democratic Bloc 80 per cent of the poll. From the official point of view, this represented an adequate if not a brilliant performance. Compared with wonders achieved by Soviet electoral managers in the Baltic States or in Lwów seven years earlier, or by Party mathematicians in 1952, it was a poor showing. But it served its purpose. The Election was neither 'free' nor 'unfettered'. The list of candidates was vetted in advance by the government. Two million voters had been struck from the register by government-controlled electoral committees. Factory workers were marched to the polls by their foremen, and told to vote for the government on pain of their jobs. The rules of secret balloting were ignored. The count was organized exclusively by government officials. The result was a foregone conclusion. The British and American governments protested against the blatant disregard for the provisions of Yalta and Potsdam. The Soviet government rejected the protests, on the grounds that western sources of information in Poland were unreliable.[17]

As a result of the Election, the PPR assumed a dominant position in Polish politics for the first time. Henceforth all business could be conducted legally and constitutionally, on the basis of a subservient majority in the Sejm, where the government held 394 seats against the PSL's 28. On 5 February, Bierut was elected President of the Republic. On 6 February a new government was sworn in with J. Cyrankiewicz as Premier. On 19 February, special powers were given to a new Council of State. From now on, all practical prospects for 'bourgeois' parties operating on the basis of popular consent came to an end. Over the next year or so, the cruder elements of the communist movement celebrated their triumph by vilifying their defeated rivals, and driving them from the scene altogether. In the Sejm, Mikołajczyk was publicly denounced as 'a foreign spy' and 'collaborator' by an ex-General recruited from the ranks of the *Sanacja*. The Censorship succeeded in censoring the Premier's protest on censorship, not only from the press but also from the minutes of the Sejm. In the courts, a group of socialist leaders were charged with treason, and removed. In the countryside, the last remnants of the anti-communist underground were destroyed. In October 1947, Mikołajczyk who, *malgré lui,* had acted as a general focus for opposition, fled for his life. In London, he was told by Churchill, who had urged him to go to Poland in the first place, that it was a surprise to see him alive.[18]

However, the mere elimination of their opponents did not automatically give the communists the means to rule and develop the country as they wished; and it is highly significant that the initiative for creating a new party organization, suited to the new conditions, came less from the PPR itself than from the pro-communist rump elements of the former radical parties. Here, the key man was Józef Cyrankiewicz, leader of the resprayed PPS, and since February, Prime Minister. In 1947, one may suppose that Cyrankiewicz faced an uncomfortable future. At any point, he could have been discarded as lightly as his predecessor, Osóbka-Morawski. He could not possibly hope to beat the communists — nor, in the Leninist game, to join them and still retain any semblance of influence. His only hope was to muscle in from the start on the creation of the new organization. He saw a ready ally in the Kremlin, which was watching Gomułka and the PPR with increasing unease. In March 1948, Cyrankiewicz travelled to Moscow to see Stalin, and it is clearly from this meeting that the project for creating a united Polish Workers Party (PZPR) reached its point of departure. Hence it is quite erroneous to imagine the PPR organizing a merger with the PPS 'in the manner of a hungry dog merging with a loaf of bread'. In this case, the weevils from the loaf walked off on their own legs and persuaded the dog's master to strap them firmly to the dog's back in a position where they could not be eaten. In this way, the PPR was linked with the PPS for the duration; the eventual emergence of the PZPR was assured; and Cyrankiewicz ensured himself a place in the sun which lasted until 1972.[19]

Over the same period, the two other elements of the government's Democratic Bloc, the bogus SL and the SD (Democratic Movement) were merging with the remnants of their anti-communist parent organizations. The SL and the SD became integral parts of the communist system in Poland, but not of the PZPR. The triumph of the one-party system was never perfectly complete.

In the economic, as in the political sphere, radical change was delayed by the lack of appropriate organizational structures and personnel. The Three Year Plan did not envisage any further industrial nationalization. There was no sign whatsoever of collectivization in agriculture. In 1947 the harvest failed, and every possible concession had to be made to the peasants in order to feed the nation. At this time, the peasant co-operative movement was flourishing. The state sector was advancing rapidly into the internal wholesale trade, reaching a virtual monopoly by the end of 1948. The retail trade, also was increasingly 'socialized'. In the countryside, it was taken over by the Peasant 'Self-help' Organizations. In Foreign Trade, the USSR's role was dramatically increased. In the era of Marshall Aid, for which Poland was a prime candidate, the Soviet Union was obliged to make a compensatory gesture. This appeared in the Trade Treaty of 28 January 1948, which provided for Polish–Soviet co-operation worth 2 million roubles over 4 years. After that, Marshall Aid was rejected out of hand.

From the communist viewpoint, the cancer in the Republic's economic life lay right at the centre, in the Central Planning Office (COP). Here the expertise was largely western trained, and was connected with the old PPS. In February 1948, a discussion meeting was convened to review its activities. To the amazement of the staff, the discussion turned into a full-scale Soviet-style pillory of their work. The Minister of Industry, Hilary Minc, denounced their efforts as 'bourgeois', 'un-Marxist', and based on false analysis. For the first time in

Poland, a public debate was conducted on the basis of who could recite the most quotations from Lenin and Stalin. It has been called 'the birth of Polish Stalinism'. Henceforth, all planning was to be undertaken in slavish imitation of Soviet methods. The Central Planning Office was abolished. Economic statistics became state secrets. Free debate ended.[20]

As the Planning affair hinted, the main crisis was looming in the ideological sphere. In the summer of 1948, a major split appeared in the ranks of the Party and government. This is sometimes explained as a rift between the advocates of the conservative 'Polish Road to Socialism' centred on Gomułka, and the adherents of a radical 'Moscow Line', headed by Bierut. Although, of course, there can be no certainty, it does seem that the standard analysis is faulty on at least three important scores. For one thing, it ignores the complexity of viewpoints and factions. Within the PPR itself at this period there were at least five main groupings. There were also the Party's close allies, especially Cyrankiewicz and his PPS and the NKVD's 'progressive Catholics'. On the Soviet side, one can identify four or five separate interests – from the Kommandatura of the Soviet Army and the security organs, to the state interest of the Soviet Ministries, the party interest of the CPSU, and last but not least the personal suspicions and whims of Stalin himself. If one perms the five or six Polish groups against the similar number of potential Soviet patrons, one immediately arrives at twenty-five or thirty important connections, some known, some hidden. The one man who does not appear to have had a definable position was Bierut. Bierut was a stool-pigeon of the most obvious ilk, quite incapable of forming a power grouping in Poland except at the end of someone else's strings. So, if Gomułka did command a solid following, dominant in the Party by 1948, the only possible source of concerted opposition lay in the Kremlin itself.

For another thing, the standard description ignores the dynamics of conflict within a totalitarian movement, where both sides are constantly on the move, each constantly shifting its ideological ground to avoid the embraces and encirclements of the other. The one thing that the weaker element must avoid at all costs is to agree publicly with the stronger

element, since 'harmonization' leads swiftly to complete submergence of its identity and separate existence. In 1944,
when the divergence between the PPR and the Soviet line was
first apparent to people in the know, it was the Soviets who
occupied the conservative position. It was Stalin who said
that 'introducing Communism to Poland was like putting a
saddle on a cow'. At that juncture, Gomułka and the PPR
with their 'homeland line' were in a leftist, messianic, 'victorio-
logical' mood, expecting to build Communism in Poland 'as
on a triumphal march'. After 1944, Stalin's confidence grew.
He began to press even more insistently for real, socialist
changes, approaching ever more nearly to Gomułka's original
position, and berating Bierut for his lack of revolutionary
ardour. Gomułka, meanwhile, faced with the practicalities of
'saddling the cow' was being pushed in the opposite direction,
expressing the opinion that he was unlikely to see true socialism, not to say communism, in Poland in his lifetime. Hence,
the ideological conflict assumed the form of a scissors movement, in which over four years the two contestants neatly
traversed from diametrically opposed positions. Gomułka in
1948 was making statements which coincided very closely
with the Soviet viewpoint in 1944, and vice versa.

The Polish comrades were bound to note changes in the
external relations of the USSR. In 1944—5, the USSR at war
was weak and courting any sort of ally who would join the
cause. Ideological divergences were permissible. By 1948, the
USSR had won the war, and made the Bomb. The schism
with Tito, the Arab—Israeli conflict, the German crisis, and
the Berlin Blockade, were all coming to a head. It was time to
close the ranks. Divergences were no longer permissible.

Thus, Gomułka's fate was sealed. As an old hand, he seems
to have sensed the danger before it arrived; but he sailed into
the storm head-on. At the June Plenum of the Party's Central
Committee, he launched into a rambling lecture on the historical traditions of Polish communism, praising the Luxemburgist flavour of the SDKPiL, the Trotskyite KPP, and even
the stand of the PPS on 'national independence'. It was an
act of open defiance. Thereon, he seems to have been put
under house arrest. His associates, Spychalski and Ochab,
were induced to denounce him, while he himself was brow-

beaten into making a public recantation. At the September Plenum, he was exposed to the insults of his friends, confessing his faults in a bitter display of self-criticism. In particular, he confessed to having grasped the importance of the USSR for the Polish Party in its immediate aspects but not 'on the higher plane'. At the end of the scene, he was replaced as General-Secretary of the Party by President Bierut, who to this point had always been presented to the world as 'a non-party man'. His departure removed the last obstacle to the formation of the PZPR in December.

Gomułka's fall was clearly the result of direct Soviet intervention in Polish Party affairs. A commentator who called it 'The Pacification of Polish Communism' was not very far from the mark. Yet to the best of their ability, Gomułka's comrades cushioned his defeat. He stayed on as Vice-Premier until January 1949, and as a member of the Central Committee until 1951. He was never put on trial, nor handed over to the mercies of Soviet justice. His act of defiance was not forgotten when the Polish Party reasserted its independence in 1956.[21]

After three-and-a-half years of peacetime, the construction of the People's Democracy in the Soviet image was virtually complete. A monolithic Leninist Party was establishing its monopoly. The identity of interests between Party and State was incarnate in the person of Bierut, who straddled the twin thrones of First-Secretary and President. The success of the communists had proved far easier than anyone in 1945 had supposed. In retrospect, it is less surprising. Contrary to what was assumed at the time in western countries, there was never a period in Poland when free competition between the communist movement and the non-communist parties was permitted. Power passed directly and smoothly from the German Occupation Forces to the Soviet Army, from the Soviet Army directly to the Soviet-controlled Provisional Government, and, at the time of Elections in 1947, from the TRJN to the PPR. For this reason, it is quite out of place to talk of a communist 'seizure of power' or a 'communist take-over'. The communists were handed Poland on a platter, and successfully obstructed all attempts to share power thereafter. Nor was there ever any need to impose Communism on Poland by force. It is quite beside the point that Stalin was a cruel, ruthless politician devoid of all sense of magnanimity or generosity. As events actually happened, all the elements which might conceivably have mounted organized resistance in Poland, had already been eliminated. They had been discredited by pre-war or wartime failures; deserted by the Allied Powers; or destroyed by the Warsaw Rising. In 1944–8 there was no one left – apart from Mikołajczyk and a few scattered and leaderless remnants of the AK – who might have opposed the communists. Stalin was given what he wanted without a struggle. Such violence as did occur, at the instigation of the NKGB, was politically superfluous. It is equally mistaken to talk of 'a concerted communist conspiracy'. Despite the affectation of monolithic solidarity, the Polish communist movement differed from the Soviets on many essential issues, and was deeply divided against itself. There was no agreement about the speed of direction of their socialist programme, still less about methods and means; no rigid conformity to a master-plan or blueprint. Both Poles and Soviets were feeling their way forward in a very uncertain and confusing situation. Indeed, one could say more. The end result, when Stalin was left ruling Poland through his reserve team of faceless puppets, was as much a failure for him as for the Polish communists themselves.

All this emphasizes that Poland's path was not the same as that of other East European countries. Poland could not be compared with neighbouring Czechoslovakia where the communists *were* strong enough to compete for a time on an open basis, but where they were then obliged to suppress the opposition by force. Nor could it be compared to Yugoslavia, where the communists possessed their own power base independent of the Soviet Army. Tito did not share the same outlook as Gomułka. Both were classified as 'rightist nationalist deviationists' simply because they happened to fall foul of the Soviets at the same time as common victims of a tack which was taken not in Poland or Yugoslavia but in the Kremlin.

The heart of the matter is that Polish political history was governed not by the Soviets alone, nor by the Polish communists alone, but by the subtle interdependence of the two.

It is true that in these early years the Polish communists could not possibly have survived without the support of the Soviet Army, and the host of Soviet advisers. But it is also true that the Soviets could not have run Poland in the way they had chosen without the co-operation of the Polish communists. In this sort of relationship, the weaker partner can often call the tune. He can threaten to collapse or to rebel. Knowing that Stalin would gain little by treating the PPR as he had treated the KPP, and that a direct Soviet takeover in Poland might well rebound against the international standing of the USSR, Gomułka manœuvred on the middle ground between open revolt and blind obedience, and established a measure of leverage. When he was removed, his Party continued to play the same game. They were not encumbered by illusions of popular support, and were able to survive with a minimum of friction. The Polish communists were able to trim quickly to Soviet demands; and yet, for reasons of their own pride, and of the national interest, were reluctant to do so. By 1948 they had successfully saddled the cow, but were not disposed to gallop.[22]

* * * * *

Stalinism — the dominant mode of Soviet-style communism from the late 1920s to the present day — has been variously described as a doctrine, a system, and as an attitude of mind. It was all of these things. In 1948, when the normal paranoia of the Kremlin was heightened to a new abnormal peak, it was hurriedly imposed on all the USSR's East European allies. Poland was no exception.

For many Poles, the main traits of Stalinism, which owe much more to ancient Russian traditions than to Marx or Engels, were all too familiar. Middle-aged people born and reared in Warsaw or Wilno in Tsarist days experienced a strong sensation of the *déjà vu*. The Stalinist psychology had been well analysed in Polish literature, notably in the work of Stanisław Ignacy Witkiewicz whose satirical novel *Nienasycenie* (Insatiability) was now proving uncomfortably prophetic. Witkiewicz had described the invasion of Europe by the Horde of Murti-Bing, a Sino-Mongolian warlord who subdues the decadent West with a well-organized sales campaign of 'philosophical pills' ensuring man's future happiness and sociability. In the last scene of the novel, the leader of the West abjectly surrenders, and is beheaded with great ceremony. In the post-war period, similar feelings were expressed by the poet and critic, Czesław Miłosz (b. 1911), whose reflections, *The Captive Mind*, were published in 1953 shortly after his defection from his post as Polish cultural attaché in Paris. Here, in one of many penetrating studies, Miłosz likens the practice of Stalinism in Poland to the 'Art of Ketman' as performed under the oriental despotism of the Shah in feudal Persia. Ketman was the art of double-think, of dissimulating, and of deceit — the profession of an army of toadies and lick-spittles, who pandered to the whims of 'Him' with limitless flattery and cynicism, simply to promote their careers or to save their skins. According to the Comte de Gobineau, who first described the Persian Court to the world at large, 'there were no true Moslems in Persia'. According to Miłosz, there were very few true communists in Poland.[23]

Ideological argument was swamped by the cult of Stalin's personality. Stalin's crude parodies of Lenin's deformation of Marx, as summarized in his *Short Course* . . . (1939) and his *Problems of Leninism* (1940) were translated into Polish, and adopted as the True Word. All discussions were brought to a close by a timely, or untimely, quotation from 'The Great Leader'. Writers of genuine talent, such as Władysław Broniewski, were reduced to writing poetic puffs and jingles:

> How beautiful to know that Stalin lives,
> How beautiful to know that Stalin thinks, etc., etc.

In the political sphere, the 'one Party state' was subject to direct Soviet control. To this end, Marshal of the Soviet Union, Konstanty Rokossowski (Rokossovskiy, 1896–1968), a Pole who had spent his entire career in the Soviet service, was installed in Warsaw in November 1949 as Vice-Premier, Minister of Defence, and member of the Political Bureau.

Militarism reared its unmistakable head. On the doubtful pretext that the socialist bloc was about to be attacked by the forces of American imperialism, the whole of Eastern Europe was turned into an armed camp. Frontiers were closed. Security was returned to wartime footing. The economy was

converted to military priorities. Military conscription, carefully avoided since 1945, was reintroduced. The Polish Army,
closely schooled by Soviet advisers, received a permanent
establishment of 400,000 men. The General Staff was poli-
ticized through the Army Political Academy created in 1951.
For several years, the earlier stage of development of the
satellite armies prevented the formation in Eastern Europe
of a Soviet military bloc in response to NATO. This short-
coming was remedied on 14 May 1955 when the Warsaw
Pact, in which the Polish Army was to take second place after
the Soviet Army, was formed.[24]

In economic affairs, absolute priority was given to heavy
industry. The revised Six-Year Plan for 1950—5 was conceived
by the so-called *metalożercy* (metal-eaters), who pressed for
unlimited production of iron and steel. In Cracow, the
ancient university city was overshadowed by the construction
and the pollution of Nowa Huta, a new suburb supporting
the Lenin Steelworks, the largest of its kind in the country.

In agriculture, absolute priority was given to forced collectivization. The campaign to deprive the peasants of their
ownership of the land, and to coral them into State Agricultural Enterprises (PGRs) and into voluntary production
co-operatives gained rapid momentum. The jargon, with its
careful avoidance of the Russian word *'kolkhoz'*, fooled no
one. Between 1950 and 1955, the number of collective farms
rose from 12,513 to 28,955. The private peasant faced the
prospect of elimination.[25]

The Roman Catholic Church was systematically attacked.
In the years after the war, the authorities had applied their
favourite 'splitting' techniques to the Church in the same way
as to the political parties. They did this partly by promoting
the schismatic Polish National Church, and partly by launching a series of anti-Catholic, pseudo-religious organizations,
such as PAX (1947), Caritas, and Veritas (1950), which
usurped the functions of the Church's former social, charitable, and cultural enterprises. Their chosen instrument in this
campaign was the former Fascist leader, Bolesław Piasecki
(1915—79), the Director of PAX, who had been spared by
the NKVD presumably on condition of his future collaboration.[26] The aim was to destroy the reputation of the Hierarchy,

and to create a bloc of Catholic opinion which was prepared to co-operate with the state on the Party's terms. When the campaign misfired, and the Hierarchy categorically forbade both priests and people to have any dealings with Piasecki or with any of his organizations, harsher methods were adopted. In 1950, all Church property with the exception of church buildings and churchyards, was confiscated. Priests were arrested in large numbers, and were harassed by the police. Arrangements for the religious education of children were interrupted. In 1953, in response to continued defiance, Cardinal Wyszyński was arrested and placed under close detention at the remote monastery of Komańcza in the Bieszczady Mountains.

The Stalinist system was formalized by the passing of the Constitution of 22 July (sic) 1952, which marked the declaration of the 'Polish People's Republic (PRL). On the model of similar communist constitutions, all citizens were guaranteed the right to work, to leisure, to health, to study, and to the freedoms of speech, assembly, and conscience, without regard to race, sex, or creed. The growth of the state's productive forces was assured on the basis of a planned economy. Supreme authority in the state was conferred to a legislative Sejm of 460 deputies, directly elected every four years by secret ballot and by universal suffrage. Executive power was to be exercised by a Council of Ministers, which together with the President and his Council of State, and the Supreme Board of Control (NIK), was to be appointed by the Sejm. Judicial authority was to reside in a Supreme Court, formed from a bench of independent judges appointed by the Council of State. The Church was separated from the State (to which, in fact, it had never been connected). On all these points, the appearance of an ideally democratic machine was carefully maintained. In practice, all chance of effective democracy was nullified by the as yet extra-constitutional 'leading role' of the Party and its National Front as the 'guardian of the state'. According to the canons of Leninist Democratic Centralism, all effective power lay in the hands of the Party's Political Bureau and of its First Secretary. All appointments within the State, and all decisions at every level, were subject to prior approval by the appropriate Party organs. All Ministries answered to corresponding departments within the Party. All candidates for election to the Sejm were to be selected in advance by the Party. In effect, 'the working people of town and countryside' whom the Constitution named as the receptacle of political power, were its helpless victims. They possessed no means whatsoever to influence the work of their nominal representatives. The People's 'Democracy' was a legal fiction. The reality lay in the Party's dictatorship over the people.[27]

The habits of Stalinism penetrated into every walk of life. Statues of Stalin appeared in public places. The Republic's leading industrial centre, Katowice, was renamed 'Stalinogród'. Everything and anything, from the Palace of Culture in Warsaw downwards, was dedicated 'to the name of J. V. Stalin'. Soviet Russian civilization was upheld as the universal paragon of virtue. An attempt was even made to modify the Polish language by introducing the Russian practice of speaking in the second person plural, per *Wy* (You) in place of the decadent Polish habit of speaking in the third person singular, per *Pan* (Sir) or *Pani* (Madam). In art, 'Socialist Realism', once described as 'the orchestra of the concentration camp', gained exclusive approval. In the sciences, Lysenko superseded Mendel, Newton, and Einstein. In the humanities, Soviet 'Diamat', the scientific analysis of all human problems, the pill of Murti-Bing, was indiscriminately applied. Nonconformity of any sort was promptly punished. The militiaman and the petty bureaucrat walked tall.

Even so, Stalinism never attained the same pitch of ferocity in Poland that reigned in neighbouring countries. Behind the scenes, the native communists of the PZPR fought a steady rearguard action against the Soviet stooges in their midst. They protected the comrades who had fallen into disfavour, and blocked any moves towards wholesale revenge. Show trials were never adopted as an instrument of policy. The security forces were not given the unlimited licence that they had enjoyed in 1944–7. Fraud and chicanery were widespread, but violence was not. The remnants of the bourgeoisie and the intellectuals, though denied all free expression, were not liquidated. The Church, though assailed on all sides, was not, as in Bulgaria or the Ukraine, suppressed.

The peasants, though deprived of legal claim to their land, were not deported. By comparison with Czechoslovakia or Eastern Germany, the progress of collectivization was slow, and incomplete.

Although the Stalinist system remained intact in Poland until October 1956, the first cracks in the monolith appeared soon after Stalin's death. Already in October 1953, the collectivization campaign, supposedly the main indicator of society's progress towards socialism, was slowed down on the Party's orders. In July 1956, it was called off altogether. In December 1954, following appalling disclosures in the West by one of its former officials, Józef Światło, the dreaded Ministry of Security was abolished, and its Director, Stanisław Radkiewicz, dismissed.[28] At the same time Gomułka and his associates were released from house arrest, though not as yet readmitted to public life. The Censorship was relaxed to the extent that one or two critical comments made their appearance. Adam Ważyk's *Poemat Dla Dorosłych* (Poem for Adults), published in July 1955, was widely taken as a sign of things to come:

> They ran to us shouting,
> 'Under Socialism
> A cut finger does not hurt.'
> But they felt pain.
> They lost faith.
> . . .
> There are overworked people;
> there are people from Nowa Huta
> who have never been in a theatre;
> there are Polish apples unavailable for children;
> there are children spurned by criminal doctors;
> there are boys forced to tell lies;
> there are girls forced to tell lies
> there are old ladies thrown out of their houses by their husbands;
> there are exhausted people dying from heart attacks;
> there are people slandered and spat upon,
> people assaulted on the streets
> by common hoodlums, for whom legal definitions can't be found;
> there are people waiting for a scrap of paper;
> there are people waiting for justice;
> there are people who wait a long time.

We should make demands on this earth
About overworked people,
About keys that fit locks,
About houses with windows,
About walls without mildew,
About the hatred of scraps of paper,
About people's precious, holy, time,
About a safe return to home,
About the simple distinction between words and deeds.
We should make demands on this earth,
which we didn't win in a game of chance,
which cost the lives of millions,
demands for the plain truth, for the harvest of freedom,
for fiery, good sense,
for fiery good sense.
We should make demands daily.
We should make demands of the Party.
. . .[29]

The clue to the poem's meaning lies in its sheer banality. In any open society, where the faults and the shortcomings of government policy are openly discussed, it could have aroused no surprise whatsoever. But in the Stalinist context, with Marshal Rokossowski still resident in Warsaw, it caused a sensation. For the first time in seven years, it hinted that something was rotten in the People's Republic and that official eulogies of the country's perfect progress would no longer be accepted. By the time that First-Secretary Bolesław Bierut left Warsaw to attend the Twentieth Congress of the Soviet Communist Party in Moscow in February 1956, the Thaw was well advanced.

The crisis of 1956 which rocked the whole communist world was launched by Krushchev's 'secret speech' to the Twentieth Congress recounting a limited selection of Stalin's crimes against the Party and the people. In Poland, it was compounded by the equally shocking news of Bierut's sudden death in Moscow, apparently, though not officially, by suicide. No one could ignore the possibility that the two events were connected. No disciplined communist could overlook the fact that what was happening in the USSR ought also to be happening in the USSR's satellites. A steadying influence was provided by Bierut's successor as Party Secretary, Edward Ochab, appointed in March 1956. Faced on the one hand by the demands of 'national communists' to shake off the Soviet yoke, and on the other by the preparations of the Stalinists to defend their position, if necessary with Soviet aid, he contrived to prevent open conflict. In April, the Minister of Culture, Sokorski, was removed. In May, discredited by the stories of tens of thousands of Poles returning from Soviet camps, the Party's ideological leader, Jakob Berman, was dismissed. In June, when the communist workers of the Zipso Locomotive Factory in Poznań rioted in the streets, under banners of 'BREAD and FREEDOM' and 'RUSSIANS GO HOME', the disturbances might well have been exploited by one faction or another for their own ends, thereby risking a direct clash. In two days' fighting between workers and the militia, 53 men died. But the workers were calmed by the intervention of Prime Minister Cyrankiewicz, and the Army was kept to a supporting role. In the course of the summer, Gomułka resurfaced in Party circles, and made his mark in a series of analytical articles privately circulated among the upper echelons. The details of the debate were superfluous. Everyone knew Gomułka's past and what he stood for; and they knew that his supporters were gaining ground over their opponents. His impending victory was signalled at the beginning of October by the resignation of Hilary Minc. An attempted coup by Rokossowski was forestalled by Party workers who circulated the Soviet Marshal's alleged list of proscribed persons. On 21 October at the 8th Plenum of the Central Committee, 'Comrade Wiesław' was unanimously elected First-Secretary on the platform of reasserting genuine Leninist principles in state and party life. His election was attended by ominous rumours that Soviet Army units were moving on Warsaw, and that Nikita Krushchev had landed at Okęcie Airport in an apoplectic mood of undisguised rage.

The confrontation between Gomułka and Krushchev was dangerous while it lasted; but it was quickly resolved on amicable lines. Gomułka could argue with reason that his loyalty to the communist movement was beyond reproach; that his brand of communism was based on a special understanding of Polish problems; and that the preservation of

Stalinism was no more justified in Poland than in the USSR. Krushchev, for his part, was furious that the decisions of the Plenum had not been cleared in advance in Moscow, and was worried lest the Polish example would trigger more serious insubordination elsewhere in the Soviet bloc. This was the first time that Moscow's claim to automatic control over the affairs of a fraternal party had ever been ignored. The lines of conflict were sharply drawn. The Soviet Army in Silesia, in former East Prussia, and in East Germany, had overwhelming force at its command. The Soviet Navy was staging a show of strength in the Bay of Gdańsk. But crack commando units of the Polish Internal Security Corps (KBW) had occupied all the approaches to Warsaw in full battle-gear and in full public view, and it was doubtful whether the Polish General-Staff would obey Rokossowski's orders. If Krushchev insisted on removing Gomułka, major bloodshed could not have been avoided. The Poles were prepared to fight, and the Soviets respected Polish courage if nothing else. There was a strong rumour that the Polish Army, if attacked, was threatening to invade East Germany, and thus to demolish the equilibrium of the entire Soviet presence in Central Europe. The Soviet leader would be seen to have coerced a fraternal party, and the myth of unanimity in the Socialist camp would be shattered for ever. So Krushchev blustered, and then relented. At one point when he began to wax eloquent about the ingratitude of the Poles towards the millions of Soviet war dead 'who had laid down their lives for Poland's freedom', he is said to have been reminded by Gomułka that 'Poles knew how to die for their country as well as anyone'. In reality there was no basis for disagreement between the two men. Both were life-long communists, with a direct, simple style. Both, in their different ways, were seeking to abolish the grosser absurdities of the Stalinist system. After two days' discussion Gomułka's election was confirmed. Rokossowski and his team were to return to the USSR. The PZPR was to take control of the People's Republic without direct supervision from Moscow. The Polish Road to Socialism was to be respected by the Soviet leaders, on condition that the unity of the bloc was not impaired. In this way, the Polish 'Spring' bloomed in October. The Polish Party achieved maturity, asserted its

independence, and freed the country from Stalinism; and it
has continued to rule the country ever since.[30]

* * * * *

Twenty years of National Communism in Poland have provided
an era of relative stability, but have failed to devise any definitive solutions to pressing political and economic problems.
The Party has had to learn the art of government the hard
way, and has had to shed some of its more fanciful ideological
vagaries. Apart from 1956, there have been serious political
crises in 1968, 1970, and 1976.

Gomułka's assumption of power was accompanied by bitter
recriminations among the Party's competing factions. If the
Soviet puppets had been re-exported, the native Stalinists
headed by Zenon Nowak still formed a powerful, if subdued,
caucus. Known henceforth as 'Natolinists', after the former
Branicki palace at Natolin where they held their meetings,
they had been thrown into direct conflict with Gomułka's
supporters, who had received the label of 'Revisionists'. Factional in-fighting rumbled on for months. The Natolinists
attempted to divert attacks against them by blaming the large
number of Jews who had prospered in the Party under the
Stalinist regime. A whispering campaign 'to oust the Abramo-
vitches' caused a number of minor casualties.[31] At the other
end of the scale, a determined attempt was launched to purge
Piasecki and his ex-Fascists, and to suppress PAX. The
November issue of *Po prostu* (Quite Simply), a radical intellectual journal, denounced PAX as an organization practising
'the powers of the Mafia', and the blind cult of the leader.
On this front, nothing happened. Despite a widespread popular
outcry, Piasecki stood firm, presumably as a result of confi-
dential Soviet lobbying on behalf of the KGB's favourite
Polish son. For this, and other offences, *Po prostu* was closed.
In January 1957, Piasecki's sixteen-year-old son, Bogdan, was
abducted on his way home from school in Warsaw by
unknown persons. His mutilated body was eventually discovered in a disused cellar.

The progress of 'Destalinization' was kept within severe
limits. A new electoral law was designed, in Gomułka's words,
'to permit the people to elect and not merely to vote'. The

General Election of 20 January 1957 offered the voters a choice between 722 candidates, some of them non-party figures, standing for 459 seats. But the Candidates' List had been drawn up, as always, by the Party: there was no possibility that the PZPR could have been defeated. The National Front, rebaptized as the 'Front of National Unity' (FJN), remained the controller and manager of political life. An important Codification Commission set to work to create the proper legal framework of public life which was lacking. Important codices of Administrative Law (1961), Family Law (1965), and Criminal Law (1969) were instituted. But there was little attempt to restrain the Party's unbridled liberties. Gomułka's regime was obviously more humane, more flexible, more independent, and more popular, than its predecessor. But those observers who expected that Gomułka would somehow 'liberalize' the People's Republic on the lines of the western democracies were due to be cruelly disillusioned.

In the affairs of the Soviet bloc, the Polish Party generally occupied a loyal, orthodox position. Its nonconformist policies at home had to be safeguarded by an ostentatiously submissive stance towards the USSR. Yet immediately after October, when the Hungarian Republic suffered the fate which Poland had so narrowly escaped, the Polish Red Cross sent medical supplies and blood plasma to Hungary in the teeth of opposition from the authorities of the intervening Czechoslovak Republic. In the General Assembly of the United Nations, the Polish Delegation's abstention from the vote on 21 November 1956 on the motion condemning Soviet intervention in Hungary, represents a solitary act of defiance in thirty years of membership.[32]

In the field of international disarmament, however, the Poles did take a number of important initiatives. On 2 October 1957, in the XII General Assembly of the United Nations, Foreign Minister Adam Rapacki (1909–70) proposed a scheme for creating a nuclear-free zone on the territories of Poland, Czechoslovakia, and the two German Republics — the so-called Rapacki Plan. Three years later, at the XV General Assembly in 1960, the Gomułka Plan proposed an over-all freeze of nuclear arms in the same area. These plans, and their numerous variants which were discussed off and on for six or seven years, clearly underlined Poland's concern to halt the arms race and to defuse tensions in Central Europe. At the same time, they represented a definite attempt by the Soviet bloc to undermine the defences of Western Germany. After 1964, when the Warsaw Pact began to enjoy military parity with NATO, attention was switched away from Disarmament to the Soviet drive for a general European Conference on Security and Co-operation – code named 'Détente'.

At home, in the period between 1961 and 1968, Gomułka gradually lost the respect and the political impetus which he had gained in 1956. In the course of the 1960s, the drive for economic self-sufficiency, especially in agriculture, ran into difficulties. The promised rise in the standard of living was slow to materialize. The Party bureaucracy prospered ostentatiously, to the disgust of ordinary people. The First-Secretary surrounded himself with a closed circle of cronies, and steadily lost contact with opinion in the Party and in the country at large. In response to neo-Stalinist noises emanating from the USSR after the fall of Krushchev in 1964, the Censorship was strengthened, and orthodox communist philistinism reasserted in cultural affairs. The students, the intellectuals, the younger, non-factional Party members known as the 'technocrats', all experienced a strong sense of frustration and disillusionment. Behind the scenes, the old factions, notably the 'Partisans' of General Moczar, now Minister of the Interior, were looking for trouble.

The crisis of 1968 was thus the result of accumulated failures. It was foreshadowed in the previous summer when a group of Polish officials and Army officers had reacted to the Israeli victory in the June War by celebrating the triumph of *'our* Jews over *their* Arabs'. By this act, a link was forged between political dissidence and pro-Israeli (and anti-Soviet) sympathies. The point was not lost on General Moczar who saw the prospect of denouncing his rivals as subversive 'Zionists'. In March 1968, a relatively trivial incident in Warsaw, where the Soviet ambassador successfully ordered the closure of a theatre performance of Mickiewicz's classic, *Dziady* (Forefather's Eve), sparked off an open clash. As the students took to the streets in protest, Moczar's militia went into action in a deliberate campaign to fan the flames of protest. The students were gratuitously beaten, and arrested in large numbers. The organs of the press called on workers to take action against 'Zionist traitors'. In Cracow, where no demonstrations had taken place, the Market Square and the student hostels were surrounded by units of the ORMO factory police, and a special riot-squad was brought into the city to attack the Jagiellonian University. The Vice-Rector joined dozens of students, employees, and cleaning women injured by the militia's clubs and tear-gas grenades. It was a classic example of political provocation so common in the annals of East European dictatorships. Its only conceivable purpose was to discredit Gomułka's leadership, and to advance the career of that watchful Minister who had taken such prompt action against the Republic's (imaginary) enemies. But Moczar was baulked. Neither the workers, nor the Army, were prepared to humour his adventures. The hunt for Zionists proved frankly puzzling to the mass of the populace who knew perfectly well that the only substantial number of Jews in Poland were to be found in the higher ranks of the Party. In Cracow, the workers of Nowa Huta disrupted a meeting called to express their (spontaneous) support for action against the students, and had themselves to be dispersed by police dogs. The Colonel of the local paratroop garrison obliged the militia to withdraw their armed cordon from the main student hostel, and sent his regimental band into the city to advertise his success. Similar confrontations undoubtedly took place in other centres, although they were never reported. In the circumstances, Gomułka was able to reassert his authority. The Party closed ranks, the militia's campaign was called off, and its authors demoted. In a broadcast speech, Gomułka appealed for national unity, and named a number of intellectuals who were supposed to have inspired the troublemakers. In this Leszek Kołakowski and Paweł Jasienica, the popular historian, joined the stream of Jewish scapegoats and refugees who were dismissed, or had resigned from their jobs, in the course of this most confusing episode.[33]

Gomułka was aided by events in Czechoslovakia. In so far as public opinion influenced the progress of the Polish crisis, the only comment relevant to Gomułka's succession was enshrined in the popular jingle:

Cała Polska czeka
Na swego Dubczeka
(The whole of Poland awaits its own Dubček)

Yet Moczar's interest in 'socialism with a human face' was still less convincing than Gomułka's. What is more, the Soviet Government, alarmed by developments in Czechoslovakia, would not have considered the moment ripe for additional changes in Poland. In the summer, the manœuvres of the Warsaw Pact in Czechoslovakia, which brought several Soviet divisions through southern Poland, served to divert attention from the Polish Party's internal problems; whilst the Invasion itself, in which Polish Army units participated from bases in East Germany, called for the strictest political vigilance. As a result, opposition to Gomułka faded. At the 5th Congress of the PZPR in November 1968, his leadership was reconfirmed.

This same Congress was attended by the Soviet Party leader, Leonid Brezhnev, who used the occasion to expound his views on the relations between socialist states. Far from apologizing for the recent invasion of Czechoslovakia, Brezhnev ominously underlined the duty of all the fraternal parties to come to the aid of any country where 'the gains of socialism' were threatened. In effect, in the clumsy euphemisms of Kremlinese, Brezhnev was signalling Moscow's determination to crush any other member of the Soviet bloc whose obedience might falter. Any fraternal party which dared to follow Dubček's example would pay the same penalty. That this so-called 'Brezhnev Doctrine' should have been formulated in Warsaw − in the capital of the USSR's largest and most suspect ally − was lost on no one. The echoes of that speech reverberate round Eastern Europe to this day.

Poland's fundamental economic and political malaise, however, had not been cured. It was merely a matter of time before Gomułka would again be challenged.

The crisis of December 1970 was provoked by the sheer clumsiness of a regime which was losing all contact with reality. Advised that a steep rise in food prices was unavoidable in view of continuing agricultural failures, the Government decided to introduce increases of up to 20 per cent at a stroke, and, of all times, in Christmas week. Having thus invited the strikes and demonstrations which ensued, the government panicked, and ordered the militia and the army to restore order with all means at their disposal. It is interesting to note that the most determined strikes occurred not among the poorest areas which would have felt the attack on their Christmas turkey most acutely, but in one of the most highly paid and traditionally communist sectors of the work-force, in the Baltic shipyards of Szczecin, Gdynia, and Gdańsk. Clearly, the root of the trouble lay much deeper than in the immediate problem of food prices; and feelings ran high. In Gdańsk, a train bringing workers to the shipyards, where a lock-out had been proclaimed, was ambushed, and fired on by armed militiamen. The workers responded with fury. Shops were looted. Party headquarters were besieged. Militiamen were lynched in the street. The Militia Training Centre at Słupsk was burned to the ground. Demonstrators were crushed by armoured vehicles. Army recruits, when ordered to fire, refused orders. In all, some three hundred people were killed. On this occasion, Gomułka was unable to defend himself. Having retired to a Party Clinic to be treated for nervous exhaustion, he rushed uninvited into the Political Bureau which was just about to depose him. His protests fell on deaf ears. On 20 December, the 7th Plenum of the Central Committee accepted Gomułka's resignation and confirmed the elevation of Edward Gierek.[34]

The terminal crisis of Gomułka's rule coincided with a great success in the realm of foreign policy. Gomułka had always known that Poland's very real fears of German revanchism perpetuated the country's humiliating dependence on the Soviet Union, and that the restoration of good relations with Western Germany would strengthen the People's Republic in the economic as well as in the purely political sphere. For many years, the intransigence of the USSR on the one side, and the influence of the *Bund der Vertrieben* (League of Expellees) with the Adenauer government on the other, had prevented any possibility of fruitful contacts between Warsaw and Bonn. But the emergence in the mid-1960s both of Soviet 'Détente' and of the German *Ostpolitik* began to foster a more favourable environment. The first moves were made by religious leaders. Early in 1965, the German Evangelical Church published an unsolicited *Memorandum . . . on the relations of the German people with their neighbours in the east*; and in May of that year a Protestant delegation from Germany, headed by Klaus von Bismarck, the Head of West German Radio, arrived in Warsaw for an exchange of views. To many people's surprise, a positive response was forthcoming from the Hierarchy of the Roman Catholic Church in Poland, whose 'Letter of the Polish Bishops' to their German counterparts dated 18 November 1965 contained a historic appeal to end the hereditary hostility of the two nations. A long rambling catalogue of past disasters, from the martyrdom of St. Adalbert to the sufferings of both Poles and Germans in the concentration camps of the Second World War, served to introduce their plea to the Germans 'to forgive and forget':

Most Reverend Brothers! We appeal to you. Let us try to forget. No more polemics. No more Cold War, but a dialogue . . . If true goodwill exists on both sides, and that cannot be doubted, then a serious dialogue must succeed, and in time must bear fruit, despite all the difficulties . . . From the tremendous moral and social dangers which threaten not only the soul of our people but also its biological existence, we can only be saved by the help and grace of our Redeemer. We ask His help, through the intercession of His Mother, the Most Blessed Virgin . . . We ask you, Catholic pastors of the German people to try in your own way to celebrate our Christian Millennium with us . . . We extend our hands to you, granting you forgiveness and asking for forgiveness . . . May the merciful Redeemer, and the Virgin Mary, Queen of Poland, Queen of the World and Mother of the Church, grant our request.[35]

At that point, in the middle of the conflict between Church and State over the celebration of the Millennium, Gomułka could not openly condone the Church's meddling in foreign policy, and Party propaganda crudely dismissed the idea of reconciliation. But the threat of a German–Soviet *rapprochement* from which Poland might be excluded was enough to overcome the Party's reluctance. In 1969, Gomułka himself launched a campaign for reaching agreement with Germany. Although there were several hiccups between the cup and its consumption — not least the one caused by Brezhnev's sudden conversion to a reconciliation policy of his own — the Treaty between the People's Republic of Poland and the Federal Republic of Germany was signed in Warsaw on 7 December

1970. It was an emotional moment. Chancellor Willi Brandt knelt in expiation before the Memorial to the Victims of Nazi Oppression. Poland's western frontier on the Odra and Lusatian Nysa was recognized by the only European power which might conceivably have entertained an interest in changing it. Henceforth, the People's Republic could go its way in the world freed from the terrible anxiety which had inhibited its freedom of action ever since the Second World War. In this way, Gomułka contrived to loosen the bonds of direct Soviet tutelage in the international, as well as in the internal, realm. This achievement of lasting importance amply compensated for the many failures of his later years.

* * * * *

To anyone who knew Poland at the end of the War, the face of the People's Republic must by now be barely recognizable. Changes, though not necessarily progress, have occurred in almost every walk of life.

For the interested observer, however, the persistence of official Censorship presents a fundamental barrier to understanding. In a country where Soviet-style controls have operated ever since the Liberation, all sources of public information must be treated as suspect. Of course, it would be idle to pretend that censorship in differing forms and in different degrees does not exist in every part of the world. But an important distinction has to be made. Whereas in most countries it is generally assumed that all information and expression of opinion is free and accessible except in those areas such as Defence or Obscenity where it is specifically proscribed, under the Soviet system of pre-emptive Censorship (*Cenzura prewencyjna*) the opposite assumption applies, where nothing is free and accessible except that which is specifically prescribed. Nothing is supposed to be known or published without the prior approval of the appropriate state authorities. In Poland, therefore, as in the Soviet Bloc as a whole, the state seeks not merely to manipulate information but actually to manufacture it, to process it, and to classify it from a position of monopolistic control. The state uses Censorship not only as an instrument of negative suppression but also and in particular as a means of active propagation. Although the self-defeating practice of falsifying government statistics appears to have been curtailed since 1956, and although the Polish censors now claim to exercise their powers in a relatively tolerant manner, it is a simple fact that the vast machinery of information control has never been dismantled. On the contrary, it is constantly expanding, and is constantly refining its techniques. From its headquarters in Warsaw, the Main Office for the Control of Press, Publications, and Public Spectacles (GUKPPiW) runs an elaborate network of local branches. Its officers, who are permanently employed on the premises of all major organizations and concerns, regulate the activities of all the media, all news and translation agencies, all publishing houses, all printing-shops, all concerts, theatres, cinemas, and exhibitions, and all other means of communication. Its approval, in the form of an authorized certificate, is required for the appearance not just of newspapers or television programmes but even of private items such as wedding invitations or funeral notices. Its instructions, which fill hundreds of pages every single week, divide information into separate categories, for foreign consumption, for mass consumption at home, for restricted circulation, for official discretion, and for suppression. Its explicit priorities concentrate on the unblemished reputation of the USSR and of the Polish Party leaders, and on sensitive subjects such as Foreign Policy, Religion and Ideology, and Military Affairs. Its targets for regular suppression start with criticism of the USSR or of the party-line of the day, all comparisons between the Soviet Union and Tsarist Russia, all civil disasters, all shortcomings in industrial safety, all defects in Polish export goods, all references to the superior economic and social standards of non-communist countries; . . . and they end, significantly enough, with all information regarding the existence of the Censorship. Here, if anywhere, is Orwell's vision of the 'Ministry of Truth'. Most seriously, the activities of the censors, although performed in the name of the State, are responsible to no one except to the Central Committee of the Party. So let all inquirers be warned. The accuracy of any information which derives from the organs of the People's Republic, including much of what follows, can never be taken for granted. Contemporary analysts of the communist world must possess a critical sense no less sharp than that of historians who delve into the mysteries of the Middle Ages.[36]

In three decades, the population has risen from 23.9 million in the first post-war census of 14 February 1946 to an estimated 35.1 million by 1979. The tremendous boost in the birth-rate, which stood at 29.1 per thousand in 1955 before falling to 16.6/00 by 1970, has caused marked 'bulges' and troughs in the demographic pattern. In 1971, people dependent on industrial employment accounted for 42 per cent of the population; those dependent on agriculture for 29.5 per cent; town-dwellers for 52.7 per cent; females for 54.2 per cent; children under 18 years for 32.2 per cent; and non-Poles for only 1.3 per cent. In contrast to earlier periods, the population of Poland is predominantly urban, and industrial; it is youthful, and is at last overwhelmingly Polish.[37]

Economic management has continued along lines laid down in the Stalinist period. Centralized state planning on the basis of Five Year Plans — 1956–60, 1961–5, 1966–70, 1971–5, 1976–80 — still governs every aspect of economic activity. Minor experiments in the 1970s in the realm of directorial responsibility and financial profitability did not involve any considerable move in the direction of a 'market economy' as practised in recent years in Hungary.[38]

Industry has developed very rapidly. The global index of industrial production (1950 = 100) rose to 200 at the end of the Six Year Plan, to 317 by 1960, to 475 by 1965, to 708 in 1970, and to 940 in 1974. Many branches of industry, such as chemicals, machine tools, electronics, and armaments, which hardly existed before the war, are now thriving. The importation of western machinery, and of western technology is increasing fast. At the same time, the endless list of negative deformations freely admitted by the Party, include 'deficient technological innovations', 'poor organization of labour', 'excessive consumption of raw materials', 'wastage of power', 'faulty co-ordination', 'inattention to quality', 'under-investment in the consumer sector', and 'poor social and work conditions'. Poland's Second Industrial Revolution has brought more comfort to the statisticians than to the ordinary consumer.[39]

Agriculture, once Poland's staple industry, has now become

the problem child of the economy. Decollectivization in 1956–7 decimated the number of collective farms, leaving 83 per cent of the arable land in the private ownership of small, ill-equipped, horse-drawn peasants. Except in the Recovered Territories where the PGRs survived in greater number, agricultural organization fell mainly to co-operative farmers' circles. Global production has improved some 70 per cent over the 1950 level. Electrification of the farms is almost complete, and, despite the Party's reluctance to construct small tractors suitable for peasant holdings, mechanization is spreading from the state to the private sector. But successive campaigns, under Gomułka for complete agricultural self-sufficiency, and under Gierek for increased deliveries, have met with successive failure. Demand outpaces supply, and food shortages, especially of meat, are still endemic.[40]

Poland's Foreign Trade is a state monopoly dominated by commerce with the socialist bloc. Although trade with the advanced industrial countries of the West rose sharply to 34.2 per cent of Export and 38 per cent of Imports in 1975 (projected figure), the Comecon countries accounted for two-thirds of Poland's foreign commercial turnover. The USSR, which supplies 42 per cent of Poland's raw materials – 80 per cent of her oil, 80 per cent of her iron ore, and 60 per cent of her cotton – and which receives over half of Poland's industrial exports, remains the largest single trading partner. Indeed, in trading terms, Poland must be rated a liability to the USSR. The imbalance of exchange has stood in Poland's favour ever since 1956. For this reason if for no other, the Soviet government has been able to insist on massive Polish investments in the Soviet economy. This investment has been effected by the introduction of (secret) preferential rates of exchange, by the transfer of ships constructed in Poland with the aid of advanced western technology, and, most recently, by the construction of the colossal Katowice Steelworks with its direct broad-gauge railway link direct to the Soviet frontier. Hence, in contrast to the pre-war period, when Polish exports were largely limited to food products and raw materials, the first place in Poland's exports is now taken by industrial products, especially by machines and semi-finished goods. Unfortunately, the technical quality of these products is not sufficient to attract many customers in the world at large. As a result, the over-all Trade Balance has been consistently negative:

	Import	Export	Balance
	(in millions of convertible złoties)		
1950	2,673	2,537	-137
1965	9,361	8,911	-450
1971	16,151	15,489	-662
1976	46,100	36,600	-9,500

What is more, any proper analysis of commercial statistics is permanently obstructed by the extraordinary demands of official secrecy. The financial principles governing calculations of the foreign account; the terms of foreign loans; and the details of foreign licence or barter contracts, are all carefully suppressed. The very existence of apparently innocuous items such as the purchase of foreign grain, the sale of meat to the USSR, the re-export of coffee, or the arms trade within Comecon, is denied. In 1976, the Censorship ruled that terms such as *Kurs* (variable rates of exchange), *obciążenia* (debit), *subwencja* (subsidy), and *dotacja* (allocation) should not be employed in textbooks dealing specifically with Polish Foreign Trade.[11]

The so-called 'specific conditions', often darkly hinted at in official apologias for the underperformance of the Polish economy, are mainly social and political in character. They refer to the historic, and apparently incurable alienation of most people from the state, and from the state-owned enterprises by which almost all of them are employed. Throughout the wars and partitions of modern times, Poles have been taught to pay authority as little respect as necessary, to slack and to cheat in their dealings with public concerns, and to reserve all their energies for the pursuit of their private welfare. They are instinctively 'agin" the system. As a result, bureaucratic controls proliferate, as management vainly opposes the ingrained habits of an endlessly ingenious workforce. Low productivity, shoddy standards, and gross inefficiency often appear for no sound technical or economic reason. In this regard, People's Poland is the heir to attitudes bred in the conditions of Tsarist Russia and multiplied by the strains of two successive German occupations.

Transport and communications have made rapid strides in certain well-defined sectors. The Polish State Airline (LOT), flying Soviet Ilyshin and Tupolev machines, covers routes totalling 49,000 kilometres, and links all the major cities and most European capitals. The merchant navy has swelled from 506,000 DWT in 1950 to 23 million in 1973, and includes an important world-wide tramp trade. The Polish State Railways (PKP) report improvements in electrification and rolling-stock. The Polish State Bus Line (PKS), provides regular services to all towns and villages. In the cities, municipal tramcars, trolleybuses, and buses offer standards of regularity if not of comfort, which are fast disappearing in Western Europe. The production of the 'Polski Fiat' under Italian licence has boosted private car ownership to 690,700 by 1973. Even so, for many Polish families, the horse-drawn cart is no less familiar than the motor-car or the aeroplane. The pre-war German steam-engine is as common as the diesel locomotive. The rolling country-road, with its carts, cobbles, drunks, and stray geese, stretches much further than the two or three lengths of bumpy motorway.

Tourism in Poland manifests all the typical weaknesses of state enterprise. Native holidaymakers are strictly segregated from foreign tourists. The former are housed in cheap, austere, communal centres administered by trade unions and places of employment. The latter are hosted by ORBIS, the State Tourist Agency, or by Youth Travel services such as ALMATUR or JUVENTUR, and are required to pay in hard currency for scarce, expensive accommodation in a small number of oversize, pretentious establishments. Private guest-houses are officially discouraged, and provisions for self-planned, family, or individual holidays hardly exist.

New social structures are rapidly emerging from the war-time levelling. Claims that Poland has a classless society are belied by the most obvious evidence. The new 'Red bour-geoisie', the 'New Class' — with their private villas, fast cars, silk suits, fashionable wives, pampered children, and foreign holidays — enjoy incomes and social benefits far beyond the reach of the working man. Their ranks are drawn from the higher levels of State, Party, and industrial management, and from the growing circle of thriving private professionals such as medical doctors or *badylarze* (market gardeners). Among this privileged élite, the prevalence of high cash incomes and low direct taxes has combined with the shortage of good quality consumer goods to encourage an extreme cult of consumerism which can only be described as 'bourgeois fetishism'. The industrial work-force has its own aristocracy, in which high-earning shipbuilders, steelworkers, and coal-miners hold a commanding position. At the bottom of the scale, in contrast, the peasants were treated for thirty years as the enemies of society, feeding the nation and paying their taxes, but not enjoying the full benefits of the Welfare State. In between the peasantry and the proletariat, a prosperous hybrid group of *chłopo-robotnicy* (peasant-workers) contrives both to own land and to earn industrial wages as well.[42]

In thirty years of constant demographic movement, over ten million people have flocked into the towns from the countryside. For the first time in 1970, the town-dwellers outnumbered the countryfolk, and by 1977 had reached 57.4 per cent of the whole. The five major cities — Warsaw (1,532,100 — population in 1977), Łódź (818,400), Kraków (712,000), Wrocław (592,500), Poznań (534,400) — and the conurbated towns of the Katowice region (3,862,000), continue to grow despite a strict system of urban planning and residence permits.[43]

Housing conditions reflect the stresses of accelerated urbanization. Well over three million housing units have been built since the War, and, notwithstanding the increase in population and the influx into the towns, have actually reduced overcrowding from 4.73 persons per unit in 1946 to 4.37 in 1970. Approximately half of the houses under construction are owned by municipal co-operatives. The rest are divided between those built directly by state concerns and those built by private owners. Building standards are extremely primitive, however. Cement, plaster, and bricks are of the poorest quality, and workmanship is notoriously shoddy. Less than one home in three possesses a bathroom, an inside lavatory, or central heating. In the countryside, less than one in twelve possesses such refinements.

Personal incomes reveal wide variations and large diffe-rentials. In so far as tax payments, pension contributions, social insurance premiums, and so forth are deducted at source, wages and salaries cannot be directly compared with their counterparts in Western countries. But by any reckoning they are extremely low. The purchasing power of the average monthly wage of 3,500 zł. (1976), which is equivalent in exchange terms to about 35 dollars US or £18 sterling, must be measured against average prices for 1 kg of bread (8 zł.), 1 kg of ham (120 zł.), for a pair of shoes (300 zł.), a gent's suit (2,000 zł.), or for a Polski Fiat 125p 1500 (225,000 zł.). Almost all families count on a second wage from the working wife, and many have to supplement their budget from un-official spare-time jobs.[44]

Unemployment is unknown. Work is both a right and a duty. The able-bodied can demand employment. The idle can be prosecuted for social parasitism. If this system avoids the scandalous insecurities and indignities of the world of free enterprise, it also encourages all forms of indiscipline in the labour force. What is more, it conceals huge areas of under-employment. The Polish employee who has little or no work to do, and who only attends in order to collect his pay packet at the end of the week, has little more real satisfaction than the members of the British and American dole queues.[45]

Trade unions in the Western sense do not exist. The Central Council of Trade Unions (CRZZ), which absorbed all the previous independent organizations in 1949, is entirely controlled by the Party and at the shop level is organized on the basis of the state enterprises by whom all its members are employed. The local branches act as a transmission belt for the official rules and conditions of work, and as an agency for enforcing productivity norms. There is no machinery for wage-bargaining. Polish workers are at the mercy of the un-seen state planners who fix both wages and prices. The non-convertibility of the currency in which they are paid puts them in the same position as that of the wage-slaves of the old capitalist truck system, which paid its labour-force in tokens from the company store. Comparative statistics about wage levels and differentials, together with adverse informa-tion about health and safety at work, are carefully withheld from the mass media. A scheme for workers' self-management, launched in 1957, has never been able to achieve its original aims. The independent role of Workers' Councils was soon muffled by their absorption into Party-controlled Committees of Self-Management (KSR).[46]

In theory, the benefits of the Welfare State are free and universal. In fact, they are subject to many limitations, and are spread thinner than in Great Britain, for example. Medical prescriptions, schoolbooks, and student hostels are just three areas where extra fees are normally charged. The National Health Service was not available to the self-employed peasantry until 1972.

Overall, the standard of living can only be described as austere. Official propaganda, which constantly harps on the advances made in relation to pre-war conditions, overlooks the fact that similar or in some cases much greater progress has been made in all European countries irrespective of the political complexion of the regime. (In this connection, it is interesting to note that at the time of the American Bicentennial in 1976 the Polish Censorship issued specific instructions to suppress all adverse comparisons between the rise in the standard of living over the last thirty years of Poles in the USA and that achieved by their relatives in Poland.) In the scale of economic priorities, consumer goods and services have always taken second place to heavy industry. Not surprisingly, therefore, there is still too much inconvertible money chasing too few goods. Unable to invest easily in private homes, in motor-cars, or in durables, the Polish consumer overspends on items of immediate consumption, especially on food and drink, thus making existing shortages more acute. Inevitably, the precious quality of life is adversely affected. Alcoholism, bad drains, long queues, peeling plaster, overcrowded homes and buses, polluted air, heavy falls of soot and chemical dust, unmade pavements, sub-standard service, endless delays and arguments with petty officials, all have to be accepted as part of everyday life. Labour alone remains cheap and readily available. All manner of personal services from nannies, domestic servants, and taxis to hairdressers, tailors, and prostitutes, are cheaper than in the Western world.[47]

The huge military establishment, whose expenditures are never disclosed but which can reliably be estimated to run at levels between two and three times above the corresponding budgets of Western Europe, provides a fundamental cause of low living standards. The Polish armed forces were designed on the Soviet model, and from 1949 to 1956 were directly subordinated to Soviet command. Since 1955, they have contributed an integral element of the Warsaw Pact. (See Diagram H.) They are divided into four services — Air Force, Air Defence, Navy, and Army — and their land forces are divided into two separate groups, one designated to home defence, the other to a strategic operational reserve. They contain a strong Frontier Defence Force (WOP) and an élite Internal Security Corps (WSW). According to the law of 21 November 1967, they are subject in the first instance to the Defence Committee of the Council of Ministers, and in times of emergency can call on the universal conscription of men between 18 and 50, and of women between 18 and 40. In peacetime, they rely partly on the professional cadres and partly on compulsory, two-year national service. Their nominal establishment (1977) stands at 15 army divisions, including one air-borne and one amphibious assault division = 3,800 tanks and 4,200 other armoured vehicles: 4 surface-to-surface missile brigades; an air-force of 55 squadrons with 745 combat aircraft, largely assigned to the interceptor role: a small navy of 25 warships, largely missile-carrying FPB and MTBs; and a total of 404,000 men plus 605,000 reservists. As demonstrated in the gigantic parade mounted in Warsaw for the Thirtieth Anniversary of the People's Republic on 22 July 1974, their equipment contains a formidable arsenal of Soviet-made guns, tanks, rockets, and missiles. Their spirit is intensely patriotic, their training is rigorous, and, with over 70 per cent of the officer corps possessing higher degrees, their technical proficiency considerable. Even so, their real capacity remains an unknown quantity. The minor Civil War of 1945–7 and the inglorious invasion of Czechoslovakia in 1968 constitute their only active engagements in thirty years. In October 1956, there were clear signs that the Polish Army would have resisted Soviet intervention. In 1968 and again in 1970, there were hints that it would not give unconditional support to political adventures emanating from the civil Militia or from the Party factions. There have been many rumours that the General Staff makes strenuous efforts to keep control of the army's political departments in its own hands. In the circumstances, the political influence of the armed forces is largely hidden from view. Their ability to act independently, against the will of the Party leadership or against the common policy of the Warsaw Pact, can only be imagined.[48]

The educational system receives high priority; and quantitative statistics are impressive. The over-all percentages of children, students, and adults attending courses of learning is higher than in Western countries. On the other hand, material conditions are often rudimentary: and teaching methods are authoritarian. Progressive education in the Western sense is unknown. Pupils are trained rather than educated, and are frequently alienated by the exhortatory tone of their teachers, by compulsory Russian lessons, and by excessive doses of political propaganda. There are now some 88 institutions of higher learning compared with 32 in 1937/8.[49]

Cultural life is closely controlled. Great advances have been made in the provision of facilities for mass culture — in libraries, theatres, concert halls, cinemas, newspapers, radio, and television; and state support has made the career of the approved artist much more secure than previously. Yet political conformity remains the touchstone of success. Although the obligatory 'Socialist Realism' of the Stalinist era has been abandoned, a representative of the official censor has a permanent office in every cultural institution. Few of the vital political or social issues of the day can be candidly discussed; many of the leading talents, such as Sławomir Mrożek (b. 1930), the dramatist, or Roman Polański (b. 1933), and Andrzej Wajda (b. 1926) the film-directors, have preferred to work abroad for long periods. As Mrożek has shown in his play *Emigranci* (The Emigrants), which consists of an unbroken conversation between a nameless intellectual and a nameless worker, Intellectual Freedom has itself become one of the burning cultural issues:

AA: It's an astonishing thing, but a man who is otherwise quite sensible, like me, does not want to see the most obvious truth when it hurts his pride. At first I jumped around like a monkey in a cage.

I swung on my tail, leaping with great speed from the bar to the
wall, or from the wall to the bar: or when given a nut, I tried to
crawl into the shell, to feel myself lord of limitless spaces. It was
a very long time before I really escaped from my illusions and
convinced myself that I really was a monkey in a cage.

XX: Monkeys are funny, I've seen them at the zoo.

AA: You're right. Monkeys in a cage can be funny. That's why, when I
finally decided that I was a monkey, I began to laugh at myself,
and I kept on laughing until the tears ran down my mush. Then I
realized that my clowning was not so hilarious, although it amused
my audience and my keepers enough for them to throw me extra
nuts and sweets. But the sweets made me sick, and I could no
longer climb into the shells. It was then that I understood how
for a monkey there was no other way but to admit that he was a
monkey . . .

XX: Of course, of course.

AA: And also, from his monkeyish, slave-like condition, to draw if not
pride then at least widsom and strength . . . For in me, in this
humiliated, imprisoned monkey, in my brutish predicament, the
entire knowledge of humanity was enshrined, fundamental knowledge, that is knowledge unspoiled by the accidents of progress or
the hazards of freedom. For this reason, I, an imprisoned monkey,
determined to write a book on Man.

XX: But monkeys can't write books.

AA: I agree, especially in a cage. But that point was only proved later
on. For the time being, I was crazed by the prospect of writing
my life's work about Man in his pure state, about Man the slave,
about myself, the first such work that the world has seen . . . As I
told myself: 'We may have nothing, but we have slavery.' That's
our treasure. What do other people know about such a theme? . . .
The entire literature of slavery is either phoney, or irrelevant; it's
written either by missionaries, or by liberators, or else by slaves
longing for Freedom, that is to say by people who have ceased to
be complete slaves. What do they know about integral slavery,
turned in on itself, self-perpetuating with no thought of being
transcended? What do they know of the joys and sorrows of a
slave, of the mysteries of slavery, of its beliefs and customs, of its
philosophy and cosmogonia, of its mathematics. They know
nothing, and I know it all. That's why I decided to write about it.

XX: And did you write it?

AA: No.

XX: Why not?

AA: I was scared. (*Pause*) . . .[50]

Despite the controls, a great deal of literature of every genre is written, published, reviewed, and openly discussed. War stories, tales of the (German) Occupation, and patriotic history are among the many themes which enjoy the encouragement of the Party; but it is not entirely profitable to divide the Polish literary scene into the official and unofficial sectors. Unlike their counterparts elsewhere in the Soviet Bloc, Polish writers have often succeeded in blurring the distinction between approved and unapproved literature; and it would be quite incorrect to suggest that the Polish Union of Writers (ZZLP) is filled exclusively with time-serving hacks or that eccentric views can only find expression in the dissident underworld. In Poland, even the Party has to accept that intelligence and slavish conformism are not compatible. Many of the most prominent and favoured figures, such as Jarosław Iwaszkiewicz (1894–1980) or Maria Dąbrowska (1889–1965) made their names before the War, whilst others — such as the Skamandrist Antoni Słonimski (1895–1976), the Catholic essayist Paweł Jasienica (1909–75), or the journalist Stefan Kisielewski (b. 1911), have contrived to steer an independent course in spite of intermittent harassment. In prose, the work of Jerzy Putrament (b. 1909), of Jerzy Andrzejewski (b. 1910), author of the novel *Popiół i diament* (Ashes and Diamonds, 1947) describing the trauma of the post-war generation, or of Tadeusz Breza (1905–70), author of *Spiżowa brama* (The Bronze Gate, 1960), describing the corridors of power in the Vatican in somewhat cynical tones, have all achieved widespread acclaim. Among the poets, representatives of the pre-war schools, such as Leopold Staff (1878–1957), Julian Tuwim (1894–1953), or the communist bard, Władysław Broniewski (1897–1962), have mingled with a cacophony of new voices including Konstanty Ildefons Gałczyński (1905–53), Julian Przyboś (1901–70), and Zbigniew Herbert (b. 1925). Polish drama was held in chains until 1956, since when it has been characterized by a vigorous revival both of the national classics and of the experimental theatre, where the names of Mrożek, of Tadeusz Różewicz (b. 1921), and of the director, Jerzy Grotowski (b. 1933), have attracted international attention. As always, Polish literature continues to be influenced by writers living abroad,

notably by the dramatist Witold Gombrowicz (1904–69),
who lived in Argentina, and by the poet and critic, Czesław
Miłosz living in California. Poland boasts a long list of literary journals headed by *Twórczość* (Creativity), *Kultura*
(Culture), and *Życie literackie* (Literary Life). The mass media
are monopolized by the State-owned and Party-controlled
radio, television, and publishing houses; but, in addition to
the more predictable categories, surprisingly wide circulation
is granted to avant-garde poetry, to belles-lettres, and above
all to foreign literature in translation. The Warsaw Centre of
the 'International PEN Club', first founded by Żeromski in
1924, contrives to operate actively, and provides an independent link with the literary profession abroad. In short, in
spite of many obstacles, Polish literary culture is thriving, and
provides clear proof of the essential 'positivism' of the authorities.[51] The trouble is, the cultural values which the Party
wishes to propagate are not shared by the people as a whole,
least of all by the cultural élite. Time and again, talented
writers who at first received official support, fall foul of their
Party sponsors only to end up in the ranks of the disaffected
and disillusioned. The tension is chronic. This is not caused,
as some would say, by the competition of rival philosophies
(to which the Poles are well accustomed); it is a matter of
style and sensitivity, of good taste, and of tone. To most
educated Poles, whom bitter experience has made infinitely
sceptical, the Party's eternal preaching, its incurable optimism,
its ineffable certainties, its busy manipulations, its habitual
patronising and, above all, its ceaseless self-congratulations,
are deeply offensive. In the eyes of the average *inteligent* of
Warsaw or Cracow, a cultural programme which tolerates
from a position of intolerance, and which ignores the essential
arts of irony, of criticism, of ambiguity, or of gentle self-
denigration, is no cultural programme at all. It recalls the
antics of 'barbarians in the Forum'. As Zbigniew Herbert has
written, with a pen which is steadily gaining worldwide
recognition, the lowest circle of Hell is not filled with fire
and brimstone, or with physical tortures:

The lowest circle of Hell. Contrary to prevailing opinion, it is inhabited
neither by despots nor matricides, nor even by those who solicit the

bodies of others. It is the refuge of artists, full of mirrors, musical instruments, and pictures. At first glance, it is the most luxurious of the infernal departments . . .

Throughout the year competitions, festivals, and concerts are held here. There is no climax to the season. The climax is permanent and almost absolute. Every few months new trends come into being; and nothing, it appears, is capable of stopping the triumphal march of the avant-garde.

Beelzebub loves art. He boasts that his choruses, his poets, and his painters are nearly superior to those of Heaven. He who has better art, has better government — that's clear. Soon they will be able to measure their strength against one another at the Festival of the Two Worlds. And then we will see what remains of Dante, of Fra Angelico, and of Bach.

Beelzebub supports the arts. He provides his artists with calm, good board, and with complete insulation against any real experience of the hellish life.[51]

The Fine Arts and Music traditionally attract the nation's brightest talents. Official preference for traditional and non-abstract forms has not been pushed to extremes. Monumental sculpture, drama, graphics, and instrumental music have reached standards of international excellence. Individuals such as Nikifor (died 1970), the primitivist painter, or the composers Witold Lutosławski (born 1913) and Krzysztof Penderecki (born 1933), enjoy worldwide reputations.[52]

Science and technology, which is taken to include all the 'humanistic' or social sciences, is controlled by the Polish Academy of Sciences (PAN). Experimental and theoretical institutes have been created for almost every conceivable branch of science, and Polish specialists participate in a full range of international ventures.

As in all communist countries, sport has been raised into a major state industry, from which the authorities hope to win popularity and prestige. Special emphasis is placed on physical fitness and hence on gymnastics, athletics, and team sports. Stadiums, coaching, and, more recently, the production of modern sports equipment all receive generous support. The defeat of England in the European Cup in 1973, and a series of creditable performances in the Olympic Games, have provoked scenes of mass rejoicing.

Political life is controlled by the ruling Party to an extent which few western observers comprehend. Indeed, the usual label of a 'One Party State' is inadequate to describe how the regime actually works. In a dual system where all organs of the state government are supervised by corresponding organs of the Party apparatus, the State must certainly be seen as the junior partner, if not just the administrative branch, of the Party. (See Diagram G.) What is more, indirect Party control by supervision from above is supplemented by direct control from within, through disciplined cells of Party activists operating in every government ministry and enterprise. Most importantly, the all-pervasive system of the *nomenklatura* or 'official nomination list' ensures that every single appointment, whether in Party, State, Armed Forces, or in social organizations such as Trade Unions or Co-operatives can only be filled on the prior recommendation of the Party. All office-holders are thus Party nominees; all elected officials and parliamentary deputies owe their position not to their election but to their nomination by the Party as candidates: all so-called 'non-party' figures are subject to Party approval. Not surprisingly, some analysts have dismissed the entire concept of 'the socialist state' as an official fiction.

Local government is firmly controlled by higher authorities. As with the central institutions of the Republic, democratic procedures at the local level are designed to perpetuate the dictatorship of the Party. There are three main administrative divisions — the *województwa* (voivodships or departments), the *powiaty* (districts), and since 1973, the *gminy* (communes). In the post-war period, the centrifugal tendencies of the individual departments began to grow alarmingly — so much so that Gierek's Silesia, for example, was dubbed the 'Polish Katanga'. These tendencies have been checked by important administrative reforms — in 1973 by the replacement of the former *gromada* (village) and *osiedla* (settlement) by the larger communes, and in 1975 by increasing the total number of departments from 17 to 49.[53] (See Map 23.)

The Constitution of 1952 has survived largely intact. The creation in 1957 of the Supreme Chamber of Control (NIK) has enabled the Sejm to exercise closer control over the organs of central and local government; but the Sejm in its turn is directly controlled by the Party and by the Party's Front of National Unity (FJN). After the slight increase of Party-sponsored 'non-Party members' in 1957, representational patterns in the Sejm have been fixed for twenty years:

Term	Front of National Unity			Non-Party members	Total
	PZPR	ZSL	SD		
I. 26 Oct '52	273	90	25	37	425
II. 20 Jan '57	239	118	39	63	459
III. 16 Apr '61	256	117	39	48	460
IV. 31 May '65	255	117	39	49	460
V. 1 Jun '69	255	117	39	49	460
VI. 15 Feb '72	255	117	39	49	460
VII. 21 Mar '79	261	113	37	49	460

Amendments to the Constitution which were voted in January 1976 aroused widespread misgivings, not so much because they changed existing practices, but because they gave the role of the Party and the Soviet Union binding and permanent legal force. By declaring the Party to be 'the Guardian of the State', nothing of substance was changed in the way that Poland had been ruled since 1948; and by raising the 'alliance with the USSR' from the realm of foreign policy to that of state law, nothing new was introduced into the external parameters of the Republic's condition as laid down in 1945. But the amendments ensure that any future attempt to release the stranglehold of the Party and the Soviet Union over Polish political life can immediately be denounced as unconstitutional. They are gestures of a purely political character and reveal the absence of true independence. They recall the baleful resolutions of the Dumb Sejm of 1717 which effectively terminated the independence of Poland—Lithuania.[54]

The Roman Catholic Church remains the sole bastion of independent thought and action. Following the unilateral renunciation of the pre-war Concordat by the TRJN in September 1945, the Polish See was cast for a long time into

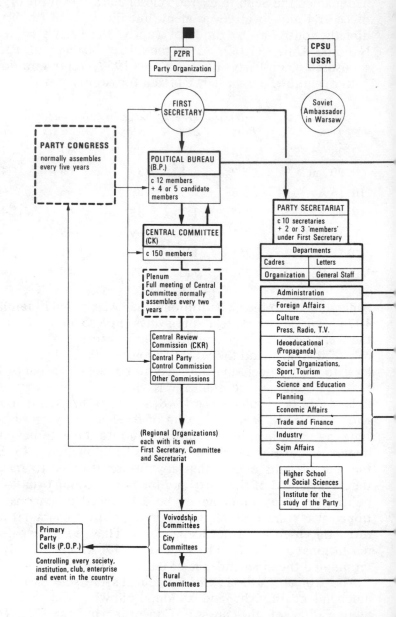

Diagram G.   Party and State Organs o

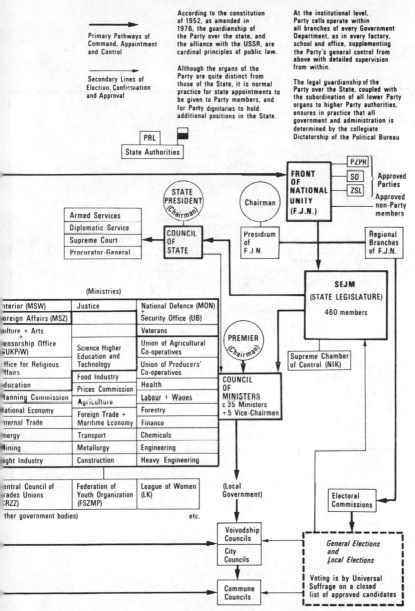

Primary Pathways of
Command, Appointment
and Control

Secondary Lines of
Election, Confirmation
and Approval

According to the constitution
of 1952, as amended in
1976, the guardianship of
the Party over the state, and
the alliance with the USSR, are
cardinal principles of public law.

Although the organs of the
Party are quite distinct from
those of the State, it is normal
practice for state appointments to
be given to Party members, and
for Party dignitaries to hold
additional positions in the State.

At the institutional level,
Party cells operate within
all branches of every Government
Department, as in every factory,
school and office, supplementing
the Party's general control from
above with detailed supervision
from within.

The legal guardianship of the
Party over the State, coupled with
the subordination of all lower Party
organs to higher Party authorities,
ensures in practice that all
government and administration is
determined by the collegiate
Dictatorship of the Political Bureau

PRL
State Authorities

FRONT
OF
NATIONAL
UNITY
(F.J.N.)

PZPR
SD — Approved Parties
ZSL

Approved
non-Party
members

STATE
PRESIDENT
(Chairman)

Chairman

Armed Services
Diplomatic Service
Supreme Court
Procurator-General

COUNCIL
OF
STATE

Presidium
of
F.J.N

Regional
Branches
of F.J.N.

SEJM
(STATE LEGISLATURE)
460 members

(Ministries)

Interior (MSW)	Justice	National Defence (MON) + Security Office (UB)
Foreign Affairs (MSZ)		Veterans
Culture + Arts + Censorship Office (GUKPiW)	Science Higher Education and Technology	Union of Agricultural Co-operatives
Office for Religious Affairs		Union of Producers' Co-operatives
Education	Food Industry	Health
Planning Commission	Prices Commission	Labour + Wages
National Economy	Agriculture	Forestry
Internal Trade	Foreign Trade + Maritime Economy	Finance
Energy	Transport	Chemicals
Mining	Metallurgy	Engineering
Light Industry	Construction	Heavy Engineering

PREMIER
(Chairman)

COUNCIL
OF
MINISTERS
c 35 Ministers
+5 Vice-Chairmen

Supreme Chamber
of Control (NIK)

| Central Council of Trades Unions (CRZZ) | Federation of Youth Organization (FSZMP) | League of Women (LK) |
| (other government bodies) | | etc. |

(Local
Government)

Electoral
Commissions

Voivodship
Councils
City
Councils

Commune
Councils

General Elections
and
Local Elections

Voting is by Universal
Suffrage on a closed
list of approved candidates

People's Republic (1979)

Map 23.　　The Polish People's Republic (1975)

legal limbo. Agreements guaranteeing freedom of worship in return for expressions of loyalty to the state were signed with governmental representatives in March 1950 and December 1956. But the Vatican's full co-operation with the People's Republic had to await the Polish—German Treaty of 1970 and the consequent apostolic constitution of 28 June 1972, 'Episcoporum Poloniae', which finally confirmed the diocesan divisions of the Western Territories. In the course of these uncertain decades, the Church was obliged to shed many of its former privileges — in 1946, its right to register legal marriages; in 1950, its landed property; and in 1961, its remaining schools. Since 1952 it has admitted the right of the state to express reservations in the matter of ecclesiastical appointments. At the same time, thanks to the legatine powers of the Primate, it has been able to centralize its jurisdiction over all Catholic organizations in Poland, including all the religious orders and the remnants of the Uniate congregations. All in all, the Church has thrived on its ordeal. An establishment which in 1972 counted 2 Cardinals, 45 seminaries, 73 bishops, 13,392 churches, 18,267 priests, 35,341 monks and nuns, and over 20 million weekly communicants, could not claim to be living out a persecuted existence among the catacombs. The Catholic University of Lublin (KUL), with over two thousand students, remains a unique institution in the communist world. Polish priests travel abroad, not only to *émigré* parishes in Europe and America but also to missionary stations in Africa and Asia.[55]

Yet the present truce between Church and State lies uneasily on both contestants. The Church resents the calculated obstructiveness of state officials in matters of education, publishing, religious processions, and church-building. The Party fears and envies the prestige and popularity of the clergy. Their rivalry, as exemplified in the divergent celebrations of the Millennium in 1966, or in the long dispute over reconciliation with Germany is the result of an irreconcilable conflict of purpose. In the latter case, the Hierarchy's Open Letter to the German bishops was taken as a direct challenge to the Party's self-instituted monopoly in political affairs. The appeal for German support against the 'social and moral dangers' besetting the Polish nation were denounced as treasonable

and inflammatory. Party slogans of 'NIE ZAPOMNIMY, NIE
WYBACZYMY' (We shall not forgive and we shall not forget)
raised emotions to a new pitch. An acrimonious exchange of
notes between the Secretary of the Episcopate and the President of the Council of Ministers led at first to the withdrawal
of the Cardinal-Primate's passport and then to the cancella-
tion of the intended visit of Pope Paul VI. It eventually led to
the realization that confrontation benefited nobody. In prevailing circumstances, the political stance of the Church must
be nicely ambivalent. On the one hand, the bishops have no
wish to encourage a direct conflict with the State. Knowing
that the logical consequence of any attempt to overthrow the
communist regime would be the immediate intervention of
the Soviet Army, they realize the dangers of popular support.
So long as their present privileges are not attacked, they will
continue to function in place of the People's Republic's only
'Loyal Opposition'. In moments of crisis, the Church will be
asked to exercise its restraining hand over political discontent.
On the other hand, the Hierarchy has learned that toughness
does pay dividends. The present position of the Church owes
much to Cardinal Wyszyński's absolute refusal to compromise
over fundamentals. Hard experience has shown that the Party
does not concede anything of substance voluntarily. Occasional gestures such as the award in 1971 of the Church's
legal titles to its property in the Western Territories, received
wide publicity in the state-controlled press, whilst the permanent deadlock on issues of more importance is studiously
avoided. The Party's continuing patronage of the schismatic
Polish National Catholic Church, and of the PAX organization,
stands as a permanent affront. Meanwhile, Cardinal Wyszyński's fearless sermons, periodically relayed from every
pulpit in the country, act as a powerful stimulant for all who
long for a non-official view of their predicament. Pronouncements to the effect that 'Polish citizens are slaves in their
own country', that 'our country did not emerge victorious
from the mass murders of the Second World War', or that 'we
shall continue to bear witness to our presence as the Antemurale of Christianity' were not designed to appease the
Party line. They occasionally worry the milder spirits on the
episcopal bench, and can sometimes disturb the Roman Curia

as much as the Central Committee. But they find their mark. They are the touchstone of a powerful and respected voice in a political wilderness where toadyism to the powers-that-be generally passes for good form.

The Roman Catholic Church in Poland has been blessed with leaders of outstanding personality. Of the two Cardinals, Stefan Wyszyński (b. 1901) is the war-horse, the doughty champion of his cause, a man of simple patriotism, of radiant piety, and of total integrity. Cardinal Karol Wojtyła (b. 1920), Metropolitan-Archbishop of Cracow since 1967, complements the Primate's virtues. Actor, poet, sportsman, philosopher, and university chaplain, he is a figure of scintillating talents and of profound spirituality. For a time, he was courted by the Party as a more malleable candidate for succession to the Primacy, but has recently given proof of his mettle by protecting dissident intellectuals. He played a prominent role in the work of the Second Vatican Council, and has strong contacts abroad, not only in Rome but also in Germany and in the USA.

At the time of the Polish October in 1956, an important experiment to heal the rift between Church and State was undertaken by an independent group of Catholic laymen based in Cracow. Through their journals *Znak* (The Sign) and *Tygodnik Powszechny* (Universal Weekly), they advanced the proposition that a distinction was to be made between the State and the Party, and that faithful Catholics could establish a working relationship with the one without admitting the atheistic ideology of the other. On this basis, their representatives were sponsored by the Front of National Unity and were elected to the Sejm. For twenty years they pursued their delicate task, denigrated by militant Catholics and communists alike, but speaking out in the name of moderation and pragmatism. In 1976, however, their one remaining deputy, Stanisław Stomma, recorded a solitary vote of protest against the constitutional amendments, and by so doing brought the experiment to an end. In the aftermath, the Party has attacked the *Znak* Group in classic fashion, by discrediting its leaders and by forming a new pressure group of the same name.

A score of other religious denominations function legally in

Poland. The Polish Autocephalous Orthodox Church, which was forced in 1948 to transfer its allegiance from the Patriarch of Constantinople to the Patriarch of Moscow, claims a membership of close to half a million. The Polish Evangelical Church of the Augsburg Confession has over 100,000 members, mainly in Cieszyn. More surprisingly, perhaps, a number of fringe sects such as the Seventh Day Adventists, the Christian Scientists, and the Mariavites, continue to attract adherents. Various attempts have been made to unite these non-Catholic Christian bodies under the aegis of a State-controlled Œcumenical Council. Pre-war Jewish, Karaite, and Muslim Leagues still exist, but have virtually no membership. In this light, the only denomination which might fairly claim to suffer from discrimination, if not from active persecution, is that of the Uniates, whose congregations were dispersed throughout the Western Territories by the resettlement of Ukrainians in 1945–7. Neglected by the Roman Catholic hierarchy and criticized by the Soviet Embassy, the one remaining Uniate See in Poland, at Przemyśl, has been left vacant since 1946. All religious bodies are subject to the Office for Denominational Affairs (USW), whose Director has ministerial rank.

The Party's losing battle with the Church has been attended by the gradual dilution of its own prestige, ideology, and morale. On the surface, of course, all is sunshine and progress. Each political crisis is followed by colossal Party rallies where tens of thousands of cheer-leaders roar their approval whilst the Party bosses denounce the 'wreckers' and the 'hooligans' who have dared to disturb the peace. They deceive no one. In reality, the Party has been gradually losing such public confidence as it possessed. Repeated economic catastrophes fuel deep-seated public mistrust. The rising membership of the PZPR, which passed the 2 million mark (or 6.5 per cent of the population) in 1970, cannot hide the fact that the Party is the resort of the most self-seeking elements of society, who see it as their passport to a successful career, to a high salary, to promotion, to privileged social benefits, and in some cases to licentious conduct, but only rarely as an opportunity for dedicated service to the community. The mercenary foundations of Party loyalty are evinced by the lavish salary supplements of Party members, by the closed clubs and shops, and by the privileged access to information, housing, health care, holidays, and education. Periodic purges of the deadwood, which occur after each change of leadership, cannot stop the rot. Recruitment from the working class has been falling ever since 1948. New members, and the upper ranks of the hierarchy, are drawn overwhelmingly from the professional, technical, and managerial classes. In this self-perpetuating bureaucracy, any pretence that the PZPR forms the 'vanguard of the workers and peasants' has long since lost all meaning. Marxism—Leninism is equally in decline. The dismissal of the country's leading Marxists in 1968 left a gap that cannot be filled. The Party spokesmen continue to mouth the empty phrases of the discarded ideology, without making any serious effort to follow its precepts. For all these reasons, the ordinary people in whose name the abuses are committed, are steadily losing patience. The gulf between Party and people, between the ruling élite and the long-suffering citizen, widens every day. When the time of reckoning comes, it may be very painful indeed.

Crime in a police state can only flourish under the patronage of the state police. In a country where state-owned property enjoys little respect, petty offences abound and are dealt with in a summary fashion; but organized crime cannot operate on the same basis as in the West. The only serious rings and rackets that exist – in the black market, in prostitution, and in drugs – are controlled by the Militia and by the other security organs. In the communist system, the idea of an impartial law enforcement agency, or of an independent judiciary, is not accepted, and the perpetrators of the worst scandals can only be brought to book by their peers in the state-and-party élite to which they themselves belong. It may be true that the streets of Polish cities, like their counterparts elsewhere in Eastern Europe, are free of many of the violences and nuisances which prevail in western cities; but the orderliness is deceptive. As a result both of their contempt for the common man, and their disregard for the law which they are supposed to uphold, the Militia are widely regarded as the true enemies of society, and official talk of 'socialist morality' rings very hollow indeed.

Indeed, the real fear amongst many thinking Poles today is the fear of 'Sovietization'. By this, they understand the onset of a social climate where the dull mass of a cowed populace is incapable of independent thought or co-ordinated action, and where the authorities can conduct themselves with impunity. Material prosperity of the sort achieved in neighbouring East Germany or Czechoslovakia, and the mindless consumerism of the conformist élite, act as powerful motors towards this end. In consequence, in the eyes of some observers, anything which militates against the reigning apathy must be welcomed. The only positive aspect of the continuing economic crisis in Poland is that it acts as a brake on the less edifying social trends of recent years.

Post-war Warsaw had to start again from scratch. The bricks that one sees today in the city's historic landmarks are not the ones that stood there throughout history. The landmarks — from the Old Town Square and St. John's Cathedral in the north to Łazienki and Wilanów in the south — are, for the most part, modern replicas. Few of the people one meets in the street, even those in middle age, were resident here before the War. Everything has had to be reconstructed afresh, and in the course of the reconstruction many important details have been changed in accordance with political considerations. The casual visitor cannot be aware of the careful way in which monuments of the past are given prominence, or are consigned to oblivion, in conformity with political criteria. There are still spots — beside the Zygmunt Column, for example, or before the Sobieski statue in Łazienki Park — where one can sense the spirits of the past. Yet all is not as it seems. Few people nowadays would know that the highly symbolic statue to Feliks Dzierżyński on the former Bank Square stands on the site of several equally symbolic predecessors. On that very spot, from 1841 to 1898 stood a monument raised by Tsar Nicholas I 'To the Poles who perished for loyalty to their Sovereign'. Few people know that the nearby shrine of the Unknown Soldier shelters the remains of one of the teenage defenders of Lwów in 1919. Few have time to compare the numerous but selective public memorials to the victims of Nazi oppression with the more telling contents of the city's cemeteries. Few of the younger generation, whilst retailing the endless jokes about the intrusive proportions of the Palace of Arts and Sciences, would realize that their grandfathers harboured exactly the same sort of feelings about the equally pretentious Russian Orthodox Cathedral of St. Alexander Nevsky before it was demolished in 1923. *Plus ça change.*

The People's Republic participates in a wide range of international organizations. As a founder member of the United Nations, Poland was the 51st nation to sign the Charter on 16 October 1945. The Polish Delegation claimed its seat on the Security Council in 1946–7, 1960, and 1970–1, and supplied the Chairman of the General Assembly in 1972. Polish representatives contribute to the work of UNESCO, FAO, WHO, UPU, and GATT, and to the International Court of Justice at The Hague.

Poland's major international commitment, however, derives from its membership of the main institutions of the Soviet Bloc — since 1949 of the Council of Mutual Economic Aid (COMECON) and since 1955 of the Warsaw Pact. Although the interdependence of these two organizations is officially denied, there can be little doubt that they form the twin pillars of the military-industrial complex on which Soviet strategic planning is based. The launching of a long-term plan for accelerated socialist integration by the XXV Session of Comecon at Bucharest in July 1971 would seem to mark a new stage in the growth of Soviet hegemony. Coupled with the Brezhnev Doctrine, which asserts the right of the USSR to oppose the secession of its allies from the Soviet Bloc, and the Helsinki Agreement, which confirmed the political and territorial status quo in Europe, it underlined the extent to which Poland's destiny is hitched to that of the Red Star. There was a time after the War, when Poland's relations with Germany had not been regulated, when it could be argued that Soviet protection was necessary. The danger now is that the Soviet net is being tightened at the very moment when Soviet protection has lost its justification.[56] (See Diagram H.)

Yet no simple description can possibly convey the complicated character of present-day Poland. Life there is not characterized by the eternal optimism of official propaganda, but by a welter of conflicting values, contradictions, and

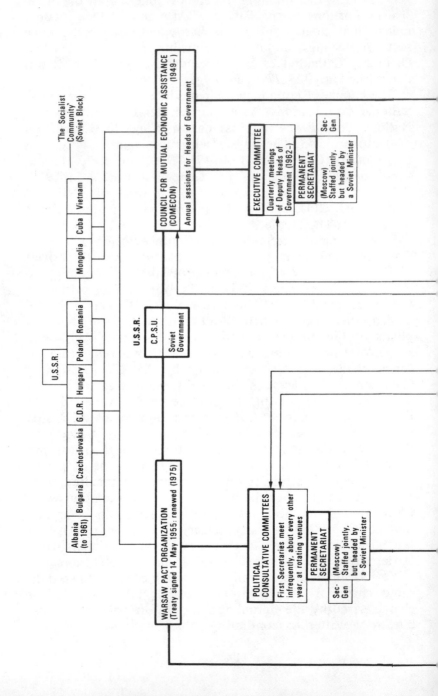

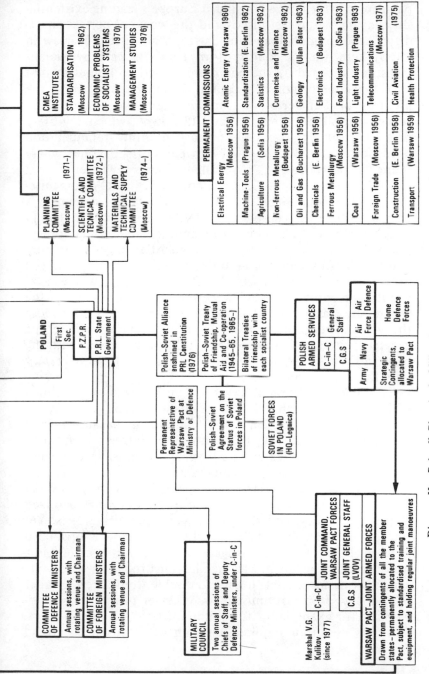

Diagram H.   Poland's Place in the Military–Industrial Complex of the Soviet Block

paradoxes, which once convinced Europe's leading existentia-
list that he had at last discovered the world of perfect absurdity. According to Jean-Paul Sartre, who visited Warsaw in
1960, here was 'a country torn from its past by violent
measures imposed by the communists, but so bound to that
past that the demolished capital is being rebuilt from the
pictures of Canaletto'; 'a capital where the citizens have
taken up residence again in the "Old Town", which is entirely
new'; 'a country where the average monthly remuneration
does not exceed the price of two pairs of shoes, but where
there is no poverty'; 'a socialist country where Church
festivals are a public holiday'; 'a country of total disorganisa-
tion, where nonetheless the trains run exactly on time'; 'a
country where the censorship and satire both flourish, and in
which every flower is subject to planning, but in which foreign
journalists can circulate without a guardian-angel'; 'the only
country of this bloc whose citizens are free to buy and sell
dollars (but not to possess them)'; 'a country, where, as a
result of terrible forces of powerlessness unparalleled in the
world, the traveller must abandon all logic if he is not to lose
the ground beneath his feet'; 'a strange country where one
can talk with the waiter in English or German, and with the
cook in French, but with the Minister and the Under-Secretary
only through an interpreter . . .'

To the Anglo-Saxon observer, Poland appears to be imbued
with the unmistakable flavour of Irishness (and not only, as
one distinguished Professor has maintained, because Poland
and Ireland are the only two Catholic countries which thrive
on a diet of potatoes and hard spirit). Whimsical anomalies
abound. Most Poles are by temperament 'agin'.

Poland vies with Ireland and Spain for the title of Most
Catholic Nation. Ninety-five per cent of Poles are baptized
Roman Catholics, and the majority are practising ones. Yet
the state is officially godless, and gives no support to organized
religion. In the resulting struggle, every citizen is caught in a
welter of divided loyalties which he must reconcile as best he
can. Split minds, double lives, and double-think, are the order
of the day. It is not unusual for younger priests to be anticlerical, for example, or for communists to be church-goers.
Workers are often required on pain of dismissal to attend

factory meetings or political rallies carefully arranged to clash with religious demonstrations. Somehow, with candle in one pocket and red flag in the other, they contrive to attend, and to be late for, both. School-children, sent on an obligatory free excursion to the mountains, learn that their home town lies on the route of a visiting Cardinal. Their coach-driver, like the good Catholic he is, will see that they return home early in order to cheer His Reverence (whose visit was the cause of their excursion in the first place). In this Slavonic Clochemerle, Don Camillo would feel perfectly at home.

The official ideology is Marxism—Leninism, which no one openly admits to believing. For Marx expressed the German view, and Lenin the Russian one, and the meeting of these particular minds has always spelled Poland's ruin. On the other hand, whereas few people bother to denounce the present ideology openly, all too many, in the eyes of the clergy, attend church as a matter of habit and social tradition, or as an assertion of their right to a life of their own.

Attitudes to Poland's neighbours are nicely ambiguous. The necessity of the 'alliance' with the Soviet Union cannot be openly questioned, but the frequency of anti-Soviet prejudices is less marked among the population at large than among the higher planes of the Party bureaucracy, who have the unenviable task of dealing with Soviet officialdom direct. Where else, if not in Poland, could one overhear a Party official describing the Russians as *untermenschen*? As some wit remarked, the Russians ought to be described as *ubermenschen*. Antipathy towards Germans is still very common, and is officially encouraged by all the media. But the contention that all evil Germans are concentrated in the Federal Republic whilst all 'good', 'democratic', 'anti-fascist' Germans have somehow been assembled in the DDR, cuts very little ice.

The Poles, above all, are patriots. It has been proved time and again that they will readily die for their country; but few will work for it. As the authorities periodically confess, 'labour problems' continually disrupt the smooth flow of economic progress. The workers feel little sense of identity with the state enterprises for which they labour, and in whose management they have no real voice. *Czy się stoi, czy się leży, dwa tysiące się należy* (Two thousand złoties are your due, whether you stand up, or whether you lie down), is the best known jingle in the land. Absenteeism and alcoholism are rife. The workers pilfer heartily and expertly, and use their winnings to support thriving private concerns. Anyone who has tried to build a private house in Poland knows that bricks, mortar, and cement are virtually unobtainable on the open market. But in most suburban areas, even casual visitors can see just how many private houses are actually built.

The outward fictions of the classless society are maintained. In all official correspondence, people are addressed in revolutionary style as 'Ob' – the accepted abbreviation of *Obywatel,* or *Obywatelka* (Citizen). But in private intercourse, the old Polish gentilities are universally cultivated. Bowing, heel-clicking, and hand-kissing remain standard form. Everyone nowadays, including the peasants, talks to each other in the third person – as *Pan* (Sir) or *Pani* (Lady): and they attach handles and titles to their name with a truly Austro-Hungarian flourish. One addresses an academic as *Panie Profesorze*! (Sir Professor), a Party official as *Panie Sekretarzu*! (Sir Secretary), and a foreman as *Panie Mistrzu*! (Sir Mastercraftsman). Even within the Party, the members choose to call each other not 'Brother' or 'Citizen', but *Towarzysz* – which is the style of the knightly companion-in-arms of the feudal gentry.

Everyone's lives are complicated by money, and in Poland by the extraordinary contortions of the currency. The *złoty* is not freely convertible. It is virtually worthless except for the purposes of internal exchange, and enjoys nobody's confidence. The US dollar, in contrast, is in universal demand. The dollar is used not only as the basis for foreign transactions, but also as the standard currency of a broad network of 'internal export' shops (PEWEX). Uniquely in Eastern Europe, Polish citizens have been permitted since 1972 to open interest-bearing dollar accounts with the State Bank. Class A accounts, with proof of the legal import of their contents, can be used for foreign travel: Class B accounts, where no such proof is available, must lie fallow for two years before being transferred to Class A. Rates of exchange make the uninitiated blink with amazement. The old official tourist rate, at 1 \$ = 19 zł., stood for years at one-third of that obtained by foreigners sending money into Poland through the

National Savings Bank (PKO), where 1 $ = 60 zł. On the black market, which is managed under cover by the Militia and the State Bank to cut their losses, 1 $ sold at 90–130 zł. In a country where the Party's official theory holds that the American dollar lies at the root of most evil, the present monetary situation is pure Alice.

This air of baffling unreality pervades Polish life from top to bottom. When foreign experts inquire how the Party can possibly escape from the present political and economic crisis, the usual answer is somewhere between a shrug and a grin. After all, as a historian would point out, the present Polish crisis has lasted for roughly 360 years, and may well go on for some time yet. The solution is ably demonstrated by the average Pole who continues to earn 4,500 zł. per month, who spends 9,000, and who, from his savings, expects in the near future to buy a motor-car. It is all part, as the posters proudly proclaim, of 'THE MAGIC OF POLAND'.[57]

*　　*　　*　　*　　*

Poland at the end of the 1970s faces an acute dilemma. Although it was the first of the East European countries to shake off direct Soviet tutelage, its national communist regime has not succeeded in creating a coherent social and political system of the sort pioneered by the Kadar regime in nearby Hungary. Policy has been characterized by the pursuit of contradictory half-measures – by support both for the Roman Catholic Church and for atheistic Marxist–Leninist ideology; by hostility both to compulsory collectivized agriculture and to the prosperity of private farming; by commitment both to the Soviet alliance and to socio-economic measures which the Soviet allies find abhorrent. Some commentators believe that Poland's unique historical development condemns her to such eternal contradictions. Others hold that the logic of the situation will eventually force the government to move in one direction or the other – either towards 'Sovietization' or else towards 'Kadarization'. The balancing act cannot go on for ever. Certainly, Gierek's gamble – to fix up a quick burst of material prosperity in place of fundamental reform – has not paid off.

Edward Gierek (b. 1913) owed his appointment to a

reputation as a practical administrator built up during his long term as Party boss in Silesia, and to his independence from the factional intrigues of the previous years. As a young man, he had spent much of his early career in the ultra-Stalinist communist parties of France and Belgium, and in the wartime Resistance. He was the first Party leader in the Soviet bloc who had never been trained in the Soviet Union. In origin a miner, he had never lost the common touch. Unlike Gomułka, he was fully aware of the gulf which separated the living standards of working people in Poland from that of their counterparts in the West, and was willing to listen to their aspirations. In all other respects, he showed few signs of originality and could be expected to tackle the country's problems with energy, if not with unorthodox ideas. His first step was to order a freeze in food prices for twelve months. His second step was to visit Gdańsk, and to talk to the ship-yard workers in person at great length. Tape-recordings of those conversations since brought to the west, show that he was fully prepared to admit to the Party's failures and to pay attention to ordinary folk. On this basis, he won respite to nurse the morale of State and Party.

Even so, under Gierek's leadership, the political situation in Poland reached the same impasse at the end of only six years that Gomułka was facing at the end of twelve. The pattern of events repeated itself in a way that suggests that the underlying causes of malaise were essentially the same. For three years, in 1971–3, as in 1956–61, the new regime radiated confidence and optimism. Free discussion, and a spirit of experimentation was in the air. At the Party's 6th Congress in December 1971, Gierek's team was approved. The workers were wooed by an increase in wages, and by proper attention to differentials. The peasants were wooed by the abolition of compulsory deliveries to the state, by the increase of prices paid for food products, and by the exten-sion of the free health service to non-state employees. The intellectuals were wooed by the easing of censorship, and by the lowering of restrictions on travel and foreign contacts. Patriotic sentiment was appeased by the rebuilding of the Royal Castle in Warsaw. Contacts with the Polish Emigration, especially in the USA, were strengthened. The weekly *Polityka*

(Politics) initiated a brand of investigative journalism which publicized scandal, corruption, and ignorance in the administration, and which was subject exclusively to the 'self-censorship' of the editor. A programme of massive investment was started in those areas of the economy which might reasonably be expected to increase trade, improve agriculture, or raise the standard of living. Licences were obtained for the construction in Poland of Fiat cars, Jones cranes, Leyland engines, Berlict buses, Grundig electronics, and more importantly of medium-size Massey Ferguson tractors suitable for the needs of peasant proprietors. Fertilizers, textiles, paper, coal, ship-building, petro-chemicals, and machine tools were all encouraged by the purchase of western technology. To finance these enterprises, debts totalling more than 6,000,000,000* dollars were quickly raised in the West on the strength of Poland's improved prospects. It was clear to all that Gierek had staked everything on economic success. Within a short time, however, there were signs that the gamble was not paying off. The oil crisis of 1974, together with the deepening recession in world trade, hit Poland at a moment of great vulnerability. Extravagant gestures of submissiveness to the USSR, not seen in Warsaw since the 1950s, could only be interpreted as the price for Soviet assistance in shoring up the Polish economy, and as a sop against Soviet fears of Poland's growing dependence on the West. On 22 July 1974, in the highspot of the military parade, Leonid Brezhnev was handed the *Virtuti Militari* medal, usually awarded for conspicuous gallantry in the field. Yet at a time when the Soviet economy itself was floundering, Moscow's assistance was of necessity strictly limited. In 1975, administrative controls were tightened. As elsewhere in the Soviet bloc in the era of 'Détente', the signing of the Helsinki Agreement was used as the occasion for increased ideological vigilance, on the grounds that greater contacts with the West would threaten the stability of the socialist camp. A major reform

---

* This key figure is never disclosed in official Polish sources, but there is no doubt that Poland's western debt has continued to multiply alarmingly throughout the 1970s. By 1979, it was certainly into eleven figures, and was accelerating beyond the 20-billion dollar mark — the estimated level of the entire foreign debt of the USSR.

of the local government system was clearly designed to enhance the leverage of the central ministries over the regions. In 1976, changes in the constitution were designed to offset fears that Poland's economic indebtedness to the West might have political repercussions. Elections were held amidst stringent security precautions, prompted by fears of popular unrest.

In this situation, in June 1976, Gierek proceeded to precisely the same confrontation with the people that had humbled Gomułka only six years before. Having repeatedly postponed the long-promised rise in food prices, he suddenly ordered that they were to be raised not by 20 per cent, but by an average of 60 per cent. The accompanying wage rises were heavily weighted in favour of the higher income groups. Strikes, protests, and demonstrations broke out in almost every town and factory in the country. In Warsaw, the workers of the Ursus tractor plant tore up the track of the railway line and captured the Paris—Moscow express. In Radom, the Party House was burned to the ground. In Nowa Huta, the army was called in to man the deserted steelworks. Then, after only one day's reflection, the government repealed its price rises. For the second time in six years, a communist government had been forced to retreat before public opinion. By the standards of the People's Democracy, this was an unacceptable defeat.

The bursting of Gierek's bubble left the policies of the PZPR in a hopeless impasse. In order to pay its steeply rising foreign debt, whose interest alone consumes over half of export income, every available item, including the food products and consumer goods which were originally destined to reward the Polish workers, had to be sold abroad. Thus, after thirty years of building socialism, the country still faces emergency austerity measures. Meat shortages and power cuts are daily facts of life. Far from deferring the need for reform, the Party's policies have made reform an urgent necessity. Yet here lie the horns of an acute dilemma. Should the Party admit its mistakes, and agree to make concessions to popular demands, it risks losing control of the political situation altogether. For the most important development of the Gierek era has been the emergence of a united political opposition.

The opposition movement coalesced in 1975 in face of the

impending constitutional amendments, and first made its presence felt in the form of several open protests — the Letter of the Eleven, the Letter of the Fifty-Nine, and the Appeal of the Thirteen. A group dedicated to the defence of human rights appeared, variously called RUCH or ROPCiO. In 1976, the *démarche* of the much respected *Znak* Group brought the Catholic intelligentsia into the fray, whilst brutal police action during the June riots inspired the formation of a Workers' Defence Committee (KOR). Very soon, each of these separate groups, and numerous spontaneous imitators, were circulating a rash of unauthorized, illegal periodicals headed by the *Zapis* (Record) and *Opinia* (Opinion), and by KOR's *Komunikaty* (Communiqués). Since then, some twenty titles have been published regularly, with a nominal imprint of 40,000 copies, each one of which is passed from hand to hand among scores of individuals. A private Society for Academic Courses (TKN) has revived the traditions of the nineteenth-century Flying University, and holds secret *komplety* or 'study classes' in each of the major cities. Despite police surveillance and harassment, and in May 1977 the apparent murder in Cracow of a student activist, Stanisław Pyjas, the opposition leaders have extended their activities at home and have kept in contact with sympathizers abroad. In one sense, they can be seen as a Polish variant of the wider movement for Human Rights which has sprung up in several countries of the Soviet bloc in consequence of the Helsinki Agreement. Like their counterparts in the USSR, or the Czechoslovak Charter 77 Group with whom they have held two or three clandestine meetings on the frontier, they cannot fairly be described as 'dissidents'. They have taken their stand on the letter of the Constitution, and demand only that the State and Party authorities honour their commitments in an open and legal manner. On the other hand, they display several features that are specifically Polish. In their pronouncements on domestic affairs, they claim to have bridged the gulf which had normally separated the radical intelligentsia both from the Catholic societies and from the workers. In their statements on foreign affairs, they have expressed the desire to move Poland in the direction of 'benevolent neutrality', akin to the position of Finland. From the viewpoint of the western journalists who report these matters, it all seems very encouraging. It looks as though Poland is moving slowly but steadily along the road to 'liberalization'. All things are possible; but a liberal, neutral, and popular regime is perhaps the least likely outcome of present developments.[58]

The western view of the Polish opposition is coloured by several fundamental misconceptions. Firstly, it is quite unrealistic to expect that the opposition leaders will ever be encouraged to negotiate their demands with the ruling Party. For the time being, in the interests of calm and order, they are tolerated, and the longer they are tolerated, the harder it will be for the Party to take effective action against them. But there can be no doubt, if ever they show signs of mobilizing active mass support, they will be ruthlessly crushed. Their leaders will be arrested, or otherwise removed. Their supporters will be attacked by a wave of police and military repression, backed up, if necessary, by Soviet forces. Even if the Party leaders in Poland, like Dubček in Czechoslovakia, were to contemplate loosening the reins of monopoly power, their Soviet masters would never permit them to do so for long.

Secondly, it is very easy to exaggerate the degree of cohesion among the various oppositionist groups. From the ideological point of view, the leaders of KOR — Adam Michnik, Jacek Kuroń, and the octogenarian economist, Edward Lipiński — hold eccentric left-wing or Marxist opinions which arouse little enthusiasm among the population at large. What is more, they are viewed with suspicion by followers of the older ROPCIO, which is associated with names such as Leszek Moczulski, Andrzej Czuma, and Wojciech Ziębiński. Even the Catholic intellectuals face considerable difficulties. In the widespread network of Catholic Societies and youth clubs, they possess a much firmer organization than any of their present allies. In writers such as Kisielewski, Mazowiecki, or Cywiński, they included men who enjoy wide popular appeal. But they have been joined by large numbers of atheist or agnostic youngsters whose political motives are entirely divorced from the interests of the Church or of Religion. The danger is obvious. If the Catholic intelligentsia is sufficiently infiltrated by non-Catholic dissidents, it stands to lose both the toleration of the Party, and the protection of the Hierarchy.

Above all, there must be doubt about the strength of the link between intellectual and working-class opposition. No one can be certain that hard-bitten dockers and miners feel very enthusiastic about their patronage by professors, journalists, and the rebellious offspring of Party functionaries. The intellectuals may see the Polish workers as the salt of the earth; but the workers often see the intellectuals as the *priviligentsia* – as privileged 'arm-chair' protesters. In a crisis the workers, not the intellectuals, would have the last word.

Clearly, the Party still retains a certain space for manœuvre. Secretary Gierek's visit to the Vatican in December 1977, and his audience with Pope Paul VI, represented a new gesture towards the Church. It could well be that a period of relaxation towards Catholic dissent might be used to mask increasing pressure on political opponents. The oppositionists command potential, but for the time being only peripheral, support. The really pressing problem concerns the effects of any serious act of repression which the Party may feel constrained to order. If the dissidents were crushed by force, the revulsion at their crushing might well provoke disaffections in areas of Polish society which could organize resistance on a really serious scale – in the Church, in the lower ranks of the Party, or most seriously in the army. The army's contempt for the People's Militia is well-known, and their reluctance to be used against the civilian population has been reinforced by its humiliating role in the invasion of Czechoslovakia and in the events in Poland in 1968, 1970, and 1976. A scenario in which the Militia loses control of a popular outburst against repressive measures, and where the army refuses to assist, could easily lead to Soviet Intervention, and hence to the next Polish Insurrection.

Seen in the context of the historical traditions of Polish politics, the present predicament of the communist movement does not inspire confidence. If the Stalinist period can be regarded as a brief reversion to the tradition of servile Loyalism, the period since 1956 has seen an episode of Conciliatory, or Realist politics of unusual longevity. But now that the communist version of Conciliation is failing to bring results, there is a real danger that the younger generation will be drawn

towards the romantic revolutionary alternative. There is plenty
in the history books, and in the legends of the Party itself, to
make such a course of action extremely appealing in conditions of extended political stagnation. The catastrophes of
1939–47 were sufficient to deter the older generation of
Poles from violent adventures for the rest of their lives. But
today, there are millions of young adults in Poland for whom
the names of Hitler and Stalin hold no terror whatsoever, and
for whom the warnings of their elders serve only to aggravate
their youthful impatience. In the eighteenth and nineteenth
centuries, the forty-one years between 1864 and 1905 formed
the longest interval between revolutionary Polish Risings. In
the twentieth century, the last such Rising occurred in 1944.
If the present regime can maintain its course until 1985 without facing a violent challenge to its supremacy, it will have
broken all records.

In this light, the crisis of 1976 may be regarded as a minor
rumbling before the major eruption which is still to come. At
all events, its eventual consequences have still to be measured.
The Party enjoys the enviable prospect of blackmailing
Moscow, in the most comradely manner, with the threat of
its own collapse. It may well oblige the Soviet leaders to
subsidize the Polish Road to Socialism, for fear of something
worse. This would be rough justice indeed, in view of the
long period after the war when the USSR mercilessly exploited
the infant Polish economy for its own ends. Neither the
USSR, nor the Party, nor the Church, nor indeed the new
Opposition have anything to gain from further disturbances
in Poland. Everyone will go to great lengths to avoid trouble.
Yet there are no signs that anything is being done to defuse
existing tensions. The longer the reckoning is delayed, the
more explosive the situation may become.

Whatever the outcome of the immediate crisis, it seems
clear that Poland's 'National Communism' contains severe
defects. Olympian pronouncements about the correctness of
'proletarian solidarity' and of 'progress in the building of
communism' do little to conceal the tremendous cost of
maintaining the present system. The high level of military
expenditure is hardly appropriate to a country with such
chronic economic problems. The low level of productivity is

hardly likely to improve living standards. The burden of foreign debt will weigh heavily on all future policies. The total absence of any institutional provision for channelling popular consent into the decision-making process is sure to accumulate popular resentments. Other parts of Europe are suffering from problems which in their way are no less acute; but recurrent crises in Poland can be safely predicted.

Postscript

It has often been said that historians should not meddle with the present, and that they are incapable of predicting the future. History can teach us little, except that there is nothing to learn from History. In one sense, this is wise advice in a country where sudden and violent charges of fortune have been commonplace, and it would be foolish to expect that the past should simply repeat itself. Yet the present is the product of the past, just as the future will be a continuation of the present. No traveller can plan the road before him if he knows not whence he came. No one can begin to contemplate things to come without a lively memory of times past. Nobody can imagine a country's destiny without a proper understanding of its growth and development. To that extent, Poland's History is a vital element in Poland's current affairs.

In many spheres, it is necessary to affirm that the life of Poles today is superior to that of previous generations. People who remember the horrors of the Second World War, or the communal and social miseries of the inter-war period, are bound to appreciate the relative security and prosperity of life in the People's Republic. Anyone who looks further back, to moments in the late nineteenth century, when Polish nationality seemed to be in danger of extinction, must necessarily admire and respect many of the Poles' present achievements. Even within the changing perspectives of the last thirty years, it is quite remarkable that Polish artists, writers, musicians, scientists, and sportspersons should now be able to play a more active part on the European scene than ever before. Given the odds against it, one is moved to view Poland's survival, and her extraordinary powers of regeneration, with wonder and admiration.

In the political field, however, any impartial observer must conclude that the present situation in Poland still contains all the ingredients of past misfortunes. Indeed, since politics

634

provides the framework within which all other social and cultural activities take place, it is impossible to ignore the omnipresent shadow which lies across Poland's path in all directions. For better or for worse, the People's Republic was created by one of the world's few remaining imperial powers, and continues to be managed in accordance with foreign priorities and foreign interests. Of course, limited sovereignty marks the condition of most nations today; and it would be idle to suppose that in this regard the countries of the Soviet bloc were somehow uniquely unfortunate. That is not the point. Poland's misfortune lies not in the fact of her patronage by one of the superpowers but rather in the nature of the political system with which she is obliged to consort. Poland's political destiny is tied to that of an empire whose communist ideology is bankrupt even in the eyes of many of the world's communists; whose unreformed internal structures reflect not Marxism or Socialism, but Russian autocracy and Stalinist tyranny; and whose external policies put their trust, as Kipling wrote, 'in reeking tube and iron shard'. Such is the constellation of political forces in East Central Europe that no improvement in Poland can be secure until fundamental improvements are also instituted in the USSR.

For the Polish historian, such a situation is depressingly familiar. It is a situation which has reigned, with many variations but with very few interruptions, since the Russians first established their baleful protectorate over Poland in the early eighteenth century. Despite her social, technical, and cultural progress, Poland's political development remains atrophied. *Mutatis mutandis*, the uneasy relationship of the present Party leadership to its current Soviet patrons is highly reminiscent of the hapless plight of the last king of Poland in his dealings with the Empress Catherine. The constitutional position of the People's Republic since 1945 is closely akin to that of the Congress Kingdom after 1815. The tactical stance of the national communist régime set up in 1956, is nothing more than a modernized version of the old theme of 'Organic Work'. So long as Poland's historic subjection to Russian power is perpetuated, it is only to be expected that the historic mechanisms of self-preservation, and the inbred habits of dissimulation and defiance, will continually reassert themselves.

Poland's uncomfortable position within the Soviet bloc is aggravated by the strength of her traditional bonds with the West. After four decades of Soviet supremacy, there are no signs that these bonds are weakening. People's Poland earns a greater proportion of its GNP from trade with Western countries than any other member of the Warsaw Pact. The Polish Emigration in Europe and America surpasses that of all of its neighbours. The flow of Polish visitors to the West, both private and official, outstrips comparable figures from anywhere else in the bloc. The percentage of practising Catholics in the population exceeds that of anywhere else in Europe. In the arts and the sciences, Poland keeps in closer touch with developments in the West than in the USSR. Soviet manufactures – from Socialist Realism, Russian folk-music, to Soviet champagne, Soviet motor-cars, or Soviet Friendship – arouse minimal enthusiasm among Polish consumers, in comparison to equivalent Western products. In those fields such as music, graphics, cinema, mathematics, dance, mime, and certain branches of the theatre and literature where the language barrier can be surmounted, Polish contributors keep company with Europe's avant-garde. In spite of many official pressures, most Poles remain more consciously 'western' in their tastes and attitudes than do the citizens of most western countries.

Poland's traditional refusal to conform to the demands of its political masters has turned it into one of Europe's perennial trouble-spots, and there is every sign that it will continue to do so. After the First World War, Aristide Briand, the French Premier, called Poland 'Europe's rheumatism'. At the end of the Second World War, President Roosevelt called it 'the world's headache'. Since then, the Polish trouble-spot has been relatively untroubled. But tensions abound beneath the surface, and Poland's reliability in any future international crisis cannot be assured. It is most unlikely that the Poles would wish to be associated with Soviet operations in Asia or Africa, and they occupy a vital and vulnerable strategic position astride the Soviets' main lines of communication with Germany and with the Iron Curtain front line. So long as the Soviet Army maintains its establishment in Eastern Europe at present levels, or, conceivably, if it engineers a strategic

withdrawal to its own frontiers, all may remain quiet for
many years to come. But in any serious confrontation,
especially within Europe, Poland's loyalty to the Soviet bloc
must remain suspect. There is undoubtedly an element of
wishful thinking in the speculations of those western strate-
gists, who see Poland as the flashpoint of the Third World
War. But the idea is not entirely without substance; and there
must be people in Moscow who also see Poland as their own
Achilles Heel.

All thoughts about Poland's future, therefore, are bound
to turn on estimates of the over-all strategic position of the
USSR. The 'primacy of foreign policy' is a maxim that has
always weighed heavily with Polish political analysts, and
contemporary pundits are no exception. The Poles are
intensely curious about the fortunes of Russia's other neighbours, and in particular about developments on the Soviet
Union's oriental borders. This curiosity is nothing new. In
the eighteenth and early nineteenth centuries, Russo-Turkish
relations provided the surest barometer of the Polish political
climate. A Russian war with the Turks usually brought
sunshine to Warsaw, whilst a Russian peace with the Porte
indicated stormy weather ahead. In the early twentieth
century, Russo-Japanese rivalry first aroused Polish dreams of
liberation. At the present time, the Sino-Soviet conflict
presents the greatest opportunities and the greatest dangers.
The outcome of Russia's differences with China and Japan is
as inscrutable as the faces of the principal contestants; but it
is certain that life in Poland could be affected as severely by
events on the Amur or the Ussuri, or in the Sea of Okhotsk,
as by anything which happens on the banks of the Oder, the
Bug, or the Vistula. Any educated Pole with the slightest
sense of history cannot possibly escape reflections of this
sort. Indeed, the recent production of the so-called 'China
card' in Washington by none other than Zbigniew Brzeziński
must surely be attributed, at least in part, to his Polish upbringing.

Poland's present predicament, however, reflects above all
the outcome of the titanic contest between Russia and
Germany which preoccupied Eastern Europe for the first
half of the twentieth century. A Nazi victory, if it had not

annihilated the Poles completely, would surely have left them as German slaves. So the fact that Stalin's victory has left them as Soviet satellites should not cause undue surprise. Things could have been worse. It is simply a fact of history that the Poles live in the heart of Europe's gangland, where the anti-social activities of their neighbours ruled out the possibility of a tranquil, independent life. The epic war between the two leading mobsters was bound to determine the fate of everyone in the area for years to come. It is true that Stalin has been dead for quarter of a century; but the ageing heirs of the Soviet Godfather are as loath to disburse his ill-gotten gains as they are to admit how he acquired them. The desperate search for respectability, which underlies so much of contemporary politics in Eastern Europe, would be seriously endangered if Stalin's victims and partners were ever to learn the truth. So the conspiracy of silence continues.

In such circumstances, it is essential that Polish youth should be given the opportunity to see the richness and the complexities of their heritage. For people beyond Poland's frontiers, Polish History is just one of Europe's many curious byways. For the Poles themselves, it is a vital aid to their self-awareness, an essential guide for their national salvation. Unfortunately, most Polish youngsters enjoy only limited access to the treasures of their past. Censors and political ideologists work unceasingly in their efforts to control, to restrict, and to deform historical knowledge. The absence of political independence inevitably cramps the right to an independent view of history. Yet in a world of increasingly sophisticated controls, few Poles are aware of the directions in which their minds are turned. Whilst most educated people repudiate the Leninist elements in present-day history-making, and whilst many question the validity of Marxist interpretations, very few are aware of the persistent Nationalism which constitutes the main strand of official ideology. It is a curious irony. Nationalism, which in the era of statelessness was used as a powerful weapon against the spurious historiography of the partitioning powers, has now been pressed into the service of Soviet imperialism. The Stalinist authors of the Soviet bloc deliberately cultivated the wounded nationalisms of each and every one of their captive peoples. Moscow's rule in post-war

East Central Europe was accompanied not just by the imposition of Communism, which Stalin himself admitted to be alien
and unsuitable, but also and in particular by the careful
cultivation of existing nationalist forces. Moscow's inimitable
policy of praising the supposedly glorious victories of Polish
Socialism, and the recovery of Poland's supposedly historic
frontiers, appeals directly to Polish vanity, and is the exact
modern equivalent of St. Petersburg's onetime policy of
praising the 'Golden Freedom' of the szlachta. All the ideologists of the bloc have been taught to maximize xenophobia
and, by inflating their citizens' sense of insecurity, to increase
their dependence on the great Soviet ally. To buttress the
rule of the imperial power by encouraging the divisive
tendencies of the subject peoples is a manœuvre as old as
Nebuchadnezzar, and the Poles have been one of its principal
victims. By exploiting and magnifying Polish resentment
against the Germans (if that were possible), the authorities
have successfully diverted attention from the comparable
evils of the Soviet record. By asserting nationalist feelings at a
juncture at which national independence had already been
formally conceded, they generated animosities which could
only work to their private advantage. By stressing the exclusiveness of the Polish heritage, and by underplaying its
links with that of the Germans, Jews, Ukrainians, Lithuanians,
Czechs, Slovaks, and Russians, they are effectively shielding
the Soviet Union from any united challenge to its imperial
supremacy. For people who know the purposes for which
nationalist ideology was first developed, this is an interesting
turnabout. Indeed, the propagation in Poland and in neighbouring countries of the sort of primitive, uncritical Nationalism, which first took shape during the Stalinist era, continues
to provide a fair measure of the health of the Soviet Union's
European empire.

As yet, few Polish commentators view things in this light,
and the average Pole-in-the-street certainly feels that his
compatriots' traditionally supercharged national consciousness forms one of the surest guarantees of the country's
survival. However, it is possible that the role of Nationalism
will be called increasingly into question. As wartime memories
fade, the old attitudes generated by fears of encirclement and

extinction are destined to fade with them. Now that Poland's existence as a distinct national community is no longer in jeopardy, public aspirations will probably move in new directions — away from nationalist obsessions and towards ideas of political freedom and international brotherhood. The feeling may well grow that Polish political life has been manœuvred into a moral cul-de-sac, from which the young and impatient will somehow have to make their escape. Nationalism — the dominant ideology of the Polish lands ever since the Partitions — will be seen at last to have played out its historic role. The post-war generation was content to find that they were still alive and that they were still Poles; their sons and daughters may well want to be Europeans, cosmopolitans, citizens of the world.

If the Poles are to escape from the mental strait-jacket imposed by their political masters, therefore, they must start, as their forebears did, by re-examining their history. Only then can they hope to relate the specific values of Individualism and Liberty that have marked the Polish spirit across the ages to their present condition. For political structures and systems, in themselves, have no virtue. The formal attainment of national independence is, in itself, of no worth, unless the energies of the state are directed towards worthwhile purposes. Now, more than ever before, the Poles need to ask what those purposes are. If their precious Republic really exists to promote the welfare of its citizens and the general progress of humanity, rather than the divisive interests of an alien empire or of the ruling élite, then all is well. If not — if the Poles have been led to think of their People's Republic as a virtuous end in itself, then they are cruelly deceived; and the impressive Sixtieth Anniversary of National Independence will have been an empty celebration.

By the same token, Poles need to realize that much of their historical writing, from the autochthonous theories of prehistory to the ethnocentric interpretations of contemporary subjects, stand fair to cause puzzlement abroad. In Great Britain, for example, where the gentle art of self-denigration is sometimes pushed to extremes, or in America, where revisionist historians frequently expose the shortcomings of the nation's past with extravagant relish, the obligatory Soviet-style optimism of official Polish historians is simply incomprehensible. No one wants to read a catalogue of other people's glorious achievements. Of course, every community must to some extent focus its historial interests on problems related to its own origins and development, and in this Poland is no exception. It is only natural that historians from a country which has been subjected to such traumatic changes, should be self-centred to a degree. It is only proper in the aftermath of the Second World War, when Poland's territorial, demographic, social, and political landscape was transformed out of all recognition, that some emphasis be placed on the study of the so-called 'Recovered Territories' and that, by way of compensation, some special search be made for themes of continuity. All that is perfectly understandable. But the apparent tendency to use historical scholarship as an instrument for reinforcing Polish national consciousness, and by extension for obliterating all memory of the non-Polish cultures of the historic Polish lands, is bound to strike a discordant note among foreign readers. Oddly enough, it is a tendency all too reminiscent of the old German School of History, whose conclusions about Eastern Europe are so earnestly contradicted by modern Polish scholars. What is more, the current habit of glossing over Poland's historic role in the East, or the view which presents the People's Republic as the crowning achievement of an organic social process, must surely be attributed to straightforward political manipulation. Poland's past is as chequered, as complicated, and in the last resort as inconclusive as anyone else's. Any pretence that it is otherwise can convince nobody.

From today's vantage point, Poland's predicament may look awfully permanent. To the faint-hearted, it would seem that no force on earth might loosen the Soviet grip on its European empire. As Alexander Solzhenitsyn is always reiterating, the Soviet system is inhumanly strong; and in the nuclear age no one can dare contemplate the benefits of armed resistance, or, like Mickiewicz, pray to God for a universal war of liberation. The Helsinki Agreement of 1975 has given but the latest expression of the Kremlin's hopes of eternalizing its supremacy. Yet the one thing that History does teach is that power is transient, and wordly success ephemeral. The captains and the commissars will one day depart. Sooner or later, Soviet pomp will surely be one with Nineveh and Tyre. In the meantime, Poland's room for manœuvre is limited.

Even so, Poles can reflect with wonder, and no small pride, on the extraordinary events which have enabled them to survive, and sometimes to flourish, in face of great adversity. Given Poland's three-hundred-year struggle for survival, it would be most inappropriate if the Poles should be judged exclusively by the standards of worldly success. For Poland, in its usual state of stabilized defeat, is not just another European country battered by war, and beset with problems of post-war adjustment. To everyone who knows its History, Poland is something more besides. Poland is a repository of ideas and values which can outlast any number of military and political catastrophes. Poland offers no guarantee that its individual citizens will observe its ideals, but stands none the less as an enduring symbol of moral purpose in European life:

> Moral right is in me, and the starry sky is above.
> So what, if the Law is disgraced by barbarity?
> Let the moons revolve in their fixed and perfect courses.
> May the sky at least retain its purity.[1]

Polish History, viewed as a scientific process or as a national crusade, carries little coherence or conviction. But viewed as the playground of mischievous fate, it does begin to assume a measure of intelligibility. Its essence cannot be properly described in a thousand pages of learned commentary but it is sometimes captured by a few frail lines of poetry:

> I built on the sand,
> And down it tumbled.
> I built on rock, and
> That, too soon crumbled.
> So now, whenever I think of building,
> Or perhaps not,
> I first plan the wisp of smoke, curling
> From the chimney-pot.[2]

Hence, the tragedies of Poland's past constantly prompt anxieties about Poland's future. For much of modern history Poles have asked themselves how Poland could be restored to its former independent condition, and, more importantly, what kind of country the independent Poland ought to be: in Lelewel's words, *Polska tak, ale jaka*? (Poland yes, but what sort of Poland?). The first question was answered by the outcome of two terrible World Wars, and more particularly by the settlement of 1945. The second question remains.

NOTES

CHAPTER 1. NARÓD

1. Not surprisingly, almost all the standard western studies of Nationalism either take a hostile stance towards Poland, relegate it to a category of 'secondary status', or else ignore it altogether. See Carlton Y. Hayes, *The Historical Evolution* of *Modern Nationalism* (New York, 1931); Elie Khedourie, *Nationalism* (London, 1960); F. Ponteil, *L'éveil des nationalités et le mouvement liberal, 1815–48* (Paris, 1960); Anthony D. Smith, *Theories of Nationalism* (London, 1971). The most accessible introduction to Polish Nationalism in English is by Peter Brock, 'Polish Nationalism', in *Nationalism in Eastern Europe*, ed. P. Sugar, I. Lederer (Seattle, 1969), 310–72. See also Konstantin Symmons-Symonolewicz, *Nationalist Movements: a comparative view* (Meadvill, Pa., 1970). Lord Acton's essay on 'Nationality' (1862), which maintained that modern Nationalism began with the Partitions of Poland, is printed in his *History of Freedom and other essays* (London, 1907). See also G. E. Fasnacht, *Lord Acton on Nationality and Socialism* (London, 1949).

2. Helmuth von Moltke, *Poland, a historical sketch* (London, 1885); Sutherland Edwards, *The Polish Captivity: an account of the present position of the Poles* (London, 1863), 2 vols.; Georg Brandes, *Poland: a study of the country, people, and literature* (London, 1903).

3. Adam Mickiewicz, *Księgi narodu polskiego i pielgrzymstwa polskiego*, ed. S. Pigoń (Cracow, 1922), 53 ff.

4. Kazimierz Brodziński (1791–1835), 'Na dzień zmartwychwstania pańskiego r 1831', *Poezje* (Wrocław, 1959), i, 239–40, quoted by W. J. Rose, *Poland* (London, 1939), 38.

5. For the most recent investigation into these problems, see Hugh Seton-Watson, *Nations and States* (London, 1977); or in Poland, Jerzy Wiatr, *Naród i państwo* (Warsaw, 1973).

6. 'Litwo! Ojczyzno maja! ty jesteś jak zdrowie', Adam Mickiewicz, *Pan Tadeusz, czyli Ostatni zajazd na Litwie: historia szlachecka z roku 1811–12 we dwunastu księgach wierszem*, ed. S. Pigoń (Wrocław, 1962), Księga I, line 1, p. 3.

7. See S. Kieniewicz, 'Rozwój polskiej świadomości narodowej w XIX wieku', *Pamiętnik X Powszechnego Zjazdu Historyków Polskich w Lublinie* (Warsaw, 1968), i. 259–70.

8. See R. F. Leslie, *The Polish Question* (Historical Association, London, 1964), with bibliography; M. Handelsman 'Sprawa polska w XIX wieku', in *Dzieje polityczne i społeczne XIX wieku*, ed. E. Driault, G. Monod (Warsaw, 1916), 521–68. Some attention to international affairs is paid by the authors of the

two standard surveys of the nineteenth century, i.e. M. Kukiel, *Dzieje Polski porozbiorowe, 1795–1921* (London, 1961); and P. Wandycz, *The Lands of Partitioned Poland, 1795–1918* (Seattle, 1975). See also H. Fraenkel, *Poland: the Struggle for Power 1772–1939* (London, 1946).

9. See W. H. Zawadzki, 'Prince Adam Czartoryski and Napoleonic France, 1801–5: a study in political attitudes', *Historical Journal*, xviii, No. 2 (1975), 245–77.

10. P. Wandycz, 'The Benes–Sikorski Agreement', *Central European Federalist*, i (1953). See Chapter 20, note 45, below.

11. Juliusz Willaume, 'Jeszcze Polska', in S. Russocki, S. K. Kuczyński, *et al.*, *Godło, Barwy, i Hymn Rzeczypospolitej: Zarys dziejów* (Warsaw, 1970), 231–314.

12. Jan Dąbrowski, *Polacy w Anglii i o Anglii* (Cracow, 1962), 188.

13. *Poezja barska*, ed. K. Kolbuszewski (Cracow, 1928). See also Janusz Maciejewski, 'Literatura barska', in *Przemiany tradycji barskiej: studia* (Cracow, 1972).

14. Alojzy Feliński (1771–1820), 'Hymn na rocznicę ogłoszenia Królestwa Polskiego: z woli Naczelnego Wodza Wojsku Polskiemu do śpiewu poddany', *Z Głębokości ... Antologia polskiej modlitwy poetyckiej*, ed. A. Jastrzębski, A. Podsiad (Warsaw, 1974), i. 254–5.

15. Peter Brock, 'Polish Nationalism', op. cit. 337–38.

16. Zenon Klemensiewicz, *Historia języka polskiego* (Warsaw, 1974), 797, especially Part III, 'Doba nowopolska'. See also A. P. Coleman, 'Language as a factor in Polish Nationalism', *Slavonic and East European Review*, xiii (37), (1934), 155–72.

17. General surveys of Polish literature in the nineteenth century include Julian Krzyżanowski, *Dzieje literatury polskiej* (Warsaw, 1969); and in English, M. Kridl, *Survey of Polish Literature and Culture* (The Hague, 1956) and Czesław Miłosz, *A History of Polish Literature* (London, 1969).

18. Claude Backvis, 'Polish Tradition and the Concept of History', *Polish Review*, vi (1961), 125–58. Maria Janion, Maria Żmigrodzka, *Romantyzm i Historia* (Warsaw, 1978).

19. Maria Czapska, 'Franciszek Xavery Duchiński', *Polski Słownik Biograficzny*, v (Cracow, 1946); F. Duchiński, *Peuples aryas et tourans* (Paris, 1864); See also H. Paszkiewicz, 'Are the Russians Slavs?', *Antemurale*, xiv (1970), 59–84.

20. Adolf Pawiński P.A., *W sprawie narodowości Kopernika* (Warsaw, 1873), Cv. Ignacy Połkowski, *Żywot Kopernika* (Gniezno, 1873); and Leopold Prowe, *Nicolaus Coppernicus* (Berlin–Leipzig, 1883).

21. See *Frederic Chopin*, ed. A. Walker (London, 1966).

22. S. Kieniewicz, 'La pensée de Mazzini et le mouvement national slave', *Atti del Convegno: Mazzini e l'Europa* (Rome, 1974), 109–23; Adam Lewak, 'Ideologia polskiego romantyzmu politycznego a Mazzini' (Warsaw, 1934), reprinted in *Przegląd Historyczny*, xxxvii (1948), 311–21.

23. e.g. W. Kuhne, *Graf August Cieszkowski: ein Schüler Hegels und des deutschen Geistes* (Leipzig, 1938).

24. Quoted by S. Blejwas, 'The Origins and Practice of Organic Work in Poland, 1795–1863', *Polish Review*, xv, No. 4 (1970), 25.

25. Stefan Kieniewicz, 'Ludwik Mierosławski (1814–78)', *Polski Słownik Biograficzny*, xx (Cracow, 1975), 812–15; *Powstanie styczniowe* (Warsaw, 1972). See also M. Żychowski. *Ludwik Mierosławski, 1814–78* (Warsaw, 1963), with summary in French.

26. Cyprian Norwid, 'Siła Ich – Fraszka', *Dzieła wybrane*, ed. J. W. Gomulicki (Warsaw, 1966), i. 310.

27. Juliusz Słowacki, from 'Poema Piasta Dantyszka herbu Leliwa o piekle' (Florence, 1838), in *Dzieła*, ed. M. Kridl, K. Piwiński (Warsaw, 1930), ii. 288.

28. K. Krzemień-Ojak, *Maurycy Mochnacki: program kulturalny i myśl krytycznoliteracka* (Warsaw, 1975). See also J. Szacki, *Historia jedynego romansu* (Warsaw, 1964).

29. André Liebich, *Selected Writings of August Cieszkowski* (New York, 1979). See also Lech Trzeciakowski, 'The Conception of Peace and Universal Peace of August Cieszkowski, 1814–94', *Polish Western Affairs*, xv (1974), 224–31; A. Cieszkowski, *The Desire of all Nations*, trans., W. J. Rose (London, 1919).

30. See A. Walicki, *Filozofia a mesjanizm: Studia z dziejów filozofii i myśli społeczno-religijnej romantyzmu polskiego* (Warsaw, 1970); F. Warrain, *L'œuvre philosophique de Hoene Wronski* (Paris, 1933).

31. Aleksandra Piłsudska, *Wspomnienia* (London, 1960), 55–7; also published in English as *The Memoirs of Mme Piłsudski* (New York, 1940).

32. W. Broniewski, 'Mazurek Szopena' (A Chopin Mazurka), from *Bagnet na broń* (1943), *Wiersze i poematy* (Warsaw, 1974), 111–12.

33. Stefan Żeromski, 'Sen o szpadzie' (Dream of the Sword), in *Sen o szpadzie. Pomyłki;* (Warsaw, 1966), 7–9.

34. Karol Swidziński, *Naprzód Pracą*, published in 'Na Dziś' (Cracow, 1872): *Zbiór poetów polskich XIX w*, ed. P. Hertz (Warsaw, 1962), iii. 665–8.

35. Aleksander Wielopolski, 'List szlachcica polskiego do księcia Metternicha' (Letter of a Polish nobleman to Prince Metternich), quoted in W. Karpiński, M. Król, *Sylwetki polityczne XIX wieku* (Cracow, 1974), 78. See W. J. Rose, 'Wielopolski to Metternich, April 1846', *Slavonic and East European Review*, xxvi (1947), 90–106.

36. Włodzimierz Spasowicz, 'Życie i polityka margrabiego Wielopolskiego (1880)', quoted in W. Karpiński, M. Król, op. cit. 100.

37. Bolesław Prus, 'Kwestyjka Żydowska' (The Minor Question of the Jews, 1875), quoted in *Polska myśl demokratyczna w ciągu wieków: antologia*, ed. M. Kridl, W. Malinowski, J. Wittlin (New York, 1945), 146–9.

38. Bolesław Prus, *Dzieci* (Children, 1909) (Jerusalem, 1944), 243–4.

39. Władysław Smoleński, 'Szkoły historyczne w Polsce: Główne kierunki poglądów na przeszłość' (Historical Schools in Poland), *Pisma historyczne* (Cracow, 1901), iii. 331 ff.

40. S. Kieniewicz, *Dramat trzeźwych entuzjastów* (Warsaw, 1964). See also S. Blejwas, 'The origins and practice of Organic Work in Poland 1795–1863', op. cit.

41. Andrzej Micewski, *Roman Dmowski* (Warsaw, 1971).

42. Quoted by A. Piłsudski, *Piłsudski – a Biography by his Wife* (New York, 1941), 191. See also T. Ładyka, *PPS (Frakcja Rewolucyjna) w latach 1906–14* (Warsaw, 1960).

43. W. F. Reddaway, *Marshal Piłsudski* (London, 1939); W. Pobóg-Malinowski, *Józef Piłsudski*, cz I 1867–1901, cz II 1901- 8 (Warsaw, 1938). The authoritative source of information on Piłsudski's career is Wacław Jędrzejewicz, *Kronika Marszałka Piłsudskiego* (New York, 1977–8), 2 vols.

44. Marian Kukiel, *Czartoryski and European Unity, 1770–1861* (Princeton, 1955).

45. See S. Małachowski-Łempicki, *Wykaz polskich lóż wolnomularskich 1738–1821* (Cracow, 1930).

46. See R. A. Rothstein, 'The Linguist as Dissenter: Jan Baudouin de Courtenay', in *For Wiktor Weintraub: Essays in Polish Literature, Language and History* (The Hague, 1975), 391–405; also 'Jan Baudouin de Courtenay 1845–1929', in *Portrety Uczonych Polskich*, ed. Λ. Biernacki (Cracow, 1974); W. Doroszewski, Jan Baudouin de Courtenay, *Z dziejów polonistyki warszawskiej* (Warsaw, 1964); I. Spustek, 'J. Baudouin de Courtenay a carska censura', *Przegląd Historyczny*, lii (1961), 112–26.

47. See *Krakowski Komisarz Policji na Służbie Carskiego Wywiadu: korespondencja . . . 1882–4*, ed. L. Baumgarten (Cracow, 1967).

48. Jan Słomka, *From Serfdom to Self-Government: memoirs of a Polish village mayor*, trans. W. J. Rose (London, 1941).

49. Georg Brandes, *Poland: a study of the land, people and literature* (London, 1903), 105, 114.

50. Gustaw Ehrenberg, 'Szlachta w roku 1831' (The Nobility in 1831), *Zbiór poetów polskich XIX w*, ed. P. Hertz (Warsaw, 1962), ii. 851–3. Ehrenberg was the son of Tsar Alexander I and of the Polish widow, Helena Rauchenstrauch. He was brought up in Warsaw, and educated in Cracow. First arrested in 1838, he returned to Poland in 1862 only to be rearrested for a second term of imprisonment. During his exile, he translated Dante and Shakespeare into Polish.

51. See S. Dubnow, *History of the Jews in Poland and Russia* (Philadelphia, 1916–20), 3 vols.

52. Quoted by R. A. Rothstein, op. cit. 399 [See note 46 above].

53. See Alfred E. Senn, *The Emergence of Modern Lithuania* (Princeton, 1959); also *Encyclopedia Lituanica*, ed. S. Suziedelis, J. Jakštas (Boston, 1970), 6 vols.

54. See Nicholas P. Vakar, *Belorussia: the making of a nation* (Cambridge, Mass., 1956).

55. See W. E. D. Allen, *The Ukraine: a History* (Cambridge, 1940); M. Hrushevsky, *A History of the Ukraine* (New Haven, 1941).

56. W. J. Rose, 'Czechs and Poles as neighbours', *Journal of Central European Affairs*, ii. (1941), 153–71.

57. See Leon Wasilewski, *Sprawy narodowościowe w teorii i w życiu* (Warsaw, 1929); K. Grunberg, *Polskie koncepcje federalistyczne 1864–1918* (Warsaw, 1971).

58. Cyprian Norwid, 'Wolność w Polsce będzie inna', from 'Pieśni społecznej cztery strony', *Dzieła*, ed. T. Pini (Warsaw, 1934), 506–11. The poem ends with the verse:

> For freedom shall be fashioned from goodwill,
> As in a well-versed melody,
> Where the thought romps along with the words
> And the words play at will with the harmony.

59. Ibid.
60. Ibid.
61. On Norwid, see George Gömöri, *Cyprian Norwid* (New York, 1974); Alicja Lisiecka. *Norwid poeta historii* (Veritas, London, 1973); Z. Łapiński, *Norwid* (Cracow, 1971); also T. Domaradzki, *Le symbolisme et l'universalisme de C. K. Norwid* (Québec, 1974).
62. Alfred Jarry, 'Ubu Roi' (1896) in *Tout Ubu* (Paris, 1962), 12; 'Quant à l'action, qui va commencer, elle se passe en Pologne, c'est-à-dire Nulle Part.'
63. Jan Reychman, *Życie polskie w Stambule w XVIII wieku* (Warsaw, 1959), Chapter VIII.
64. Stanisław Mackiewicz (Cat), *Historia Polski od 11 listopada do września 1939 r* (London, 1941), 347.

CHAPTER 2. ROSSIYA

1. Since the whole of the Russian Partition eventually became an integral part of the Russian Empire, any balanced understanding of the subject requires a knowledge both of general Russian History and of Polish affairs. For English-speaking students, the standard introductions are: Hugh Seton-Watson, *The Russian Empire, 1806–1917* (Oxford, 1967); and Piotr Wandycz, *The Lands of Partitioned Poland, 1795–1918* (Seattle, 1975).
2. Quoted by N. Riasanovsky, *Nicholas I and Official Nationality in Russia, 1825–55* (Berkeley, 1959), 70 ff.
3. Ibid. 127.
4. Feodor I. Tyutchev, (1803–73), in *The Penguin Book of Russian Verse* (London, 1967), 187.
5. Pyotr Y. Chaadayev (1793–1856) in his 'Philosophic Letter' (1836). See R. Hare, *Pioneers of Russian Social Thought* (London, 1951).
6. Szymon Tokarzewski, *Pamiętniki*, (Warsaw 1907–9), 2 vols.; (Vol. I, *Siedem lat katorgi*, Vol. II, *Ciernistym szlakiem*).
7. Wacław Lednicki, *Russia, Poland and the West: essays in literary and cultural history* (London, 1954), Chapter VI, 'Dostoevsky and Poland'.
8. Quoted by Riasanovsky, op. cit. 219–20.
9. Eve Curie, *Madame Curie: the biography by her daughter* (London, 1938), 19–21.
10. Karl Baedeker, *Russia with Teheran. Port Arthur and Peking: a Handbook for Travellers* (Leipzig–London, 1914), 9–12.
11. Adam Mickiewicz, 'Do przyjaciół Moskali' (To my Muscovite Friends). See W. Lednicki, 'Pushkin, Tyutchev, Mickiewicz and the Decembrists: legends and facts', *Slavonic and East European Review*, xxix, 73 (1951), 375–402.
12. Quoted by A. Bromke, *Poland's Politics: Idealism versus Realism* (Cambridge, Mass., 1967), 26.
13. Adam Mickiewicz, 'Stepy Akermańskie', *Dzieła poetyckie* (Warsaw, 1965), i. 259.
14. Alexander Blok, 'Voz'mediye' (Retribution), Chapter 3, lines 4–13, in *Stikhotvoreniya*, ed. V. Orlov (Leningrad, 1955), 560 ff. See Lednicki, op. cit. Chapter VII, 'Blok's Polish poem'.

CHAPTER 3. PREUSSEN

1. Since the Polish provinces became an integral part of the Prussian Kingdom and of the German Empire, their history can only be understood in conjunction with that of Prussia in general. In English see W. A. Carr, *A History of Germany, 1815–1945* (London, 1969); H. W. Koch, *A History of Prussia* (London, 1978); A. J. P. Taylor, *Bismarck* (London, 1955); and E. J. Feuchtwanger, *Prussia – myth and reality: the role of Prussia in German History*, (London, 1970). See also M. Laubert, *Die preussische Polenpolitik von 1772–1914* (Berlin, 1920), and H.-U. Wehler, 'Die Polenpolitik in deutschen Kaisscrreich, 1871–1918', in *Politische Ideologien und national-staatliche Ordnung*, ed. K. Knixen, W. J. Mommsen (Munich, 1968); M. Broszat, *200 Jahre deutsche Polenpolitik* (Munich, 1963); and Werner Grauendienst, 'Prussian Civic Consciousness and Polish Nationalism', in *Eastern Germany*, ed. Göttingen Research Committee (Würzburg, 1963). Contemporary Polish views on the subject are regularly expressed in the monthly, *Polish Western Affairs* (Poznań, 1959); see Lech Trzeciakowski, *Pod pruskim zaborem, 1850–1918* (Warsaw, 1973).

2. Oswald Spengler, *Prussianism and Socialism* (1919), quoted by Feuchtwanger, op. cit. 7.

3. C. E. Black, 'Poznań and Europe in 1848', *Journal of Central European Affairs*, viii (1948), 191–206. S. Kieniewicz, *Społeczeństwo polskie w powstaniu polskim 1848 roku* (Warsaw, 1935).

4. Quoted by W. Jakobczyk, *Studia nad dziejami Wielkopolski w XIX wieku* (Poznań, 1967), and by P. Wandycz, *The Lands of Partitioned Poland, 1795–1918* (Seattle, 1975), 229.

5. Moritz Busch, *Our Chancellor – sketches for a historical picture*, trans. W. Beatty-Johnson (London, 1884), ii. 146–57. The marginal nature of the Polish question in Bismarck's thinking can be judged from the fact that in A. J. P. Taylor's study, it is not even mentioned. Cv J. Feldman, *Bismarck a Polska* (Warsaw, 1966; Cracow, 1937).

6. Busch, op. cit. 157–62.

7. J. Krasuski, *Kulturkampf, katolicyzm i liberalizm w Niemczech XIX wieku* (Poznań, 1963); Erich Schmidt-Volkmar, *Der Kulturkampf in Deutschland, 1871–90*, (Göttingen, 1962).

8. See H. Neubach, *Die Ausweisungen von Polen und Juden aus Preussen 1885–6: ein Beitrag zu Bismarcks Polenpolitik, und zur Geschichte des deutsche–polnischen Verhaltnisses* (Wiesbaden, 1967).

9. Lech Trzeciakowski, 'The Prussian in state and the Catholic Church in Prussian Poland, 1871–1914', *Slavic Review*, xxvi (1967), 618–37.

10. Karl Baedeker, *Northern Germany . . .* (Leipzig–London, 1890), 250–3.

11. A. Wojtkowski, *Działalność Pruskiej Komisji Kolonizacyjnej* (Toruń, 1932); Witold Jakobczyk, *Pruska Komisja Osadnicza, 1886–1919* (Poznań, 1976).

12. A. Basiński, 'Michał Drzymała (1857–1937)', *Polski Słownik Biograficzny*, v (Cracow, 1946), 424–5. In 1939, the village of Podgradowice was re-named Drzymałowo in his honour. Few Polish accounts mention the fact that the idea of living in a caravan to beat the regulations came from a local German, one Neldner, who helped Drzymała to fight the Prussian authorities.

13. Edward Martuszewski, *Polscy i nie polscy Prusacy: szkice z historii Mazur i Warmii* (Olsztyn, 1974), 8–9.
14. Marx (1848) quoted by M. Serejski, *Europa a rozbiory Polski* (Warsaw, 1970), 239–40: Engels (1851) quoted by Edmund Wilson, *To the Finland Station* (London, 1962), 232. General works on Marx's and Engels's views on Poland include the documentary collection *Marks i Engels o Polsce* (Warsaw, 1960), 2 vols; Celina Bobińska, *Marks i Engels a sprawa polska* (Warsaw, 1955); idem. *Marksa spotkania z Polską* (Cracow, 1971), with extensive English summary. Marx maintained his support for Polish independence even when his opinions were increasingly unpopular in radical circles.
15. R. Tims, *Germanising Prussian Poland: the H-K-T Society and the struggle for the Eastern Marches in the German Empire, 1894–1919* (New York, 1941); also I. D. Morrow, 'The Prussianisation of the Poles', *Slavonic and East European Review*, xv (1936), 153–64; M. Dufourmantelle, *La Politique de germanisation en Pologne prussienne* (Bruxelles, 1922); A. Galos, F. Gentzen, W. Jakobczyk, *Dzieje Hakaty, 1894–1934* (Poznań, 1966).
16. Max Weber, 'Der Nationalstaat und die Volkswirtschaftspolitik (1895)', in *Gesammelte Politische Schriften* (Munich, 1971), 8.
17. Maria Konopnicka, 'Rota' (The Oath), *Wybór poezji*, ed. J. Karłowicza (Chicago, 1945), 320. See J. Słomczyńska, *Maria Konopnicka: życie i twórczość* (Łódź, 1946).
18. See Richard Blanke, 'The development of Loyalism in Prussian Poland, 1886–90', *Slavonic and East European Review*, lii (1974), 548–65.
19. *Powstanie wielkopolskie 1918–19*, ed. K. Piwarski (Poznań, 1958).

CHAPTER 4. GALICIA

1. The Austrian framework of Galician history can be traced in H. Wickham Steed, *The Habsburg Monarchy* (London, 1914), and E. A. Kann, *The Multinational Empire: Nationalism and National Reform in the Habsburg Monarchy 1848–1918* (New York, 1950), 2 vols. On the Poles, see P. Wandycz, 'The Poles in the Austrian Empire', and H. Wereszycki, 'The Poles as an integrating and disintegrating factor', both in *Austrian History Yearbook* iii, Part 2 (1967), 261–313. Two recent studies of Galician affairs are: Konstanty Grzybowski, *Galicja 1848–1914* (Wrocław, 1959), and S. Grodziski, *W królestwie Galicyi i Lodomerii* (Cracow, 1976).
2. S. Szczepański, *Nędza Galicyjska w cyfrach* (Lwów, 1888).
3. See T. W. Simons, 'The Peasant Revolt of 1846 in Galicia: some recent Polish historiography', *Slavic Review*, xxx (1971), 795–817; S. Kieniewicz, *Ruch chłopski w Galicji w 1846 roku* (Wrocław, 1951); M. Żychowski, *Rok 1846 w Rzeczypospolitej Krakowskiej i Galicji* (Warsaw, 1956).
4. Karl Baedeker, *Austria–Hungary* (Leipzig–London, 1905), 283–4.
5. Peter Brock, 'B. Wysłouch: founder of the Polish Peasant Party', *Slavonic and East European Review*, xxx (74), (1951), 139–63; and 'The Early years of the Polish Peasant Party, 1895–1907', *Journal of Central European Affairs*, xiv (1954), 219–35. K. Dunin-Wąsowicz, *Dzieje Stronnictwa Ludowego w Galicji* (Warsaw, 1958).

6. W. J. Rose, 'Wincenty Witos', *Slavonic and East European Review*, xxv (1946), 39–54.

7. W. J. Rose, 'Ignacy Daszyński, 1886–1936', *Slavonic and East European Review*, xv (1937), 445–8.

8. Attributed to Viceroy Sanguszko. S. Grodziski, *W Królestwie Galicji i Lodomerii* (Cracow, 1976), 265.

9. Jan Hulewicz, *Polska Akademia Umiejętności 1873–1948: Zarys dziejów* (Cracow, 1948).

10. Tadeusz Boy-Żeleński (1874–1941); A. Stawar, *Boy* (Warsaw, 1958); S. Sterkowicz, *Boy: Dr. T. Żeleński* (Warsaw, 1960); B. Winklowa, *T. Żeleński: twórczość i życie* (Warsaw, 1967); W. Borowy, 'Boy jako tłumacz', *Studia i rozprawy* (Wrocław, 1952), ii.

11. N. Andrusiak, 'The Ukrainian Movement in Galicia', *Slavonic and East European Review*, xiv (1935–6), 163–75, 372–9.

12. M. Król, 'Michał Bobrzyński', in *Sylwetki polityczne XIX wieku* (Cracow, 1974), 105–10.

13. Tadeusz Boy-Żeleński, 'Historia Prawicy Narodowej' (The History of the National Right-wing), from Piosenki Zielonego Balonika, *Boy: Słówka*, (8th Edition, Cracow, 1973), 177–9.

CHAPTER 5. FABRYKA

1. Irena Pietrzak-Pawlikowska, 'Uprzemysłowienie ziem polskich na tle europejskim', *Pamiętnik X Powszechnego Zjazdu Historyków Polskich w Lublinie 1968: Referaty* (Warsaw, 1968), i. 313–33.

2. R. Luksemburg, *Die industrielle Entwicklung Polens* (Leipzig, 1898).

3. Oskar Lange, *Political Economy*, trans., A. H. Walker (Oxford, 1963–71), 2 vols.

4. See W. W. Rostow, *The Process of Economic Growth* (Oxford, 1953).

5. See Antonina Keckowa, *Żupy krakowskie w XVI–XVIII wieku, (do 1772 roku)* (Wrocław, 1969), 'Opieka społeczna', 257–62.

6. W. Rozdzieński, *'Officina Ferraria abo Huta y Warstat z Kuzniami szlachetnego dzieła żelaznego'*, (Officina Ferraria or the Workshop and Forges of the noble iron industry), (Cracow, 1612).

7. See B. Zientara, *Dzieje małopolskiego hutnictwa żelaznego XIV–XVII wieku* (Warsaw, 1954).

8. See K. Bajer, *Przemysł włókienniczy na ziemiach polskich od początku XIX wieku do roku 1939* (Łódź, 1939).

9. See S. Bartoszewicz, 'Przemysł naftowy w Polsce', in *Bilans gospodarczy 10-lecia Polski odrodzonej* (Poznań, 1929).

10. See J. Pazdur. *Zakłady metalowe w Białogonie, 1614–1914* (Wrocław, 1957), which cites instances of early Victorian engineers in Poland.

11. J. Gieysztor, *Koleje żelazne na ziemiach polskich* (Warsaw, 1918); H. Hilchen, *Historia drogi Warszawsko-Wiedeńskiej, 1835–98* (Warsaw, 1912); Feliks Filipek, *Kolej Warszawsko-Wiedeńskiej, 1895–98* (Warsaw, 1912); Feliks Filipek, *Kolej Warszawsko-Terespolska* (Warsaw, 1972).

12. J. Bankiewicz, B. Domosławski, 'Zniszczenia i szkody wojenne', *Polska w czasie wielkiej wojny, t III, Historia Ekonomiczna* (Warsaw, 1936).

CHAPTER 6. LUD

1. Virtually all official histories in present-day Poland regarding the nineteenth and early twentieth centuries are based on the assumption of an organic social process determining the development of a well-defined Polish nation under the conditions of 'Capitalism' and 'Imperialism' -- see the forewords to ii, Part 1, and iii, Part 1 of the *Historia Polski (PAN)*.

2. Irena Gieysztor, 'Research into the Demographic History of Poland: a provisional summing-up', *Acta Poloniae Historica*, xviii (1968), 5--17.

3. See K. Dunin-Wąsowicz, 'Struktura demograficzna narodu polskiego 1864--1914', *Historia Polski* (PAN), iii, Part 1 (Warsaw, 1967), 92--110.

4. Harold Nicolson, *Peacemaking* (London, 1964), 332. On Paderewski's life see Mary Lawton, I. Paderewski, *The Paderewski Memoirs* (New York and London, 1939).

5. Stefan Kieniewicz, *The Emancipation of the Polish Peasantry* (Chicago, 1969).

6. From W. Reymont, *Chłopi: powieść współczesna* (Peasants: a contemporary tale) (Warsaw, 1909), 4 vols.; Ladislas Reymont, *The Peasants: Autumn--Winter--Spring--Summer: a tale of our own time* (New York, 1937).

7. A. Świętochowski, *Historia chłopów polskich w zarysie*, ii (Lwów, 1928).

8. See M. Kridl, J. Wittlin, *et al.*, *The Democratic Heritage of Poland: For Your Freedom and Ours: an Anthology* (London, 1944), 122--27.

9. Jan Borkowski *et al.*, *Zarys historii polskiego ruchu ludowego*, 2 vols. (Warsaw, 1970); see also Olga Narkiewicz, *The Green Flag: Polish Populist Politics, 1867--1970* (London, 1976).

10. See Ryszard Kołodziejczyk, *Kształtowanie się burżuazji w Królestwie Polskim, 1815--50* (Warsaw, 1957); Ireneusz Ihnatowicz, *Burżuazja warszawska* (Warsaw, 1972); *Obyczaj wielkiej burżuazji warszawskiej w XIX wieku* (Warsaw, 1971).

11. A. Gella, 'The Life and Death of the old Polish Intelligentsia', *Slavic Review*, xxx (1970), 1--27.

12. Władysław Reymont, *Ziemia obiecana* (The Promised Land), (Warsaw, 1899), 29--33.

13. B. Kłapkowski, *Ruch zawodowy robotników i pracowników na ziemiach polskich w czasie zaborów* (Warsaw, 1939); I. Orzechowski, A. Kochański, *Zarys dziejów ruchu zawodowego 1905--18* (Warsaw, 1964).

14. See Lidia and Adam Ciołkosz, *Zarys dziejów socjalizmu polskiego*, i (London, 1966).

15. J. Peterkiewicz, Burns Singer, *Five Centuries of Polish poetry* (London, 1960), 83.

16. Stefan Żeromski, *Ludzie bezdomni* (Homeless People) (Warsaw, 1928), 36--40.

CHAPTER 7. KOŚCIÓŁ

1. Bp Wincenty Urban, *Ostatni etap dziejów kościoła w Polsce przed nowym tysiącleciem, 1815--1965* (Rome, 1966) 555; the authoritative survey with extensive bibliographies.

2. A. de Koskowski, *La Pologne Catholique* (Couvin, Belgium, 1910); see also J. J. Zatko, 'The organisation of the Catholic Church in Russia, 1772–84', *Slavonic and East European Review*, xliii (1965), 303–13; and Z. Olszamowska, 'Tentatives d'introduire la langue russe dans les églises latines de la Pologne orientale', *Antemurale*, ii (1967), 25–169.

3. J. A. White, *The Occupation of West Russia after the First Partition of Poland* (New York, 1940).

4. The Revd Martinoff SJ, 'Le Brigandage de Chelm', in *Études Réligieuses*, Brussels (June 1875), 952–3: quoted by Koskowski, op. cit. 94–5.

5. Ks. Edward Likowski, *Dzieje kościoła unickiego na Litwie i Rusi* (Warsaw, 1906), 2 vols.

6. See *Papiestwo wobec sprawy polskiej w latach 1772–1864: Wybór źródeł*, ed. O. Beiersdorf (Wrocław, 1960); also A. Tamborra, 'Catholicisme et le Monde Orthodoxe à l'époque de Pie IX', *Miscellanea Historiae Ecclesiasticae*, nr. 4 (Louvain, 1972), 179–93.

7. Juliusz Słowacki, *Kordian*, Act II, lines 174–217.

8. Emanuel Rostworowski, 'Ksiądz Marek i proroctwa polityczne doby radomskobarskiej', in the collective work, *Przemiany tradycji barskiej: studia* (Cracow, 1972), 29–57.

9. Włodzimierz Djaków, *Piotr Ściegienny i jego spuścizna* (Warsaw, 1972); Text of *List ojca świętego Papieża Grzegorza do rolników i rzemieślników z Rzymu przysłany*, 248–64; T. Rek, *Ksiądz Eugeniusz Okon* (Warsaw, 1962).

10. On Feliński, see Bohdan Cywiński, *Rodowody niepokornych* (Cracow, 1970), 247–51, which includes the text of his letter to *Le Moniteur* of 15 March 1862. Cywiński optimistically characterizes the condition of the Polish Church in the nineteenth century as 'Julianist', stoutly resisting the oppression of apostate secular authorities: ibid. 262 ff.

11. See J. Kucharzewski, *Od białego caratu do czerwonego* (Warsaw, 1925), 2 vols.; C. M. Young, *The Moscow Trial of Archbishop Cieplak* (Chicago, 1957).

12. N. Cieszyński, *Uniwersytet lubelski: jego powstanie i rozwój* (Poznań, 1924).

13. Ct. Bniński 1923. See S. Bross, *Akcja Katolicka w Polsce* (Poznań, 1929); F. Machay, *Dogmatyczne podstawy Akcji Katolickiej* (Poznań, 1934).

14. St. Mystkowski, *Polski Kościół Narodowy* (Warsaw, 1923).

15. O. Honorat, *Prawda o Mariawitach* (Warsaw, 1906); M. Skrudlik, *Zbrodnie mariawitów w świetle dokumentów* (Warsaw, 1927); G. Skwara, *Mariawici: szkic historyczny* (Płock, 1925).

16. Z. J. Sochocki, *Rycerz niepokalanej: Ojciec Maksymilian Kolbe* (London, n.d.). See also Jan Sziling, *Polityka okupanta hitlerowskiego wobec Kościoła katolickiego 1939–45* (Poznań. 1970).

CHAPTER 8. KULTURA

1. There are many surveys of Polish cultural history, including, in English, Manfred Kridl, *A Survey of Polish Literature and Culture* (The Hague, 1956); Wacław Lednicki, *The Life and Culture of Poland as reflected in Polish Literature* (New York, 1944); and Czesław Miłosz, *A History of Polish Literature* (London, 1969). On the History of Polish Education, see *Historia*

wychowania, ed. L. Kurdybacha (Warsaw, 1965), 2 vols.; S. Wołoszyn, *Dzieje wychowania i myśli pedagogicznej w zarysie* (Warsaw, 1964). By far the most interesting and provocative study of the Polish cultural crusade in the late nineteenth century is Bogdan Cywiński, *Rodowody niepokornych* (Warsaw, 1971).

2. See A. Brückner, *Dzieje języka polskiego* (Warsaw, 1925). See also A. P. Coleman, 'Language as a factor in Polish nationalism', *Slavonic and East European Review*, xiii, 37 (1934), 155–72.

3. W. J. Rose, *Stanislas Konarski, Reformer of Education in Eighteenth Century Poland* (London, 1929).

4. Tadeusz Mizia, *O Komisji Edukacji Narodowej* (Warsaw, 1972); Renata Dutkowa, *Komisja edukacji narodowej: zarys działalności, wybór materiałów źródłowych* (Wrocław, 1973); A. Jobert, *La Commission d'Éducation Nationale en Pologne, 1773–94* (Dijon, 1941); L. Kurdybacha, 'The Commission of National Education in Poland, 1773–94', *History of Education*, ii, No. 2 (1973), 133–46.

5. Stanisław August Poniatowski, *Pamiętnik polityczno-historyczny, rok 1783*, 329–332, quoted by Dutkowa, op. cit. 134–7.

6. See W. Tokarz, 'Komisja Edukacyjna a Uniwersytet Jagielloński' *Przegląd Warszawski* vol. 3 (1923), 285–319; also M. Chamcówna, *Uniwersytet Jagielloński w dobie Komisyi Edukacyjnej* (Wrocław, 1957, 1959), 2 vols.

7. N. Hans, 'Polish schools in Russia, 1772–1831', *Slavonic and East European Reviews*, xxxviii (1959), 394–414.

8. Cywiński, op. cit. 79 ff.

9. H. Ceysingerówna, 'Tajne nauczanie w Warszawie, 1894–1906/7', *Niepodległość*, (1930) ii. 95–103.

10. Quoted by Cywiński, op. cit. 104–5.

CHAPTER 9. ŻYDZI

1. The most convenient source of reliable information on Polish Jewry is to be found in the articles of the *Encyclopaedia Judaica* (Jerusalem, 1971), especially under 'Poland', xiii. 710–90. The standard work, S. M. Dubnow, *The History of the Jews in Russia and Poland* (Philadelphia, 1916–20), 3 vols., is still useful, if somewhat tendentious. See also Michel Borwicz, *A Thousand Years of Jewish Life in Poland* (Paris, 1955); Bernard Weinryb, *The Jews of Poland* (Philadelphia, 1973); and Irving Howe, *World of our Fathers: the Jews of Eastern Europe* (New York, 1976).

2. Markus Wischnitzer, *To dwell in safety: the story of Jewish migration since 1800* (Philadelphia, 1948).

3. See H. M. Rabinowicz, *The World of Hasidism* (New York, 1970), idem, *Guide to Hassidism* (New York, 1960); S. H. Dresner, *The Zaddik* (New York, 1960).

4. J. S. Raisin, *The Haskalah Movement in Russia* (1913; republished, Westport, 1972).

5. A. Duker, 'The Polish Insurrection's missed opportunity, 1830–1', *Jewish Social Studies*, xxviii (1966), 212–32.

6. Artur Eisenbach, 'Les droits civiques des Juifs dans le Royaume de Pologne,

1815–63', *Revue d'Études Juives*, cxxiii (1964), 19–84; idem, *Kwestia Równouprawnienia Żydów w Królestwie Polskim* (Warsaw, 1972).

7. See E. Mendelsohn, 'From Assimilation to Zionism in Lvov', *Slavonic and East European Review*, xlix (1971), 521–34.

8. Dubnow, op. cit. ii. 213.

9. Menachem Ribalow, *The Flowering of Modern Hebrew Literature* (New York, 1959).

10. Charles Madison, *Yiddish Literature: its scope and major writers* (New York, 1971). See also *A Treasury of Yiddish Stories*, ed. I. Howe, E. Greenberg (New York, 1958), and *Voices from the Yiddish* (Ann Arbor, Mi., 1972); *The Golden Tradition: Jewish Life and Thought in Eastern Europe*, ed. Lucy S. Dawidowicz (New York, 1967); M. Samuel, *Prince of the Ghetto* (New York, 1973), (on I. J. Peretz); I. B. Singer, *Of a World that is no more* (New York, 1970), etc.

11. J. Frumkin *et al.*, *Russian Jewry 1860–1917* (New York, 1966).

12. See Walter Laqueur, *A History of Zionism* (New York, 1972).

13. *The Zionist Idea*, ed. A. Hertzberg (New York, 1966), 401–4.

14. Mark Zborowski, Elizabeth Herzog, *Life is with People: the Jewish Little-town of Eastern Europe* (New York, 1952); A. Ain, 'Swisłocz: Portrait of a Jewish Community in Eastern Europe', *Yivo Annual of Jewish Social Sciences*, iv (1949), 86–114.

15. H. J. Tobias, *The Jewish Bund in Russia from its origins to 1905* (Stanford, 1972).

16. B. K. Johnpoll, *The Politics of Futility: the General Jewish Workers Bund of Poland, 1917–43* (Ithaca, N.Y., 1967).

17. Adapted from an English translation in M. Kridl, W. Malinowski, *For Your Freedom and Ours: The Democratic Heritage of Poland: an Anthology* (London, 1944), 77–9.

18. Published as a separate broadsheet in a sort of English and entitled *First Congress of the Founders of the Association of the Poles' Jewish Confession* (Warsaw, May 1919). For a personal account of the confused state of affairs at this juncture, see I. Cohen, 'My mission to Poland, 1918–19', *Jewish Social Studies*, xiii (1951), 149–72; also C. S. Heller, 'Assimilation: a deviant pattern among the Jews of inter-war Poland', *Jewish Journal of Sociology*, xv, nr. 2 (1973), 221–37.

19. Antoni Słonimski, 'Na drażliwość żydów', in *Wiadomości Literackie* (Literary News) (Warsaw, 1925) nrs. 6, 14, 16, 18.

20. Lucjan Blit, *The Eastern Pretender* (London, 1965), 38–9.

21. In his covering letter to the Samuel Report, June 1920. See Norman Davies, 'Great Britain and the Polish Jews, 1918–21', *Journal of Contemporary History*, viii, nr. 2 (1973), 119–42.

22. See Yehudah Bauer, *The Holocaust in Historical Perspective* (London, 1978).

23. G. Reitlinger, *The Final Solution: an attempt to exterminate the Jews of Europe, 1939–45* (London, 1953); *Martyrs and Fighters*, ed. P. Friedman (New York, 1954); Reuben Ainsztein, 'The Jews in Poland – need they have died?', *Twentieth Century*, clxiv, No. 979 (Sept, 1958), and Lucjan Blit, ibid., clxiv, No. 980 (Oct, 1958); Michal Borwicz, 'Spekulanci żydowską krwią', *Unser Wort – Notre Parole* (Paris), Nos. 8, 10 (1958); Joseph Lichten,

'Some aspects of Polish–Jewish Relations during the Nazi Occupation', *Studies in Polish Civilisation*, ed. D. Wandycz (New York, 1966), 154–75; *Righteous among nations: how Poles helped the Jews, 1939–45*, ed. W. Bartoszewski, Z. Lewin (London, 1972); S. Krakowski, 'The Slaughter of Polish Jewry: a Polish "re-assessment"', *Wiener Library Bulletin*, cxxi (May 1973), 293–401; *Polacy i Żydzi, 1939–45*, ed. S. Wroński, M. Zwałakowa (Warsaw, 1971); E. Ringelblum, *Polish–Jewish Relations during the Second World War* (Jerusalem, 1974), etc.

CHAPTER 10. WOJSKO

1. Marian Kukiel, *Zarys historii wojskowości w Polsce* (Cracow, 1929; republished, London, 1949) is one of the few surveys of the subject to cover the whole of the modern period. For obvious reasons, most histories of Polish military affairs, like T. Korzon, *Dzieje wojen i wojskowości* (Lwów, 1923), 3 vols., stop short at the Partitions. See also *Histoire militaire de la Pologne: problèmes choisis*, ed. Witold Biegański (Varsovie, 1971).

2. See Leonard Ratajczyk, *Wojsko i obronność Rzeczypospolitej, 1788–92* (Warsaw, 1975).

3. Jerzy Kowecki, *Pospolite ruszenie w insurekcji kościuszkowskiej* (Warsaw, 1964).

4. Marian Kukiel, *Dzieje wojska polskiego w dobie napoleońskiej* (Warsaw, 1920); Jan Pachoński, *Legiony polskie 1794–1807* (Warsaw, 1971), 3 vols.

5. Mieczysław Chojnacki, *Wojska Królestwa Polskiego 1815–31* (Warsaw, 1961).

6. M. Kukiel, 'Problèmes des guerres d'insurrection au XIX siècle', *Antemurale* ii (1959), 70–9. K. Wyczańska, *Polacy w Komunie Paryskiej 1871 r* (Warsaw, 1958).

7. On the history of the Legions, see H. Bagiński, *U podstaw organizacji Wojska Polskiego 1908–1914* (Warsaw, 1935); A. Garlicki, *Geneza Legionów* (Warsaw, 1964); Wacław Lipiński, *Walka zbrojna o niepodległość Polski 1905–18* (2nd Edition, Warsaw, 1935); S. Arski, *My, Pierwsza Brygada* (Warsaw, 1963).

8. The main sources for the Polish military contribution to the Second World War are: *Polskie Siły Zbrojne w Drugiej Wojnie Światowej* (London, 1959), 2 vols.; and *Polski czyn zbrojny w II wojnie światowej – Ludowe Wojsko Polskie 1943–5* (Warsaw, 1973). See also W. Anders, *An Army in Exile: the Story of the Second Polish Corps* (London, 1949); Cz. Podgórski, *Lenino* (Warsaw, 1972); Charles Cannell, *Monte Cassino: the Historic Battle* (London, 1963); Melchior Wańkowicz, *Monte Cassino* (Warsaw, 1972).

9. J. Piłsudski, *Year 1920* (London, 1972), (includes the text of M. Tukhachevsky, *Advance to the Vistula*); W. Sikorski, *La campagne polono-russe de 1920* (Paris, 1928); Norman Davies, *White Eagle, Red Star – the Polish–Soviet War, 1919–20* (London, 1972); N. E. Kakurin, A. Melikov, *Voyna s Belopolyakami, 1920 g* (Moscow, 1925); *La Guerre polono–sovietique de 1919–20*, Collection Historique de l'Institut d'Études Slaves, No. XXII (Paris, 1975).

10. J. Bednarowicz, S. Werner, eds., *Żołnierska rzecz: zbiór pieśni wojskowych* (Warsaw, 1965), 57.

11. Several versions of the lyric exist, the first one dating from 17 July 1917. See Tadeusz Biernacki, *My Pierwsza Brygada* . . . *Powstanie i historia pieśni* (Warsaw, 1929).

12. J.-J. Rousseau, from *Remarques sur le gouvernement polonais* (1771).

CHAPTER 11. EMIGRACJA

1. Research into this subject has received strong official support in Poland in recent years. See *Dzieje Polonii w XIX i XX wieku: referaty i komunikaty*, ed. M. Drozdowski (Toruń, 1974); also R. Bierzanek, 'Stan i potrzeby badań naukowych nad problematyką polonijną', *Problemy Polonii Zagranicznej*, v (1966/7), J. Zubrzycki, 'Emigration from Poland in the nineteenth and twentieth centuries', *Population Studies*, vi (1953), 248–72; B. P. Murdzek, *Emigration in Polish Social–Political Thought, 1870–1914* (Boulder–New York, 1977).

2. S. Kalembka, *Wielka Emigracja a Polskie uchodźstwo 1831–62* (Warsaw, 1972; Jerzy Borejsza, *Emigracja polska po powstaniu styczniowym* (Warsaw, 1966).

3. Halina Janowska, 'Research on economic emigration', *Acta Poloniae Historica*, xxvii (1973), 187–208; C. Bobińska, ed., *Emigracje zarobkowe na tle wschodnioeuropejskich i polskich struktur społeczno-ekonomicznych: tezy i streszczenia referatów i komunikatów* (Toruń, 1974).

4. Wincenty Witos, *Jedna wieś* (One Village), (Chicago, 1955). The classic work on peasant emigration is Wm. Thomas, Florian Znaniecki, *The Polish Peasant in Europe: monograph of an immigrant group* (Boston, 1918–20), 5 vols.

5. *The Church Records of Panna Maria (Texas)*, ed. J. Dworaczyk (Chicago, 1945), 8. See also A. Brożek, *Ślązacy w Teksasie* (Warsaw, 1972); J. Przygoda, *Texas pioneers from Poland: a study in ethnic history* (San Antonio–Los Angeles, 1971).

6. See Andrzej Brożek, *Polonia amerykańska, 1854–1939* (Interpress, Warsaw, 1977), which has an extensive bibliography; also P. Fox, *The Poles in America* (New York, 1922); M. Haiman, *The Polish past in America, 1608–1865* (Chicago, 1939).

7. Helena Znaniecki-Łopata, 'Polish Immigration to the United States of America: problems of estimation and parameters', *Polish Review*, xxi, nr. 4 (1976), 85–107. See also Alina Baran, 'Distribution of Polish Origin Population in the USA', *Polish Western Affairs*, xvii, nr. 1–2 (1976), 139–44.

8. J. S. Wordsworth, *Strangers within our gates* (Toronto, 1972), 114.

9. 'Throughout the century men of the sturdy stocks of north of Europe had made up the main strain of foreign blood . . . but now there came multitudes of men from the lowest class from the south of Italy and men of the meaner sort out of Hungary and Poland, men out of the ranks where there was neither skill nor energy nor any initiative or quick intelligence . . .' T. Woodrow Wilson, *A History of the American People* (New York, 1902) v, 212.

10. Irwin T. Sanders, Ewa T. Morawska, *Polish–American Community Life: a survey of research*, The Community Sociology Monograph Series, ii (Boston–New York, 1975), which contains an extensive bibliography. See also S. Włoszczewski, *A History of Polish American Culture* (Trenton, 1946);

J. A. Wytrwal, *America's Polish Heritage: a social history of the Poles in America* (Detroit, 1961).

11. W. B. Makowski, *The History and Integration of the Poles in Canada* (Niagara Falls, 1967); *Past and Present: Selected Topics on the Polish Group in Canada*, ed. Benedikt Heydenkorn (Toronto, 1974); A. Kapiszewski, 'Problems in Multiculturalism and the Polish Canadian Community', *Polish Western Affairs*, xvii, No. 1–2 (1976), 145–51.

12. Krzysztof Groniowski, 'The Main Stages in the History of Polish Immigrants in South America', *Polish Western Affairs*, xvii, No. 1–2 (1976), 152–60; R. Stemplowski, 'Enlistment in Brazil to the Polish Armed Forces, 1940–44', ibid., 161–72. See also the collective work, *Emigracja polska w Brazylii: 100 lat osadnictwa* (Warsaw, 1971).

13. Krystyna Murzynowska, *Polskie wychodźstwo zarobkowe w Zagłębiu Ruhry w latach 1880–1914* (Wrocław, 1972); R. Clemens, *L'Assimilation culturelle des immigrants en Belgique; Italiens et polonais dans la région liégoise* (Liége, 1953); H. Janowska, *Polska emigracja zarobkowa we Francji* (Warsaw, 1964).

14. See J. Zubrzycki, *Polish Immigrants in Britain* (The Hague, 1956); and especially Sheila Patterson, 'The Poles: an exile community in Britain', in *Between Two Cultures*, ed. J. L. Watson (Oxford, 1977), 214–41; also B. Czajkowski, B. Sulik, *Polacy w Wielkiej Brytanii* (Paris, 1961).

15. The persistence of a substantial Polish community in the USSR is not advertised by the Soviet authorities, and Soviet Poles are conspicuous by their absence from almost all the official activities arranged in Poland for Polish *émigrés*. Soviet sources, which put Soviet citizens of Polish nationality at about 1.5 million, are widely believed to underestimate their true numbers.

16. n.b. The great majority of Polish-speaking Israelis would never admit to being 'Poles' but merely to being 'Jews from Poland'.

17. George Orwell, *Homage to Catalonia* (London, 1975), 246. This verse, inspired by the defeat of the Republicans in the Spanish Civil War, rings very true to the Polish socialists and radicals who were the main target for Stalinist repression.

18. From Lord Byron, *Childe Harolde's Pilgrimage*, Canto I, xiii. Mickiewicz's translation, 'Pożegnanie Czajld Harolda' is in his *Poezje*, ed. J. Kallenbach (Wrocław, 1949), i, 165–8.

19. Julian Ursyn Niemcewicz, 'Wygnańcy' (The Exiles), 12 May 1841.

20. Composed by Kajetan Koźmian and Franciszek Morawski.

CHAPTER 12. VARSOVIE

1. The standard work on this period is undoubtedly S. Askenazy, *Napoleon a Polska*, translated as *Napoléon et la Pologne* (Brussels, 1925), 3 vols.; see also B. Grochulska, *Księstwo Warszawskie* (Warsaw, 1966); W. Sobociński, *Historia ustroju i prawa Księstwa Warszawskiego* (Warsaw, 1964).

2. There is some controversy over the authorship of this pamplet, but the identity of views between Kościuszko and Pawlikowski renders any speculation superfluous. On the Napoleonic legend in Poland, see A. Zahorski, *Z dziejów legendy napoleońskiej w Polsce* (Warsaw, 1971).

3. W. H. Zawadzki, 'Prince Adam Czartoryski and Napoleonic France, 1801–5: a study in political attitudes', *Historical Journal*, xviii (1975), 245–7; see also E. Halicz, *Geneza Księstwa Warszawskiego* (Warsaw, 1962).

4. B. Grochulska, 'Sur la structure économique du Duché de Varsovie 1807–13', *Annales Historiques de la Révolution Française*, xxxvi (1964), 349–63; Marian Kallas, *Konstytucja Księstwa Warszawskiego* (Toruń, 1970).

5. See Zbigniew Załuski, *Siedem polskich grzechów głównych i inne polemiki* (Warsaw, 1973), 'Z szablami na baterie', 52–60.

6. Adam Mickiewicz, *Pan Tadeusz, or the Last Foray in Lithuania* adapted from the English translation by George Rapall Noyes (London, 1917), Book XI, 278 ff.

7. Ibid.

8. Kajetan Koźmian, *Pamiętniki* (Wrocław, 1972), ii, 189.

9. Szymon Askenazy, *Książę Józef Poniatowski, 1763–1813* (Warsaw, 1922; republished, Warsaw, 1973).

CHAPTER 13. KONGRESÓWKA

1. On the diplomatic origins of the Congress Kingdom, see K. Bartoszewicz, *Utworzenie Królestwa Kongresowego* (Cracow, 1916); also W. H. Zawadzki, 'Adam Czartoryski: an advocate of Slavonic solidarity at the Congress of Vienna', *Oxford Slavonic Papers* (New Series), x (1977), 73–97; C. K. Webster, 'England and the Polish–Saxon problem at the Congress of Vienna', *Transactions of the Royal Historical Society*, vii (1913), 49–101.

2. P. Rain, 'Alexandre I et la Pologne: un essai en gouvernement constitutionel', *Revue d'histoire diplomatique*, xxvi (1912), 74–101; L. Pingual, 'L'Empereur Alexandre I, roi de Pologne', ibid., xxxi–ii (1917/18), 513–40.

3. S. K. Potocki, *Podróż do Ciemnogrodu, Świstek krytyczny*, ed. E. Kipa (Wrocław, 1955), with extensive introduction.

4. See R. F. Leslie, 'Politics and economics in Congress Poland 1815–65', *Past and Present*, No. 8 (1955), 43–63; S. Smolka, *Polityka Lubeckiego przed powstaniem listopadowym* (Cracow, 1907), 2 vols.

5. M. Chojnacki, *Wojska Królestwa Polskiego, 1815–31* (Warsaw, 1961).

6. S. Askenazy, *Łukasiński* (Warsaw, 1929), 2 vols.; W. Łukasiński (*Pamiętnik*), ed. E. Gerber (Warsaw, 1960); H. Dylągowa, *Towarzystwo Patriotyczne i Sąd Sejmowy 1821–9* (Warsaw, 1970).

7. W. L. Bleckwell, 'Russian Decembrist views of Poland', *Polish Review*, iii, nr. 4 (1958), 30–54. L. Baumgarten, *Dekabryści a Polska* (Warsaw, 1952).

8. M. Kukiel, 'Lelewel, Mickiewicz and the underground movement of European Revolution, 1816–33', *Polish Review*, v. nr. 3 (1960), 59–76.

9. See R. F. Leslie, *Polish Politics and the Revolution of November 1830* (London, 1956).

10. Casimir Delavigne, 'La Varsovienne', *Œuvres complètes* (Paris, 1855), 522–3. Translated into Polish by Karol Sienkiewicz as 'Warszawianka' and set to music by Karol Kurpiński, this poem has become the most popular of Polish revolutionary anthems.

11. Popular views of the episode owe more to Wyspiański's idealized play, *Noc*

Listopadowa (1904), than to reality. See Artur Śliwiński, *Powstanie listo-padowe* (Cracow, 1911).

12. Wacław Tokarz, *Wojna polsko-rosyjska, 1830–1* (Warsaw, 1930).

13. This is the subject of a popular poem by Słowacki, 'Sowiński w okopach Woli', *Wiersze i poematy (Wybór)* (PIW, Warsaw, 1971), 57–9.

14. F. I. Tyutchev (1803–73), 'Na vzyatie Varshavy 26 avgusta 1831g', *Polnoe Sobranie Sochinenii*, ed. P. V. Bykov (St. Petersburg, 1911), 277–8.

15. Alexander Pushkin, 'Klevetnikam Rossii – vox et praeterea nihil'. *The Oxford Book of Russian Verse* (2nd Edition, Oxford, 1948), 73–4.

16. *Selected Correspondence of Fryderyk Chopin*, ed. A. Hedley (London, 1962), Nos. 48, 96.

17. Casimir Delavigne, 'La Dies Irae de Kościuszko', op. cit. 522.

18. August von Platen, 'Wiegenlied einer polnischen Mutter', (Cradle song of a Polish Mother, 7 Nov. 1831), in *Polenlieder deutscher Dichter* (Lemberg, n.d.).

19. Thomas Campbell, *The Complete Poetical Works*, ed. J. Logie Robertson (London, 1907), 'Lines on Poland (1831)', 'The Power of Russia' etc, 218–26.

20. *The Wrongs of Poland: a poem in three cantos comprising The Siege of Vienna*, by the author of 'Parental Wisdom' (London, 1849), 149. On British attitudes, see H. G. Weisser, 'Polonophilism and the British Working Class', *Polish Review*, xii (1967), 78–96; T. Grzebieniowski, 'The Polish Cause in England a century ago', *Slavonic and East European Review*, ii (1832), 81–7.

21. Richard Cobden, *Russia: by a Manchester manufacturer* (Edinburgh, 1836), especially Chapter II, 'Poland, Russia and England', 15–25. Cobden, basing his opinions on the work of Rulhière and Heeren, wrote of 'Poland, upon which has been lavished more false sentiment, deluded sympathy and amiable ignorance than on any other subject of the present age'.

22. Quoted by N. Riasanovsky, *Nicholas I and Official Nationality in Russia 1825–55* (Berkeley, 1959), 230; Nicholas I/Pashkievich, September 1831, in N. Schilder, *Imperator Nikolai Pervyi*, (St. Petersburg 1901), ii. 589–92.

23. See C. Morley, 'The European significance of the November Uprising', *Journal of Central European Affairs*, ii (1952), 407–16.

CHAPTER 14. CRACOVIA

1. S. Kieniewicz, 'The Free State of Cracow, 1815–46', *Slavonic and East European Review*, xxvi (1946–8), 69–89. Janina Bieniarzówna, *Rzeczpos-polita Krakowska, 1815–46* (Cracow, 1948); M. Żychowski, *Rok 1846 w Rzeczypospolitej Krakowskiej i w Galicji* (Warsaw, 1956).

2. *The Cracow Manifesto*, 1846. Quoted by V. Heltman, *Demokracja Polska na emigracji* (Leipzig, 1866), 87–8. See also J. Bieniarzówna, *Rzeczpospolita Krakowska, 1815–46: Wybór źródeł* (Wrocław, 1951).

3. K. Marx, 22 Feb. 1848. Celina Bobińska, *Marksa spotkania z Polską*, op. cit. 69 ff. See Chapter 21, note 14 above.

4. Kornel Ujejski (1823–97), 'Z dymem pożarów', published in *Skargi Jeremiego* (1847) in Paris, although deliberately misattributed to London, 1847.

Z Głębokości ... Antologia polskiej modlitwy poetyckiej, op. cit., i. 424–6.

CHAPTER 15. WIOSNA

1. L. B. Namier, *1848: The Revolution of the Intellectuals,* British Academy: Raleigh Lecture, 1946 (London, 1947); J. A. Hawgood, '1848 in Central Europe', *Slavonic and East European Review,* xxvi (1948), 314–28; *W stulecie Wiosny Ludów, 1848,* ed. N. Gąsiorowska (Warsaw, 1935), 5 vols.
2. N. Gąsiorowska, op. cit. i. 'Wiosna ludów na ziemiach polskich'; and Irena Koberdowa, *Polska Wiosna Ludów* (Warsaw, 1967) tend to maximize the Polish contribution to 1848.
3. H. Batowski, *Legion Mickiewicza w kampanii włosko-austriackiej* (Warsaw, 1956); S. Kieniewicz, *Legion Mickiewicza* (Warsaw, 1955).
4. J. Hermant, *La Révolution hongroise de 1848: l'intervention russe et l'intervention polonaise* (Paris, 1901). Eligiusz Kozłowski, *Generał Józef Bem* (Warsaw, 1958).
5. See H. Batowski, 'The Poles and their fellow Slavs in 1848', *Slavonic and East European Review,* xxvii (1949), 404–13.
6. Paul Henry, 'Le gouvernement provisoire et la question polonaise en 1848', *Revue Historique,* lxi (1936), 198–240; P. Quentin-Bauchart, *Lamartine et la politique étrangère de la Révolution de Février* (Paris, 1913).
7. See J. Kucharzewski, 'The Polish Cause at the Frankfurt Parliament of 1848', *Bulletin of the Polish Institute of Arts and Sciences in America,* i. (1942–3), 11–73. See also Chapter 3, note 3 above.

CHAPTER 16. RÊVERIES

1. On the Polish Question during the Crimean War, see M. Kukiel, *Czartoryski and European Unity, 1770–1861* (Princeton, 1955); also M. Handelsman, 'La Guerre de Crimée: la question polonaise . . . ', *Révue Historique,* lvii (1932), 270–315.
2. See R. F. Leslie, *Reform and Insurrection in Russian Poland 1856–65* (London, 1965).
3. Irene Roseveare, 'From Reform to Rebellion: A. Wielopolski and the Polish Question, 1861–3', *Canadian Slavic Studies,* iii (1969), 163–5; S. J. Zyzniewski, 'The Futile Compromise Reconsidered: Wielopolski and Russian policy 1861–3', *American History Review,* lxx (1965), 395–412; Zbigniew Stankiewicz, *Dzieje wielkości i upadku Aleksandra Wielopolskiego* (Warsaw, 1967).
4. See S. Kieniewicz, *Powstanie styczniowe* (Warsaw, 1972); also W. Rudzka, 'Studies on the Polish Insurrectionary Government in 1863–4', *Antemurale,* viii (1967), 397–481.
5. See J. Piłsudski, 'Zarys historii militarnej powstania styczniowego', *Pisma Zbiorowe,* iii (Warsaw, 1937), 82–141; S. Zieliński, *Bitwy i potyczki 1863–4* (Rapperswil, 1913).
6. See E. H. Carr, 'Poland: or the cruise of the "Ward Jackson" ', in *Romantic Exiles: a Nineteenth Century Portrait Gallery* (London, 1949), 204–17.
7. J. H. Gleason, *The Genesis of Russophobia in Great Britain: a study of the*

interaction of policy and opinion (Cambridge, Mass., 1950); W. E. Mosse, 'England and the Polish Insurrection of 1863', *English Historical Review,* lxxi (1956), 28–55. See also M. K. Dziewanowski, 'Herzen, Bakunin and the Polish Insurrection of 1863', *Journal of Central European Affairs,* viii (1948), 58–78.

8. See S. Kieniewicz, 'Polish Society and the Insurrection of 1863', *Past and Present,* No. 37 (1967), 130–38; idem, *Sprawa włościańska w powstaniu styczniowym* (Wrocław, 1953).

9. M. Dubiecki, *Romuald Traugutt i jego dyktatura podczas powstania styczniowego 1863–4* (Poznań, 1925).

10. *Traugutt: Dokumenty, Listy, Wspomnienia, Wypisy,* ed. J. Jarzębowski (London, 1970), 200. See E. Halicz, 'Proces Romualda Traugutta', *Wojskowy Przegląd Historyczny,* ii (1957), 242–65.

11. Adapted from related documents referring to Court Martial, Appeal, and Viceroy's Report, Traugutt: *Dokumenty* . . . 215–28.

12. See *Pamiętniki hr. Michała Mikołajewicza Murawiewa (Wieszatela), 1863–5,* trans. into Polish by J. Cz. (Cracow, 1897).

13. See G. Kennan, *Siberia and the exile system* (New York, 1891), 2 vols. See also Chapter 2, note 6 above.

CHAPTER 17. REWOLUCJA

1. M. K. Dziewanowski, 'The Polish Revolutionary Movement and Russia, 1904–7', *Harvard Slavic Studies,* iv (1957), 375–95; Stanisław Kałabiński, Feliks Tych, *Czwarte powstanie czy pierwsza rewolucja: lata 1905–7 na ziemiach polskich* (Warsaw, 1969). See also *Rok 1905 na ziemiach polskich: szkice i obrazki'* ed. B. Krauze (Warsaw, 1955).

2. Wacław Jędrzejewicz, *Sprawa Wieczoru: J. Piłsudski a Wojna Rosyjsko-Japońska, 1904–5* (Paris, 1974), 45.

3. See 'Revolution', Joseph Piłsudski, *The Memories of a Polish Revolutionary and Soldier,* translated and edited by D. R. Gillie (London, 1931), 151–78.

4. See Andrzej Micewski, *Roman Dmowski* (Warsaw, 1971): Chapter II, 'Bezwzględny przeciwnik Rewolucji, 1905–6'; Chapter III, 'O kierunek polityki polskiej, 1907–11'.

5. *Źródła do dziejów rewolucji 1905–7 w okręgu łódzkim,* ed. N. Gąsiorowska, i, Part 2 (Warsaw, 1958), nr. 229. See P. Korzec, *Walki rewolucyjne w Łodzi i okręgu łódzkim w latach 1905–7* (Warsaw, 1956).

6. See A. Żarnowska, *Geneza rozłamu w PPS 1904–6* (Warsaw, 1965).

CHAPTER 18. FENIKS

1. On the Eastern Front, see Alan Clark, *Suicide of the Empires: the battles on the Eastern Front, 1914–18* (London, 1971); Norman Stone, *The Eastern Front, 1914–17* (London, 1975).

2. See T. Komarnicki, *The Rebirth of Poland: a Study in the Diplomatic History of Europe, 1914–20* (London, 1957); J. Holzer, J. Molenda, *Polska w Pierwszej Wojnie Światowej* (Warsaw, 1967); *La Pologne: sa vie économique et sociale pendant la Guerre* ed. M. Handelsman (Paris, 1933–8), 2 vols.

3. Edward Słoński, 'Ta co nie zginęła' (That which has not perished, 1914). *Zbiór poetów polskich XIX w'* (Warsaw, 1965), iv, 855–6: Słoński's first poems were composed in Russian.

4. K. Srokowski, *NKN – Zarys historii* (Cracow, 1923); See also J. Dąbrowski: *Dziennik, 1914–18*, ed. Jerzy Zdrada (Cracow, 1977).

5. M. Leczyk, *Komitet Narodowy Polski a Ententa i Stany Zjednoczone, 1917–19* (Warsaw, 1966); Janusz Pajewski, *Wokół sprawy polskiej: Paryż-Lozanna-Londyn 1914–18* (Poznań, 1970).

6. Norman Davies, 'The Poles in Great Britain, 1914–19', *Slavonic and East European Review*, 1 (1972), 63–89.

7. See Chapter 10, note 7 above.

8. W. Lipiński, 'Polska Organizacja Wojskowa', *Bellona*, xxxvii (1931), 171–95.

9. W. Lipiński, *Walka zbrojna o niepodległość Polski, 1905–18* (2nd Edition, Warsaw, 1935), with bibliographies, surveys the history of Polish formations on all fronts.

10. See S. Dąbrowski, *Walka o rekruta polskiego pod okupacją* (Warsaw, 1922).

11. See S. Arski, *Galicyjska działalność wojskowa J. Piłsudskiego 1906–14* (Warsaw, 1967).

12. K. Kumaniecki, *Odbudowa państwowości polskiej. Najważniejsze dokumenty* (Warsaw–Cracow, 1924), 12.

13. W. Conze, *Polonische Nation und deutsche Politik im Ersten Weltkrieg* (Cologne, 1958); E. R. Burke, *The Polish policy of the Central Powers during the World War* (Chicago, 1936); Leon Grosfeld, 'La Pologne dans les plans imperialistes allemands, 1914–18', *La Pologne au X Congrès International des Sciences Historiques à Rome* (Warsaw, 1955), 327–55.

14. I. Geiss, *Der Polnische Grenzstreifen, 1914–18: ein Beitrag zur deutschen Kriegspolitik im Ersten Weltkrieg,* (Lübeck–Hamburg, 1960); P. R. Sweet, 'Germany, Austria, and Mitteleuropa, 1915–16', in *Festschrift für Heinrich Benedikt*, ed. H. Hansch, A. Novotny (Vienna, 1957).

15. J. W. Wheeler-Bennett, *Brest-Litovsk: the Forgotten Peace, March 1918* (London, 1938).

16. MS Autobiography of Ignacy Mościcki, 129–30, in Archive of Józef Piłsudski Institute of America Inc., New York.

17. R. Dmowski, *Problems of East and Central Europe* (London, 1916). See Davies, op. cit., note 6 above.

18. A. Dallin, 'The Future of Poland', in *Russian Diplomacy and Eastern Europe 1914–17* (New York, 1963). For the text of the Provisional government's Declaration, 29 March 1917, see *Dokumenty i Materiały do historii stosunków polsko-radzieckich,* i (Warsaw, 1962), 18–20.

19. For the Bolshevik statement, 27 March 1917, ibid. i, 8–9.

20. Louis Gerson, *Woodrow Wilson and the Rebirth of Poland, 1914–20* (New Haven, 1953); V. Mamatey, *The United States and East Central Europe, 1914–20: a study in Wilsonian Diplomacy and Propaganda* (Princeton, 1959).

21. Leon Grosfeld, *Polskie reakcyjne formacje wojskowe w Rosji, 1917–19* (Warsaw, 1956); H. Bagiński, *Wojsko polskie na wschodzie, 1914–20* (Warsaw, 1921); S. Żbikowski, 'Zachodnia Dywizja Strzelców', *Z Pola Walki* R 3 (1960), 329–59; M. Wrzosek, *Polskie Korpusy Wojskowe w Rosji w latach 1917–18* (Warsaw, 1969).

22. See Chapter 21, note 6 above.
23. M. Stachiw, J. Sztendera, *Western Ukraine at the turning point of Europe's History* (Scranton, Penn., 1969) 1, (1918–May 1919); Rosa Bailly, *A City fights for its freedom: the rising of Lwów in 1918–19* (London, 1956); Józef Bendow, *Der Lemberger Judenpogrom, 1918–19* (Vienna, 1919); S. Skrzypek, *The Problem of East Galicia* (London, 1948).
24. Official historians in present-day Poland wilfully exaggerate the role of Daszyński's embryonic 'People's Government' in Lublin in order to detract from Piłsudski's subsequent achievement in forming the first effectively independent government. See H. Jabłoński, *Narodziny Drugiej Rzeczypospolitej, 1918–19* (Warsaw, 1962).
25. Józef Iwicki, *Z myślą o Niepodległej: Listy Polaka, żołnierza armii niemieckiej z okopów I wojny światowej, 1914–18*, ed. Adolf Juzwenko (Wrocław, 1978).

CHAPTER 19. NIEPODLEGŁOŚĆ

1. It is unfortunate that the most recent survey of inter-war Poland in English, Antony Polonsky, *Politics in Independent Poland, 1921–39: the Crisis of Constitutional Government* (Oxford, 1972), omits the three formative years of the Republic's existence. J. Rothschild, *East Central Europe between the two World Wars* (Seattle, 1975), puts Poland into the broader, regional context. In Polish, important introductions to the period include A. Micewski, *Z geografii politycznej II Rzeczypospolitej* (Cracow, 1965); M. M. Drozdowski, *Społeczeństwo-Państwo Politycy II Rzeczypospolitej* (Cracow, 1972); J. Żarnowski, *Społeczeństwo drugiej Rzeczypospolitej, 1918–39* (Warsaw, 1973); W. Pobóg-Malinowski, *Najnowsza historia polityczna Polski 1865–1945* (Paris–London, 1953–6), 2 vols.; S. Mackiewicz, *Historia Polski 11 xi 1918–17 ix 1939* (London, 1941). See also the collective work: *Pologne 1918–39* (Neuchâtel, 1946–7), 3 vols.
2. This is an eccentric view. Other partisan introductions can be found in Pobóg-Malinowski, op. cit. or A. Ajnenkiel, *Od rządów ludowych do przewrotu Majowego* (Warsaw, 1968).
3. Adam Przybylski, *La Pologne en lutte pour ses frontières* (Paris, 1931); S. Pomarański, *Pierwsza wojna polska, 1918–20* (Warsaw, 1920), (War communiqués).
4. Norman Davies, *White Eagle, Red Star*. See Chapter 10, note 9 above.
5. Lord D'Abernon, *The Eighteenth Decisive Battle of World History* (London, 1931), 49 ff. D'Abernon, HM Ambassador in Berlin, was one of the leading eye-witnesses of the Battle of Warsaw.
6. Izaak Babel', *Zamost'* (Zamość) in *Konarmiya, Odesskiye razskazy, p'esy*, introduction by A. B. Murphy (Letchworth, 1965). See Norman Davies, 'Izaak Babel's Konarmiya Stories and the Polish–Soviet War, 1919–20', *Modern Languages Review*, xxiii (1972), 845–57.
7. Piotr Wandycz, *Soviet–Polish Relations, 1917–21*, (Cambridge, Mass., 1969). See also S. Dąbrowski, 'The Peace Treaty of Riga', *Polish Review*, v (1960), 3–34.
8. D'Abernon, op. cit. 8–9.

9. Clara Zetkin, *Reminiscences of Lenin* (London, 1929), 19–22. See also S. W. Page, *Lenin and World Revolution* (New York, 1959), 154–76.

10. Piotr Wandycz, 'General Weygand and the Battle of Warsaw', *Journal of Central European Affairs*, xix (1960), 357–65; also his *France and her Eastern Allies, 1919–25* (Minneapolis, 1965).

11. *The Democratic Heritage of Poland*, op. cit. 143–4. See also *Historia państwa i prawa Polski, 1918–39*, ed. F. Ryszka, Part one (Warsaw, 1962).

12. On the question of integration, see *Drogi integracji społeczeństwa w Polsce XIX–XX*, ed. H. Zieliński (Wrocław, 1976), including Piotr Sławecki, 'Kilka uwag o roli wojska w procesach integracyjnych i dezyintegracyjnych II Rzeczypospolitej', ibid. 193–215.

13. S. Horak, *Poland and her national minorities, 1919–39* (New York, 1961). See A. Groth, 'Dmowski, Piłsudski and ethnic conflicts in pre-1939 Poland', *Canadian Slavic Studies*, iii (1969), 69–91; *La Pologne et le problème des minorités: recueil d'informations*, ed. S. J. Paprocki (Warsaw, 1935).

14. W. Napier, 'The Ukrainians in Poland: an historical background', *International Affairs*, xi (1932), 391–421; M. Feliński, *The Ukrainians in Poland* (London, 1931). See also: E. Reviuk, *Polish Atrocities in the Ukraine* (New York, 1931); W. Szota, 'Zarys rozwoju OUN i UPA', *Wojskowy Przegląd Historyczny*, viii (1963), 163–218.

15. For a martyrological assessment of pre-war Polish Jewry, see C. S. Heller, *On the Edge of Destruction* (New York, 1977). A more convincing introduction to the subject is contained in the illustrated album, *Image before my eyes: a photographic history of Jewish life in Poland, 1864–1939*, eds. L. Dobroszycki, B. Kirschenblatt-Gimblett (YIVO, New York, 1977–8), 2 vols. See also H. M. Rabinowicz, *The Legacy of Polish Jewry: a History of Polish Jews in the Inter-war Years, 1919–39* (New York, 1965).

16. N. Vakar, *Belorussia: the making of a nation* (Cambridge, Mass., 1956). Stanisław Ełski (pseudonym), *Sprawa białoruska zarys historycznopolityczny* (Warsaw, 1931).

17. J. C. Hesse, 'The Germans in Poland', *Slavonic and East European Review*, xvi (1937), 93–101. See also *The German Fifth Column in Poland* (Poland: Ministry of Information, London, 1941); S. Potocki, *Położenie mniejszości niemieckiej w Polsce 1918–38* (Gdańsk, 1938).

18. Modestino Carbone, *La questione agraria in Polonia, 1918–39* (Naples, 1976). See also M. Mieszczankowski, *Struktura agrarna Polski międzywojennej* (Warsaw, 1960); J. Ciepielewski, *Wieś polska w latach wielkiego kryzysu 1929–35, Materiały i dokumenty* (Warsaw, 1965); Z. Landau, 'The Polish Countryside in the years 1929–35', *Acta Poloniae Historica*, ix (1964), 28–47.

19. From the memoir of J. Guzik in *W dwudziestolecie wielkiego strajku chłopskiego, 1937–57* (The twentieth anniversary of the great Peasants' Strike, Warsaw, 1957), 185–8.

20. J. Żarnowski, 'Robotnicy', in *Społeczeństwo Drugiej Rzeczypospolitej* op. cit. 48–113.

21. On the pre-war economy, see F. Zweig, *Poland between Two Wars* (London, 1944); and J. J. Taylor, *The Economic Development of Poland, 1919–50* (Ithaca, NY, 1952); also Zbigniew Landau, 'Poland's Economy against the

background of the World Economy, 1913–38', *Acta Poloniae Historica*, xx (1969), 75 ff.; idem., 'The Influence of Foreign Capital on the Polish Economy, 1918–39', *La Pologne au XII Congrès des Sciences Historiques à Vienne* (Warsaw, 1965), 133–145.

22. M. M. Drozdowski, *Polityka gospodarcza rządu polskiego 1936–39* (Warsaw, 1963); idem., 'Geneza i rozwój Centralnego Okręgu Przemysłowego', *Najnowsze Dzieje Polski*, ii (Warsaw, 1959), 35–73.

23. Stanisław Manersberg, 'Wpływ oświaty na integrację społeczeństwa II Rzeczypospolitej, 1918–39', *Drogi integracji* . . . op. cit. 57–107.

24. Stanisław Feret, *Polska sztuka wojenna, 1918–39* (Warsaw, 1972); E. Kozłowski, *Wojsko Polskie 1936–9* (Warsaw, 1964).

25. For a hostile but informative account of the Church's position, see Janina Barycka, *Stosunek kleru do państwa i oświaty; fakty i dokumenty* (Warsaw, 1934).

26. R. Dębicki, *Foreign Policy of Poland, 1919–32* (New York, 1962); J. Korbel, *Poland between East and West: Soviet and German Diplomacy towards Poland 1919–33* (New York, 1963); J. Rothschild, 'Poland between Germany and USSR, 1926–39: the Theory of Two Enemies', Piłsudski Institute Symposium, *Polish Review*, xx (1975), 3–63.

27. Joseph Rothschild, *Piłsudski's Coup d'État* (New York, 1966); see also Andrzej Garlicki, *Przewrót majowy* (Warsaw, 1978).

28. Edward D. Wynot Jr., *Polish politics in transition: the Camp of National Unity and the struggle for power, 1935–9* (Athens, Georgia, 1974); T. Jędruszczak, *Piłsudczycy bez Piłsudskiego* (Warsaw, 1963).

29. Quoted in *The Democratic Heritage of Poland*, 161–2. On the opposition to the *Sanacja* regime, see A. Czubiński *Centrolew* . . . *1926–30* (Poznań, 1963); T. Smoliński, *Dyktatura J. Piłsudskiego w świetle konstytucji marcowej* (Poznań, 1970).

30. Quoted in *The Democratic Heritage of Poland*, 195 ff.

31. Roman Knoll, commenting less on the coup itself than on the resultant influx of military officers into the Civil Service; quoted by Polonsky, op. cit. 333.

32. See R. Dyboski, *Poland in World Civilisation* (New York, 1950). Chapters 8 and 9; On Witkiewicz, see the symposium comprising the first volume of *Polish Review* (1973) nos. 1–2, 1–157.

33. Marian Marek Drozdowski, *Warszawiacy i ich miasto w latach Drugiej Rzeczypospolitej* (Warsaw, 1973).

34. On Beck's policy, compare H. L. Roberts, 'The Diplomacy of Colonel Beck', in *The Diplomats*, ed. G. Craig, F. Gilbert (Princeton, 1953); idem, with Anna Cienciała, *Poland and the Western Powers, 1938–9* (London, 1968). Key memoirs of the period include: J. Beck, *Final Report* (New York, 1957); *Diplomat in Berlin: the papers of J. Lipski, 1933–9*, ed. W. Jędrzejewicz (New York, 1968); *Diplomat in Paris 1936–9: the papers and memoirs of J. Lukasiewicz*, ed. W. Jędrzejewicz (New York, 1970); J. Szembek, *Journal 1933–9* (Paris, 1952); Leon Noel, *Une Ambassade à Varsovie, 1935–9* (Paris, 1946). Recent studies from Poland include H. Batowski, *Kryzys dyplomatyczny w Europie, 1938–9* (Warsaw, 1962); idem, *Ostatni tydzień pokoju* (Poznań, 1964); Stefania Stanisławska, *Polska a Monachium* (Warsaw, 1964).

35. E. Kozłowski, *Wojna obronna Polski 1939: wybór źródeł* (Warsaw, 1968), 36–8.
36. Karol Lapter, 'Les garanties anglaises accordées à la Pologne en 1939', *Annuaire Polonais des affaires internationales*, ii (1961), 192–221; Simon Newman, *March 1939: The British Guarantee to Poland* (Oxford, 1976).
37. *Ciano's Diaries, 1939–43*, ed. Malcolm Muggeridge (London, 1947), 71, 72.
38. *Nazi–Soviet Relations, 1939–41: Documents from the Archives of the German Foreign Office*, ed. R. J. Sonntag, J. S. Beddie (Washington, 1948), 78. On the history of the Nazi–Soviet Pact, see G. L. Weinberg, *Germany and the Soviet Union, 1939–41* (Leiden, 1954); J. W. Brugel, *Stalin und Hitler: Pakt gegen Europa* (Vienna, 1973); Aleksander Bergman, *Najlepszy sojusznik Hitlera* (4th Edition, London, 1974).
39. Cf. J. Rothschild's conclusions: 'Despite all the . . . failures of the *Sanacja* regime . . ., Piłsudski must in justice be acknowledged as meriting the primary credit for the fact that today the notion of a Europe without a Polish state is no longer conceivable.' op. cit. 371.

CHAPTER 20. GOLGOTA

1. (US Chief of Counsel for Prosecution of Axis Criminality) *Nazi Conspiracy and Aggression*, vi (Washington 1948), 390–2, cites Naujock's own deposition.
2. Heinz Guderian, *Panzer Leader* (London, 1952), 38.
3. Nicholas Bethell, *The War Hitler Won* (London, 1972), describes the political background to the September campaign. Clare Hollingworth, *The Three Weeks' War in Poland* (London, 1940) provides an eye-witness account. Military studies include R. M. Kennedy, *The German Campaign in Poland* (Washington, 1956); M. N. Neugebauer, *The Defence of Poland, September 1939* (London, 1942); John Kimche, *The Unfought Battle* (London, 1968); *The German Invasion of Poland (The Polish Black Book)*, Poland Ministry of Information (London, 1940); *Polskie Siły Zbrojne w drugiej wojnie światowej*, Sikorski Institute, i (London, 1951); T. Jurga, *Wrzesień 1939* (Warsaw, 1970); Z. Flisowski, *Westerplatte* (Warsaw, 1971); T. Kutrzeba, *Bitwa nad Bzurą: 9–22 września 1939* (Warsaw, 1958); M. Zgórniak, 'A German general on the September Campaign', *Polish Western Affairs*, iii (1962), 353–72; M. M. Drozdowski, *Alarm dla Warszawy* (Warsaw, 1975).
4. See Zbigniew Załuski, *Siedem grzechów polskich* (Warsaw, 1973), 'Grzech czwarty: z lancami na czołgi', 60–4.
5. Adrian Carton de Wiart, *Happy Odyssey* (London, 1950), Foreward by Winston S. Churchill.
6. Stanisław Piotrowski, *Hans Frank's Diary* (Warsaw, 1961; in English tr.) 299–300.
7. The two comprehensive studies of Nazi policy in occupied Poland are M. Broszat, *Nationalsozialistische Polenpolitik, 1939–45* (Revised Edition, Frankfurt–Hamburg, 1965); Cz. Madajczyk, *Polityka III Rzeszy w okupowanej Polsce* (Warsaw, 1970), 2 vols: (also in German, as *Die deutschen Besatzungspolitik in Polen, 1939–45* (Wiesbaden, 1967).
8. *Krushchev Remembers*, trans. Strobe Talbot, with an introduction, com-

comentary, and notes by Edward Crankshaw (London, 1971), 128–9. In this same passage, Krushchev recalls making friends with Wanda Lvovna Wassilevska (Wanda Wasilewska), 'who helped us to get through to those Poles who were clinging irrationally to the idea that we had negotiated the Ribbentrop–Molotov Pact at their expense'.

9. *Documents on German Foreign Policy (1918–45)*, Series D, xi (London, 1961, No. 638, 1068.

10. See Chapter 19, note 38 above.

11. Willi Frischauer, *Himmler: the evil genius of the Third Reich* (London, 1953), 135–6. See *German Crimes in Poland* (Warsaw, 1946–7), 2 vols.

12. See K. M. Pospieszalski, *Hitlerowskie prawo okupacyjne w Polsce: dokumenty* (Poznań, 1952–8), 2 vols.; T. Cyprian, *Wehrmacht: Zbrodnia i kara* (Warsaw, 1972); A. Konieczny, *Pod rządami wojennego prawa karnego Trzeciej Rzeszy, Górny Śląsk 1939–45* (Warsaw, 1972); J. T. Gross, *Polish Society under German Occupation, 1939–44*, Princeton 1979.

13. See G. R. Reitlinger, *The Final Solution: an attempt to exterminate the Jews of Europe, 1939–45* (London, 1953). Some technical details, and the timing of the operation are in dispute. See above Chapter 9, note 23.

14. See E. Duraczyński, *Wojna a okupacja* (Warsaw, 1973).

15. T. Esman, W. Jastrzębski, *Pierwsze miesiące okupacji hitlerowskiej w Bydgoszczy w świetle źródeł niemieckich* (Bydgoszcz, 1967); C. Łuczak, *Kraj Warty, 1939– 45* (Poznań, 1972).

16. Order 0054, 28 November 1940 signed by Gusevitius, People's Commissar for the Interior, Lithuanian SSR. quoted in *The Dark Side of the Moon*, prefaced by T. S. Eliot (New York, 1947), 51. Under Soviet practice, a deportation order normally included all the immediate relatives of the named deportee.

17. Anon., ibid. 143–8. *The Dark Side of the Moon* is one of the few accounts published in English, but there is much *émigré* material in Polish: See *Polacy w ZSSR 1939–42: Antologia*, ed. M. Czapska (Paris, 1963). A rare discussion of the problem in post-war Poland is in Krystyna Kersten, *Repatriacja ludności polskiej po II wojnie światowej* (Warsaw, 1974), subsequently withdrawn by the Censorship. Estimates of the numbers of Poles involved vary from a minimum of 800.000 to a maximum of over 2 million. See also R. Conquest, *Kolyma* (London, 1978), and Edward Buca, *Vorkuta* (London, 1976). Solzhenitzyn, whose sources of information were personal and fragmentary, writes little about the Poles; but his description of the deportation of the 'special settlers' from Estonia in 1940 matches the Polish case; see *The Gulag Archipelago* (London, 1978), iii Part VI, Chapter 4, 'The Nations in Exile'.

18. J. K. Zawodny, *Death in the Forest: the story of the Katyń Forest Massacre* (London, 1971). See also J. Mackiewicz, *The Katyń Wood Murders* (London, 1950); Louis Fitzgibbon, *Katyń: Crime without parallel* (London, 1971); Sir Owen O'Malley, *Katyń: Dispatches of Sir Owen O'Malley to the British Government* (Chicago, 1973); ed. W. Anders, *Zbrodnia katyńska w świetle dokumentów* (London, 1962).

19. C. Madajczyk. 'Generalplan Ost', *Polish Western Affairs*, iii (1962), nr. 2, 391–442.

20. See J. Billig, *Les camps de concentration dans l'économie du Reich hitlérien* (Paris, 1973).

21. C. Madajczyk. 'Deportation in the Zamość Region in 1942 and 1943 in the light of German Documents', *Acta Poloniae Historica*, i (1958), 75−106; idem, *Hitlerowski terror na wsi polskiej 1939−45* (Warsaw, 1965).

22. See E. Kogen, *The Theory and Practice of Hell: the German concentration camps and the system behind them* (New York, 1973).

23. Jan Sehn, *The Concentration Camp Oświęcim-Brzezinka* (Auschwitz-Birkenau), (Warsaw, 1957); J. Garliński, *Fighting Auschwitz* (London, 1975).

24. From Tadeusz Borowski, *Proszę państwa do gazu* (To the gas, ladies and gentlemen!). Quoted by C. Miłosz, *The Captive Mind* (New York, 1953), 120 1.

25. *International Military Tribunal* (Nürnberg, 1946), viii, 324−9, 27 Feb. 1946.

26. Rudolf Hoess, *Commandant of Auschwitz; The Autobiography of Rudolf Hoess* (London, 1959), 144−57.

27. Quoted by George H. Stein, *The Waffen SS* (New York, 1966), 88.

28. See R. Nurowski, ed., *1939−45 War losses in Poland* (Warsaw, 1960). See also Chapter 9, note 23 above.

29. Tadeusz Wyrwa, *W cieniu legendy majora Hubala* (London, 1974); Melchior Wańkowicz, *Hubalczycy* (Warsaw, 1959).

30. On the Polish Resistance, see T. Pełczyński *et al.*, eds., *Armia Krajowa w dokumentach 1939−45* (London, 1970−4), 2 vols.; T. Bór-Komorowski, *The Secret Army* (London, 1950); S. Korboński, *Fighting Warsaw: the Story of the Polish Underground State 1939−45* (London, 1956); J. Karski, *Story of a Secret State* (London, 1945); J. Garliński, 'The Polish Underground State 1939−45', *Journal of Contemporary History*, x (1975), 219−59; Jerzy Mond, O sztuce przemilczania: kilka uwag o pracy płk, T. Jędruszczaka, 'Les organisations de la Resistance antihitlerienne en Pologne,' *Zeszyty Historyczne (Kultura)*, nr. 39 (Paris, 1977), 229 31.

31. J. Garliński, *Poland, SOE and the Allies* (London, 1969); idem, *Hitler's Last Weapons: The Underground War against the V1 and the V2* (London, 1978); G. Bertrand, *Énigme* (Paris, 1973); F. Winterbotham, *The Ultra Secret* (London, 1975).

32. W. Bartoszewski, Z. Lewin eds., *Righteous Among Nations: How Poles helped the Jews, 1939−45*, (London, 1972).

33. L. Tushnet, *To Die with Honour: the Uprising of the Jews of the Warsaw Ghetto* (New York, 1965); A. ben Bernfes, *The Warsaw Ghetto no longer exists: in their own words and photographs* . . . (London, 1970); Jurgen Stroop, *The Report of Jurgen Stroop* . . . , (Warsaw, 1958).

34. USSR People's Commissariat of Justice, *Trial of the Organisers, Leaders and Members of the Polish Diversionist Organisations* . . . *June 18−21, 1945* (Moscow−London, 1945), 240; Z. Stypułkowski, *Invitation to Moscow* (New York, 1962).

35. Despatch from Bór to C.-in-C., 22 July 1944: quoted by Jan Ciechanowski, *The Warsaw Rising of 1944* Cambridge, 1974), 217−18.

36. Ciechanowski, ibid., is the authoritative study of the genesis of the Warsaw Rising; also published in Polish as *Powstanie Warszawskie* (London, 1971).

37. Joanna K. Hanson, 'The Civilian Population and the Warsaw Uprising 1944'

(Unpublished Ph.D. Thesis; University of London, 1978). See also E. Serwański ed., *Życie w powstańczej Warszawie; relacje – dokumenty* (Warsaw, 1965).

38. J. K. Zawodny, *Nothing but Honour* (New York, 1977). See also G. Bruce, *The Warsaw Rising: 1 August to 2 October 1944* (London, 1972); G. Deschner, *The Warsaw Rising* (London, 1972); H. von Krannhals, *Der Warschauer Aufstand – 1944* (Frankfurt-am-Main, 1962).

39. Winston S. Churchill, *The Second World War*, vi (London, 1954), Chapter IX, 'The Martyrdom of Warsaw', 126, 127.

40. K. F. Grau, *Silesian Inferno: War Crimes of the Red Army on its march into Silesia, 1945: a collection of documents* (Cologne, 1970).

41. Alexander Solzhenitsyn, *Prussian Nights: a Narrative Poem*, trans. Robert Conquest (London, 1977), 33, 41–3, 49–53.

42. A. Polonsky ed., *The Great Powers and the Polish Question, 1941–5: a documentary study in Cold War origins*, (London, 1976). See also E. J. Rozek, *Allied Wartime Diplomacy: a Pattern in Poland* (New York, 1958).

43. See Edward Raczyński, *In Allied London* (London, 1963).

44. S. Kot, *Conversations with the Kremlin and Despatches from Russia* (London, 1963), 112–14, 141–3.

45. See Piotr Wandycz, *Czechoslovak–Polish Confederation and the Great Powers, 1940–3* (Bloomington, Ind., 1956); also L. L. Barrell, 'Poland and East European Union 1939–45', *Polish Review*, iii (1958), 87–127; E. Taborski, 'Polish–Czechoslovak Federation: the story of the first Soviet veto', *Journal of Central European Affairs*, ix (1949–50), 379–85.

46. *Documents of Polish–Soviet Relations, 1939–45*, Sikorski Institute (London, 1961), 2 vols. For widely differing evaluations of Stalin's policies, see B. Kuśnierz, *Stalin and the Poles: an indictment of the Soviet leaders* (London, 1949), and Włodzimierz T. Kowalski, *Walka dyplomatyczna o miejsce Polski w Europie, 1939–45* (Warsaw, 1970).

47. W. Sworakowski, 'An error regarding East Galicia in Curzon's Note to the Soviet Government', *Journal of Central European Affairs*, iv (1944), 3–26. See also R. Yakemtchouk, *La Ligne Curzon et la deuxième guerre mondiale* (Paris, 1957).

CHAPTER 21. GRANICE

1. The territorial issue looms large in most contemporary summaries of Polish History. See O. Halecki, 'Poland's Place in Europe, 966–1906' in D. Wandycz ed., *Studies in Polish Civilisations* (New York, 1966), 15–22; J. H. Retinger, *Poland's Place in Europe* (London, 1947); L. H. Woolsey, 'The Polish Boundary Question: *American Journal of International Law* (1944), xxxviii, 441–8; H. Bagiński, *Poland and the Baltic* (Edinburgh, 1942); A. Żółtowski, *Border of Europe* (London, 1950).

2. On the Paris Peace Conference and its aftermath, see H. W. V. Temperley, *A History of the Peace Conference of Paris* (London, 1920–4), 6 vols.; Sarah Wambaugh. *Plebiscites since the World War* (Washington, 1933), 2 vols.; also J. Blociszewski, *La Restauration de la Pologne et la Diplomatie Européenne* (Paris, 1927); 'Poland', in *Some Problems of the Peace Conference*, ed. C. M.

Haskins, R. H. Lord (Cambridge, Mass., 1920); S. Kozicki, *Sprawa granic Polski na konferencji pokojowej w Paryżu* (Warsaw, 1921).

3. Norman Davies, 'Lloyd George and Poland, 1919–20', *Journal of Contemporary History*, vi (1971), 132–54.

4. G. M. Gaythorne-Hardy, *A Short History of International Affairs 1920–39* (London, 1950), 95.

5. P. Wandycz, 'Pierwsza Republika a Druga Rzeczpospolita: szkic', *Zeszyty Historyczne* (Paris), 28 (1974), 3–20; W. J. Rose, 'Czechs and Poles as neighbours', *Journal of Central European Affairs*, xi (1951), 153–71; Vaclav Benes, 'The Psychology of Polish–Czechoslovak Relations', *Central European Federalist*, xv (1967), 21–8; J. Kozeński, *Czechosłowacja w polskiej polityce zagranicznej w latach 1932–9* (Poznań, 1964). See also C. M. Nowak, *Czechoslovak–Polish Relations 1919–39: a selected and annotated Bibliography* (Stanford, 1976).

6. J. Chlebowczyk, *Nad Olzą: Śląsk cieszyński w wiekach XVIII, XIX, i XX* (Katowice, 1971). See also Norman Davies, 'Wielka Brytania a plebiscyt cieszyński, 1919–20', *Sobótka*, xxi (1972), 139–65; K. Witt, *Die Teschener Frage* (Berlin, 1935); V. Tapie, *Le Pays de Teschen et les rapports entre la Pologne et la Tchecoslovaquie* (Paris, 1936).

7. K. Tymieniecki, *The History of Polish Pomerania* (Poznań, 1929).

8. S. Askenazy, *Danzig and Poland* (London, 1932); C. M. Kimmich, *The Free City of Danzig and German Foreign Policy, 1919–34* (New Haven, 1968); J. B. Mason, *The Danzig Dilemma* (Stanford, 1946).

9. See J. D. F. Morrow, *The Peace Settlement in the Polish–German Borderland* (London, 1936).

10. See Z. Wieliczka, *Wielkopolska a Prusy, 1918–19* (Warsaw, 1933).

11. Wambaugh, op. cit. i. Chapter 6. See also F. G. Campbell, 'The Struggle for Upper Silesia, 1919–22', *Journal of Modern History*, xlii (1970), 361–85; H. Zieliński, 'The Social and Political Background to the Silesian Risings', *Acta Poloniae Historica*, xxvi (1972), 73–108.

12. *Foreign Relations of the United States* Potsdam II, 1579–80. See also W. Wagner, *The Genesis of the Oder–Neisse Line: a study of diplomatic negotiations during World War Two* (Stuttgart, 1957); G. Bluhm, *Die Oder–Neisse Frage* (Hanover, 1967); A. Błoński, *Wracamy nad Odrę: historyczne, geograficzne i polityczne podstawy zachodnich granic Polski* (London, 1942); W. M. Drzewieniecki, *The German–Polish Frontier* (Chicago, 1959); Z. Jordan, *The Oder–Neisse Line* (London, 1952); J. Kokot, *The Logic of the Oder–Neisse Line* (Poznań, 1959). B. Wiewora, *The Polish–German Frontier from the standpoint of international law* (Poznań, 1964).

13. T. Derlatka *et al.* eds., *Western and Northern Poland*, (Poznań, 1962); cf. Charles Wassermann, *Europe's Forgotten Territories* (Copenhagen, 1960).

14. Polska Akademia Nauk, Akademia Nauk ZSRR, *Dokumenty i Materiały do Historii Stosunków Polsko-Radzieckich*, ii (Warsaw, 1961), No. 311. This collection is notable for the boldness of its omissions.

15. See Chapter 20, note 47 above.

16. S. Grabski, *The Polish–Soviet Frontier* (London, 1943); J. Dąbski, *Pokój Ryski* (Warsaw, 1931).

17. On Piłsudski's federalist policies, see M. K. Dziewanowski, *Joseph Piłsudski:*

a *European Federalist, 1918–22* (Stanford, 1969). More hostile accounts of the subject include J. Lewandowski, 'Prometeizm – koncepcja polityki wschodniej piłsudczyzny', *Biuletyn WAP*, seria historyczna I, II, nr. 2/12 (1958): nr. 1/14 (1959); idem, *Imperializm słabości* (Warsaw, 1967); Aleksy Deruga, *Polityka wschodnia Polski wobec ziem Litwy, Białorusi i Ukrainy, 1918–19* (Warsaw, 1969); Sergiusz Mikulicz, *Prometeizm w polityce II Rzeczpospolitej* (Warsaw, 1971). The most thorough study of Polish policy towards Russia in this period is to be found in Adolf Juzwenko, *Polska a biała Rosja: od listopada 1918 do kwietnia 1920* (Wrocław, 1973).

18. P. Łossowski, *Stosunki polsko-litewskie w latach 1918–20* (Warsaw, 1966); A. F. Senn, *The Great Powers, Lithuania and the Vilna Question, 1920–8* (Leiden, 1966); Richard C. Lukas, 'The Seizure of Vilna, October 1920', *Historian*, xxiii (1961), 234–46.

19. See Chapter 18, note 23 above.

20. See 'Mikołajczyk and Churchill', in Jan Ciechanowski, op. cit. 27–51, with references.

21. Kazimierz Rosen-Zawadzki, 'Karta Buduszczej Jewropy, *Studia z dziejów ZSRR i Europy Środkowej*, viii (Wrocław, 1972), 141–5, with map.

22. See H. Batowski, *Słownik nazw miejscowych Europy Środkowej i wschodniej XIX i XX wieku* (Warsaw, 1964), which includes historical and linguistic introductions to the subject.

23. Karl Baedeker, *Northern Germany* . . . (Leipzig–London, 1890), 255–61.

24. *Poland – Travel Guide (Sport i Turystyka)*, (Warsaw, 1970), 'Wrocław', 132–9.

25. On Mikołajczyk's dealings with Stalin, see 'Rozmowa T. Arciszewskiego, 15 ego stycznia 1945r,' in *Zeszyty Historyczne* (Paris), No. 1, 1947.

26. *Festung Breslau: dokumenty oblężenia 1945* (Wrocław, 1962); R. Majewski, T. Sozańska, *Bitwa o Wrocław* (Wrocław, 1975).

27. Mieczysław Orłowicz, *Guide Illustré de la Pologne* (Varsovie, 1927), 197–208.

28. M. Rudnitskiy, 'L'viv Vchora i S'yogodni' (L'viv yesterday and today)', in *L'viv–Lvov: Maliy Ilustrovaniy Putivnik*, ed. A. Pashuk, I. Derkach (L'viv, 1962), 5–6; cf. the entry under 'Lvov', in the *Great Soviet Encyclopaedia.*

29. For Polish views on the History of Lwów, see S. Mękarski (J. Rudnicki), *Lwów: a page of Polish History* (London, 1943); ibid., *Lwów and the Lwów Region,* (Polish Ministry of Information, London, 1945); also J. Mękarska, *Wędrówka po ziemiach wschodnich Rzeczpospolitej* (London, 1966).

30. See notes 17 and 18 above.

31. A. E. Senn, *The Emergence of Modern Lithuania* (Princeton, 1959).

32. Nicholas P. Vakar, *Belorussia: the making of a nation* (Cambridge, Mass., 1956).

33. J. Reshetar, *The Ukrainian Revolution 1917–20* (Princeton, 1952).

34. See Chapter 18, note 23 above.

35. See P. Wandycz, 'Z zagadnień współpracy polsko–ukraińskiej w latach 1919–20', *Zeszyty Historyczne*, nr. 12 (Paris, 1967).

36. Nicholas Bethell, *The Last Secret: the delivery to Stalin of over two million Russians by Britain and the United States* (New York, 1974); Nikolai Tolstoy, *Victims of Yalta* (London, 1971), 321.

37. Mykhailo Hrushevskyi, *A History of Ukraine*, ed. O. J. Frederiksen (Hamden, Conn., 1970); Oleh Martovych, *The Ukrainian Liberation Movement in modern times* (Edinburgh, 1972).

38. Henryk Sienkiewicz, 'Nienawiść wrosła w serca i zatruła krew pobatrymczą.', being the final sentence of *Ogniem i mieczem* (By Fire and Sword, Warsaw, 1894) iv, 240.

39. A chvanytes', shcho my Pol'shchu/Kolys' zavalyly! .../Pravda vasha: Pol'shcha vpala,/Ta i vas rozdavyla./'I mertvym i zhyvym,' (1845), lines 186–9.

40. P. Hoffmann, *The History of the German Resistance, 1933–45* (London, 1977), 33 ff., 192–7; also *A German of the Resistance: the Last Letters of Count von Moltke* (Oxford, 1946).

41. Joseph, Freiherr von Eichendorff, lines from 'Der Zebrochene Ringlein' (The Broken Ring), 'Abschied' (Farewell) and 'Der Umkehrende' (The Return), in *The Penguin Book of German Verse*, ed. L. Forster (Harmondsworth, 1959), 311–17. See Roger Cardinal, 'Joseph Freiherr von Eichendorff', in *The German Romantics in Context* (London, 1975), 134–43.

42. Georg Heym, lines from 'Der Krieg' (War, 1911) in *The Oxford Book of German Verse*, ed. E. L. Stahl (3rd Edition, Oxford, 1967), 457–8.

43. Guenther Grass, 'Ich sag es immer, Polen sind begabt . . .,' trans. Norman Davies, 'Pan Kichot', *Gedichte* (Neuwied/Berlin, n.d.), 27.

44. See *The German Eastern Territories beyond Oder and Neisse in the light of the Polish Press* (Goetingen Research Committee; Würzburg, 1958); Z. Kaczmarczyk, 'One Thousand Years of the History of the Polish Western Frontier,' *Acta Poloniae Historica* (1962), v. 79–106; P. Lysek, *Poland's Western and Northern Territories: a Millennium of Struggle* (New York, 1973), etc. Although Polish scholarship has done much in recent years to defuse the cruder claims of German nationalism, it has done little to question the equally exaggerated claims of Polish nationalist interpretations. The work of centres such as the Institute of Western Affairs in Poznań, which is devoted to the study of German relations, is permanently crippled by the activities of the Censorship, whose simplified view of German aggression in the past and of German revanchism at present prevents any impartial discussion of the subject.

45. From 'Elegie auf dem Schlachtfelde bei Kunersdorf', by Christian Tiegde, *Penguin Book of German Verse*, ed. L. Forster (London, 1959), 235–41.

CHAPTER 22. PARTIA

1. M. K. Dziewanowski, *The Communist Party of Poland: an outline history*, (Cambridge, Mass., 1959: 2nd edition, 1976); Richard R. Starr, 'The Polish Communist Party 1918–48', *Polish Review*, i (1956), 41–59.

2. P. Brock, 'Polish Socialists in early Victorian England', *Polish Review*, vi (1961), 33–53.

3. K. J. Cottam, 'Bolesław Limanowski: a Polish theoretician of agrarian socialism', *Slavonic and East European Review*, ii (1973), 58–75.

4. Lucjan Blit, *The Origins of Polish Socialism: The History and Ideas of the first Polish Socialist Party, 1878–86* (London, 1971). F. Perl, *Dzieje ruchu socjalistycznego w zaborze rosyjskim do powstania PPS* (Warsaw, 1932).

5. J. P. Nettl, *Rosa Luxemburg* (London, 1966), 2 vols. See also Horace B. Davis, *The National Question: Selected Writings by Rosa Luxemburg* (New York, 1976).

6. L. Wasilewski, *Zarys dziejów PPS* (Warsaw, 1925); H. Jabłoński, *Polityka PPS w czasie wojny 1914–18* (Warsaw, 1958); T. Daniszewski, *Zarys historii ruchu robotniczego*, Part 1, 1864–1917 (Warsaw, 1956); A. Kochański, *SDKPiL w latach 1907–10* (Warsaw, 1971); W. Najdus, 'Z historii kształtowania się poglądów SDKPiL w kwestii narodowej', *Z pola walki*, v (1962), nr. 3.

7. F. Swietlikowa, 'Powstanie KPRP', *Z pola walki* i (1958), 1051–75; also R. Solchanyk, 'The Foundation of the Communist Party in Eastern Galicia, 1919–21', *Slavic Review*, xxx (1971), 774–94.

8. On the Provisional Polish Revolutionary Committee (TKRP), or 'Polrevkom', see Norman Davies, *White Eagle, Red Star*, 150–9, with references.

9. Trotsky Archive (Harvard), T 546, quoted by P. Wandycz, *Soviet–Polish Relations, 1917–21* (Cambridge, Mass., 1969), 230; also V. I. Lenin, *Sochineniya* (5th Edition, Moscow, 1958), li. 266.

10. See J. A. Reguła *Historia K.P.P. w świetle faktów i dokumentów* (2nd Edition, Warsaw, 1934), 169–288.

11. Eighteenth Congress of the CPSU: Report given by Comrade D. Manuilsky, *World News and Views* (6 April 1939), 382, quoted by M. K. Dziewanowski, op. cit. 151–2. See I. Deutscher, 'The Tragedy of Polish Communism between Two World Wars', in *Marxism in our Time* (London, 1972); also J. Kowalski, *K.P.P. 1935–8: Studium historyczne* (Warsaw, 1975).

12. See A. Korboński, 'The Polish Communist Party, 1938–42', *Slavic Review*, xxvi (1966), 430–44.

13. W. Broniewski, 'Rozmowa z historią' (A Conversation with History). English text adapted from a translation by Burns Singer in *Five Centuries of Polish Poetry*, ed. J. Peterkiewicz (London, 1970), 106.

14. See *Szkice z dziejów polskiego ruchu robotniczego w latach okupacji hitlerowskiej, 1939–45, Zarys historii* (Warsaw, 1964).

15. The full story of Gomułka's career, and especially of his ambiguous relations with Russian communism, has not yet been written, but there are two clear introductions: N. Bethell, *Gomułka: his Poland and his Communism* (London, 1969); and P. Raina, *Gomułka: eine politische Biographie* (Köln, 1970).

16. See Norman Davies, 'Poland' in Martin McCauley ed., *Communist Rule in Europe, 1944–9* (London, 1977), 39–57; Among several authorized versions of this period is W. Góra *et al.*, *Zarys Historii Polskiego Ruchu Robotniczego, 1944–47* (Warsaw, 1971); N. Kolomejczyk, B. Szydek, *Polska w latach 1944–9* (Warsaw, 1971).

17. Adam Schaff, *A Philosophy of Man* (London, 1963).

18. Leszek Kołakowski, 'Katolicyzm a humanizm', in *Światopogląd i życie codzienne* (Warsaw, 1957); 'Jezus Chrystus – Prorok Reformator', *Argumenty*, nr. 12 (1965).

18. Leszek Kołakowski, 'Katolicyzm a humanizm', in *Światopogląd i życie codzienne* (Warsaw, 1957); 'Jezus Chrystus – Prorok Reformator', *Argumenty*,

20. Stanisław Ossowski, 'Teoretyczne zadania marksismu', *Myśl współczesna*, nr. 1 (1948).

21. Henryk Skolimowski, *Polski Marksism* (London, 1969); also in the original English edition as *Polish Marxism* (London, 1967).

CHAPTER 23. POLSKA LUDOWA

1. General studies of People's Poland include R. Hiscocks, *Poland: Bridge for the Abyss? An interpretation of developments in post-war Poland* (London, 1963); J. F. Morison, *The Polish People's Republic* (Baltimore, 1968); H. J. Stehle, *The Independent Satellite: Society and Politics in Poland since 1945* (London, 1965). See also T. N. Cieplak ed., *Poland since 1956: Readings and Essays on Polish Government and Politics* (New York, 1972).
2. See T. Żenczykowski, 'Geneza i kulisy PKWN', *Kultura* (Paris, 1974), George H. Janczewski, 'The Origin of the Lublin Government', *Slavonic and East European Review*, i (1972); Scaevola (pseudonym), *The Lublin Committee: a study in forgery* (London, 1945). For an authorized version of the construction of communist rule, see W. Góra *et al.*, also N. Kolomejczyk, B. Szydek, opera cit, see Chapter 22, note 16 above.
3. The symposium, *Polska Ludowa* (Warsaw, 1964), edited by Cz. Madajczyk for the twentieth anniversary of the PKWN contains much factual detail but little pertinent comment on the central political issues.
4. See A. Polonsky, B. Drukier eds., *The Beginnings of Communist Rule in Poland, December 1943–July 1945*, (London, to be published), *passim*.
5. Ibid., Minutes of the PPR Central Committee, 9 October 1944.
6. J. Ciechanowski, *Defeat in Victory* (London, 1968); A. B. Lane, *I Saw Freedom Betrayed* (London, 1949); Stanisław Mikołajczyk, *The Rape of Poland: the Pattern of Soviet Domination* (New York, 1948); Jean Malora, *La Pologne d'une occupation à l'autre, 1944–52* (Paris, 1952).
7. Andrzej Korboński, *The Politics of Socialist Agriculture in Poland, 1945–60* (New York, 1964); see also H. Słabek, *Dzieje polskiej reformy rolnej, 1944–8* (Warsaw, 1972).
8. See Z. Stypułkowski, *Invitation to Moscow* (New York, 1962), *passim*.
9. Stanisław Kluz, *W potrzasku dziejowym* (London, 1978).
10. On the civil war see *W walce ze zbrojnym podziemiem*, ed. M. Turlejska (Warsaw, 1972); more specifically on UPA, A. B. Szczesniak, W. Szopa, *Droga do nikąd: działalność OUN i ich likwidacja w Polsce* (Warsaw, 1973): and the semi-fictional account by J. Gerhard, *Łuny w Bieszczadach* (Warsaw, 1968). The second of these volumes was withdrawn from circulation. The author of the third was murdered in mysterious circumstances.
11. S. Banasiak, 'The Settlement of the Polish Western Territories, 1945–7', *Polish Western Affairs*, vi (1965), 121–49; Krystyna Kersten, 'The Transfer of German Population from Poland, 1945–7', *Acta Poloniae Historica*, x (1964), 27–47; J. B. Schechtman, 'The Polish–Soviet Exchange of Population', *Journal of Central European Affairs*, ix (1949), 289–314; Krystyna Kersten, *Repatriacja Ludności polskiej po II wojnie Swiatowej* (Warsaw, 1974).
12. B. R. von Oppen, *Documents on Germany under Occupation 1945–54*, Royal Institute of International Affairs (London, 1955), 107–10. These published documents can now be supplemented by reference to the archival material recently made available at the Public Record Office for the period 1945–8.

13. See S. Schimitzek, *Truth or conjecture: German civilian war losses in the East*, (Poznań, 1966). For a pro-German account, see Alfred M. de Zayas, *Nemesis at Potsdam: the Anglo Americans, and the Expulsion of the Germans: Background, Execution, Consequences* (Revised Edition, London 1979).

14. See note 7 above.

15. Maria Turlejska, *Zapis pierwszej dekady, 1945–54* (Warsaw, 1972), 71–3. This study, written by a former party activist with inside knowledge, is one of the very few of its kind to admit to the real problems of the era – namely, how to construct a communist government without the backing of public support.

16. See J. Pawłowicz, *Strategia frontu narodowego PPR* (Warsaw, 1965).

17. A. Bregman ed., *Faked Elections in Poland* (London, 1947).

18. On the destruction of the democratic opposition see Mikołajczyk op. cit.; also Karol Popiel, *Na mogiłach przyjaciół* (London, 1966); Franciszek Wilk, 'Lista członków PSL zamordowanych, 1944–64', *Zeszyty Historyczne* (Paris), VI (1964).

19. For an official version of the merger of the PPS and the PPR, see B. Syzdek, *Polska Partia Socjalistyczna, 1944–8* (Warsaw, 1974). David Klin, 'Dwudziesta rocznica likwidacji PPS', *Zeszyty Historyczne* (Paris), xv (1969), 209–12.

20. Jan Drewnowski, 'The Central Planning Office on Trial: an Account of the Beginnings of Stalinism in Poland', *Soviet Studies*, xxxi, No. 1 (1979), 23–42 (a revised version of an article in *Zeszyty Historyczne*, xxviii (Paris), (1974)).

21. Adam Ulam, 'Crisis in the Polish Communist Party', *Titoism and the Comintern* (Cambridge, Mass., 1953), 146–88; R. Wraga, 'Pacyfikacja polskiego komunizmu', *Kultura* (Paris), No. 9/26 (1948), 5–12.

22. For a fuller treatment of this period, see Norman Davies, 'Poland' in M. McCauley ed., *Communist Power in Europe 1944–9* (London, 1977), 39–57.

23. Czesław Miłosz, *The Captive Mind* (New York, 1953).

24. B. Meissner, *Der Warschauer Pakt: Dokumentensammlung* (Cologne, 1963); NATO Information Service, *The Atlantic Alliance and the Warsaw Pact: case studies in communist conflict resolution* (Cambridge, Mass., 1971); F. Wiener *Der Armeen der Warschauer-Pakt Staaten* (Vienna, 1971).

25. See I. T. Sanders ed, *The Collectivisation of Agriculture in Eastern Europe* (Lexington, Kentucky, 1958).

26. Lucjan Blit, *The Eastern Pretender: Bolesław Piasecki, his life and times* (London, 1965); and especially Andrzej Micewski, *Współrządzić czy nie kłamać* (Paris, 1978).

27. Cf. A. Burda, *Polskie prawo państwowe* (Warsaw, 1969); and J. Triska *Constitutions of the Communist Party States* (Stanford, 1968). See also R. C. Gripp, *The Political System of Communism* (London, 1973).

28. J. Światło, *Za kulisami bezpieki i partii* (New York, 1955).

29. Adam Ważyk, 'Poemat dla dorosłych', *Nowa Kultura* (Warsaw, 21 Aug. 1955). See J. Mieroszewski, *Kultura* (Paris), No. 9/191 (1963), 122–7.

30. Flora Lewis, *A Case History of Hope: the story of Poland's Peaceful Revolution* (Garden City, 1958); Konrad Syrop, *Spring in October* (New York, 1957); P. E. Zinner ed., *National Communism and Popular Revolt in Eastern Europe: a selection of documents on events in Poland and Hungary, February–*

November 1956 (New York, 1956); George Sakwa, 'The Polish October: a reappraisal through historiography', *Polish Review*, xxiii (1978), nr. 3, 62–78.

31. See W. Jedlicki, 'Chamy i Żydzi', *Kultura* (Paris), No. 12/182 (1962), 3–41.

32. On Polish sympathies for Hungary, see Adam Bromke, 'Poland', in *The Hungarian Revolution in Retrospect*, ed. B. Kiraly, P. Jonas, Brookly College Studies in Social Change No. 6 (New York, 1978), 87–94.

33. Wydarzenia Marcowe, 1968 r. *Kultura* Instytut Literacki, Seria Dokumenty, clxvii (Paris, 1969); W. Bieńkowski, *Motory i hamulce socjalizmu*, ibid. clxxxiii (Paris, 1969).

34. *Canadian Slavonic Papers*, xv (1973), was devoted entirely to the events of 1970 and their effects on all aspects of contemporary Polish life. Ed. Ewa Wacowska, *Rewolta szczecińska i jej znaczenie* (Paris, 1971). See also A. Bromke, J. W. Strong, *Gierek's Poland* (New York, 1973).

35. From an English translation in *Inter-Catholic Press Agency Inc. News Bulletin* (New York), xx, No. 23, 20 December 1965. *The German–Polish Dialogue: Letters of the Polish and German Bishops* (Bonn, 1966). See also André Liebich, 'La lettre des évêques: une étude sur les réactions polonaises à la Ostpolitik de la RFA', *Études Internationales* (Montreal), vi, nr. 4 (1975), 501 28. On post war diplomatic relations, see W. W. Kulski, *Germany and Poland: from war to peaceful relations* (Syracuse, 1976).

36. *Czarna księga cenzury PRL 1*, ed. T. Strzyżewski (Aneks), (London, 1977), contains a detailed collection of regulations and decisions of the censorship in the period 1974–7.

37. See E. Rosset, 'The Demography of the New Poland', *Acta Poloniae Historica*, xvi (1967), 109–38; L. Kosiński, *Demographic Developments in the Soviet Union and Eastern Europe* (New York, 1976).

38. J. H. Montias, *Central Planning in Poland* (New Haven, 1952); M. Kaser, J. G. Zieliński, *Planning in Eastern Europe* (London, 1970); G. R. Feiwel, *Problems in Polish Economic Planning: Continuity, Change and Prospects* (London, 1971); and A. Korboński, 'Gospodarka polska na bezdrożach planowania', *Kultura* (Paris), No. 6/188 (1963), 153–55.

39. A. Zauberman, *Industrial Progress in Czechoslovakia, Poland, and East Germany, 1937–62* (London, 1964); G. R. Feiwel, *Poland's Industrialisation Policy: a current analysis* (London, 1971); J. G. Zieliński *Economic Reforms in Polish Industry* (London, 1973); S. Leszczyński, T. Lijewski, *Geografia Przemysłu Polski* (Warsaw, 1974); and M. C. Ernst, *Indexes of Polish industrial production, 1937–60*, ed. T. P. Alton (New York, 1967); idem, 'Overstatement of industrial growth in Poland', *Quarterly Journal of Economics* (November 1965), xxix. 623–41.

40. Korboński, op. cit.; see note 7 above. W. Bieńkowski, 'Katechizm rolniczy', *Kultura* (Paris), No. 11/278 (1970), 81–94.

41. *Czarna księga* . . . op. cit. 31–8. On Foreign Trade in general see J. Wilczyński, *The Economics and Politics of East–West Trade* (London, 1969); G. P. Lauter, P. M. Dickie, *Multinational Corporations and East European Socialist Economies* (New York, 1975); and R. Skalski, 'Rzeczywistość handlu zagranicznego PRL', *Kultura* (Paris) No. 6/285 (1971), 101–7.

42. David Lane, George Kolankiewicz eds., *Social Groups in Polish Society* (London, 1972). See also Jan Szczepański, *Polish Society* (New York, 1970),

and Alexander Matejko, *Social Change and Stratification in Eastern Europe* (New York, 1974), for contrary interpretations.

43. W. Kalinkowski, 'Poland' in E. A. Gutkind ed, *Urban Development in East Central Europe,* (London, 1972).

44. See B. Mieczkowski, 'Szacunki zmian w płacach realnych w latach 60-tych', *Kultura* (Paris), No. 12/291 (1971), 93 ff.

45. See B. Mieczkowski, 'Bezrobocie w systemie komunistycznym', *Kultura* (Paris), No. 11/254 (1968), 92–100.

46. Janina Miedzińska, 'Likwidacja samorządu robotniczego', *Kultura* (Paris), No. 6/128 (1958), 105–13; Paul Barton, *Misère et révolte de l'ouvrier polonais: 25 ans du syndicalisme d'état: les 74 jours du proletariat* (Paris, 1971); A. Litwin, 'Prawda o Radach Robotniczych', *Zeszyty Historyczne* (Paris), xxiv (1973), 52–67.

47. B. Brodziński, *Stopa życiowa w Polsce, 1945–63* (London, 1965). Since 1975, the over-all situation has again deteriorated dramatically.

48. See *'20 Lat Ludowego Wojska Polskiego* (Warsaw (MON), 1967), reviewed by T. Nowacki, *Zeszyty Historyczne* (Paris), xii (1968), 203–6, with references; also E. Żółtowski, *Kto kiedy, dlaczego o wojsku i obronności kraju* (Warsaw, 1973). *The Military Balance,* International Institute of International Affairs (London, 1977), Poland, 14–15.

49. J. R. Fiszman, *Revolution and Tradition in People's Poland: Education and Socialisation* (Princeton, 1972); G. Singer, *Teacher Education in a Communist State: Poland 1956–61* (New York, 1965); Z. Skubarski, Z. Tokarski, *Polish Universities* (Warsaw, 1959). See also Aleksander Gella, 'Student Youth in Poland: four generations, 1945–70', in *Youth and Society,* vi, nr. 3, (1975), 309–43.

50. Sławomir Mrożek, *Utwory sceniczne nowe* (Cracow, 1975), 126–7. The Intelligentsia provides a theme of constant controversy, e.g. A. Gella, 'The Life and Death of the old Polish intelligentsia', *Slavonic Review,* xxx (1970), 1–27; A. Matejko, Świadomość inteligencka', *Kultura* (Paris), Nos. 7/286, 8/287 (1971), 126–37; Wojciech Rysak, 'Inteligencja polska: rzeczywistość czy mit', *Kultura* (Paris), Nos. 7/298, 8/299 (1972), 178–85; Georges Mond, 'The Role of the Intellectuals', *Canadian Slavonic Papers,* xv (1973), 122–33.

51. Zbigniew Herbert, from 'Pan Cogito': 'What Mr. Cogito thinks about hell', in English translation in *Selected Poems,* Oxford 1977, pp. 60–1. Contemporary Polish literature is not very accessible to English readers, although some works and anthologies have been published in translation: see *Polish Writing Today,* ed. Celina Wieniawska (Penguin, Harmondsworth, 1967); A. Gillon, L. Krzyżanowski, *An Introduction to Modern Polish Literature* (New York, 1964).

52. See B. M. Maciejewski, *Twelve Polish Composers,* London 1976.

53. J. Piekalkiewicz, *Communist Local Government: a study of Poland* (Ohio, 1977).

54. W. Sokolewicz, 'Changes in the structure and functions of the Polish Sejm', *East Central Europe,* ii (1975), 78–91. On the constitutional amendments of 1976, see *Dziennik Ustaw,* nr. 7, poz 36 of 21 Feb. 1976. The main changes are in Article 1 which declares the Polish People's Republic to be a 'socialist state' instead of a 'people's democracy'; in Article 3.1 which describes the Polish United Workers' Party as 'the leading political force of

society'; and in Article 6.2, which declares that the Polish People's Republic 'is strengthening friendship and co-operation with the USSR and other socialist countries.'

55. V. Gsovski, *Church and State behind the Iron Curtain* (New York, 1955). For more recent comments see articles by J. Turowicz, L. Dembiński, and S. Staron, in *Canadian Slavonic Papers*, xv (1973), 151–83. Two papal biographies – Mary Craig, *Man from a far country* (London, 1979), and George Blazynski, *Pope John Paul II* (London, 1979) – give vivid insights into contemporary Polish Catholicism.

56. Zbigniew Brzeziński, *The Soviet Bloc: Unity and Conflict* (Cambridge, Mass., 1960); Adam Bromke, 'Polish Foreign Policy in the 1970's', *Canadian Slavonic Papers*, xv (1973), 192–204.

57. Norman Davies, 'Magical Mystery Tour of Poland', *The Times*, Friday, 27 October 1972.

58. *Dissent in Poland: reports and documents in translation, December 1975– July 1977*, Association of Polish Students and Graduates in Exile (London, 1977); Peter K. Raina, *Political Opposition in Poland, 1955–77* (London, 1978).

POSTSCRIPT

1. Antoni Słonimski, 'Obrona księżyca,' (The Defence of the Moon): 'Prawo moralne we mnie, . . .'; *Poezje zebrane* (PIW, Warsaw, 1970), 535.

2. Leopold Staff, 'Podwaliny' (Foundations): 'Budowałem na piasku . . .'; *Wybór poezji*, ed. M. Jastruń (Wrocław, 1970), 224.

SUGGESTIONS FOR FURTHER READING

Although most of the leading works on Polish History are written in Polish, a surprising number have been translated, and it is now standard practice for academic monographs published in Poland to contain a short summary in English, French, or German. The quarterly journal *Acta Poloniae Historica* (Warsaw, 1959–   ) is devoted to presenting recent historical research in translation.

The standard works on Polish historical bibliography – H. Madurowicz-Urbańska ed, *Bibliografia Historii Polski* (Warsaw, 1965–7), 2 vols. in eight parts; and J. Baumgart, S. Głuszek eds., *Bibliografia historii polskiej za lata 1944–66* (Wrocław Cracow, 1952–68) with annual continuations – assume a knowledge of Polish. A convenient guide for the English reader is provided by Norman Davies, *Poland, Past and Present: a Select Bibliography of Works in English,* Oriental Research Partners (Newtonville, Mass., 1977).

The leading Polish historical journals include:

Kwartalnik Historyczny (Warsaw, 1889–   )
Przegląd Historyczny (Warsaw, 1905–   )
Studia Historyczne (Cracow, 1967–   )
Dzieje najnowsze (Warsaw, 1969–   )
Zeszyty Historyczny (*Kultura*) (Paris, 1962–   )

The following periodicals regularly contain articles on Polish History in English:

Acta Poloniae Historica (Warsaw, 1959–   )
Antemurale (Rome, 1954–   )
Bulletin of the Polish Institute of Arts and Sciences in America (New York, 1943–   )
California Slavic Studies (Berkeley, 1960–7)
Canadian Slavic Studies (Montreal, 1967–   )
(now *Canadian–American Slavic Studies,* Pittsburg, Pa.)
Canadian Slavonic Papers (Ottawa, 1957–69)
East European Quarterly (Boulder, Colorado, 1967–   )
Jahrbucher für Geschichte Osteuropas (Breslau, 1926–   ; Munich, 1953–   )
Jewish Social Studies (New York, 1939–   )

Journal of Central European Affairs (Boulder, Colorado, 1941–64)
Lituanus: the Lithuania Quarterly (New York, 1954–   )
Poland and Germany (London, 1957–67)
Polish–American Historical Association Bulletin (Orchard Lake, Mich., 1946–   )
Polish Perspectives (Warsaw, 1957–   )
Polish Review (New York, 1941–   )
Polish Western Affairs (Poznań, 1959–   )
Slavic and East European Studies (Montreal, 1956–   )
Slavic Review (Washington, 1941–   )
Slavonic and East European Review (London, 1922–   )
Soviet Jewish Affairs (London, 1971–   )
Ukrainian Quarterly (New York, 1944–   )

Among many modern titles, the following works would serve to introduce the most important topics:

W. E. D. Allen, *The Ukraine: a History* (Cambridge, 1940).

Władysław Anders, *An Army in Exile: the Story of the Second Polish Corps* (London, 1949).

Anon., *The Dark Side of the Moon*, Preface by T. S. Eliot (London, 1946).

Angus Armitage, *The World of Copernicus* (East Ardsley, 1971).

Karl Baedeker, *Russia with Teheran, Port Arthur and Peking* (Leipzig, 1914, reprinted, Newton Abbot, 1971); *Northern Germany* (10th Edition, London, 1890); *Austria–Hungary* (10th Edition, London, 1905).

R. N. Bain, *The Last King of Poland and his contemporaries* (London, 1909).

W. Bartoszewski, *Warsaw Death Ring 1939–44* (Warsaw, 1968).

V. Benes, N. Pounds, *Poland* (London, 1970).

Nicholas Bethell, *Gomułka: his Poland and his Communism* (London, 1969).

—, *The War Hitler Won* (London, 1972).

Georg Brandes, *Poland, a study of the Land, People and Literature* (London, 1903).

Peter Brock, *Polish Nationalism* (New York, 1968).

—, *Nationalism and Populism in partitioned Poland: Selected Essays* (London, 1973).

Adam Bromke, *Poland's Politics: Idealism versus Realism,* (Cambridge, Mass., 1967).

Zbigniew K. Brzezinski, *The Soviet Bloc – Unity and Conflict* (Cambridge, Mass., 1960).

Jan. M. Ciechanowski, *The Warsaw Rising* (London, 1974).

Anna Cienciała, *Poland and the Western Powers, 1938–9* (London, 1968).

Mary Craig, *A Man from a Far Country* (London, 1979).

Norman Davies, *White Eagle, Red Star: The Polish–Soviet War, 1919–20* (London, 1972).

The Democratic Heritage of Poland: For Your Freedom and Ours: an Anthology, M. Kridl, J. Wittlin, and W. Malinowski (London, 1944).

M. K. Dziewanowski, *The Communist Party of Poland: an outline of History* (Cambridge, Mass., 1976).

Eva Fournier, *Poland* (Vista Books, London, 1964).

Paul Fox, *The Reformation in Poland* (Baltimore, 1924; republished, 1970).

J. Garlicki, *Fighting Auschwitz* (London, 1976).

A. Gella, 'The Life and Death of the old Polish Intelligentsia', *Slavic Review*, xxx (1970), 1–27.

A. Gieysztor, S. Kieniewicz, *et al.*, *A History of Poland* (Warsaw, 1968).

Maria Gimbutas, *The Slavs*, Ancient Peoples and Places (London, 1971).

O. Halecki, *A History of Poland* (Revised Edition, London, 1977).

Witold Hensel, *The Beginnings of the Polish State* (Warsaw, 1960).

K. Jazdżewski, *Poland*, Ancient Peoples and Places (London, 1965).

C. R. Jurgela, *History of the Lithuanian Nation* (New York, 1948).

S. Kieniewicz, *The Emancipation of the Polish Peasantry* (Chicago, 1969).

Paul W. Knoll, *The Rise of the Polish Monarchy, 1320–70* (Chicago, 1972).

Brian Knox, *The Architecture of Poland*, with 216 plates (London, 1971).

S. Kot, *Socinianism in Poland* (Boston, 1957).

M. Kukiel, *Czartoryski and European Unity, 1770–1861* (Princeton, 1955).

Wacław Lednicki, *The Life and Culture of Poland as reflected in Polish Literature* (New York, 1944).

——, *Russia, Poland and the West: Essays in Literature and History* (New York, 1954).

——, *Reminiscences: the adventures of a modern Gil Blas during the last war* (The Hague, 1971).

R. F. Leslie, *Polish politics and the Revolution of November, 1830* (London, 1956).

——, *Reform and the Insurrection in Russian Poland, 1856–65* (London, 1963).

Lucjan Lewitter, 'Poland, the Ukraine and Russia in the seventeenth century', *Slavonic and East European Review*, xxvii (1948–9), 157–71, 414–29.

——, 'Peter the Great and the Polish Election of 1697', *Cambridge Historical Journal*, xii (1956), 126–43.

——, 'Russia, Poland and the Baltic, 1697–1721', *Historical Journal*, xi (1968), 3–34.

——, 'The Partitions of Poland', *History Today*, viii (1958), 873–82; ix (1959), 30–9.

R. H. Lord, *The Second Partition of Poland: a study in diplomatic history* (Cambridge, Mass., 1915).

Marian Małowist, 'The economic and social development of the Baltic countries from the fifteenth and sixteenth centuries', *Economic History Review*, xii (1959–60), 177–89.

Czesław Miłosz, *A History of Polish Literature* (London, 1969).

——, *The Captive Mind* (London, 1953).

S. Mikołajczyk, *The Rape of Poland: the Pattern of Soviet domination* (New York, 1948).

Stefan Mizwa, ed., *Great Men and Women of Poland* (New York, 1942).

J. F. Morrison, *The Polish People's Republic* (Baltimore, 1968).

J. B. Morton, *Sobieski: King of Poland* (London, 1932).

L. B. Namier, *The Revolution of the Intellectuals, 1848* (London, 1946).

Jan Chrystostom Pasek, *Memoirs of the Polish Baroque*, trans. Catherine B. Leach (Berkeley Ca., 1975).

Sheila Patterson, 'The Poles: an exile community in Britain', in J. L. Watson ed., *Between Two Cultures* (Oxford, 1977), 214–41.

Jozef Piłsudski, *Memoirs of a Polish revolutionary and soldiers*, trans. D. R. Gillie (London, 1931).

Antony Polonsky, ed., *The Great Powers and the Polish Question, 1941–5: a documentary in Cold War origins* (London, 1976).

——, *Politics in Independent Poland: the Crisis of Constitutional Government, 1921–39* (London, 1971).

——, 'Libraries and Archives: Poland', *History*, lvi (3), (1971), 408–10.

J. Pomian, ed., *Joseph Retinger: memoirs of an eminence grise* (London, 1972).

W. J. Reddaway, ed., *The Cambridge History of Poland* (Cambridge, 1941–50), 2 vols.

Hans Roos, *A History of Modern Poland* translated from the German by J. R. Foster (London, 1966).

W. J. Rose, 'Polish Historical Writing', *Journal of Modern History*, ii (1930), 569–85.

W. J. Rose, *The Rise of Polish Democracy* (London, 1944).

—, *The Drama of Upper Silesia: a regional study* (London, 1936).

Joseph Rothschild, *Piłsudski's Coup d'État* (New York, 1966).

Irwin Sanders, Ewa T. Morawska, *Polish–American Community Life: a survey of research*, Polish Institute of Arts and Sciences in America Inc. and Dept. of Sociology, Boston University (Boston–New York, 1975).

Samuel Sharpe, *White Eagle on a Red Field* (Cambridge, Mass., 1953).

Jan Slomka, *From Serfdom to Self-government; Memoirs of a Polish village mayor, 1842–1927*, trans. W. J. Rose (London, 1941).

W. I. Thomas and F. Znaniecki, *The Polish Peasant in Europe and America* (Boston, 1918–20), 5 vols.

Piotr Wandycz, *The Lands of Partitioned Poland, 1795–1918* (Seattle, 1975).

Bernard Weinryb, *The Jews of Poland* (Philadelphia, 1973).

Wiktor Weintraub, 'Tolerance and Intolerance in Old Poland', *Canadian Slavonic Papers*, xiii (1971), 21–43.

David Welsh, *Adam Mickiewicz* (New York, 1966).

Edward D. Wynot, *Polish politics in transition: the camp of national unity and the struggle for power, 1935–39* (Athens, Georgia, 1974).

J. K. Zawodny, *Death in the Forest: the Story of the Katyn Forest Massacre* (London, 1971).

S. Żółkiewski, *Expedition to Moscow, a Memoir (1609–17)* (London, 1959).

A. Żółtowski, *Border of Europe: a Study of the Polish Eastern Provinces* (London, 1950).

Index

(NB. The entries are in English alphabetical order, not Polish. Place-names are entered in their present-day form.)

685

SOLIDARITY, 1980-1981

Although some sort of major crisis in Poland had been confidently predicted for several years (see pp. 632–3), no one foresaw the particular course of recent events. Few people would have guessed that the political initiative would have been taken not by the Church or by the reformers in the Party, and not by the dissident intellectuals, but by the Polish working class and by an entirely new crop of hitherto unknown and untried proletarian leaders. Few people would have banked on an orderly confrontation between the authorities and the opposition. Until the Independent Trades Union movement surfaced in July 1980, no one in the world at large had ever heard of it. Indeed, the prime mover of the organization, a thirty-seven-year-old unemployed electrician from Gdańsk called Lech Wałęsa, when interviewed in June about his 'discussion group', had no idea as to when or how it might produce any concrete results. All he knew himself, just one month before the eruption, was that the cause was worth striving for.

The summer crisis developed with dizzy acceleration. At first, in July, a rash of local strikes seemed to be heading in the same direction as their predecessors in 1970 and 1976. Protests over food shortages fuelled a plethora of minor grievances directed against all manner of hardships and abuses. One might have expected the Party to respond with a matching set of promises and wage rises, a cosmetic change of government, an attempt to raise further foreign loans, a new reformist strategy at the most. But soon it became clear that on this occasion the worke s would not be fobbed off. In mid-August, the strike committee in the vast Lenin Shipyards of Gdańsk rejected a favourable settlement of their own local claim, on the grounds that to do so would have betrayed their fellow strikers elsewhere. It was the moment of truth. The realization dawned that the Party's monopoly of power was being challenged by the concerted action of workers up and down the country – under the ironic slogan of 'WORKERS OF ALL ENTERPRISES – UNITE'. On 31 August, in the Gdańsk Agreement, and later in a separate agreement signed at Jastrzembie in Silesia, government negotiators were obliged to meet the most important of the strikers' demands. In return for confirmation of the Party's leading role, they formally accepted a long list of concessions including the workers' right to strike, their right to organize themselves into free trades unions, their right to construct a monument to colleagues killed in 1970, and a relaxation of censorship. In direct consequence of these agreements, representatives of strike committees from every province of Poland joined together as the National Co-ordinating Committee of a new Independent Self-Governing Trades Union (NSZZ). They called their new organization 'Solidarność' (SOLIDARITY); and they elected as their chairman the man who had led the crucial strike in Gdańsk – Lech Wałęsa.

In retrospect, one can see that all the main elements of the crisis had been fermenting over a long period of time. The bankruptcy of the official ideology (see pp. 551–5, 623), the corruption of officialdom and the growing gulf between Party and people (pp. 616–17) have been known facts of life for decades. The low level of industrial productivity (p. 595), and the stagnation of the standard of living (pp. 597, 599, 600–1), had apparently become permanent features of the system. The failure to support peasant agriculture (p. 596), and the resultant food shortages (pp. 590–1, 628) had persisted throughout the 1970s. The collapse of the Party's economic strategy was demonstrated as early as 1976 (pp. 626–8), whilst the leadership's inability to implement effective reforms increased with every year that passed. The strength of the Roman Catholic Church (pp. 613–15), the ambiguous stance of the armed forces (pp. 602–3), and the growth of a dissident opposition (pp. 628–31) had all been widely reported. In this scene of mounting chaos and disillusionment, all that was needed was some spark, some catalyst, which could mobilize people's feelings and turn the smouldering mood of discontent into open demands for reform of the political order.

In the view of many observers, this spark was provided by

the visit to Poland in June 1979 of Pope John Paul II. The election of the Polish Pope eight months earlier had already injected a new spirit of self-esteem into the private lives of many Poles; but his triumphant return to an adoring homeland, amidst scenes of fervent rejoicing, transformed the tone of public life as well. During the five days of his visit the communist authorities suspended many of their usual practices. Religion monopolized the media. The Catholic mass was televised, for the first time ever in Poland. A towering symbolic cross was erected in Warsaw's Victory Square. The Citizens' Militia retired from view, whilst millions of orderly pilgrims were marshalled by thousands of volunteer stewards. The leaders of an atheist Government, which had spurned Poland's national faith for thirty-five years, were obliged to pay their respects to the father of the Universal Church. Here was a spiritual experience, and an exercise in self-discipline, which no one in Poland could easily forget. The contrast between the overwhelming prestige of the Church and the disrepute of the ruling Party needed no commentary. After that, the rottenness of the system was revealed for all to see. The population did not break into open revolt; but henceforth the vast majority of men, women, and children knew in their hearts that the Party and all it stood for was irrelevant to their real interests. It was then, in the momentous days of June 1979, that the people's sense of moral superiority, their quiet resolve, their religious identity – in short, the spirit of 1980 – was born.

The emergence of SOLIDARITY, therefore, must be seen as the culmination of a long process. It is the agency of a spontaneous movement for national revival, whose seeds were sown in a fertile soil many years ago and which came to life through the warmth generated by a Polish Pope. Its symbols, like its motivation, are religious and patriotic. Its aims, against a fossilized and uncaring system, are for simple justice. It does not wish to overthrow the Party, but merely to overcome the forces of reaction and inertia within the ruling apparatus. There is no reason to doubt the desire for a genuine partnership which SOLIDARITY shares with the new Party leaders. The slogan of *Odnowa* (Renewal) is something to which everyone, from the Pope to the new First Secretary, Stanisław Kania (born 1927), appointed 6 September 1980, publicly subscribe.

However, the rush of popular support has inevitably driven SOLIDARITY into association with all sorts of non-party, and oppositionist, organizations. It works in close contact with the Church hierarchy, and claims the Pope as its chief patron. It has intervened on behalf of KOR, and has rescued these self-appointed defenders of the workers from official harassment. Whether its founders intended it or not, SOLIDARITY was bound to act as an umbrella for anyone and everyone, from students to old-age pensioners, who wish to pursue their interests free from Party control.

In this light, SOLIDARITY cannot be classified as a mere labour movement in the familiar western sense. The fact that it has to operate in an arena where the ruling Party continues to claim a monopoly of power, is bound to give it a political function in the broad sense. In a totalitarian environment, no independent organization can avoid some sort of competition with the government. Nor can it avoid becoming the host for all sorts of camp-followers and parasite bodies who are drawn to it by impulse, simply because they have nowhere else to exist. A bright light in a dark room is bound to attract moths.

Other organizations in Poland's past have had the same problem. One need look no further than the Warsaw Agricultural Society of 1858–61 (see pp. 348–9), which quickly became the centre of national political life not because its founders were ambitious extremists but because there was no other forum where Poles in Russia could meet to express their independent views.

There is a fascinating historical parallel, too, for SOLIDARITY's organizational structure. At an early stage, Wałęsa rejected the concept of a centralized organization based on a powerful central executive issuing directives to its regional branches. Instead, he argued in favour of the sovereignty of the existing regional (strike) committees, whose delegates to the National Co-ordinating Committee would be free to approve or to ignore its recommendations. Such a system may have difficulties in formulating a coherent policy, but it is well designed to resist any outside attack on its central organs. It is strangely reminiscent of the *Sejm,* and the *Sejmiki* of the old Republic. Wałęsa, like the old Polish nobleman whom he so uncannily resembles, seems to have perceived

instinctively that the main danger lay in the absolutist pretensions of state power. If this is so, the Polish working class can
be seen to be reviving the political traditions of the Noble
Democracy — traditions which appear to have survived almost
two centuries of suppression.

At the same time it must be stressed that the Party's claims
to absolute power have always been more myth than reality.
The established position of the Roman Catholic Church in
People's Poland contradicts the most fundamental tenets of
communist doctrine; but the Party has had no alternative but
to reach a working compromise with the Hierarchy. No intelligent Polish communist can have serious illusions about the
limits of Party power; and one can reasonably suppose that
necessity could inspire a *modus vivendi* with SOLIDARITY
similar to the arrangement agreed with the Church.

For SOLIDARITY, unlike the Party, which was imposed
without reference to popular demand (see pp. 548–51, 556–
77), enjoys genuine legitimacy. By recognizing the Party's
leading role, and by signing solemn agreements with the
Government, SOLIDARITY has actually served to shore up
the authorities' failing powers. It is a curious situation, but
through its association with SOLIDARITY, the PZPR is gaining its first measure of legitimacy in the thirty-three years of
its existence. This development provides some basis for their
mutual partnership. It certainly provides the last chance for
the reformers within the Party itself.

In fact, the fate of the Party hangs in the balance. Initially,
it was thought that SOLIDARITY was at risk through its
infiltration by one million Party members. Now, it appears,
the Party is more at risk through its penetration by one million
members of SOLIDARITY. It is difficult to see how these
rank-and-file communists, who have sensed the elation of
genuine democratic debate in their SOLIDARITY meetings,
can readily accept the reimposition of Party discipline and
Leninist controls in their other role as Party activists.

Much depends on the actions of the Soviet Union, whose
dilemma is as obvious as its intentions are obscure. If the
Soviet Union intervenes by force, to reassert what it is pleased
to consider 'socialist norms', it may regain control of Poland
for a season; but it will earn the undying contempt of the Poles

and lose their support forever. Poland would rapidly become
an intolerable burden for the whole Soviet empire. On the
other hand, if the USSR withholds its forces and chooses the
path of restraint, there is no way that the Polish Party can
reassert its former position. Whatever happens, therefore,
there can be no return to the *ancien régime* as practised in
Poland by Gomułka and Gierek since 1956.

It is a bad moment for a historian. At the growing point of
History, historians are no more prescient than anyone else.
What is more, a knowledge of Polish History is apt to inspire
a note of pessimism, at least in any short-term forecast. No
nation is ever so vulnerable as at the time when it tries to
reform itself; and Polish History is strewn with movements
for reform which provoked internal dissension and preceded
external intervention. However, everyone in Poland is well
aware of the consequences of disorder, and all parties in the
current confrontations have displayed remarkable skill and
circumspection. Unless driven to desperation by unrepentant
hardliners, or by a Warsaw Pact invasion, there are few signs
that SOLIDARITY might turn to violence. To date, there has
been no recourse to the Polish insurrectionary tradition waiting in the wings. Even so, one way or the other, SOLIDARITY
has already ensured its place in one more honourable chapter
of Poland's unfinished History.